THE ROUTLEDGE HANDBOOK
OF TOURISM IN ASIA

Asia is regarded as the fastest growing area for international and domestic tourism in the world today and over the next 20 years. Given the economic, social and environmental importance of tourism in the region, there is a need for a comprehensive and readable overview of the critical debates and controversies in tourism in the region and the major factors that are affecting tourism development both now and in the foreseeable future.

This Handbook provides a contemporary survey of the region and its continued growth and development as a key destination and generator of tourism, which is marked by a high proportion of intra-regional travel. The book is divided into five sections. This first section provides an introduction to the region and context to the nationally focused chapters. The next three sections are then broadly based on the three UNWTO Asian regions: South-East Asia, South and Central Asia, and East and North-East Asia, providing readers with a valuable snapshot of tourism at various scales, and from various approaches and positions. The concluding section considers future prospects for tourism in Asia. The handbook is interdisciplinary in coverage and is also international in scope through its authorship and content. It presents a range of perspectives and understanding of the processes and forces that are shaping tourism in this fascinating and dynamic region that is one of the focal points of global tourism.

This is essential reading for students, researchers and academics interested in tourism in the growth region of Asia now and in the future.

C. Michael Hall is Professor of Marketing, University of Canterbury, New Zealand; Docent in Geography, Oulu University; Visiting Professor, Linneaus University; and Senior Research Fellow, University of Johannesburg. Author and editor of over 80 books, he has published widely on tourism, sustainability, governance and food issues.

Stephen J. Page is Professor of Tourism, School of Tourism, Bournemouth University; author and editor of 36 books on tourism, leisure and events; and Associate Editor of the journal *Tourism Management*.

T0384005

THE ROUTLEDGE HANDBOOK OF TOURISM IN ASIA

Edited by C. Michael Hall and Stephen J. Page

Routledge
Taylor & Francis Group

LONDON AND NEW YORK

First published 2017 by Routledge

2 Park Square, Milton Park, Abingdon, Oxon OX14 4RN
605 Third Avenue, New York, NY 10017

Routledge is an imprint of the Taylor & Francis Group, an informa business

First issued in paperback 2022

Publisher's Note

The publisher has gone to great lengths to ensure the quality of this reprint but points out that some imperfections in the original copies may be apparent.

British Library Cataloguing in Publication Data
A catalogue record for this book is available from the British Library

Library of Congress Cataloging in Publication Data
Names: Hall, Colin Michael, 1961- editor. | Page, Stephen J., editor.
Title: The Routledge handbook of tourism in Asia / edited by C. Michael Hall and Stephen J. Page.
Other titles: Handbook of tourism in Asia
Description: New York, NY : Routledge, 2016. | Includes bibliographical references and index.
Identifiers: LCCN 2016013753| ISBN 9781138784581 (hardback) | ISBN 9781315768250 (ebook)Subjects: LCSH: Tourism--Asia. | Tourism--Social aspects--Asia.
Classification: LCC G155.A74 R68 2016 | DDC 338.4/7915--dc23
LC record available at https://lccn.loc.gov/2016013753

ISBN: 978-1-138-78458-1 (hbk)
ISBN: 978-1-03-233991-7 (pbk)
DOI: 10.4324/9781315768250

Typeset in Bembo
by Saxon Graphics Ltd, Derby

CONTENTS

Contents

FIGURES

PLATES

TABLES

BOXES AND CASES

CONTRIBUTORS

Jayatilleke S. Bandara, Department of Accounting, Finance and Economics, Griffith Business School, Griffith University, Queensland, Australia.

Murat Alper Başaran, Department of Management Engineering, Alanya Alaaddin Keykubat University, Alanya, Sigorta Caddesi, 07425, Turkey.

T.C. Chang, Department of Geography, National University of Singapore, 1 Arts Link, Kent Ridge, Singapore 117570.

Julian Clifton, School of Earth and Environment, The University of Western Australia, 35 Stirling Highway, Crawley WA 6009, Australia.

Chris Cooper, Department of Business and Management, Business School, Oxford Brookes University, Wheatley Campus, Wheatley, Oxford, OX33 1HX, UK.

Subhajit Das, Department of Geography, Presidency University, 86/1 College Street, Kolkata, 700073 India.

David Timothy Duval, Faculty of Business and Economics, University of Winnipeg, Winnipeg, Manitoba, Canada.

Sriyantha Fernando, Department of Accounting, Finance and Economics, Griffith Business School, Griffith University, Queensland, Australia.

Carolin Funck, Hiroshima University, Faculty of Integrated Arts and Sciences, Graduate School of Integrated Arts and Sciences, 1-7-1 Kagamiyama, 739-8521 Higashi-Hiroshima-shi, Japan.

C. Michael Hall, Department of Management, Marketing and Entrepreneurship, University of Canterbury, Christchurch, New Zealand; Department of Geography, University of Oulu,

Oulu, Sweden; School of Business and Economics, Linneaus University, Kalmar, Sweden; School of Tourism and Hospitality, University of Johannesburg, South Africa.

Mark P. Hampton, Kent Business School, Parkwood Road, University of Kent, Canterbury, Kent, CT2 7PE, UK.

Kashif Hussain, Center for Research and Innovation in Tourism, School of Tourism, Hospitality and Culinary Arts, Taylor's University, No. 1, Jalan Taylor's, 47500 Subang Jaya, Selangor Darul Ehsan, Malaysia.

Kemal Kantarci, Department of Tourism, Alanya Alaaddin Keykubat University, Alanya, Sigorta Caddesi, 07425, Turkey.

Heidi Karst, University of Waterloo, Waterloo, ON N2L, Canada.

Nick Kontogeorgopoulos, International Political Economy, University of Puget Sound, 1500 N. Warner St., Tacoma, WA 98416, USA.

Anh Le, Department of Hotel Management, Vietnam National Administration of Tourism, Vietnam and Department of International Economics, National Economics University, Hanoi, Vietnam.

Timothy Jeonglyeol Lee, Cluster of Tourism and Hospitality, Ritsumeikan Asia Pacific University, Beppu 874-8577, Japan.

Alan A. Lew, Department of Geography and Public Planning, Northern Arizona University, Flagstaff, AZ 86011 5016, USA.

Zhifei Li, Department of Tourism Management, Hubei University, Wuhan, China.

Vincent Magnini, Hospitality and Tourism Management, Pamplin College of Business, Virginia Polytechnic Institute and State University, Blacksburg, VA 24060, USA.

Paolo Mura, School of Hospitality, Tourism and Culinary Arts, Taylor's University, No. 1 Jalan Taylor's, 47500 Subang Jaya, Selangor Darul Ehsan, Malaysia.

Ghazali Musa, Department of Business Strategy and Policy, Faculty of Business and Accountancy, University of Malaya, 50603 Kuala Lumpur, Malaysia.

Sanjay Nepal, Department of Geography and Environmental Management, University of Waterloo, Waterloo, ON N2L, Canada.

V. Manh Nguyen, Department of Tourism and Hospitality, National Economics University, 207 Giai Phong, Hanoi, Vietnam.

Stephen J. Page, Faculty of Management, Bournemouth University, Talbot Campus, Poole, BH12 5BB, Dorset, UK.

Girish Prayag, Department of Management, Marketing and Entrepreneurship, University of Canterbury, Christchurch, New Zealand.

Lisa Ruhanen, UQ Business School, Colin Clark Building, Blair Drive, The University of Queensland, St. Lucia, QLD 4072, Australia.

Daniela Schilcher, EU Business School, Theresienhöhe 28, 80339 Munich, Germany.

Aishath Shakeela, Department of Tourism, Sport and Hotel Management, Griffith University, Gold Coast, Queensland, 4222, Australia.

Elmarie Slabbert, Tourism Programme, School of Business Management, North-West University, Potchefstroom Campus, South Africa.

Christine Smith, Department of Accounting, Finance and Economics, Nathan Campus, Griffith University, 170 Kessels Road QLD 4111, Australia.

Wantanee Suntikul, School of Hotel and Tourism Management, The Hong Kong Polytechnic University, 17 Science Museum Road, TST East, Kowloon, Hong Kong.

Thinaranjeney Thirumoorthi, Department of Marketing, Faculty of Business and Accountancy, University of Malaya, 50603 Kuala Lumpur, Malaysia.

Dallen J. Timothy, School of Community Resources and Development and Global Institute of Sustainability, College of Public Service & Community Solutions, Arizona State University, 411 N. Central Ave. Suite 550, Phoenix, AZ 85004-0685-4020, USA.

V. Dao Truong, Tourism Research in Economic Environs and Society (TREES), North-West University, Potchefstroom Campus, South Africa, and Department of Tourism and Hospitality, National Economics University, 207 Giai Phong, Hanoi, Vietnam.

Muzaffer Uysal, Hospitality and Tourism Management, Pamplin College of Business, Virginia Polytechnic Institute and State University, Blacksburg, VA 24060, USA.

Andrea Valentin, Tourism Transparency, Shwe Gone Daing, Bahan Township, Yangon, Myanmar.

Adam Weaver, School of Management, Victoria University of Wellington, PO Box 600, Wellington, 6140, New Zealand.

David Weaver, Department of Tourism, Sport and Hotel Management, Griffith University, Gold Coast Campus, Southport, Queensland, 4222, Australia.

Tim Winter, Alfred Deakin Institute for Citizenship and Globalisation, Melbourne Burwood Campus, 221 Burwood Highway, Burwood, Victoria 3125, Australia.

ACKNOWLEDGEMENTS

Stephen would like to thank Jo, Rosie and Toby for their support and good humour during writing.

Michael would like to thank Nicole Aignier, Tim Baird, Tim and Vanessa Coles, David and Melissa Duval, Jamie Gillen, Martin Gren, Stefan Gössling, Johan Hultman, Michael James, John Jenkins, Dieter Müeller, Lara Penke, Yael Ram, Jarkko Saarinen, Anna-Dora Saetorsdottir, Dan Scott, Dallen Timothy, Tim Winter and Maria-Jose Zapata Campos, who have all recently contributed in various ways to some of the ideas contained within, although the interpretation of their thoughts is, of course, his own. Paul Buchanan, Nick Cave, Bruce Cockburn, Elvis Costello, Ebba Forsberg, Fountains of Wayne, Lotte Kestner, Laura Marling, Yael Naim, Vinnie Reilly, Glen Tilbrook, Loudon Wainwright, and BBC Radio 6 and KCRW were also essential to the writing process. Finally, Michael would like to thank the many people who have supported his work over the years, and especially to the Js and the Cs who stay at home and mind the farm.

We would all like to extend our grateful thanks to Jody Cowper-James for her assistance with editing as well as to our editor Emma Travis at Routledge and to Pippa Mullins for her shepherding as well as to the rest of the Routledge team who have supported us during the project.

ABBREVIATIONS AND ACRONYMS

ABTC	APEC Business Travel Card
ABTO	Association of Bhutanese Tour Operators
ADB	Asian Development Bank
ADS	Approved Destination Status
AEC	ASEAN Economic Community
AITD	Asian Institute of Transportation Development
APEC	Asia-Pacific Economic Cooperation
ASEAN	Association of Southeast Asian Nations
ATF	ASEAN Tourism Forum
bn	billion
BPC	Bangladesh Parjatan Corporation
CA	Central Asian (countries)
CBS	Centre for Bhutan Studies
CBT	community-based tourism
CCP	Chinese Communist Party
CCZ	Civilian Control Zone
CEPAR	ARC Centre of Excellence in Population Ageing Research
CHA	Cultural Heritage Administration of Korea
CITES	Convention on International Trade in Endangered Species of Wild Fauna and Flora
CNTA	China National Tourism Administration
DASSK	Daw Aung San Suu Kyi (Myanmar)
DfID	Department for International Development (UK)
DMZ	Demilitarised Zone
ETC	European Travel Commission
FAO	Food and Agriculture Organization of the United Nations
FDI	foreign direct investment
GATS	General Agreement on Trade in Services
GHG	greenhouse gas
GMS	Greater Mekong Subregion

GNH	gross national happiness
GNHC	Gross National Happiness Commission
GNI	gross national income
HDI	Human Development Index
HFCs	hydrofluorocarbons
IATA	International Air Transport Association
ICAO	International Civil Aviation Organisation
ICCA	International Congress and Convention Association
ICOMOS	International Council on Monuments and Sites
IEA	International Energy Agency
ILO	International Labour Organization
IMS GT	Indonesia–Malaysia–Singapore Growth Triangle
IPCC	Intergovernmental Panel on Climate Change
ISIS	Islamic State of Iraq and Syria
ITDC	Indian Tourism Development Corporation
IUCN	International Union for Conservation of Nature
IVS	Individual Visit Scheme
JCI	Joint Commission International
JSA	Joint Security Area
JTA	Japan Tourism Agency
KTO	Korea Tourism Organization
LCC	low-cost carrier
m	million
MAS	Malaysian Airline System
MDG	Millennium Development Goal
MDL	Military Demarcation Line
MDS	multi-dimensional scaling
MICE	meetings, incentives, conventions and exhibitions
MM2H	Malaysia My Second Home
MOAF	Ministry of Agriculture and Forests
MOHT	Myanmar Ministry of Hotels and Tourism
MPA	marine protected area
MTCE	Ministry of Tourism and Creative Economy (Indonesia)
MTI	Ministry of Trade and Industry (Singapore)
NGO	non-governmental organisation
NIE	newly industrialised economy
NKEA	National Key Economic Area
NLD	National League For Democracy (Myanmar)
NSR	northern sea route
NTB	Nepal Tourism Board
ODA	Official Development Assistance
PA	protected area
PATA	Pacific Asia Travel Association
PFCs	perfluorocarbons
PPP	public–private partnerships
PPT	pro-poor tourism
PRC	People's Republic of China
PTDC	Pakistan Tourism Development Corporation

RCI	Royal Caribbean International
RF	radiative forcing
RFE	Russian Far East
RGoB	Royal Government of Bhutan
ROK	Republic of Korea (South Korea)
SAARC	South Asian Association for Regional Cooperation
SAR	Special Administrative Region
SATIS	SAARC Agreement on Trade in Services
SCCI	SAARC Chamber of Commerce and Industry
SCO	Shanghai Cooperation Organization
SLR	sea level rise
SMEs	small and medium enterprises
STB	Singapore Tourism Board
ST-EP	Sustainable Tourism–Eliminating Poverty
STPB	Singapore Tourist Promotion Board
TALC	Tourism Area Life Cycle
TAT	Tourism Authority of Thailand
TCB	Tourism Council of Bhutan
TDS	tourism development strategy
TSA	Tourism Satellite Account
UNDESA	United Nations Department of Economic and Social Affairs
UNDP	United Nations Development Programme
UNESCAP	United Nations Economic & Social Commission for Asia and Pacific
UNESCO	United Nations Educational, Scientific and Cultural Organization
UNHabitat	United Nations Human Settlements Programme
UNP	United National Party (Sri Lanka)
UNWTO	United Nations World Tourism Organization
USSR	Union of Soviet Socialist Republics
VFR	visiting friends and relations
WEF	World Economic Forum
WTM	World Travel Market
WTTC	World Travel and Tourism Council
WWF	World Wildlife Fund
ZSL	Zoological Society of London

PART 1

Introduction

Region and context

1

INTRODUCTION

Tourism in Asia: region and context

C. Michael Hall & Stephen J. Page

Introduction

Growth in Asian tourism since the early 1990s has been little short of astonishing in terms of levels of growth, the expansion of new markets, new destinations and the creation of the world's most dynamic and growth-oriented inbound and outbound region for global tourism. Similarly, domestic tourism has mirrored this growth but evidence and data remain less clear in relation to the scale and extent of such growth (Singh 2009). In the case of international tourism, the UNWTO reported in 2015 that China had become the top source market and, as earlier commentators (e.g. Hall 1994) observed, this was a sleeping giant about to awaken. It has now not only awoken but become the trendsetter in terms of the pace of growth and change. In 2014–15 alone, it accelerated its expenditure abroad by 27% to US$165 billion. Whilst its contribution to Asian tourism as a whole is significant, countries within the region received 263 million international arrivals, earned US$377 billion in receipts and accounted for 23% of worldwide receipts (UNWTO 2015).

China's rise in tourism reflects the overall importance of Asia for international tourism. According to the UNWTO (2016a), international tourist arrivals grew by 4.4% in 2015 to reach a total of 1,184 million in 2015. Asia's growth continued to be above the global average. Asia and the Pacific recorded 13 million more international tourist arrivals last year to reach 277 million, an overall increase of 5%. Within the region South-East Asia (+5%) led growth, while South Asia and North-East Asia recorded an increase of 4% from the previous year. This compared favourably to other developing regions. For example, arrivals to the Middle East increased by 3% while Africa was estimated to have a 3% decrease in international arrivals in 2015 (UNWTO 2016b) (Table 1.1).

However, such is the wider economic importance of Asia, and of the Chinese economy in particular, that changes in the region and their effects now have major repercussions on confidence in the global economy. For example, forecasts of slower economic growth in China in early 2016 had a knock-on effect on global share prices that reflects the increasing globalisation not only of the economy, but also of communication, information, trade, human mobility and, of course, tourism. Asia has become a major region in the world economy and is increasingly integrated with the developed economies of Europe and North America, as well as developing

Table 1.1 International arrivals and market share by region, 2000–2015

UNWTO region	2000 ('000)	Share (%)	2005 ('000)	Share (%)	2010 ('000)	Share (%)	2015 ('000)*	Share (%)
Europe	386.6	57.36	453.2	56.02	489.4	51.52	609.1	51.4
Northern Europe	44.8	6.65	59.9	7.40	62.8	6.61	75.3	6.4
Western Europe	139.7	20.73	141.7	17.52	154.4	16.25	180.9	15.3
Central/Eastern Europe	69.6	10.33	95.3	11.78	98.9	10.41	127.8	10.8
Southern/Mediterranean Europe	132.6	19.67	156.4	19.33	173.3	18.24	225.1	19.0
of which EU-28	330.5	49.04	367.9	45.48	384.3	40.45	478.3	40.4
Asia and the Pacific	110.4	16.38	154.0	19.04	205.5	21.63	277.0	23.4
North-East Asia	58.3	8.65	85.9	10.62	111.5	11.74	142.3	12.0
South-East Asia	36.3	5.39	49.0	6.06	70.5	7.42	102.2	8.6
Oceania	9.6	1.42	10.9	1.35	11.4	1.20	14.2	1.2
South Asia	6.1	0.91	8.2	1.01	12.1	1.27	18.3	1.5
Americas	128.2	19.02	133.3	16.48	150.2	15.81	190.7	16.1
North America	91.5	13.58	89.9	11.11	99.5	10.47	126.2	10.7
Caribbean	17.1	2.54	18.8	2.32	19.5	2.05	23.8	2.0
Central America	4.3	0.64	6.3	0.78	7.9	0.83	10.3	0.9
South America	15.3	2.27	18.3	2.26	23.2	2.44	30.3	2.6
Africa	26.2	3.89	34.8	4.30	50.4	5.31	53.1	4.5
North Africa	10.2	1.51	13.9	1.72	19.7	2.07	18.8	1.6
Sub-Saharan Africa	16.0	2.37	20.9	2.58	30.8	3.24	34.2	2.9
Middle East	22.4	3.32	33.7	4.17	54.7	5.76	54.1	4.6
World	674	100	809	100	950	100	1,184	100

Source: based on UNWTO 2016b.
Note
* Provisional figures.

economies. Furthermore, there has been an intensification of intra-regional linkages as trade and investment within the region have grown, strengthening the way in which tourism has become a more interconnected aspect of the regional economy (Hall & Page 2000). In this environment tourism, for long one of the mainstays of the region's economy, has now become an even more important source of economic development and foreign exchange, as well as a mechanism for employment generation. However, tourism in Asia is also facing numerous environmental, social and political challenges (Barclay & Smith 2013; Frost, Laing & Beeton 2014; Henderson 2015; King 2015; see also the following chapters in this volume).

Defining Asia

On the surface the task of defining Asia would appear to be a simple one. For many academic and armchair geographers, and readers of Wikipedia, Asia is traditionally defined as the landmass to the east of the Suez Canal and the Ural Mountains, and south of the Caucasus Mountains and the Black and Caspian Seas. To the east it is bound by the Pacific Ocean and the Bering Strait, to the south by the Indian Ocean, and to the north by the Arctic Oceans (Lew *et al.* 2015) (Figure 1.1). Although the physiographic dimensions of such a definition are somewhat problematic, given that Europe and Asia share the same continental landmass, the historical convention has been that they are treated separately, although this may also be as much for political and cultural reasons as spatial concerns (Hall 2009). However, such an approach tells us little of the way the concept of Asia has come to be socially constructed in space and time (Roy 2015; Sheppard 2015), and the implications that it has for economic and social relationships, identity, governance and, of course, tourism.

The concept of Asia is usually regarded as a Western construct. It appears that the word 'Asia' has its origins in Ancient Greece, where the term was used to describe the region of Anatolia in present-day Turkey. In the *Iliad* Homer refers to an ally of the Trojans named Asios that may be associated with a confederation of states in Western Anatolia. However, the term was clearly in common use by about 2450 BP when Herodotus used the word to refer to Anatolia or, with respect to the description of the Persian Wars, to differentiate the Persian Empire from Egypt and Greece. Herodotus was also curious as to why different women's

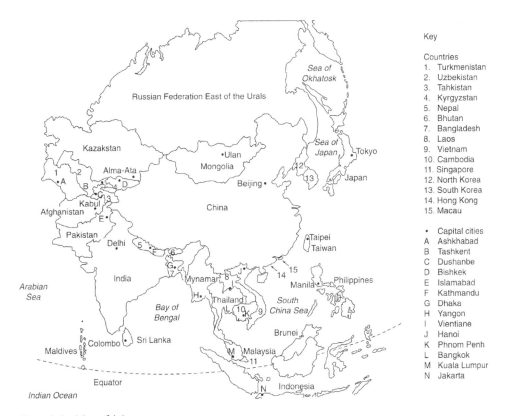

Figure 1.1 Map of Asia.

names (Asia, Europa and Libya [with respect to Africa]) were used to describe the landmass surrounding the Mediterranean. Nevertheless, within the history of European thought the concept of Asia has clearly long been significant within a process of geographic, cultural and political "othering" (Yapp 1992), although the continental affiliations of countries that cross geographic and cultural boundaries may be quite problematic as in the case of Russia, and more recently countries such as Turkey, Georgia and Armenia, which have either applied or expressed interest in applying for membership of the European Union, and which are seen as having both European and Asian identities, or at least being clearly "different" (Hall 2009). Similarly, the position of Australia and New Zealand, as well as many of the Pacific Islands, with respect to Asia also presents interesting issues of how identity is positioned given the increasingly strong economic and tourism ties, as well as a significant ethnic Asian population (Keating 2000; Broinowski 2003). However,

> Although there has been little consensus about what constitutes Asia, many in the international community perceived ... that the Asia economies were growing at such a vast scale that the 21st century would be marked by the ascendance of Asia – possibly a Pax Asiana.
>
> *(Jain 2004: 1)*

The notion of a regional or a political space is as much a social construct as it is a representation of physical geography. In the same way that the orient was constructed as an "other" by various European imperial powers, so also has the notion of Asia been influenced by European and Northern American constructs. However, 'Asia is a contested notion with different meanings and associations for different people in different places, even within Asian societies' (Jain 2004: 3). The construction and perception of Asia are different within India (Deshingkar 1999) and Japan (Suehiro 1999), as well as being influenced by historical and political events. The concept of an Asian identity is therefore as much being constructed from within as it is from without. For example, in the 1990s considerable political attention was being given to the notion of Asian values (Chong 2004; Beeson & Yoshimatsu 2007), particularly by Prime Ministers Mahathir bin Mohamad of Malaysia (1999) and Lee Kuan Yew of Singapore (Barr 2000). Asian values have been defined as emphasising a consensual approach, communitarianism rather than individualism, social order and harmony, respect for elders, discipline, a paternalistic State and the primary role of government in economic development, linked to the premise that 'there are values and patterns of behaviour that are common to Asian countries and peoples' (Han 1999: 4; see also Yang & Lim 2000). In contrast, Han (1999: 7) associates "Western values" with transparency, accountability, global competitiveness, a universalistic outlook and universal practices, and an emphasis on private initiatives and the independence of the private sector. Even though the religious, cultural, ethnic and political diversity of Asia or even East Asia seems to belie the notion of Asian values, the concept still has influence in Asia and beyond in the same way that the notion of European values is used in discussions within the European Union (Patten 1998; Glassman 2015). Empirical evidence for shared Asian values is also mixed. Kim (2010) examined the extent to which Asians shared four different Asian values discourses: familism, communalism, authority orientations and work ethic. He found that although East Asian respondents exhibited strong work-related values compared to other regions, commitment to familial values and authoritarian values was actually lower. In addition, while preference for strong leadership and parental duty did form distinct sets of attitudes among South and South-East Asians, the four dimensions did not constitute a clear value complex in the minds of East Asians (Kim 2010). However, the fact that they are often perceived to exist may be more important than the realities of their existence. As Milner (2000, 2003) noted, the Asian values concept, although at times confused and contradictory, is part of a much larger and longer process of cultural refiguration that however problematic it might be in cultural and political terms, is attracting substantial and growing emotional investment. Some of the elements of the supposed "Asian" and "anti-Asian" values are indicated in Table 1.2.

Table 1.2 Arguments for and against the exceptionalism of "Asian values"

Elements of Asian values	Anti-Asian values elements
• A set of values as shared by people of many different nationalities and ethnicities living in East Asia. These values include a stress on the community rather than the individual, the privileging of order and harmony over personal freedom, refusal to compartmentalise religion away from other spheres of life, a particular emphasis on saving and thriftiness, an insistence on hard work, a respect for political leadership, a belief that government and business need not necessarily be natural adversaries, and an emphasis on family loyalty. • In seeking to understand the economic success of certain Asian societies credit must be given to the role of "Asian values". It is not sufficient to analyse such economic success in culture-free economic terms, or as a result of the adoption of specifically Western values. • In the process of developing modern political systems in Asian societies, due recognition must be given to the specific Asian cultures in which they are to be situated. It is not acceptable to reform or criticise such societies solely on the basis of Western liberal-democratic practice. • A belief that a major political and economic international shift is underway, involving the rise of "the East" and the fall of "the West". • An expression of disquiet and misgivings regarding certain "Western values", especially related to a perceived excessive stress on the individual rather than the community, a lack of social discipline and too great an intolerance for difference in social behaviour. The suggestion is sometimes present that Western countries would do well to learn from "Asian values". • A style of policy delivery marked by strong central leadership and very close relations between government and business.	• The suggestion that a set of "Asian values" operates throughout Asia, or even just in East Asia, contradicts what we know about the presence of long-standing religious (Islamic, Buddhist, Hindu, Confucian) and other divisions in the region, and of the ongoing major social and cultural transformation of the region. • Many so-called "Asian values" are equally Western values, and, in some cases, they have been deliberately inculcated in Asian societies as a consequence of the influence on Asian elites of Western models and colonial legacies. • The role in social and economic analysis of "Asian values", "Western values" or "culture" in general can be questioned: economic change may in fact be the result of other, deeper processes. Cultures are often (re)constructed, constructed or invented to serve the specific purposes of their inventors. • The specific purpose of promoting "Asian values" in the case of a number of Asian regimes is that of defending illiberal forms of government by cloaking authoritarian strategies and tactics in arguments of cultural exceptionalism. • "Asian values" are the ideological constructs of Asian leaderships rather than the genuinely held beliefs of their subjects. • The ideology of "Asian values" is a radical conservatism that serves the needs of neoliberal capitalism at a particular stage of its development in specific Asian societies; it is an ideology that combines organic statism with market economies. • There is disagreement within the Asian region about "Asian values". NGOs and even some political leaders, are powerful advocates of "universal", "liberal" values. • As a unifying ideological system in the region, the notion of "Asian values", like the idea of "Asia" itself, has proved of little value. • "Asian values" are based on double standards. For example, those claiming the West is materialistic are accused of being engaged in enriching themselves.

Sources: Han 1999; Milner 2000; Jain 2004; Kingsbury 2008; Hall 2009; Kim 2010; Glassman 2015.

Such debates are not just part of an intellectual argument, they also have an extremely practical effect on how policy is made (de Jong 2012; Yung 2012; Glassman 2015), particularly with respect to international trade, investment and the mobility of capital, transport and the mobility of people. In addition, they also raise issues of different ways of doing business, the meaning of work (Parfitt & Wysocki 2012), the nature of innovation (Goxe 2012) and human rights (Kingsbury 2008; Pisanò 2014). Moreover, despite claims as to the diminished role of the state given the rate of contemporary economic globalisation, it is nevertheless essential to recognise that the state is the foundation of regulatory regionalism via the bilateral and multilateral series of political and economic relations established by states under international law.

Asian regulatory spaces are the product of the large number of political agreements covering economic, cultural, governance and environmental activities between countries that specifically use Asia as an identifying term (Barclay & Smith 2013). For example, agreements under APEC (Asia-Pacific Economic Cooperation) gives support for the creation of a specific set of transnational relations and flows within the regulatory spaces of APEC members. Such spaces are not anonymous or blank, but are identified with a geographical space which, in turn, has its own implications for the social, economic and political construction of particular identities, as noted at the start of this chapter.

The shift from national to supranational identities of regulation and control is arguably part of a broader process of the development of post-sovereign governance (MacCormick 1996; Morales-Moreno 2004) in which the creation of supranational governance structures arguably goes hand-in-hand with the formation of new sets of political identities and, potentially in the longer term, social identities. The formation of an Asian identity, albeit highly contested, therefore runs parallel to the development of a series of transnational political spaces. For example, it can be argued that the development of new sets of visa and border agreements between countries as a result of the development of new regulatory spaces also encourages the development of new understandings of citizenship not only with respect to belonging and identity but also with mobility. For Isin and Wood (1999: 4), modern citizenship is no longer exclusively tied to membership of a nation-state; that is, restricted to 'legal obligations and entitlements which individuals possess by virtue of their membership in a state'. Instead, citizenship is a more complex form of identity which is distinctive because it is based on reciprocal social relations and common interests among a particular group that new Asian supranational regulatory spaces serve to enhance and reinforce. Although notions of "expanded citizenship" (van Steenbergen 1994) or cosmopolitan citizenship have tended to be applied more to the European sphere (Coles 2008), there is no reason not to consider the development of an Asian cosmopolitan citizenship, given the extent to which accessibility and mobility of certain groups in society is being afforded by structures such as APEC or ASEAN (Bianchi & Stephenson 2014).

The new regulatory spaces of Asia not only serve to encourage new Asian mobile identities for some groups by virtue of new forms and rights of citizenship, but also provide the political means for influencing the direction of flows and connections between places (Winter *et al.* 2008). For example, the capacity for flying between international destinations or for crossing borders via particular modes of transport is enabled by the political agreements that exist between countries with respect to air rights, transport connections and networks, and border crossings. All of these factors therefore influence the capacity of destination development and international mobility within Asia, as well as in terms of long-distance travel. Indeed, intra-regional travel has become proportionately more important over time with respect to tourism growth.

Membership of Asian political institutions is therefore an important element in the development of Asian identities, as well as a signifier of Asian space. Table 1.3 records a number of these institutions and their memberships. One of the notable observations is that there has been a far longer tradition of international cooperation in supranational bodies among European nations as compared to Asia, but to a great extent this may be a reflection of the relatively short history of nationhood and the influence of colonial powers on international relations in Asia. Nevertheless, the development of "Asian" institutions has historically tended to be more focused on East Asia than on western Asia. Indeed, it is noticeable that the United Nations has a separate economic and social commission for West Asia which, with the exception of the Islamic Republic of Iran and, to an extent, Turkey, comprises those countries that in European parlance would be described as the "Middle East".

The break-up of the former Soviet Union has led to the emergence of a number of new states that have now become members of the Asian Development Bank (ADB) and the UN Economic and Social Commission for the Asia-Pacific (UNESCAP). Several of these states have also joined the central and western Asian economic grouping known as the Economic Cooperation Organization and the interregional Black Sea Economic Cooperation group, while the Gulf States excluding Iran and Iraq have their own economic grouping. But the confused nature of cultural and geographical identity is illustrated by the fact that several of the countries of western Asia that were formerly part of the Soviet Union – Armenia, Azerbaijan, Georgia and Kazakhstan – are playing in the UEFA (Union of European Football Associations) nations championship, while Georgia and Armenia have expressed interest in becoming members of the European Union. It is also worth noting that with respect to the Olympic sports movement, only Kazakhstan of the above-mentioned nations participates in the Asian Games run under the auspices of the Olympic Council of Asia (OCA).

To the east there is also confusion as to the extent to which the Pacific Islands (sometimes referred to, together with Australia and New Zealand, as Oceania) and the Pacific Rim are also a part of the Asian experience (Hall & Page 1996). The APEC forum is perhaps the clearest example of these institutional linkages, although the extent to which observer status of ASEAN and the East Asia Summit has been extended also illustrates the expansion of the concept of Asia. Here again, sport indicates some interesting changes, as in 2007 Australia competed in the Asian Nations Cup after shifting in 2006 from the Oceania Football Federation. Although Australia is unlikely to compete in the Asian Games in the foreseeable future, the shift to playing football in an Asian context for both club and country raises interesting issues of identity for such a sports-focused country. In one sense a shifting in sporting focus follows changes in political focus. As Jain (2004) observed, the 2002 Bali bombings forced the conservative Australian government under Prime Minister John Howard to engage with Asia in a much more involved way that it had previously espoused under its foreign policy settings. Nevertheless, Howard's clear alignment with the United States and, to a lesser extent, the United Kingdom means that, as with Australia playing football in Asia, involvement in Asia is presently based on highly pragmatic as opposed to ideological grounds. As Jain (2004: 13) noted, Howard's 'government seeks little convergence between Australian values and Asian values and appears to be blind to the strategic value of goodwill that Australia had finally managed to begin building under the previous administration, which has now been squandered'.

There are also significant changes in terms of the growing interrelationships between Asian countries. Although the countries of South Asia have been especially slow in achieving economic integration as compared to those of ASEAN, it is noticeable that India and Pakistan have been given a stronger role in ASEAN affairs as well as being invited to participate in Asia–Europe meetings; therefore, potentially providing something of a complementary role to that played by China, Japan and South Korea in East Asian affairs.

Table 1.3 Membership of select Asian political, economic and sporting institutions

Institution	Description	Member countries
Association of Southeast Asian Nations (ASEAN)	Originally a 1967 defence agreement between the original members of ASEAN: Indonesia, Malaysia, Philippines, Singapore and Thailand. The association was transformed into a trade relationship in 1992.	Brunei, Cambodia, Indonesia, Laos, Malaysia, Myanmar, Philippines, Singapore, Thailand, Vietnam. Observers at ASEAN meetings include Australia, China, India, Japan, New Zealand, Pakistan and South Korea. Bangladesh and Fiji have sought observer status. Timor-Leste and Papua New Guinea are ASEAN candidate/observer states.
ASEAN Plus Three	Forum that functions to assist cooperation between ASEAN and three East Asian nations.	ASEAN nations and China, Japan and South Korea.
Asia–Europe Meeting (ASEM)	Interregional forum established in 1996 between the European Union and the members of the ASEAN Plus Three grouping.	India, Pakistan and Mongolia were invited to participate in the 2006 and future meetings. Further additions have been Australia and New Zealand in 2010, and Bangladesh in 2012.
Asia Europe Foundation	Cultural and education complement to the Asia–Europe Meeting.	Asia–Pacific countries include: Australia, Bangladesh, Brunei, Cambodia, China, India, Indonesia, Japan, Kazakhstan, Korea, Lao PDR, Malaysia, Mongolia, Myanmar, New Zealand, Pakistan, Philippines, Russian Federation, Singapore, Thailand, Vietnam.
East Asia Summit	Pan-Asian forum first held in 2005.	The ASEAN Plus Three plus Australia, India and New Zealand. In 2010 it was discussed that the roles for Russia and the United States may be to create a new grouping "ASEAN + 8" including the East Asia Summit members together with the United States and Russia. Proposed members currently include Papua New Guinea and Timor-Leste.
Asia-Pacific Trade Agreement (APTA)	Commenced 1975. China joined 2001.	Bangladesh, China, India, Lao PDR, Republic of Korea, Sri Lanka, Mongolia.
Asia-Pacific Economic Cooperation (APEC)	Economic forum established in 1989.	Australia, Brunei, Canada, Chile, Chinese Taipei (Taiwan), Hong Kong China, Indonesia, Japan, Malaysia, Mexico, New Zealand, Papua New Guinea, People's Republic of China, Peru, Philippines, Russia, Singapore, South Korea, Thailand, United States, Vietnam.

Organization	Description	Members
Asia Development Bank	Regional development bank established 1966.	Afghanistan, Armenia, Australia, Azerbaijan, Bangladesh, Bhutan, Brunei Darussalam, Cambodia, Cook Islands, Federated States of Micronesia, Fiji, Georgia, Hong Kong China, India, Indonesia, Japan, Kazakhstan, Republic of Korea, Kyrgyz Republic, Lao People's Democratic Republic, Kiribati, Malaysia, Maldives, Marshall Islands, Mongolia, Myanmar, Nauru, Nepal, New Zealand, Pakistan, Palau, Papua New Guinea, People's Republic of China, Philippines, Samoa, Singapore, Solomon Islands, Sri Lanka, Taipai China (Taiwan), Tajikstan, Thailand, Timor-Leste, Tonga, Turkmenistan, Tuvalu, Uzbekistan, Socialist Republic of Vietnam, Vanuatu. Countries from other regions: Austria, Belgium, Canada, Denmark, Finland, France, Germany, Ireland, Italy, Luxembourg, Netherlands, Norway, Portugal, Spain, Sweden, Switzerland, Turkey, United Kingdom, United States.
UN Economic and Social Commission for Asia and the Pacific (ESCAP)		Afghanistan, Armenia, Australia, Azerbaijan, Bangladesh, Bhutan, Brunei Darussalam, Cambodia, Federated States of Micronesia, Fiji, France, Georgia, India, Indonesia, Islamic Republic of Iran, Japan, Kazakhstan, Kiribati, Republic of Korea, Kyrgyz Republic, Lao PDR, Malaysia, Maldives, Marshall Islands, Mongolia, Myanmar, Nauru, Nepal, Netherlands, New Zealand, North Korea, Pakistan, Palau, Papua New Guinea, People's Republic of China, Philippines, Russian Federation, Samoa, Singapore, Solomon Islands, Sri Lanka, Tajikstan, Thailand, Timor-Leste, Tonga, Turkey, Turkmenistan, Tuvalu, United Kingdom, United States of America, Uzbekistan, Socialist Republic of Vietnam, Vanuatu. Associate members: American Samoa, Commonwealth of the Northern Mariana Islands, Cook Islands, French Polynesia, Guam, Hong Kong China, Macao China, New Caledonia, Nuie.
Economic Cooperation Organization	Founded by Iran, Pakistan and Turkey in 1995.	Afghanistan, Azerbaijan, Islamic Republic of Iran, Kazakhstan, Kyrgyzstan, Pakistan, Tajikstan, Turkey, Turkmenistan, Uzbekistan.
Black Sea Economic Cooperation	Founded 1992.	Albania, Armenia, Azerbaijan, Bulgaria, Georgia, Greece, Republic of Moldova, Romania, Russian Federation, Turkey, Ukraine.
Gulf Cooperation Council	Founded 1981.	Bahrain, Kuwait, Oman, Qatar, Saudi Arabia, United Arab Emirates.

(Continued overleaf)

Table 1.3 (continued)

Institution	Description	Member countries
UN Economic and Social Commission for Western Asia	Founded 1973.	Bahrain, Egypt, Iraq, Jordan, Kuwait, Lebanon, Libya, Mauritania, Morocco, Oman, Palestine, Qatar, Saudi Arabia, Sudan, Syrian Arab Republic, Tunisia, United Arab Emirates, Yemen.
South Asian Association for Regional Cooperation (SAARC)	Founded 1985.	Afghanistan, People's Republic of Bangladesh, Kingdom of Bhutan, Republic of India, Republic of Maldives, Kingdom of Nepal, Islamic Republic of Pakistan, Democratic Socialist Republic of Sri Lanka.
Asian Football Confederation	Founded in 1954, it is the governing body of association football (soccer) in Asia and Australia (joined 2006). Azerbaijan, Armenia, Georgia, Israel, Kazakhstan, Russia and Turkey are members of UEFA (Europe).	West Asian Football Federation (WAFF): Bahrain, Iraq, Jordan, Kuwait, Lebanon, Oman, Palestine, Qatar, Saudi Arabia, Syria, United Arab Emirates, Yemen. Central Asian Football Association (CAFA): Afghanistan, Iran, Kyrgyzstan, Tajikistan, Turkmenistan, Uzbekistan. South Asian Football Federation (SAFF): Bangladesh, Bhutan, India, Maldives, Nepal, Pakistan, Sri Lanka. East Asian Football Federation (EAFF): China, Guam, Hong Kong, Japan, North Korea, South Korea, Macau, Mongolia, Northern Mariana Islands, Chinese Taipei. ASEAN Football Federation (AFF): Australia, Brunei, Cambodia, Indonesia, Laos, Malaysia, Myanmar, Philippines, Singapore, Thailand, Timor-Leste, Vietnam.

Tourism-specific bodies for the region tend to have a marked East Asia–Pacific Rim orientation. The United Nations World Tourism Organization (UNWTO) organises member states by six regions – Africa, Americas, East Asia and the Pacific, Europe, Middle East and South Asia (Table 1.4). As of November 2007 there were 16 full members and two associate members of the UNWTO East Asia and the Pacific region, nine full members of South Asia, and 12 full members of the Middle East and one observer. Unlike the UN categories for the social and economic commissions, Libya is included in the Middle East region by the UNWTO. Western Asian countries such as Armenia, Azerbaijan, Georgia, Kazakhstan, Kyrgyzstan, Turkmenistan and Uzbekistan are members of the UNWTO's Europe region, along with countries such as the Russian Federation and Turkey that occupy both European and Asian geographical, economic and political space. The self-declared leader of the tourism industry in the Asia-Pacific region is PATA, the Pacific Asia Travel Association. Established in 1952 at the First Pacific Area Travel Conference the association is an organisation that represents a range of industry sector, government and other interests, e.g. education, financial services and media, in tourism. According to PATA (2007a), its goal 'is to help members develop and increase business opportunities through a wide array of products, such as events, market intelligence, communications, networking and industry-wide recognition and exposure through the prestigious PATA brand'. However, in governmental terms PATA primarily consists of East Asian, Australasian and Pacific Island members (Table 1.4) although the Asia-Pacific map on its website (PATA 2007b) records a sphere of interest ranging from the Americas (although Hawaii is the only government which has an organisation representing it) through to Pakistan in the west (a member), and Russia and the central Asian republics of Kyrgyzstan, Kazakhstan and Turkistan, none of which have government agencies as members of PATA.

The "Asian" political and economic community is therefore increasingly centred on East Asia, with growing interconnections with South Asia and Australia, and to a lesser extent New Zealand and other members of the Pacific community. The growing economic interdependence between these countries and regions, including tourism, has been mooted as heralding the potential development of an Asian economic community to rival that of the European Union. Although the Asian process lies many years behind the European experience of economic integration, the identification of an "Asian" community and its associated new regulatory space remains an important component of the reorganisation of economic space in Asia and the Pacific Rim (Park 2003). Moreover, such economic and political relations have considerable potential to influence the cultural sphere and the development of new mobilities within Asia. East Asian geographies and regulatory spaces in particular, along with associated travel flows, are being increasingly extended to South Asia and to Australia and New Zealand. However, institutionally, western Asia is only weakly linked to southern and eastern Asia and is not a part of discourses on Asian identity, instead tending to participate more in discourses with respect to Islamic and Arabic identity (Hall 2009). The concept of an Asian identity is primarily being constructed by the countries and institutions of East and South Asia, particularly through the Asia–Europe meeting, ASEAN and, to a lesser extent, APEC. However, the new institutions of Asia are also representative of a rapidly growing dense set of new regulatory spaces that espouse Asian identity which not only serve to reinforce the social construction of Asia but have a very practical effect on mobilities and citizenship. Such institutions are significant in terms of media representation and notions of otherness but, more particularly, may have a long-term influence of flows of tourists to and from Asia, given that the political-economic frameworks that facilitate international trade also facilitate flows of tourists thereby further leading to changes in understanding of identity and region.

Table 1.4 Membership of tourism bodies

Organisation	Members
UNWTO	
East Asia and the Pacific	Australia, Brunei Barussalam, Cambodia, China, Democratic People's Republic of Korea (North Korea), Fiji, Indonesia, Japan, Lao PDR, Malaysia, Mongolia, Myanmar, Papua New Guinea, Philippines, Republic of Korea, Samoa, Thailand, Timor-Leste, Vanuatu, Vietnam. Associate members: Hong Kong, China; Macao, China
South Asia	Afghanistan, Bangladesh, Bhutan, India, Islamic Republic of Iran, Maldives, Nepal, Pakistan, Sri Lanka
Middle East	Bahrain, Egypt, Iraq, Jordan, Kuwait, Lebanon, Libyan Arab Jamahiriya, Oman, Qatar, Saudi Arabia, Syrian Arab Republic, United Arab Emirates, Yemen. Observer: Palestine
PATA (Pacific Asia Travel Association)	Abu Dhabi Tourism & Culture Authority, Bangladesh Tourism Board, Canadian Tourism Commission, China National Tourism Administration, Consulate General of the Republic of Indonesia, Cook Islands Tourism Corporation, Fiji Visitors Bureau, FSM Visitors Board – Department of Resources & Development Micronesia, Government of India Tourist Office, Government of Timor-Leste, Guam Visitors Bureau, Hong Kong Tourism Board, India Tourism Development Corporation Ltd (ITDC), India Tourism, Indonesia Tourism Authority Office, Japan Travel Bureau, Korea International Travel Company Office, Korea National Tourism Organization, Macao Government Tourism Office, Marianas Visitors Authority, Ministry of Foreign Affairs, Government of Pakistan, Ministry of Hotels & Tourism, Republic of the Union of Myanmar, Ministry of Information, Culture and Tourism Lao, Ministry of Tourism Indonesia, Ministry of Tourism Cambodia, Ministry of Tourism Government of India, Ministry of Tourism Maldives, National Tourism Administration DPR Korea, Nepal Tourism Board, Office du Tourisme de Tahiti, Pakistan Tourism Development Corporation, Palau Visitors Authority, Papua New Guinea Tourism Promotion Authority, Philippine Department of Tourism, Samoa Tourism Authority, Solomon Islands Visitors Bureau, Sri Lanka Tourism, Sri Lanka Tourist Board, Tahiti Tourisme, Taiwan Tourism Bureau, Thailand Convention & Exhibition Bureau, Tibet Tourism Development Committee, Tonga Visitors Bureau, Tourism Australia, Tourism Authority of Thailand, Tourism Bureau, Chinese Taipei, Tourism Commission the Government of the Hong Kong Special Administrative Region, Tourism Council of Bhutan, Tourism Fiji, Tourism Infrastructure and Enterprise Zone Authority (TIEZA) Philippines, Tourism Malaysia, Tourism New Zealand, Vietnam National Administration of Tourism (VNAT)

Context and issues

Tourism in Asia has undergone a dramatic growth and significant change since its recognition by governments as an economic development mechanism from the 1970s onwards (Hall & Page 2000; Dolezal & Trupp 2015). Nevertheless, the understanding of tourism in Asia must go hand-in-hand with other significant social, political, economic and environmental changes in the region. Many of these elements are discussed in chapters in this first section of the volume. However, several overarching elements will be briefly discussed here.

Economy

The Asia economy, and particularly the South and East Asian economies, has been among the best performing in the world in terms of GDP growth since the 1980s. However, after 2012 economic growth in the region began experiencing a "new normal" in terms of somewhat lower growth than had been the case previously. Although economic growth in Asia still generally remains higher than that of any other region in the world, after a strong initial recovery in 2010/11 from the global financial and economic crises that began in 2008, growth has been considerably lower compared with the pre-crisis average. Economic growth in the period 2012–2014 averaged 5.2% annually, while the average in the period 2005–2007 was 9.4% (UNESCAP 2016). China has also become increasingly critical to the regional economy, accounting for 40% of the GDP in the Asia-Pacific, as UNESCAP (2016: 4) noted: 'even a small change in its GDP growth estimates will result in a considerable impact on the region's growth outlook'.

Population and urbanisation

The twenty-first century is the urban century: the first in which the number of people living in towns and cities is greater than those living in rural areas. In 2014, 55% of the global urban population was living in Asia and the Pacific. Although urbanisation rates in Asia are lower than in other parts of the world (North America 81.5%, Latin America and the Caribbean 79.5%, Europe 73.4%), by 2018 the population of Asia is expected to become more than 50% urban. The speed of population increase and urbanisation in Asia is unprecedented. The urban population of the region more than doubled between 1950 and 1975, and doubled again between 1975 and 2000. It is projected to almost double once more between 2000 and 2025 (UNHabitat & UNESCAP 2015). Between 1980 and 2010, the region's cities grew by around one billion people. United Nations projections show they will add another one billion by 2040. By 2050, urban areas will account for nearly two out of three people in Asia (UNHabitat & UNESCAP 2015). However, as has been long noted (Asian Development Bank 1998), the region's:

> impressive urban façades often mask enormous vulnerabilities and inequalities. It is no secret that the region is home to some of the world's most polluted and unhealthy cities. Moreover, its cities are among the most vulnerable to natural disasters and the projected impacts of climate change. Almost three-quarters of the worldwide fatalities of disasters between 1970 and 2011 occurred in the Asia and Pacific region.
>
> *(UNHabitat & UNESCAP 2015: 10)*

Megacities (cities exceeding ten million inhabitants) are becoming increasingly commonplace, with Asia being home to 17 megacities, three of them the world's largest: Tokyo, Delhi and Shanghai. By 2030 Asia is projected to have at least 22 megacities. However, as UNHabitat and UNESCAP (2015: 12) note, 'contrary to common perception, only a little over 10 percent of the Asia and Pacific region's urban population actually lives in megacities'.

The region's urbanisation also has important direct and indirect implications for tourism: direct in that cities are significant destinations (Table 1.5) and tourist-generating regions as well as being vital transport hubs, and indirect through the development of urban policies that affect tourism, the role of formal and informal employment in tourism and hospitality, contribution to economic development, and the role of the urban environment in attraction, experience and competitiveness. The relationship between the level of urbanisation and the level of domestic economic development in Asia indicates a strong correlation, although the causal link between the two is not clear-cut, and the benefits of economic development are also unevenly distributed (UNHabitat & UNESCAP 2015). For example, in examining urban tourism in Asia the UNWTO (2009) noted that up to 40% of the population of large urban centres in Asia were living in poverty. In extreme cases, cities like Mumbai, with 18 million people, had 54% of its population living in poverty.

Table 1.5 Asia's top ten destination cities by international overnight visitors

Rank	City	Estimated population ('000)*	International overnight visitors (million)					Change 2013–14 (%)	Estimated visitor spending 2014 (US$ billion)
			2010	2011	2012	2013	2014*		
1	Bangkok	14,998	10.4	13.8	15.8	18.5	16.4	−11.0	13.00
2	Singapore	5,625	8.8	10.1	11.1	12.1	12.5	3.1	14.30
3	Kuala Lumpur	7,088	8.9	9.0	9.3	9.6	10.8	13.1	8.10
4	Hong Kong	7,246	8.1	8.4	8.4	8.3	8.8	7.0	8.30
5	Seoul	23,480	6.1	6.6	7.5	8.2	8.6	4.7	11.50
6	Taipei	7,438	3.5	4.0	4.7	5.8	6.3	8.4	10.80
7	Shanghai	23,416	6.7	6.2	6.0	5.7	6.1	7.6	5.30
8	Tokyo	37,843	4.5	2.9	4.1	5.0	5.4	6.5	7.40
9	Mumbai	20,741	4.0	3.8	4.0	4.6	4.9	5.9	3.30
10	Beijing	19,520	4.5	4.8	4.6	4.0	4.4	9.2	4.20

Sources: Demographia 2015; MasterCard, Global Destination Index 2014 in UNHabitat & UNESCAP 2015; UNDESA 2014.
Note
* Using urban area population estimates; may differ from administrative area estimates.

Population growth itself also has implications for tourism growth. The UNWTO (2010) observed that by 2030, the world population will have reached 8.3 billion, and 18% of that growth will have come from Asia. The report suggested that in 2030, China will comprise 17% of the world population and India 17.9%, which will alter the global dynamic of outbound tourism, especially at an intra-regional level. From a tourism perspective, Ashworth and Page (2011: 13) argued that:

> Global change and capital is altering the landscape and rationale of many cities but the emergence of world cities also has profound implications for tourism as both an industry, support for world city status and as a tool used by the public and private sector to competitively raise the global position of a world city. The scale of world cities and their built environment gives rise to a complex mosaic of microgeographies of tourism which are emerging, in part, based on notions such as cultural quarters, districts and areas with common characteristics for consumption by specific user groups (which sometimes blur the distinction between tourist, day tripper and resident).

Consequently, many Asian world cities as gateways to the wider sub-regions of tourism within different countries are developing distinctive geographies and characteristics within these emergent global city landscapes.

Plate 1.1 Tourism, leisure and the creation of new spaces of urban consumption I: Sun City, Kuala Lumpur.

Plate 1.2 Tourism, leisure and the creation of new spaces of urban consumption II: Fisherman's Wharf, Macau.

Plate 1.3 Tourism, leisure and the creation of new spaces of urban consumption III: Christmas shopping in Singapore.

Plate 1.4 Tourism, leisure and the creation of new spaces of urban consumption IV: cosmopolitan eating options in Da'an district, Taipei.

Box 1.1 The Asian economy: a snapshot in 2016

Economic growth in the Asia-Pacific region is markedly less robust compared to the years before and immediately after the global financial and economic crisis that started in 2008. Developing economies in the Asia-Pacific region grew by an estimated 4.5% in 2015, the lowest rate since 2010, and only a modest rebound to 5% growth is forecast for 2016.

Rapid increases in household and corporate debt in some economies pose risks for financial stability and economic growth prospects. Thailand's household debt is on a par with OECD levels and China now holds more corporate debt than the United States.

Despite much progress having been achieved in poverty reduction, significant inequalities of incomes and opportunities remain in many economies of the region, hampering the achievement of broader development goals.

Source: UNESCAP 2016: iii–iv

The Handbook and its structure and content

The Handbook is an ambitious survey of the region and its continued growth and development as a key tourism region as a receiver and generator of tourism, with a high proportion of intra-regional travel. The book is divided into five sections. This first section provides an introduction to the region and offers a context to the nationally focused chapters. The next three sections are then broadly based on the three UNWTO Asian regions: South-East Asia, South and Central Asia and East and North-East Asia. As noted above, these three regional units also relate strongly to growth economic regionalism, political differences over territory and assertions of nationalism notwithstanding.

Douglas and Douglas (2000) highlighted the term Asia and its mystical alternative to European eyes at least – "the Orient". This European construct illustrates the powerful influence of colonial powers and the past on modern-day tourism. The history of travel to the region dates to at least Marco Polo's thirteenth-century travel, with its focus on trade. Other studies like Shackley (2006) highlight the historical development of global tourism, and its link to voyages of discovery, conquest, sequestration and subjugation as part of European colonisation and mercantilism. Asia was no exception to this and despite the post-war decolonisation of Asia, the history of conflict (and examples of re-colonisation by Western tourism), trade and resources exploitation epitomise the history of travel and tourism in Asia prior to the boom in international arrivals in the 1980s and 1990s. Initial travel to the region by sea, steamships and more latterly on cruise ships depicts the changing impact of technology on travel. Other advances in land-based transport, especially the European-sponsored railways, to carry the spoils of Empire have subsequently been turned to mass forms of domestic tourist travel, most notably in India. The growth of hospitality and hosting generated a new dimension to colonialism and was the root of the modern-day tourism and hospitality sector. Colonisation, with road and rail construction, created opportunities for mobility that pre-date modern-day tourism and yet the colonial infrastructure often has a key role to play in shaping modern-day tourism patterns.

It is therefore apposite that this section of the book should be focused on the impact and implications of this historical growth and development of tourism through Asia's colonial and post-colonial path to independence and globalisation (Lo & Marcotullio 2000). Chapter 2 is a fresh and provocative survey of the political issues around Asian tourism, highlighting the key themes of heritage and diplomacy. Chapter 3 analyses the fundamental importance of transport, accessibility and mobility within tourism. The focus on air travel underpins the key driver of mass international inbound and outbound travel. Yet running in parallel to this is the importance of the major consequences of motorisation of transport within the destination and impact on urban and destination pollution. In many Asian high-density cities, debates are long running on the constrained transport choices for residents and tourists alike. As Schafer and Victor (2000) argued, these limited choices meant that many localised and entrepreneurial solutions emerged. Importantly, these could also accommodate both tourists and locals. For example, in India's largest cities motorised and non-motorised options are extremely important (e.g. buses, auto-rickshaws and cycle rickshaws, minivans and taxis). However, in many of Asia's rapidly expanding and most high-density cities, many of the traditional modes of transport are being affected by cars, changes in consumer preferences and a drive for modernity. As urban populations grow, this is creating a crisis of urban transport and mobility that is impacting on local populations as well as urban tourism and the wider environment (Singh, 2006; Reddy & Balachandra, 2012; Loo & Li, 2012).

From a development perspective, the implications of the major growth spurt generated by the tourism arrivals since the 1980s has created a demand for high-skilled labour to service tourist needs. This is the subject of Chapter 4, analysing the challenges within Asia. This in itself is increasingly interconnected with Chapter 5, focusing on policy and political issues, since the impact of foreign direct investment to facilitate tourism development and growth does not always benefit local people in terms of employment growth as much as had been expected (Sheng 2011). This is often highlighted when mega-events are hosted and new infrastructure built without a substantive long-term impact on employment and economic growth (Colantonio *et al.* 2013). An important corollary of the failure of policy and planning is the environmental impact of tourism development in Asia. As Chapter 6 demonstrates, growth at a rapid pace, especially in many dense urban areas and countries such as China, has had a detrimental and irreversible impact on nature and the environment. In Chapter 7, the counter-balance to the environmental impact of tourism development is the impact on people and society. The chapter addresses the consequences of rapid growth on the society and culture, where contributing to natural economic development objectives outweighs the needs of preserving local identities, culture and heritage. One controversial and yet increasingly popular strategy being pursued in many Asian destinations to justify tourism and the creation of benefits for local people is pro-poor tourism (PPT) (Phommavong & Sörensson 2014; Truong *et al.* 2014). This is the focus of Chapter 8, which critiques this PPT approach that seeks to harness the benefits of tourism to address the endemic poverty that exists in many parts of Asia.

In any one book, it is impossible to realistically separate out the holistic nature of the impact and overall consequences of the changes induced by tourism from those arising from other social, economic, political and environmental forces, particularly in a region such as Asia which is undergoing rapid change. However, for the purposes of understanding the intricacies, effects and significance of tourism in different regions, countries, places and in different times, one is usually forced to look at the existing model of tourism development in a regional and global context and the various facets and systematic dimensions of the "tourism experience" and development in the region. Only by segmenting tourism into various facets (e.g. historical dimensions, social and cultural impacts, economics, policy, transportation, politics, environment) can one begin to appreciate how the development patterns of tourism have emerged in the different countries and regions. In this respect, the chapters which follow examine tourism in more detail within particular different spatial, economic, political, environmental and cultural contexts to begin to reconstruct the patterns of tourism development that have occurred, what is currently happening and some of the prospects for future growth and development in the region.

This book, like tourism itself, is spatially and temporally uneven with respect to what can be covered. Nevertheless, the ensuing chapters seek to provide readers with a valuable snapshot of tourism at various scales, and from various approaches and positions. The breadth of the chapters and the range of subjects and authors are therefore part of this desire to present a range of perspectives and understanding of the processes and forces shaping tourism in this fascinating and dynamic region of global tourism activity.

Key reading

UNESCAP (2016) *Economic and Social Survey of Asia and the Pacific 2015: Year-End Update.* Bangkok: United Nations.

United Nations Human Settlements Programme (UNHabitat) and United Nations Economic and Social Commission for Asia and the Pacific (UNESCAP) (2015) *The State of Asian and Pacific Cities 2015: Urban Transformations Shifting from Quantity to Quality.* Bangkok: UNESCAP.

Winter, T. (2009) 'Asian tourism and the retreat of Anglo-western centrism in tourism theory', *Current Issues in Tourism*, 12(1): 21–31.

Winter, T., Teo, P. and Chang, T.C. (eds) (2008) *Asia on Tour: Exploring the Rise of Asian Tourism.* London: Routledge.

Pacific Asia Travel Association (founded in 1951, the Pacific Asia Travel Association (PATA) is a not-for-profit membership-based organisation promoting tourism and the interests of the tourism industry in the Asia-Pacific region): www.pata.org

UNWTO: www.unwto.org

World Travel & Tourism Council: www.wttc.org

Acknowledgement

A much earlier version of the section on 'Defining Asia' was presented at the conference 'Of Asian origin: Rethinking tourism in contemporary Asia' by Michael Hall, which took place at the National University of Singapore in Singapore in 2006. Feedback received at the conference and subsequently is gratefully acknowledged.

References

Ashworth, G. and Page, S.J. (2011) 'Urban tourism research: Recent progress and current paradoxes', *Tourism Management*, 32(1): 1–15.

Asian Development Bank (1998) *The Development and Management of Asian Megacities.* Manila: Asian Development Bank.

Barclay, K. and Smith, G. (2013) 'Introduction: The international politics of resources', *Asian Studies Review*, 37(2): 125–140.

Barr, M.D. (2000) 'Lee Kuan Yew and the "Asian values" debate', *Asian Studies Review*, 24(3): 309–334.

Beeson, M. and Yoshimatsu, H. (2007) Asia's odd men out: Australia, Japan and the politics of regionalism. *International Relations of the Asia-Pacific*, 7(2): 227–250.

Bianchi, R. and Stephenson, M. (2014) *Tourism and Citizenship: Rights, Freedoms and Responsibilities in the Global Order.* Abingdon: Routledge.

Broinowski, A. (2003) *About Face: Asian Accounts of Australia.* Melbourne: Scribe Publications.

Chong, A. (2004) 'Singaporean foreign policy and the Asian values debate, 1992–2000: Reflections on an experiment in soft power', *The Pacific Review*, 17(1): 95–133.

Colantonio, A., Burdett, R. and Rode, P. (2013) *Transforming Urban Economies: Policy Lessons from European and Asian Cities.* Abingdon: Routledge.

Coles, T. (2008) 'Citizenship and the state: Hidden features in the internationalisation of tourism', in T. Coles and C.M. Hall (eds), *Tourism and International Business* (pp. 55–69). London: Routledge.

de Jong, M. (2012) 'The pros and cons of Confucian values in transport infrastructure development in China', *Policy and Society*, 31(1): 13–24.

Demographia (2015) *Demographia World Urban Areas*, 11th annual edition. Belleville: Demographia.

Deshingkar, G. (1999) 'The construction of Asia in India', *Asian Studies Review*, 23(2): 173–180.

Dolezal, C. and Trupp, A. (2015) 'Tourism and development in Southeast Asia', *Austrian Journal of South-East Asian Studies*, 8(2): 117–124.

Douglas, N. and Douglas, N. (2000) 'Tourism in South and Southeast Asia: Historical dimensions', in C.M. Hall and S. Page (ed.), *Tourism in South and Southeast Asia: Issues and Cases* (pp. 29–44). Oxford: Butterworth Heinemann.

Frost, W., Laing, J. and Beeton, S. (2014) 'The future of nature-based tourism in the Asia-Pacific region', *Journal of Travel Research*, 53(6): 721–732.

Glassman, J. (2015) 'Emerging Asias: Transnational forces, developmental states, and "Asian values"', *The Professional Geographer*, DOI: 10.1080/00330124.2015.1099185.

Goxe, F. (2012) 'Innovation with "Chinese" characteristics? Reflecting on the implications of an ethnic-based paradigm of management and innovation', *Prometheus*, 30(2): 155–168.

Hall, C.M. (1994) *Tourism in the Pacific Rim*, 1st edn. South Melbourne: Longman Cheshire.

—— (2009) 'A long and still-unfinished story: Constructing and defining Asian regionalisms', in T. Winter, P. Teo and T.C. Chang (eds), *Asia on Tour: Exploring the Rise of Asian Tourism* (pp. 21–33). London: Routledge.

Hall, C.M. and Page, S.J. (eds) (1996) *Tourism in the Pacific*. London: International Thomson Publishing.

—— (eds) (2000) *Tourism in South and South-East Asia*. Oxford: Butterworth-Heinemann.

Han S.-J. (1999) 'Asian values: An asset or a liability', in Han Sung-Joo (ed.), *Changing Values in Asia: Their Impact on Governance and Development* (pp. 3–9). Tokyo: Japan Center for International Exchange.

Henderson, J.C. (2015) 'The new dynamics of tourism in South East Asia: Economic development, political change and destination competitiveness', *Tourism Recreation Research*, 40(3): 379–390.

Isin, E.F. and Wood, P.K. (1999) *Citizenship and Identity*. London: Sage.

Jain, P. (2004) *Asia, Asian Values and Australia*, Asia Pacific Research Centre, Asia Pacific Papers No. 3.

Keating, P. (2000) *Engagement: Australia Faces the Asia-Pacific*. Sydney: Macmillan.

Kim, S.Y. (2010) 'Do Asian values exist? Empirical tests of the four dimensions of Asian values', *Journal of East Asian Studies*, 10(2): 315–344.

King, V.T. (2015) 'Encounters and mobilities: Conceptual issues in tourism studies in Southeast Asia', *SOJOURN: Journal of Social Issues in Southeast Asia,* 30(2): 497–527.

Kingsbury, D. (2008) 'Universalism and exceptionalism in "Asia"', in D. Kingsbury and L. Avonius (eds), *Human Rights in Asia* (pp. 19–39). New York: Palgrave Macmillan.

Lew, A.A., Hall, C.M. and Timothy, D.J. (2015) *World Regional Geography: Human Mobilities, Tourism Destinations, Sustainable Environments*, 2nd edn. Phoenix: Kendall Hunt.

Lo, F.C. and Marcotullio, P.J. (2000) 'Globalisation and urban transformations in the Asia-Pacific region: A review', *Urban Studies*, 37(1): 77–111.

Loo, B.P. and Li, L. (2012) 'Carbon dioxide emissions from passenger transport in China since 1949: Implications for developing sustainable transport', *Energy Policy*, 50: 464–476.

MacCormick, N. (1996) 'Liberalism, nationalism and the postsovereign state', *Political Studies,* 44(3): 553–567.

Milner, A. (2000) 'What's happened to Asian values?' in D. Goodman and G. Segal (eds), *Towards Recovery in Pacific Asia* (pp. 56–68). London: Routledge.

—— (2003). 'Asia-Pacific perceptions of the financial crisis: Lessons and affirmations'. *Contemporary Southeast Asia: A Journal of International and Strategic Affairs*, 25(2): 284–305.

Mohamad, M. (1999) *A New Deal For Asia*, Selang Darul Ehsan: Pelanduk Publications.

Morales-Moreno, I. (2004) 'Postsovereign governance in a globalizing and fragmenting world: The case of Mexico', *Review of Policy Research*, 21(1): 107–117.

Parfitt, T. and Wysocki, J. (2012) 'The meaning of work in neoliberal globalisation: The Asian exception?', *Third World Quarterly*, 33(1): 37–53.

Park, S.O. (2003) 'Economic spaces in the Pacific Rim: A paradigm shift and new dynamics', *Papers in Regional Science*, 82: 223–247.

PATA (2007a) 'Join PATA: Serious about the travel and tourism industry in Asia Pacific?' www.pata.org/patasite/index.php?id=13 (accessed 13 November 2007).

—— (2007b) 'About Asia Pacific'. www.pata.org/patasite/index.php?id=36 (accessed 13 November 2007).

Patten, C. (1998) *East and West*. London: Macmillan.

Phommavong, S. and Sörensson, E. (2014) 'Ethnic tourism in Lao PDR: Gendered divisions of labour in community-based tourism for poverty reduction', *Current Issues in Tourism*, 17(4): 350–362.

Pisanò, A. (2014) 'Human rights and sovereignty in the ASEAN path towards a human rights declaration', *Human Rights Review*, 15(4): 391–411.

Reddy, B.S. and Balachandra, P. (2012) 'Urban mobility: A comparative analysis of megacities of India', *Transport Policy*, 21: 152–164.

Roy, A. (2015) 'When is Asia?', *The Professional Geographer*, DOI:10.1080/00330124.2015.1099183.

Schafer, A. and Victor, D.G. (2000) 'The future mobility of the world population', *Transportation Research Part A: Policy and Practice*, 34(3): 171–205.

Shackley, M. (2006) *Atlas of Travel and Tourism Development*. Oxford: Butterworth-Heinemann.

Sheng, L. (2011) 'Foreign investment and urban development: A perspective from tourist cities', *Habitat International*, 35(1): 111–117.

Sheppard, E. (2015) 'Emerging Asias: Introduction', *The Professional Geographer*, DOI:10.1080/00330124.2015.1099182.

Singh, S.K. (2006) 'The demand for road-based passenger mobility in India: 1950–2030 and relevance for developing and developed countries', *European Journal of Transport and Infrastructure Research*, 6(3): 247–274.

Singh, S. (ed.) (2009) *Domestic Tourism in Asia: Diversity and Divergence*. London: Earthscan.

Suehiro, A. (1999) 'A Japanese perspective on the perception of "Ajia" from Eastern to Asian studies', *Asian Studies Review*, 23(2): 153–172.

Truong, V.D., Hall, C.M. and Garry, T. (2014) 'Tourism and poverty alleviation: Perceptions and experiences of poor people in Sapa, Vietnam', *Journal of Sustainable Tourism*, 22(7): 1071–1089.

UNESCAP (2016) *Economic and Social Survey of Asia and the Pacific 2015: Year-End Update*. Bangkok: United Nations.

United Nations Department of Economic and Social Affairs (UNDESA) (2014) *World Urbanisation Prospects: The 2014 Revision, Highlights*. New York: UNDESA.

United Nations Human Settlements Programme (UNHabitat) and United Nations Economic and Social Commission for Asia and the Pacific (UNESCAP) (2015) *The State of Asian and Pacific Cities 2015: Urban Transformations Shifting from Quantity to Quality*. Bangkok: UNESCAP.

UNWTO (2009) *Managing Metropolitan Tourism: An Asian Perspective*. Madrid: UNWTO.

—— (2010) *Demographic Change and Tourism*. Madrid: UNWTO.

—— (2015) *Tourism Highlights 2015*. Madrid: UNWTO.

—— (2016a) 'International tourist arrivals up 4% reach a record 1.2 billion in 2015', Press Release 16008, 18 January. Madrid: UNWTO.

—— (2016b) 'International tourist arrivals up 4% and reach a record 1.2 billion in 2015', *UNWTO Tourism Barometer* (Advance release), 14 (January). Madrid: UNWTO.

van Steenbergen, B. (1994) 'The condition of citizenship: An introduction', in B. van Steenbergen (ed.), *The Condition of Citizenship* (pp. 1–9). London: Sage.

Winter, T., Teo, P. and Chang, T.C. (eds) (2008) *Asia on Tour: Exploring the Rise of Asian Tourism*. London: Routledge.

Yang, J. and Lim, H.C. (2000) 'Asian values in capitalist development revisited', *Asian Perspective*, 24(3): 23–40.

Yapp, M.E. (1992) 'Europe in the Turkish mirror', *Past and Present*, 137: 134–155.

Yung, B. (2012) 'Road to good governance and modernization in Asia: "Asian values" and/or democracy?' *Journal of Asian Public Policy*, 5(3): 266–276.

2

Heritage diplomacy and tourism in Asia

Tim Winter

Introduction

This chapter explores the theme of heritage diplomacy in Asia in relation to the ongoing growth of intra-regional tourism. Today, cultural heritage is playing an increasingly important role in mediating relations between nations and states. Indeed, the desire to preserve and curate material culture has at once brought countries across the region together and simultaneously kept them apart. While extensive attention has been given to the ties between heritage and politics, the majority of the focus has been given to themes like conflict, destruction, post-war recovery and nationalism, with much less known about the ways in which the cultural past figures into diplomacy and diplomatic relations, both bilateral and multilateral. This chapter picks up such questions and highlights the role tourism – both domestic and intra-regional – plays in this space.

I suggest that increasing levels of Asian tourism since the early 2000s have been a contributing factor to the rise of cultural aid in the region. It will be seen that a number of countries have created programmes and institutions dedicated to heritage diplomacy, such that cultural sector assistance is now a feature of development aid and foreign policy strategies of governments. Fascinatingly, however, at the same time, the very idea of what constitutes "heritage" in Asia continues to expand, incorporating sites that are diplomatically sensitive. With Asia's growing cross-border mobility, the diplomatic entanglements between tourism and heritage thus become ever more complex. To explore such themes, the chapter presents a number of examples from South-East and East Asia, tracing the threads of diplomatic cooperation and contestation, and the role tourism plays therein.

Heritage tourism diplomacy

As we stood in line waiting for our turn at the lunch buffet, upon noticing that my conference badge indicated I was from the UK, the ambassador to the Government of Thailand enquired as to which temple I was adopting. Bemused and amused by the question, I indicated I wasn't actually planning to "adopt" any temple. It was 2000 and the conversation took place during one of the annual meetings of the International Coordinating Committee for the Safeguarding and Development of Angkor. As I learned over lunch, the Thai delegation had joined the Committee with the intention of assisting the Royal Government of Cambodia with the conservation and management of its premier archaeological site, hence the idea of "adopting" one of its temples. In equal measure, the ambassador was also bemused and somewhat amused by my interests, which centred around trying to understand what was going on in this space of cooperation, how it was politically configured, and the more abstract questions of how cultural aid figured into the reconstruction of a country ravaged by conflict and genocide. The cooperation between the Thais and Cambodians went ahead, and stones were "adopted". But less than ten years later things had changed dramatically. As relations broke down, the two countries started their own conflict over the ownership of antiquity, and the territorial significance of archaeological remains located on a shared border. The addition of Preah Vihear to the World Heritage List in July 2008 under controversial circumstances reignited tensions that had rumbled on for a century. The site's listing came at a politically charged moment for both countries, as each headed towards national elections. Inflammatory language by politicians meant the issue featured heavily in political campaigns on either side of the border. Over the following weeks tensions escalated and the two countries moved hundreds of troops and heavy military equipment into the border area. The standoff lasted several months, and in October the two sides exchanged fire, resulting in the death of three Cambodians and the wounding of seven Thai soldiers. Over the coming months and years fighting continued, with flash points and more deaths occurring during 2009 and 2010. The following year fighting intensified and spread further along the border, with hundreds more civilian and military deaths reported. Tanks, rocket launchers and even cluster munitions were among the weapons deployed during the fighting. The election of a new government in Thailand in August 2011 marked a release in the tensions and a significant drop in violence, and a resumption of more peaceful, albeit fragile, relations. It was a situation that had multiple contributory factors that lay far beyond domestic politics including a desire by both sides to control the development of the site as a high-value tourist destination.

Not surprisingly, Preah Vihear garnered considerable media and academic attention (e.g., see Buss 2010; Silverman 2011; Tanaka 2012; Wagener 2011). In that respect it was yet another example of cultural heritage in conflict; a theme that has become the subject of numerous conferences, books, PhDs and documentaries since the late 1990s. Interest has been fuelled by global media coverage of the destruction of material culture under conditions of conflict in the Balkans, Iraq and Afghanistan, to name a few. Within academia, such events have been interrogated via the frameworks of critical archaeology theory, heritage and museum studies, whereby interest has primarily revolved around reading the political in, and of, material culture through the lenses of contestation, dissonance and conflict (Bevan 2006; Holtorf & Kristensen 2015). By contrast, much less critical scrutiny has been given to the complex role heritage plays in international relations and cooperation, and the politics at play in one country "adopting" a temple owned by another. Indeed, and as I have argued elsewhere, there is a real need to better understand the multitude of ways in which the governance and conservation of the cultural past have been internationalised over the last 150 years or so, through complex structures of cooperation that emerged within and via shifting geopolitical and institutional conditions. UNESCO has become both the metaphor and metonym of the globalisation of heritage, understood as both discourse and material practice; a situation that has led to the complex interplay between the national and the international, and the cultural economies that shape these relations too often being missed.

For a variety of reasons, the last decade or so has seen a dramatic rise in heritage diplomacy in Asia. First, culture increasingly features within the discourses of developmental aid, and as such has become part of both bilateral agreements and multilateral structures of assistance. Second, huge investments have been undertaken to increase the level of economic and physical integration of the region. Trade has been the primary driver of cross- and sub-regional investments in rail, road, telecommunications and the infrastructure associated with a fast-growing international energy economy (Calder 2012). A third factor contributing to the emergence of new modes of cooperation has been the rise of interregional tourism and the growth of interest in culture and heritage from a rapidly expanding middle class.

The role tourism plays in this space requires careful consideration, and to begin exploring such issues it is first helpful to consider heritage diplomacy as a form of cultural diplomacy. For cultural diplomacy is the attempt 'to manage the international environment through making its (that nation's) cultural resources and achievements known overseas and/or facilitating cultural transmissions abroad' (Gienow-Hecht & Donfried 2010: 13). Indeed, in the international diplomatic arena, culture is used to convey affinities, bonds, dialogue, mutuality and other such values. Whilst acknowledging such factors, Albro (2012) suggests that we also need to consider cultural diplomacy in terms of cultural display. And it is the coupling of these various features that leads to the intertwining of heritage diplomacy and tourism. A careful reading of Angkor reveals this point, in that the network of international heritage conservation aid that solidified from the mid-1990s onwards reflected, in part, the dynamics of international tourism in the country. Key donors such as Japan, India, France, the US and Italy were also the countries that featured heavily in the visitor arrival statistics. More interestingly though – and an issue rarely acknowledged in the public discussion about the selection of sites for conservation assistance at Angkor – was the level of tourist visibility they offered. Structures such as carved walls, statues or individual buildings were often much more attractive for international conservation agencies if they were located on or close to tourist walkways or were popular as photographic spots. The most heavily visited, iconic temple complexes were also the sites that received the most international assistance. In such an arena of competition and cooperation, heritage diplomacy since World Heritage Listing has involved a politics of display. Signboards, scaffolding, vehicles and staff uniforms emblazoned with logos, along with visitor centres, have highlighted and explained not just the works being undertaken, but also the precise details of the financial assistance provided by governments or private donors from more than 15 countries. As the profile of international tourist arrivals changed – through the rise of an intra-regional tourism industry, most notably from South Korea and China – so too did the profile of international conservation assistance. With Angkor far from unique, this entangling between state-based cultural aid and intra-regional tourist mobility has been replicated elsewhere in the region, as Akagawa (2014) has demonstrated.

Indeed, in recent years, heritage conservation is fast emerging as an important component of the intra-regional economic and political ties that are binding states and populations in the Asia region. For a number of decades Japan has successfully utilised culture and cultural heritage as a mechanism for advancing its foreign policy and soft power strategy (Akagawa 2014). Within South and Southeast Asia alone, Japan currently has heritage-related projects in Afghanistan, Bangladesh, Cambodia, China, India, Laos, Mongolia, Myanmar, Nepal, Pakistan and Vietnam. Today, however, they are far from alone in folding heritage diplomacy into their bilateral and multilateral programmes of cooperation and aid. China, India and South Korea are among those spending heavily on heritage diplomacy to secure influence in the region. South Korea, for example, is investing in a number of institutions designed to provide expertise both domestically and overseas. The National Research Institute of Cultural Heritage now includes a division dedicated to international exchanges. Through a focus on Buddhist archaeological sites, collaborations with Mongolia, China and Japan have been underpinned by a discourse of shared heritage. Since 2005 the institute has been running a series of training programmes, with participants travelling from more than 15 Asian countries (e.g., see Sojung 2014). The Cultural Heritage Administration of Korea (CHA), an independent government agency since 1999, has also moved beyond its original domestic remit by signing nearly 60 bilateral agreements with organisations in 14 countries over the last decade or so. And in Doha in July 2014, representatives of the Ministry of Foreign Affairs and Korea ICOMOS used the opportunity of the World Heritage Committee meeting, attended by nearly 190 countries, to showcase a new strategy for international cooperation centred around embedding heritage into existing Official Development Assistance (ODA) strategies.

India is similarly expanding its cultural interests in Southeast Asia. For a number of years India has provided assistance to Indonesia, Thailand, Cambodia and Laos in an array of heritage sectors, including archaeology, textiles, museums and modern urban architecture (Chapman 2013). More recently, however, such forms of cooperation have been more explicitly mobilised as a mechanism for promoting economic and diplomatic relations, with Myanmar offering a case in point. Concerned by the growing influence of China in the country, the Indian government began folding archaeology into its official diplomatic visits from 2010 onwards, invoking ideas of mutual pasts to build trust and diplomatic ties. The Archaeological Survey of India offered assistance at Pagan, declaring it to be a sacred site 'whose architecture is similar to temples in Bengal and Orissa'. With the opening up of Myanmar's economy, the Indian government stepped up its trade and assistance packages, with Manmohan Singh being the first Indian prime minister to visit the country in 25 years in May 2012. While much of the talk focused on bilateral trade and cooperation in the agriculture, transportation and energy sectors, such proposals were couched in a wider context of cultural and political affinities. As noted above, this embedding of heritage aid is occurring in tandem with a rise in intra-regional aid and trade. The economic and political ascendency of the region over the last decade or so, most notably in East Asia and India, has been accompanied by a growth in intra-regional aid and soft loans, supplanting previous arrangements with governmental and non-governmental bodies located outside the region. As the volume by Dent and Dosch (2012) notes, a discourse of development driven primarily by bilateral and multilateral agencies headquartered in Europe or North America is being complemented, and in some cases replaced, by new forms of intra-regional cooperation. As a result, the cartographies of influence and power across the networks of heritage diplomacy are shifting steadily.

For all these countries, heritage tourism delivers significant opportunity. Each country in the region has a foreign policy agenda that revolves around a particular narrative image. As Anholt (2006) and Frew and White (2011) note, countries have come to see and advance themselves as brands. One of the ways in which states enact this is through using and constructing a cultural identity and national heritage. For a number of countries, including China, India, Saudi Arabia and Sri Lanka, to cite just a few, this sense of heritage extends far beyond the boundaries of the modern nation-state, and revolves around ideas of religion or civilisation that are defined by much larger geographies. Such cultural pasts can thus serve as a form of soft power, and heritage sites in other countries are among the places where this can be made visible. Both China and India, for example, have long looked to Southeast Asia as a region that carries legacies of their cultural and religious influences, with its archaeological sites and museums providing evidence of that. The provision of assistance with conservation is thus often driven and supported by strategies conceived back in Beijing and Delhi. For various reasons, World Heritage Sites offer particular opportunities. Invariably, they are among the most spectacular legacies of previous civilisations or cultural traditions, and have thus acquired considerable prestige internationally. As a result they are also likely to be pivotal in the cultural narrative of the host nation and state, and therefore carry considerable diplomatic benefit. But equally, they also tend to be the most popular tourist sites. More precisely, tourism is beneficial due to the variegated nature of the audiences it delivers. For countries such as India and Japan, heritage diplomacy enables them to communicate a message to the populations of countries like Indonesia, Laos, Myanmar and Cambodia via domestic tourism. In the case of India, this message might revolve around a sense of religious and civilisational affinity associated with histories of Buddhism and Hinduism. For Japan, while such cultural affinities might also be in play, providing aid in conservation and restoration enables them to present an image of peaceful engagement and a respect for the host culture. As others have documented, the concept of peace has been a central canon of Japanese government policy since World War II, and heritage diplomacy is merely one manifestation of a much larger programme. And as we shall see later, the idea of linking peace and heritage has also been adopted by the state for public diplomacy purposes within Japan itself. But with these same Japanese audiences travelling to other countries in the region, undertaking projects in South-East Asia also enables the state to communicate to its own citizens that it is acting responsibly in the region. Such gifts thus bestow honour and respect between states and citizens in multiple directions. Of course, the audiences for projects undertaken at sites like Angkor, Pagan and Borobudur are not limited to Japanese and domestic tourists. High-visibility heritage diplomacy projects reach a host of touristic audiences, communicating messages to tourists from China, the United States, Europe, Australia and elsewhere; visitors from countries and regions that are of strategic diplomatic importance.

Entangled diplomacies

One of the reasons why heritage diplomacy in Asia and its associations with tourism have received less attention than themes like contestation and conflict is in part down to the nature of the "heritage" deemed to be of national or "global" value. As countries in the region began adopting the prevailing international discourses, conventions and ideas about heritage of recent decades, they typically identified and promoted historically distant archaeological pasts, significant monuments or urban quarters as their heritage. For those countries undergoing the various transformations and social changes associated with post-colonial nation building, neoliberal globalisation, or disaster and conflict recovery, such processes have invariably been embedded with the narratives of ethnocultural nationalism. Whilst I recognise there are a number of notable exceptions, a broad survey of the modern heritage industry – as it emerged in the mid- to late twentieth century in Asia – reveals that the vast majority of these archaeological remains, architectural icons, and forms of "intangible heritage" have not been the subject of diplomatic tensions or international disputes.

However, in recent years this balance has begun to change in interesting and important ways, as more contentious and politically complex landscapes, buildings and other cultural forms have been put forward for national and world heritage status. The growing recognition of the material culture of the twentieth century is also bringing into focus histories of war and hostility which remain in the living memory, and thus fuel deep feelings of anger, fear and hatred. With ever-increasing levels of cross-border mobility, the entanglements between tourism and heritage are thus becoming ever more complex at the diplomatic level (Kim *et al.* 2007). Recent developments in East Asia are illustrative of this trend. As noted earlier, Japan has been at the forefront of using heritage and conservation aid as part of a post-Second World War foreign policy oriented by a discourse of peace. At the same time, however, the Japanese state has also extensively officiated the commemoration of the war at home to advance a sense of civic honour and pride. Given the atrocities Japan inflicted upon its regional neighbours, this has not surprisingly been the source of contention and tense international relations. One site in particular, the Yasukini Shrine in Tokyo, has remained highly controversial with successive prime ministers honouring those that died in the service of the Empire of Japan, including over a thousand war criminals. South Korea, China and Taiwan have all vocally criticised the Japanese government's approach to the shrine, arguing it represents a revisionist and unapologetic perspective towards the war.

With the tensions surrounding Yasukini extensively covered by media outlets outside the region, including those in the West, Allen and Sakamoto (2013) point to other lesser known sites that have also sparked controversy for similar reasons. To cite a few examples, the film about the battleship Yamato was released to cinemas across Japan in 2005 to coincide with the anniversary of its sinking. Much like other World War II films produced domestically, the storyline focused on the suffering and sacrifice of the Japanese, in this case the ship's crew, rather than their victims. In the same year, a new museum opened under controversial circumstances in Kure, Hiroshima, the shipyard where the Yamato was built. Elsewhere, the Chiran Peace Museum For Kamikaze Pilots in Chiran, Kyushu has long been a source of diplomatic tension in the region for the way it has recognised and bestowed honour upon the lives and deaths of Japan's World War II suicide pilots (Ohnuki-Tierney 2002). Although first opened in the mid-1970s, the museum's exhibitions have more recently been reworked to align with the national narrative of peace. Akiko Takenaka has documented similar processes for the Osaka International Peace Centre, commonly referred to as Osaka Peace, arguing that a redesign of the museum to remove 'any traces of aggressive behaviour by the Japanese military' (Takenaka 2014: 75) forms part of a larger neo-revisionism about the war. To substantiate this argument, she points to exhibits that have been reconceived in order to focus on the victims of Osaka's air raids, leading to the removal of display panels and film footage which detail the war against China. These museums, along with the various buildings and material culture preserved as part of the memory of war found elsewhere in the country, have been developed as part of a domestic tourist industry. A number of sites such as Chiran might also be categorised as pilgrimage sites, where the "spirits" of the dead have come to be revered as they take on sacred-like qualities.

Interestingly, however, as these sites move "out" of their national context, and into a more international space, fresh diplomatic controversies arise. As China and South Korea's middle class travel around the region in increasingly large numbers, Japan's museums and landscapes associated with the war become more than just destinations of domestic and Western tourism. The growth in inbound Chinese tourism to Japan has been dramatic, rising more than 70 per cent year on year between 2012 and 2014 to nearly 2.5 million annually (for further details see Murphy 2015). As a higher proportion of these visitors travel independently, beyond the confines of carefully configured package tours, some have expressed shock and anger at the portrayal of the war within the country. In a parallel case, the lobbying by Japanese war veterans for the letters of kamikaze pilots written to their families and friends to be internationally recognised under UNESCO's Memory of the World initiative caused considerable controversy in early 2014. Taking place against a backdrop of the tense diplomatic standoff between China and Japan over the disputed Diaoyu or Senkaku islands (as named by the two countries respectively), the idea of a UN agency endorsing such a controversial form of cultural heritage was not surprisingly met with considerable resistance and expressions of deep concern (Tian & Wuyong 2014).

This entanglement between diplomatically sensitive heritage sites and regional tourism is likely to develop considerably with the addition of "The Modern Industrial Heritage Sites in Kyûshû and Yamaguchi" to the World Heritage List in 2015. The nomination centres around a number of factories, warehouses and other buildings serving as testimony to the speed of Japan's industrialisation in the mid- to late nineteenth century and the flows of culture and technology which shaped the country's Westernisation during that period. With efforts to have the island sites recognised by UNESCO's premier convention having commenced more than a decade earlier, the narrative was carefully crafted around the transitions of culture and technology associated with iron making, shipbuilding and coal mining industries from the late nineteenth century onwards in an effort to depoliticise the process. Despite this, the path towards World Heritage nomination spawned debate and expressions of anger, particularly in South Korea where civil society groups highlighted the use of war-time Korean forced labour at the factories. Objections to the nomination even came directly from the prime minister's office, which, according to the Northeast Asia History Foundation, gathered data on the number of Korean victims:

> The Korean government protested and demanded withdrawal of the decision [to nominate the sites], stressing that 'the effort to register the facilities where the people of neighbouring countries suffered as a World Heritage site does not serve the World Heritage List's purpose of honouring universal value to humanity.' The Korean Prime Minister's Investigation Committee to Identify and Support the Korean Victims of Forced Labor during the Period of Resistance against Japan gathered information on the forced-labor camps and the status of forced labor in the areas that the Japanese government is promoting as a UNESCO World Heritage site, and submitted it to the Korean National Commission for UNESCO. According to the data, the Kyushu and Yamaguchi prefectures, which Japan is promoting to register on the UNESCO World Heritage List, include 845 forced-labor camps, of which up to 140 being war factories. The data also confirms that there were 37,393 victims of forced labor, 2,512 people who died locally, and 675 missing people. Many of the representative companies in this region responsible for forced labor, such as Mitsubishi Heavy Industries, Mitsubishi Materials Corporation, Nippon Steel, Sumitomo, and Hitachi, are on the "List of War Criminal Companies" confirmed by the Korean National Assembly, a list of Japanese companies to be restricted from bidding on Korean national or public projects.
>
> *(Yoo 2013)*

What we see here, then, is a situation that lies in distinct contrast to the structures of cooperation above. The theme of heritage diplomacy helps reveal the divergent and contradictory ways in which selected narratives of the past, and the material culture that surrounds and enables them, become entangled in the arena of international politics. But rather than this merely occurring as a dynamic between states, we see how the desire to promote particular messages to audiences folds tourism into the picture. By citing the ongoing expansion of intra-regional mobilities, it has been suggested that this situation is becoming increasingly complex and in some cases fraught.

Conclusion

In exploring such themes this chapter has thus aimed to open up the analysis of heritage and tourism beyond the more familiar themes of development, conflict or the localised identity issues associated with globalisation or the domestic cultural policies of states. I have suggested that we are now witnessing a series of interlocked, and yet seemingly paradoxical, developments in Asia today. At a time when greater attention is being given to the history and memory of twentieth-century conflict, resulting in the solidification of internationally divisive forms of heritage, the scale of bilateral and multilateral cooperation focused on the cultural past is increasing rapidly. To analytically consider such developments as heritage diplomacy reveals the complexities at play here, and the reasons why the past comes to be framed as heritage in certain ways in the international arena. In the case of Japan, for example, it has been seen how a narrative of peace has articulated both programmes of overseas cultural aid and the memory of conflict at home. In both cases, tourism has been a key vehicle for the Japanese state to communicate such messages and ideas. Yet, by turning to the sensitivities which now surround the cultural past in East Asia, it also becomes apparent that the pursuit of a peace narrative for sites associated with World War II is triggering diplomatic difficulties for Japan with its regional counterparts. While such a narrative framing has worked successfully to date for a domestic tourist audience, the arrival of visitors from neighbouring countries, most notably China, significantly complicates the picture for the Japanese state. My pursuit of this analytical framework here then stems from a sense that the long-term growth of intra-regional tourism in Asia will continue to figure in an arena of international relations that is increasingly invoking the cultural past as heritage to mediate the politics of the present.

Key reading

Akagawa, N. (2014) *Heritage Conservation and Japan's Cultural Diplomacy: Heritage, National Identity and National Interest*. London: Routledge.

Allen, M. and Sakamoto, R. (2013) 'War and peace: War memories and museums in Japan', *History Compass*, 11(12): 1047–1058.

Holtorf, C. and Kristensen, T.M. (2015) 'Heritage erasure: Rethinking "protection" and "preservation"', *International Journal of Heritage Studies*, 21(4): 313–317.

Takenaka, A. (2014) 'Reactionary nationalism and museum controversies', *The Public Historian*, 36(2): 75–98.

References

Akagawa, N. (2014) *Heritage Conservation and Japan's Cultural Diplomacy: Heritage, National Identity and National Interest*. London: Routledge.

Albro, R. (2012) *Cultural Diplomacy's Representational Conceit, USC Annenberg*. Online. Available: http://uscpublicdiplomacy.org/index.php/newswire/cpdblog_detail/cultural_diplomacys_representational_conceit (accessed 16 November 2014).

Allen, M. and Sakamoto, R. (2013) 'War and peace: War memories and museums in Japan', *History Compass*, 11(12): 1047–1058.

Anholt, S. (2006) *Competitive Identity: The New Brand Management for Nations, Cities and Regions*. Basingstoke: Palgrave Macmillan.

Bevan, R. (2006) *The Destruction of Memory: Architecture at War*. London: Reaktion Books.

Buss, A.E. (2010) 'The Preah Vihear case and regional customary law', *Chinese Journal of International Law*, 9(1): 111–126.

Calder, K.E. (2012) *The New Continentalism: Energy and Twenty-First-Century Eurasian Geopolitics*. New Haven: Yale University Press.

Chapman, W. (2013) *A Heritage of Ruins: The Ancient Sites of Southeast Asia and Their Conservation*. Honolulu: University of Hawai'i Press.

Dent, C. and Dosch, J. (eds) (2012) *The Asia-Pacific: Regionalism and the Global System*. Cheltenham: Edward Elgar.

Frew, E. and White, L. (eds) (2011) *Tourism and National Identities: An International Perspective*. Routledge: London.

Gienow-Hecht, J. and Donfried, M. (2010) 'The model of cultural diplomacy: Power, distance, and the promise of civil society', in J. Gienow-Hecht and M. Donfried (eds), *The Model of Cultural Diplomacy: Power, Distance, and the Promise of Civil Society* (pp. 13–32). New York: Berghahn Books.

Holtorf, C. and Kristensen, T.M. (2015) 'Heritage erasure: Rethinking "protection" and "preservation"', *International Journal of Heritage Studies*, 21(4): 313–317.

Kim, S., Prideaux, B. and Prideaux, J. (2007) 'Using tourism to promote peace on the Korean Peninsula', *Annals of Tourism Research*, 34(2): 291–309.

Murphy, C. (2015) 'Japan tries to persuade Chinese tourists to go off the beaten path', *Wall Street Journal: China Realtime*. Online. Available: http://blogs.wsj.com/chinarealtime/2015/02/19/japan-tries-to-persuade-chinese-tourists-to-go-off-the-beaten-path (accessed 10 March 2015).

Ohnuki-Tierney, E. (2002) *Kamikaze, Cherry Blossoms, and Nationalisms: The Militarization of Aesthetics in Japanese History*. Chicago: University of Chicago Press.

Silverman, H. (2011) 'Border wars: The ongoing temple dispute between Thailand and Cambodia and UNESCO's World Heritage List', *International Journal of Heritage Studies*, 17(1): 1–21.

Sojung, Y. (2014) 'Korea, Asia share cultural heritage management knowhow', Korea.net. Online. Available: www.korea.net/NewsFocus/Policies/view?articleId=121427 (accessed 5 November 2014).

Takenaka, A. (2014) 'Reactionary nationalism and museum controversies', *The Public Historian*, 36(2): 75–98.

Tanaka, Y. (2012) 'A new phase of the Temple of Preah Vihear dispute before the International Court of Justice: Reflections on the indication of provisional measures of 18 July 2011', *Chinese Journal of International Law*, 11(1): 191–226.

Tian, L. and Wuyong F. (2014) 'Kamikaze letters' bid for world memory disgraces Japan itself', *Xinhuanet*. Online. Available: http://news.xinhuanet.com/english/indepth/2014-02/06/c_133095392.htm (accessed 10 March 2015).

Wagener, M. (2011) 'Lessons from Preah Vihear: Thailand, Cambodia, and the nature of low-intensity border conflicts', *Journal of Current Southeast Asian Affairs*, 30(3): 27–59.

Yoo, J. (2013) 'Does Japan's forced labor camp carry any outstanding universal value to humanity? On Japan's move to include its modern industrial heritage sites on the UNESCO World Heritage List: History Q & A', *Northeast Asia History Foundation Newsletter*. Online. Available: www.nahf.or.kr/Data/Newsletterlist/1311_en/sub08.html (accessed 1 February 2015).

3

TRANSPORT AND INFRASTRUCTURE ISSUES IN ASIAN TOURISM

David Timothy Duval & Adam Weaver

Introduction

Asia represents one of the fastest growing regions in the world with respect to both tourism and transport. Forecasts from airframe manufacturers such as Boeing and Airbus continue to point to the Asia-Pacific region as one with significant and sustainable growth potential. Many Asian destinations are benefiting from major shifts in markets and market access, including large intercontinental growth by China, India and Japan, substantially more connections between the Middle East and India, and the growth of secondary airports in China (e.g., Hangzhou, Chengdu) (*Flightglobal* 2014).

Hall and Page (2000) acknowledge the deep relationship between tourism and transport in the region, and various scholars have demonstrated significant linkages between the provision of transport and the rate of development of tourism (e.g., Lohmann 2003; Henderson 2009). Globally, the trend of enhanced access continues, with adjustments and refinements to existing business models for air services, cruise tourism and the degree to which some forms of land transport (e.g., self-drive tourism (Denstadli & Jacobsen 2011)) are integrated in tourism experiences. In Asia, the competitiveness of tourism destinations is acknowledged to be contingent upon the provision of transport (Leung & Baloglu 2013). As a consequence of the strong role that transport plays in economic development, it is not terribly unusual to see innovations in transportation be first manifested in the Asian region. One example is the development of the Airbus A380, which was delivered first to Singapore Airlines in October 2007.

This chapter offers a restricted overview of transportation and infrastructure issues in Asia. Our focus is largely modes of transport that have had the most visible and significant impact on tourism development and government policy, namely air and marine transport. Our treatment of air transport reviews issues of liberalization and protectionism and assesses new and emerging business models in commercial air transport within the region. Our attention to marine tourism assesses the region's cruise sector. The dominant theme of this chapter is that air carriers and cruise lines operating in Asia are adapting to a business environment that is sometimes unfamiliar and uneven, but is no doubt changing dramatically. There are uncertainties to consider, arising from, for instance, the development of markets and organizational structures tied to governance and, to be discussed briefly later in the chapter, uncertainties associated with global challenges such as greenhouse gas emissions. The chapter concludes with a case study that highlights the implications of a sudden, tragic event – namely, the means by which such an event can illustrate recent (but hitherto not widely publicized) changes to the way in which an industry functions and, furthermore, can trigger regulatory responses that have far-reaching consequences, including those that generate short-term uncertainties.

Not unlike other geographic regions – and even global systems – of trade and commerce, connectivity is a paramount issue in Asia. A report by Gautrin (2014) offers a synopsis of the means by which connectivity can be fostered through ground transport linkages between South Asia and Southeast Asia. Importantly, Gautrin (2014) signals the value in tourism from improving such linkages, but also cautions that obstacles exist such as the high cost of infrastructure development, wider connectivity imperatives (as policy issues), uneven demand and the challenges of incongruent networks (World Bank 2014). The Asian Development Bank (ADB) and the ADB Institute (2014) released an interim report on connectivity which noted that "Rail transport is an underutilized transport mode in South and Southeast Asia because of serious limitations in the rail network, particularly in facilitating regional connectivity."

While the range of transport options in Asia is vast, there is an argument to be made following studies elsewhere (e.g., Stubbs & Jegede 1998) that, unlike some air cargo services (Lin & Chen 2003), the wider region struggles with multi-modal integration (see also Das 2004). This assists the seamless movement of goods in the context of international trade. It also aids in ensuring that passenger services are not rendered inefficient as tourism development expands outward from major centres to include more remote regions. Transport networks, then, need to have planning imperatives and milestones that incorporate modal use by tourists (Koo *et al.* 2010). Doing so would reduce what Graham (1998) identified, in the case of the EU, as disparities in accessibility. Indeed, the rapid growth trajectory of economies in the region makes integration a problematic issue (UNESCAP & AITD 2007: 134):

> the dynamic economic, trade, investment and tourism development in the region since the 1980s, as well as the concomitant adoption of outward-looking policies, positive changes in the political environment and the advent of container technology, have resulted in the revival of a keen interest in regional cooperation as a means of improving and developing interregional land transport linkages.

Solutions are not always apparent to ensure transport and tourism are linked in future development implementations. De Alwis (2010), however, offers a prescription to foster enhanced tourism development in Southeast Asia, some elements of which focused specifically on transport initiatives, including the further liberalisation of access between countries and the support for fast ferry and cruise options for tourist movement.

Air transport issues

The scale and scope of commercial aviation in the region has grown significantly in recent decades. The industry is project to earn a net post-tax profit in 2015 of US$5 billion with a 7.7 per cent growth in the number of passenger kilometres over 2014 (International Air Transport Association (IATA) 2014a). IATA released a series of 20-year projections in October 2014 (IATA 2014b). Most notable in the report was the fact that the size of the commercial passenger market in China is expected to overtake that of the United States by 2030. Furthermore, strong economic and demographic trajectories and the Asian and South American markets will result in the fastest growth, according to IATA (2014b).

While the broader Asian region is largely robust in terms of air services from a business and geographic scope, there are nonetheless significant challenges. Here, we consider three, each of which have complex interrelationships with each other. For instance, the business models of subsidiary airlines can have an important effect on forward planning at regional airports, as well as considerations by regional governments with respect to market access.

Liberalisation of air services

One of the more complex and long-standing issues with respect to commercial passenger air services is the liberalisation of those services. This is especially relevant in the Southeast Asian region, where slow ("inching" as described by Chin 1997) progress is sought toward an Association of Southeast Asian Nations (ASEAN) single aviation market. The approach ASEAN governments have taken with respect to developing a single market for access and connectivity is largely economic, and thus to secure long-term development opportunities and regional growth (Yue 1998). In this sense, the intent is not dissimilar to the regional liberalisation approach in the 1990s in Europe (Forsyth *et al.* 2006), with an intentional design of a staged approach. A 2008 multilateral agreement by the ten member states of ASEAN served as a precursor to a planned future implementation of the single market. As Tan (2010: 289) notes, the multilateral agreement is limited:

> For now, the Agreement goes only as far as providing market access relaxations for certain key routes, principally between the ASEAN capital cities. At the same time, it seeks to relax airline ownership and control requirements beyond the traditional substantial ownership and effective control rule.

The wider agreement for a single aviation market is scheduled for full implementation in 2015, despite the fact that, at the time of writing, the Philippines had not fully adopted the full list of principles of the agreement (Tan 2014). Various news reports in the early part of 2015 cast doubt over whether an agreement is even likely. As Tan (2009) argues, the ASEAN approach to liberalisation can sit alongside the Philippines' approach to aviation policy, but the country may be reluctant to fully adopt the stated principles of open market access for fear of reducing the competitiveness of its own national carrier.

In East Asia, the same fundamental elements of liberalisation as outlined by Tan (2010), namely market access and ownership, are also debated. Wang and Heinomen (2015) argue that the aeropolitical landscape has largely been shaped by fundamental changes in economic orientation in states such as Hong Kong, China and South Korea, but the wider political framework is responsible for these changes. Oum and Lee (2002) consider the restrictive bilateral relations between China, South Korea and Japan, arguing that a pan-national committee would seek to help liberalise these markets. Today, however, several Chinese airlines, for instance, have been actively seeking new routes through the southern Asian region, including further into Australia and New Zealand in order to support growing tourism demand.

Air access agreements have important implications for tourism. For one, they allow for a more seamless flow and allow for passengers to undertake multi-destination itineraries. This, in turn, can lead to more even, and perhaps positive, economic impacts from tourism receipts. Liberal agreements also present countries with more problematic economies an opportunity to use tourism to further economic growth. That said, it can be difficult to craft a multilateral agreement in complex regions such as Asia that touches various types of economic development so deeply and has general support from all parties. Tan (2009, 2010) signals multiple political and economic roadblocks that have challenged the seamless implementation of the approach to ASEAN open skies. Most of these relate to the perceived imposition of a regional open skies approach on a nation's desire to ensure its own airlines are protected.

Airports

Infrastructure in support of tourism is often overlooked in the assessment of transport and tourism. While airlines provide the business case for the mobility of international and domestic tourists, it is the airport infrastructure which facilitates such mobility. Airports in the region are actually very much competitive. They exist within a marketplace where profits can often be quite thin, customers are varied and numerous, and there are extensive performance expectations and metrics. Airports should be seen as the vectors by which economic development is fostered, and thus their ownership structures (as strategic assets) offers some unique regulatory perspectives given many (if not most) are expected to operate as profitable entities (Gillen 2011).

De Wit *et al.* (2009: 640) note that "airline networks are progressively transforming into hub-and-spoke networks, as international aviation markets become increasingly liberalized". On this basis, they (de Wit *et al.* 2009) measure the performance of Asia-Pacific airports by incorporating the supply elements (whereas other studies have used demand) of airline schedules and resulting hub performance. They find that Chinese airports have a significant number of direct connections, but Sydney and Tokyo had the highest overall hub performance. The airports in the de Wit *et al.* (2009) study were, however, primary airports. With the overall increase in air service growth, including the growth in low-cost carriers, it is important to consider the impact on secondary ports. Zhang *et al.* (2008) argue that, interestingly, a regional response to the growth in low-cost services has been the construction of secondary terminals (e.g., AirAsia's terminal at Kuala Lumpur) as opposed to the direct utilisation of scarce secondary airports:

> as availability of secondary airports seems to be a key requirement for the implementation of the LCC business model, how to deal with the scarcity of secondary airports in Asia appears to be a major problem for airports, airlines, and governments.
>
> *(Zhang et al. 2008: 37)*

Airline business models

Finally, a number of alternative business models have arisen in the region with respect to air transport. Two are prominent. The first is the carrier-within-carrier (or airline-within-airline) concept (Gillen & Gados 2008), where separate firms are created for specific competitive markets, often a response to the presence of strong low-cost carriers (Graham & Vowles 2006). Gross and Lück (2013) identify over a dozen airline brands in the region which are subsidiaries of parent firms. The second is the low-cost, long-haul model. Francis *et al.* (2007) and Morrell (2008) correctly question whether such a model could function profitably. Despite this, attempts have been made. Several carriers in the region already operate relatively long-haul routes on a low-cost model. Scoot, a subsidiary of Singapore Airlines, offers services from Singapore to Hong Kong and Nanjing, for instance, and Cebu Pacific, based in the Philippines, also targets cities such as Hong Kong, Beijing and Bangkok. AirAsiaX, perhaps the most successful, boasts a substantial route map and a growing fleet.

Case study 3.1 Indonesia AirAsia flight 8501

Indonesia AirAsia flight 8501 was announced as missing in January 2014 on a flight from Indonesia to Singapore. All 155 passengers were killed. In the weeks that followed, a number of issues were raised. Chief among these was the question of the safety of airlines in the region, specifically low-cost airlines, despite the fact that low-cost carriers are often credited with facilitating and spawning substantial growth in tourism numbers (e.g., Chung & Whang 2011; see also Lawton & Solomko 2005). Many of these concerns were raised in the popular press following revelations of problems relating to scheduling and authorisations.

The integration of safety and security mechanisms into an airline's operation is largely the responsibility of the aviation regulatory authorities in that airline's home country (Broderick & Loos 2002). With respect to Indonesia, the wider concern was the fact that a number of Indonesian airlines have been blacklisted by major markets such as Europe (see Reitzfeld & Mpande 2008 for an overview of the legislation enacted). Henderson (2009) explored the impact of the European ban on Indonesian airlines, noting that "defects" in suitable transport between source markets and destinations can have severe repercussions, especially given the relative popularity of nearby countries like Malaysia and Singapore.

Beyond the tragic human loss and the wider regulatory concerns regarding safety, the loss of flight 8501 also raised a number of issues with respect to air access within the region. The first of these is how airline branding fits within a single brand operating across multiple jurisdictions of regulatory oversight. In the case of Indonesia AirAsia, the airline itself was majority owned by a private company in Indonesia. However, the brand AirAsia was utilised via a 49 per cent ownership stake in the airline by the AirAsia group. The reason for this is that Indonesia, not unlike most countries around the world, requires that the majority ownership of a particular airline must be vested in nationals or citizens of that country. This presents some fairly unique business model issues. One of these is the complex nature of branding of airlines with multiple-ownership structures, where the brand may be seen throughout the region but is licensed by multiple operators. In incidents such as flight 8501, the ability for a wider airline group, which manages multiple airlines in multiple countries, to respond to crises becomes paramount.

The second issue is safety. It is well known that consumer perceptions of airline disasters are somewhat sticky in that they are perpetuated for quite some time after a disaster (Siomkos 2000). In some instances, governments are proactive, as in the case of Japan restricting the number of flights that Thai airlines can operate to its airports in March 2015 (*Reuters* 2015). Citing safety concerns, the Japanese Civil Aviation Bureau effectively banned on 27 March 2015 any increase in the number of flights operated by an airline designated by Thailand, and prohibited Thai airlines from changing aircraft type or routings. Thailand's Transport Minister responded by indicating that "This seriously affects Thailand's tourism sector" (*Bangkok Post* 2015). Following this, the International Civil Aviation Organisation (ICAO) downgraded the Thailand Department of Civil Aviation, arguing that it is not in compliance with international safety regulations. This could have significant repercussions for Thailand's tourism sector given its overall importance to the country (see Kontogeorgopoulos, Chapter 11, this volume).

Marine and cruise tourism issues

Not entirely like air transport serving the growth of tourism in the region overall, the popularity of cruise travel is spreading to Asian markets (Mondou & Taunay 2012; Sun *et al.* 2014). There are multiple reasons for the increasing volume of Asian cruise travellers, many of which also account for the overall growth of outbound travel from Asia: increasing affluence and more free time in the region, the rising availability of affordable international travel, the development of (more suitable) infrastructure, and the positive support and national significance accorded by governments to tourism development. As well as an expanding source of outbound travellers, Asia has emerged as a prominent destination for a rising number of inbound travellers. Redeploying ships to Asia has enabled cruise lines to offer novel products to repeat customers in a range of markets, including the United States, and to entice first-time Asian passengers. The recent "discovery" of Asia as a cruise destination coincides with its growth as a market. Several issues are defining the development of cruise travel in Asia: the characteristics of Asian tourists, the importance of infrastructure and political relationships between countries.

Bold projections have been made regarding the future growth of the Asian cruise market. Asian travellers are by no means peripheral to the concerns of the global cruise industry. Pier Luigi Foschi – the former chief executive officer of Carnival Asia, a subsidiary of Carnival Corporation – predicts that "Asian passengers will account for one in every five cruisers" by 2020, nearly double the number in 2013 (Stieghorst 2013: 1). Chinese consumers, in particular, will contribute substantially to the anticipated expansion of the Asian cruise market. The rising demand for cruise travel among Asian travellers has prompted a range of supplier responses. Shorter cruises that are three to five days in duration, for example, are preferred (Mondou & Taunay 2012; Stieghorst 2013; Sun *et al.* 2014). The dining experience typically offered to cruise passengers is modified to suit Asian travellers. These travellers "prefer not to be assigned to a table with total strangers" (Bachman 2014: 21), a common practice on board cruise ships. Themed dinners – and meal menus more broadly – require adjustment. A Carnival cruise ship that sailed with Chinese passengers featured a "presidential menu" (Shao 2014: 18). The dishes served were those that China's former president, Hu Jintao, received during a 2011 visit to the White House.

Shipboard environments are being altered to accommodate Asian travellers. Princess Cruises "has added a 66-seat sushi restaurant" on board one of its vessels that sailed from Japan in 2014 as well as "a huge bathing complex to cater to the Japanese enjoyment of onsen, or dips in hot springs" (Bachman 2014: 21). The Japan-oriented thrust of Princess Cruises' recent activities in Asia contrasts with the China-focused endeavours of Royal Caribbean International (RCI) and Carnival Corporation. In order to attract Chinese passengers – namely, families with children – RCI has "partnered with DreamWorks Animation to feature the studio's animated characters onboard" (Stieghorst 2012: 14). The characters from the film *Kung Fu Panda* are prominently featured – that is, vessels are populated with images of, and people dressed as, cartoon animals – because this motion picture is "one of the highest-grossing movies of all time in China" (Stieghorst 2012: 14). In the near future, more radical changes to the cruise-ship environment are forecast. The types of onboard revenue generated by cruise lines has historically had implications for ship design. There is speculation "that ships built for a Chinese or Asian passenger may eventually look quite different from the US model, in the same way that ships built for German lines are different" (Stieghorst 2012: 14).

However, despite the differences between Asian and Western consumers, adapting "the onboard experience to Chinese tastes" must be balanced with retaining a company's "brand identity" (Stieghorst 2012: 14) and the distinctive appeal of cruise travel. There are established features of the shipboard experience that will probably remain unchanged. Consumers in

China, for example, are thought to be "keen to sample chocolate buffets and stroll the lido deck" (Bachman 2014: 20). When RCI redeployed *Voyager of the Seas* to China, the on-board Italian-themed restaurant was "sold out every night" (Stieghorst 2012: 14). Chinese passengers "don't want to go on Chinese product [sic]" because they are "enamored with Western culture" (Stieghorst 2012: 14). The gastronomic profile of Chinese travellers is different from that of Americans, but there are similarities worthy of note.

"[T]rial-and-error discoveries" (Stieghorst 2013: 1) occur, and sometimes they inform cruise-industry product development. Princess Cruises expected its Japanese itineraries in 2013 to appeal to mainly Japanese consumers. In fact, the number of reservations made by Americans and Europeans prompted the company to hire "English-speaking tour guides for its shore excursions" (Stieghorst 2013: 1). A product developed for an Asian market became popular with the company's more established markets that were seeking an alternative to the types of mass-market cruise itineraries often available. RCI, according to its vice president for commercial development, is "at an experimental stage" (Stieghorst 2013: 1) with respect to the adaptations it is making for Asian passengers. "[T]he initial burst of gold-rush enthusiasm about China's staggering potential" (Weissmann 2014: 12) is accompanied by an acknowledgement that a carefully considered mixture of Chinese and Western shipboard amenities is a potential recipe for success.

Steps have been taken by cruise lines to develop their own administrative infrastructure in response to the growth of the Asian market. These companies have, in recent years, built this infrastructure by expanding the presence of their organizations in Asia. RCI has opened a corporate office in Shanghai (Christoff 2013). Carnival Asia, a subsidiary of Carnival Corporation, was established in Singapore (Stieghorst 2012). Princess Cruises has sales offices in a number of Asian countries (Mathisen 2014). In addition to sales, corporate offices in Asia are used by cruise lines for purposes related to strategy and logistics. Propinquity with respect to the Asian market and potential business partners is seen as a necessity for cruise lines wanting to reap the benefits of operating in the region.

Also, port-based infrastructure has been built in order to accommodate the expansion of cruise tourism in Asian destinations. Port development is crucial to accommodating more – and larger – cruise ships (Sun *et al.* 2014). Cruises lines are demonstrating a willingness to have some of their larger vessels operate in Asia during certain times of the year. Expanded port facilities have been built in Hong Kong and Singapore. Singapore is seen by Carnival Asia as "fortunately situated" and a home port from which a cruise line "can go to Thailand, Malaysia and Indonesia" (Weissmann 2014: 12). However, there is still scope to build better port facilities in a number of destinations. A regional vice president for the parent company that owns RCI has noted that "[t]he lack of destination ports [in Asia] with the capability to handle big ships may be the biggest challenge" (Stieghorst 2013: 1). Serving more cruise passengers in the region at an appropriate standard inevitably involves creating more suitably sized and equipped port facilities in more places.

Support for the cruise industry in Asia through the development of infrastructure has occurred at the same time that regional tensions pose challenges. Tourism typically flourishes in the context of political stability and harmony. Simmering conflicts create complications. Territorial disputes between China and Japan are an ongoing concern. In the middle of 2014, "China informed … cruise lines that ships leaving Chinese ports could no longer include Japan on their itineraries" (Weissmann 2014: 12). Political relations between China and Taiwan have been strained from decades. Cruise lines are acutely aware of these issues and ship itineraries could feasibly include more private island stops should circumstances dictate that some Asian ports of call had to be dropped. Private islands are a means of providing passengers with a visit to a bubble environment that conforms to passengers' perceptions of a remote, exotic paradise, but they have also been described as "a hedge against the vagaries of Asian government policies" (Weissmann 2014: 12).

Despite the influence of globalization and international market forces, the policies and practices of national governments continue to have implications for transnational enterprises.

Conclusion

Future trends in global transport will undoubtedly have an impact on tourism in Asia given the projections for growth and business model innovations already witnessed in the region. Several global trends can be highlighted. The first is the role of emissions in transport, especially with respect to aviation. What is still unclear is whether regional and/or global approaches to emissions mitigation and externality internalisation will have an impact on the cost of transport, and whether this increase in cost will ultimately have an impact on tourist flows to, from and within Asia (Veryard 2010; Steppler & Klingmüller 2009).

While transport accounts for a substantial proportion of greenhouse gas emissions in international tourism (Dubois *et al.* 2011), the relationship between specific countries or regions and their national emissions profile is still a slowly emerging (and necessarily precise) area of enquiry (e.g., Pentelow & Scott 2011). Gössling, Scott and Hall (2015), for instance, note that some countries may positively change their overall emission intensity by specifically targeting visitors from markets where associated emissions are fewer. It is more likely, however, that initiatives such as efficient flight paths and continuous descent will be attempted first. The so-called "Seamless Asia Sky" project from IATA is attempting to have air traffic managed regionally, thus saving considerable fuel and reducing emissions.

Another trend that will impact on tourism in Asia is the shifting business models of transport providers in the region. As the case study in this chapter demonstrates, large brands circumvent ownership restrictions in order to ensure seamless service expectations and delivery. The air transport and cruise tourism sectors have demonstrated a desire to adapt their activities in Asia by catering to consumers with different needs and tastes, developing organizational structures that are specific to the region, and – initially – tailoring their activities so that they are compatible with the infrastructure that is available. A final trend to be identified involves the linkage and alignment of the broader economic policies for the region and the overall approach that individual, and collective, governments take with respect to access (Grosso 2012). It will be important that economic development initiatives take into account the role of transport in the trade of goods and services (see Moore & Heeler 1998). In the case of tourism, the liberalisation of access will need to closely follow desired economic development trajectories. The risk of not aligning these could be risky as other regions in the world (e.g., South America, Africa) build on existing liberalised and common market policies. The benefits of alignment will ensure that tourism is assured a meaningful place within a wider economic development trajectory of the region.

Key reading

Chung, J.Y. and Whang, T. (2011) 'The impact of low cost carriers on Korean Island tourism', *Journal of Transport Geography*, 19(6): 1335–1340.

Sun, X., Feng, X. and Gauri, D. (2014) 'The cruise industry in China: Efforts, progress and challenges', *International Journal of Hospitality Management*, 42: 71–84.

Tan, A.K.-J. (2010) 'The ASEAN multilateral agreement on air services: En route to open skies?', *Journal of Air Transport Management*, 16: 289–294.

Wang, J.J. and Heinomen, T.H. (2015) 'Aeropolitics in East Asia: An institutional approach to air transport liberalisation', *Journal of Air Transport Management*, 42: 176–183.

References

Asian Development Bank (ADB) and ADB Institute (2014) *Connecting South Asia and Southeast Asia: Interim report*. Online. Available: www.adbi.org/files/2013.05.05.book.connecting.south.asia.southeast. asia.interim.report.pdf (accessed 13 December 2015).

Bachman, J. (2014) 'Asia is getting its own love boats', *Bloomberg Business*, 2 June, 20–21.

Bangkok Post. (2015) 'Japan caps Thai air services amid safety concerns'. Online. Available: www. bangkokpost.com/news/transport/509357/japan-caps-thai-air-services-amid-safety-concerns (accessed 27 March 2015).

Broderick, A.J. and Loos, J. (2002) 'Government aviation safety oversight: Trust, but verify', *Journal of Air Law and Commerce*, 67: 1035–1056.

Chin, A.T.H. (1997) 'Implications of liberalisation on airport development and strategy in the Asia Pacific', *Journal of Air Transport Management*, 3(3): 125–131.

Christoff, J. (2013) 'Cruising the Far East', *TravelAge West*, 48(9): 12–15.

Chung, J.Y. and Whang, T. (2011) 'The impact of low cost carriers on Korean Island tourism', *Journal of Transport Geography*, 19(6): 1335–1340.

Das, D.K. (2004) 'Structured regionalism in the Asia-Pacific: Slow but sure progress', *Asia Pacific Viewpoint*, 45(2): 217–233.

de Alwis, R. (2010) 'Promoting tourism in South Asia', in S. Ahmed, S. Kelegama and E. Ghani (eds), *Promoting Economic Cooperation in South Asia* (pp. 259–278). London: Sage.

Denstadli, J.M. and Jacobsen, J.K.S. (2011) 'The long and winding roads: Perceived quality of scenic tourism routes', *Tourism Management*, 32(4): 780–789.

de Wit, J., Velduis, J., Burghouwt, G. and Matsumoto, H. (2009) 'Competitive position of primary airports in the Pacific Rim', *Pacific Economic Review*, 14(5): 639–650.

Dubois, G., Peeters, P., Ceron, J.-P. and Gössling, S. (2011) 'The future tourism mobility of the world population: Emission growth versus climate policy', *Transportation Research Part A: Policy and Practice*, 45(10): 1031–1042.

Flightglobal (2014) 'Analysis: Asia-Pacific looks north as market dynamics shift'. Online. Available: www. flightglobal.com/news/articles/analysis-asia-pacific-looks-north-as-market-dynamics-402768 (accessed 31 August 2014).

Forsyth, P., King, J. and Rodolfo, C.L. (2006) 'Open Skies in ASEAN', *Journal of Air Transport Management*, 12: 143–152.

Francis, G., Dennis, N., Ison, S. and Humphreys, I. (2007) 'The transferability of the low-cost model to long-haul airline operations', *Tourism Management*, 28(2): 391–398.

Gautrin, J.-F. (2014) *Connecting South Asia to Southeast Asia: Cross-border infrastructure investments*, ADBI Working Paper 483. Tokyo: Asian Development Bank Institute. Online. Available: www.adbi.org/ working-paper/2014/05/27/6271.connecting.south.asia.southeast.asia (accessed 13 December 2015).

Gillen, D. (2011) 'The evolution of airport ownership and governance', *Journal of Air Transport Management*, 17: 3–13.

Gillen, D. and Gados, A. (2008) 'Airlines within airlines: Assessing the vulnerabilities of mixing business models', *Research in Transportation Economics*, 24(1): 25–35.

Gössling, S., Scott, D. and Hall, C.M. (2015) 'Inter-market variability in CO_2 emission-intensities in tourism: Implications for destination marketing and carbon management', *Tourism Management*, 46: 203–212.

Graham, B. (1998) 'Liberalization, regional economic development and the geography of demand for air transport in the European Union', *Journal of Transport Geography*, 6(2): 87–104.

Graham, B. and Vowles, T. (2006) 'Carriers within carriers: A strategic response to low-cost airline competition', *Transportation Review*, 26(1): 105–126.

Gross, S. and Lück, M. (eds) (2013) *The Low Cost Carrier Worldwide*. Surrey: Ashgate.

Grosso, M.G. (2012) 'Air passenger transport in the APEC: Regulatory impacts and prospects for Asia Pacific integration', *Journal of Economic Integration*, 27(2): 312–327.

Hall, C.M. and Page, S. (eds) (2000) *Tourism in South and Southeast Asia*. London: Routledge.

Henderson, J. (2009) 'Transport and tourism destination development: An Indonesian perspective', *Tourism and Hospitality Research*, 9(3): 199–208.

International Air Transport Association (IATA). (2014a) 'Industry statistics', December 2014. Online. Available: www.iata.org/pressroom/facts_figures/fact_sheets/Documents/industry-facts.pdf (accessed 27 March 2015).

—— (2014b) '20 year passenger forecast'. Online. Available: www.iata.org/publications/Pages/20-passenger-forecast.aspx (accessed 27 March 2015).

Koo, T.T.R., Wu, C.-L. and Dwyer, L. (2010) 'Transport and regional dispersal of tourists: Is travel modal substitution a source of conflict between low-fare air services and regional dispersal?', *Journal of Travel Research*, 49(1): 106–120.

Lawton, T.C. and Solomko, S. (2005) 'When being the lowest cost is not enough: Building a successful low-fare airline business model in Asia', *Journal of Air Transport Management*, 11(6): 355–362.

Leung, X.Y. and Baloglu, S. (2013) 'Tourism competitiveness of Asia Pacific destinations', *Tourism Analysis*, 18(4): 371–384.

Lin, C.-C. and Chen, Y.-C. (2003) 'The integration of Taiwanese and Chinese air networks for direct air cargo services', *Transportation Research Part A: Policy and Practice*, 37(7): 629–647.

Lohmann, G. (2003) 'The role of transport in tourism development: Nodal functions and management practices', *International Journal of Tourism Research*, 5(5): 403–407.

Mathisen, O. (2014) 'Love boat to Asia', *Cruise Industry News Quarterly*, 24(98): 76.

Mondou, V. and Taunay, B. (2012) 'The adaptation strategies of the cruise lines to the Chinese tourists', *Tourism*, 60(1): 43–54.

Moore, K. and Heeler, R. (1998) 'A globalization strategy for subsidiaries: Subsidiary specific advantages', *Journal of Transnational Management Development*, 3(2): 1–14.

Morrell, P. (2008) 'Can long-haul low-cost airlines be successful?', *Research in Transportation Economics*, 24(1): 61–67.

Oum, T.H. and Lee, Y.H. (2002) 'The Northeast Asian air transport network: Is there a possibility of creating Open Skies in the region?', *Journal of Air Transport Management*, 8: 325–337.

Pentelow, L. and Scott, D.J. (2011) 'Aviation's inclusion in international climate policy regimes: Implications for the Caribbean tourism industry', *Journal of Air Transport Management*, 17(3): 199–205.

Reitzfeld, A.D. and Mpande, C.S. (2008) 'EU regulation on banning of airlines for safety concerns', *Air and Space Law*, 33(2): 132–154.

Reuters. (2015) 'China, Japan, South Korea halt Thai air route expansion on safety concerns'. Online. Available: www.reuters.com/article/2015/03/30/us-thailand-aviation-idUSKBN0MQ1ZM20150330 (accessed 30 March 2015).

Shao, H. (2014) 'Fast sailing', *Forbes Asia*, 10(6): 18–20.

Siomkos, G.J. (2000) 'Managing airline disasters: The role of consumer safety perceptions and sense-making', *Journal of Air Transport Management*, 6(2): 101–108.

Steppler, U. and Klingmüller, A. (2009) 'EU emissions trading scheme and aviation quo vadis?', *Air and Space Law*, 34(4): 253–260.

Stieghorst, T. (2012) 'Playing to Asia', *Travel Weekly*, 71(45): 14.

—— (2013) 'Asia cruise market prediction: 7m passengers a year by 2020', *Travel Weekly*, 72(4): 1.

Stubbs, J. and Jegede, F. (1998) 'The integration of rail and air transport in Britain', *Journal of Transport Geography*, 6(1): 53–67.

Sun, X., Feng, X. and Gauri, D. (2014) 'The cruise industry in China: Efforts, progress and challenges', *International Journal of Hospitality Management*, 42: 71–84.

Tan, A.K.-J. (2009) 'Aviation policy in the Philippines and the impact of the proposed South East Asian Single Aviation Market', *Air and Space Law*, 34(4/5): 285–308.

—— (2010) 'The ASEAN multilateral agreement on air services: En route to open skies?', *Journal of Air Transport Management*, 16: 289–294.

—— (2014) 'As 2015 nears, ASEAN's single aviation market must gear up for new but harder phase', *Airline Leader*, 25. Online. Available: www.airlineleader.com/categories/feature/as-2015-nears-aseans-single-aviation-market-must-gear-up-for-new-but-harder-phase-193965 (accessed 12 December 2015).

United Nations Economic and Social Commission for Asia and the Pacific (UNSCAP) and Asian Institute of Transportation Development (AITD) (2007) *Toward an Asian Integrated Transport Network*. Online. Available: http://unohrlls.org/UserFiles/File/LLDC%20Documents/MTR/Toward%20integrated%20highway.pdf (accessed 13 December 2015).

Veryard, D. (2010) 'Tourism impacts in South-East Asia from aviation carbon pricing', *Road and Transport Research: A Journal of Australian and New Zealand Research*, 19(4): 51–65.

Wang, J.J. and Heinomen, T.H. (2015) 'Aeropolitics in East Asia: An institutional approach to air transport liberalisation', *Journal of Air Transport Management*, 42: 176–183.

Weissmann, A. (2014) 'Eastern Caribbean or Caribbean East?', *Travel Weekly*, 73(33): 12.

World Bank (2014) *Regional Economic Impact Analysis of High Speed Rail in China, Main Report*. Report No: ACS9734, China and Mongolia Sustainable Development Sector Unit, East Asia and Pacific Region. Online. Available: www-wds.worldbank.org/external/default/WDSContentServer/WDSP/IB/2014/07/16/000333037_20140716143756/Rendered/PDF/ACS97340WP0P140a0Box385238B00OUO090.pdf (accessed 6 November 2014).

Yue, C.S. (1998) 'The ASEAN free trade area', *The Pacific Review*, 11(2): 213–232.

Zhang, A., Hanaoka, S., Inamura, H. and Ishikura, T. (2008) 'Low-cost carriers in Asia: Deregulation, regional liberalization and secondary airports', *Research in Transportation Economics*, 24(1): 36–50.

4

HUMAN RESOURCE AND LABOUR ISSUES IN ASIAN TOURISM

Lisa Ruhanen & Chris Cooper

Introduction

Employment is the vehicle through which a country's economic growth is transferred to its citizens. The tourism sector, which already constitutes one in every eleven jobs around the world (United Nations World Tourism Organization (UNWTO) 2014a), is widely acknowledged as a key source of employment opportunities in both developed and developing countries. As such, national governments have pursued tourism as a high-potential economic growth option, and the employment it creates as a way of ensuring that economic growth translates into poverty reduction among those most in need.

In the continuously developing Asian region, a focus on physical development and capital investment has overshadowed labour market and employment issues in the tourism sector (UNWTO 2002a). However, recognising the service orientation of the sector and the need to deliver unique, memorable and competitive experiences vis-à-vis other destinations have led governments in the region to examine more closely the issues around human capital.

Indeed, the tourism labour market is affected by both general employment issues (including finding and retaining key talent, constantly upgrading workers' skills and coping with rising labour costs) and the inherent features of the tourism sector, including, for example, the fragmented nature of the sector, the dominance of small to medium enterprises (SMEs), a predominance of short-term and/or casual work, low wages and seasonality of demand. Combined, these present a range of unique challenges. Indeed, such challenges only add to the difficulties already faced by the tourism sector, including its exposure to global crises, incidents and fluctuations in the global economy. They also inhibit the capacity of the sector to maximise its poverty alleviation potential.

Perhaps due to the nature of the sector and the aforementioned challenges, many countries do not have a complete picture of the employment situation in their tourism industries. In both developed and developing countries, the conditions and characteristics of the tourism labour market are not clearly identified, and the variables which may affect it are not comprehensively understood. As noted by the UNWTO and the International Labour Organization (ILO) (2008:v):

the world of work in tourism is generally not well-known because reliable data on employment in the tourism industries are not properly identified separately or poorly

45

done. For this reason, only a limited number of countries produce meaningful statistics on employment in the tourism industries. [This] only confirm[s] that the world of work in tourism, in general, and the economic value of tourism in terms of employment, as a source of productive labour in particular, remain inadequately measured and insufficiently studied.

In light of this, the Tourism Satellite Account (TSA) was launched as a standard statistical framework and tool for measuring the economics of tourism, thereby establishing a clear sectoral identity for the tourism industries. Today, the TSA includes tourism labour statistics, though this has not always been the case. It could be said that the lack of statistical data – due predominantly to the fragmented nature of the tourism industries – has been the reason why tourism, in policy terms, has not always been considered as an employment-generating sector (UNWTO & ILO 2008).

The rapid growth of the Asian region, particularly over recent decades, has not made it immune to the aforementioned challenges. Meeting increasing levels of tourist demand and overcoming both internal and external obstacles means that the need for skilled labour and an improvement of the quality of tourism-related jobs is more pertinent than ever.

Supply and demand issues in the tourism labour market

Due to their capacity and effectiveness in generating employment, the tourism industries are seen as valuable economic development tools for many countries. The economic advantages of tourism and its benefits for a country's labour market are comprehensively documented in the literature (e.g., see Ball 1988; Briedenhann & Wickens 2004; Choy 1995; Dwyer & Forsyth 1993; Lee & Warner 2006; Liu & Wall 2006; Lourens 2007; UNWTO 2002b). Several characteristics of tourism – especially its potential to create jobs and boost employment among various levels of society – make the sector an attractive economic development option. However, some facets of the tourism industry can also be inhibitors to tourism being a source of decent work. These facets include tourism's seasonality, the mobility of the labour force, the dominance of SMEs in the tourism industry, education and training and ongoing technological changes.

Employment options in the tourism sector range from professional, skilled positions to semi-skilled and unskilled jobs. Workers could be owners of SMEs, entrepreneurs or paid on a full-time, part-time, casual or temporary basis (Marchante *et al.* 2006; Szivas *et al.* 2003). The variety of positions available in the sector, particularly at the low- or semi-skilled level, make it a viable and attractive option for entry-level employees and groups prone to unemployment, such as women, youth and those with minimal formal education or qualifications. It is for this reason that the tourism sector has been acknowledged as a valuable tool for contributing to poverty alleviation, as it provides realistic employment options to key groups in society and can contribute to social inclusion and personal development (De Lacy *et al.* 2002; UNWTO 2006).

Despite the multifaceted nature of the tourism sector and the variety of employment options available (including large numbers of well-paid and desirable jobs (Baum 1995)), the sector's main employers (i.e. the accommodation and food and beverage sectors) are often associated with poor working conditions such as low pay, long working hours, low skills and a lack of career advancement opportunities. Though in some countries, such as China, working for a large international company such as a hotel chain carries with it a certain status due to its international exposure (ILO 2003), the tourism sector is often viewed unfavourably in comparison with other industries in which the wages and conditions are seen as more appealing (ILO 2003).

Perhaps unsurprisingly, labour market mobility is a key concern for the tourism sector. From high turnover rates among the low-/semi-skilled and casual workers dominating the hotel and food and beverage sectors to high-level employees moving between organisations to progress their career, it can be argued that in general there is minimal attachment to positions within the sector. If conditions do not meet an employee's expectations, they are likely to seek alternative positions, even in other industries.

Further compounding the issues surrounding tourism labour market instability is the lack of focus on education and training in the tourism sector. This is particularly the case for SMEs, where seasonality, part-time and casual employment and significant turnover are not conducive to offering career development-focused training and education possibilities. When training is offered, it is commonly focused on teaching staff how to improve their current job function with minimal time investment (Baum 1995). Despite this commonly criticised lack of focus on training at the lower skill levels of the tourism sector, larger organisations, particularly accommodation providers, often have well-established training programmes for existing staff (Ruhanen & Cooper 2009). As well as this, increasing attention has been given to training and education at the higher academic levels in response to the worldwide demand for skilled labour, and indeed, many countries today have an extensive education system which includes various tourism industry-related qualifications, even up to the postgraduate level. However, the development of these has not quite kept up with the rapid development of the tourism sector (Ruhanen & Cooper 2009; UNWTO 2002a). Nevertheless, aside from increased wages, it is suggested that the best strategy to address skills shortages and labour supply issues is through training, education and skills development, including in languages (ILO 2003; Ruhanen & Cooper 2009).

A final issue impacting supply and demand of labour in the tourism industries is the issue of continuous technological changes. Technology has changed the type of work undertaken and the skills needed to perform certain roles, made some positions redundant and yet created new, previously non-existent jobs in areas such as website development and technical operations management (Baum 2007a, 2007b). However, while technological advancements have caused major changes to some industries – such as transport – they have had less impact on others – such as customer service (Ruhanen & Cooper 2009).

The Asian tourism labour market

The Asian region has focused on tourism as a source of economic growth and development, particularly since the end of the 1997 Asian Economic Crisis (Briedenhann & Wickens 2004). Today, the region is the world's fastest growing tourism region in relative terms, attracting some 248 million international arrivals in 2013, accounting for US$359 billion in tourism-related earnings (UNWTO 2014a). This growth has been robust for the last four years and is predicted to continue despite continued economic, environmental and health-related challenges. This strong and sustained growth shows the growing political commitment to the tourism sector in many countries and an acknowledgement of tourism's potential to be a stimulus for investment, foreign exchange earnings and employment creation (Ruhanen & Cooper 2009; UNWTO 2014b)

The tourism sector in the region currently supports approximately 146.9 million jobs (8.2 per cent of total employment), a figure expected to rise to 196.8 million (9.7 per cent of total employment) in 2024 (World Travel and Tourism Council (WTTC) 2014). Despite this, the tourism labour market situation varies from country to country. Challenges for individual countries range from a need to utilise imported labour because of an internal labour shortage, to shifting demographic structures causing fewer young people to enter the market and oversupplies of unskilled workers to fill entry-level positions (UNWTO 2002a; ILO 2003; Ruhanen & Cooper 2009).

As in other tourism regions around the world, the region must grapple with the challenges impacting the labour market in order to maintain competitiveness and retain market share in the face of often difficult economic conditions. Impacted by such demographic trends as ageing populations, increased participation of women in the workforce, mobility and immigration, changing wages and a focus on global change initiatives like the Millennium Development Goals, and in the context of technological advancements and continuing globalisation, skilled labour shortages remain the most pressing issue for the tourism industries in the Asia region (Ruhanen & Cooper 2009).

Demographic trends

Perhaps the most pressing concern for a sustainable tourism labour market in Asia is the issue of region-wide ageing populations. It is expected that within the next 30 years, Asia will add one billion people to the world's population. By 2040, half of these one billion extra people will be over 65 years of age. Adding to this, the ratio of older (65 years and over) people to working-age (15–64 years) people will be more than triple in many East and South-East Asian countries by 2050, and China's whole population will be older than that of Australia or the United States (ARC Centre of Excellence in Population Ageing Research (CEPAR) 2013). Similarly, Japan's population statistics have been the cause of media attention for many years. With a consistent decline in population (the country's head count declined for the third year in a row in 2013–2014, by 217,000, or 17 per cent), low fertility rates and an increasingly ageing population (25.1 per cent of the population was 65 or over in 2013–2014), Japan is facing an acute labour market shortage over the coming years and decades (Miyamoto 2014). Indeed, "the Asian century will also be the ageing century" (CEPAR 2013: i), and this demographic change will impact both the size and productivity of the labour force – and inevitably alter its nature and composition.

The career progression of "Generation Y" employees (those born between 1978 and 1994) and the entrance of "Generation Z" (born 1995–2009) into the global workforce will also bring new challenges. While Generation Y employees are characterised by their high demands and expectations regarding salaries, benefits and opportunities, different work habits and technological literacy (Burke & Ng 2006), Generation Z employees will value work–life balance, flexibility, innovation and empowerment, a global working atmosphere and ownership (McCrindle 2015). An Adecco study of 15–18-year-old Generation Z members in Asia examined the employment preferences and workplace attitudes of this cohort and concluded that Generation Z is entrepreneurial, values flexibility in the workplace and ranks job security as the most important employment attribute (*The Nation* 2014). These characteristics will present new challenges and opportunities for the region's tourism labour market.

The third demographic trend impacting the tourism labour market is the growing percentage of women in the workforce. According to a 2015 study by the ILO, there has been a surge in the number of women employed in senior and middle management positions over the past two decades. Women also own and manage over 30 per cent of all businesses, although these are more likely to be micro and small enterprises (ILO 2015). Nevertheless, the "glass ceiling" for women in the workforce still exists, and only 5 per cent or less of the CEOs of the world's largest corporations are women (ILO 2015).

Political factors

In recent decades, many countries in Asia – most recently Myanmar – have transitioned from centrally organised economies to private markets, opening the door to increased numbers of private sector jobs (Gammack *et al.* 2004; ILO 2007a). A shift away from agriculture and commodities to service-based industries (such as tourism) and an increasing push towards urban centres has opened new avenues for employment in the tourism industry, and has seen many countries target the tourism sector as a strategic way of boosting economic growth, social development and job creation (Baum & Thompson 2007; Bowden 2005; UNWTO 2002a).

A relaxation of immigration policies such as those allowed by the Association of South-East Asian Nations' (ASEAN) visa-free zone for member country nationals (UNWTO 2007) has been identified as a priority for the region to meet tourism labour market needs, particularly at management and professional levels (Ruhanen & Cooper 2009). Though in many countries employers must demonstrate that it is not possible to fill a vacant position with a qualified local candidate before being allowed to employ a foreign worker (ILO 2003), labour migration is on the increase.

Migrant labour

Although the region is made up of countries with large populations, demographic changes – such as the ageing population – are likely to have significant effects on the region's long-term tourism labour supply and increase the need to examine other source markets, such as migrant labour. Indeed this must be the case if the situation of the European Union is anything to go by, where countries will need up to 20 million migrants over the next 25 years to cover the decline of its economically active population (Commission of the European Communities 2005).

However, the use of migrant labour to address skilled labour shortages in tourism is not seen as equally important by all countries. In Malaysia, for example, migrant labour is already being used to meet skills shortages, and many other countries have policies allowing 'imported' labour to meet certain skills gaps. Yet for other countries in the region, amending immigration laws to increase the participation of unskilled migrant workers in the tourism labour market is not a priority. Instead, large populations with relatively high unemployment rates already supplied a large pool of candidates for general labour and these countries place more value on attracting skilled migrant labour, particularly when such migrants could transfer skills to local employees (Ruhanen & Cooper 2009).

Labour market practices and wages

In 2014, the APEC Human Resources Development Ministerial meeting identified a number of key issues related to the region's general labour market practices, including the need to focus on improving the wellbeing of workers and their families, strengthening social protection mechanisms and providing equal employment opportunities, particularly to vulnerable economic groups (APEC 2014). Previous APEC studies have found that short-term cost-cutting is prevalent during times of economic insecurity, leading to increased unemployment and reduced skills in the labour force. Taking into account the inherent characteristics of the tourism sector mentioned earlier, synergies arise in terms of financial and time constraints limiting investments in HR practices and employee skills development.

Indeed, in a 2009 survey of the region it was found that there was general consensus among opinion leaders in the region that salaries and working conditions, limited career opportunities and negative perceptions of employment in the tourism industries had a large part to play in the lack of labour supply (Ruhanen & Cooper 2009). Though wages in the tourism industries are generally aligned with the country's minimum wage level, employees often do not believe that the wages offered are reflective of the work required; nor do low wages increase the appeal of long, irregular and anti-social working hours common especially in the food and beverage and accommodation industries. These issues increase the risk that skilled and highly qualified workers will leave the tourism sector and move to new industries that offer more stable, social working hours and higher wages.

While some governments in the region have addressed minimum wage levels and workforce policies to improve employment conditions, boost productivity and enhance stability in the labour market (Ruhanen & Cooper 2009), the issue remains that many jobs offered in the tourism sector are basic, frontline service positions which do not necessarily warrant higher wages. Even if a desire exists to offer higher wages to retain quality staff, low profit margins of many tourism businesses – particularly SMEs – decrease their ability to do so.

The tourism labour market in Asia is also dominated by part-time, casual and temporary employees. This working structure does little to enhance job security and can thus adversely impact commitment to and performance on the job. While creating flexibility for employers, a continual loss of knowledge through staff turnover can impact on the competitiveness of an organisation and lower morale among workers. High turnover or labour mobility has been identified by many countries in Asia as a key issue for the tourism sector, raising the need for improved recruitment and retention strategies, particularly if businesses want to maintain their profitability and competitiveness (Ruhanen & Cooper 2009).

Negative perceptions of tourism sector employment

Along with the low wages and unfavourable working conditions commonly associated with the tourism sector, a lack of career advancement opportunities is a further deterrent to labour market entrants. For tertiary-qualified employees, for example, the types of tasks required to work in the tourism sector may be considered too menial and not in line with their high levels of education (Ruhanen & Cooper 2009). In addition, the drive for "Generation Y" employees to rapidly advance their career rather than gradually work their way up an organisation creates challenges. As Baum (2007a, 2007b) notes, tourism is sometimes also not even seen as a "real" or "serious" industry to work in, let alone viewed as providing a promising long-term career option for skilled workers. Service-based roles can be considered demeaning, though work in high-end hotels and executive air travel can carry a level of esteem.

A labour market study undertaken in the region (Ruhanen & Cooper 2009) found that the most pressing concern for the tourism labour market was the negative perception of working in the tourism industries and the resulting high unmet demand, particularly for skilled labour. This lack of supply to meet demand is especially felt at the professional and managerial levels and in the accommodation and food and beverage sectors because of the significant number of workers required for these roles and the conditions associated with this type of work.

Human resource development

Imperative to attracting skilled workers and combating supply and demand gaps in the tourism industries is the development of human resource capacity. In order to counteract negative perceptions of tourism sector employment and make employment in the tourism industries attractive, despite low wages and unfavourable working conditions, human resource professionals must work even harder on demand-side strategies. As APEC (1999) notes, an "assets" approach to human resources – one which is focused on investment in skills development, continual learning and training or development to improve productivity – is essential for reducing long-term costs, increasing efficiency and increasing innovation to benefit tourism businesses. For employees, such an approach can improve wages and working conditions, provide employment security and boost skill levels (APEC 1999).

A study of tourism policy makers from a number of countries in Asia identified a number of the key labour market skill shortages. Clear skills gaps were identified by respondents, though responses varied from country to country (Table 4.1). The most common skills gaps identified were management skills (particularly in terms of human resources development and management) and communication and language skills.

Table 4.1 Identified future skills required by tourism industries

China	• Innovation and entrepreneurship to improve product development • Executive management and organisational leadership • Communication skills and language capabilities, particularly English, for frontline service positions • Niche tourism market capabilities such as business/exhibitions, cultural, eco-tourism, adventure, etc.
India	• Destination management capabilities • Management skills, particularly for the accommodation sector • Specialists and guides to meet niche markets such as adventure tourism and eco-tourism • Marketing capabilities • Service delivery and quality standards • Improved capabilities and skills of frontline employees
Indonesia	• Managerial skills • Entrepreneurship • Information technology • English-language capabilities • General business skills/professionalism
Iran	• HR management in the tourism industries • Practical and vocational skills, particularly in the accommodation and F&B sectors • Marketing and market research capabilities to identify and target emerging tourist markets
Japan	• Improved linguistic skills • Management skills • General ongoing education and training programmes to provide employees with a range of skills such as customer service
Malaysia	• Further development of communication skills and languages • Service skills to ensure high service quality • Functional flexibility of employees in the tourism labour market
Korea	• Language skills to meet emerging visitor markets such as Thailand and Vietnam • Marketing and promotion skills • Improved communication skills, particularly for multicultural awareness and understanding • Customer service and service quality • Computer and technical skills
Sri Lanka	• Specific training for niche markets such as adventure tourism, as well as travel agents and the transportation sector • Management training • Service quality • Business skills including professionalism
Thailand	• Good communication and language skills, particularly Chinese and English • Management and professional skills • Skills for niche markets such as eco-tourism • Technical and operational skills

Future needs and challenges

Looking ahead to the future trends of the tourism labour market in Asia, it is certain that countries will continue to face a plethora of challenges, but also opportunities. Increasing connectivity, especially through the establishment of the ASEAN Economic Community (AEC), will result in a freer flow of goods, services, investment capital and skilled labour in the region (ILO & ADB 2014). However, it will also increase the need for inclusive policies, balanced growth across the region, better jobs and shared prosperity (ILO & ADB 2014). The opportunities presented by the AEC will not be the same across all countries involved, nor across all industries. In the tourism labour market specifically, a number of trends and issues have been identified which are likely to likely have an impact on the tourism labour market to 2020, with considerable similarities between countries (Ruhanen & Cooper 2009) (Table 4.2).

Table 4.2 Identified future trends and challenges in the tourism labour market

China	• Ongoing challenges of attracting sufficient skilled labour to meet demand in the tourism industries • Continued high levels of labour mobility as a result of reduced job security and tenure • Developing and nurturing local talent for professional-/managerial-level positions • Obtaining standardised education and training systems for the tourism industries • Overall financial/economic situation of the country • Continued poor perception of tourism as a career option or desirable employer given wage levels and working conditions
India	• Ongoing challenge of obtaining sufficient skilled labour to meet required service standards of the tourism industries, particularly in language capabilities • Continued competition for skilled labour with other industries which are more appealing to the labour market because of wages and working conditions • Coordination and engagement of the tourism industries to improve their HR practices • An aversion to continuous training within the sector by SMEs due to investment costs
Indonesia	• Movement of cross-border labour both within the country and internationally • Reinstatement of high visitor demand for Indonesia providing stimulus for the tourism industries but creating further labour market shortages • Ongoing skills shortages and capabilities particularly at management level • New investment and development of education and training institutes • Continued lack of standardisation in HR competencies in the sector • Shortage of labour with skills in communication, IT and languages • Impact and recovery from global financial crisis
Iran	• Ongoing lack of skilled labour to meet the demand of the tourism industries • Continued challenge of low wages and salaries in the tourism industries relative to other major industries • Training and further education for educators and trainers in the tourism industries to meet international standards and practices • Improving access to educational resources and research on the tourism industries and tourism labour market • Reforms to the tourism labour market structure including trade associations to cooperate and engage in policies and strategies for enhancing the tourism industries • Rectify current marketing activities to offset low inbound arrivals
Japan	• To maintain and grow the availability of skilled labour in the tourism industries
Malaysia	• Continued general and skilled labour shortages in the tourism industries, particularly in the accommodation sector • Increasing labour costs in order to attract and retain skilled or experienced employees in the tourism industries

Korea
- The impact of changes to the immigration law for foreign labour
- The increased outsourcing and use of temporary labour
- Increasing gap in wages between highly skilled employees such as professionals and specialists as compared to those with low skills
- Continued changes to the country's economic base from manufacturing to service industries

Sri Lanka
- Tourism visitation improvement, leading to increased demand for skilled labour
- Lack of skilled labour at the professional and management levels
- Fewer young people choosing to enter the tourism industries
- Continued low salaries and unfavourable working conditions
- Continued high labour mobility and "drain" of skilled employees seeking employment in other industries and overseas because of wages and working conditions in the tourism industries

Thailand
- Ongoing shortage of skilled labour in the tourism industries
- Lack of appropriately skilled labour at the professional and management levels
- Increased capacity within the existing education and training system to meet demand for skilled labour in the tourism industries

Case study 4.1 Tourism employment and poverty alleviation

The Millennium Development Goals (MDGs) were officially adopted by the international community at the Millennium Summit in 2000, under the leadership of the United Nations. The first of these goals, to halve the proportion of the population living on less than US$1 per day, aimed to: "make the goals of full and productive employment and decent work for all, including women and young people, a central objective of our relevant national and international policies and our national development strategies" (ILO 2007b).

The ILO (2007a) identified that the realisation of full and productive employment and decent work is the principal way for people to escape poverty. Since the implementation of the MDGs, the number of workers living below the poverty line decreased dramatically, to 384 million workers in 2011 – a reduction of 294 million since 2001. However, the gender gap in employment remains an issue worldwide (United Nations n.d.), and global economic downturns continue to exert pressure on the labour market, including in the tourism industries.

In Asia, significant levels of poverty and inequality prevail despite countries' commitment to the MDGs. This is because economic growth is not generating sufficient productive and decent employment (UNESCAP *et al.* 2013), which is in part due to technological change and in part due to a lack of multiplier effect. In countries which rely heavily on extractive industries, for example, rural populations and farmers often do not reap the benefits of economic growth and are frequently neglected. This can lead to increased numbers of people entering vulnerable employment. In fact, in South Asia, it is estimated that almost 80 per cent of the workforce are in vulnerable employment, and in East Asia, which has witnessed rapid economic growth, 50 per cent of workers are. Many of these workers, predominantly women, still live on less than US$1.25 per day (UNESCAP *et al.* 2013).

Nevertheless, tourism and the resulting employment created are still widely regarded as a significant vehicle for poverty alleviation. Indeed, maximising the number of local workers employed in technical, supervisory and managerial levels can help to retain income domestically and reduce leakage (UNWTO 2006). SMEs especially can have a positive economic impact on poor communities because they are generally locally owned and operated, buy from local suppliers, have fewer negative socio-cultural impacts, are adaptable and fill market gaps with small products mostly overlooked by large organisations (Echtner 1995).

Conclusion

The issues presented in this chapter highlight the strengths and weaknesses of the tourism sector, and the resulting challenges and opportunities for labour markets. Because the sector is often perceived to be associated with poor working conditions, unsociable hours, low wages and a lack of career progression opportunities, it often fails to attract a pool of skilled workers who are committed to remaining in the tourism industries. Likewise, shifting demographic trends and the changing nature of Asia's political and economic connectivity pose new challenges that have yet to be fully understood by labour market researchers. While employment in the tourism sector has been shown to have potential in terms of poverty alleviation (see case study), especially though its accessibility to women and new workforce entrants, this potential can be hampered by government policy, a lack of recognition of the value of work in the sector and a limited focus on good human resource management, adequate training and opportunities to progress upwards to succeed.

In summary, if the tourism sector continues to grow at its current rate, there is strong potential for it to have a real and lasting impact on the communities and lives it impacts, particularly those that are most vulnerable. However, further research is needed into the challenges and opportunities of individual countries, the influence of technological and demographic changes, and how to change the general perception of work in the tourism sector.

Acknowledgement

The authors gratefully acknowledge the contribution and assistance of Lina Cronin of the University of Queensland in the preparation of this chapter.

Key reading

Baum, T. (2007) 'Human resources in tourism: Still waiting for change', *Tourism Management*, 28: 1383–1399.

International Labour Organization (ILO) (2003) *Employment and Human Resources in the Tourist Industry in Asia and the Pacific*. Geneva: ILO.

Ruhanen, L. and Cooper, C. (2009) *The Tourism Labour Market in the Asia Pacific Region: Final Report to the UNWTO Regional Representation for Asia and the Pacific*. Madrid: World Tourism Organization.

Szivas, E., Riley, M. and Airey, D. (2003) 'Labor mobility into tourism: Attraction and satisfaction', *Annals of Tourism Research*, 30(1): 64–78.

United Nations World Tourism Organization (UNWTO) and International Labour Organization (ILO). (2008) *Sources and Methods: Labour Statistics – Employment in the Tourism Industries (Special Edition)*. Madrid: World Tourism Organization.

References

ARC Centre of Excellence in Population Ageing Research (CEPAR). (2013) *Asia in the Ageing Century: Part 1 – Population Trends*. Sydney: CEPAR.

Asia-Pacific Economic Cooperation (APEC) (1999) *Successful Practices in Human Resources Development in the Workplace: Contributions from Labour, Management and Government*. Singapore: Asia-Pacific Economic Cooperation Secretariat.

—— (2014) *Sixth APEC Human Resources Development Ministerial Meeting: Joint Statement*. Ha Noi, Vietnam Asia-Pacific Economic Cooperation. Online. Available: www.apec.org/Meeting-Papers/Ministerial-Statements/Human-Resources-Development/2014_hrdmm.aspx (accessed 2 February 2015).

Ball, R.M. (1988) 'Seasonality: A problem for workers in the tourism labour market?' *The Service Industries Journal*, 8(4): 501–513.

Baum, T. (1995) *Managing Human Resources in the European Tourism and Hospitality Industry: A Strategic Approach*. London: Chapman & Hall.

—— (2007a) 'Human resources in tourism: Still waiting for change', *Tourism Management*, 28: 1383–1399.

—— (2007b) 'Skills and the hospitality sector in a transition economy: The case of front office employment in Kyrgyzstan', *Asia Pacific Journal of Tourism Research*, 12(2): 89–102.

Baum, T. and Thompson, K. (2007) 'Skills and labour markets in transition: A tourism skills inventory of Kyrgyzstan, Mongolia and Uzbekistan', *Asia Pacific Journal of Human Resources*, 45(2): 235–255.

Bowden, J. (2005) 'Pro-poor tourism and the Chinese experience', *Asia Pacific Journal of Tourism Research*, 10(4): 379–398.

Briedenhann, J. and Wickens, E. (2004) 'Tourism routes as a tool for the economic development of rural areas: Vibrant hope or impossible dream?' *Tourism Management*, 25: 71–79.

Burke, R.J. and Ng, E. (2006) 'The changing nature of work and organizations: Implications for human resource management', *Human Resource Management Review*, 16: 86–94.

Choy, D.J.L. (1995) 'The quality of tourism employment', *Tourism Management*, 16(2): 129–137.

Commission of the European Communities (2005) *Green Paper on EU Approach to Managing Economic Migration*. Online. Available: http://ec.europa.eu/justice_home/doc_centre/immigration/work/doc/com_2004_811_en.pdf (accessed 31 December 2009).

De Lacy, T., Battig, M., Moore, S. and Noakes, S. (2002) *Public/Private Partnerships for Sustainable Tourism: Delivering a Sustainability Strategy for Tourism Destinations*. Gold Coast: Sustainable Tourism Cooperative Research Centre.

Dwyer, L. and Forsyth, P. (1993) 'Assessing the benefits and costs of inbound tourism', *Annals of Tourism Research*, 20: 751–768.

Echtner, C.M. (1995) 'Entrepreneurial training in developing countries', *Annals of Tourism Research*, 22(1): 119–134.

Gammack, J., Asia Pacific Economic Cooperation Tourism Working Group, Griffith University School of Management and Asia Pacific Economic Cooperation International Centre for Sustainable Tourism (2004) *Development Needs of Small to Medium Size Tourism Businesses*. Report prepared for APEC Tourism Working Group, School of Management, Griffith Business School, Griffith University, Queensland, Australia.

International Labour Organization (ILO) (2003) *Employment and Human Resources in the Tourist Industry in Asia and the Pacific*. Geneva: ILO.

—— (2007a) *Key Indicators of the Labour Market* (5th edn). Geneva: ILO.

—— (2007b) 'Almost half of Thai workers are putting in "excessive" hours'. Press release. Online. Available: www.ilo.org/asia/info/public (accessed 2 February 2015).

—— (2015) *Women in Business and Management: Gaining Momentum*. Geneva: International Labour Organisation Bureau for Employers' Activities.

International Labour Organization (ILO) and Asian Development Bank (ADB) (2014) *ASEAN Community 2015: Managing Integration for Better Jobs and Shared Prosperity*. Bangkok: ILO and ADB.

Lee, G.O.M. and Warner, M. (2006) 'The impact of SARS on China's human resources: Implications for the labour market and level of unemployment in the service sector in Beijing, Guangzhou and Shanghai', *The International Journal of Human Resource Management*, 17(5): 860–880.

Liu, A. and Wall, G. (2006) 'Planning tourism employment: A developing country perspective', *Tourism Management*, 1(1): 159–170.

Lourens, M. (2007) 'Route tourism: A roadmap for successful destinations and local economic development', *Development Southern Africa*, 24(3): 475–490.

McCrindle, M. (2015) 'Generation Z: employees'. Online. Available: http://generationz.com.au/employees (accessed 2 February 2015).

Marchante, A.J., Ortega, B. and Pagan, R. (2006) 'Determinants of skills shortages and hard-to-fill vacancies in the hospitality sector', *Tourism Management*, 27: 791–802.

Miyamoto, H. (2014) 'Japan must work hard to solve labour crisis', *East Asia Forum*. Online. Available: www.eastasiaforum.org/2014/08/05/japan-must-work-hard-to-solve-labour-crisis (accessed 2 February 2015).

The Nation (2014) 'Gen Z workers will rewrite job market demand and supply in Asia', *The Nation*, 7 April. Online. Available: www.nationmultimedia.com/business/Gen-Z-workers-will-rewrite-job-market-demand-and-s-30231016.html (accessed 2 February 2015).

Ruhanen, L. and Cooper, C. (2009) *The Tourism Labour Market in the Asia Pacific Region: Final Report to the UNWTO Regional Representation for Asia and the Pacific.* Madrid: World Tourism Organization.

Szivas, E., Riley, M. and Airey, D. (2003) 'Labor mobility into tourism: Attraction and satisfaction', *Annals of Tourism Research*, 30(1): 64–78.

United Nations (n.d.) *Millennium Development Goals and Beyond 2015.* Online. Available: www.un.org/millenniumgoals/poverty.shtml (accessed 2 February 2015).

United Nations Economic and Social Commission for Asia and the Pacific (UNESCAP), Asian Development Bank (ADB) and United Nations Development Programme (UNDP) (2013) *Asia-Pacific Aspirations: Perspectives for a Post-2015 Development Agenda.* Bangkok: UNESCAP, ADB and UNDP.

United Nations World Tourism Organization (UNWTO) (2002a) *Human Resources in Tourism: Towards a New Paradigm.* Madrid: World Tourism Organization.

—— (2002b) *Enhancing the Economic Benefits of Tourism for Local Communities and Poverty Alleviation.* Madrid: World Tourism Organization.

—— (2006) *Poverty Alleviation through Tourism: A Compilation of Good Practices.* Madrid: World Tourism Organization.

—— (2007) *Policies, Strategies and Tools for the Sustainable Development of Tourism.* Madrid: UNWTO.

—— (2014a) *UNWTO Tourism Highlights 2014 Edition.* Madrid: UNWTO.

—— (2014b) *International Tourism on Track to End 2014 with Record Numbers.* Madrid: UNWTO.

United Nations World Tourism Organization (UNWTO) and International Labour Organization (ILO) (2008) *Sources and Methods: Labour Statistics – Employment in the Tourism Industries (Special Edition).* Madrid: UNWTO.

World Travel and Tourism Council (WTTC) (2014) *Travel and Tourism Economic Impact 2014: Asia Pacific.* London: WTTC.

5

TOURISM POLICIES AND POLITICS IN ASIA

C. Michael Hall & Wantanee Suntikul

Introduction

While the politics of international trade, especially with respect to commodities such as fuels, receives a significant amount of attention, partly because of its impacts on global and regional geopolitics, but also because of its flow-on effects on economic and environmental policy making, the politics of tourism are nowhere nearly as well considered. Nevertheless, the politics of international tourism are a vital dimension of world tourism, and government policy is an important determinant of the character and possibilities for expansion in global and regional tourism (Matthews 1978; Elliot 1983; Richter 1989; Butler & Suntikul 2010; Timothy & Kim 2015). Issues of political stability and political relations within and between states are also extremely important in determining the image of destinations in tourist-generating regions and, of course, the real and perceived safety of tourists (Hall 2005). A government's position on the role and appropriate nature of tourism is an important component of that government's foreign policy and is usually indicative of the ideological and economic alignment of the nation. However, it should also be noted that the dynamics and trajectories of tourism are not only affected by tourism policy but also by other policy areas (Bramwell & Lane 2013; Truong 2013). Indeed, Hall (2005) has suggested that policy making in areas such as the economy, especially exchange rate policy, employment law, and the environment, may be more important for what happens in tourism development than tourism policy, although this clearly depends on the policy mix in specific jurisdictions. For example, in discussing the role of tourism in negotiations on international trade in services and their implications for tourist mobility, Hall (2008: 50) argued,

> it is extremely difficult to separate the tourism services policy arena from other policy areas related to such issues as migration or international trade in general ... tourism policy per se only represents a very small proportion of the overall number of policy fields that affect tourism and for which decisions are made often with little consideration of the impacts on trade in tourism services.

This chapter provides a general overview of tourism and political issues in the Asian context. It first provides a broad introduction to some of the main themes in studies of the politics of tourism before looking more specifically at issues of the politics of mobility, tourism in bilateral and multilateral agreements, and tourism and political instability and security.

Tourism and politics in Asia

Tourism can be used as a political instrument in relations between states, and travel restrictions were especially prevalent during the Cold War, between countries of the socialist and capitalist blocs. Restrictions on the travel of their citizens has been used by countries such as China and the United States as a political tool for many years. For example, in the Asian context the ease of tourist movement between Taiwan and mainland China has long been an element in the countries' political relations (Guo *et al.* 2006; Chiang 2012). Importantly, tourism is also a significant beneficiary of peaceful relations between and within countries (Pratt & Liu 2016).

Case study 5.1 Relationships between neighbouring countries: Thailand, Cambodia and the Preah Vihear Temple

The case of the Preah Vihear Temple exemplifies the complex interrelations between politics, national identity, heritage and tourism. The Khmer temple complex of Preah Vihear lies in Cambodia, just a few hundred metres from the current border with Thailand. The location of this border has shifted repeatedly over the years. The current boundary was drawn in 1907, as the outcome of a Franco-Siamese treaty, placing the temple complex within the French colony of Cambodia. However, the territorial right over this site has continued to be a point of perennial dispute between Cambodia and Thailand. In 2008, UNESCO's ratification of Cambodia's application for World Heritage Listing for the Preah Vihear Temple was met with public protests in Thailand and a denouncement by Thai Prime Minister Abhisit Vejjajiva, fearing that ratification of this application would legitimize Cambodian claims to the site. From 2009, the dispute escalated to a series of military skirmishes at or near the temple site, culminating in a four-day battle in February 2011, which killed, injured or financially ruined a number of local people and damaged structures.

Because of the conflict, no tourists visited the site in February 2011 (Makara 2011), and in the first six months of 2011 only 27,980 tourists came, compared to 46,400 in the first half of 2010 (Say 2011). However, once the site was again perceived as "safe", foreigners were drawn by curiosity to see the impact of the conflict on the site, while domestic tourists began to return out of a sense of solidarity (Kunthear 2013), such that tourism to Preah Vihear recovered very quickly after the conflict. In the third quarter of 2012, the number of domestic tourists had increased by 57.7 per cent from the previous year, to 142,910. The number of foreign tourists had increased by over 77 per cent, to 13,140 (Reuy 2012). The belligerence between the two national governments was in contrast with the attitudes of local people on both sides of the border. The headman of one local *Tambon* (group of villages) on the Thai side of the border said that his main concern was to re-establish relations with people on the Cambodian side to perform a joint religious ceremony to "improve the atmosphere" (Kanparit 2013). As Suntikul and Butler (2014: 222) concluded,

> the views of local participants in such issues is often more appropriate than official political positions taken in capital cities unaffected by such local conflicts. The sharing of tourism-generated revenues and employment is seen as being of greater local benefit by residents on opposite sides of the border than continued hostilities at the national level.

Further reading

Suntikul, W. and Butler, R. (2014) 'War and peace: and tourism in Southeast Asia', in C. Wohlmuther and W. Wintersteiner (eds), *International Handbook on Tourism and Peace* (pp. 216–229). Klagenfurt: Drava.

An appreciation of the political context of tourism is critical to an understanding of the complex nature of tourism, particularly in Asia where political effects have had dramatic impacts on tourism flow, labour flow, investment, development and policy making (Nyaupane & Timothy 2010; Kim & Prideaux 2012; Bendle 2015; Henderson 2015). Richter's seminal works on the politics of tourism in Asia have been extremely influential (e.g. Richter 1980, 1989, 1999). Since then, there has been a range of research on the politics of tourism in Asia at both a macro-level (e.g. Elliot 1997; Hall & Oehlers 2000; Butler & Suntikul 2010) and at a national or thematic level, e.g. the Korean peninsula (Henderson 2002; Kim, Timothy & Han 2007; Timothy & Kim 2015); the politics of tourism in Myanmar and issues of boycotts and sanctions (Philp & Mercer 1999; Henderson 2003; Hudson 2007); the political economy of Asian sex tourism (Leheny 1995; Jeffreys 2008); and the politics of culture, identity and branding (Jeong & Santos 2004; Henderson 2007; Winter 2007; Geary 2013; Zhang *et al.* 2015).

Tourism also requires a degree of cooperation between the governments of tourist-generating countries and those of destination countries. Currency exchange rates, taxes, duties and customs, transport routes, immigration policies and diplomatic agreements each play a part in this. Even for non-governmental ventures, successful business efforts depend on political relations in dealing with authorities in host nations. However, such ventures are often framed by the broader set of trade agreements in which countries are engaged (Hall & Coles 2008). This is of particular importance in the Asian context because of the growing significance of bilateral and multilateral trade agreements.

Tourist flows between two countries provide a de facto measurement of the state of their political relations. A government can choose to construct political barriers against travel by its nation's own citizens to a particular foreign country as a way of indicating its antipathy towards that country's regime or people. In addition, personal or economic travel restrictions, e.g. how much money can be taken out of a country, were historically used as a means to retain scarce economic resources within a country. For example, Japan had such restrictions in place until the hosting of the 1964 Tokyo Olympics. Similarly, South Korea had restrictions on its citizens' travel outside the country until 1988, when the country hosted the Seoul Summer Olympics (Hall 1997). The relationship with mega-events is also no coincidence as their media profile means countries will often want to cast themselves in as positive a light as possible. Both the Tokyo and Seoul Olympics were regarded as opportunities to showcase the countries and the cities as modern and contemporary societies. For example, a study by Jeong (1988) indicated that the 1988 Summer Olympics in Seoul were perceived as a means to overcome the poor image of Korea in the international tourism market as a "dangerous place to visit" (Jeong 1988: 176). Indeed, tourism, together with the hosting of events, has long been an important mechanism of para-diplomacy (Soldatos 1993).

The politics of mobility

Although there is much emphasis on mobility in tourism, states have the power to render their citizens and visitors immobile (Figure 5.1). Although travel may be positioned as a fundamental

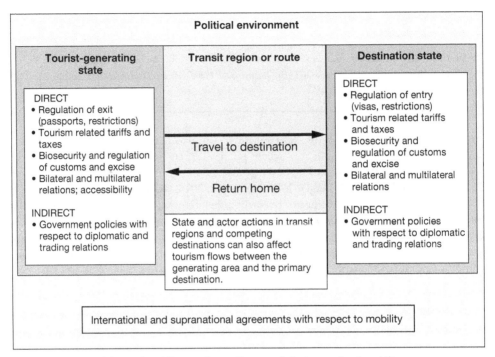

Figure 5.1   Constraining and enabling regulatory framework for international mobility.
Source: adapted from Hall 2008.

human right by a supranational body such as the UNWTO, it is rarely enshrined in law by states. Indeed, the right to control and restrict entry into state territory has "historically been viewed as inherent in the very nature of sovereignty" (Collinson 1996: 77). The capacities of the state to constrain or enable mobility can generally be classified as tariff or non-tariff barriers. Non-tariff barriers include restrictions on entry through screening by nationality or other criteria (e.g. prior criminal or medical condition or some other measure of unsuitability), cost of application for visa, travel allowance restrictions, restrictions on credit card use, and advance-import-deposit-like measures (e.g. compulsory deposits prior to travel). Tariff barriers include import-duty measures, airport departures or airport taxes, and subsidies (e.g. a consumer-subsidy measure such as an official preferential exchange rate for foreign tourists or price concessions) (Hall 2008). Tariff barriers may be managed through bilateral agreements as well as through multilateral negotiations, such as within ASEAN (UNWTO 2013).

Nowhere in international law is there enshrined a right to enter foreign spaces. For example, the advisory *Universal Declaration of Human Rights* only postulates a right of exit and entry to one's own country and freedom of mobility within a citizen's own country. Article 13 states:

(1) Everyone has the right to freedom of movement and residence within the borders of each state.
(2) Everyone has the right to leave any country, including his [sic] own, and to return to his country.

(United Nations 1948)

Article 8 of the *Global Code of Ethics for Tourism* with respect to liberty of tourist movements also notes Article 13 (Table 5.1). However, these are only recommendations and, especially in the

Table 5.1 Liberty of tourist movements (Article 8) of UN Global Code of Ethics for Tourism

1	Tourists and visitors should benefit, in compliance with international law and national legislation, from the liberty to move within their countries and from one state to another, in accordance with Article 13 of the Universal Declaration of Human Rights; they should have access to places of transit and stay and to tourism and cultural sites without being subject to excessive formalities or discrimination.
2	Tourists and visitors should have access to all available forms of communication, internal or external; they should benefit from prompt and easy access to local administrative, legal and health services; they should be free to contact the consular representatives of their countries of origin in compliance with the diplomatic conventions in force.
3	Tourists and visitors should benefit from the same rights as the citizens of the country visited concerning the confidentiality of the personal data and information concerning them, especially when these are stored electronically.
4	Administrative procedures relating to border crossings, whether they fall within the competence of states or result from international agreements, such as visas or health and customs formalities, should be adapted, so far as possible, so as to facilitate the maximum freedom of travel and widespread access to international tourism; agreements between groups of countries to harmonise and simplify these procedures should be encouraged; specific taxes and levies penalising the tourism industry and undermining its competitiveness should be gradually phased out or corrected.
5	So far as the economic situation of the countries from which they come permits, travellers should have access to allowances of convertible currencies needed for their travels.

Source: adapted from United Nations (2001).
Note
The Global Code of Ethics for Tourism was initially adopted by resolution A/RES/406(XIII) at the Thirteenth World Tourism Organization General Assembly (Santiago, Chile, 27 September–1 October 1999). It was then adopted as a resolution of the United Nations General Assembly, 21 December 2001.

case of the Global Code, carry very little weight in international law. Although many nation-states have entered into bilateral and multilateral agreements that facilitate mobility between state parties, the prerogative to control entry remains firmly with each nation-state (Neumayer 2006; Coles & Hall 2011). For example, arguably the most important direct measure by government on mobility is the provision of passports and travel documents (Neumayer 2006, 2010, 2011). In order to enter foreign territories, travellers require passports or other documentation, which only nation-states have the right to issue, together with a valid visa depending on which passport they hold and where they want to travel to (see also Coles 2008). Without such documentation an individual becomes stateless in an international regulatory system that is founded on the recognition of state authority (Hess 2006).

"The capacity of gaining access to foreign spaces is … highly unequal" (Hall 2008: 38). The extent to which access to travel documentation is a right varies because of different national laws. However, even where rights exist, such documentation is not provided for free and the financial cost of passport provision may deter some potential travellers (Neumayer 2006; Coles & Hall 2011; UNWTO 2013, 2014). Furthermore, in many Asian jurisdictions citizenship by itself does not confer a right to a passport as the state may have a number of political reasons not to grant passports. Recognition of passports by destination authorities also affects travel decision making as acceptance is embedded within a complex set of bilateral and multilateral arrangements with respect to recognition of various nation-states; visa provision to provide for entry; and even sanctions on those who come from or visit some states. For example, Israeli citizens may not be able to gain entry to a number of predominantly Muslim Asian countries, such as Indonesia. Many countries also require the issuance of visas as a provision for entry, although these can sometimes be purchased or obtained at the border. In many cases visa-granting regulations require the temporary surrender of a passport to an embassy (or other authority) of the destination country, as well as other documentation relating to identity and purpose of visit and the payment of a fee (Whyte 2008; UNWTO 2014). Economic measures may also affect travel flows. For example, many jurisdictions impose a departure tax or other taxes on international visitors or nationals, often for revenue-raising purposes, while others seek to reduce the extent of illegal immigration by having more rigorous and/or restrictive visa access for nationals of some countries (Thunø 2003).

Chinese Approved Destination Status (ADS) programme

A good example of the ways in which regulatory requirements can affect travel flows is the Chinese Approved Destination Status (ADS) programme (Neumayer 2006; Arita *et al.* 2011; Arita *et al.* 2014; Ma *et al.* 2015). Although travel for sightseeing was long frowned upon in state communist China, post-1978 and the "open-door" policy, international leisure tourism has become recognised as being an extremely significant part of the economy, an important symbol of Chinese modern economic development, and a mechanism of Chinese diplomacy and international relations. In 1981 Chinese citizens were only allowed to undertake group leisure trips to selected countries in southeast Asia (Hong Kong, Macau, Thailand and Singapore). In 1983 private travel with the purpose of visiting friends and relations (VFR) overseas was allowed. Since the early 1990s the Chinese government has enacted a number of policy changes in order to encourage outbound tourism (Zhang and Han 2004):

- The State Council enacted the *Measures on Management of Outbound Tourism by Chinese Citizens*, which have improved the management system of outbound tourism, seeking to protect the rights of outbound tourists and enterprises running outbound business. The measures stipulate the approved destination countries and regions; the qualifications, approval procedures and business processes of travel agencies running outbound business; the responsibilities of tour leaders; the rights and obligations of tourists; and penalties for not meeting legal obligations.
- The application process for passports was simplified.
- Foreign currency exchange management and control were adjusted.

ADS is a bilateral programme developed by the People's Republic of China (PRC) to manage the international group leisure travel of its citizens to recipient destinations. Each destination country negotiates separately with the China National Tourism Administration (CNTA) and the Chinese government with respect to their specific ADS agreement. Unlike Japan and South Korea, which placed no restrictions on where their citizens could visit after their travel bans were lifted, China's outbound tourism policy is selective and therefore, as Arita *et al.* (2014) note, is both liberalizing and restricting.

Introduced in 1995, the ADS programme enables citizens of the PRC to use personal passports and apply for tourism visas to countries approved for visitation. For national destinations approved under ADS, mainland Chinese no longer have to contact embassies or consulates in order to obtain a visa. Instead, visas for leisure group travel are provided by outbound travel agencies that have been authorised by the CNTA. However, the visas are restricted by the itinerary, which must be fixed at the beginning of the trip. Travellers are also obliged to travel in a tour group (minimum of five people including a tour leader) and are not allowed to extend their stay or apply for other types of visas. The destination tourist authority must provide a list of approved tour operators that can handle land arrangements for tour groups. Travel solely for pleasure is not allowed to non-ADS countries. If mainland Chinese wish to travel to non-ADS countries their trip must be for business, education, or family (VFR) purposes in order to gain a departure visa.

Achievement of ADS is now recognised as crucial to the development of tourism, transport and aviation relations with China and has become a significant economic aspect of China's foreign relations, particularly with respect to smaller economies, such as those in the Pacific (Windybank 2005; Shie 2007; Arita *et al.* 2014). The ADS is also significant because, as well as providing for tourist entry into the destination country, it also allows the destination country to open a tourist office in China and conduct marketing activities, thereby potentially encouraging further demand from Chinese tourists (King *et al.* 2006). Arita *et al.* (2014) argue that since the Chinese government regards granting ADS to a country as a concession favouring the grantee country, China may be seen as using ADS as an instrument of "soft power" to gain political concessions from potential grantee countries. They cite the example of Fiji, noting that it was widely reported that China granted ADS to the South Pacific island nation in return for Fiji not recognizing Taiwan diplomatically, and highlight that the Dominican Republic is the only country that currently recognises Taiwan that has successfully negotiated an ADS agreement with China (2009) (China granted ADS to Taiwan in 2008).

The significance of bilateral and multilateral agreements

In the Asian context bilateral agreements such as the ADS appear to have had a far greater direct impact on travel flows than multilateral agreements (Neumayer 2010, 2011). Multilateral agreements have been important for the investment regime under which countries operate and may have also facilitated the opening up of aviation routes. However, individual leisure tourist mobility is unlikely to be further substantially liberalised in the foreseeable future, although some specific market segments may benefit. For example, Asia-Pacific Economic Cooperation (APEC) members created an APEC Business Travel Card (ABTC) which is designed to facilitate short-term entry through pre-clearance measures between participant countries (Hall 2008).

The Preah Vihear case, discussed above, provides a clear illustration of the contentious and counterproductive facets of nationalism that regional organizations and supranational alliances seek to overcome. Ideally, such organizations aim to build on shared assets to achieve co-prosperity (rather than quarrelling over them in a zero-sum game). Supranational alliances are both economic and political in nature, and membership in such blocs is becoming increasingly important for nations to manage economic and political relations in an increasingly globalised world, where many policy issues, such as the environment, cross international boundaries (Hall 2005). In terms of economics and trade, such alliances can range from free trade agreements to customs unions to common markets to economic unions, and may involve a pair of national governments or a regional or global bloc of nations. Such economic relations always entail political relations and with greater degrees of economic cooperation and integration increasing levels of political co-dependency and trust are also required to fully leverage the value of such relationships.

Many changes in tourism patterns in Asia are emerging as a result of the shifting economic landscape and trade policy in the region. The relationship between China and Vietnam provides an illustration. The normalization of relations between China and Vietnam in 1991 can be seen as one facet of the opening-up of both nations' economies (Womack 2006). This led to an opening of their mutual border for trade purposes, which also allowed easier passage of tourists between the two countries. Especially with the growing affluence of some sectors of Chinese society, Vietnam became a near-at-hand and low-priced destination, leading to 12.77 million border crossings between the two countries from 1993 to 1998 (Xiaosong & Womack 2000). However, disputes between China and Vietnam over the conduct of Chinese firms doing business in Vietnam (Chan 2013), and territorial disputes regarding oil drilling rights in the South China Sea, led to anti-Chinese riots in Vietnam in 2014, which killed several Chinese citizens, causing the Chinese government to issue a "yellow" travel warning for Vietnam, leading to an almost 50 per cent drop in Chinese visitors from April to June 2014 (Thu 2014; see also Lamb & Dao 2015 for a discussion of broader anti-Chinese sentiment in south-east Asia). This is an example of the established Chinese government practice of restricting outbound tourism of its citizens to a country as a "negative sanction" in political disputes (Tse & Hobson 2008; Tse 2015).

A number of the bilateral and regional trade relationships and alliances in Southeast Asia originated in political alliances forged during the Cold War. Close Vietnam–China relations in the 1970s were driven by China's support of Vietnam's communist government in the war against the United States (Womack 2006). Similarly, the initial impetus for the founding of ASEAN in 1967 was apprehension among non-communist (some Western-aligned, some Muslim) countries of Southeast Asia (Thailand, Singapore, Malaysia, the Philippines and Indonesia) to join forces to strengthen themselves against the rising tide of communism in the region, which had led to the toppling of regimes in Vietnam, Laos and Cambodia (Hall 1997). This is in contrast to the current manifestation of ASEAN, which now counts all of the countries of Southeast Asia among its members, and has an agenda that has shifted to building co-prosperity of the member nations.

Tourism is an increasingly prominent element of this integration. The removal of barriers (economic, political and perceptual) that comes with growing economic and political integration between countries, and the formation of international economic unions, is generally associated with an increase in tourism (Timothy 2003; UNWTO 2013). Though the economic integration of ASEAN was originally based on trade of raw materials and manufactured goods, by the early 1990s tourism had become an important aspect of the organization's consideration (Hall, 1994). For example, 1992 was declared "Visit ASEAN Year" and the member countries cooperated to promote the region as an integrated destination, to encourage tourists to stay longer. The ASEAN Tourism Strategic Plan 2011–2015 (ASEAN Secretariat 2011) focuses on the development of "regional products" to attract a greater share of the global tourism market, including raising the quality of human resources, services and facilities, and especially connectivity and coordination between member nations. The plan calls for increased government spending on tourism from all of its members, and establishes visitor arrivals as an essential indicator of progress towards ASEAN's overall goals (ASEAN Secretariat 2011).

SAARC (the South Asian Association for Regional Cooperation), founded in 1985, counts as its members Bangladesh, Bhutan, India, the Maldives, Nepal, Pakistan and Sri Lanka. It plays a similar role to ASEAN in promoting the integrated social and economic co-development among its members. Tourism has been an element of this integration nearly since the organization's inception; the SAARC Technical Committee on Tourism was founded in 1991, and in 1999 a Tourism Council was established under the SAARC Chamber of Commerce and Industry in an attempt to try to unify tourism promotion for the member countries (Hall & Page 2000). Timothy (2003) remarked that this organization has the added challenge of promoting political and economic integration and cooperation between countries with even longer-standing and continuing histories of dispute and antagonism, if not outright conflict, than those of ASEAN, and the lack of progress in SAARC tourism initiatives is indicative of this (Rasul & Manandhar 2009).

The integration brought by such supranational alliances is not without its problems. While bringing economic and social benefits to participating nations, loosening control on flows of money, people and goods can also make it more difficult to control flows of drugs, terrorists and other undesirable elements, uneven distribution of benefits among member countries, and the exploitation of weaker partner countries by stronger ones (Timothy 2003).

Tourism and political instability

Political instability refers to a situation in which conditions and mechanisms of governance and rule are challenged as to their political legitimacy by elements operating from outside of the normal operations of the political system (Hall 2005). When challenge occurs from within a political system and the system is able to adapt and change to meet the demands placed on it, it can be regarded as stable. However, when forces for change are unable to be satisfied from within a political system and the consequence is the use of what the specific jurisdiction regarded as non-legitimate means, such as protest, violence, or even civil war to seek change, then a political system can be described as being unstable. Clearly, the notion of what constitutes legitimate political actions will vary from state to state. While protests such as street marches or publications critical of the incumbent government or rulers may be permitted in one country, they may not in another. For example, in Thailand there are very severe penalties for the crime of lese-majeste, including significant jail terms for criticising the monarchy or their pets (Holmes 2015).

Nevertheless, there are also degrees of political instability, with perceptions often being more important for tourist decision making than political realities or human rights issues. For example, Thai governments have tended to have very short life-spans due to the nature of their political and electoral system, including a long history of military takeovers of government. The PRC, on the other hand, has been reasonably stable even as other former state communist regimes collapsed in Eastern Europe. Political stability is therefore not a value judgment as to the democratic nature, or otherwise, of a state. Indeed, it may well be the case that some authoritarian states in Asia which limit formal opposition to government may provide extremely stable political and economic environments in which tourism may flourish, and may even promote tourism as a means of bringing in foreign exchange and improving their public image (Hall & Ringer 2000; Ghimire 2001; Sofield 2009). By their very nature, authoritarian regimes do not have to go through the public consultation measures that are in place in most Western democracies and which affect planning and development decision making (Hall 1994). Whether a political regime is repressive or not from a human rights perspective may not matter very much at all. What is far more significant from the perspective of most tourists is the extent to which a location is regarded as secure and stable. It is only when places become unstable for extended periods of time and there is media coverage that affects tourist awareness and perceptions that visitor flows change.

The role that authoritarian states have played in tourism development highlights the importance of government, media and tourist perceptions of destinations in determining attitudes towards the political characteristics of the destination and the creation of its tourist image. Figure 5.2 provides a model of some of the factors identified in this chapter and elsewhere that lead to the creation of images of the political stability of a destination region in tourist-generating regions, as well as potential reactions in the tourism destination region. As noted above, critical to market reactions to instability is the role of the media as they play a major part in conveying the relative safety or security of a destination to the market, along with word-of-mouth, and advertising campaigns sponsored by the government(s) of the tourist-generating region. For example, in 2015 the Tourism Authority of Thailand (TAT) won awards for

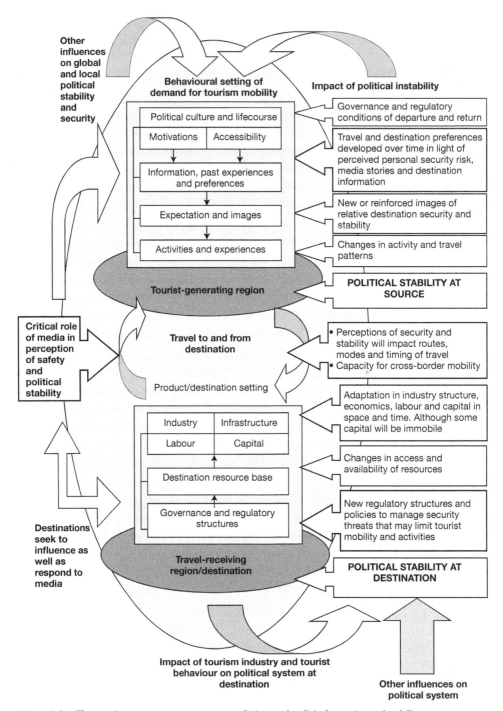

Figure 5.2 The tourism system, governance, regulation and political security and stability.

advertising campaigns that provided a completely different portrayal of the country to that seen in many Western media accounts of the country's political troubles. The YouTube video "I Hate Thailand", which is a story of an independent traveller's experiences of the kingdom after losing his belongings, in which frustration is replaced by love for the nation thanks to the help of the local people, received the Gold Award for Marketing in the Social Media Category. A second PATA Gold Award went to the "Discover Thainess" campaign in the Promotional Travel Video category. The video shows different aspects of Thai culture, including Thai boxing, Thai massage, Thai cooking, and Thai classical dance (*Tourism News* 2015). The TAT campaign is also of significance not only because of negative images of political instability in Thailand, but also stories in some markets with respect to attacks on tourists. For example, the British media have run a series of stories over the rape and murder of backpacker Hannah Witheridge in Koh Tao in September 2014. Concerns have been raised over the Thai police investigation of the murder as well as their use of media to portray their own investigation – which was substantially criticised in the British media – in a more positive light. In a post covered by the *Guardian* after the conviction of Burmese migrant bar workers who denied the charges, the sister of the murdered tourist said that "those who still think Thailand is a safe travel destination should watch a recent video produced by the cyber activist collective Anonymous that accuses the Thai police of a cover-up in the Koh Tao and other murder cases" (Holmes 2016a). Anonymous also suggested that the Thai police "would rather blame foreigners or migrants for such crimes so as to protect their tourism industry than accuse their own Thai locals, that may deter tourists from choosing Thailand as their holiday destination" (quoted in Holmes 2016b).

The issue of attacks on tourists is something that can have a dramatic impact on perceptions of a destination. For example, a series of high-profile attacks on female tourists in India as well as greater coverage of attacks on Indian women in Western media had a substantial effect on perceptions of the safety of India as a place to travel, especially for women, at a time when India was seeking to further promote the country as a destination through the "Incredible India" campaign (Mundkur 2011; Gupta 2014). For example, after the widely publicised gang rape, and later death, of a female physiotherapy intern in New Delhi in December 2012, Khan (2015: 219) suggested that after the coverage of the incident "the image of 'Incredible India' has been broken into pieces". Khan (2015) also noted that according to a report published in the *Hindustan Times* at the end of March 2013 the incident resulted in foreign tourism falling by 25 per cent on average, with an even greater drop of around 35 per cent in female tourists.

However, while direct media coverage is clearly important with respect to perceptions of security, governments also strongly affect travel flows via their communications to the media and individual travellers. Governments, through their foreign policy, can also impact on perceptions of potential destinations and capacity to travel, especially through the contents of travel advisories which not only provide travel advice on the safety of particular destinations but can also affect the price of travel insurance (Lovelock 2004; Löwenheim 2007). Although the clearest link between tourism policies and international diplomacy is seen in the extent to which freedom of movement is enabled between countries by visa and passport policies, travel advisories and short-term policy changes can nevertheless have significant impacts, especially in response to terrorism, health and other threats (Hall, Timothy & Duval 2004; Henderson 2004; Löwenheim 2007; McCartney 2014).

Conclusion

This chapter has provided a brief overview of some of the main features of the politics of tourism in Asia. A key point is that there is no inherent right to international travel under international law. The vast majority of statements and politics from organisations such as the UNWTO are regarded as "soft" international law and therefore do not carry the same legal weight as the international conventions surrounding international trade, for example. In Asia a number of governments still retain tight control on their nationals' international mobility and use tourism as a tool of "soft power" diplomacy. Tourism is also incorporated in bilateral and multilateral agreements, with the former seemingly having the most impact on mobility, usually as a result of changes in visa requirements.

However, despite greater economic and political integration in Asia, significant political disagreements and conflicts still occur to the detriment of tourist flows – examples were given from the relationship between China and Vietnam, as well as that between Cambodia and Thailand. The significance of political instability for tourism was therefore also noted, as well as issues of security. The role of the media in influencing consumer perceptions of security was highlighted, with examples from Thailand in particular, although the ongoing role of government in influencing tourist flows and perceptions remains a critical element of the politics of tourism.

Key reading

Butler, R. and Suntikul, W. (eds) (2010) *Tourism and Political Change*. Oxford: Goodfellow Publishers.

Chan, Y.W. (2013) *Vietnamese–Chinese Relationships at the Borderlands: Trade, Tourism and Cultural Politics*. London: Routledge.

Coles, T. and Hall, C.M. (2011) 'Rights and regulation of travel and tourism mobility', *Journal of Policy Research in Tourism, Leisure and Events*, 3(3): 209–223.

Neumayer, E. (2011) 'On the detrimental impact of visa restrictions on bilateral trade and foreign direct investment', *Applied Geography*, 31: 901–907.

Pratt, S. and Liu, A. (2016) 'Does tourism really lead to peace? A global view', *International Journal of Tourism Research*, 18(1): 82–90.

References

Arita, S., Edmonds, C., La Croix, S and Mak, J. (2011) 'Impact of Approved Destination Status on Chinese travel abroad: An econometric analysis', *Tourism Economics*, 17(5): 983–996.

Arita, S., La Croix, S. and Edmonds, C. (2014) 'Effect of Approved Destination Status on mainland Chinese travel abroad', *Asian Economic Journal*, 28(3): 217–237.

ASEAN Secretariat (2011) *ASEAN Tourism Strategic Plan 2011–2015: ASEAN Tourism*. Jakarta: Association of Southeast Asian Nations (ASEAN).

Bendle, L.J. (2015) 'The structures and flows of a large tourist itinerancy network', *Current Issues in Tourism*, DOI:10.1080/13683500.2015.1092948.

Bramwell, B. and Lane, B. (eds) (2013) *Tourism Governance: Critical Perspectives on Governance and Sustainability*. Abingdon: Routledge.

Butler, R. and Suntikul, W. (eds) (2010) *Tourism and Political Change*. Oxford: Goodfellow Publishers.

Chan, Y.W. (2013) *Vietnamese–Chinese Relationships at the Borderlands: Trade, Tourism and Cultural Politics*. London: Routledge.

Chiang, M.H. (2012) 'Tourism development across the Taiwan strait', *East Asia*, 29(3): 235–253.

Coles, T. (2008) 'Citizenship and the state: Hidden features in the internationalisation of tourism', in T. Coles and C.M. Hall (eds), *International Business and Tourism: Global Issues, Contemporary Interactions* (pp. 55–69). London: Routledge.

Coles, T. and Hall, C.M. (2011) 'Rights and regulation of travel and tourism mobility', *Journal of Policy Research in Tourism, Leisure and Events*, 3(3): 209–223.

Collinson, S. (1996) 'Visa requirements, carrier sanctions, safe third countries and readmission – the development of an asylum buffer zone in Europe', *Transactions of the Institute of British Geographers*, 21(1): 76–90.

Elliot, J. (1983) 'Politics, power, and tourism in Thailand', *Annals of Tourism Research*, 10(3): 377–393.

—— (1997) *Tourism: Politics and Public Sector Management*. New York: Taylor & Francis.

Geary, D. (2013) 'Incredible India in a global age: The cultural politics of image branding in tourism', *Tourist Studies*, 13(1): 36–61.

Ghimire, K.B. (2001) 'Regional tourism and South–South economic cooperation', *Geographical Journal*, 167(2): 99–110.

Guo, Y., Kim, S.S., Timothy, D.J. and Wang, K.C. (2006) 'Tourism and reconciliation between mainland China and Taiwan', *Tourism Management*, 27(5): 997–1005.

Gupta, P. (2014) 'Frozen vodka and white skin in tourist Goa', in D. Picard and M. Di Giovine (eds), *Tourism and the Power of Otherness: Seductions of Difference* (pp. 95–109). Bristol: Channel View.

Hall, C.M. (1994) *Tourism and Politics: Power, Policy and Place*. Chichester: John Wiley.

—— (1997) *Tourism in the Pacific Rim: Development, Impacts and Markets* (2nd edn). South Melbourne: Addison-Wesley Longman.

—— (2005) *Tourism: Rethinking the Social Science of Mobility*. Harlow: Pearson.

—— (2008) 'Regulating the international trade in tourism services', in T. Coles and C.M. Hall (eds), *International Business and Tourism: Global Issues, Contemporary Interactions* (pp. 33–54). London: Routledge.

Hall, C.M. and Coles, T. (2008) 'Introduction: tourism and international business – tourism as international business', in T. Coles and C.M. Hall (eds), *International Business and Tourism: Global Issues, Contemporary Interactions* (pp. 1–25). London: Routledge.

Hall, C.M. and Oehlers, A. (2000) 'Tourism and politics in South and Southeast Asia: Political instability and policy', in C.M. Hall and S.J. Page (eds), *Tourism in South and South-East Asia: Critical Perspectives* (pp. 79–84). Oxford: Butterworth-Heinemann.

Hall, C.M. and Page, S.J. (2000) 'Developing tourism in South Asia: India, Pakistan and Bangladesh: SAARC and beyond', in C.M. Hall and S.J. Page (eds), *Tourism in South and South-East Asia: Critical perspectives* (pp. 197–224). Oxford: Butterworth-Heinemann.

Hall, C.M. and Ringer, G. (2000) 'Tourism in Cambodia, Laos and Myanmar: From terrorism to tourism', in C.M. Hall and S.J. Page (eds), *Tourism in South and South-East Asia: Critical perspectives* (pp. 178–194). Oxford: Butterworth-Heinemann.

Hall, C.M., Timothy, D.J. and Duval, D.T. (2004) 'Security and tourism: Towards a new understanding?' *Journal of Travel & Tourism Marketing*, 15(2–3): 1–18.

Henderson, J.C. (2002) 'Tourism and politics in the Korean Peninsula', *Journal of Tourism Studies*, 13(2): 16–27.

—— (2003) 'The politics of tourism in Myanmar', *Current Issues in Tourism*, 6(2): 97–118.

—— (2004) 'Managing the aftermath of terrorism: The Bali bombings, travel advisories and Singapore', *International Journal of Hospitality & Tourism Administration*, 4(2): 17–31.

—— (2007) 'Communism, heritage and tourism in East Asia', *International Journal of Heritage Studies*, 13(3): 240–254.

—— (2015) 'The new dynamics of tourism in South East Asia: Economic development, political change and destination competitiveness', *Tourism Recreation Research*, 40(3): 379–390.

Hess, J.M. (2006) 'Statelessness and the state: Tibetans, citizenship, and national activism in a transnational world', *International Migration*, 44(1): 79–103.

Holmes, O. (2015) 'Thai man faces jail for insulting king's dog with "sarcastic" internet post'. *Guardian*, 15 December. Online. Available: www.theguardian.com/world/2015/dec/15/thai-man-faces-jail-insulting-kings-dog-sarcastic-internet-post

—— (2016a) 'Corrupt police make Thailand a "dangerous trap", says sister of murdered British tourist', *Guardian*, 12 January.

—— (2016b) 'Anonymous hacks Thai police sites over Burmese jailings for British backpacker murders', *Guardian*, 6 January.

Hudson, S. (2007) 'To go or not to go? Ethical perspectives on tourism in an "outpost of tyranny"', *Journal of Business Ethics*, 76(4): 385–396.

Jeffreys, S. (2008) *The Industrial Vagina: The Political Economy of the Global Sex Trade*. New York: Routledge.

Jeong, G.-H. (1988) 'Tourism expectations on the 1988 Seoul Olympics: A Korean perspective', in *Tourism Research: Expanding Boundaries, Travel and Tourism Research Association, Nineteenth Annual*

Conference (pp. 175–182). Salt Lake City: Bureau of Economic and Business Research, Graduate School of Business, University of Utah.

Jeong, S. and Santos, C.A. (2004) 'Cultural politics and contested place identity', *Annals of Tourism Research*, 31(3): 640–656.

Kanparit, S. (2013) 'A mediator named ASEAN: Lessons from Preah Vihear', *ASEAN News*. Online. Available: www.aseannews.net/a-mediator-named-asean-lessons-from-preah-vihear (accessed 30 July 2013).

Khan, A.R. (2015) 'A chronicle of the global movement to combat violence against women: The role of the second-wave feminist movement and the United Nations – the perspective of Bangladesh'. *Journal of International Women's Studies*, 16(2): 213–244.

Kim, S. and Prideaux, B. (2012) 'A post-colonial analysis of bilateral tourism flows: The case of Korea and Japan', *International Journal of Tourism Research*, 14(6): 586–600.

Kim, S., Timothy, D.J. and Han, H.C. (2007) 'Tourism and political ideologies: A case of tourism in North Korea', *Tourism Management*, 28(4): 1031–1043.

King, B., Dwyer, L. and Prideaux, B. (2006) 'An evaluation of unethical business practices in Australia's China inbound tourism market', *International Journal of Tourism Research*, 8(2): 127–142.

Kunthear, M. (2013) 'Preah Vihear visits on the up', *Phnom Penn Post*. Online. Available: www. phnompenhpost.com/business/preah-vi-hear-visits (accessed 30 July 2013).

Leheny, D. (1995) 'A political economy of Asian sex tourism', *Annals of Tourism Research*, 22(2): 367–384.

Lamb, V. and Dao, N. (2015) *Perceptions and Practices of Investment: China's Hydropower Investments in Mainland Southeast Asia*. BRICS Initiative for Critical Agrarian Studies (BICAS) Working Paper No. 11.

Lovelock, B. (2004) 'New Zealand travel agent practice in the provision of advice for travel to risky destinations', *Journal of Travel & Tourism Marketing*, 15(4): 259–279.

Löwenheim, O. (2007) 'The responsibility to responsibilize: Foreign offices and the issuing of travel warnings', *International Political Sociology*, 1(3): 203–221.

Ma, E., Qu, C., Hsiao, A. and Jin, X. (2015) 'Impacts of China tourism law on Chinese outbound travelers and stakeholders: An exploratory discussion', *Journal of China Tourism Research*, 11(3): 229–237.

McCartney, G. (2014) 'Get out of jail! Locked up and detained abroad – when tourists become prisoners', *Current Issues in Tourism*, 17(7): 561–575.

Makara, K. (2011) 'Preah Vihear tourism drop', *Phnom Penh Post*, www.phnompenhpost.com/business/preah-vihear-tourism-drop (accessed 13 July 2011).

Matthews, H.G. (1978) *International Tourism: A Social and Political Analysis*. Cambridge: Schenkman.

Mundkur, B. (2011) 'Incredible India: the inconvenient truth', *Asian Affairs*, 42(1): 83–97.

Neumayer, E. (2006) 'Unequal access to foreign spaces: How states use visa restrictions to regulate mobility in a globalized world', *Transactions of the Institute of British Geographers*, 31(1): 72–84.

—— (2010) 'Visa restrictions and bilateral travel', *The Professional Geographer*, 62(2): 171–181.

—— (2011) 'On the detrimental impact of visa restrictions on bilateral trade and foreign direct investment', *Applied Geography*, 31: 901–907.

Nyaupane, G.P. and Timothy, D.J. (2010) 'Power, regionalism and tourism policy in Bhutan', *Annals of Tourism Research*, 37(4): 969–988.

Philp, J. and Mercer, D. (1999) 'Commodification of Buddhism in contemporary Burma', *Annals of Tourism Research*, 26(1): 21–54.

Pratt, S. and Liu, A. (2016) 'Does tourism really lead to peace? A global view', *International Journal of Tourism Research*, 18(1): 82–90.

Rasul, G. and Manandhar, P. (2009) 'Prospects and problems in promoting tourism in South Asia: A regional perspective', *South Asia Economic Journal*, 10(1): 187–207.

Reuy, R. (2012) 'Border row hurts tourists numbers in Preah Vihear', *Phnom Penh Post*. Online. Available: www.phnompenhpost.com/business/border-row-hurts-tourist-numbers-pre-ah-vihear (accessed 20 July 2012).

Richter, L.K. (1980) 'The political uses of tourism: A Philippine case study', *Journal of Developing Areas*, 14: 237–257.

—— (1989) *The Politics of Tourism in Asia*. Honolulu: University of Hawai'i Press.

—— (1999) 'After political turmoil: The lessons of rebuilding tourism in three Asian countries', *Journal of Travel Research*, 38(August): 41–45.

Say, S. (2011) 'Preah Vihear Temple waiting for sustained tourism recovery', *Phnom Penh Post*. Online. Available: www.phnompenh-post.com/business/preah-vihear-temple-waiting-sustained-tourism-recovery (accessed 13 July 2011).

Shie, T.S. (2007) 'Rising Chinese influence in the South Pacific: Beijing's "island fever"', *Asian Survey*, 47(2): 307–326.

Sofield, T.H. (2009) 'The political economy of tourism development in the Greater Mekong Sub-region', *Tourism Recreation Research*, 34(3): 255–267.

Soldatos, P. (1993) 'Cascading subnational paradiplomacy in an interdependent and transnational world', in D.M. Brown and E.H. Fry (eds), *States and Provinces in the International Economy*. Berkeley: Institute of Governmental Studies Press.

Suntikul, W. and Butler, R. (2014) 'War and peace: and tourism in Southeast Asia', in C. Wohlmuther and W. Wintersteiner (eds), *International Handbook on Tourism and Peace* (pp. 216–229). Klagenfurt: Drava.

Thu, H.L. (2014) *The Anti-Chinese Riots in Vietnam: Responses from the Ground*. Institute of Southeast Asian Studies, ISEAS Perspective No. 32. Singapore: ISEAS.

Thunø, M. (2003) 'Channels of entry and preferred destinations: The circumvention of Denmark by Chinese immigrants', *International Migration*, 41(3): 99–133.

Timothy, D.J. (2003) 'Supranationalist alliances and tourism: Insights from ASEAN and SAARC', *Current Issues in Tourism*, 6(3): 250–266.

Timothy, D.J. and Kim, S. (2015) 'Understanding the tourism relationships between South Korea and China: A review of influential factors', *Current Issues in Tourism*, 18(5): 413–432.

Tourism News (2015) '"I Hate Thailand" campaign wins award at PATA Travel Mart 2015', *Tourism News*, 11 September.

Truong, V.D. (2013) 'Tourism policy development in Vietnam: A pro-poor perspective', *Journal of Policy Research in Tourism, Leisure and Events*, 5(1): 28–45.

Tse, T.S. (2015) 'A review of Chinese outbound tourism research and the way forward', *Journal of China Tourism Research*, 11(1): 1–18.

Tse, T.S. and Hobson, J.P. (2008) 'The forces shaping China's outbound tourism', *Journal of China Tourism Research*, 4(2): 136–155.

United Nations (1948) *Universal Declaration of Human Rights*, Adopted and Proclaimed by General Assembly Resolution 217 A (III) of 10 December 1948. New York: United Nations. Online. Available: http://daccessdds.un.org/doc/RESOLUTION/GEN/NR0/043/88/IMG/NR004388.pdf?OpenElement.

—— (2001) *Global Code of Ethics for Tourism*, A/RES/56/212. New York: United Nations.

United Nations World Tourism Organization (UNWTO) (2013) 'Visa facilitation: Stimulating economic growth and development through tourism'. Online. Available: http://dtxtq4w60xqpw.cloudfront.net/sites/all/files/docpdf/visafacilitationrevisedweb.pdf (accessed 3 March 2015).

—— (2014) *Visa Openness Report 2014*. Online. Available: http://dtxtq4w60xqpw.cloudfront.net/sites/all/files/docpdf/2014visaopennessreport2ndprintingonline.pdf (accessed 3 March 2015).

Whyte, B. (2008) 'Visa-free travel privileges: An exploratory geographical analysis', *Tourism Geographies*, 10(2): 127–149.

Windybank, S. (2005) 'The China syndrome', *Policy*, 21(2): 28–33.

Winter, T. (2007) *Post-conflict Heritage, Postcolonial Tourism: Tourism, politics and Development at Angkor*. London: Routledge.

Womack, B. (2006) *China and Vietnam: The Politics of Asymmetry*. Cambridge: Cambridge University Press.

Xiaosong, G. and Womack, B. (2000) 'Border cooperation between China and Vietnam in the 1990s', *Asian Survey*, 40(6): 1042–1058.

Zhang, C.X., Decosta, P.L.E. and McKercher, B. (2015) 'Politics and tourism promotion: Hong Kong's myth making', *Annals of Tourism Research*, 54: 156–171.

Zhang, W. and Han, Y. (2004) 'An analysis on China's international tourism development and regional cooperation', *Conference Proceedings, Sixth Asian Development Research Forum General Meeting*, Siam City Hotel, Bangkok, Thailand, 7–8 June 2004.

6

TOURISM AND ENVIRONMENTAL CHANGE IN ASIA

C. Michael Hall

Introduction

Asia has been the fastest growing economic region in the world since the 1970s. Economic development has primarily been driven by adopting a labour-intensive, export-oriented industry development strategy, including tourism, that has been supported by substantial exploitation of both human resources and natural resources (United Nations, Economic and Social Commission for the Asia and the Pacific (UNESCAP) 2012). Asian populations are regarded as having a strong intrinsic environmental ethic (Yencken 2000), yet despite this, environmental losses in the region have been profound with respect to deforestation and desertification, pollution, extinction and biodiversity loss (UNESCAP & ADB 2000; Hubacek *et al.* 2009; Avishek *et al.* 2012; Galli *et al.* 2012; Shively & Smith 2014). As Barua and Khataniar (2015: 23) note specifically with respect to the policies of national governments in relation to sustainability in the Asian context, 'in their pursuit of achieving higher economic growth and standards of living, resources have been exploited at a rate much faster than the regenerative capacity of nature'.

Tourism, impacts and environmental change

Tourism is deeply embedded in economic and environmental change in Asia. Its role as a significant foreign exchange earner and employment generator means that in many countries in Asia tourism has been an important contributor to land use change. However, tourism is not evenly distributed and has particularly significant impacts in high amenity environments, especially on some coastal and marine environments. Nevertheless, systematic assessments of the environmental effects of tourism in Asia are limited, with much of the environmentally related research based on case studies and perceptual studies (Li 2002; Davenport & Davenport 2006; Zhong *et al.* 2011; Leung 2012; Wan & Li 2013). This is not, of course, to suggest that visitor or community perceptions of environmental change are unimportant, especially given their role in decision making. However, it does highlight the difficulties that exist in separating out the effects of tourism from other contributors to environmental change. Although it has long been recognised that tourism has a wide range of effects on the physical environment, several significant methodological problems exist in understanding the relationship between tourism and environmental change. These include (Hall & Lew 2009):

- the difficulty of distinguishing between changes induced by tourism and those induced by other activities;
- the lack of information on conditions prior to the advent of tourism and, hence, the lack of a baseline against which change can be measured;
- the paucity of information on the numbers, types and tolerance levels of different species of flora and fauna; and
- the concentration of research on particular environments, such as beaches and coral reefs, with there being extremely limited research in most arid and semi-arid environments.

Trying to assess tourism's "impacts" is also difficult because tourism both influences and is influenced by the environment and notions of the natural. The notion of tourism or tourist impact on the environment is strongly embedded in tourism and wider discourse (Hall & Lew 2009). Yet, this approach is problematic because the emphasis on the moment(s) of collision between two separate entities (e.g. the "impact" between tourism and the environment) has favoured explanations and methods that depend on correlation in time and space (Weyl 2009), to the detriment of the search for mechanisms of connection and causation rather than simple correlation (Head 2008).

The emphasis on moment(s) of impact also assumes a stable environmental baseline (Hall & Lew 2009), which as we know with respect to environmental change is not the case over longer time periods. Of great influence is the way in which the terms "tourism impacts" or "tourist impacts" position tourism and tourists as somehow being "outside" the system under analysis, as outside of nature (or whatever it is that is being impacted) (Hall 2016). This is also ironic given that research on global climate and environmental change demonstrates just how deeply entangled tourism is in environmental systems (Gössling and Hall 2006), yet the metaphor remains in widespread use. This is not to suggest that tourism does not have effects. Some sites of tourism production, such as resort areas or specific attractions, have clear implications for the environment as a result of clearing of vegetation and land use change, while the addition of transient visitor populations to the permanent population and their associated waste products (Manomaivibool 2015) can also help indicate the effects of tourism consumption and production. Nevertheless, the environmental dimensions of tourism are certainly not all negative as tourism can provide an economic justification for conserving biodiversity, landscapes and specific flora and fauna (Fennell 1999; Frost & Hall 2009; Hall 2006). Tourism therefore provides both positive and negative contributions to environmental conservation (Table 6.1) (Hall 2006). Unfortunately, the full evaluation of the contribution of tourism to environmental change and conservation is hindered by insufficient consideration of the spatial and temporal scales and connections at which effects occur (Hall 2016).

As Table 6.1 indicates, many of the usually described positive benefits of tourism for biodiversity and natural ecosystems are relatively immediate, i.e. the economic and employment benefits of tourist expenditure or the construction of tourist infrastructure. The difficulty is that most positive assessments of the benefits of tourism (e.g. Christ *et al.* 2003) rest on it being a better economic alternative than other development options, such as forest clear felling for the establishment of palm oil plantations or conversion of land to agriculture (Barbier, Burgess & Markandya 1991; Abram *et al.* 2014; Yong & Peh 2014), and do not recognise a number of the longer-term negative contributions of tourism to environmental change processes. These include tourism acting as a means of artificial selection, for example, because it provides a utilitarian focus on conserving charismatic species that possess public relations and tourism value, e.g. in the case of Asia giant bamboo, panda and orang-utan, above other species that do not have such attraction (Hall *et al.* 2011). Tourism's contribution to climate change and the

Table 6.1 Positive and negative contributions of tourism to environmental change

Nature of effect	Time scale in which observed	Comments
Usually regarded as positive		
• An economic justification for biodiversity and landscape conservation practices, including the establishment of national parks and reserves (public and private)	Short to long term	Provides for the conservation of certain landscapes and associated ecosystems, although these are usually characterised by low utilitarian values for exploitative economic development, e.g. agriculture, forestry.
• A source of financial and political support for biodiversity and landscape maintenance and conservation	Short term	Dependent on ongoing tourist and industry interest; also contributes to the ongoing commodification of nature by which value is primarily accrued in economic terms rather than with respect to the intrinsic value of nature, i.e. saving nature for its own sake.
• An economic alternative to other forms of development that negatively impact biodiversity, landscape and the environment	Short term	Generally short term as conservation actions are only maintained while tourism is more economically attractive than other options. Should conditions change other options will dominate.
• A mechanism for educating people about the benefits of biodiversity conservation	Short to long term	May have immediate impact on environmental behaviour but long-term maintenance of behaviour is unknown.
• Involves local people in conservation management and incorporates local ecological knowledge in environmental management practices	Short term. Longer term unknown	May have immediate impact on environmental behaviour but long-term maintenance of that behaviour in the face of other economic and behavioural alternatives is unknown.
Portrayed as both positive and negative		
• Focus on charismatic mega-fauna and flora	Short and long term	Focus on individual species may fail to appreciate broader ecosystem significance though may assist specific species to survive in the short term. May be regarded as a form of artificial selection by which species with some attributes (e.g. "cuteness") are favoured to survive over others.
Usually regarded as negative		
• Outside of national parks and reserves contributes to the fragmentation of natural areas and a reduction in their size	Long term	Can lead to isolation of gene pools and species loss and provides opportunities for introductions of invasive species.
• Contributes to changes in environmental conditions, particularly in high-value amenity areas such as the coast, as well as localised effects such as trampling	Short to long term	Direct contributor to ecosystem change and loss, e.g. replacement of dune systems or wetlands with golf courses or mangroves with marinas. Environmental change will directly affect some plant and animal species.

• Is a major vector for the introduction of exotic species and diseases. In some cases introductions may be deliberate, e.g. for hunting, fishing or aesthetic reasons	Short to long term	Some disease introductions may have immediate impact. The effects of the introduction of competing exotic species usually take years to be fully appreciated but can lead to significant long-term ecosystem change.
• Is a significant contributor to climate change	Long term	The effects of climate change will be experienced over centuries.
• The presence of tourists can lead to changes in animal behaviour	Medium term	Animals will modify behaviours to avoid tourists, or in the case of feeding, potentially respond to them.
• Consumptive tourism such as hunting and fishing if poorly managed can lead to species loss	Long term	Hunting and fishing may act as a form of artificial selection in evolutionary terms; over-exploitation will also affect gene pools.

Source: after Hall 2010, 2016.

introduction of alien species also constitute a long-term effect on biodiversity that is not usually accounted for in terms of tourism impact (Hall 2015). The specific loss of ecosystems and species as a result of tourism-related development tends to occur in amenity areas such as the coast, although even here long-term change is likely to come as much from ecosystem fragmentation as from direct ecosystem change (e.g. Lynam *et al.* 2013).

Environmental change in Asia

Recognition of the importance of understanding the temporal dimensions of change reinforces the lack of detailed knowledge of the extent of tourism's contribution to environmental change in the Asian context, although the overall pattern of environmental change is well recognised (Table 6.2). Since the 1970s Asia has seen substantial deforestation; agricultural intensification leading to an increase in the extent of degraded land; biodiversity loss; decline in water quality; increased urbanisation; increased degradation of coastal and marine environments; a reduction in air quality; and a growing contribution to climate change (Shively & Smith 2014). Tourism is a direct and indirect contributor to these factors, although it has also been used as a justification to establish protected areas under national legislation, although the implementation of conservation measures within them is often relatively weak and previous practices that existed before the establishment of a national park or reserve often continue. This can be particularly important for the wildmeat and medicinal trade in endangered wildlife (Donovan 2004; Drury 2011) (see case study on rhinoceros conservation).

Table 6.2 Key environmental indicators for tourism and environmental change in Asia

Country	HDI ranking (2015)[a]	CO₂ emissions per capita (tonnes) (2011)[b]	CO₂ emissions per capita (annual average growth 1970–2011)[c]	Natural resource depletion (% of GNI 2008–13)[d]	Freshwater withdrawals (% of total renewable water resources 2005–14)[e]	Population living on degraded land (% 2010)[f]	Population affected by natural disasters 2005–12 (average %)[g]	Land area where elevation is below 5m (% of total land area 2000)[h]	Population occupying land area where elevation is below 5m (% of total population 2000)[h]	Land protected area 2009 (%)[i]	Marine protected area 2009 (%)[j]	International tourist arrivals 2013 (mn)[k]	% change previous year
Very high human development													
Singapore	11	4.3	-2.3	–	–	–	0.00	8.1	12.1	5.4	1.6	11.899	7.2
Hong Kong, China (SAR)	12	5.7	3.2	–	–	–	0.02	24.6	26.2	41.8	0.0	25.661	8.0
Korea (Republic of)	17	11.8	6.5	0.0	–	2.9	0.02	4.3	5.0	2.4	5.3	12.176	9.3
Japan	20	9.3	0.8	0.0	–	0.3	0.09	5.9	16.2	16.3	5.6	10.364	24.0
Brunei Darussalam	31	24.0	-3.1	29.8	–	11.4	0.00	3.3	9.2	42.9	0.1	0.225	7.7
High human development													
Russian Federation	51	12.6	–	11.8	–	3.1	0.02	1.9	2.9	9.0	9.1	30.792	9.3
Kazakhstan	56	15.8	–	17.2	18.4	23.5	0.06	6.7	3.9	2.5	–	4.926	2.5
Malaysia	62	7.8	5.9	8.1	1.9	1.2	1.02	3.0	9.0	17.9	1.6	25.715	2.7
Sri Lanka	73	0.7	3.1	0.4	24.5	21.1	4.65	3.9	5.4	20.8	1.1	1.275	26.7
China[1]	90	6.7	6.5	4.2	19.5	8.6	7.33	1.4	8.1	16.6	1.4	55.686	-3.5
Mongolia	90	6.9	3.7	19.8	1.6	31.5	2.92	0.0	0.0	13.4	–	0.418	-12.2
Thailand	93	4.6	8.0	4.7	13.1	17.0	7.07	4.2	13.8	19.6	4.3	26.547	18.8
Maldives	104	3.3	–	0.0	15.7	–	0.09	100.0	100.0	–	–	1.125	17.4

Medium human development

Turkmenistan	109	12.2	–	37.0	–	11.1	0.00	0.0	0.0	3.0	–	–	–
Indonesia	110	2.3	6.7	4.8	–	3.1	0.43	5.5	11.2	14.1	1.9	8.802	9.4
Uzbekistan	114	3.9	–	13.8	100.6	27.0	0.00	0.1	0.0	2.3	–	1.969	–
Philippines	115	0.9	0.7	2.2	17.0	2.2	10.59	6.0	10.5	10.9	1.5	4.681	9.5
Vietnam	116	2.0	3.6	6.7	9.3	8.0	2.01	17.5	42.8	6.2	2.1	7.572	10.6
Kyrgyzstan	120	1.2	–	7.9	32.6	9.7	3.86	0.0	0.0	6.9	–	3.076	27.8
Tajikistan	129	0.4	–	1.3	51.1	10.5	3.86	0.0	0.0	4.1	–	0.208	–14.8
India	130	1.7	5.2	3.6	33.9	9.6	1.20	1.4	3.8	5.3	1.7	6.968	5.9
Bhutan	132	0.8	14.2	16.5	0.4	0.1	0.28	0.0	0.0	28.3	–	0.116	10.5
Timor Leste	133	0.2	–	–	–	–	0.10	2.9	4.4	6.0	6.7	0.058	13.7[m]
Lao People's Democratic Republic	141	0.2	–0.5	8.3	1.1	4.1	2.23	0.0	0.0	16.3	–	2.510	17.3
Bangladesh	142	0.4	–	2.8	2.9	11.3	2.81	14.1	14.0	1.6	0.8	0.148	18.4
Cambodia	143	0.3	2.0	2.5	0.5	39.3	2.88	3.8	10.6	24.0	0.9	4.210	17.5

Low human development

Nepal	145	0.2	7.0	4.2	4.5	2.3	0.84	0.0	0.0	17.0	–	0.798	–0.6
Pakistan	147	0.9	2.7	3.1	74.4	4.5	2.90	1.4	1.3	10.3	1.8	0.966	–16.8[m]
Myanmar	148	0.2	0.5	–	–	19.2	0.64	4.6	14.0	6.3	0.3	2.044	93.0
Afghanistan	171	0.4	3.3	1.2	–	11.0	1.73	0.0	0.0	0.4	–	–	–

(Continued overleaf)

Table 6.2 Continued

Country	HDI ranking (2015)[a]	CO₂ emissions per capita (tonnes) (2011)[b]	CO₂ emissions per capita (annual average growth 1970–2011)[c]	Natural resource depletion (% of GNI 2008–13)[d]	Freshwater withdrawals (% of total renewable water resources 2005–14)[e]	Population living on degraded land (% 2010)[f]	Population affected by natural disasters 2005–12 (average %)[g]	Land area where elevation is below 5m (% of total land area 2000)[h]	Population occupying land area where elevation is below 5m (% of total population 2000)[h]	Land protected area 2009 (%)[i]	Marine protected area 2009 (%)[j]	International tourist arrivals 2013 (mn)[k]	% change previous year
Other countries or territories													
Korea (Democratic People's Rep. of)	3.0	–	–	11.2	2.9	2.22	2.4	5.3	4.0	0.1	–	–	
Macao SAR, China							35.4	79.9			14,268	5.1	
World		4.6	–0.9	4.0	–	10.2	–	1.8	6.6	–	–	1,123,200	4.8

Notes

a   Human Development Index (HDI) for 2014. The HDI is a composite index measuring average achievement in three basic dimensions of human development: a long and healthy life, knowledge and a decent standard of living (UNDP 2015).

b   Carbon dioxide emissions per capita: anthropogenic carbon dioxide emissions stemming from the burning of fossil fuels, gas flaring and the production of cement, divided by mid-year population. Includes carbon dioxide emitted by forest biomass through depletion of forest areas (World Bank World Development Indicators database in UNDP 2015).

c   UNDP (2015) calculations based on data on carbon dioxide emissions per capita from World Bank World Development Indicators database.

d   Natural resource depletion: monetary expression of energy, mineral and forest depletion, expressed as a percentage of gross national income (GNI) (World Bank World Development Indicators in UNDP 2015).

e   Freshwater withdrawals: total fresh water withdrawn, expressed as a percentage of total renewable water resources (FAO 2015b in UNDP 2015).

f   Population living on degraded land: percentage of the population living on severely or very severely degraded land. Land degradation estimates consider biomass, soil health, water quantity and biodiversity (unpublished 2011 Food and Agricultural Organization (FAO) data in UNDP 2015).

g   Population affected by natural disasters: average annual percentage of people requiring immediate assistance during a period of emergency as a result of a natural disaster, including displaced, evacuated, homeless and injured people (derived by UNDP (2015) from Centre for Research on the Epidemiology of Disasters database and United Nations Department of Economic and Social Affairs (UNDESA) (2013). The World Bank World Development Indicators only provide data for percentage of population affected by droughts, floods and extreme temperature for a single year. Although UNDP figures also include earthquake and related non-anthropogenic disasters it therefore provides better coverage over time.

h   Percentage area and population figures for 2000 from World Bank World Development Indicators (http://data.worldbank.org).

i   The definition of a "protected area" is that adopted by the International Union for Conservation of Nature (IUCN): 'an area of land and/or sea especially dedicated to the protection and maintenance of biological diversity, and of natural and associated cultural resources, and managed through legal or other effective means' (IUCN 1994). Proportions are calculated as the total terrestrial protected area extent divided by the total country (surface) area (includes total land area and inland waters). Figures are for 2009 and are available in UNStatistics UNSD Millennium Development Goals Indicators database (http://unstats.un.org/unsd/ENVIRONMENT/qindicators.htm).

j   The definition of a "marine protected area" (MPA) is that adopted by the IUCN as 'any area of intertidal or sub tidal terrain, together with its overlying water and associated flora, fauna, historical and cultural features, which has been reserved by law or other effective means to protect part or all of the enclosed environment' (IUCN 1988). Proportions are calculated as the total marine protected area extent divided by the area of territorial waters (up to 12 nautical miles). Figures are for 2009 and are available in UNStatistics UNSD Millennium Development Goals Indicators database (http://unstats.un.org/unsd/ENVIRONMENT/qindicators.htm).

k   Based on UNWTO figures and derived from World Bank World Development Indicators database (http://data.worldbank.org).

l   Data for China do not include Hong Kong Special Administrative Region of China, Macao Special Administrative Region of China or Taiwan.

m   International arrivals figures for Pakistan and Timor Leste are for 2012, with change shown for the previous year.

Case study 6.1 Rhinoceros conservation

C. Michael Hall and V. Dao Truong

During the past century all rhinoceros populations have decreased, with some critically endangered, and some becoming extinct. Although the global focus is on the African rhinoceros species, Asia also has an indigenous species. However, two rhinoceros subspecies, the Javan rhinoceros in Vietnam (*Rhinoceros sondaicus annamiticus*) and the Indian Javan rhinoceros (*Rhinoceros sondaicus inermis*), became extinct in the 20th century, while the Indian rhinoceros, or greater one-horned rhinoceros (*Rhinoceros unicornis*) (now limited to India, Nepal and Pakistan), the Sumatran rhinoceros (*Dicerorhinus sumatrensis*) (Sumatra and Borneo) and the Javan rhinoceros (*Rhinoceros sondaicus*) (limited to Ujung Kulon National Park, Java, Indonesia) are all extremely threatened. In order to reduce poaching there has been extensive emphasis on reframing rhinoceros as a valuable economic resource via tourism (e.g. Mazur & Stakhanov 2008; Steinmetz *et al.* 2014). Nevertheless, as with many transnational environmental problems, regulatory and legal approaches undertaken in isolation limit both the range and the level of success of any intervention that may seek to alter poaching and consumer behaviour. Therefore, there are attempts to reduce both consumer demand and supply throughout the international trafficking system which is closely overlaid on the international tourism and transport system (Figure 6.1).

Vietnam is currently recognised as the world's largest market for illicit trade in South African rhino horns (Brook *et al.* 2014). The extinction of the Vietnamese rhinoceros population did not stop local demand for rhino horn. Instead, Asian-sourced rhino horn was substituted with African rhino horn (Brook *et al.* 2014). The use of rhino horn for medicinal purposes is hundreds of years old. Perhaps just as importantly, a dinner of exotic meats and expensive alcohol together with gifts of rhino horn is often regard as essential for major business dinners (Donovan 2004; Truong *et al.* 2016). Tourism and hospitality are embedded in the traffic in rhino horn in several ways. It is part of the attempt to prevent poaching; it is part of the transnational mobilities in which smuggling or illegal transfer occurs, including as souvenirs; and the use of rhino horn, along with other endangered species, is often part of business-related hospitality.

The Convention on International Trade in Endangered Species of Wild Fauna and Flora (CITES) entered into force in Vietnam in 1994. The Government of Vietnam has developed numerous policies with respect to conservation and trade to respond to the illegal trade in rhino horn and promulgated a variety of laws and decrees to govern the export, import, re-export, and reintroduction of wild fauna and flora. Depending on the severity of the infringement, violations of laws and regulations with respect to endangered species can be regard as a criminal act or incur a substantial fine. A number of campaigns have been undertaken by the Vietnamese government in collaboration with international NGOs to raise public awareness of wildlife conservation laws and regulations (Truong & Hall 2013). Unfortunately, these have largely been ignored, given that the profits derived from the illicit wildlife trade are much higher than the penalties enforced, although there are signs that demand is gradually falling as a result of health- and status-related social marketing campaigns (Truong *et al.* 2016).

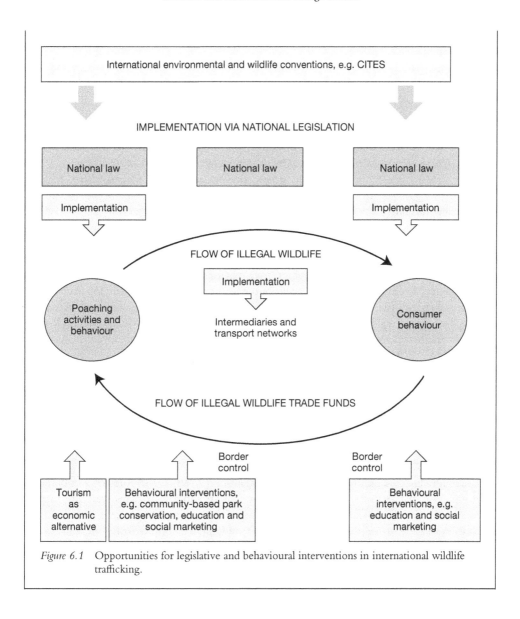

Figure 6.1 Opportunities for legislative and behavioural interventions in international wildlife trafficking.

Biodiversity loss and conservation

According to Christ *et al.* (2003: 41), 'Biodiversity is essential for the continued development of the tourism industry', although there is 'an apparent lack of awareness of the links—positive and negative—between tourism development and biodiversity conservation'. Certainly, the extinction of individual charismatic species that are desirable from a tourism perspective, such as the rhinoceros, is often a public focal point for biodiversity loss. However, the extent of loss is much greater than individual mega-fauna. In 2014 the Zoological Society of London (ZSL) and World Wildlife Fund (WWF) (2014) reported that global wild animal populations had declined in absolute numbers by 52 per cent in the previous 40 years. There were half as many mammals, birds, reptiles, amphibians and fish in 2010 as there were in 1970 and populations of freshwater species had suffered an even worse fall of 76 per cent. Similarly, the fourth iteration of the global biodiversity outlook of the Secretariat of the Convention on Biological Diversity (2014), also reported that progress with respect to government implementation of measures to reduce biodiversity loss was poor:

> Despite individual success stories, the average risk of extinction for birds, mammals and amphibians is still increasing … Genetic diversity of domesticated livestock is eroding, with more than one-fifth of breeds at risk of extinction and the wild relatives of domesticated crop species are increasingly threatened by habitat fragmentation and climate change.
>
> *(Secretariat of the Convention on Biological Diversity 2014: 14)*

Nevertheless, it is important to recognise that the extent of loss is not so great in protected areas, with an estimated global loss of −18 per cent of global vertebrates (Milligan *et al.* 2014). Although countries such as India and Pakistan have experienced over a 25 per cent loss of vertebrates, and China, Thailand and Vietnam over a 5 per cent loss, other Asian countries, such as Japan, Mongolia and the Philippines, have experienced considerable gains (Table 6.3).

Importantly, ecotourism is a major contributor to the economic rationale for maintaining protected areas in Asia (e.g. Nault & Stapleton 2011; Yamada 2011), although terrestrial protected areas are much more established than marine protected areas (MPAs) (see Table 6.2). Given the significance of coastal and marine areas, such as coral reefs, for tourism in Asia, the relative lack of MPAs may be relatively surprising. However, the export-oriented fishing sector has a major political interest in restricting the establishment of marine reserves, although the state of the region's fisheries are now leading to a rethink in conservation strategies. For example, sea cucumbers are a luxury food item in Asia. Yet many populations have been overfished, causing knock-on effects in the ecosystem. This is because sea cucumbers fill a similar ecological niche to ants and worms in terrestrial ecosystems, as sea cucumbers turn over sand by feeding on organic matter mixed within it, and the nutrients they excrete can then be taken up again by algae and corals. As a result of their decline, some areas without sea cucumbers have therefore become uninhabitable for other organisms (WWF 2015). Another area of major environmental change in Asia is that of mangrove forest. More mangroves were lost in Asia between 1980 and 2005 than any other continent, of the order of 25 per cent (WWF 2015); much of this has been lost to aquaculture, resort development and urbanisation, yet mangroves are an important fish nursery and have high biodiversity, while also being an important barrier to the effects of storm surges and coastal erosion.

Table 6.3 Average abundance change between 1970 and 2010 for all species populations monitored inside protected areas – select countries

Average abundance change	Asian countries for which data exists
−25% to −50%	India, Pakistan
−5% to −25%	China, Thailand, Vietnam
−5% to +5%	Nepal
5% to 25%	Indonesia, South Korea
25% to 50%	Bangladesh, Russian Federation, Uzbekistan
50% to 100%	Malaysia
>100%	Japan, Mongolia, Philippines

Source: derived from Milligan *et al.* 2014.

The Coral Triangle

The Coral Triangle, an area which covers the ocean spanning Indonesia, Malaysia, the Philippines, Papua New Guinea, Solomon Islands and Timor-Leste, is regarded as being richer in marine natural capital than any other place on earth. The area is home to three-quarters of all known coral species, six of the world's seven species of marine turtles, 27 marine mammal species and 3,000 species of fish (WWF 2015).

More than 120 million people – one-third of the inhabitants of the region – depend directly on local marine and coastal resources for their income and livelihoods (ADB 2014). In 2011 fisheries exports from Coral Triangle countries were worth nearly US$5.2 billion. Nature-based tourism in Coral Triangle countries is worth US$12 billion annually (WWF 2015). Since 1970, over 40 per cent of the region's coral reefs and mangroves have disappeared (Hoegh-Guldberg *et al.* 2009), while more than 85 per cent of its remaining reefs are threatened, with nearly 45 per cent at high or very high threat levels (Burke *et al.* 2011).

In 2009 the six Coral Triangle countries launched an initiative to sustainably manage the marine resources of the region, including the development of MPAs (Weeks *et al.* 2014). One of the most significant of these is the Tun Mustapha Park, an MPA encompassing almost 1 million hectares and 50 islands off Sabah, Malaysia. The marine resources of the MPA are being managed collaboratively with local people so as to conserve the seascape as well as seek to maintain sustainable fish production, currently approximately of 100 tonnes per day, which supports the livelihoods and food security of many people in the region. In addition, the MPA is also serving as a tourist attraction (Teh & Cabanban 2007) and as a model for the adoption of appropriate marine conservation practices in the region (Weeks *et al.* 2014).

Conserving biodiversity and the environment

Although the creation of terrestrial and marine protected areas are significant, they are by no means the only way that tourism assists biodiversity conservation efforts. Table 6.4 details some of the in-situ and ex-situ ways in which tourism promotes environmental conservation, using examples from throughout Asia. Altering tourist behaviours and providing substitute attractions are also ways of reducing tourist pressures on the environment (Hall 2014), although an increasingly common thread in all measures is greater collaboration with local communities (Andrade & Rhodes, 2012; Hakim *et al.* 2012). Nevertheless, understanding of the approaches in terms of tourism is primarily seen in short time frames. In contrast, arguably one of the major challenges to the tourism and environment relationship in Asia is that of climate change, which operates at time scales far greater than those by which the effects of tourism are usually assessed, and to which tourism is a significant contributor (Scott *et al.* 2012).

Table 6.4 Tourism in relation to major strategies of biodiversity conservation

Strategy	Element	Role of tourism	Examples
In-situ conservation (on site)	Establish protected area network, e.g. national parks and reserves, with appropriate management practices, corridors to link fragments; restore degraded habitats within and outside protected areas	Tourism economic justification for protected area framework given their role as attractions; domestic and international volunteer tourism may also assist in protected area management. Tourism also important for development of environmental knowledge which may have implications for long-term behaviours	Ranthambore National Park, India; Khan Khentii Strictly Protected Area, Mongolia
Ex-situ conservation (off site)	Establish botanical and zoological gardens; conservation stands; banks of germplasm, pollen, seed, seedlings, tissue culture, gene and DNA	Botanical and zoological gardens are significant tourism attractions; volunteer tourism also significant; significant educational tourism function	Singapore Night Zoo, Singapore; Ueno Zoo, Tokyo, Japan
Reduction of anthropogenic pressure	Reduce anthropogenic (human) pressure on natural species populations by altering human activities and behaviours. May also include cultivating species elsewhere to remove visitor pressure	Species populations may have role as tourism attractions; some species which can be sustainably harvested may also be used for hunting and fishing	Sustainable hunting of Suleiman Markhor (*Capra falconeri jerdoni*), a wild goat and Afghan Urial (*Ovis orientalis cycloceros*), a wild sheep in Torghar, Balochistan, Pakistan
Reduction of biotic pressure	Removal or reduction of invasive exotic species and pests that compete with indigenous species	Ensure good biosecurity practice; interpretation programmes to support eradication of invasive species and pests	Removal of paper mulberry (*Broussonetia papyrifera*) and mahogany from native forests in the Philippines
Rehabilitation	Identify and rehabilitate threatened species; launch augmentation, reintroduction or introduction programmes	Species may become tourism attractions; volunteers also significant in management	The Bohorok Orangutan Rehabilitation Centre, Sumatra and Ketapang Rescue Center, West Kalimantan, Indonesia

Tourism and climate change

The reality of climate change is no longer open to scientific dispute. The most recent IPCC report on the physical science of climate change concluded in its summary for policy makers:

> Warming of the climate system is unequivocal, and since the 1950s, many of the observed changes are unprecedented over decades to millennia. The atmosphere and ocean have warmed, the amounts of snow and ice have diminished, sea level has risen, and the concentrations of greenhouse gases have increased.
>
> *(IPCC 2013a: 2)*

They go on to emphasise: 'Human influence on the climate system is clear. This is evident from the increasing greenhouse gas concentrations in the atmosphere, positive radiative forcing, observed warming, and understanding of the climate system' (IPCC 2013a: 13).

The physical impacts and science of climate change present a number of significant challenges for tourism with respect to its effects on destinations, infrastructure and resources, generating regions, competitiveness, and tourist flows and behaviours as well as adaptation and mitigation. As with other economic sectors, tourism therefore both contributes to and is affected by climate change. However, tourism is often regarded as being among the more vulnerable sectors because of its dependence on the environment as a factor in the attractiveness of destinations (Scott *et al.* 2012), although the long-term effects of climate change on tourist decision making are relatively unknown given the adaptive capacity of tourists (Gössling *et al.* 2012).

Tourism and travel contribute to climate change through emissions of GHGs, including in particular CO_2, as well as methane (CH_4), nitrous oxides (NOx), hydrofluorocarbons (HFCs), perfluorocarbons (PFCs) and sulphur hexafluoride (SF_6) (Scott *et al.* 2012). There are also various short-lived GHGs that are important in the context of aviation (Lee *et al.* 2009). Tourism transport, accommodation and activities were estimated by independent assessments for the UNWTO *et al.* (2008) and World Economic Forum (WEF) (2009) to contribute approximately 5 per cent to global anthropogenic emissions of CO_2 in the year 2005. Most CO_2 emissions are associated with transport, with aviation accounting for 40 per cent of tourism's overall carbon footprint, followed by car transport (32 per cent) and accommodation (21 per cent) (UNWTO *et al.* 2008). Cruise ships are included in "other transport" and account for approximately 1.5 per cent of global tourism emissions (Eijgelaar *et al.* 2010). The UNWTO *et al.* (2008) and WEF (2009) assessments of tourism's contribution to climate change do not include the impact of non-CO_2 short-lived GHGs. A more accurate assessment of tourism's contribution to global warming should be made on the basis of radiative forcing (RF) (IPCC 2013b). Given the range of uncertainty with respect to RF, especially for aviation emissions, Scott, Peeters and Gössling (2010) estimated that tourism contributed between 5.2 and 12.5 per cent of all anthropogenic forcing in 2005, with a best estimate of approximately 8 per cent (Gössling *et al.* 2013).

Tourism and emissions growth in Asia

Tourism's emissions contribution is expected to continue into the foreseeable future, given that tourism growth, and especially growth in aviation, is increasing far greater than any efficiency gains. The International Air Transport Association (IATA 2009) suggests that air travel will almost quadruple between 2005 and 2050, with a tripling of energy use and emissions. Significantly, much of this growth will occur in the Asia-Pacific, which is the fastest growing region for international tourism and is predicted to achieve a 30 per cent global market share by 2030 (UNWTO 2012). As a result, the Asia-Pacific region is, for example, forecast to have the highest rate of accommodation emissions growth, increasing from 29 per cent of all accommodation emissions in 2005 to 40 per cent in 2035 (WEF 2009), while up to one-third of all new commercial jet aircraft are expected to be used in Asia (Su & Hall 2014). Carbon emissions from the accommodation sector depends on the level of energy consumption, which varies with floor area, room number, occupancy rate, facility standard, service quality, energy source, energy price and climatic location of hotels; water and material usage; and level of waste production (Su *et al.* 2013). Asian three- to five-star lodging facilities generally have higher energy consumption levels than European hotels with a key reason being the extensive use of air-conditioning (Su & Hall 2014).

Asian tourism is especially vulnerable to climate change since many tourism businesses and destinations are extremely dependent on natural resources, such as coral reefs, forests, alpine areas and beaches, and, in many cases, also demonstrate a relative lack of adaptive capacity (Su & Hall 2014). However, despite its economic significance, very few systematic assessments have been done on the relationships between tourism and climate change in an Asian context at a regional or national level (Hall 2008; UNWTO 2014; Scott *et al.* 2016).

Tourism and climate change in Asia

IPCC (2012) climate predictions for Asia indicate that the temperature increase for Asian sub-regions is generally higher than the global average (1.8–4 °C) by 2100. The highest increase is projected for North Asia (+4.3 °C), followed by Central and West Asia (+3.7 °C), East and South Asia (+3.3 °C) and Southeast Asia (+2.5 °C). Temperature increases are likely to lead to increased glacier and permafrost melt in the Himalayas, Xizang Autonomous Region and the northwestern part of China, with potential consequences for water availability in the long term (ADB 2012) as well as for tourism development. The melting of mountain permafrost will increase natural hazards for mountain communities and infrastructure (Nyaupane & Chhetri 2009). Asia is already extremely susceptible to climate-related disasters and climate change is expected to exacerbate risk levels (ADB 2012). Heatwave events are likely to increase in frequency and duration region-wide and become more intense in some areas, such as East, Central and West Asia (IPCC 2012). There is also an increasing trend of more intense tropical cyclones (typhoon or hurricane) in East Asia, South Asia and Southeast Asia, and higher precipitation events in all sub-regions. Regional sea level rise (SLR) is also potentially higher than the estimated global average, meaning that the combination of SLR and more intense high-magnitude weather events poses significant challenges to the low-lying areas and populations of Eastern and South Asia (IPCC 2013b) (see also Table 6.2 for the percentage of countries and their populations below 5m).

With a coastal erosion rate of up to four to six metres per year in some locations (Cruz *et al.* 2007), Asian megacities (also recognised as major tourist destinations, transport hubs and source regions), including Tokyo, Shanghai, Guangzhou, Seoul, Taipei, Bangkok, Ho Chi Minh City, Jakarta, Manila, Dhaka, Kolkata, Mumbai, Chennai and Karachi, will be potentially highly affected by climate change, including flooding and landslides (ADB 2012). Approximately 88 per cent of regional coral reef is also likely to disappear because of the multiple effects of climate change by 2035 (Cruz *et al.* 2007; Scott *et al.* 2012), creating significant issues for a number of coastal destinations. However, it is important to stress that the impacts of climate change will affect tourism not just because of their impact on destinations, but also because of their capacity to reduce economic growth and per capita income, thereby affecting tourism demand as well (Su & Hall 2014; UNWTO 2014).

Although some sustainable tourism policies have been adopted in the region (Nyaupane & Timothy 2010), few countries, such as Laos and Vietnam, have introduced specific climate-change adaptation strategies into tourism legislation. Most Asian countries utilise soft instruments to manage climate change-related issues in tourism, such as voluntary energy-saving and green hotel practices (Su & Hall 2014). The potential success of such an approach is not helped by the generally low level of public awareness of climate change issues in Asia. Citizens of Asian countries generally have a lower support for climate change policies and lifestyle adjustment than other areas, except Africa and the Middle East (Kim 2011). Brouwer, Brander and Van Beukering (2008) found that Asian air passengers had the lowest recognition of the relation between flying and climate change, its related problems, Kyoto protocol, carbon tax as well as their willingness to pay among global air travellers. A Hong Kong Household study found that frequent travellers had a lower willingness to voluntarily modify their travel behaviours than inactive travellers, even though they were highly aware of climate change issues (McKercher *et al.* 2010). Chen, Hsu and Lin (2011) suggested that Taiwanese air travellers had moderate to high environmental knowledge and positive attitude towards environmental issues, especially female, older and well-educated customers. However, they rarely considered environmental factors in their travel decisions, even though they perceived pro-environmental behaviour as part of their daily life.

Conclusions

Economic growth has been the primary policy focal point for the majority of Asian countries since the 1970s. Tourism has been an integral component of this strategy, given its capacity to attract foreign exchange as well as its broader contributions to economic development and employment. The overall approach has meant a substantial decline in natural capital for Asian countries. Tourism has been both a contributor to decline and an economic justification for its conservation, although most studies of tourism in the region usually do not systematically identify these two contributions occurring simultaneously in the tourism system. Overall, many Asian countries, especially middle-income ones for which data is readily available, appear to be following a path of weak sustainability. Weak sustainability is characterised by a non-declining combined stock of capital and assumes that man-made capital can be replaced with natural capital. Strong sustainability, on the other hand, implies that natural capital cannot be replaced by any other capital (Barua & Khataniar 2015).

Asian tourism is characterised by forecasts of high levels of tourism growth over the next 20–30 years. The long-term implications of such growth rates reflect the complexities of the tourism system. Although some forms of tourism may encourage some environmental conservation measures, such as support for protected areas and voluntary industry and visitor conservation actions, including attempts to reduce water and energy usage, the overall situation reflects the potential further rundown of natural capital. Growth in domestic and international tourism in Asia will be a major contributor to greenhouse gas emissions. The Asian tourism industry will also be profoundly affected by climate change, including higher temperatures, SLR and extreme weather events. However, despite the significance of tourism to many of the region's economies there is a relative dearth of research on climate and environmental change in Asia (Hall 2008; Scott *et al.* 2016). This relative lack of knowledge characterises both the production and supply dimensions of tourism as well as consumer understanding of climate and environmental change and the long-term implications of increased levels of demand for long-haul travel. Arguably the most urgent and critical issue in assessing tourism and environmental change in Asia is therefore the need for comprehensive and systematic research that provides a basis for sustainable tourism policy making that goes beyond short-term responses and that meets the needs of industry stakeholders.

Key reading

Hall, C.M. (2016) 'Loving nature to death: Tourism consumption, biodiversity loss and the Anthropocene', in M. Gren and E.H. Huijbens (eds), *Tourism and the Anthropocene* (pp. 52–73). Abingdon: Routledge.

Nyaupane, G.P. and Chhetri, N. (2009) 'Vulnerability to climate change of nature-based tourism in the Nepalese Himalayas', *Tourism Geographies* 11: 95–119.

Su, Y.-P., Hall, C.M. and Ozanne, L. (2013) 'Hospitality industry responses to climate change: A benchmark study of Taiwanese tourist hotels', *Asia Pacific Journal of Tourism Research*, 18: 92–107.
UNWTO (2014) *Responding to Climate Change: Tourism Initiatives in Asia and the Pacific*. Madrid: UNWTO.
Weeks, R., Aliño, P.M., Atkinson, S., Beldia, P., Binson, A., Campos, W., Djohani, R., Green, A., Hamilton, R., Horigue, V., Jumin, R., Kalim, K., Kasasiah, A., Kereseka, J., Klein, C., Laroya, L., Magupin, S., Masike, B., Mohan, C., Da Silva Pinto, R., Vave-Karamui, A., Villanoy, C., Welly, M. and White, A. (2014) 'Developing marine protected area networks in the Coral Triangle: Good practices for expanding the Coral Triangle marine protected area system', *Coastal Management*, 42(2): 183–205.

References

Abram, N.K., Meijaard, E., Ancrenaz, M., Runting, R.K., Wells, J.A., Gaveau, D., Pellier, A.S. and Mengersen, K. (2014) 'Spatially explicit perceptions of ecosystem services and land cover change in forested regions of Borneo', *Ecosystem Services*, 7: 116–127.
Andrade, G.S. and Rhodes, J. (2012) 'Protected areas and local communities: An inevitable partnership toward successful conservation strategies?' *Ecology and Society*, 17(4): 14.
Asian Development Bank (ADB) (2012) *Addressing Climate Change and Migration in Asia and the Pacific*. Mandaluyong City: ADB.
—— (2014) *Regional State of the Coral Triangle: Coral Triangle Marine Resources – Their Status, Economies, and Management*. Manila: ADB.
Avishek, K., Yu, X. and Liu, J. (2012) 'Ecosystem management in Asia Pacific: Bridging science–policy gap', *Environmental Development*, 3: 77–90.
Barbier, E., Burgess, J. and Markandya, A. (1991) 'The economics of tropical deforestation', *Ambio*, 20(2): 55–58.
Barua, A. and Khataniar, B. (2015) 'Strong or weak sustainability: A case study of emerging Asia', *Asia-Pacific Development Journal*, 22(1): 1–31.
Brook, S.M., Dudley, N., Mahood, S.P., Polet, G., Williams, A.C., Duckworth, J.W., Van Ngoc, T. and Long, B. (2014) 'Lessons learned from the loss of a flagship: The extinction of the Javan rhinoceros, *Rhinoceros sondaicus annamiticus* from Vietnam'. *Biological Conservation*, 174: 21–29.
Brouwer, R., Brander, L. and Van Beukering, P. (2008) '"A convenient truth": Air travel passengers' willingness to pay to offset their CO_2 emissions', *Climate Change*, 90: 299–313.
Burke, L., Reytar, K., Spalding, M. and Perry, A. (2011) *Reefs at Risk Revisited*. Washington, DC: World Resources Institute.
Chen, F.Y., Hsu, P.Y. and Lin, T.W. (2011) 'Air travelers' environmental consciousness: A preliminary investigation in Taiwan', *International Journal of Business and Management*, 6(12): 78–86.
Christ, C., Hilel, O., Matus, S. and Sweeting, J. (2003) *Tourism and Biodiversity: Mapping Tourism's Global Footprint*. Washington, DC: Conservation International.
Cruz, R.V., Harasawa, H., Lal, M., Wu, S., Anokhin, Y., Punsalmaa, B., Honda, Y., Jafari, M., Li, C. and Huu Ninh, N. (2007) 'Asia', in M.L. Parry, O. Canziani, J. Palutikof, P. van der Linden and C. Hanson (eds), *Climate Change 2007: Impacts, Adaptation and Vulnerability* (pp. 469–506). Cambridge: Cambridge University Press.
Davenport, J. and Davenport, J. (2006) 'The impact of tourism and personal leisure transport on coastal environments: A review', *Estuarine, Coastal and Shelf Science*, 67(1): 280–292.
Donovan, D.G. (2004). Cultural underpinnings of the wildlife trade in Southeast Asia. In J. Knight (ed.), *Wildlife in Asia: Cultural Perspectives* (pp. 88–111). London: Routledge.
Drury, R. (2011) 'Hungry for success: Urban consumer demand for wild animal products in Vietnam', *Conservation and Society*, 9(3): 247–257.
Eijgelaar, E., Thaper, C. and Peeters, P. (2010) 'Antarctic cruise tourism: The paradoxes of ambassadorship, "last chance tourism" and greenhouse gas emissions', *Journal of Sustainable Tourism*, 18: 337–354.
Fennell, D. (1999) *Ecotourism: An Introduction*. London: Routledge.
Frost, W. and Hall, C.M. (eds) (2009) *Tourism and National Parks: International Perspectives on Development, Histories and Change*. London: Routledge.

Galli, A., Kitzes, J., Niccolucci, V., Wackernagel, M., Wada, Y. and Marchettini, N. (2012) 'Assessing the global environmental consequences of economic growth through the ecological footprint: A focus on China and India', *Ecological Indicators*, 17: 99–107.

Gössling, S. and Hall, C.M. (eds) (2006) *Tourism and Global Environmental Change*. London: Routledge.

Gössling, S., Scott, D., Hall, C.M., Ceron, J-P. and Dubois, G. (2012) 'Consumer behaviour and demand response of tourists to climate change', *Annals of Tourism Research*, 39: 36–58.

Gössling, S., Scott, D. and Hall, C.M. (2013) 'Challenges of tourism in a low-carbon economy', *Wiley Interdisciplinary Reviews: Climate Change*, 4(6): 525–538.

Hakim, L., Soemarno, M. and Hong, S. (2012) 'Challenges for conserving biodiversity and developing sustainable island tourism in North Sulawesi Province, Indonesia', *Journal of Ecology and Environment*, 35(2): 61–71.

Hall, C.M. (2006) 'Tourism, biodiversity and global environmental change', in S. Gössling and C.M. Hall (eds), *Tourism and Global Environmental Change: Ecological, Economic, Social and Political Interrelationships* (pp. 211–226). Abingdon: Routledge.

—— (2008) 'Tourism and climate change: Knowledge gaps and issues', *Tourism Recreation Research*, 33: 339–350.

—— (2010) 'Tourism and biodiversity: More significant than climate change?' *Journal of Heritage Tourism*, 5(4): 253–266.

—— (2014) *Tourism and Social Marketing*. Abingdon: Routledge.

—— (2015) 'Tourism and biological exchange and invasions: A missing dimension in sustainable tourism?' *Tourism Recreation Research*, 40(1): 81–94.

—— (2016) 'Loving nature to death: Tourism consumption, biodiversity loss and the Anthropocene', in M. Gren and E.H. Huijbens (eds), *Tourism and the Anthropocene* (pp. 52–73). Abingdon: Routledge.

Hall, C.M. and Lew, A. (2009) *Understanding and Managing Tourism Impacts: An Integrated Approach*. London: Routledge.

Hall, C.M., James, M. and Baird, T. (2011) 'Forests and trees as charismatic mega-flora: Implications for heritage tourism and conservation', *Journal of Heritage Tourism*, 6(4): 309–323.

Head, L. (2008) 'Is the concept of human impacts past its use-by date?' *The Holocene*, 18(3): 373–377.

Hoegh-Guldberg, O., Hoegh-Guldberg, H., Veron, J., Green, A., Gomez, E., Lough, J., King, M., Ambariyanto, Hansen, L., Cinner, J., Dews, G., Russ, G., Schuttenberg, H., Peñaflor, E., Eakin, C., Christensen, T., Abbey, M., Areki, F., Kosaka, R., Tewfik, A. and Oliver, J. (2009) *The Coral Triangle and Climate Change: Ecosystems, People and Societies at Risk*. Brisbane: WWF-Australia.

Hubacek, K., Guan, D., Barrett, J. and Wiedmann, T. (2009) 'Environmental implications of urbanization and lifestyle change in China: Ecological and water footprints', *Journal of Cleaner Production*, 17(14): 1241–1248.

International Air Transport Association (IATA) (2009) *Aviation and Climate Change Pathway to Carbon-Neutral Growth in 2020*. Geneva: IATA.

International Union for Conservation of Nature (IUCN) (1988) *Resolution 17.38 of the 17th General Assembly of the IUCN*. Gland: IUCN.

—— (1994) *Guidelines for Protected Areas Management Categories*. Gland: IUCN.

IPCC (2012) *Managing the Risks of Extreme Events and Disasters to Advance Climate Change Adaptation: A Special Report of Working Groups I and II of the Intergovernmental Panel on Climate Change*. Cambridge: Cambridge University Press.

—— (2013a) 'Summary for policymakers', in T. Stocker, D. Qin, G.-K. Plattner, M. Tignor, S. Allen, J. Boschung, A. Nauels, Y. Xia, V. Bex and P. Midgley (eds), *Climate Change 2013: The Physical Science Basis. Contribution of Working Group I to the Fifth Assessment Report of the Intergovernmental Panel on Climate Change*. Cambridge: Cambridge University Press.

—— (2013b) *Working Group I Contribution to the IPCC Fifth Assessment Report Climate Change 2013: The Physical Science Basis. Contribution of Working Group I to the Fifth Assessment Report of the Intergovernmental Panel on Climate Change*. Cambridge: Cambridge University Press.

Kim, S.Y. (2011) 'Public perceptions of climate change and support for climate policies in Asia: Evidence from recent polls', *The Journal of Asian Studies* 70: 319–331.

Lee, D.S., Fahey, D., Forster, P., Newton, P., Wit, R., Lim, L., Owen, B. and Sausen, R. (2009) 'Aviation and global climate change in the 21st century', *Atmospheric Environment*, 43(22): 3520–3537.

Leung, Y.F. (2012) 'Recreation ecology research in East Asia's protected areas: Redefining impacts?' *Journal for Nature Conservation*, 20(6): 349–356.

Li, Y. (2002) 'The impact of tourism in China on local communities', *Asian Studies Review*, 26(4): 471–486.

Lynam, A.J., Bradshaw, C.J., He, F., Bickford, D.P., Woodruff, D.S., Bumrungsri, S. and Laurance, W.F. (2013) 'Near-complete extinction of native small mammal fauna 25 years after forest fragmentation'. *Science*, 341(6153): 1508–10.

McKercher, B., Prideaux, B., Cheung, C. and Law, R. (2010) 'Achieving voluntary reductions in the carbon footprint of tourism and climate change', *Journal of Sustainable Tourism*, 18: 297–317.

Manomaivibool, P. (2015) 'Wasteful tourism in developing economy? A present situation and sustainable scenarios', *Resources, Conservation and Recycling*, 103: 69–76.

Mazur, R.E. and Stakhanov, O. (2008) 'Prospects for enhancing livelihoods, communities, and biodiversity in Africa through community-based forest management: a critical analysis', *Local Environment*, 13(5): 405–421.

Milligan, H., Deinet, S., McRae, L. and Freeman, R. (2014) *Protecting Species: Status and Trends of the Earth's Protected Areas. Preliminary Report*. London: Zoological Society of London.

Nault, S. and Stapleton, P. (2011) 'The community participation process in ecotourism development: A case study of the community of Sogoog, Bayan-Ulgii, Mongolia', *Journal of Sustainable Tourism*, 19(6): 695–712.

Nyaupane, G.P. and Chhetri, N. (2009) 'Vulnerability to climate change of nature-based tourism in the Nepalese Himalayas', *Tourism Geographies* 11: 95–119.

Nyaupane, G.P. and Timothy, D.J. (2010) 'Power, regionalism and tourism policy in Bhutan', *Annals of Tourism Research*, 37: 969–988.

Scott, D., Peeters, P. and Gössling, S. (2010) 'Can tourism deliver its aspirational greenhouse gas emission reduction targets?' *Journal of Sustainable Tourism*, 18: 393–408.

Scott, D., Hall, C.M. and Gössling, S. (2012) *Tourism and Climate Change: Impacts, Adaptation and Mitigation*. Abingdon: Routledge.

—— (2016) 'A review of the IPCC 5th Assessment and implications for tourism sector climate resilience and decarbonization', *Journal of Sustainable Tourism*, 24(1): 8–30.

Secretariat of the Convention on Biological Diversity (2014) *Global Biodiversity Outlook 4*. Montréal: Secretariat of the Convention on Biological Diversity.

Shively, G. and Smith, T. (2014) 'Natural resources, the environment and economic development in Southeast Asia', in I. Coxhead (ed.), *Handbook of Southeast Asian Economics* (pp. 114–135). London: Routledge.

Steinmetz, R., Srirattanaporn, S., Mor-Tip, J. and Seuaturien, N. (2014) 'Can community outreach alleviate poaching pressure and recover wildlife in South-East Asian protected areas?' *Journal of Applied Ecology*, 51(6): 1469–1478.

Su, Y.-P. and Hall, C.M. (2014) 'Climate change and tourism in Asia: A review', in United Nations World Tourism Organization, *Responding to Climate Change: Tourism Initiatives in Asia and the Pacific* (pp. 27–40). Madrid: UNWTO.

Su, Y.-P., Hall, C.M. and Ozanne, L. (2013) 'Hospitality industry responses to climate change: A benchmark study of Taiwanese tourist hotels', *Asia Pacific Journal of Tourism Research*, 18: 92–107.

Teh, L. and Cabanban, A. (2007) 'Planning for sustainable tourism in southern Pulau Banggi: An assessment of biophysical conditions and their implications for future tourism development', *Journal of Environmental Management*, 85(4), 999–1008.

Truong, V.D. and Hall, C.M. (2013) 'Social marketing and tourism: What is the evidence?' *Social Marketing Quarterly*, 19(2): 110–135.

Truong, V.D., Dang, V.H.N. and Hall, C.M. (2016) 'The marketplace management of illegal elixirs: Illicit consumption of rhino horn', *Consumption Markets & Culture*, DOI:10.1080/10253866.2015.1108915.

United Nations Department of Economic and Social Affairs (UNDESA) (2013) *World Population Prospects: The 2012 Revision*. New York: UNDESA.

United Nations Development Programme (UNDP) (2015) *Human Development Report 2015: Work for Human Development*. New York: UNDP.

United Nations, Economic and Social Commission for the Asia and the Pacific (UNESCAP) (2012) *Green Growth, Resources and Resilience: Environmental Sustainability in Asia and the Pacific*. Bangkok: UNESCAP and ADB.

United Nations, Economic and Social Commission for the Asia and the Pacific (UNESCAP) and Asian Development Bank (ADB) (2000) *State of the Environment in Asia and the Pacific 2000*. New York: UNESCAP and ADB.

United Nations World Tourism Organization (UNWTO) (2012) *UNWTO Tourism Highlights: 2012 Edition*. Madrid: UNWTO.

—— (2014) *Responding to Climate Change: Tourism Initiatives in Asia and the Pacific*. Madrid: UNWTO.

United Nations World Tourism Organization, United Nations Environment Programme, and World Meterological Organization (UNWTO, UNEP, WMO) (2008) *Climate Change and Tourism: Responding to Global Challenges*. Madrid: UNWTO.

Wan, Y.K.P. and Li, X. (2013) 'Sustainability of tourism development in Macao, China', *International Journal of Tourism Research*, 15(1): 52–65.

Weeks, R., Aliño, P.M., Atkinson, S., Beldia, P., Binson, A., Campos, W., Djohani, R., Green, A., Hamilton, R., Horigue, V., Jumin, R., Kalim, K., Kasasiah, A., Kereseka, J., Klein, C., Laroya, L., Magupin, S., Masike, B., Mohan, C., Da Silva Pinto, R., Vave-Karamui, A., Villanoy, C., Welly, M. and White, A. (2014) 'Developing marine protected area networks in the Coral Triangle: Good practices for expanding the Coral Triangle marine protected area system', *Coastal Management*, 42(2): 183–205.

Weyl, H. (2009) *Philosophy of Mathematics and Natural Science*, revised and augmented English edition based on a translation of Olaf Helmer. Princeton: Princeton University Press.

World Economic Forum (WEF) (2009) *Towards a Low Carbon Travel & Tourism Sector*. Davos: World Economic Forum.

WWF (2014) *Living Planet Report 2014: Species and Spaces, People and Places*. Gland: WWF.

—— (2015) *Living Blue Planet Report: Species, Habitats and Wellbeing*. Gland: WWF and Zoological Society of London.

Yamada, N. (2011) 'Why tour guiding is important for ecotourism: Enhancing guiding quality with the ecotourism promotion policy in Japan', *Asia Pacific Journal of Tourism Research*, 16(2): 139–152.

Yencken, D. (2000) 'Attitude to nature in the East and West', in J. Fien, H. Sykes and D. Yencken (eds), *Environment, Education and Society in the Asia-Pacific: Local Traditions and Global Discourses* (pp. 4–27), New York: Routledge.

Yong, D.L. and Peh, K.S.H. (2014) 'South-east Asia's forest fires: Blazing the policy trail', *Oryx*, DOI:10.1017/S003060531400088X.

Zhong, L., Deng, J., Song, Z. and Ding, P. (2011) 'Research on environmental impacts of tourism in China: Progress and prospect', *Journal of Environmental Management*, 92(11): 2972–2983.

7

TOURISM, SOCIO-CULTURAL CHANGE AND ISSUES

Paolo Mura

Introduction

As I drive through the neighbourhood (which I will refer to as *Area Asia*), my eyes are wide-open as they gaze upon the luxury of the exaggeratedly baroque villas, the grandeur of fake Roman-style swimming pools, the extravagance of high-end shops, and the seductive look of food outlets selling luscious food. I am not in Beverly Hills or Bel Air. Instead, this time I am a tourist exploring one of the most renowned areas of an emerging Asian megalopolis, which I would refer to as *Asiana City*. *Area Asia* is an evident tourist enclave, a temple of consumption where visitors wander around with their cameras and enjoy their expensive beers and Italian Pizzas al fresco. Here tourists are visibly amazed by their surroundings and look (and sound) very happy. As I turn right, I take a one-way road, which leads me to an intersection not so far from *Area Asia*. I suddenly find myself lost in a labyrinth of small streets and turn left and right a bit randomly while the radio plays Asian punk-rock music. Surprisingly, the scenario around me has totally changed. What my eyes see now is a group of barefooted children running on a rather dirty street, an old woman begging for money, and a middle-aged man selling food by the roadside. Based on the clothes they wear, I can assume that these people are not wealthy. They do not look happy either. The smell of the drainage canals is pungent and well perceptible inside my car. There are no tourists or al fresco outlets here, only visible signs of poverty and misery. I instinctively reverse the car and drive back to *Area Asia* to enjoy a beer with other tourists and locals.

(Notes taken during fieldwork conducted in Asia)

It would not be surprising to begin a book chapter on tourism by presenting numbers and figures about tourism's contribution to national GDPs and economies worldwide as this politically and socio-culturally constructed "grand narrative" is often reiterated in the literature (Durbarry 2004; Seetanah 2011; Akkemik 2012). Also, highly repeated by tourism scholars is the recurrent narrative portraying tourism as a catalyst for socio-cultural development (Farsani *et al.* 2011). Indeed, the idea that tourism may act as an instrument for fostering peace (Salazar

2006), social cohesion (Kamble 2013) and social capital (Mura & Tavakoli 2014) contemplates the positive role of tourism on people's economic and socio-cultural conditions. In many cases tourism development is linked to economic and socio-cultural change; yet, the question arises as to whether tourism-related socio-cultural change is positive or negative. Moreover, it is unclear whether and how tourism contributes to widening or reducing already existing socio-economic inequalities in Asian developing economies.

This chapter explores the relationship between tourism and socio-cultural change in Asia. It is based on ethnographic fieldwork I have conducted in the last five years in Asia as a tourist and researcher. As an Italian scholar who has lived in Malaysia since 2010, I have had the opportunity of "being a tourist" in almost all the Asian countries. My journeys throughout Asia include multiple and diverse experiences in Malaysia, Thailand, Singapore, Indonesia, India, Sri Lanka, Vietnam, Cambodia, Hong Kong and South Korea. Being a fervent writer, I have accumulated pages and pages of observational notes and memos, which often inform (and are informed by) my academic writings in the field I am mostly interested in, namely sociology of tourism. Based on my observations and the existing academic literature, in this chapter I will discuss whether and how tourism has contributed to socio-cultural change in Asia.

First, I will critically analyse the historical, political and socio-cultural events that have shaped the current Asian scenario. In doing so, I will place emphasis on the colonial and post-colonial forces that have constructed "Asia". Second, I will discuss how colonialism and its post-colonial legacies have influenced people's patterns of mobilities as well as tourists' flows and experiences. Third, I will examine the role played by tourism in the politics of identity (trans)formation and nation building in many Asian countries. Finally, in the concluding remarks I will discuss whether the development of tourism in the region has led to positive or negative socio-cultural changes.

Understanding Asia: a diverse and complex universe

The term "Asia" refers to a politically and socially constructed artificial entity that includes a number of diverse realities (Hitchcock *et al.* 2008). It is a wide and heterogeneous region in which the interplay of global and local trends has produced differences between countries and among different areas within each country (Piper & Rother 2011). These differences involve the linguistic, religious, political, economic and socio-cultural spheres (Houben & Rehbein 2011). For example, Malaysia and Thailand are characterised by profound political, religious and socio-cultural differences, despite being neighbouring countries. Also, Malaysia presents a complex and varied socio-cultural fabric due to local differences among the various states and regions (e.g. between Peninsular Malaysia and the part of Borneo belonging to Malaysia) (Andaya & Andaya 1982).

A number of factors have contributed to shaping the geo-political context of the region. Undoubtedly, historical events like colonialism and its post-colonial legacies have played a major role in "constructing" Asia (Nyaupane & Budruk 2009). Indeed, with few exceptions (e.g. Thailand, China and Japan), the majority of Asian countries were under the control of Western powers by the 1930s (Loomba 1998). One of the effects of colonialism has been the development of diverse educational systems in the various Asian countries (Altbach 1989). Anglo-Saxon educational paradigms, for example, are still dominant in India, Malaysia and Singapore, despite variations due to local adaptations. Also, earlier historical events have played a role in the establishment of religious values, such as Islam in Malaysia, Indonesia and Brunei, and Christianity in the Philippines.

Alongside historical factors, different political events have also contributed to shape the context of the region. While countries like Malaysia and Singapore have achieved independence from the colonisers and established relatively democratic societies since the second half of the 20th century (Andaya & Andaya 1982), others have been ruled by autocratic regimes until recent times. For example, Cambodia's Khmer Rouge regime, led by Pol Pot, only ended in 1975. Moreover, Myanmar (or Burma) was under the control of military rule until 2011. Also, political factors have influenced the degree of openness to Western capitalist and globalising forces and consequent consumerist practices. As such, while the so-called "Asian tigers" (Singapore, Hong Kong, Taiwan, South Korea) have enjoyed (relatively) stable economies for the last 50 years (Kim 1998), some parts of Asia are still characterised by more volatile economic scenarios. Historical, political and economic factors have also led to various socio-cultural changes. In this regard, the emergence of an Asian middle class (Robison & Goodman 1996) has transformed the social fabric of the region, despite the fact that visible differences between the rich and the poor still exist. Indeed, economic and socio-cultural inequalities are strikingly obvious in almost any of the Asian countries (Houben & Rehbein 2011). The question arises as to whether and how tourism has contributed (or not contributed) to power imbalances in the region.

Tourism and (post-)colonial forces in Asia

The complex historical, political, economic and socio-cultural factors discussed in the previous paragraph have played a crucial role in influencing patterns of mobilities (which also include the flow of migrants and tourists) between Asian and non-Asian countries as well as between the different regions of Asia. Colonialism is not a phenomenon of modern history as it already occurred in classical antiquity. Alexander the Great's Greek Empire and Augustus' Roman Empire are early examples of Western imperialist attempts to colonise parts of Africa and Asia during ancient times (Webster & Cooper 1996). However, European nation-states' hegemonic desire to establish commercial and cultural colonies outside Europe (including Asia) became more pronounced since the 16th century, also due to the complex interplay between imperialist and capitalist forces (Loomba 1998). According to King *et al.* (2010), by 1914 about 200,000 British citizens had already migrated to India while 20,000 French nationals had moved to French Indochina permanently. Besides strengthening commercial exchanges of goods between Europe and Asia, this phenomenon also encouraged intensified patterns of mobilities (including tourism) between the "West" and the "East".

Importantly, colonial and post-colonial forces, together with environmentalist and conservationist Western impulses seeking paradisiac geographical spaces (Shepherd 2011), have played a crucial role in influencing past and present Westerners' practices of gazing upon Asians. More specifically, the Western gaze has been mainly fuelled by the mythical, mystical and romantic aspects attached to the "exotic other" (Hall 2009), which has often been admired with a sort of flirtatious attitude by European tourists and travellers. This desire for seeking the "non-ordinary" has led to the development of specific forms of tourist practices in Asia, mainly related to the consumption of local heritage and indigenous cultures (Henderson 2009). Also, post-colonial gendered structures of power have contributed to specific patterns of mobility from the West to the East, such as sex tourism in Thailand (Hitchcock *et al.* 2008).

While complex patterns of tourist mobility from the West to the East have been the norm, recently new tourist flows (of different direction) have emerged, such as Asians visiting or migrating to other Asian countries (Winter 2007). An example of such a trend is the Japanese and South Koreans migrating to Malaysia, who are attracted by special programmes like "Malaysia My Second Home" (see Malaysia My Second Home Program, 2014). Also, new social trends such as South Korean K-pop and TV dramas have become popular within the young Asian market, which in turn have generated interest in, and subsequent patterns of mobility within, the region (Chan 2007). In addition, the post-colonial survival of pseudo-Anglo-Saxon educational systems in some Asian countries has influenced Asian people's mobilities within the region (Pyvis & Chapman 2007). Malaysia and Singapore, for example, attract many students from other Asian countries, such as China, Indonesia and South Korea, as they are recognised as international (Anglo-Saxon) educational hubs. Internal patterns of mobility have also been influenced by the rise of a solid Asian middle class (Robison & Goodman 1996), which in turn has contributed to the development of domestic tourism within each country.

Tourism and the politics of identity formation in Asia

The intensification of tourists' patterns of mobility in Asia (between and within countries) has not occurred without socio-cultural implications (Henderson 2009). To a certain extent, tourism has tended to reinforce socio-cultural stereotypes. In this respect, tourism has played a major role in the politics of identity formation and transformation (Hitchcock *et al.* 2008) as it has helped to "construct" idealised and commoditised images of the local community. These stereotypical images are often based on (post-)colonial representations of Asians, who are usually portrayed as "primitive" and "pre-modern" to satisfy Western desires and fantasies (Hall 2009). Moreover, stereotypical Asian representations are also driven by Westerners' quest (at times an obsession) for "authenticity". Indeed, past and present studies (Cohen 1982; MacCannell 1976; Wang 1999; Brown 2013) show that seeking objective, perceived and existential 'authentic' experiences is still one of the reasons behind tourist consumption, especially within the context of Asian societies.

I have observed this process of "commoditisation" of people and places during my tourist experiences in Asia. In general, I have observed that tourism and non-tourism related promotional material tends to reiterate these post-colonial images as it often portrays Westerners in modern settings and Asians in more "traditional" contexts. Throughout my trips and my daily routines in Asia, I have observed (with few exceptions) that the majority of billboards promoting fashion items and educational products (or other "modern" items) portray Caucasians, while billboards "selling" culture and heritage (or items perceived as "pre-modern") tend to represent Asians. By denying the plurality and complexity of postmodern (Western and Asian) identities, tourism promotional material also tends to re-emphasise (post-)colonial images that portray Westerners as "conquerors" and Asians as "conquered" (Hall & Tucker 2004). I have noticed that these representations play an important role in shaping perceptions concerning how they (Asians) "see" us (Westerners) and vice versa. I have also observed that local communities play an active role in constructing these images (Tucker 2001) and, subsequently, re(producing) their identities (and others' identities). In other words, both tourists and locals actively participate in the process of identity formation, negotiation and representation.

Importantly, the persistence of (post-)colonial discourses of power (co-created and promulgated by both tourists and locals) tends to reinforce socio-economic inequalities between tourists and locals as the latter can rarely afford the luxurious experiences consumed by the former. In this regard, the scenario portrayed by my field notes at the beginning of the chapter is not unusual within many Asian tourist contexts. Tourism thus provides a "stage" in which (Asian) locals play subordinated socio-economic roles and (Western) tourists perform hegemonic wealthy characters. Yet, throughout my journeys I have also observed that structures of power not only exist between Westerners and Asians but also within Asians. As Asian middle classes become more visible (Robison & Goodman 1996), an increasing number of people can afford to travel within and between Asian countries. As such, sharp inequalities also exist between Asian tourists and Asian locals. Within the context of Malaysian urban areas, for example, I have observed that exclusive tourist (and non-tourist) "bubbles" are patronised by European, North American, Japanese, South Korean and some Malaysian tourists. At the same time, these areas are unknown or unaffordable to other Malaysian and Asian groups. Within this complex scenario, tourism should not be considered as the only culprit, as multiple socio-economic forces triggered by capitalism and globalisation contribute to widen these disparities. Yet, by encouraging social and cross-cultural contact, tourism makes these inequalities more visible spatially and temporally due to the proximity between "tourist bubbles" and non-tourist areas.

At a macro-level, the role of tourism in shaping identities and building national identity should also be contemplated (Butler *et al.* 2014; Picard 1997). As Leong (1997: 72) points out, 'elements of tourism are at the same time the ingredients of nationalism: the identification with a place, a sense of historical past, the revival of cultural heritage, and the national integration of social groups'. Obviously, this phenomenon has not occurred without significant social and ethical issues. Driven by political structures of power, social interactions between tourists and locals are monitored and mediated by nation-state policies (Wood 1997), which encourage representations of selected ethnicities in multicultural and multi-ethnic societies. Importantly, in this process of homogenisation of places and people, economic and socio-cultural minorities are silenced. This in turn tends to emphasise already existing socio-cultural inequalities and power imbalances. Paradoxically, it has been argued that this phenomenon also has positive effects due to the visibility it gives to threatened ethnic minorities. As Lanfant (1995: 6) points out

> Tourism is a double-edged sword. In certain cases it contributes towards repressing, marginalizing and neutralizing autonomous or resistance movements. In other cases it allows ethnic minorities that have been cut off from international decision-making to claim and assert their identities.

Studies about tourism and social cohesion in Sri Lanka (Kamble 2013) and social capital in Malaysia (Mura & Tavakoli 2014) have highlighted the important role of tourism in building social relationships among different ethnicities. However, this has also unveiled how simplistic representations of ethnicities are socially and politically "produced" by the nation-state and represented in tourism promotional material. The socio-cultural fabric of Malaysia, for example, is often portrayed as constituted by three main ethnicities, despite being more complex (Shamsul 1996). In this respect, the homestay programme in many Asian countries is an example of promotion of a "simplified and commoditised ethnic fabric" as it projects national identities as homogeneous. However, it is also true that the simplification of ethnic diversity may be used as an "easier" tourism promotional tool. Leong (1997: 93) claims that '[m]ass tourists are not anthropologists who seek a textured understanding of another culture; rather, they often want a formula of an abbreviated culture'. As such, the simplification of culture may lead to positive financial outcomes as it facilitates the process of commoditisation of cultures. This phenomenon leads to the creation of what Shepherd (2011: 5) refers to as 'global non-place[s]' or 'utopias that depend on the words spoken about them for their existence as destinations'.

Case study 7.1 Tourism and alcohol consumption in Asian Muslim countries

Despite the plethora of studies on tourism and religion, little is known about the relationship between locals' religious values and socio-cultural tourist practices. In this regard, there is a paucity of empirical material on the complex relationship between Islamic religious values and tourists' consumption of alcohol. While the Islamic Law prohibits its followers to consume alcohol (and this rule is strictly enforced in some countries, such as Brunei), alcoholic beverages are commonly served to tourists in some Asian Muslim countries, especially within confined "tourist bubbles". For example, alcohol cannot be imported in the Republic of the Maldives, but its consumption is allowed in certain tourist resorts. Also, alcohol in Malaysia and Indonesia is sold in many tourist and non-tourist areas, also due to the fact that minorities (such as Chinese and Indians) are allowed to drink alcohol. The provision of wine, beer and spirits in public spaces has not occurred without complications and socio-cultural issues. In some instances, clashes of values have occurred in tourist (and non-tourist) spaces between locals and tourists, as well as among more progressive and more conservative locals. Importantly, it needs to be emphasised that "tourist bubbles" are not totally detached from locals' areas. Indeed, as tourist areas are often patronised by locals (and locals' areas are often patronised by tourists in search of "authenticity"), problematic socio-cultural encounters cannot be avoided.

Issues have arisen as locals have not always compromised their religious values and accepted alcohol consumption. Some locals have accepted tourists' alcohol consumption, lured by its financial benefits. Others have taken a more conservative stance by embracing the idea that Muslims should not even be allowed to work in environments where alcohol is served. This has also created problems for the hospitality industry due to issues related to lack of available human resources and manpower. A degree of ambiguity has also been created by the lack of clear boundaries between Islamic dogmas and secular laws, which have not been capable of reducing the gap between religious dogmas and more secular social practices. Also, the messages sent by the media have often reproduced the "normality" of consuming alcohol in a globalised world. Within this complicated scenario, locals (especially those working in tourism-related businesses) have learnt mechanisms that allow them to negotiate their different identities (as Muslims, employees, tourism entrepreneurs, hosts) and values (religious, personal, societal, professional) in different performative contexts (at work, at home, in public spaces). However, this has not occurred without personal and public crises as what is (and what is not) allowed within these buffer zones remains unclear.

Conclusion

Does tourism influence socio-cultural change? Perhaps it would not be erroneous to answer "yes" to this question (Henderson 2009). However, how and in which circumstances tourism plays a major role in socio-cultural change in Asia remains open to debate. Certainly the change promoted by tourism and non-tourism related forces is not homogeneous across the many countries and regions of Asia. While "tourist bubbles" are visibly present in selected and preferred areas, there are many places and people that remain relatively untouched by tourism. As a highly localised phenomenon, tourism has not had the influencing role that other factors have had in promoting change, such as the internet and social media. Rather, tourism has exacerbated issues concerning environmental and socio-cultural sustainability due to its localised effects.

With regard to the areas were tourist bubbles have been created, the question arises as to whether they contribute to socio-cultural local development. It needs to be noted that tourist and local "bubbles" are not totally separated. Rather, they have "points of contact" in which contrasting values, beliefs and patterns of behaviour meet (and often clash due to cross-cultural differences). In this respect, the development of tourist bubbles in some areas has not helped to ease more traditional socio-cultural issues between hosts and guests. Despite this, much literature emphasises the positive outcomes of tourism for the locals in these "contact points", without taking into consideration whether the word "locals" refers to selected members of the community or the whole community. In fact, many members of local communities are excluded by tourism development plans. The development of tourism is driven by discourses of power in which political forces, rather than locals' interests, tend to play a major role.

Importantly, through my observations I have realised that the locals play a very active role in the reiteration of tourism and non-tourism related socio-cultural inequalities. Through discourses and practices local communities often tend to reproduce established structures of power. However, I have also experienced situations in which social hierarchies were challenged, sometimes in a very subtle manner. In many homestay programmes in which I have participated, I was often reminded of my role as "guest", whose performance includes acceptance of the "host" rules. Also, despite the stereotype of Asians as being remissive and powerless, I have witnessed cases of violence perpetrated against Western tourists, which certainly question the idyllic images of "weak" and overly tolerant Asians portrayed by tourism promotional material. This reminds us that the politics of identity are rather dynamic and should not be taken for granted by Western tourists. Furthermore, episodes of intolerance against the tourists highlight that political and socio-cultural structures of power are not static but very dynamic according to different performative contexts. I believe that it is a responsibility of the tourism academic community to continue exploring the societal (macro) and individual (micro) socio-cultural implications of tourism-related structures of power in Asian countries for both tourists and locals. Indeed, only an in-depth analysis of these structures will allow us to understand whether and how tourism influences socio-cultural change in Asia.

Key reading

Hall, C.M. and Tucker, H. (eds) (2004) *Tourism and Postcolonialism*. London: Routledge.

Lanfant, M.F., Allcock, J.B. and Bruner E.M. (eds) (1995) *International Tourism: Identity and Change*. London: Sage Publications.

Picard, M. and Wood, R.E. (eds) (1997) *Tourism, Ethnicity, and the State in Asian and Pacific Societies*. Honolulu: University of Hawai'i Press.

Rehbein, B. (ed.) (2011) *Globalization and Inequality in Emerging Societies*, New York: Palgrave Macmillan.

Shepherd, R. (2011) *Partners in Paradise: Tourism Practices, Heritage Policies, and Anthropological Sites*. New York: Peter Lang Publishing.

Timothy, D.J. and Nyaupane, G.P. (eds) (2009) *Cultural Heritage and Tourism in the Developing World*. Florence, KY: Routledge.

References

Akkemik, K.A. (2012) 'Assessing the importance of international tourism for the Turkish economy: A social accounting matrix analysis', *Tourism Management*, 33(4): 790–801.

Altbach, P.G. (1989) 'Twisted roots: The Western impact on Asian higher education', *Higher Education*, 18(1): 9–29.

Andaya, B.W. and Andaya, L.Y. (1982) *A History of Malaysia*. London: Macmillan Press.

Brown, L. (2013) 'Tourism: A catalyst for existential authenticity', *Annals of Tourism Research*, 40: 176–190.

Butler, G., Khoo-Lattimore, C. and Mura, P. (2014) 'Heritage tourism in Malaysia: Fostering a collective national identity in an ethnically diverse country', *Asia Pacific Journal of Tourism Research*, 19(2): 199–218.

Chan, B. (2007) 'Film-induced tourism in Asia: A case study of Korean television drama and female viewers' motivation to visit Korea', *Tourism Culture & Communication*, 7(3): 207–224.

Cohen, E. (1982) 'Marginal paradises: Bungalow tourism on the islands of Southern Thailand', *Annals of Tourism Research*, 9(2): 189–228.

Durbarry, R. (2004) 'Tourism and economic growth: The case of Mauritius', *Tourism Economics*, 10(4): 389–401.

Farsani, N.T., Coelho, C. and Costa, C. (2011) 'Geotourism and geoparks as novel strategies for socio-economic development in rural areas', *International Journal of Tourism Research*, 13(1): 68–81.

Hall, C.M. (2009) 'Heritage tourism in the Pacific: Modernity, myth, and identity', in D.J. Timothy and G.P. Nyaupane (eds), *Cultural Heritage and Tourism in the Developing World* (pp.109–126). Florence, KY: Routledge.

Hall, C.M. and Tucker, H. (2004) 'Tourism and postcolonialism: An introduction', in C.M. Hall and H. Tucker (eds,), *Tourism and Postcolonialism* (pp. 1–24). London: Routledge.

Henderson, J.C. (2009) 'The meanings, marketing, and management of heritage tourism in Southeast Asia', in D.J. Timothy and G.P. Nyaupane (eds), *Cultural Heritage and Tourism in the Developing World* (pp. 73–92). Florence, KY: Routledge.

Hitchcock, M., King, V. and Parnwell, M. (2008) 'Introduction: Tourism in Southeast Asia revisited', in M. Hitchcock, V.T. King and M. Parnwell (eds), *Tourism in Southeast Asia: Challenges and Directions* (pp. 1–42). Copenhagen: Nordic Institute of Asian Studies Press.

Houben, V. and Rehbein, B. (2011) 'The persistence of sociocultures and inequality in contemporary Southeast Asia', in B. Rehbein (ed.), *Globalization and Inequality in Emerging Societies* (pp. 11–30). New York: Palgrave Macmillan.

Kamble, Z. (2013) 'Special interest tourism as a catalyst to social cohesion in fragmented societies', in *Proceedings of the International Conference on Tourism and Hospitality Management, Colombo, 8th–10th December 2013* (pp. 45–54). Malabe, Sri Lanka: International Center for Research and Development.

Kim, E.M. (1998) *The Four Asian Tigers: Economic Development and the Global Political Economy*. New York: Academic Press.

King, R., Black, R., Collyer, M., Fielding, A. and Skeldon, R. (2010) *People on the Move: An Atlas of Migration*. Berkeley: University of California Press.

Lanfant, M.F. (1995) 'International tourism, internationalization and the challenge to identity', in M.F. Lanfant, J.B. Allcock and E.M. Bruner (eds), *International Tourism: Identity and Change* (pp. 24–43). London: Sage.

Leong, L.W.T. (1997) 'Commodifying ethnicity: State and ethnic tourism in Singapore', in M. Picard and R.E. Wood (eds.), *Tourism, Ethnicity, and the State in Asian and Pacific Societies* (pp. 71–98). Honolulu: University of Hawai'i Press.

Loomba, A. (1998) *Colonialism-Postcolonialism*. London: Routledge.

MacCannell, D. (1976) *The Tourist: A New Theory of the Leisure Class*. London: Macmillan Press.

Malaysia My Second Home Program (2014) *Malaysia*. Ministry of Tourism and Culture Malaysia. Online. Available: www.mm2h.gov.my/index.php/en (accessed 4 December 2014).

Mura, P. and Tavakoli, R. (2014) 'Tourism and social capital in Malaysia', *Current Issues in Tourism*, 17(1): 28–45.

Nyaupane, G.P. and Budruk, M. (2009) 'South Asian heritage tourism: Conflict, colonialism, and cooperation', in D. Timothy and G.P. Nyaupane (eds), *Cultural Heritage and Tourism in the Developing World* (pp. 127–145). New York: Routledge.

Picard, M. (1997) 'Cultural tourism, nation-building, and regional culture: The making of a Balinese identity', in M. Picard and R.E. Wood (eds), *Tourism, Ethnicity, and the State in Asian and Pacific Societies* (pp. 81–214). Honolulu: University of Hawai'i Press.

Piper, N. and Rother, S. (2011) 'Transnational inequalities, transnational responses: The politicization of migrant rights in Asia', in B. Rehbein (ed.), *Globalization and Inequality in Emerging Societies* (pp. 235–255). New York: Palgrave Macmillan.

Pyvis, D. and Chapman, A. (2007) 'Why university students choose an international education: A case study in Malaysia', *International Journal of Educational Development*, 27(2): 235–246.

Robison, R. and Goodman, D.S.G. (1996) *The New Rich in Asia: Mobile Phones, McDonald's and Middle-Class Revolution*. London: Routledge.

Salazar, N.B. (2006) 'Building a "culture of peace" through tourism: Reflexive and analytical notes and queries', *Universitas Humanistica*, 62: 319–333.

Seetanah, B. (2011) 'Assessing the dynamic economic impact of tourism for island economies', *Annals of Tourism Research*, 38(1): 291–308.

Shamsul, A.B. (1996) 'Debating about identity in Malaysia: A discourse analysis', *Southeast Asian Studies*, 34(3): 476–499.

Shepherd, R. (2011) *Partners in Paradise: Tourism Practices, Heritage Policies, and Anthropological Sites*. New York: Peter Lang Publishing.

Tucker, H. (2001) 'Tourists and troglodytes', *Annals of Tourism Research*, 28(4): 868–891.

Wang, N. (1999) 'Rethinking authenticity in tourism experience', *Annals of Tourism Research*, 26(2): 349–370.

Webster, J. and Cooper, N.J. (1996) *Roman Imperialism: Post-Colonial Perspectives*. Leicester: School of Archaeological Studies, University of Leicester.

Winter, T. (2007) 'Rethinking tourism in Asia', *Annals of Tourism Research*, 34(1): 27–44.

Wood, R.E. (1997) 'Tourism and the state: Ethnic options and constructions of otherness', in M. Picard and R.E. Wood (eds), *Tourism, Ethnicity, and the State in Asian and Pacific Societies* (pp. 1–34). Honolulu: University of Hawai'i Press.

8

POVERTY IN TOURIST PARADISE?

A review of pro-poor tourism in South and South-East Asia

V. Dao Truong, Elmarie Slabbert & V. Manh Nguyen

Introduction

Poverty is complex, multi-dimensional, multi-scale, and affects many countries. The elimination of poverty requires multiple approaches that are flexible to local contexts and embrace a diversity of knowledge and values. To achieve this, tourism has been increasingly embedded into national and international policy. One outcome of this policy relationship was the emergence of the pro-poor tourism (PPT) concept in 1999, which was defined as tourism that

> generates benefits for the poor. Benefits may be economic, but they may also be social, environmental or cultural... [A]s long as poor people reap net benefits, tourism can be classified as "pro-poor" (even if richer people benefit more than poorer people)
>
> *(Ashley et al. 2000: 2)*

The PPT concept has been rapidly advocated, as reflected by the endorsement of the United Nations World Tourism Organization's (UNWTO) Sustainable Tourism–Eliminating Poverty (ST-EP) Initiative and Foundation. The governments of many developing countries (e.g. South Africa, Vietnam) have incorporated tourism as a key component of poverty reduction strategies (Goodwin 2008; Truong 2013). PPT has also been advocated by non-governmental organisations (NGOs) and international development agencies, such as SNV Netherlands Development Organisation and GIZ German Agency for International Development (Truong *et al.* 2014). It is often argued that tourism has greater potential for poverty alleviation than other sectors because of its particular characteristics. Primary among these is the provision of job and income opportunities, particularly for women (Mitchell & Ashley 2010). However, such claims are not always tested (Croes 2014), and there is growing scepticism among tourism academics and practitioners who have failed to see these claims realised (Holden 2013; Pleumarom 2012; Truong 2015). Efforts therefore have been made to quantify the impacts of tourism on poor people, for example, through the value chain approach (Mitchell 2012). More recently a participatory approach has been adopted, which allows poor people to give their "voice" regarding the effects of tourism on their lives (Holden *et al.* 2011).

This chapter aims to examine evidence for the claims made for and against PPT in South and Southeast Asia that has been described as a "tourist paradise" (Yamashita 2009) but where a substantial proportion of the population live below the international poverty line of US$1.25 per day (UN Development Programme (UNDP) 2014). This chapter begins with a brief history of PPT and the debates that have arisen around the concept. Next, the regional tourism and poverty situation is analysed. The claims that have been made for and against PPT are then presented. The chapter concludes with discussion of avenues for further PPT research and practice.

Pro-poor tourism: history and debates

Although the role of tourism in economic development has long been recognised (de Kadt 1979) and research into the importance of tourism to national economies has an established legacy (Holden *et al.* 2011), the contribution of tourism to poverty alleviation is a relatively recent topic in the extant literature (Holden 2013). Academic literature on the role of tourism has evolved from the expectations in the 1950s–1960s that tourism could make significant contributions to modernisation, whose profits would trickle down to benefit poor segments of society; through the realisation in the 1970s that tourism did not bring about expected economic achievements, but instead increased dependency, inefficiency and slower economic growth; to the increased awareness in the 1980s–1990s of the environmental consequences of tourism and the need to engage host communities in tourism development; and to the recognition in the late 1990s of the relationship between tourism and poverty alleviation (Harrison & Schipani 2007; Holden *et al.* 2011; Holden 2013).

The past decade has witnessed an increase in academic studies of tourism and development that place a greater focus on the benefits that tourism may bring about for poor people (Truong 2015). The term "pro-poor tourism" emerged following the change in the British government in the late 1990s when the Overseas Development Administration was separated from the Foreign and Commonwealth Office and renamed as the Department for International Development (DfID) (Goodwin 2008, 2009). With poverty elimination as its key purpose, the DfID commissioned a discussion paper on *Tourism and Poverty Elimination* (Goodwin 1998) and later another paper by Deloitte and Touche on *Sustainable Tourism and Poverty Elimination* (Bennett *et al.* 1999). These were followed by a series of research projects undertaken to investigate mechanisms through which tourism could improve the livelihoods of poor people in Africa, America, and Asia (Ashley 2005; Ashley & Wolmer 2003). The British government's adoption of poverty reduction as a key goal of development policy reflected the international community's growing consensus on the elimination of poverty (Goodwin 2009). Indeed, at the 2000 Millennium Summit the UN identified poverty alleviation as one of the most crucial tasks and established the Millennium Development Goals (MDGs), where the first goal was to halve the number of people living on less than US$1.25 per day by 2015. The UNWTO promptly embraced this challenge, adopting the PPT concept and endorsing the ST-EP Initiative and Foundation. In particular, it considered 2007 a critical year where tourism was recognised as a key agent in poverty alleviation (UNWTO 2007). Support for PPT has also been reflected by the inclusion of tourism as a component of poverty reduction policies in many developing countries (Truong 2013) and the implementation of PPT projects by NGOs and international development agencies such as SNV and GIZ (Hummel *et al.* 2013; Hummel & van der Dium 2012).

Advocates of PPT claim that PPT is potentially a human-centred and holistic approach because it aims to increase not only economic impacts but also non-financial livelihood effects of tourism on poor people. Three types of PPT strategies have been proposed (Roe & Khanya 2002). The first strategy concentrates on increasing the economic profits of tourism for poor people through expansion of local employment and income opportunities, expansion of local enterprise opportunities (e.g. food supply, tourist guiding), and development of collective income sources (e.g. revenue shares, equity dividends). The second strategy seeks to enhance the non-economic livelihood impacts of tourism for poor people with such measures as capacity building, training, mitigating environmental impacts, improving social and cultural impacts, and increasing local access to infrastructure and services provided for tourists (e.g. roads, transport). The third strategy focuses on enhancing poor people's participation and partnerships where a supportive regulatory framework is established to enable poor people's participation in decision-making processes and meaningful collaboration with relevant stakeholders in the tourism development process (Roe & Khanya 2002).

Mitchell and Ashley (2010) suggest three main channels through which tourism impacts poverty. The first involves the direct effects of tourism, which include labour income and other forms of earnings such as craft selling. The second concerns secondary effects that embrace indirect earnings from tourism activities and induced effects from tourism workers re-spending their earnings in the local economy. The third channel involves long-term changes in the macro-economy due to tourism growth. However, such channels are essentially not different from any other kind of tourism-related economic impact (Truong *et al.* 2014), and reflect criticisms that a focus on international tourism development as a means of creating jobs for poorer people and issues of mobility disguise broader issues of wealth distribution, with tourism not necessarily being more effective in alleviating poverty than other sectors (Hall 2007). In addition, such channels presume that a link readily exists between tourism and poverty, and attention is thus given to finding "pathways" and making the link stronger. Meanwhile, any link between tourism and poverty is not automatic, and is instead strongly dependent on specific conditions or policies that are put in place (Croes 2014; Hall 2007; Truong 2013).

Although there is increased awareness of the importance of evaluation studies in development projects and interventions (Rutkowski & Sparks 2014), the PPT literature is lacking evidence to demonstrate that poor people's livelihoods are improved due to tourism (Goodwin 2009; Holden 2013; Mitchell & Ashley 2010). This is despite the use of related new approaches, such as a value chain approach (Mitchell 2012), having highlighted ways in which the benefits of tourism can be maximised and better targeted as tourism spend flows through the economy. More recently, attention has turned towards a participatory, interpretative approach that gives "voice" to poor people regarding the impacts of tourism on their lives (Holden *et al.* 2011; Islam & Carlsen 2012; Truong *et al.* 2014).

A large number of PPT studies and initiatives have been undertaken within the African contexts and societies (Goodwin 2008, 2009; Truong *et al.* 2014). In contrast, there is relatively little research into the evolution of PPT in other regions, such as South and Southeast Asia, that have a large or potentially large tourism market (UNWTO 2015) but where a considerable proportion of the population lives below internationally or nationally recognised poverty lines (UNDP 2014). The tourism and poverty situation in South and Southeast Asia is discussed next.

South and Southeast Asia in context

South and Southeast Asia is arguably one of the world's largest and most populous regions. It comprises South (or Southern) Asia, which covers the countries of Afghanistan, Bangladesh, Bhutan, India, the Maldives, Nepal, Pakistan, and Sri Lanka; and Southeast Asia, which consists of Brunei, Cambodia, Indonesia, Lao PDR, Malaysia, Myanmar, the Philippines, Singapore, Thailand, Timor-Leste, and Vietnam. The region covers about 8.9 million km², which is approximately 20% of the Asian continent's surface land area. In terms of population, it is home to some 2.2 billion people (World Bank 2013), accounting for half of Asia's total population. Of the ten most populous Asian countries, six are in South and Southeast Asia: India, Indonesia,

Pakistan, Bangladesh, the Philippines, and Vietnam (World Population Statistics 2013). The region is also home to a vast array of ethnic groups, whose populations range from hundreds of millions to small tribal groups.

The region boasts a wide variety of resources for tourism development, which range from sandy beaches in the Maldives, Thailand, and Vietnam to spectacular mountains in the Himalayas and cultural and religious heritages in India, Lao PDR, and Cambodia (Boniface & Cooper 2009). In 2005, the region received 56.6 million international tourists who generated US$44.5 billion in gross revenue. The number of international tourists to the region almost doubled in 2014, with 117.3 million arrivals, around 10% of the world's total international tourist figure (Table 8.1). While many countries attracted significant numbers of international tourists, others were less successful. For example, Thailand was the world's tenth largest destination in terms of international tourists (27 million) and seventh in terms of tourism receipts (US$42 billion) in 2013 (UNWTO 2014a). By contrast, Pakistan, although having a diverse resource base and extensive coastline, attracted limited international tourist arrivals due to poor infrastructure, security concerns, and strict cross-border control (Boniface & Cooper 2009).

The governments of most regional countries have realised the importance of tourism and adopted different approaches to tourism development. In India, tourism is the third largest earner of foreign exchange and creates jobs for millions of people (Michot 2010). Tourism development thus becomes an important part of the Indian government's action plans. The Indian government has endorsed a liberal open skies policy, allowing foreign charter airlines to fly directly from Europe to resort areas such as Goa (Boniface & Cooper 2009). Similarly, the Vietnamese government has recognised tourism as a spearhead sector and a means of poverty alleviation, and has signed visa exemption agreements with more than 80 countries worldwide (Truong 2013). By contrast, the government of Bhutan imposes tight restrictions on visitor numbers in order to preserve the country's natural and cultural resources. Until 2001, access

Table 8.1 International tourism in South and South-East Asia, 2005–2014

	South Asia			South-East Asia			Total		
	International tourist arrivals[a]	Share (%)[b]	Receipts[c]	International tourist arrivals	Share (%)	Receipts	International tourist arrivals	Share (%)	Receipts
2005	8.1	–	9.6	48.5	–	34.9	56.6	–	44.5
2006	–	–	11.4	–	–	43.6	–	–	55.0
2007	10.1	–	13.9	59.7	–	55.3	69.8	–	69.2
2008	10.3	1.1	15.4	61.8	6.7	61.6	72.1	7.8	77.0
2009	9.9	1.1	15.6	62.1	7.1	54.3	72.0	8.2	69.9
2010	11.1	1.2	18.9	69.9	7.4	68.6	81.0	8.6	87.5
2011	13.8	1.4	23.1	77.5	7.8	81.9	91.3	9.2	105.0
2012	14.6	1.4	22.9	84.2	8.2	96.0	98.8	9.6	118.9
2013	15.5	1.4	24.3	93.1	8.6	107.4	110.2	10.0	131.7
2014	17.1	1.5	27.2	96.6	8.5	106.8	113.7	10.0	134.0

Sources: Data aggregated from UNWTO 2009a, 2009b, 2009c, 2009d, 2010, 2012, 2013, 2014a, 2014b, 2015.
Notes
a Million.
b Percentage of the world's total numbers.
c Billion US$.

was restricted to a limited number of accredited tour operators offering tours to small groups of tourists (Nyaupane & Timothy 2010).

Many of the regional countries also have a national tourism management agency in place. The Tourism Authority of Thailand, which was set up in 1960, is one of the oldest agencies in the region. The Ceylon Tourism Board (presently Sri Lanka Tourist Board) was established in 1966. In 1978 the Vietnam National Administration of Tourism was formed (Truong 2013). The Maldives Tourism Promotion Board was created much later, in the late 1990s, to promote the islands internationally (Boniface & Cooper 2009). In terms of international and regional tourism cooperation, in Southeast Asia, the Association of Southeast Asian Nations (ASEAN) has formalised regional cooperation in tourism since 1976. The Greater Mekong Subregion (GMS) was formed in 2001 to enable an effective regulatory framework and infrastructural linkages that would facilitate cross-border trade, investment, tourism, and other forms of regional cooperation. It has received funding from the Asian Development Bank (ADB) to promote regional tourism development. A GMS tourism strategy was formulated for the period 2006–2015 with the goal of 'promoting the Mekong as a single destination, offering a diversity of good quality and high yielding subregional products' so that 'all regional countries and tour operators earn more from tourism and over a long period of time' (ADB 2008: ii). A revised "road map" for the period 2011–2015 was approved at the GMS 2011 Tourism Ministers' Meeting, focusing on the development of multi-country tour circuits along the GMS Economic Corridor and the Mekong River Tourism Corridor (ADB 2008). Furthermore, many of the regional countries have joined other membership-based associations such as the Pacific Asia Travel Association (PATA) to promote tourism development within the region and internationally. In contrast, the South Asian Association for Regional Cooperation's (SAARC) initiatives in tourism have not been so well developed (Chapter 16).

South and Southeast Asia has substantial levels of poverty. South Asia alone accounts for more than 40% of the world's population living on US$1.25–2.5 per day (UNDP 2014). In 2011, almost half of Bangladesh's population lived on less than US$1.25 per day. The number of poor people was also high in Laos and India, who accounted for 33.9% and 32.7% of the population, respectively. In Singapore, a developed country with a very high level of human development (UNDP 2014), an estimated 12% of the local people earned less than US$1.25 per day in 2011. By contrast, Thailand and Malaysia, both of which had a lower level of human development (UNDP 2014), reportedly had the smallest proportion of people living below the poverty line of US$1.25 per day, with 0.4% and 0.5% respectively (Table 8.2).

Table 8.2 also shows that the proportion of multi-dimensionally poor people is much higher than that of people living on less than US$1.25 per day. The multi-dimensional poverty index was introduced by the UNDP in 2010, which measures poverty in the dimensions of health, education, and living standards (UNDP 2014). In Pakistan, half of the population was identified as multi-dimensionally poor although only 21% lived on less than US$1.25 per day. Similarly, only 1.7% of Bhutan's population earned less than US$1.25 per day but 43.5% lived in multi-dimensional poverty. The proportion of the income-poor and the multi-dimensionally poor may be declining in some countries. However, sizeable proportions of the regional population are close to the poverty threshold. This means that a large number of people may fall back into poverty if they are affected by, for example, natural disasters, social unrest, or economic turmoil.

Given the growth in visitor numbers and total tourism receipts, the governments of many regional countries have considered tourism a tool of economic development and a contributor to poverty alleviation, as mentioned earlier. The next section examines evidence for the claims that have been made for and against PPT in the region.

Table 8.2 Multi-dimensional poverty in South and South-East Asia by country

	Year and survey	Population in multi-dimensional poverty				Population below income poverty line (%)	
		Headcount[b] (thousands)	Intensity of deprivation[c] (%)	Population near multi-dimensional poverty[d] (%)	Population in severe poverty[e] (%)	PPP $1.25 per day	National poverty line
Afghanistan	2010/2011	17,116	49.9	16.0	29.8	–	36.0
Bangladesh	2011	75,610	47.8	18.8	21.0	43.3	31.5
Bhutan	2010	211	43.5	18.0	8.8	1.7	12.0
Brunei	–	–	–	–	–	–	–
Cambodia	2010	6,721	45.1	20.4	16.4	18.6	20.5
India	2005/2006	631,999	51.1	18.2	27.8	32.7	21.9
Indonesia	2012	14,574	41.3	8.1	1.1	16.2	12.0
Lao PDR	2011/2012	2,447	50.5	18.5	18.8	33.9	27.6
Malaysia	2004	–	–	–	–	0.5	3.8
Maldives	2009	6	37.5	8.5	0.1	1.5	–
Myanmar	–	–	–	–	–	–	–
Nepal	2011	11,255	47.4	18.1	18.6	24.8	25.2
Pakistan	2012/2013	83,045	52.0	14.9	26.5	21.0	22.3
Philippines	2008	6,559	51.9	12.2	5.0	18.4	26.5
Singapore	2011	–	–	–	–	12.0	–
Sri Lanka	2003	–	38.7	14.4	0.6	14.0	22.7
Thailand	2005/2006	664	38.8	4.4	0.1	0.4	13.2
Timor-Leste	2009/2010	694	50.1	21.4	31.5	–	49.9
Vietnam	2010/2011	5,796	40.7	8.7	1.3	16.9	20.7

Sources: Data aggregated from Donalson *et al.* 2013; Oxford Poverty and Human Development Initiative 2015; UNDP 2014.

Notes

a The multi-dimensional poverty index identifies poor populations across the dimensions of health, education and living standards. It is measured on the scale of 0 (not deprived) to 1 (deprived).

b Population with a weighted score of at least 33%.

c Average percentage of deprivation experienced by multi-dimensionally poor people.

d Percentage of population at risk of suffering from multiple deprivations (having a deprivation score of 20–33%).

e Percentage of population in severe multi-dimensional poverty (having a deprivation score of 50% or higher).

PPT in South and Southeast Asia: evidence for the claims?

The many claimed benefits of PPT have to some extent driven its widespread incorporation into national and international policy. At the same time, scepticism has been growing among tourism academics and practitioners who have failed to see the benefits of PPT realised. These claims can be broadly categorised under outcome- and process-based arguments for tourism as a means of poverty alleviation. While outcome-based claims tend to be positive, those based on a process approach appear to report relatively limited impact of tourism on poor people. In both categories, the reporting of quantitative analyses and techniques was rare. As will be analysed below, contradictory evidence may be found regarding the efficacy of tourism in poverty alleviation within a country or even a single tourist destination (e.g. Michot 2010; Pleumarom 2012).

Outcome-based claims focus on the benefits that tourism brings about for poor people and these are primarily made through the measurement of financial income. For example, Anand *et al.* (2012) indicate that each household in Korzo village in India earned between US$700 and US$1,200 per month by providing homestay service as a result of a homestay development initiative implemented, where local people also worked as porters, cooks, and tourist guides. In this way, homestay owners were able to improve their living standards. They could buy "expensive" assets such as televisions and vehicles that they could not afford before (Anand *et al.* 2012). In Laos, the ADB's Mekong Tourism Development Programme implemented in Luang Namtha, Luang Prabang, Khammouane, and Champassak contributed to generating gross revenue of about US$474,596 after only one year, wherein nearly half (US$260,947) was realised at the village level (Harrison & Schipani 2007). Hummel *et al.* (2013) applied a value chain approach that consisted of accommodation, food and beverage, handicrafts, and excursions as key elements, and found that in Laos an estimated US$6 million per year of tourist expenditure flowed directly to the local poor. Poor people benefited the most from food and beverage (45%; US$3 million), followed by handicrafts (US$1.8 million) with 40% of souvenir spending accruing to poor people. In Bhutan, a pro-poor sustainable tourism project led to an increase of over US$100 per household during its first four years of operation. However, limited impact of tourism on poor people was reported (Hummel *et al.* 2013).

A survey conducted in 1996 suggested that tourism-related activities were the main source of income for 78% of the local residents in Namche Bazaar, Nepal (Sharma 2002). An estimated 90% of the income of the Khumbu region in north-eastern Nepal was attributed to tourism development (Nepal *et al.* 2002). It is argued that in such cases the local poor are definitely the beneficiaries (Sharma 2002). Shahia and Smith (2005) indicate that the benefits of the *Annapurna Conservation Area* project in Nepal were used to build schools for children, upgrade infrastructure, protect natural and cultural resources, and thereby contribute to improving the living conditions of local poor people as a whole. In northern Thailand, Suriya and Gruen (2012) suggest that revenues earned from souvenir production are distributed to poor communities in Mae Kam Pong village, given that the production does not require high skills, it is open to all villagers who can join at any time, the local market is large enough, and the production is innovative in that it often creates new product designs.

Simply calculating the amount of income poor people earn from tourism is perhaps too simplistic. A number of studies have examined the process through which poor people participate in tourism and the extent to which their quality of life is improved by tourism. This approach often involves in-depth research into the perceptions and experiences of poor people in relation to tourism and poverty alleviation. For example, Brickell (2008) indicates that some Cambodian women who migrate from rural areas to work as waitresses in restaurants in Krobei Riel and Slorkram near the Angkor Wat World Heritage Site earn about US$50 a month, of which about one-third (US$15) is paid for accommodation. It is suggested that although tourism helps alleviate their income poverty, in multi-dimensional terms their emotional well-being is compromised by their ability to lead a fulfilling life. Many of them feel uncomfortable for having to leave their small children in the countryside. In addition, their work is not highly regarded by local people who associate women working after dark in restaurants and bars with immorality and shame (Brickell 2008). The situation appears to be worse for a number of

Filipino women who migrate from rural areas to the capital city of Manila to work as street vendors. Although selling stuff to tourists is allowed in Rizal Park, it only earns these immigrants a meagre income. Many of them cannot afford to rent a room and thus have to sleep in the park (Yotsumoto 2013).

Taking a participatory approach to PPT allows for meaningful reflections on barriers that poor people confront in participating in tourism-related activities. It offers the reader a unique opportunity to glance into poor people's perceptions and interpretations of tourism as a means of poverty alleviation. Islam and Carlsen (2012) indicate that a number of challenges are facing poor people in Bangladesh who wish to participate in tourism, including lack of financial and technical support from governmental and non-governmental organisations, dominance of intermediaries and wealthy elites in the tourism market, and poor knowledge and skills. Likewise, Mao *et al.* (2013) suggest that tourism has provided job and business opportunities for poor people in Siem Reap who, however, earn extremely low incomes from tourism because they do not have, among others, financial resources, business knowledge, market access, or good foreign language skills (see also Mao *et al.* 2014). It is also found that poor people in Sapa, Vietnam are not the main beneficiaries of tourism. Instead, a large proportion of tourism profits accrue to the tour operators who dominate the local tourism market. Although a number of poor people can increase their income by selling handicrafts, most others lack capital and foreign language proficiency to establish homestays or to become tourist guides (Truong *et al.* 2014).

Despite the rhetoric and the concerns that have been expressed, there have been few attempts to quantify the impact of tourism on poor people. For example, Thomas (2014) estimates that the pro-poor impact of Laos' tourism ranges from 1.9% to 79.8% and that at least 60% of the local tourism workers earn less than US$2 per day. Wattanakuljarus and Coxhead (2008) analysed the distribution of Thailand's tourism income using a general equilibrium model and indicated that there was an increase in aggregate household income due to the growth in inbound tourism demand, but that this increase worsened the distribution of income between rich and poor households. These attempts have tended to focus on evaluating the outcomes rather than the process. They have also relied on secondary data instead of primary data that are, for example, provided by poor people. This is partly due to the challenge of collecting data over an extended period of time and selecting appropriate evaluation criteria. Holden *et al.* (2011) argue that the evaluation of PPT's efficacy should itself be a participatory process, with poor people giving voice to the impact of tourism development on their lives. Truong *et al.* (2014) go further, claiming that the identification of poor people who are supposed to give their voice should even be undertaken by poor people. This is because poor people's perception of poverty may be different from that of academics and governments (Pleumarom 2012; Suntikul 2009).

Claims over the efficacy of PPT diverge not only across and within countries, but also within a single destination where a tourism initiative is implemented. For example, the *Kerala Responsible Tourism* initiative was launched in 2008 by the Indian Tourism Department in collaboration with the Indian section of the International Centre for Responsible Tourism. It aimed to promote eco- and responsible tourism practices that are viable for businesses while also providing employment and income-earning opportunities for local poor people. The initiative was awarded the UNWTO's Ulysses Award for Innovation in Public Policy and Governance and was considered by the Indian government to be a responsible tourism model (Goodwin 2014; see also Michot 2010). However, local poor people claimed that 'Kerala was not a model of "sustainable" or "responsible tourism" by any international standard' because 'it contributed little, if anything, to ensure "maximum positive benefit" to and "minimum negative impact" on local communities' (Pleumarom 2012: 5). It is notable that neither the claims for nor those against the initiative were substantiated by quantitative evidence.

This section has shown that although theoretical perspectives give rise to the number of studies on the role of tourism in poverty alleviation, there appear to be divergent views and even contradictory evidence concerning the contribution that tourism makes to poverty alleviation in South and Southeast Asian countries. Through a combination of quantitative evaluations (which are rare) and insights from qualitative studies and case studies (which are far more abundant), suggestions are emerging for best practice in PPT, which are reviewed below.

Best practice PPT in South and Southeast Asia

Given the controversies over the contribution of tourism to poverty alleviation, much disagreement exists among tourism academics and practitioners concerning what constitutes "best practice" in PPT. For example, Hummel *et al.* (2013) called for the incorporation of PPT into national policy and the formulation of an appropriate method that is capable of measuring the impact of tourism on poor people. Meanwhile, Truong *et al.* (2014) highlighted the importance of giving voice to poor people over the course of tourism planning and development if tourism was to make meaningful contributions to their livelihoods. However, such views are not mutually exclusive, and a review of the literature suggests that a broad consensus over key features of best practice PPT is emerging.

A theme running through this literature is the need to shift from the "outcome-based" approach, which measures the income benefits that poor people earn from tourism, towards an approach that considers PPT as a process through which poor people participate in tourism and improve their living standards. This view places poor people in the context of a long-term relationship where stakeholders develop mutual trust and respect as they learn from each other to negotiate potential solutions. To be successful, this process needs to be underpinned by an appropriate philosophy, and consider how to engage the relevant stakeholders at the most appropriate time and in a manner that will enable them to effectively shape PPT policies and decisions. The rest of this section reviews four key features of best practice PPT that have emerged from a grounded theory analysis of the literature. Grounded theory is a qualitative method used to systematically analyse large bodies of literature in order to construct theoretical models that are "grounded" in the text (Corbin & Strauss 1990). It is conducted through a process of reviewing texts with specific questions in mind, coding passages and dividing them into concepts and then into themes from which theory can be derived.

PPT needs to be underpinned by a philosophy that emphasises representation, empowerment, and equity

The first component of this philosophy that is emphasised in the literature is the need to empower poor people through participation and representation. This takes two forms: (1) ensuring that poor people have the power to influence the decision making and project design and implementation processes (Anand *et al.* 2012; Holden *et al.* 2011; Truong *et al.* 2014); and (2) ensuring that poor people have the technical capability to participate in these processes (Suntikul 2007; Tolkach *et al.* 2012; Yotsumoto 2013). If a decision has already been made or cannot be influenced by poor people, their participation in any PPT initiatives may not be effective. This situation has been seen in Sapa in north-western Vietnam where some poor ethnic minorities merely follow decisions and regulations made by the majority Kinh who have better education, knowledge, skills, and market information. Those poor ethnic minorities thus have little influence on decisions that affect their lives (Truong *et al.* 2014).

It is not sufficient simply to provide poor people with the opportunity to participate in decision making or project design and implementation, though; they must actually be able to participate (Sharma 2002). This would involve the removal of the barriers that prevent the participation of poor people, including gender inequality, social discrimination, and unequal distribution of resources (Islam & Carlsen 2012; Mao *et al.* 2013, 2014; Sharma 2002). When decisions are highly technical, this may entail training poor people, developing knowledge and skills as well as confidence that is necessary for them to engage meaningfully in the process. For example, the *Tourism for Rural Poverty Alleviation* project in Nepal provided education and training workshops where poor communities were able to determine for themselves their capacity to develop a tourism project, defined by themselves on the basis of their resources and designed with technical assistance from the project consultants (Rossetto *et al.* 2007).

Power inequalities within and between different groups of poor people represent an equally important barrier to meaningful participation. It is necessary to consider how inequalities in age, gender, and ethnic background can be overcome to enable poor people to participate meaningfully in and benefit from PPT. Phommavong and Sorensson (2014) suggest that ethnic women in Akha village of Laos have the opportunity to work in different positions in tourism as a result of the community-based PPT projects implemented. However, for religious reasons they do not have access to education and therefore they often do not get promoted to equal management positions and income levels to men. In Sapa, Vietnam, the H'Mong are the largest ethnic group whose language is the second most widely spoken after Vietnamese (Vietnam's national language). Therefore, the number of H'Mong people working as tourist guides and handicraft sellers far outweighs that of the other ethnic groups such as Red Dzao and Dzay. The H'Mong also tend to support members of their own group and this increases the likelihood that they can earn more from tourism than the other ethnic groups (Truong *et al.* 2014).

Where relevant, participation and support of relevant stakeholders should be considered as early as possible and throughout the process

PPT initiatives are often funded or implemented by foreign NGOs or international development agencies in collaboration with local governments and institutions (Harrison & Schipani 2007; Hummel *et al.* 2013; Hummel & van der Dium 2012). Foreign NGOs are not only important sources of funding, but also have been frequently cited as essential contributors to strengthening the capacity of local civil organisations, redefining poverty and making it a policy priority (Phommavong 2011; Truong & Hall 2013), motivating poor people to participate in PPT initiatives (Sharma 2002), as well as facilitating communication between local communities and other stakeholders such as the private sector (Islam & Carlsen 2012). Their advantages include, but are not limited to, independence from formal state structures, wide community outreach, and ability to work creatively and negotiate with local governments (Truong & Hall 2013).

Foreign NGOs' experience and expertise is not sufficient to ensure the long-term success of PPT initiatives though; increasingly it is indicated that the participation and support of local-level organisations should be considered right from the outset, from concept development and planning, through implementation, to monitoring and evaluation of PPT's outcomes. In former and transitioning socialist state countries (e.g. Laos, Cambodia, Vietnam) community organisations, such as Women's Unions that are often run by state funding, play an important role in supporting local governments in community management. With respect to tourism development, it has been demonstrated that members of local Women's Unions are useful channels through which information about PPT initiatives is disseminated to the wider community and meaningful contacts are established between the project funding agency, local government, the private sector, and community members (Phommavong 2011; Phommavong & Sorensson 2014; Theerapappisit 2009; Truong *et al.* 2014). Local Women's Unions play a particularly important role when community support is sought for tourism development due to their ability to mobilise, persuade, and motivate community members (Harrison & Schipani 2007; Phommavong 2011; Sharma 2002). Truong and Hall (2013, 2015) present one of the few documented examples of PPT projects undertaken in Vietnam where members of local Women's Unions (alongside poor people themselves) were engaged right from the development of the initial concept. This was made possible through the adoption of theories of community organisation and participation in project design and implementation (Truong & Hall 2013, 2015).

However, there is also a danger that the engagement of local Women's Unions in PPT projects may bias decisions and result in unexpected conflicts and tensions. This is particularly the case in multi-ethnic communities where an ethnic group may have more advantages than the others due to population size or prevalence of language. For example, Truong *et al.* (2014) describe the failure of the *Handicrafts for Women* project that was implemented in Ta Phin village in north-western Vietnam by the Canadian Capilano University and the Hanoi Open University. The head of the local Women's Union was in charge of the handicraft production process. Those who participated in the project were not happy because they were underpaid. If they produced a piece of handicraft and sold directly, they could earn a minimum of US$2.3. However, the project only paid them about US$0.5. As a result, most women in Ta Phin left the project and started to sell handicrafts to tourists in the streets (Truong *et al.* 2014).

Financial support to poor people is essential

In PPT, sustained efforts are usually made to ensure that poor people are able to participate in tourism-related activities and that the benefits of tourism are distributed less unequally through communities (Ashley *et al.* 2000). The success of such efforts is not always apparent and is strongly dependent on the financial capability of poor people. Indeed, the lack of financial resources has been cited by a large number of authors as being among the most critical barriers preventing poor people's engagement in tourism (Hummel *et al.* 2013; Hummel & van der Dium 2012; Islam & Carlsen 2012; Shahia & Smith 2005; Truong *et al.* 2014). For example, Mao *et al.* (2013, 2014) indicate that many poor people in Siem Reap cannot start up their own tourism businesses because they do not have money, alongside business knowledge and skills. Those in other countries such as Bangladesh, India, and Vietnam are also having financial difficulty in establishing their homestays and other forms of tourism enterprises (Islam & Carlsen 2012; Roy, Roy & Saha 2010; Truong *et al.* 2014). It is thus essential that financial support be provided and this can be taken in various ways. Village/community funds can be established, with contributions by both state- and private-owned tourism enterprises such as in Laos (Harrison & Schipani 2007) or by entrance ticket fees in the case of Sapa in Vietnam (Truong *et al.* 2014). Although these funds can be used to upgrade community infrastructure (e.g. roads and trekking trails), they can also be lent to poor households in the form of microloans that would then be used to build homestays or other types of tourism business (Roy *et al.* 2010; Shahia & Smith 2005; Truong *et al.* 2014). The case of the Bangladeshi Grameen Bank may offer useful suggestions for PPT initiatives. A microfinance programme can be established, where groups, each of five poor households, are formed. The poorest two households would get the loans first. The other three could not receive their own loans until the first two have begun to repay the loans. This mechanism not only ensures that the borrowers would be able to pay back the loans (under peer pressure), but also offers the opportunity for members in and between groups to learn from one another (Yunus 2007).

PPT needs to be institutionalised

Much of the PPT literature has presumed that the connection between tourism and poverty alleviation is readily available, and has focused on identifying "pathways" or "channels" through which that link can be strengthened (e.g. Shahia & Smith 2005; Suriya & Gruen 2012). However, before this can be done, an appropriate policy framework needs to be put in place. Although PPT has become increasingly embedded into national and international policy, as discussed earlier, specific measures or regulations guiding the implementation of such policy are generally missing, particularly at the local level (Truong 2013). The need for a concrete local-level regulatory framework has been identified by many authors as an essential ingredient for ensuring the long-term success of any tourism initiatives aimed to benefit poor people (Mao *et al.* 2013, 2014; Phommavong 2011; Sharma 2002; Suntikul 2007; Tolkach *et al.* 2012; Truong 2013). Such a framework needs to place an explicit focus on poverty and ensure that poor people benefit from tourism (Hummel *et al.* 2013). It may cover issues such as tax deductions or exemptions for private businesses that provide skills training and job opportunities for poor people (Harrison & Schipani 2007), flexible regulations concerning international tourist guides who are ethnic minorities (Truong 2013), and empowerment of women (Phommavong 2011). Sharma (2002: 239) argues that this requires significant institutional reform:

> Empowerment of the poor does not happen in isolation. It is the creation of a political, legal, socio-cultural, and economic environment that facilitates, encourages, and enables the powerless (i.e., the poor) to influence policies, decisions, and actions on their behalf.

Case study 8.1 Nam Ha Ecotourism Project

The Nam Ha Ecotourism Project was launched in 1999 in Nam Ha National Protected Area (NPA) in Laos' northern province of Luang Namtha. It aimed to develop community-based ecotourism to mitigate pressures on the NPA's forest resources, and generate income and employment opportunities for local people. The project covered 57 villages that were home to 3,451 households with a population of 21,227 residents. It began with the NPA Management Unit's identification and assessment of threats to the ecological integrity of the NPA, which included local people's slash-and-burn agricultural practice, harvesting of non-timber forest products for sale and consumption, and hunting of wildlife for consumption.

Extensive ecotourism information and education campaigns were implemented, targeting policy-makers, the private sector, and local communities. These campaigns resulted in close collaboration between the NPA's various stakeholders in creating regulations to protect the cultural and natural resources that underpin the province's growing and profitable ecotourism sector. Local communities worked closely with the NPA management personnel to create cooperative agreements that defined stakeholder responsibilities in protecting the NPA's resources, provided guidance on the harvesting of non-timber forest products and other forest resources, prohibited the unlicensed hunting or sale of wildlife, and set aside tracts of village-managed forests as bird, wildlife and plant sanctuaries. The Nam Ha eco-guides also worked with the Nam Ha NPA management to introduce a "trekking and NPA user permit" fee system that was the first of its kind in Lao PDR.

The project contributed to the conservation and sustainable use of the NPA's resources in many ways. Through the development of alternative livelihood opportunities, the project reduced pressures on the natural resources of the NPA, with over 100 local people employed as guides, cooks, handicraft makers, and accommodation and transportation providers in the 17 villages where community-based ecotours were hosted. Ecotourism also generated funds for protected area management and conservation extension work, wherein more than US$8,000 was contributed by the guide service and over US$10,000 by tour operators in Luang Namtha in the form of NPA user fees. Community eco-guides and associated service providers received over US$600,000 from the Eco-Guide Service Unit treks alone.

Tourism helped diversify local traditional livelihoods, offering community members the opportunity to have more occupations, save money, purchase household items and pay school fees. More than 300 people were employed in the accommodation sector in Luang Namtha, while 172 people worked as full- and part-time tourist guides in the province. Hundreds of other community members derived part-time employment from community-based tourism activities as food and accommodation providers. Throughout the province, the tourism sector generated more than 1,000 additional jobs in restaurants, on tourism-related construction projects, in travel agencies, transportation, producing handicrafts, or supplying agricultural products to the tourism supply chain.

Source: UNDP (2012) *Nam Ha Ecotourism Project.*
Equator Initiative Case Study Series. New York: UNDP

Conclusion

South and Southeast Asia represents one of the world's most important tourism markets. In 2014, the region received 113.7 million international tourists, which accounted for 10% of the world's total international tourists (Table 8.1). This number is forecast to increase to 144 million and 223 million in 2020 and 2030, respectively (UNWTO 2014c). On the other hand, this "tourist paradise" is home to a substantial proportion of the population living on less than US$1.25 per day. The governments of most regional countries have attached importance to tourism development, with some considering tourism a tool of poverty alleviation (Harrison & Schipani 2007; Mao *et al.* 2013, 2014; Truong 2013). The many claimed benefits of tourism for poverty alleviation have to some extent driven its increased incorporation into national and regional policy.

Although few efforts have been made to quantify the beneficial impact of tourism on poverty alleviation (Thomas 2014; Wattanakuljarus & Coxhead 2008), there is little empirical evidence to demonstrate that poor people's lives are improved due to tourism. While some studies have indicated that there are significant increases in poor people's income due to tourism development, those that draw upon a participatory approach tend to suggest that tourism's contribution to poverty alleviation is limited, particularly when poor people's perceptions and experiences are taken into account. Contradictory evidence may even be found within a single tourist destination, such as Kerala, where the *Kerala Responsible Tourism* initiative was implemented. This finding suggests that tourism may not be an effective means of poverty alleviation in all countries and contexts. Therefore, the conditions that make tourism an effective means of poverty alleviation offer an interesting avenue for future research.

It is argued that PPT needs to be underpinned by a philosophy that emphasises participation, representation, and equity. Where relevant, participation and support of relevant stakeholders needs to be considered as early as possible and throughout the design, implementation, and evaluation of PPT initiatives. Financial support is essential to ensuring that poor people can participate meaningfully in tourism-related activities. Finally, it has been argued that PPT needs to be institutionalised and that concrete regulatory measures need to be underlined, particularly at the local level. In the broader area of PPT research, there has been a perceived need for the formulation of an appropriate method or tool that is capable of measuring the impact of tourism on poor people (Goodwin 2009; Truong 2015). It is interesting, however, that this issue has only been discussed by a couple of authors in South and Southeast Asia (Hummel *et al.* 2013; Tolkach *et al.* 2012). This represents a potential gap that future research needs to fill.

This chapter has attempted to provide a systematic review of PPT research with a focus on South and Southeast Asia. It is not aimed to capture the whole of Asia, which is in geographical terms too broad for a book chapter. Although every effort has been made to cover as many regional countries as possible, there is limited discussion of PPT in some countries such as Afghanistan and Pakistan due to the lack of literature, even though these are some of the countries that most need poverty reduction assistance. Nevertheless, the insights gained from this study may still offer useful implications for further PPT research and practice in the region and internationally.

Key reading

Goodwin, H. (2009) 'Reflections on 10 years of pro-poor tourism', *Journal of Policy Research in Tourism, Leisure and Events*, 1(1): 90–94.

Hall, C.M. (2007) 'Pro-poor tourism: Do "tourism exchanges benefit primarily the countries of the South"?' *Current Issues in Tourism*, 10(2–3): 111–118. This is the introduction to a special issue of the journal on pro-poor tourism.

Hummel, J., Gujadhur, T. and Ritsma, N. (2013) 'Evolution of tourism approaches for poverty reduction impact in SNV Asia: Cases from Lao PDR, Bhutan and Vietnam', *Asia Pacific Journal of Tourism Research*, 18(4): 369–384.

Phommavong, S. and Sorensson, E. (2014) 'Ethnic tourism in Lao PDR: Gendered divisions of labour in community-based tourism for poverty alleviation', *Current Issues in Tourism*, 17(4): 350–362.

Truong, V.D. (2015) 'Pro-poor tourism: Reflections on past research and directions for the future', in C.M. Hall, S. Gössling and D. Scott (eds), *The Routledge Handbook of Tourism and Sustainability* (pp. 127–139). Abingdon: Routledge.

Truong, V.D., Hall, C.M. and Garry, T. (2014) 'Tourism and poverty alleviation: Perceptions and experiences of poor people in Sapa, Vietnam', *Journal of Sustainable Tourism*, 22(7): 1071–1089.

References

Anand, A., Chandan, P. and Singh, R.B. (2012) 'Homestays at Korzok: Supplementing rural livelihoods and supporting green tourism in the Indian Himalayas', *Mountain Research and Development*, 32(2): 126–136.

Ashley, C. (2005) *Facilitating Pro-Poor Tourism with the Private Sector: Lessons Learnt from 'Pro-Poor Tourism Pilots in Southern Africa'*. London: Overseas Development Institute.

Ashley, C. and Wolmer, W. (2003) 'Transforming or tinkering? New forms of engagement between communities and the private sector in tourism and forestry in Southern Africa'. Online. Available: www.ids.ac.uk/env/slsa/index.html (accessed April 2013).

Ashley, C., Roe, D. and Goodwin, H. (2000) *Pro-Poor Tourism Strategies: Making Tourism Work for the Poor*. London: Pro-poor Tourism Partnership.

Asian Development Bank (ADB) (2008) *Tourism Sector in the Greater Mekong Subregion*. Manila: ADB.

Bennett, O., Roe, D. and Ashley, C. (1999) 'Sustainable tourism and poverty elimination study'. A report to the Department for International Development. Online. Available: www.propoortourism.info (accessed April 2013).

Boniface, B. & Cooper, C. (2009) *Worldwide Destinations: The Geography of Travel and Tourism* (5th edn). Oxford: Butterworth-Heinemann.

Brickell, K. (2008) 'Tourism-generated employment and intra-household inequality in Cambodia', in J. Cochrane (ed.), *Asian Tourism: Growth and Change* (pp. 299–310). Oxford: Elsevier.

Corbin, J. and Strauss, A.L. (1990) 'Grounded theory research: Procedures, canons and evaluative criteria', *Qualitative Sociology*, 13: 3–21.

Croes, R. (2014) 'Tourism and poverty reduction in Latin America: Where does the region stand?' *Worldwide Hospitality and Tourism Themes*, 6(3): 293–300.

de Kadt, E. (1979) 'Social planning for tourism in the developing countries', *Annals of Tourism Research*, 6(1): 36–48.

Department for International Development (DfID) (1999) *Tourism and Poverty Elimination: Untapped Potential*. London: DfID.

Donalson, J.A., Loh, J., Mudaliar, S., Kadir, M.Md., Biqi, W. and Keong, Y.L. (2013) 'Measuring poverty in Singapore: Frameworks for consideration', *Social Space*, 6: 58–66.

Goodwin, H. (1998) *Sustainable Tourism and Poverty Elimination*. Discussion paper for the Department for the Environment, Transport and the Regions and the Department for International Development. Online. Available: www.propoortourism.info (accessed May 2014).

—— (2008) 'Tourism, local economic development, and poverty reduction', *Applied Research in Economic Development*, 5(3): 55–64.

—— (2009) 'Reflections on 10 years of pro-poor tourism', *Journal of Policy Research in Tourism, Leisure and Events*, 1(1): 90–94.

—— (2014) 'Kerala tourism honoured for achievements in Responsible Tourism'. Online. Available: http://blog.wtmresponsibletourism.com/2014/01/27/kerala-tourism-unwto-award (accessed June 2015).

Hall, C.M. (2007) 'Pro-poor tourism: Do "tourism exchanges benefit primarily the countries of the South"?' *Current Issues in Tourism*, 10(2–3): 111–118.

Harrison, D. and Schipani, S. (2007) 'Lao tourism and poverty alleviation: Community-based tourism and the private sector', *Current Issues in Tourism,* 10(2–3): 194–230.

Holden, A. (2013) *Tourism, Poverty and Development*. London: Routledge.

Holden, A., Sonne, J. and Novelli, M. (2011) 'Tourism and poverty reduction: An interpretation by the poor of Elmina, Ghana'. *Tourism Planning & Development*, 8(3): 317–334.

Hummel, J. and van der Dium, R. (2012) 'Tourism at work: 15 years of tourism and poverty reduction within the SNV Netherlands Development Organisation', *Journal of Sustainable Tourism*, 20(3): 319–338.

Hummel, J., Gujadhur, T. and Ritsma, N. (2013) 'Evolution of tourism approaches for poverty reduction impact in SNV Asia: Cases from Lao PDR, Bhutan and Vietnam', *Asia Pacific Journal of Tourism Research*, 18(4): 369–384.

Islam, F. and Carlsen, J. (2012) 'Tourism in rural Bangladesh: Unlocking opportunities for poverty alleviation?' *Tourism Recreation Research*, 37(1): 37–45.

Mao, N., DeLacy, T. and Grunfeld, H. (2013) 'Local livelihoods and the tourism value chain: A case study in Siem Reap-Angkor region, Cambodia', *International Journal of Environment and Rural Development*, 4(2): 20–26.

Mao, N., Grunfeld, H., DeLacy, T. and Chandler, D. (2014) 'Agriculture and tourism linkage constraints in the Siem Reap-Angkor region of Cambodia', *Tourism Geographies*, 16(4): 669–686.

Michot, T. (2010) 'Pro-poor tourism in Kumarathorn, Kerala, South India: Policy implementation and impacts', *Journal of Alternative Perspectives in the Social Sciences*, 7: 1–24.

Mitchell, J. (2012) 'Value chain approaches to assessing the impact of tourism on low-income households in developing countries', *Journal of Sustainable Tourism*, 20(3): 457–475.

Mitchell, J. and Ashley, C. (2010) *Tourism and Poverty Reduction: Pathways to Prosperity*. London: ODI & Earthscan.

Nepal, S., Kohler, T. and Banzhaf, B. (2002) *Great Himalaya: Tourism and the Dynamics of Change in Nepal.* Berne: Swiss Foundation for Alpine Research.

Nyaupane, G.P. and Timothy, D.J. (2010) 'Power, regionalism and tourism policy in Bhutan', *Annals of Tourism Research*, 37: 969–988.

Oxford Poverty and Human Development Initiative (2015) *Sri Lanka Country Briefing*. Online. Available: www.ophi.org.uk/multidimensional-poverty-index/mpi-2014-2015/mpi-country-briefings (accessed May 2015).

Phommavong, S. (2011) 'International tourism development and poverty reduction in Lao PDR', Doctoral Dissertation, University of Umea, Sweden.

Phommavong, S. and Sorensson, E. (2014) 'Ethnic tourism in Lao PDR: Gendered divisions of labour in community-based tourism for poverty alleviation', *Current Issues in Tourism*, 17(4): 350–362.

Pleumarom, A. (2012) *The Politics of Tourism, Poverty Alleviation and Sustainable Development*. Penang: Third World Network.

Roe, D. and Khanya, U. (2002) *Pro-poor Tourism: Harnessing the World's Largest Industry for the World's Poor.* London: IIED.

Rossetto, A., Li, S. and Sofield, T. (2007) 'Harnessing tourism as a means of poverty alleviation: Using the right language or achieving outcomes?' *Tourism Recreation Research*, 32(1): 49–58.

Roy, P.B., Roy, T.B. and Saha, S. (2010) 'Pro-poor tourism as an approach towards community development: A case study', *South Asian Journal of Tourism and Heritage*, 3(2): 90–98.

Rutkowski, D. and Sparks, J. (2014) 'The new scalar politics of evaluation: An emerging governance role for evaluation', *Evaluation*, 20: 492–508.

Shahia, M. and Smith, F. (2005) 'Tourism, poverty and sustainable development: Observations from Nepal', *Journal of Public Administration*, 40: 512–521.

Sharma, P. (2002) 'Tourism as an instrument for area development and poverty alleviation with focus on Nepal', in N. Jodha, B. Bhadra, N. Khanal and J. Richter (eds), *Poverty Alleviation in Mountain Areas of China* (pp. 10–15). Kathmandu: ICIMOD.

Suntikul, W. (2007) 'The effects of tourism development on indigenous populations in Luang Namtha provinces, Laos', in R. Butler and T. Hinch (eds), *Tourism and Indigenous Peoples: Issues and Implications* (pp. 128–140). Oxford: Butterworth-Heinemann.

—— (2009) 'Pro-poor tourism in Viengxay, Laos: Current state and future prospects', *Asia Pacific Journal of Tourism Research*, 14(2): 153–168.

Suriya, K. and Gruen, C. (2012) 'Souvenir production in community-based tourism and poverty reduction in Thailand', *The Empirical Econometrics and Quantitative Economics Letters*, 1(1): 1–4.

Theerapappisit, P. (2009) 'Pro-poor ethnic tourism in the Mekong: A study of three approaches in northern Thailand', *Asia Pacific Journal of Tourism Research*, 14(2): 201–221.

Thomas, F. (2014) 'Addressing the measurement of tourism in terms of poverty reduction: Tourism value chain analysis in Lao PDR and Mali', *International Journal of Tourism Research*, 16(4): 368–376.

Tolkach, D., Pearlman, M. and King, B. (2012) 'Key implementation factors in pro-poor tourism', *Tourism Recreation Research*, 37(1): 3–13.

Truong, V.D. (2013) 'Tourism policy development in Vietnam: A pro-poor perspective', *Journal of Policy Research in Tourism, Leisure and Events*, 5(1): 28–45.

—— (2015) 'Pro-poor tourism: Reflections on past research and directions for the future', in C.M. Hall, S. Gössling and D. Scott (eds), *The Routledge Handbook of Tourism and Sustainability* (pp. 127–139). Abingdon: Routledge.

Truong, V.D. and Hall, C.M. (2013) 'Social marketing and tourism: What is the evidence?' *Social Marketing Quarterly*, 19(2): 110–135.

—— (2015) 'Exploring the poverty reduction potential of social marketing in tourism development', *ASEAS: Austrian Journal of South-East Asian Studies*, 8(2): 125–142

Truong, V.D., Hall, C.M. and Garry, T. (2014) 'Tourism and poverty alleviation: Perceptions and experiences of poor people in Sapa, Vietnam', *Journal of Sustainable Tourism*, 22(7): 1071–1089.

United Nations Development Programme (UNDP) (2014) *Human Development Report 2014: Sustaining Human Progress – Reducing Vulnerabilities and Building Resilience*. New York: UNDP.

United Nations World Tourism Organization (UNWTO) (2007) *Increase Tourism to Fight Poverty: New Year Message from UNWTO*. Madrid: UNWTO.

—— (2009a) *UNWTO World Tourism Barometer 9(3)*. Online. Available: www.unwto.org (accessed May 2015).

—— (2009b) *UNWTO World Tourism Barometer (Interim Update)*. Online. Available: www.unwto.org (accessed May 2015).

—— (2009c) *UNWTO World Tourism Barometer 7(1)*. Online. Available: www.unwto.org (accessed May 2015).

—— (2009d) *UNWTO World Tourism Barometer 7(2)*. Online. Available: www.unwto.org (accessed May 2015).

—— (2010) *UNWTO World Tourism Barometer 8(3)*. Online. Available: www.unwto.org (accessed May 2015).

—— (2012) *UNWTO World Tourism Barometer 10*. Online. Available: www.unwto.org (accessed May 2015).

—— (2013) *UNWTO World Tourism Barometer 11*. Online. Available: www.unwto.org (accessed May 2015).

—— (2014a) *UNWTO World Tourism Barometer 12 (April)*. Online. Available: www.unwto.org (accessed May 2015).

—— (2014b) *UNWTO World Tourism Barometer 12 (August)*. Online. Available: www.unwto.org (accessed May 2015).

—— (2014c) *UNWTO Tourism Highlights*. Online. Available: www.unwto.org (accessed May 2015).

—— (2015) *UNWTO World Tourism Barometer 13*. Online. Available: www.unwto.org (accessed May 2015).

Wattanakuljarus, A. and Coxhead, I. (2008) 'Is tourism-based development good for the poor? A general equilibrium analysis for Thailand', *Journal of Policy Modelling*, 30: 929–955.

World Bank (2013) 'World population'. Online. Available: http://data.worldbank.org/indicator/SP. POP.TOTL (accessed May 2015).

World Population Statistics (2013) 'Asia population 2013'. Online. Available: www.worldpopulation statistics.com/asia-population-2013 (accessed May 2015).

Yamashita, S. (2009) 'Southeast Asian tourism from a Japanese perspective', in M. Hitchcock, V. King and M. Parnwell (eds), *Tourism in Southeast Asia: Challenges and New Directions* (pp. 189–205). Copenhagen: NIAS Press.

Yotsumoto, Y. (2013) 'Formalization of urban poor vendors and their contributions to tourism development in Manila, Philippines', *International Journal of Japanese Sociology*, 22(1): 128–142.

Yunus, M. (2007) *Creating a World Without Poverty: Social Business and the Future of Capitalism*. New York: Public Affairs.

PART 2

Tourism in South-East Asia

9

TOURISM IN SOUTHEAST ASIA

C. Michael Hall & Stephen J. Page

Introduction: becoming southeast Asia

The notion of south-east Asia is a rather recent geographical construction (Acharya 2013).

> Before world war II South East Asia was scarcely even a geographical expression. For the west, it was little more than an undifferentiated part of Monsoon Asia, the teeming eastern and southern margins of the great Asian continent; for Asians themselves it had no significance at all.
>
> *(Fryer 1970: 1)*

However, as Dwyer (1990: 1) noted 'although the concept of South East Asia as a geographical region is relatively recent, in terms of international relationships its significance in the world today is profound'.

One of the most influential studies of the post-war period, at least in Western terms, was Fisher's (1962) assessment of South East Asia as the Balkans of the Orient, in which he depicted the region as an area of transition, geographic variation and potential instability. In the post-World War II period, Fisher (1962) identified the implications of post-colonial transition from subjugation under colonial rule to nation status, where many states contained an enormous diversity of population with varied cultures and religions. Fisher highlighted the role of economic development in determining the political future of most states. In his highly influential 831-page seminal study on Southeast Asia, Fisher (1964) depicts the spatial delimitation of Southeast Asia in that

> it is only since the second world war that the term South-east Asia has been generally accepted as a collective name for the series of peninsulars and islands which lie to the east of India and Pakistan and to the south of China. Nor is it altogether surprising that the West should have been slow to recognise the need for some common term for this area, which today comprises Burma [Mynamar], Thailand, Cambodia, Laos, Vietnam, the Federation of Malaysia, Singapore, Brunei, Indonesia and the Philippines.
>
> *(Fisher 1964: 3)*

In fact, one of the unifying features that, in part, explains the common development histories of many of the countries within the region is their different links to European imperial ambition and mercantilism (with the exception of Thailand), which played an important role in fixing the region in the Western imagination. For the purpose of this book, Fisher's (1964: 5) poignant comments of 1964 still hold true in that 'from a geographical point of view South East Asia must be accounted a distinctive region within the larger unity of the Monsoon lands ... and worthy to be ranked as an intelligible field of study on its own'.

Kirk (1990) explored the colonial past of Southeast Asia, building on the excellent historical analysis of the region's development by Fisher (1964), to indicate that a series of core areas developed prior to and during the period of European colonisation and mercantilism (1500–1950) (see also Tarling 2003). These core areas were largely established prior to European rule and accentuated the existing patterns of core and periphery so that a series of patterns emerged, as illustrated in Figure 9.1. Kirk (1990) examined the core areas in Thailand, British Burma, India, the Malayan west coast core, Dutch Indonesia and French Indochina. These processes of colonialism did little to reduce regional inequalities. In fact Dixon and Smith (1997: 4) argue that

> The incorporation of Southeast Asia into the emergent global capitalist system took place under the auspices of colonial economic and, except for Thailand, political control. By the end of the colonial period for much of South East Asia an extremely uneven pattern of development had emerged. The post-colonial states were characterised by high levels of ethnic diversity, limited national integration, little contact with their neighbours, unbalanced urban hierarchies and unevenly developed economies, both spatially and by sector. These situations have had a profound impact on both the subsequent development of the region's economies and on economic policies that have followed.

Thus, the decolonisation era saw many of the former colonies become nation-states with very little adjustment of political boundaries. Likewise, many of the new states inherited the development problems of the former colonies, not the least of which were some of the divisive social structures fostered by colonial rule. Nevertheless, the colonial period shaped much of the development trajectory for the region as a result of transport route, diasporas, the primacy of a number of colonial cities and the initial construction of regional identity (Tarling 2003; Acharya 2013). In economic terms, Kirk (1990: 44–45) argued that following the colonial era, 'over-dependence on a few commodities to earn foreign exchange ... [with] ... foreign capital still prominent in new forms of dependency'. This virtually encouraged a greater core–periphery pattern of neo-colonial development. In fact 'the core infrastructures built during the colonial era, have provided the main attraction to new industrial and commercial developments, and central governments, whatever their political policies and ideals' (Kirk 1990: 45–46). This point is developed by Dixon and Smith (1997: 5) who argue that

> the emergence and/or intensification of core areas during the colonial era was closely associated with the development of a series of major port cities – Bangkok, Jakarta, Manila, Rangoon, Saigon-Cholon and Singapore. These centres became the major focus for their respective national economies and the principal interface with the international economy. The emergence of these major cities has resulted in the South East Asian region exhibiting high levels of urban primacy and remarkably unbalanced urban hierarchies.

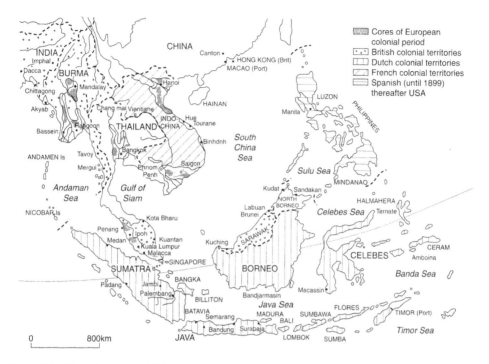

Figure 9.1 Map of southeast Asia's colonial past.

Nevertheless, while certain aspects of the trajectory of economic development for Southeast Asia were framed during the colonial period, others have been reset more recently as the region started to develop its own identity. In great part the contemporary construction of Southeast Asia following the end of the Vietnam War and the end of the Cold War – in which the region was marked by the construction of an intra-regional "otherness" – has come to be replaced by a rethinking of Southeast Asia as a region.

Intraregional linkages in the region have been transformed. These include transport and economic linkages, that also include tourism – which has shown significant growth in international tourism arrivals since 1990 (Table 9.1). Much of the growth in arrivals is intra-regional; Table 9.2, for example, indicates that within the Association of Southeast Asian Nations (ASEAN), which includes every country in the region except Timor-Leste (Box 9.1), which has applied for membership (see Chapter 1), intra-ASEAN travel by ASEAN nationals accounts for approximately 47% of all international tourist arrivals. ASEAN itself is also central to intraregional linkage. As Acharya (2013: 3–4) comments:

> For the first time in its history, there is a regional organization that claims to represent the "entire" region of Southeast Asia. The political division of Southeast Asia – based on the relative intensity of nationalism and competing ideological orientations of regimes that characterized intraregional relations after the end of World War II – has come to an end. Notwithstanding differences among Southeast Asian states in terms of their openness to the global economy, their domestic social and political organization, and their relationship with outside powers, Southeast Asia today arguably displays far more homogeneity and convergence than at any other time in the modern era.

Table 9.1 International tourism in South-East Asia

Country		1995	2000	2005	2010	2011	2012	2013
Brunei Darussalam	Number of arrivals			126,000	214,000	242,000	209,000	225,000
	Receipts (% of total exports)			2.79			0.69	
	Number of departures							
	Expenditures (% of total imports)			14.83			8.75	
Cambodia	Number of arrivals	220,000	466,000	1,422,2000	2,508,000	2,882,000	3,584,000	4,210,000
	Receipts (% of total exports)			23.07	28.00	29.08	30.18	28.90
	Number of departures	31,000	41,000	568,000	505,000	710,000	792,000	872,000
	Expenditures (% of total imports)			3.00	4.16	4.17	4.22	4.17
Indonesia	Number of arrivals	4,324,000	5,064,000	5,002,000	7,003,000	7,650,000	8,044,000	8,802,000
	Receipts (% of total exports)			5.38	4.57	4.24	4.48	5.02
	Number of departures		2,205,000	4,106,000	6,235,000	6,750,000	7,454,000	7,973,000
	Expenditures (% of total imports)			5.49	5.80	4.58	4.25	4.87
Lao PDR	Number of arrivals	60,000	191,000	672,000	1,670,000	1,786,000	2,140,000	2,510,000
	Receipts (% of total exports)			18.88	17.06	17.18	16.19	20.13
	Number of departures							
	Expenditures (% of total imports)			1.09	9.25	9.01	7.10	11.28
Malaysia	Number of arrivals	7,469,000	10,222,000	16,431,000	24,577,000	24,714,000	25,033,000	25,715,000
	Receipts (% of total exports)			6.44	7.85	7.42	7.63	8.12
	Number of departures	20,642,000	30,532,000					
	Expenditures (% of total imports)			3.32	4.39	4.69	5.03	5.17
Myanmar	Number of arrivals	194,000	416,000	660,000	792,000	816,000	1,059,000	2,044,000
	Receipts (% of total exports)			2.19	1.18	3.95	5.82	8.27

Country	Indicator							
	Number of departures							
	Expenditures (% of total imports)			1.69	1.14	1.54	2.92	1.20
Philippines	Number of arrivals	1,760,000	1,992,000	2,623,000	3,520,000	3,917,000	4,273,000	4,681,000
	Receipts (% of total exports)			8.48	6.31	7.09	7.43	8.25
	Number of departures	1,615,000	1,670,000	2,144,000				
	Expenditures (% of total imports)			7.51	9.08	8.53	8.97	10.70
Singapore	Number of arrivals	6,070,000	6,062,000	7,079,000	9,161,000	10,390,000	11,098,000	11,899,000
	Receipts (% of total exports)			2.16	3.01	3.26	3.34	3.29
	Number of departures	2,867,000	4,444,000	5,159,000	7,342,000	7,753,000	8,048,000	8,647,000
	Expenditures (% of total imports)			4.03	4.58	4.46	4.72	4.83
Thailand	Number of arrivals	6,952,000	9,579,000	11,567,000	15,936,000	19,230,000	22,354,000	26,547,000
	Receipts (% of total exports)			9.36	10.54	11.86	13.71	16.21
	Number of departures	1,820,000	1,909,000	3,047,000	5,451,000	5,397,000	5,721,000	5,970,000
	Expenditures (% of total imports)			3.70	3.46	2.88	2.89	3.06
Timor-Leste	Number of arrivals				40,000	51,000	58,000	79,000
	Receipts (% of total exports)				25.29	17.78	20.45	33.01
	Number of departures	—						
	Expenditures (% of total imports)				5.06	3.32	5.54	4.73
Vietnam	Number of arrivals	1,351,000	2,140,000	3,477,000	5,050,000	6,014,000	6,848,000	7,572,000
	Receipts (% of total exports)			6.28	5.58	5.40	5.52	5.28
	Number of departures							
	Expenditures (% of total imports)			2.29	1.68	1.57	1.58	1.52

Source: UNWTO 2015; World Bank 2016a, 2016b, 2016c, 2016d.

Table 9.2 Tourist arrivals in ASEAN 2010–14 ('000)

Country	2010			2011			2012			2013			2014		
	Intra-ASEAN	Extra-ASEAN	Total	Intra-ASEAN	Extra-ASEAN	Total	Intra-ASEAN	Extra-ASEAN	Total	Intra-ASEAN	Extra-ASEAN	Total	Intra-ASEAN	Extra-ASEAN	Total
Brunei Darussalam[a]	109.9	104.4	214.3	124.2	117.9	242.1	115.9	93.2	209.1	3,053.5	225.6	3,279.2	3,662.2	223.4	3,885.5
Cambodia	853.2	1,655.1	2,508.3	1,101.1	1,780.8	2,881.9	1,514.3	2,070.0	3584.3	1,831.5	2,378.7	4,210.2	1,991.9	2,510.9	4,502.8
Indonesia	2,338.5	4,664.4	7,002.9	3,258.5	4,391.2	7,649.7	2,607.7	5,436.8	8,044.5	3,516.1	5,286.1	8,802.1	3,683.8	5,751.6	9,435.4
Lao PDR	1,990.9	522.1	2,513.0	2,191.2	532.3	2,723.6	2,712.5	617.6	3,330.1	3,041.2	738.3	3,779.5	3,224.1	934.6	4,158.7
Malaysia	18,937.2	5,640.0	24,577.2	18,885.3	5,829.0	24,714.3	18,809.7	6,223.0	25,032.7	19,105.9	6,609.6	25,715.5	20,372.8	7,064.5	27,437.3
Myanmar	512.3	279.2	791.5	100.4	716.0	816.4	151.1	907.9	1,059.0	218.7	1,825.6	2,044.3	1,598.3	1,483.2	3,081.4
The Philippines	298.2	3,222.3	3,520.5	331.7	3,585.8	3,917.5	375.2	3,897.6	4,272.8	422.1	4,259.2	4,681.3	461.5	4,371.9	4,833.4
Singapore	4,779.6	6,859.0	11,638.7	5,372.2	7,799.1	13,171.3	5,732.7	8,758.5	14,491.2	6,114.7	9,453.2	15,567.9	6,113.0	8,982.1	15,095.2
Thailand	4,534.2	11,402.2	15,936.4	5,529.9	13,568.4	19,098.3	6,462.6	15,891.3	22,353.9	7,410.4	19,136.3	26,546.7	6,620.2	18,159.5	24,779.8
Vietnam	688.7	4,361.1	5,049.9	838.4	5,175.6	6,014.0	1,363.8	5,483.9	6,847.7	1,440.3	6,132.1	7,572.4	1,495.1	6,379.2	7,874.3
ASEAN	35,042.8	38,709.8	73,752.6	37,732.9	43,496.1	81,229.0	39,845.5	49,379.8	89,225.2	46,154.4	56,044.6	102,199.0	49,223.0	55,860.8	105,083.8

Source: ASEAN Statistics (2015). A tourism statistics database compiled from AMS data submissions publications/reports and/or websites of national tourism organisations/agencies and/or national statistical offices.

Notes

Details may not add up to totals due to rounding errors.

a Prior to 2013 Brunei Darussalam data only cover visitor arrivals by air transport.

These shifts are important because the political, economic and military actions of China and the United States in the region, and especially in the China Sea, notwithstanding, to a great extent the political affairs of Southeast Asia are being shaped by the interaction of local actors. This is, of course, not to argue that differences do not exist. Acharya (2013), for example, highlights the differences between mainland and maritime or archipelagic areas of the region for understanding the different sources of diversity. Political systems in maritime South-East Asia have been much more fragmented and volatile than on the mainland, with the divide illustrating substantial differences in state formation (Lieberman 1997, 2003, 2009), with the Indo-Malay world experiencing much less political integration – a legacy which lasts to the present given various independence movements and demands for greater autonomy in a number of regions. Another aspect of diversity in Southeast Asia includes religion and ethnic and language diversity. These aspects of cultural diversity have also proven significant for tourism with, for example, Malaysia positioning itself as a halal tourism hub, and ethnic identity becoming a significant dimension of tourism promotion.

Box 9.1 Tourism in Timor-Leste

C.M. Hall

Timor-Leste is the newest nation in Southeast Asia. Formerly the Portuguese colony of East Timor, the country was invaded by Indonesia on 7 December 1975 after independence from Portugal was declared on 28 November 1975. Following a long struggle against the Indonesian occupying forces and the United Nations-sponsored act of self-determination in 1999, Indonesia relinquished control of the territory. The country became independent again in May 2002. West Timor is now part of the province of Nusa Tenggara Timur, Indonesia, and was formally Dutch Timor until Indonesian independence.

After the Indonesian withdrawal, according to the World Bank (2015) 'nearly 70 percent of all buildings, homes and schools [were] destroyed, and an estimated 75 percent of the population displaced'. The country has a population of approximately 1.21 million people of which 60% are under 25 years of age. The post-conflict situation together with one of the fastest growing populations in Asia means that Timor-Leste is attempting to tackle major issues of unemployment, poverty, education and food security, especially in rural areas where the majority of the population live. In 2014 GDP was $1.417 billion and was growing at an annual rate of 7%; however, the volatility in the global oil and gas markets poses a significant threat to the economy.

The country has one of the most oil-dependent economies in the world and one of the least diversified (UNDP 2011). Other significant sectors include coffee, cocoa and cinnamon production. As a result of its oil dependence, tourism has been identified under the Timor-Leste Strategic Development Plan 2011–2030 as one of the most important sectors for developing the non-energy sector economy (Quintas 2015). A number of studies have identified the significant potential for coastal and marine ecotourism development in the country (Dutra *et al.* 2011), with a substantial focus on community-based approaches (Tolkach & King 2015; Vong *et al.* 2015). The country has passed a number of laws with respect to environmental and biodiversity conservation; however, major challenges are faced in their implementation. The capital, Dili, is the gateway to the country and has direct flights from Darwin (Australia), Denpasar (Bali) and Singapore. The country attracted 79,000 international arrivals in 2013 and 60,000 in 2014. In 2014 international tourism receipts amounted to US$35 million (UNWTO 2015).

- Government website: www.easttimorgovernment.com/tourism.htm
- Lonely Planet: www.lonelyplanet.com/east-timor

ASEAN and political regionalism

Political regionalism has also become extremely significant in the formation of a southeast Asian identity. Foremost here is the creation of ASEAN and its expansion from a defence alliance to a political and economic relationship between member countries. Founded in 1967 as a non-communist bloc of East Asian countries, ASEAN plays a major role in the region's economic, social and political development. In the 50 years of its existence, ASEAN has gone through three distinct stages (Wah 1995). The first decade was characterised by intra-regional political confidence building with only rudimentary economic cooperation. The second decade was marked by the consolidation of a distinct political community, particularly in the face of external problems posed by the status of Cambodia, and gradual movement on economic cooperation. From the late 1980s on, ASEAN demonstrated substantial commitment to economic cooperation and the development of a free trade area which arguably culminated with the ASEAN Economic Community (AEC) that came into effect at the end of 2015.

On 22 November 2015 the ten members of ASEAN signed a declaration on the formal establishment of the ASEAN Community, a broad framework of regional integration made up of three pillars: the AEC, which is the focus for economic integration; the Political-Security Community, which aims to link up the region's foreign affairs and security interests; and the Socio-Cultural Community, which seeks to build people-to-people connections. The AEC aims to reduce barriers to trade, services, investment and the mobility of skilled labour across ASEAN, with the goal of making the region more economically competitive. Seven nations – Brunei, Indonesia, Malaysia, the Philippines, Singapore, Thailand and Vietnam – are full members of the AEC, whilst the three remaining nations of Cambodia, Laos and Myanmar have a two-year extension to work on meeting certain requirements, primarily a greater reduction of existing trade restrictions. As a single economy the AEC would be the seventh largest in the world. However, the establishment of the AEC does not mean that the region will begin to act as a completely integrated economic bloc along the lines of the European Union. There are four key strands of the AEC: creating a single-market production base; forming a competitive economic region; facilitating equitable economic growth; and, eventually, deeper integration with the rest of the global economy.

The AEC is implemented through the signing of various agreements and legally binding contracts between the ASEAN member states. However, as *The Economist* (2015a) emphasises, the existence of the AEC's legal agreements alone is unlikely to ease local implicit barriers to business and free trade in individual countries as implementation of these agreements is relatively uneven among ASEAN member states, given that no ASEAN supranational body exists to enforce implementation. The next stage will be the ASEAN Community Vision 2025. Yet as *The Economist* (2015a) highlights:

> Regardless of how ambitious ASEAN's agenda is in the period to 2025, the next decade is likely to be the same as the previous ten years in that ASEAN integration will remain slow. For a start, the still-wide disparity in terms of the levels of economic development between the member states means that priorities will continue to clash.

In addition to the economic disparities between members, other factors limiting ASEAN economic integration include ASEAN's consensus approach to decision making, which make it difficult to find agreed responses to transnational problems such as China's geo-strategic threat in the South China Sea, refugee flows and transboundary haze from forest burning and clearance (see also Hall, Chapter 6, this volume).

ASEAN has long identified tourism as a service sector with the "highest priority" for liberalisation within the ASEAN region (Hall 1997). However, negotiations on the ASEAN Trade in Services Agreement are still underway as of early 2016, although the ASEAN open skies policy has started to be implemented (see Duval & Weaver, Chapter 3, this volume). The policy links three previous multilateral agreements among ASEAN members (general protocols on air services, passenger services and air freight) with lifting the limitations on how many carriers may shuttle between ASEAN capitals and international airports and enabling so-called fifth freedom rights, by which carriers may combine three destinations as part of a single route (Tan 2009, 2010). Nevertheless, infrastructure constraints and reluctance among members to harmonise rules governing safety and operations mean that the policy falls far short of establishing a single aviation market. There remains substantial protectionism and a reluctance to give up regulatory authority among various members. For example, Indonesia will not open domestic routes to foreign carriers or permit majority foreign ownership of domestic carriers, while the Philippines limits foreign ownership of its airlines to 40% (*The Economist* 2015b). The continued restrictions in the ASEAN market are all the more remarkable given tourist growth in the region as well as financial difficulties of some carriers. As *The Economist* (2015b) commented, only five of the 22 low-cost carriers that operate in the region were profitable in the year to December 2014:

> Nevertheless, low-cost carriers are planning to triple their fleet of aircraft with orders of just fewer than 1,200 jetliners at end-2014. US-based Boeing itself says that it expects passengers in the region to grow by an average of 6.5% a year over the next two decades.

The development of greater economic cooperation within the region clearly has substantial implications for tourism, which is of significant economic importance for the ASEAN members (Tables 9.3 and 9.4). Apart from aviation and cross-border transport agreements, the most obvious area of tourism-related economic cooperation is joint marketing campaigns such as Visit ASEAN Years. Joint cross-border economic development strategies have also been undertaken, which also have substantial implications for tourism – for example, the "growth triangle" between the Malaysian State of Johor, Singapore, and the Indonesian Province of Riau (Henderson 2001). Nevertheless, tourism in the ASEAN countries has grown rapidly and has become a vital source of foreign exchange and an essential element in government economic strategies for all except oil-rich Brunei, which itself is now starting to pay more attention to tourism, given volatility in oil prices (see Box 9.2).

Table 9.3 ASEAN international tourism overview

Country	Slogan	Tourism arrivals (2014)	Revenue generated (US$ billion) (2014)	Travel and tourism's direct contribution to GDP (US$ billion) (2014)	Travel and tourism's direct contribution to employment ('000 jobs) (2014)	Top source markets by volume (2014)		
Malaysia	Truly Asia	27,437,315	16.69	18.6	724.3	Singapore	Indonesia	China
Thailand	Amazing Thailand	24,779,668	38.4	31.9	2,210.2	China	Malaysia	Russia
Singapore	YourSingapore	15,095,152	17.44	14.8	152.7	Indonesia	China	Malaysia
Indonesia	Wonderful Indonesia	9,435,411	10.69	27.5	3,325.8	Singapore	Malaysia	Australia
Vietnam	Vietnam. Timeless charm	7,874,312	–	8.6	1,963.5	China	South Korea	Japan
Philippines	It's more fun in the Philippines	4,833,368	4.84	12.0	1,259.8	South Korea	USA	Japan
Cambodia	Kingdom of Wonder	4,502,800	3*	2.3	985.4	Vietnam	China	South Korea
Laos	Simply Beautiful	4,158,719	0.641	0.6	129.7	Thailand	Vietnam	China
Brunei	A kingdom of unexpected treasures	3,885,500	–	0.3	5.0	Malaysia	China	
Myanmar	Let the journey begin	3,081,400	1.14	1.4	505.2	Thailand	China	Japan

Source: ASEAN Statistics 2015; WTTC 2015a, 2015b.
Note
* Estimate only.

Table 9.4 Economic contribution of tourism to ASEAN member states

Country	International tourism receipts as percentage of total exports (2013)	Travel and tourism's direct contribution to GDP (US$ bn) (2014)	Travel and tourism's direct contribution to GDP (% share) (2014)	Travel and tourism's direct contribution to employment ('000 jobs) (2014)	Travel and tourism's direct contribution to employment (% share) (2014)
Brunei	3.5	0.3	1.5	5.0	2.4
Cambodia	24.5	2.3	13.5	985.4	11.7
Indonesia	4.9	27.5	3.2	3 325.8	2.9
Laos	20.3	0.6	5.0	129.7	4.2
Malaysia	8.4	18.6	5.7	724.3	5.3
Myanmar	5.0	1.4	2.2	505.2	1.8
Philippines	6.9	12.0	4.2	1 259.8	3.3
Singapore	3.5	14.8	4.9	152.7	4.3
Thailand	16.0	31.9	8.6	2 210.2	5.8
Vietnam	4.7	8.6	4.6	1 963.5	4.7

Source: WTTC 2015a, 2015b.

Box 9.2 Tourism in Brunei

C.M. Hall

With an area of 5,765km² and a population of 400,000, Brunei is one of the smallest countries in Southeast Asia. Yet Brunei is also one of the richest countries in the world on a per capita basis because of its oil and gas wealth. Because of its dependence on energy resources, Brunei is one of the few countries in Asia which historically has not actively pursued tourism development. The majority of travel to Brunei is business-oriented, although oil price volatility has led to increased interest in trying to encourage tourism to the sultanate. At the 2016 ASEAN Tourism Forum the Brunei Ministry of Primary Resources and Tourism (MPRT) stated that it was committed to developing the country's tourism industry, now that the government has given more weight to the sector, as a measure to diversify the economy from oil and gas, and particularly in light of the fall in oil prices (Zaili 2016). In addition to encouraging further cross-border travel with Malaysia, this is likely to be in specialist areas such as Islamic tourism and medical tourism, the latter also potentially attractive to the region's Islamic community. For example, the Jerudong Park Medical Centre and the Brunei Neuroscience, Stroke and Rehabilitation Centre in particular have been identified as having the potential to attract medical tourists seeking treatment (Thein, 2014).

Visitor arrivals were 377,000 in 1990 and 557,000 in 1994 (Hall 1997), yet figures barely passed the 250,000 mark annually during most of the years between 2003 and 2012, with a peak of 944,000 tourist arrivals in 2003 (Kasim 2014). In 2012 total arrivals (including air arrivals and other arrivals) fell by 11.7% year on year, to 241,000, and in 2007–2012 total growth in arrivals averaged only 3.1% per year, raising substantial questions about Brunei's ability to meet its goal of 400,000 visitor arrivals by 2016. However, one bright spot in tourist growth was the increase in cruise arrivals, with an expectation of approximately 90,000 arrivals in 2014 (*The Economist* 2013). The WTTC (2015a) estimated that the direct contribution of travel and tourism to GDP in 2014 was

BND317.0m (1.5% of GDP). This is forecast to rise by 2.5% to BND324.8m in 2015. The total contribution of travel and tourism to Brunei's GDP (including wider effects from investment, the supply chain and induced income impacts) was BND1,402.5m in 2014 (6.8% of GDP) and is expected to grow by 1.2% to BND1,419.0m (6.8% of GDP) in 2015. The WTTC (2015a) forecast the direct contribution to GDP to rise by 4.1% pa to BND2,117.5m by 2025 (7.5% of GDP), supporting 20,000 jobs (7.7% of total employment). Malaysia is by far the major source of visitors in great part as a result of cross-border tourism. This market is likely to become even more important as a result of the Brunei government extending the times for which the border is open as well as the development of improved road access. However, it should also be noted that many of the Malaysian cross-border visitors were not counted in official tourism arrival statistics until recently. Singapore, one of Brunei's major trading partners, is the second most important market, with the United Kingdom the only regular non-Asian market that is usually listed in the top six visitor-generating countries.

Box 9.3 Tourism in the Philippines

C.M. Hall

From being regarded as one of the wealthiest Asian countries during the 1950s, the Philippines has been subject to a succession of economic, social, environmental and political crises since the 1970s (Henderson 2011). Natural disasters, rampant political corruption and poor economic growth for much of this time meant that the country has slumped substantially in economic and social indices. In the 1970s, during the Marcos regime, international tourism was seen as both a contributor to the country's ills, through sex tourism, corruption and the provision of tacit support for authoritarian rule, and as a solution, because of tourism's ability to generate foreign exchange and employment (Hall 1997). When President Corazon Aquino came to power in 1986 she

> inherited a bankrupt nation with a negative growth rate, a $26 billion foreign debt, 70 percent of the population at or below the poverty line, and a country that lost between 10 and 20 billion dollars to the systematic plundering of the Marcos government.
>
> *(Richter 1989: 51)*

Nevertheless, tourism is a major component in the country's overall economic strategy (Maguigad 2013; Dela Santa 2015; Dela Santa & Saporsantos 2016), although has never reached its potential promise (Henderson 2011).

Although issues of accessibility and infrastructure have influenced tourism development, most notable of which was the US FAA downgrade of the Philippine civil aviation system in 2008 and the EU ban of Philippine carriers in 2010 (Manuela & de Vera 2015), political issues are paramount, even affecting how the country is marketed. For example, when a new secretary of tourism is installed, the ongoing marketing programme is invariably replaced with a new one, notwithstanding the huge costs involved. Thus, it was the "Best of the Islands" campaign under the Ramos administration in 1992–1998, "Rediscovery Philippines" under the Estrada administration from 1998 to 2001, "Wow Philippines" under the Arroyo Administration from 2001 to 2010 (Dela Santa 2015), and the current "It's more fun in the Philippines", with Manila being promoted as "the capital of fun" and Boracay as "Asia's 24/7 Island". In 2007 tourism contributed around 6.2%

to the national GDP, and the direct employment in tourism totalled 3.25m, representing a 9.7% share of the country's total employment (Department of Tourism (DOT) 2009). For 2014 the WTTC estimated that tourism's direct contribution to GDP was 4.2%, with a direct employment in tourism totalling 1.26m, equivalent to 3.3% of total employment (see Table 9.3).

Tourism in the Philippines is tied up in its short- and long-term political stability (Henderson 2011). The country desperately needs stability in order to attract foreign investment with which to establish the required tourism infrastructure and also to improve the image of the country in the international marketplace, particularly given the ongoing conflicts with the independence movement in the primarily Muslim south of the country. The Philippines has also experienced a sequence of natural disasters in recent decades in the form of typhoons, earthquakes and volcanic eruptions, all of which have further affected the country's infrastructure and image. Nevertheless, the climate, culture and natural landscape make it attractive to overseas leisure tourists, particularly coastal and marine tourism, although tourism development has also competed with other resource users as well as environmental constraints (Teh & Cabanban 2007; Lucas & Kirit 2009; Fabinyi 2010; Smith *et al.* 2011; Porter *et al.* 2015).

Environmental conservation represents a major long-term challenge for the Philippines as it is vital not only for tourism, but also as a means of climate change adaptation and mitigation. The Philippines is one of the "hottest" of the 34 terrestrial hotspots in the world in terms of high vulnerability and irreplaceability of threatened species, and is also on the top of the list of the 18 global marine hotspots (Catibog-Sinha & Heaney 2006). However, the major tourism attractions in the Philippines are concentrated in natural heritage areas and key biodiversity sites (Catibog-Sinha 2010). A *National Integrated Protected Areas System (NIPAS) Act* was passed in 1992 and requires the tourism industry to comply with the Philippine Environmental Impact Assessment (EIA) system regarding any proposed developmental activity within NIPAS sites (Catibog-Sinha 2010). The Philippines has been a pioneer of community-based marine protection areas (MPAs), with a major focus on coral reefs given their significance to both fishing and tourism. However, because of the different motives (i.e. conservation vs economics) and perspectives about the nature and extent of benefit-sharing from tourism revenue and the associated social equity implications (i.e. "poor" fishers vs "rich" tourists), not all MPAs have been successful in delivering their intended objectives and in facilitating the promotion of sustainable tourism and marine conservation (Catibog-Sinha 2010). Similar issues have plagued the national ecotourism strategy which was launched by the government in 1999. More than three-fifths of the 32 "banner sites" (key ecotourism areas) identified in the national ecotourism programme are in protected areas. Catibog-Sinha (2010) notes that in implementing the strategy there is a major challenge in ensuring that tourism developments are appropriately located while the provision of alternative livelihoods to host communities so as to reduce their natural resource use has been limited despite the overall economic impact (Gallato *et al.* 2012).

The image of the Philippines being regarded as a major international sex tourism destination appears to have waned. However, the fundamental inequalities that exist between classes and regions and which force people into prostitution still need to be addressed, while new forms of mobility-related exploitation of the poor have developed, such as the trafficking in organs for transplant tourism (Alburo 2007; Mendoza 2010; Yea 2010, 2015; De Castro 2013; Gatarin 2014). This is not to suggest that medical tourism is an inappropriate area of tourism development and promotion, rather, it is to highlight the difficulties of regulating the field as well as the ethical issues that are associated with it.

From 1991 on, tourism development in the Philippines was guided by a 20-year master plan (Hall 1997; Dela Santa 2015). Funded by the UN Development Programme and executed by the WTO and the DOT, the plan was given the support of President Fidel Ramos. The key elements of the master plan were to improve the country's image overseas and make better use of existing facilities and infrastructure within the framework of deregulated civil aviation and generous incentives for overseas investors (DOT 1995). A total of P52 billion (US\$2 billion) was required to implement the plan, including P22.8 billion (US\$912 million) for accommodation, P18 billion (US\$720 million) for infrastructure, P5.6 billion (US\$224 million) for transport, and P5.4 billion (US\$216) for education, training and other programmes. Seven areas were identified as priority areas for tourism development under the master plan (DOT 1995):

1   Samal Island

2   Panglao Island

3   Northern Palawan

4   Tagaytay, Tall, Batangas

5   Baguio, La Union, Ilocos Norte, Ilocos Sur, Pangasinan

6   Boracay

7   Bicol.

Examples of development include the Boracay Service Infrastructure Project for the construction of sewerage, waste-water treatment and solid-waste disposal systems so as to avert further deterioration of the environment in the region and the development of an airport on Panglao Island (DOT 1995). The visitor arrival targets under the plan are far more realistic than the goals of the 1989 plan discussed above, and were set at 1.5m in 1993, 1.7m in 1996 and 5.3m in 2010. The actual total for 2010 was 3.52m (DOT 2011). International arrivals reached 4,833,368 in 2014, which was 3.25% higher than the previous year's 4,681,307 arrivals. However, the target had been five million. The DOT had set a target of six million arrivals in 2015 and ten million in 2016 (Torres 2015). The country recorded 5.36m international arrivals in 2015; of these almost half came from the East Asian region. The country's top five markets are South Korea, USA, Japan, China and Australia, with China soon to overtake Japan in terms of numbers of arrivals.

In 2009 a new *Tourism Act* was passed which restructured tourism policy making in the Philippines. The Act restructured the offices and agencies attached to the DOZ, increased its budget, rationalised tourism zones, provided generous fiscal incentives to investors, and encouraged public–private partnerships. Sustainable tourism was a significant part of the agenda although the institutional model provided for far more influence by the private sector and the regions in policy making than had previously been the case. The Act created a Tourism Congress, composed of accredited tourism enterprises to serve as a consultative body to assist government in policy making. One way by which this was undertaken was by nominating representatives to the governing boards of the Philippine Tourism Board, Tourism Infrastructure and Enterprise Zone Authority, and Duty Free Philippines (Dela Santa 2015). In addition, a Tourism Coordinating Council composed of other government agencies was established, which was also envisioned to help the DOT in formulating and implementing tourism policies and programmes. Although such a whole-of-government approach to tourism together with a strong focus on public–private partnerships may assist in encouraging information flow and improving decision making in an ideal situation, Dela

Santa (2015) suggests that the institutionalised nature of clientelistic relations and converging personal and official interests may negatively affect intended outcomes. Indeed, the openness the government seeks to encourage in its tourism policy making does not appear to be extended internationally. The Philippines had not adopted the full list of principles in the ASEAN "open skies" agreement (discussed above). As Tan (2009) argues, the ASEAN approach to liberalisation can sit alongside the Philippines' approach to aviation policy, but the country may be reluctant to fully adopt the stated principles of open market access for fear of reducing the competitiveness of its own national carrier and the impacts this would have on associated economic and political interests.

The WTTC (2015c) predict that the direct contribution of travel and tourism to the Philippines' GDP, which was 4.2% of total GDP in 2014, will rise by 5.6% pa from 2015 to 2025, to 4.4% of total GDP in 2025. The direct contribution of tourism to employment is expected to stay the same proportion of total employment over this period (3.3%) but add just over 400,000 more jobs in absolute terms. Perhaps most significantly, the value of visitor exports is expected to rise from the 6.9% of total exports in 2014 and grow by 6.6% pa from 2015 to 2025, to become 9.9% of the total. However, these forecasts require the political and economic stability that has eluded the country for much of the past four decades to be in place.

- Website of the Philippines Statistics Authority that provides a profile of
  - domestic tourism: https://psa.gov.ph/tags/local-travel-and-tourism
  - international tourism: www.nscb.gov.ph/secstat/d_tour.asp
- The Philippines national tourism promotion website: http://itsmorefuninthephilippines.com

Conclusions

This chapter has provided a brief overview of some of the issues associated with the construction of the southeast Asian region. In so doing it has also highlighted the central role of ASEAN in the political and economic development of the region. However, it has also noted that there are significant differences both between and within the 11 countries that make up Southeast Asia, and especially the historical divide between the mainland and archipelagic areas with respect to state formation (Acharya 2014). The implications of this divide still affect the region to the present day, particularly with respect to regional demands for greater autonomy. Nevertheless, it is also true that, as Weatherbee (2014: 17) observes,

> What we might call the Southeast Asian "virtual" or "imagined" region is a product of a process that is as much ideational as institutional. In fact, the term "ASEAN" itself is often used as a synonym for geographic Southeast Asia, even though Timor is excluded.

Significantly, tourism has also had a part to play in the construction of Southeast Asia through its critical role in transport connectivity, as well in the role of tourism promotion in encouraging both tourists (actual and potential) and those who live within destinations to construct the mental map of a region. As the following chapters of this section highlight, tourism's role is therefore not just economic, as important as that is given population and urban growth, but also profoundly political and cultural.

Key readings

Acharya, A. (2013) *The Making of Southeast Asia: International Relations of a Region*. Ithaca: Cornell University Press.
Acharya, A. (2014). *Constructing a Security Community in Southeast Asia: ASEAN and the Problem of Regional Order* (3rd edn). Abingdon: Routledge.
Dela Santa, E. (2015) 'The evolution of Philippine tourism policy implementation from 1973 to 2009', *Tourism Planning & Development*, 12(2): 155–175.
Manuela, W.S. and de Vera, M.J. (2015) 'The impact of government failure on tourism in the Philippines', *Transport Policy*, 43: 11–22.
Weatherbee, D.E. (2014) *International Relations in Southeast Asia: The Struggle for Autonomy*. New York: Rowman & Littlefield.

References

Acharya, A. (2013) *The Making of Southeast Asia: International Relations of a Region*. Ithaca: Cornell University Press.
—— (2014). *Constructing a Security Community in Southeast Asia: ASEAN and the Problem of Regional Order* (3rd edn). Abingdon: Routledge.
Alburo, K.Z.K. (2007) 'Kidneys for sale: Regulating bodies through medical tourism in the Philippines', *Philippine Quarterly of Culture and Society*, 35(3): 196–212.
ASEAN Statistics (2015) 'Tourist Arrivals in ASEAN as of 30 September 2015'. Online. Available: www.asean.org/storage/2015/11/tourism/Table_28.pdf (accessed 1 February 2015).
Catibog-Sinha, C. (2010) 'Biodiversity conservation and sustainable tourism: Philippine initiatives', *Journal of Heritage Tourism*, 5(4): 297–309.
Catibog-Sinha, C. and Heaney, L. (2006) *Philippine Biodiversity: Principles and Practice*. Quezon City: Haribon Foundation.
De Castro, L.D. (2013) 'The declaration of Istanbul in the Philippines: Success with foreigners but a continuing challenge for local transplant tourism', *Medicine, Health Care and Philosophy*, 16(4): 929–932.
Dela Santa, E. (2015) 'The evolution of Philippine tourism policy implementation from 1973 to 2009', *Tourism Planning & Development*, 12(2): 155–175.
Dela Santa, E. and Saporsantos, J. (2016) 'Philippine Tourism Act of 2009: Tourism policy formulation analysis from multiple streams', *Journal of Policy Research in Tourism, Leisure and Events*, 8(1): 53–70.
Department of Tourism (Philippines) (DOT) (1995) *Annual Report 1994*. Manila: DOT.
—— (2009) *Philippine Tourism: Stable Amidst a Global Tourism Downturn*. Manila: DOT.
—— (2011) *Visitor Arrivals to the Philippines by Country of Residence, January–December 2010*. Manila: DOT. Online. Available: www.visitmyphilippines.com/images/ads/b0f324c05c9579967ae340820bb397bd.pdf (accessed 1 April 2015).
Dixon, C. and Smith, D. (eds) (1997) *Uneven Development in South East Asia*. Aldershot: Ashgate.
Dutra, L.X., Haworth, R. and Taboada, M.B. (2011) 'An integrated approach to tourism planning in a developing nation: A case study from Beloi (Timor-Leste)', in D. Dredge and J. Jenkins (eds), *Stories of Practice: Tourism Policy and Planning* (pp. 269–293). Farnham: Ashgate.
Dwyer, D. (ed.) (1990) *South East Asian Development*. Harlow: Longman.
The Economist (2013) 'Strong growth in visitor arrivals', *The Economist*, 31 December.
—— (2015a) 'ASEAN economic integration: Steady as we go', *The Economist*, 26 November.
—— (2015b) 'Opening the ASEAN skies', *The Economist*, 12 October.
Fabinyi, M. (2010) 'The intensification of fishing and the rise of tourism: Competing coastal livelihoods in the Calamianes Islands, Philippines', *Human Ecology*, 38(3): 415–427.
Fisher, C. (1962) 'South East Asia: The Balkans of the Orient', *Geography*, 47: 347–367.
—— (1964) *South-East Asia*. London: Methuen.
Fryer, D. (1970) *Emergent South East Asia: A Study in Growth and Stagnation*. London: Philip.
Gallato, C.G., Gallato-Reamillo, K.A., Valdez, N.P., Warokka, A. and Hilman, H. (2012) 'Eco-tourism in the Philippines: Educational and recreational value of the Alayan cave systems', *Journal for Global Business Advancement*, 5(2): 169–178.

Gatarin, G.R. (2014) 'Masculine bodies in the biocapitalist era compromising human rights of commercial kidney donors in the Philippines', *Gender, Technology and Development*, 18(1): 107–129.

Hall, C.M. (1997) *Tourism in the Pacific Rim* (2nd edition). South Melbourne: Longmans.

Henderson, J. (2001) 'Regionalisation and tourism: The Indonesia–Malaysia–Singapore growth triangle', *Current Issues in Tourism*, 4: 78–93.

—— (2011) 'Tourism development and politics in the Philippines', *Tourismos: An International Multidisciplinary Journal of Tourism*, 6(2): 159–173.

Kasim, L. (2014) 'Brunei tourist arrivals remain stagnant', *The Brunei Times*, 16 December. Online. Available: www.bt.com.bn/business-national/2014/12/16/brunei-tourist-arrivals-remain-stagnant (accessed 14 February 2016).

Kirk, W. (1990) 'South East Asia in the colonial period: Cores and peripheries', in D. Dwyer (ed.), *South East Asian Development* (pp. 15–47), Harlow: Longman.

Lieberman, V. (1997) 'Transcending East–West dichotomies: State and culture formation in six ostensibly disparate areas', *Modern Asian Studies*, 31(3): 463–546.

—— (2003) *Strange Parallels: Southeast Asia in Global Context, c. 800–1830. Vol. 1 Integration on the Mainland*. Cambridge: Cambridge University Press.

—— (2009) *Strange Parallels: Southeast Asia in Global Context, c. 800–1830. Vol. 2 Mainland Mirrors: Europe, Japan, China, South Asia, and the Islands*. Cambridge: Cambridge University Press.

Lucas, E.Y. and Kirit, R. (2009) 'Fisheries–marine protected area–tourism interactions in Moalboal, Cebu, Philippines', *Coastal Management*, 37(5): 480–490.

Maguigad, V.M. (2013) 'Tourism planning in archipelagic Philippines: A case review', *Tourism Management Perspectives*, 7: 25–33.

Manuela, W.S. and de Vera, M.J. (2015) 'The impact of government failure on tourism in the Philippines', *Transport Policy*, 43: 11–22.

Mendoza, R.L. (2010) 'Kidney black markets and legal transplants: Are they opposite sides of the same coin?' *Health Policy*, 94(3): 255–265.

Porter, B.A., Orams, M.B. and Lück, M. (2015) 'Surf-riding tourism in coastal fishing communities: A comparative case study of two projects from the Philippines', *Ocean & Coastal Management*, 116: 169–176.

Quintas, J.F.D. (2015) 'Sustainable tourism and alternative livelihood development on Atauro Island, Timor-Leste, through pro-poor, community-based ecotourism', Master's thesis, Charles Darwin University, Darwin.

Richter, L.K. (1989) *The Politics of Tourism in Asia*. Honolulu: University of Hawai'i Press.

Saddique, I. (2015) 'Malaysia keeps topping ASEAN tourism arrivals', *Investvine*, 22 April.

Smith, R.A., Henderson, J.C., Chong, V., Tay, C. and Jingwen, Y. (2011) 'The development and management of beach resorts: Boracay Island, the Philippines', *Asia Pacific Journal of Tourism Research*, 16(2): 229–245.

Tan, A.K.-J. (2009) 'Aviation policy in the Philippines and the impact of the proposed South East Asian Single Aviation Market', *Air and Space Law*, 34(4/5): 285–308.

—— (2010) 'The ASEAN multilateral agreement on air services: En route to open skies?', *Journal of Air Transport Management*, 16: 289–294.

Tarling, N. (2003) *Imperialism in Southeast Asia*. London: Routledge.

Teh, L. and Cabanban, A.S. (2007) 'Planning for sustainable tourism in southern Pulau Banggi: An assessment of biophysical conditions and their implications for future tourism development', *Journal of Environmental Management*, 85(4): 999–1008.

Thein, R. (2014) 'Brunei has potential to attract medical tourists', *The Brunei Times*, 16 December. Online. Available: www.bt.com.bn/news-national/2014/12/16/brunei-has-potential-attract-medical-tourists (accessed 14 February 2016).

Tolkach, D. and King, B. (2015) 'Strengthening community-based tourism in a new resource-based island nation: Why and how?' *Tourism Management*, 48: 386–398.

Torres, T. (2015) '2014 tourist arrivals up 3.25% to 4.8 M', *The Philippine Star*, 18 February. Online. Available: www.philstar.com/business/2015/02/18/1424847/2014-tourist-arrivals-3.25-4.8-m (accessed 1 April 2015).

UNDP (2011) *Towards Human Resilience: Sustaining MDG Progress in an Age of Economic Uncertainty*. New York: UNDP.

UNWTO (2015) *Tourism Highlights*. Madrid: UNWTO.

Vong, M., Silva, J.A. and Pinto, P. (2015) 'Local leaders' perceptions about sustainable tourism development in Timor-Leste', *Journal of Spatial and Organizational Dynamics*, 3(2): 85–98.

Wah, C.K. (1995) 'ASEAN: consolidation and institutional change', *The Pacific Review*, 8(3), 424–439.

Weatherbee, D.E. (2014) *International Relations in Southeast Asia: The Struggle for Autonomy*. New York: Rowman & Littlefield.

World Bank (2015) 'Timor-Leste'. Online. Available: www.worldbank.org/en/country/timor-leste (accessed 14 February 2016).

—— (2016a) 'World Bank Data: International tourism, number of arrivals'. Online. Available: http://data.worldbank.org/indicator/ST.INT.ARVL (accessed 14 February 2016).

—— (2016b) 'World Bank Data: International tourism, receipts (% of total exports)'. Online. Available: http://data.worldbank.org/indicator/ST.INT.RCPT.XP.ZS (accessed 14 February 2016).

—— (2016c) 'World Bank Data: International tourism, number of departures'. Online. Available: http://data.worldbank.org/indicator/ST.INT.DPRT (accessed 14 February 2016).

—— (2016d) 'World Bank Data: International tourism, expenditures (% of total imports)'. Online. Available: http://data.worldbank.org/indicator/ST.INT.XPND.MP.ZS (accessed 14 February 2016).

World Travel & Tourism Council (WTTC) (2015a) *Travel & Tourism Economic Impact Brunei 2015*. London: WTTC.

—— (2015b) *Travel & Tourism Economic Impact Singapore 2015*. London: WTTC.

—— (2015c) *Travel & Tourism Economic Impact Philippines 2015*. London: WTTC.

Yea, S. (2010) 'Trafficking in part(s): The commercial kidney market in a Manila slum, Philippines', *Global Social Policy*, 10(3): 358–376.

—— (2015) 'Masculinity under the knife: Filipino men, trafficking and the black organ market in Manila, the Philippines', *Gender, Place & Culture*, 22(1): 123–142.

Zaili, Z. (2016) 'MPRT affirms commitment to develop tourism sector', *The Brunei Times*, 22 January. Online. Available: www.bt.com.bn/business-national/2016/01/22/mprt-affirms-commitment-develop-tourism-sector (accessed 25 January 2016).

10

SINGAPORE TOURISM

T.C. Chang

Introduction

Country atlases, by and large, do not usually bear unusual descriptors and titles. De Koninck's two-part atlas of Singapore is an exception. The first volume was titled *An Atlas of the Revolution of Territory* (De Koninck 1992), while the second is called *An Atlas of Perpetual Territorial Transformation* (De Koninck *et al.* 2008). Singapore, according to De Koninck, is an environment in constant evolution, with the pace and direction of change controlled tightly by the state. 'The permanent overhaul of the Singaporean environment, whether one calls it development, improvement or upgrading, still seems to be a way of life, or rather a way of managing a country – since some may call it governance' (De Koninck *et al.* 2008: 2).

The titles of the atlases are extremely telling and an appropriate way to conceive of Singapore's transformation over the years and, more specifically, changes that have taken place in its tourism industry. This chapter offers an overview of Singapore's tourism through the narrative of change. In particular, two aspects are examined alongside each other: *policy* changes and transformation of *place*. The policy–place nexus is a natural one in a development-state like Singapore where the government wields considerable power not only over planning and regulation, but also in terms of land rights and uses (the government being the largest landowner in the country).

The chapter begins with an overview of tourism over the years in order to contextualise the spectrum of changes that have taken place. Recent tourism statistics will reveal a thriving industry in terms of international tourist arrivals and revenues generated. This is followed by a three-part discussion of the key policies that have shaped the country's tourism development and environment. The three policy plans "escalate in scale" from parochial local concerns in the 1980s to regional/Asian concerns in the 1990s and finally global-city ambitions in the new millennium. Under each policy regime, the resultant tourism geographies will also be identified and discussed.

Singapore tourism in numbers: a numerical revolution

Under British colonial rule since 1819, Singapore achieved self-government in 1959; six years later in 1965 it became an independent state. In its formative years, tourism was never regarded as a viable economic avenue; if anything, tourism was seen as a source of unwanted social values associated with hippies, "yellow culture" and other undesirable traits of Westernisation (Fontaine 1999). However, the economic imperatives of becoming an independent state and the urgent need to create new streams of revenues and employment saw the establishment of the Singapore Tourist Promotion Board (STPB) in 1964. In the view of the government, tourism was a necessary sector to develop primarily for its economic benefits, even if its social impacts remain suspect. In the year of independence in 1965, the number of international visitors to the country was 98,481. In 1971, tourism revenues stood at S$333 million (or approximately US$246 million in 2015).

The scale of change is evident when we compare statistics over the years. Some 30 years later in 1995, the number of international visitors to Singapore was 7.14 million visitors, generating a revenue base of US$7.55 billion. This ranked Singapore as the world's tenth largest tourism earner just ahead of Switzerland and Canada (Chang 1996: 11). By 2013, the tourist arrival figure had swelled to 15.6 million, and total tourism revenues stood at S$23.5 billion, contributing about 4 per cent to the country's GDP. Singapore compares extremely well with its regional neighbours. The top Asian destinations in 2013 were China with over 55 million international tourist arrivals followed by Thailand at 26.6 million, Malaysia and Hong Kong both at 25.7 million and Singapore (UNWTO 2014). In terms of tourism receipts, Singapore was ranked fifth after China, Thailand, Hong Kong and Malaysia, and ahead of Japan and South Korea.

The rapid expansion in Singapore's tourism, particularly in the 1970s, was due to its liberal tourism and aviation policies. There were no visa or foreign currency restrictions in the 1970s, even if strict rules were enforced regarding male visitors with long hair in the 1970s and the country-wide ban on chewing gum in 1992. In the area of aviation, there were also few restrictions on landing rights and on the operation of chartered flights. These policies helped to increase the growth of air travel and establish Singapore as an aviation hub. In the 1990s, growth was spurred by Singapore's involvement in bilateral and multilateral tourism projects with neighbouring countries. As a small country at just over 700km^2 (the smallest in Southeast Asia), it leverages on its central location and transport hub status to attract cruise visitors and transit passengers. Marketing Indonesia, Malaysia and Singapore as a single destination also supplemented its own resource inadequacies, benefiting as a result from the tourism markets of its immediate neighbours.

The Tourism Product Development Plan (1986): a celebration of the local

Since the establishment of the STPB in 1964, there have been three large-scale tourism plans in 1986, 1996 and 2005. (In 2010, a tourism plan called *Tourism Compass 2020* was launched as a supplement to Tourism 2015 in order to ensure the latter was on track. This plan is not made publicly available by the Singapore Tourism Board and hence is not the subject of this discussion.) Each plan outlined a vision statement on how the tourism industry is to develop over a roughly ten-year time span. In this section, a broad overview of the plans is outlined with a particular focus on their evolving "scales". As we shall see, while the 1986 policy focused on developing local sites and landscapes, the 2005 plan envisioned Singapore as a global city with iconic and worldly attractions. This escalation of scale speaks of the evolving ambitions of Singapore as a tourist destination over time. It also reflects the imperatives of a country grappling with its limitations of size and resource endowment.

In 1986, the first ever tourism masterplan was conceived by the Ministry of Trade and Industry (or MTI, within which the STPB resides). The *Tourism Product Development Plan* (or Development Plan for short) was conceived jointly by the MTI, STPB and 11 other statutory boards (MTI, 1986). Five themes were chosen for development:

1   "Exotic East": a total of S$187 million was pledged for the redevelopment of ethnic-historic zones such as Chinatown, Kampong Glam, Little India and the Singapore River.
2   "Colonial Heritage": S$260 million for the Civic District, museums and Raffles Hotel.
3   "Tropical Island Resort": S$470 for the enhancement of Sentosa and other offshore islands.
4   "Clean Green Garden City": S$30 million for gardens, parks and nature-based sites.
5   "International Sporting Events': S$1 million for sports events and projects.

The urgency to develop the local tourism product was prompted by a dip in tourism numbers in 1983 and continued stagnation in 1984/85. The dip in tourist arrivals (-3.5 per cent compared to 1982) was particularly severe as Singapore's performance was worst among ASEAN countries. A Tourism Task Force was convened in 1984 to consider the reasons for the poor performance and concluded that rather than a 'cyclical problem' that would solve itself over time, the decline was the outcome of a 'structural' condition that hints at a 'deeper malaise' (MTI 1984: 13).

   This deeper malaise turned out to be a combination of regional economic circumstances and local product shortcomings. Regionally, protectionist policies in countries like Indonesia (Singapore's largest tourist market), Malaysia and Thailand made regional travel more expensive and hence, less attractive. While regional factors were harder to control, local product shortcomings were also blamed for the decline. In particular, the dearth of cultural and historical attractions and the misguided perception that tourists were attracted to Singapore because of its modernity were highlighted. As the Tourism Task Force warned, 'in our effort to build a modern metropolis, we have removed aspects of our Oriental mystique and charm which are best symbolised in old buildings, traditional activities and bustling roadside activities such as the "*pasar malam*"' (MTI 1984: 15).

   The tourism plan to redevelop the historic neighbourhoods came alongside the Urban Redevelopment Authority's (URA) conservation plans. In 1988, Conservation Manuals were published to explain why and how restoration of historic buildings in Chinatown, Little India and Kampong Glam are to be undertaken. A year later, these three precincts, along with three others, were officially gazetted as "historic conservation areas". A list of desirable new uses (and also prohibited activities) was drawn up for the "cores" of these neighbourhoods to prevent further dilution of their architectural heritage and land uses. Like the URA's plan, the Development Plan was pragmatic in its stance on traditional-versus-new activities. Where it was not possible to retain uneconomic traditional activities, dilapidated old buildings or original tenants, adaptive reuse and reconstruction of buildings were permitted. New but compatible activities for historic areas included food stalls and handicraft shops. Adaptive reuse of buildings for museums/interpretive centres, hotels and restaurants were also permitted.

   Apart from local landscapes, the "celebration of the local" also refers to the safeguarding of local community needs. The Development Plan stressed that tourism development must also benefit Singaporeans:

> Generally, tourists are inclined to go where locals go and enjoy what locals enjoy. Attractions built specially for tourists are not, by and large, of special interest to them. Therefore, while the projects outlined have the tourists in mind, they are likely to form a leisure and entertainment base, enjoyed and patronised also by Singaporeans.
>
> *(MTI 1986: 6)*

The de-differentiation of tourism spaces and local recreational places is necessary, given the small size of Singapore, where consolidation of multiple land uses is preferred over exclusive right to space by any one particular user group.

The existence of historic neighbourhoods in Singapore today is the direct outcome of the Development Plan. Apart from Chinatown, Little India and Kampong Glam, other heritage sites include the Civic and Colonial District (also the museum belt), Emerald Hill and Joo Chiat (Peranakan-themed neighbourhoods) and the historic Singapore River waterfront. This is not to say, however, that conservation is an uncontested phenomenon. What constitutes heritage and what new activities to introduce into a historic zone are often subject to vociferous debates. Different studies on various heritage zones reveal conflicting opinions on the success of conservation and tourism appeal of the final product (e.g. Chang *et al.* 2004; Yeoh and Huang 1996).

A case in point is the "Exotic East" image that historic zones are supposed to embody. The adjective "exotic" appears extremely archaic today, but in the 1980s it served as a rallying point to "Asianise" what the STPB feared was the emergence of an increasingly "pseudo-Western" environment in Singapore. In their study on urban conservation policies, Kong and Yeoh (1994) argued that while the majority of Singaporeans recognised the importance of conservation, many valid concerns were also raised. While some feared that 'conserved environments quickly lose their authenticity', others lamented that 'conservation benefits tourists rather than Singaporeans' (Kong & Yeoh 1994: 255). In a survey of 373 residents in Chinatown, Little India and Kampong Glam, it was revealed that 84.0 per cent of respondents felt that conservation had become too commercialised. This is evidenced by the disappearance of traditional (even if unprofitable) trades and the introduction of activities to attract "external" audiences (such as cafes, souvenir shops and boutiques). The result, in the eyes of residents, is the erosion of "cultural essence" and the "spiritual, aesthetic aspects" of place, and the concomitant rise of commercialised environments to capture the tourist dollar (Kong & Yeoh 1994: 261).

Tourism 21: envisioning Singapore as a tourism capital

In 1996, the Singapore Tourism Board (STB, renamed from STPB) outlined a new plan titled *Tourism 21: A Vision of a Tourism Capital* aimed at developing Singapore as a tourism capital (STB 1996). Just as Paris is a fashion capital or New York a cultural capital, a tourism capital is recognised for its innovation in tourism concepts and global influence. Apart from attracting visitors, a tourism capital must also be a choice location for tourism businesses and a gateway for visitors and capital entering the region. Six specific strategies were outlined:

1   Redefining tourism: apart from foreign visitors to a country, tourism is also about business investments and tourism expertise/knowledge.
2   Reformulating product: enhancing the tourism environment along thematic zones so that similarly themed attractions may be clustered together.
3   Configuring new tourism space: to develop Singapore's complementarity with the region by encouraging cross-border investments and marketing neighbouring countries as single destination zones.
4   Developing tourism as an industry: to develop Singapore as a base for tourism enterprises and to ensure optimal operating conditions through refinement of government regulations and tax incentives.
5   Partnering for success: the STB to partner private enterprises in developing the industry, and adopting a regional approach to market Singapore as a tourism hub and business centre.
6   Championing tourism: the STB to spearhead a tourism resource centre and foster a culture of tourism research.

While the Development Plan sought to enhance the local tourism environment, Tourism 21 had a wider regional focus. Having developed the national product, there is now a need to re-define Singapore's tourism environment beyond its immediate borders. The STB explained that Singapore needs to break free from 'traditional thinking which limits our tourism activities to the resources we possess ... adopting a transborder approach in going beyond physical boundaries, to participate in the growth of the Asia Pacific region' (STB 1996: 16). This transborder approach offered a 'new way for Singapore to look at itself, as well as the world', calling in particular for greater partnership with neighbouring countries and 'creating new economic space for everyone through leveraging resources regionally and globally' (STB 1996: 16). Four regions were identified for special attention: Southeast Asia, North Asia, South Asia and Oceania (Tham 2001).

In 1995, the STB established a Regional Tourism Division devoted to facilitating overseas expansion of Singaporean companies and advising on regional investment opportunities. The STB also set up its in-house consultancy division devoted to selling its own expertise in feasibility studies, tourism planning and institution building (Lee 2004). Regional consultancy projects were subsequently undertaken in Cambodia, China, India, Laos, Mauritius and Vietnam. Following the lead by STB, private sector operators were also encouraged and incentivised to start their own consultancy services. A good example is the Wildlife Reserves Singapore (the parent company of the Singapore Zoo, Night Safari and Jurong Bird Park), which set up its consultancy company in 1995 specialising in zoo design, management and landscape construction. Since its launch, Wildlife Reserves had conceived plans for a new zoo in Surabaya, Indonesia (1996), conceptualised masterplans for Bintan's Wildlife Sanctuary (1996), Cambodia's Phnom Tamao Zoo (1996), Chennai's Dizzee Animal Kingdom, India (1998), as well as provided landscaping advice for wildlife reserves in China and the Seychelles.

Another outcome of Tourism 21 was strategic partnerships across national borders. The goal was to enlarge tourism geographies by conjoining proximate destinations as single destination areas. Singapore's involvement in regional tourism was evident in two ways. At the formal level, its membership within ASEAN saw its involvement in various regional initiatives such as the Visit ASEAN Campaign, the ASEAN Tourism Agreement Plan (2002) and ASEAN Tourism Vision (2004–10) (Ghimrie 2001; Timothy 2002). Strategic partnerships were also forged at intra-regional levels, such as through the creation of the Indonesia Malaysia Singapore Growth Triangle (IMS GT). With its efficient airport and harbour, Singapore served as the transportation gateway to the triangle; with their ample land and labour, Malaysia and Indonesia provided the resources for development of beach resorts, marinas and golf courses. Through the IMS GT, access to Indonesian and Malaysian coastal resorts also allowed Singapore to market itself as a cruise centre. Cruise tourism was non-existent in Singapore in the 1980s. By 1992, cruise passengers numbered over 190,000, with 350 ships calling at port. In 2013 there were 1.03 million cruise passengers to the country.

Regional tourism development is not without challenges and conflicts. In the IMS GT, for example, Singapore's economic dominance and the "trickle down" effects in Indonesia have been noted (Chang 2001). With tourists spilling into the Riau islands of Indonesia (over 70 per cent being Singaporeans), rising crime rates, congestion, poor housing and environmental deterioration have also been noticed (Lim 1999). Despite the setting up of a Thematic Tours Subworking Group in 1997 by the IMS GT Tourism Sector Working Group to develop itineraries combining all three countries, tangible benefits are questionable. Henderson (2001: 87), for example, argues that 'actual cooperation in development and promotion involving all three poles is uncommon and the most productive arrangements have been those bilateral ones between Singapore and the Riau islands'. Others have also noted the "differentiated mobilities" and "unevenness of transnational flows" across borders, with Singaporean tourists and capital passing through easily to Riau, compared to the difficulties Riau islanders encounter trying to enter Singapore either for work or leisure (Ford and Lyons 2006: 257–258). While it is beyond the scope of this chapter to fully address the inequities of the IMS GT, it suffices to say that regional tourism plans inevitably encounter inter-country conflicts and disagreements, a problem that the earlier nationalistic plan was not subjected to.

Tourism 2015: a global city in the making

In 2005, the STB unveiled its new Tourism 2015 masterplan. Three specific targets were set for the ten-year plan; they included tourism receipts of S$30 billion, tourist arrivals of 17 million and tourism employment of 250,000 by the year 2015. A S$2 billion Tourism Development Fund was also established for infrastructural development and capability/product enhancement. While the 1986 Development Plan focused on enhancing Singapore's local cultural and natural assets, and the 1996 Tourism 21 plan emphasised regional collaboration, the ambitions of Tourism 2015 are clearly international and global.

Tourism 2015 identified four avenues for development:

1   Strengthen Singapore as a convention and exhibition hub: already Asia's leading convention centre, the goal is to further target the BT-MICE market (Business Travellers and Meetings, Incentive, Convention and Exhibition tourists).
2   Provide enriching experience to visitors: the goal is to develop quality tourism experiences for different travel segments.
3   Establish Singapore as a global service centre: target services include health and education in order to entice education and medical travellers.
4   Create iconic events and landmarks: to develop Singapore as a world-class city with an "X factor".

In a study of Tourism 2015, Sin (2013: 245) identifies the main geographic outcome to be the development of "spectacular tourism landscapes" comprising iconic events and landmarks. Events such as "Singapore 2006" (a series of high-profile meetings such as the Annual Meetings of the International Monetary Fund (IMF) and World Bank Group), the Formula 1 Singtel Singapore Grand Prix (inaugurated in 2008) and the Youth Olympic Games (2010) were organised to project Singapore as a city with international capabilities. Landmark projects include the Singapore Flyer, the two integrated resorts of Marina Bay Sands and Resorts World Sentosa, and Gardens by the Bay, all of which fundamentally changed Singapore's skyline and waterfront. Not only attractive to tourists, these global city-making projects were also aimed at international capital and foreign talent, as well as local citizens.

Tourism 2015 may be better understood when contextualised against Singapore's larger planning agendas in the 2000s. At a World Conference on Model Cities held in Singapore in 2000, then Prime Minister Goh Chok Tong envisioned Singapore as a cosmopolis with a global and local identity. He said:

> This cosmopolis or world city will be a clean and safe city set in a pleasant, tropical garden environment. It will be a cosmopolitan city with a Singapore flavour, a forward-looking modern city with a rich diversity of eastern and western cultures.
>
> *(Goh 2000: 3)*

Five years later and with a new leader at the helm, Prime Minister Lee Hsien Loong spoke of Singapore at the National Day Rally 2005 as a 'vibrant, global city' that is attractive to global talent and investors, but also 'anchor[ing] Singaporeans in Singapore' (cited in Li 2005: u.p.). It is clear that as Singapore embarks on globalisation plans, caution is exercised to ensure that these plans do not alienate local citizens.

The development of the Marina Bay Sands and Resorts World Sentosa Integrated Resorts may be the most dramatic landscape change to ever take place in Singapore. After two decades of outlawing casino gambling, the Singapore government made an about-turn in 2005 by approving not one but two casinos to be built within two integrated resorts. Both resorts are to comprise a range of leisure and entertainment facilities such as hotels, food/beverage services, museums, parks and theatres, in addition to the casinos. To allay fears of the social harm brought about by the casinos, the government also set up a National Council on Problem Gambling in 2005, introduced an entry levy of S$100 for Singaporean citizens and permanent residents, and established a register of exclusion orders barring people who are 'vulnerable or are undesirable … from stepping into the casino' (Sin 2013: 249). Social impacts aside, the casinos were seen as necessary in augmenting Singapore's tourism environment, ensuring that it kept abreast of global competition, particularly from other Asian cities.

In addition to iconic landscapes, mega-events such as the F1 Grand Prix and Youth Olympic Games are the other major outcomes of Tourism 2015. It is estimated, for example, that F1 draws about 110,000 international visitors to the country annually, generating a total of more than S$420 million between 2008 and 2010. However, it should be noted that organising the race costs an approximate S$150 million each year, 60 per cent of which is borne by the government and hence tax payers (Sin 2013: 250). This is a huge expense for a three-day event in which only a small segment of Singaporeans are involved as on-site spectators. A study of Singaporeans' perceptions of the Grand Prix showed that many felt the F1 tickets were exorbitant, as were the food, drinks and accommodation in and around the circuit (Singh 2011). In the eyes of many, the F1 races are geared to elite tourists rather than entertainment for the masses. Others lamented that historical sites near to the track are sullied each year during the F1 season. For example, the War Memorial Park adjacent to the track (commemorating those who died in Singapore during World War II) are always filled with tourists eating, drinking, sleeping and littering (Singh 2011: 81). The free flow of alcohol publicly and the ubiquitous advertisements of tobacco companies on race cars (contravening the ban on all such advertisements in Singapore) have also been questioned.

Case study 10.1 Singapore's ever-evolving marketing image

In line with this chapter's emphasis on policy changes and spatial effects, it is appropriate to consider Singapore's evolving marketing images. Rather than regard "image" as a frivolous output of creative advertisers, the ever-changing tourism marketing campaigns help to shed light on Singapore's self-image and its evolving socio-cultural and economic priorities over time.

In the 1970s, "Instant Asia" projected Singapore as a destination that combined the cultures, sights and artefacts of Asia's dominant groups: the Chinese, Malay and Indian communities. For the time-strapped and cost-conscious traveller, Singapore served as a convenient all-in-one Asian destination. Because of its compact urban form, tourists could experience Chinatown, rural Malay *kampongs* (villages), Little India and the Colonial and Civic District in a single place. The Instant Asia theme was also in line with the government's push for multiculturalism in the newly independent nation. If Singapore can be successfully projected to the world as a harmonious community of different ethnic groups, the chances of its own citizens believing in and upholding the multicultural ethos would be enhanced (Chang 1997).

In 1984, a new marketing image was introduced – "Surprising Singapore: A Magic Place of Many Worlds". With rapid development since the 1970s, Singapore has been transformed with highways, shopping malls and high-rise buildings. At the same time, increasing concerns about the need to conserve heritage were voiced by many Singaporeans. The marketing image thus portrayed Singapore at a crossroads – modern yet historic, a cultural destination filled with parks and gardens. The juxtaposition of old and new was also aligned with broader urban conservation agendas outlined by the URA that permitted retention of select buildings and economic trades, while doing away with dilapidated structures, slums and defunct activities (Kong & Yeoh 1994).

A new tourism campaign was launched in 1997 to showcase "New Asia-Singapore: So Easy to Enjoy". Unlike Instant Asia's stereotype of Asian exotica, New Asia portrayed a destination that is modern and progressive, and an embodiment of an equally progressive continent (Chang & Lim 2004). While Instant Asia projected a self-sufficient country, New Asia took a different approach by representing Singapore as integrally connected to the region. While not possessing either the scenic resources or market size of other countries, Singapore is imagined to have both the cultural and economic resources that enable access to the rest of Asia. With its continental connections and cultural affinities, Singapore presented itself as an entry point for visitors and tourism enterprises entering into Asia.

In 2004, yet another marketing campaign was launched, this time showcasing "Uniquely Singapore". As the country embarked on its globalisation agenda through landmark projects like the Integrated Resorts and F1 Grand Prix, extra care was taken to ensure that the country's unique appeal was not compromised. It was hence under the "Uniquely Singapore" mantle that one-of-a-kind, original-to-Singapore tourism concepts were born such as the first ever F1 night-race, the inaugural Youth Olympic games and the Integrated Resorts that combined multiple entertainment options from casinos to museums, theme parks and gardens.

In March 2010, STB launched "YourSingapore", a campaign that revolves around an interactive website where travellers can customise their itineraries, book flights and hotels, and have their travel plans sent to their mobile phones and other communicative devices. As part of the move to keep up with creative technologies, "YourSingapore" deploys social media and viral marketing to entice web-savvy visitors. At the same time, digital media allows for the "personalisation" of experiences so that individual travellers are able to craft itineraries for themselves.

Conclusion

This chapter has spotlighted Singapore's tourism through the narrative of change. It highlighted three key tourism plans in the 1980s, 1990s and 2000s, and noted the escalation of scale across the decades. From the emphasis on local cultural and natural sites in the Development Plan (1986) to regional agendas in Tourism 21 (1996) and global ambitions under Tourism 2015 (2005), the broadening of goals is as much a reflection of Singapore's growth trajectory as it is the need to compete with other tourist destinations. Apart from policy shifts, this chapter has also considered the concomitant spatial effects of changes. While urban heritage conservation was the focus of tourism plans in the 1980s, regional projects and trans-border collaborations were emphasised in the 1990s. The outward-looking posture continued into the new millennium with Singapore's global-city quest epitomised by iconic buildings, landmark events and mega-million dollar infrastructure. The policy–place nexus provides readers with an insight into how government plans can and do shape spaces, environments and societies. It is precisely for this reason that tourism policies are so often contested grounds upon which differing ideologies about change and development come to a head. How such policies are harnessed for local societal good apart from economic demands must certainly be closely monitored.

Key reading

Chang, T.C. and Teo, P. (2001) 'From rhetoric to reality: cultural heritage and tourism in Singapore', in L. Low and D.M. Johnston (eds), *Singapore Inc. Public Policy Options in the Third Millennium* (pp. 273–303) Singapore: Asia Pacific Press.

De Koninck, R., Drolet, J. and Girard, M. (2008) *Singapore: An Atlas of Perpetual Territorial Transformation*. Singapore: NUS Press.

Lee, P. (2004) *Singapore, Tourism & Me*. Singapore: Pamelia Lee Pte. Ltd.

Sin, H.L. (2013) 'Tourism 2015: Making your Singapore', in E. Ho, C.Y. Woon and K. Ramdas (eds), *Changing Landscapes of Singapore: Old Tensions, New Discoveries* (pp. 237–256). Singapore: NUS Press.

STB (2013), *Navigating the Next Phase of Tourism Growth*. Tourism Industry Conference 2013, Discussion Paper. Online. Available: www.stb.gov.sg/news-and-publications/publications/Documents/TIC%20Discussion%20Paper%202013.pdf.

Relevant websites

Singapore Tourism Board: www.stb.gov.sg
Tourism statistics for Singapore: www.stb.gov.sg/statistics-and-market-insights

References

Chang, T.C. (1996) 'Local uniqueness in the global village: heritage tourism in Singapore'. Unpublished doctoral dissertation, McGill University, Montreal.

—— (1997) 'From "Instant Asia" to "Multi-faceted Jewel": urban imaging strategies and tourism development in Singapore', *Urban Geography*, 18: 542–562.

—— (2001) '"Configuring new tourism space": exploring Singapore's regional tourism forays', *Environment and Planning A*, 33: 1597–1619.

Chang, T.C. and Lim, S.Y. (2004) 'Geographical imaginations of "New Asia-Singapore"', *Geografiska Annaler*, 86B: 165–185.

Chang, T.C., Huang, S. and Savage, V. (2004) 'On the waterfront: Globalization and urbanization in Singapore', *Urban Geography*, 25: 413–436.

De Koninck, R. (1992) *Singapour: Un atlas de la revolution du territoire/Singapore: An Atlas of the Revolution of Territory*. Montpellier: RECLUS.

De Koninck, R., Drolet, J. and Girard, M. (2008) *Singapore: An Atlas of Perpetual Territorial Transformation*. Singapore: NUS Press.

Fontaine, G. (1999) 'Singapore, tourism and world', *Asia Pacific Journal of Tourism Research*, 4: 30–38.

Ford, M. and Lyons, L. (2006) 'The borders within mobility and enclosure in the Riau Islands', *Asia Pacific Viewpoint*, 47: 257–271.

Ghimrie, K. (2001) 'Regional tourism and south–south economic cooperation', *The Geographical Journal*, 167: 99–110.

Goh, C.T. (2000) 'Cities: leading the way to the next millennium', address at the World Conference on Model Cities, Singapore, 19–21 April 2000.

Henderson, J. (2001) 'Regionalisation and tourism: The Indonesia–Malaysia–Singapore growth triangle', *Current Issues in Tourism*, 4: 78–93.

Kong, L. and Yeoh, B.S. (1994) 'Urban conservation in Singapore: A survey of state policies and popular attitudes', *Urban Studies*, 31(2): 247–265.

Lee, P. (2004) *Singapore, Tourism & Me*. Singapore: Pamelia Lee Pte. Ltd.

Li, X. (2005) 'S'pore set to be "sparkling jewel" in 10 years' time', *The Straits Times*, 22 August.

Lim, L.H. (1999) 'A triangle love affair? Tourism in the Indonesia–Malaysia–Singapore Growth Triangle', unpublished honours thesis, Department of Geography, National University of Singapore, Singapore.

Ministry of Trade and Industry (MTI) (1984) *Tourism Task Force*. Singapore: MTI and Singapore Tourist Promotion Board (STPB).

—— (1986) *Tourism Product Development Plan*. Singapore: MTI and Singapore Tourist Promotion Board (STPB).

Sin, H.L. (2013) 'Tourism 2015: Making your Singapore', in E. Ho, C.Y. Woon and K. Ramdas (eds), *Changing Landscapes of Singapore: Old Tensions, New Discoveries* (pp. 237–256). Singapore: NUS Press.

Singh, S. (2011) 'Need for speed: Urban entrepreneuralism and the F1 spectacle in Singapore', unpublished honours thesis, Department of Geography, National University of Singapore, Singapore.

STB (1996) *Tourism 21: Vision of a Tourism Capital*. Singapore: Singapore Tourism Board and National Tourism Plan Committees.

Tham, E. (2001) 'Regionalisation as a strategy for Singapore's tourism development', in E.S. Tan, B.S.A. Yeoh and J. Wang (eds), *Tourism Management and Policy: Perspectives from Singapore* (pp. 50–54). Singapore: World Scientific.

Timothy, D. (2002) 'Tourism planning in Southeast Asia: Bringing down borders through cooperation', in K. Chon (ed.), *Tourism in Southeast Asia: A New Direction* (pp. 2–38). New York: Haworth Hospitality Press.

UNWTO (United Nations World Tourism Organization) (2014) *UNWTO Tourism Highlights, 2014 Edition*. Spain: WTO.

Yeoh, B.S.A. and Huang, S. (1996) 'The conservation–redevelopment dilemma in Singapore: The case of the Kampong Glam historic district', *Cities*, 13: 411–422.

11

TOURISM IN THAILAND

Growth, diversification and political upheaval

Nick Kontogeorgopoulos

Introduction

In the span of just a few decades, Thailand has emerged as a major international tourism destination. Steady growth has characterized the tourism industry in Thailand since at least the 1960s when its cooperation with the United States during the Vietnam War led to foreign investment, improved infrastructure, and exposure to an international audience. In the mid-1980s, as Thailand entered a period of rapid economic transformation, its tourism industry began to undergo a "touristic transition" (Cohen 2001). In particular, like many other once remote destinations that become affordable and accessible to mass tourists, Thailand experienced a change in the motivation, composition, and distribution of international tourists. Moreover, as the pre-existing natural attractions of Thailand, including cultural and historical sites, inevitably changed in response to rising tourist demand and visitation, 'new, contrived attractions [were] created to enhance the attractiveness of the destination and to deflect tourists from the declining natural attractions, or even to substitute for the latter' (Cohen 2001: 155). This touristic transition towards mass tourism and the creation or modification of original events and sites has continued since the mid-1980s, and has accelerated at an even great pace in the past few years; the explosive growth of international tourism since 2009 in particular has now made Thailand a top-ten global destination.

There are currently two dominant trends in Thai tourism. First, the diversification of source markets, particularly China and Russia, have enabled Thailand to intensify and expand its mass, package tourism industry. Second, in response to slower, albeit still moderate, rates of growth in Western tourism markets, Thailand has actively promoted small-scale, niche tourism activities such as wildlife tourism, volunteer tourism, and community-based tourism. It is tempting to see these bifurcated tourism products as mutually exclusive and oppositional, but one is in fact related to the other in that an intensification of mass tourism from new source markets motivates some tourists to spatially and discursively distance themselves from conventional tourists. Although there are both immediate and long-term threats to further expansion of tourism in Thailand, most notably the ongoing political crisis, it is likely that mass tourism, and its alternatives, will continue to grow in the coming years.

Thailand's emergence as a top international destination

International tourism arrivals and revenues in Thailand have grown steadily in recent decades, but the past few years have seen an especially dramatic uptick in the number of people travelling to Thailand (Figure 11.1).

As Figure 11.1 indicates, rates of growth for international tourism have grown consistently, with two points in time when the slope of the line increases noticeably. The first discernible increase in the slope of the data line comes in 1985, and continues until 2009, when the slope takes another sharp turn upwards. These two years mark the boundaries of different periods of growth for the tourism industry in Thailand. The first period, which spans the 1960s until the mid-1980s, was characterized by growth in Western tourist markets such as Australia, Europe, and North America. The emergence of an international tourism industry during these early decades had its roots in the military involvement of the United States in Vietnam, which induced foreign direct investment in the construction and service industries, and led to the development of Bangkok as an international air transportation hub (Ouyyanont 2001). The seeds of future tourism development were sown at this time due to the need for businesses and services that could meet the leisure demands of the 322,000 American soldiers stationed in military bases in Thailand, as well as the 310,000 GIs that visited the country between 1966 and 1974 on rest and recreation (R&R) trips (Meyer 1988). The presence of American troops and the international media coverage of the war in Southeast Asia also enhanced global awareness of the region and led indirectly to increased visitation, especially by male travellers from Western countries (Cohen 1996).

Beginning in the mid-1980s, international arrivals from traditional tourist markets continued to grow, but were supplemented with growing numbers of tourists from East Asian countries

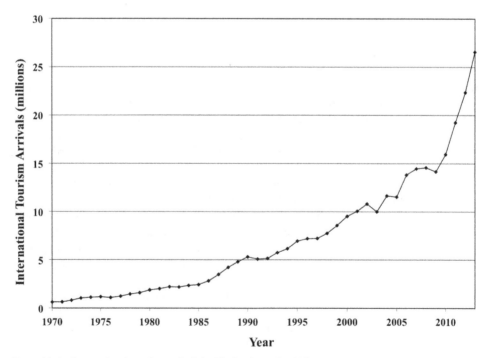

Figure 11.1   International tourism arrivals in Thailand, 1970–2013.
Source: TAT (1998, 2015a).

such as Japan. The rapid influx of foreign direct investment from East Asia following the Plaza Accord of 1985, which led to the devaluation of the Japanese yen and therefore the pursuit of offshore manufacturing opportunities in Southeast Asia on the part of Japanese investors, had a similar effect as the investment related to US military involvement two decades earlier. Further, with burgeoning prosperity within the South-East Asian region, the number of tourists visiting from neighboring countries such as Malaysia also increased from the mid-1980s onwards. During the 1980s and 1990s, the guiding hand of the Thai state that had steered tourism development in the past was joined by the Thai private sector, which worked together with government agencies to boost tourism. One such collaborative effort was the highly successful 1987 campaign titled "Visit Thailand Year," which led to a 24% increase in international tourism arrivals (Chon *et al.* 1993). As Cohen (1996) argues, the tourism industry of Thailand came to take its current characteristics during this period. In addition to moving towards structured mass tourism, Thailand also experienced the dispersion of arrivals and activities along a north–south corridor, which helped to spread tourism to destinations that continue to this day to attract the majority of international arrivals.

The final period, from 2009 onwards, features the most dramatic growth in tourist arrivals of any period in Thailand's recent history. In just four years, arrivals almost doubled, going from 14.1 million to 26.5 million. As Table 11.1 illustrates, the rate of growth stayed relatively similar between 1970 and 2009, but shot up beginning in 2009. However, the magnitude of growth is thrown into even starker relief when considering the additional *number* of tourists per year who decided to travel to Thailand each year between 2009 and 2013.

For many years, Thailand remained in the list of the top 20 international tourism destinations in the world, sitting at 16th, 18th, and 16th in 1995, 2005, and 2010, respectively (World Bank 2015), but its recent growth in tourism arrivals has catapulted Thailand into the list of the top ten tourist destinations in the world in 2013 (UNWTO 2014: 6). In 2013, Thailand also surpassed Malaysia as Southeast Asia's top tourism destination. Partly as a result of Thailand's rapid ascent to the group of countries receiving the most international tourism arrivals, Southeast Asia was the fastest growing region of the world in both 2012 and 2013. It is obvious when considering these data and patterns that Thailand has recently undergone a continued intensification and expansion of conventional mass tourism and everything that this involves, including consolidated transportation and communication networks, global promotional campaigns, and the packaging of travel services for very large groups of tourists.

The astonishing expansion of tourism since 2009 is largely attributable to the surge in arrivals from China (discussed later), and points to the importance of diversified markets in extending the period of "development" identified in Butler's (1980) Tourism Area Life Cycle (TALC). According to Butler's model, the development stage, which in Thailand's case seems to have begun in the mid-1980s, is normally followed by consolidation (with a slowing down of arrivals), stagnation, and then either rejuvenation or decline. Instead of reaching the consolidation stage, as one would expect based on the characteristics of growth from the mid-1980s onwards,

Table 11.1 Historical patterns of growth for international tourism arrivals in Thailand, 1970–2013

Time period	Average annual increase (%)	Average number of additional tourists each year
1970–1985	9.84	120,600
1985–2009	7.91	487,993
2009–2013	17.07	3,099,221

Source: TAT (1998, 2015a).

Thailand has instead extended the development period itself by tapping into new markets, thereby delaying the consolidation and then stagnation stages. This is true even despite the likely decline in tourism caused by the 2014 military coup, because past declines in tourism caused by natural disasters such as the Boxing Day Tsunami in December 2004 or previous military coups have been followed immediately by a resumed expansion of tourism. In any case, it remains to be seen if the growth of the past few years will pick up where it left off before 2014, or whether the slight decline likely to occur in 2015 is a harbinger of imminent consolidation and stagnation.

Tourism's economic importance

Tourism became Thailand's number one source of foreign exchange revenue in 1982, and has remained the top earner since then (Chancharat 2011). Due to its importance in generating revenues for the state as well as for individual Thai workers and businesses, it is no surprise that Thailand has heavily promoted the expansion of international tourism. Revenues from international tourism have exhibited patterns similar to those found for arrivals. For example, in the ten years between 1985, when tourism arrivals began to start taking off, and 1995, international tourism revenues to Thailand increased by 503% compared to 234% for the world as a whole (WTO 1996). Since that time, revenues have continued to rise at a similar pace, with a sharp rise in growth rates beginning in 2009 (Figure 11.2).

In the four years since 2009, at the same time that Thailand was experiencing a dramatic surge in international tourism arrivals, revenues grew by 2.6 times, going from $14.9 billion to $39.3 billion and resulting in Thailand occupying the number-seven spot in the world in 2013 when it comes to international tourism receipts (UNWTO 2014: 6). Thailand now receives more revenue from international tourism than such well-established and popular destinations as Germany and the United Kingdom. Enhanced revenues have certainly raised the profile of the tourism industry in Thailand, but by global standards, Thailand cannot yet be characterized as

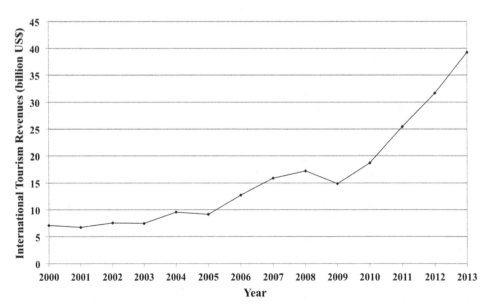

Figure 11.2 International tourism revenues in Thailand, 2000–2013.
Source: TAT (2015b).

a country dependent on tourism. According to the World Travel and Tourism Council (WTTC), tourism in 2013 directly accounted for 9% of Thailand's GDP and 6.6% of total employment: this ranks 25th and 38th, respectively, on a global scale (WTTC 2014: 8). Nevertheless, by regional standards, Thailand depends more on international tourism as a percentage of total export revenues than all but two other Southeast Asian countries (see Chapter 10). Further, unlike other countries in Southeast Asia, where the contribution of tourism to export earnings has either remained flat or grown very slowly in the past few years, tourism's contribution to Thailand's exports has risen from 10.4% in 2010 to 16% in 2013: this represents a 53.8% increase in just three years (WTTC 2015).

Regional distribution of tourism benefits

It is obvious that Thailand has benefitted economically from international tourism, both in terms of income as well as employment and export earnings. These benefits are not, however, distributed evenly throughout the entire country. Domestic travel undertaken by Thais tends to occur in a wide number of destinations throughout Thailand, but international tourism is spatially concentrated in four specific locations (Figure 11.3). First, Bangkok is the entry point for the majority of tourists arriving in Thailand by air, and has long represented the central hub of the Thai tourist economy. As mentioned earlier, investment in construction, services, and

Figure 11.3 Map of Thailand with regions and key tourism destinations.

transportation in the Bangkok area spurred a nascent tourism industry in the 1960s and 1970s, and although Bangkok's legendary traffic problems and poor air quality serve as a deterrent for some, the sprawling capital continues to attract many visitors. In 2013, 17.5 million tourists stayed at least one night in Bangkok: this represents 66% of all tourists visiting Thailand that year.

Second, the beach resort of Pattaya, located along Thailand's Eastern Seaboard, first emerged as a tourism destination when it served as a popular R&R stop for American servicemen during the Vietnam War. As a result of being located less than two hours from Bangkok, Pattaya is often included in tour packages for those visiting Bangkok, and currently attracts approximately nine million international tourists each year (Amnatcharoenrit 2014). Third, marketed for decades as the "Pearl of the Andaman," the island of Phuket in southern Thailand received eight million tourists in 2013, making it the third most popular destination in Thailand, after Bangkok and Pattaya (Department of Tourism 2015a). Lastly, the ancient city of Chiang Mai now hosts over two million tourists each year. Tourists are attracted to the area because the mountainous landscapes of northern Thailand provide the setting for popular activities such as visits to elephant camps, national parks, famous Buddhist temples, and indigenous "hilltribe" communities. Other than these four locations, there are also several minor destinations throughout the country that attract, in some cases, hundreds of thousands of annual visitors.

The concentration of international tourism in the handful of sites mentioned above is the primary reason why there are wide discrepancies in the number of tourists received by each region of Thailand (Figure 11.4). In addition to some regions benefiting more than others from tourism, there is also inequality *within* each region since tourist arrivals, and therefore revenues, are usually heavily concentrated in just one key location. For example, northern Thailand consists of 17 provinces, but just one province, Chiang Mai, accounts for 66% of all international tourists in the region (Department of Tourism 2015a). Similarly, Phuket alone attracts 49% of all tourists in southern Thailand. The key point to draw from these data is that tourism, while beneficial overall to the country, nevertheless reflects and contributes to the uneven regional development that has long characterized Thailand (Doner 2009).

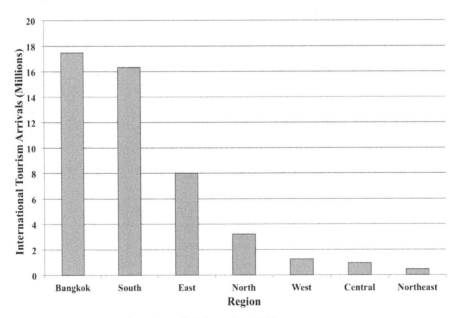

Figure 11.4 International tourism arrivals by region, 2013.
Source: Department of Tourism (2015a).

Diversification of source markets

As mentioned above, the post-war tourism industry in Thailand was heavily oriented towards visitors from high-income countries in Europe, North America, and Oceania. This began to change in the 1980s, as East Asian tourists and tourists from neighboring Southeast Asian countries such as Malaysia began to visit Thailand in ever-increasing numbers. Currently, Thailand attracts tourists from a diverse range of source markets, but the majority (60%) of international tourists come from East Asian countries (Table 11.2).

Table 11.2 International tourism arrivals by nationality, 2013

Nationality	Number	% share	Nationality	Number	% share
East Asia	15,911,375	59.94	United Kingdom	905,024	3.41
ASEAN	7,282,266	27.43	East Europe	346,230	1.30
Brunei	14,205	0.05	Others	138,688	0.52
Cambodia	481,595	1.81	The Americas	1,166,633	4.39
Indonesia	594,251	2.24	Argentina	21,035	0.08
Laos	976,639	3.68	Brazil	37,263	0.14
Malaysia	3,041,097	11.46	Canada	229,897	0.87
Myanmar	172,383	0.65	United States	823,486	3.10
Philippines	321,571	1.21	Others	54,952	0.21
Singapore	955,468	3.60	South Asia	1,347,585	5.08
Vietnam	725,057	2.73	Bangladesh	82,418	0.31
China	4,637,335	17.47	India	1,050,889	3.96
Hong Kong	588,335	2.22	Nepal	25,455	0.10
Japan	1,536,425	5.79	Pakistan	78,986	0.30
Korea	1,295,342	4.88	Sri Lanka	76,260	0.29
Taiwan	502,176	1.89	Others	33,577	0.13
Others	69,496	0.26	Oceania	1,021,936	3.85
Europe	6,305,945	23.75	Australia	900,460	3.39
Austria	106,278	0.40	New Zealand	118,395	0.45
Belgium	101,109	0.38	Others	3,081	0.01
Denmark	163,186	0.61	Middle East	630,243	2.37
Finland	141,692	0.53	Egypt	28,175	0.11
France	611,582	2.30	Israel	134,874	0.51
Germany	737,658	2.78	Kuwait	71,173	0.27
Ireland	63,522	0.24	Saudi Arabia	21,452	0.08
Italy	207,192	0.78	UAE	123,926	0.47
Netherlands	218,765	0.82	Others	250,643	0.94
Norway	154,049	0.58	Africa	163,008	0.61
Russia	1,746,565	6.58	South Africa	75,748	0.29
Spain	123,084	0.46	Others	87,260	0.33
Sweden	341,398	1.29			
Switzerland	199,923	0.75	Grand total	26,546,725	100.00

Sources: Department of Tourism (2015b); TAT (2015a).

Table 11.2 reveals that six countries – Malaysia, China, Japan, Korea, Russia, and India – each send more than one million annual visitors to Thailand, with several other countries (Laos, Singapore, the United States, and Australia) each sending more than 800,000 tourists. This list not only reflects the ongoing importance of Asian and European markets (and, concurrently, the rather insignificant role played by regions such as South Asia, the Middle East, and Africa), but also the emergence of China and Russia as key tourist markets for the Thai tourism industry. When examining the top sources of international tourism in Thailand, it is obvious that although there are some consistent patterns across time, Thailand has successfully diversified its tourism industry by expanding into new markets (Table 11.3).

Among the trends displayed in Table 11.3, three stand out in particular. First, the role of Malaysia has changed over the past 20 years. Despite being the leading source of tourists in Thailand since the late 1980s, Malaysia lost its top spot to China in 2012. Even though the number of Malaysian tourists visiting Thailand annually tripled between 1995 and 2013, Malaysia's share of all tourists slipped from 15.8% to 11.5% during that span. It should be noted, however, that if it were not for the meteoric rise of Chinese tourism in Thailand, Malaysia would still occupy the top spot and command a large share of the total. Second, certain markets that have for many years provided tourists to Thailand appear to be reaching saturation, or at least growing at much slower rates than the newer markets into which Thai tourism is now reaching. In particular, countries such as Japan, Korea, Taiwan, Germany, and the United Kingdom have indeed increased the number of tourists visiting Thailand, but the slowing of growth rates indicates that new opportunities for expansion are to be found mostly in alternative markets. Third, the most stark and significant trend illustrated in Table 11.3 is the rapid ascent of the Chinese and Russian tourist markets.

The sudden emergence of Russia and especially China as key tourist-generating countries is a principal reason why the number of international arrivals in Thailand has recently experienced such a steep climb. It is also clear evidence that Thailand has intensified its orientation towards conventional mass tourism, despite both the well-documented problems associated with

Table 11.3 Top ten international tourist markets in Thailand, various years

	1995			2005			2013	
Country	*Number*	*% share*	*Country*	*Number*	*% share*	*Country*	*Number*	*% share*
Malaysia	1,101,670	15.8	Malaysia	1,373,946	11.9	China	4,637,335	17.5
Japan	840,186	12.1	Japan	1,196,654	10.4	Malaysia	3,041,097	11.5
Taiwan	475,523	6.8	Korea	815,512	7.1	Russia	1,746,565	6.6
Korea	446,222	6.4	China	776,792	6.7	Japan	1,536,425	5.8
China	380,619	5.5	United Kingdom	773,843	6.7	Korea	1,295,342	4.9
United Kingdom	359,456	5.2	Singapore	650,559	5.6	India	1,050,889	4.0
Germany	355,076	5.1	United States	639,658	5.6	Laos	976,639	3.7
Singapore	346,917	5.0	Germany	441,827	3.8	Singapore	955,468	3.6
United States	328,260	4.7	Australia	428,521	3.7	United Kingdom	905,024	3.4
Hong Kong	220,791	3.2	India	381,471	3.3	Australia	900,460	3.4

Source: TAT (2015a).

package tourism in Thailand and the rhetoric of sustainability and sufficiency espoused by Thai tourism officials. In 1995, Russia was the 26th most important tourist market in Thailand, and this barely changed ten years later in 2005 when Russia sat in 25th place and accounted for only 0.89% of the share of all tourists (TAT 2015a). Nevertheless, in a span of less than a decade, Russia became the third largest source market and, in 2013, featured a 6.6% market share. As of late 2014, however, Russian tourism had declined by 5.5% from the previous year due to the falling value of the ruble, and this has had an immediate impact on areas popular with Russian tourists, such as Phuket and Pattaya (Spector 2014).

Even more spectacular than the rise of Russian tourism in Thailand is the dominant role played by China in the current inbound tourist market. In 2013 there were 11 times more arrivals from China than in 1995; with a 17.5% market share, China is now coming close to providing one-fifth of all international tourists in Thailand. Aside from rising prosperity in China, which has boosted outbound tourism and made China a rising source of international tourism generally, another reason for the additional interest in Thailand is the popular Chinese film *Lost in Thailand*, which was released in December 2014 and became the highest grossing domestic film in Chinese history. The comedy, which depicts a search by two businessmen, and a tourist they meet along the way, for their boss in Thailand, greatly enhanced familiarity with Thailand among Chinese travellers and led to an immediate increase in Chinese tourism, particularly in Chiang Mai where much of the filming took place.

The success of *Lost in Thailand* corroborates the point made by several film-tourism scholars (Grihault 2003; Hudson & Ritchie 2006) that product placement in a successful film, with the destination serving as the product itself, can be a highly effective means of generating additional tourism. However, despite its positive economic implications, the influx of Chinese tourists has been met with concern among Thai commentators and locals residents. After reviewing social networks and online forums, Li (2013) points out several complaints made about Chinese tourists in Thailand, including communication problems, littering, ignoring posted rules at tourist sites, spitting in public, and a perceived tendency to be loud or rude. In a survey of 2,220 Chiang Mai residents conducted in early 2014, 80% of respondents complained about problems caused by Chinese tourists, while 70% reported a loss of privacy and peacefulness in public areas (Zander 2014).

What is interesting about these criticisms of Chinese tourists, aside from the possibly racist underpinnings that motivate them among some observers, is that they mirror criticisms made in the 1960s and 1970s of Western mass tourists, who were likened to barbarians and golden hordes (Turner and Ash 1975). Much like other low- and middle-income countries that have had to rely on early mass tourism for economic growth, Thailand must nevertheless accept various problems associated with large groups of Chinese tourists because they will ultimately help to compensate for the maturation of traditional markets, as well as the steep decline expected in Russian tourism in 2015 due to the depreciation of the ruble in 2014–2015 (Phillips 2014).

Diversification of tourism products

The sun, sea, and sand formula of mass tourism is clearly working for Thailand, as it continues to attract large numbers of pleasure-seeking tourists. The addition of "sex" to the triple-S formula above also applies quite strongly to Thailand, which for many decades has represented the quintessential example of a sex tourism destination, particularly to those that do not know very much about the country beyond hackneyed media or popular culture depictions. While there continues to exist a very visible sex trade aimed at foreign tourists, Thailand has in recent years deliberately moved away from this type of tourism in favor of tourism products that attract a wider range of visitors, including female travellers and families. In addition to efforts to make mass tourists aware of aspects of Thai culture and society that counter the stereotypical eroticized depictions of the past, Thai government planners and entrepreneurs have also begun to promote services that broadly fall into the category known as alternative tourism. Consequently, just as there has been an intensification and expansion of package tourism in Thailand, there has also occurred a simultaneous move towards alternative tourism products aimed at long-established tourism markets in Europe, North America, and Oceania.

Alternative tourism activities seek to provide visitors with experiences that go beyond the packaged resort experience sold to millions of mass tourists. Such activities can be grouped, on the one hand, into niche activities that often enhance or supplement the mass tourism experience, thereby perpetuating rather than challenging the industry as a whole, and on the other hand, those that actually serve as viable alternatives to mass tourism. Medical tourism, whereby visitors travel to Thailand to receive specialized medical care or procedures that are much more expensive or inaccessible at home (Cohen 2008), is a niche form of tourism that contributes to the existing tourism industry, albeit in a minor way: there are roughly 400,000 medical tourists in Thailand, which not only represents a small percentage of all tourist arrivals, but is also probably an inflated number since it counts foreigners already living in Thailand that seek medical treatment (Connell 2013). Another alternative to standard 4-S tourism activities is wildlife tourism, which in Thailand involves tourist engagement with 'captured wild animals in "semi-contrived" settings, like zoos, and especially with tamed, trained or humanized ones in "fully-contrived" settings, like establishments offering elephant shows' (Cohen 2009: 100). In many ways, heightened tourist demand for experiences with animals has improved the welfare of elephants by creating income-earning opportunities for their owners (Kontogeorgopoulos 2009), but wildlife tourism is certainly far from ideal as a conservation strategy and, at a broader level, illustrates the neoliberal repackaging of nature for global consumption (Duffy & Moore 2010).

In contrast to medical and wildlife tourism, which have merely supplemented existing offerings available to conventional tourists, activities such as volunteer tourism and community-based tourism (CBT) represent more genuine alternatives to mass tourism, both in how they are framed discursively as well as practiced on a day-to-day basis. Tourists who volunteer for short periods of time (typically, two weeks to three months) interact with locals in everyday, "backstage" settings that are inaccessible to typical mass tourists. While legitimate criticisms have been leveled against volunteer tourism in Thailand, most notably its inability to tackle the structural causes of poverty and inequality in Thai society (Mostafanezhad 2013), it nonetheless stands as a possible antidote to the highly scripted and superficial nature of many (but not necessarily all) tourist–host encounters. Similarly, small-scale tourism in rural communities pursuing CBT provide tourists with intimate experiences, such as homestays, while also creating economic opportunities for locations normally bypassed by the conventional tourism industry. However, as Case study 11.1 illustrates, successful CBT in Thailand depends on several specific factors that make it difficult for many rural communities to participate.

Case study 11.1 Mae Kampong Village: a successful model of community-based tourism

In order to counter the negative consequences associated with mass tourism, Thai non-governmental organizations (NGOs), in concert with rural communities, have over the past decade pursued CBT, which aims to transfer ownership, control, and benefits of tourism to locals. For many communities, remoteness and a lack of knowledge, capital, and experience have made it difficult to participate in tourism, community-based or otherwise. One community that has overcome such challenges is Mae Kampong, a village located 50 kilometers from Chiang Mai, northern Thailand's largest city and a key national tourism destination. Mae Kampong is located 1,100 meters above sea level, which ensures a cool climate that attracts middle class Thais living in congested urban environments. Visitors are also drawn by the bucolic surroundings of the village, as well as opportunities to participate in jungle treks, watch traditional music and dance performances, and observe local religious rituals and activities. Despite containing only 312 people, and not having a paved road until 2000, Mae Kampong today receives close to 5,000 annual visitors, 80% of whom stay overnight in homestay programs. In the past decade or so, tourism activities have tripled individual incomes in Mae Kampong while also allowing village revenues to rise from US$2,730 in 2000 to US$88,737 in 2012.

Most assessments of CBT indicate that success depends on outcomes such as community ownership, environmental sustainability, cooperative profit sharing, and mutual learning, but recent studies of Mae Kampong point to three success factors not often mentioned in other studies: luck, external support, and individual leadership. Mae Kampong is lucky in both its geographical location and recent history. Mae Kampong's close proximity to a major tourist hub and its lush, tranquil surroundings make it an attractive destination, while an existing profit-sharing system established before the arrival of tourism facilitated the implementation of community participation and shared benefits. Aside from fortunate pre-existing circumstances, Mae Kampong also received external support in the form of training, marketing, and funding support from Thai government agencies. Mae Kampong also received ample support from NGOs such as the Thailand Community Based Tourism Institute, which brought the first homestay visitors and continues today to provide marketing and promotional assistance. Finally, the transformational leadership of the long-time village headman has been indispensible in the establishment and ongoing success of the village's CBT program. The leader managed a thorough and deliberate process of consultation, coordinated the efforts of external actors, and gained the trust of the villagers by demonstrating fairness, competence, and vision. Mae Kampong demonstrates that successful CBT in Thailand is indeed possible, but remains difficult for those rural communities that lack particular circumstances.

Sources: Boonratana (2011); Kontogeorgopoulos et al. (2014); Leksakundilok & Hirsch (2008); Suansri & Richards (2013)

Thailand's concurrent and sometimes contradictory promotion of both mass tourism and alternative tourism is reflected in government planning and marketing materials. Thailand's National Tourism Development Plan for 2012–2016 centers mostly around the maximization of tourism arrivals and spending through several strategies, including the development of infrastructure, the rehabilitation of tourist sites in order to accommodate more tourist arrivals, and the improvement of Thailand's international image 'so that the country will welcome a greater number of tourists who will spend more in Thailand' (Thai Foreign Office 2011). Meanwhile, the Tourism Authority of Thailand (TAT), which is the agency responsible for marketing and promotion, mentions in its 2015 Tourism Marketing Plan the need to promote 'Thainess, happiness, sustainability, as well as balanced and equitable growth' (TAT 2014). Building on the highly successful Amazing Thailand campaign first initiated in the late 1990s, the TAT in 2015 launched a campaign titled "Amazing Thailand: Discover Thainess." This latest campaign clearly targets alternative tourists interested in escaping the very same mass tourists currently being lured by other Thai government bodies. For example, the opening page of the *Discover Thainess* online promotional booklet states that

[f]or "tourists," a week might suggest days on the beach and partying by night with some sightseeing stops here and there...But for a "traveller" who looks beyond just having fun, Thailand has much more to offer such a discerning spirit.

(TAT 2015c: 2)

It would seem, therefore, that Thai tourism planners are trying to have it both ways by attracting greater numbers of mass tourists from new markets while simultaneously trying to convince "discerning" travelers from mostly Western countries that this influx of tourists has not yet managed to tarnish Thailand's attractiveness as a destination.

Conclusion

This chapter has argued that Thailand has undergone a transformation of sorts in recent years, as new source markets such as China and Russia have boosted international arrivals dramatically, thereby allowing the tourism industry to continue its decades-long trajectory of expansion and consolidation. At the same time, though, Thailand's tourism planners have countered this growth in conventional 4-S tourism with an effort to appeal to alternative tourists interested in more personalized, novel, and authentic experiences. Mass and alternative tourism may be positioned in promotional materials as dissimilar, and may draw from different tourist markets, but all international tourism in Thailand, whether it is the standard "sun, sea, sand, and sex" variety or small-scale alternative tourism, relies in many ways on a particular view of Thailand as an exotic, enchanting, and enticing destination. Further, rather than indicating contradictory market trends or diverging directions for the Thai tourism industry, the intensification of mass tourism and the development of niche alternatives have in fact gone hand in hand.

The greatest similarity or connection between the various types of tourism in Thailand is that they share several common threats to their further growth and success. First, tourism in Thailand has suffered from a lack of thoughtful environmental planning or adequate consideration of carrying capacity (Cohen 2005). As a result, the natural environments of popular tourism destinations such as Pattaya and Phuket have declined significantly in the past several decades, and in sites such as these that depend on natural resources to draw tourists, this poses a potential threat to future growth. In theory, ecotourism offers a possible way of ameliorating, or at least not further contributing to, these environmental problems, but much of what is advertised as ecotourism in Thailand fails in practice to fulfill the goals of all but the loosest definition of the term. Second, even though Thailand is generally considered a safe travel destination, recurring media accounts of tourists being robbed, cheated, or harassed has perhaps begun to threaten Thailand's otherwise safe reputation (Chinmaneevong & Siripunyawit 2014). Particularly damaging, especially in European markets, was the grisly murder in September 2014 of two British backpackers on the southern island of Koh Tao. This incident, the botched investigation, and the government's reaction (which included a proposal, never actually implemented, for tourists to wear identification bracelets) tarnished the country's image and was partly blamed for an anticipated decline in tourist arrivals in 2014.

In the immediate future, and perhaps over the long term depending on how events unfold, the greatest threat to the further growth of international tourism in Thailand is the ongoing political crisis, the roots of which lie in the 2006 military coup that ended the elected rule of Prime Minister Thaksin Shiniwatra. Since 2006, opponents of Thaksin, known as the "yellow shirts," have clashed with his "red shirt" supporters, with the highest level of violence coming in 2010 when at least 90 people died after the Thai military cracked down on red-shirt protestors calling for the government at the time to hold elections. Since 2006, Thaksin-affiliated parties have won elections twice, including in 2011 when Thaksin's sister Yingluck Shiniwatra won power in a landslide victory. In May 2014, after Yingluck was removed by Thailand's Constitutional Court from office due to allegations of corruption and abuse of power, the military acted again and dissolved the National Assembly, repealed the constitution, and declared martial law.

The current regime, known as the National Council for Peace and Order, has cracked down on dissent and, for the first month of its rule, imposed an overnight curfew. The curfew, international publicity about the coup, and the sight of military personnel in popular tourist sites scared off potential tourists and temporarily halted the rapid growth of tourism in Thailand. As a result, according to preliminary data published at the very beginning of 2015, international tourism arrivals declined in 2014 by 6.6% (*Bangkok Post* 2015). Nonetheless, if the past is any guide, this latest downturn will be followed by renewed growth, at least until the next crisis occurs. International tourist arrivals in Thailand have never, since at least 1970, declined for two straight years, and overall numbers declined on an annual basis only seven times in the past 45 years. In short, although the 2014 military coup may have dampened the explosive growth of recent years, the Thai tourism industry will likely follow its familiar pattern of two steps forward and one step back in the near future.

Key reading

Cohen, E. (2001) 'Thailand in "touristic transition",' in P. Teo, T.C. Chang and K.C. Ho (eds), *Interconnected Worlds: Tourism in Southeast Asia* (pp. 155–175). London: Routledge.

Cohen, E. (2009) 'The wild and the humanized: Animals in Thai tourism,' *Anatolia*, 20(1): 100–118.

Kontogeorgopoulos, N., Churyen, A. and Duangsaeng, V. (2015) 'Homestay tourism and the commercialization of the rural home in Thailand,' *Asia Pacific Journal of Tourism Research*, 20(1): 29–50.

Mostafanezhad, M. (2014) 'Tourism, visual culture, and the state in northern Thailand,' *Tourism Culture & Communication*, 14(1): 27–39.

Wongkit, M. and McKercher, B. (2013) 'Toward a typology of medical tourists: A case study of Thailand,' *Tourism Management*, 38: 4–12.

Relevant websites

Department of Tourism, Ministry of Tourism and Sports, Government of Thailand: www.tourism. go.th/home/content

Tourism Authority of Thailand (TAT): www.tourismthailand.org

Tourism Authority of Thailand Newsroom: www.tatnews.org

Thailand Community Based Tourism Network Coordination Center: http://cbtnetwork. org/#sthash.sxxiiUyj.dpuf: http://cbtnetwork.org

References

Amnatcharoenrit, B. (2014) 'Pattaya sees drop in 2014 tourists to 7m,' *The Nation (Bangkok)*. 12 March 12. Online. Available: www.nationmultimedia.com/business/Pattaya-sees-drop-in-2014-tourists-to-7m-30228975.html (accessed 20 November 2014).

Bangkok Post (2015) 'Tourist arrivals fall 6.6% in 2014,' *Bangkok Post*, 8 January. Online. Available: www.bangkokpost.com/business/tourism/455288/tourist-arrivals-fall-6-6-in-2014 (accessed 11 January 2015).

Boonratana, R. (2011) 'Sustaining and marketing community-based tourism: Some observations and lessons learned from Thailand,' *ABAC Journal*, 31(2): 48–61.

Butler, R.W. (1980) 'The concept of a tourist area cycle of evolution: Implications for management of resources,' *The Canadian Geographer*, 24(1): 5–12.

Chancharat, S. (2011) 'Thai tourism and economic development: The current state of research,' *Kasetsart Journal (Soc. Sci)*, 32: 340–351.

Chinmaneevong, C. and Siripunyawit, S. (2014) 'Greed: Calls for return to Thai values,' *Bangkok Post*, 6 October. Online. Available: www.bangkokpost.com/news/social/436070/greed-calls-for-return-to-thai-values. (accessed 15 December 2014).

Chon, K.S., Singh, A. and Mikula, J. (1993) 'Thailand's tourism and hotel industry,' *Cornell Hotel and Restaurant Administration Quarterly*, 34(3): 43–49.

Cohen, E. (1996) *Thai Tourism: Hill Tribes, Islands, and Open-Ended Prostitution*. Bangkok: White Lotus.

—— (2001) 'Thailand in "touristic transition",' in P. Teo, T.C. Chang and K.C. Ho (eds), *Interconnected Worlds: Tourism in Southeast Asia* (pp. 155–175). London: Routledge.

—— (2005) 'The beach of "The Beach": The politics of environmental damage in Thailand,' *Tourism Recreation Research*, 30(1): 1–17.

—— (2008) 'Medical tourism in Thailand,' in E. Cohen (ed.), *Explorations in Thai Tourism* (pp. 225–255). Bingley: Emerald.

—— (2009) 'The wild and the humanized: Animals in Thai tourism,' *Anatolia*, 20(1): 100–118.

Connell, J. (2013) 'Contemporary medical tourism: Conceptualisation, culture and commodification,' *Tourism Management*, 34: 1–13.

Department of Tourism (2015a) 'Internal tourism 2013 (by region),' *Visitor Statistics 2013*, Ministry of Tourism and Sport, Government of Thailand. Online. Available www.tourism.go.th/home/details/11/221/621 (accessed 2 January 2015).

—— (2015b) 'International tourist arrivals to Thailand 2013 (by nationality),' *Visitor Statistics 2013*, Ministry of Tourism and Sport, Government of Thailand. Online. Available: www.tourism.go.th/home/details/11/221/621 (accessed 2 January 2015).

Doner, R.F. (2009) *The Politics of Uneven Development: Thailand's Economic Growth in Comparative Perspective*. Cambridge: Cambridge University Press.

Duffy, R. and Moore, L. (2010) 'Neoliberalising nature? Elephant-back tourism in Thailand and Botswana,' *Antipode*, 42(3): 742–766.

Grihault, N. (2003) 'Film tourism: The global picture,' *Travel & Tourism Analyst*, 5: 1–22.

Hudson, S. and Ritchie, J.B. (2006) 'Promoting destinations via film tourism: An empirical identification of supporting marketing initiatives,' *Journal of Travel Research*, 44(4): 387–396.

Kontogeorgopoulos, N. (2009) 'Wildlife tourism in semi-captive settings: A case study of elephant camps in northern Thailand,' *Current Issues in Tourism*, 12(5–6): 429–449.

Kontogeorgopoulos, N., Churyen, A. and Duangsaeng, V. (2014) 'Success factors in community-based tourism in Thailand: The role of luck, external support, and local leadership,' *Tourism Planning & Development*, 11(1): 106–124.

Leksakundilok, A. and Hirsch, P. (2008) 'Community-based ecotourism in Thailand,' in J. Connell and B. Rugendyke (eds), *Tourism at the Grassroots: Villagers and Visitors in the Asia-Pacific* (pp. 214–235). London: Routledge.

Li, A. (2013) 'Chiang Mai locals shocked by "rude" Chinese tourists,' *South China Morning Post*, 28 February. Online. Available: www.scmp.com/news/china/article/1162131/chiang-mai-locals-shocked-rude-chinese-tourists?page=all (accessed 15 December 2014).

Meyer, W. (1988) *Beyond the Mask*. Saarbrticken: Verlag Breitenbach.

Mostafanezhad, M. (2013) 'The politics of aesthetics in volunteer tourism,' *Annals of Tourism Research*, 43: 150–169.

Ouyyanont, P. (2001) 'The Vietnam War and tourism in Bangkok's development, 1960–70,' *Southeast Asian Studies*, 39(2): 157–187.

Phillips, J. (2014) 'Chinese tourists to bring smiles back to Thailand,' *CNBC Travel*, 23 December. Online. Available: www.cnbc.com/id/102287777# (accessed 20 November 2014).

Spector, D. (2014) 'The Russians aren't feasting like monarchs in Thailand anymore,' *Business Insider*. 18 December. Online. Available: www.businessinsider.com/russian-tourists-market-slumps-in-thailand-2014-12 (accessed 20 November 2014).

Suansri, P. and Richards, P. (2013) 'A case study of community-based tourism in Thailand,' in World Tourism Organization, *Domestic Tourism in Asia and the Pacific* (pp. 529–551). Madrid: UNWTO.

Thai Foreign Office (2011) 'Thailand's national tourism development plan,' Government Public Relations Department, Office of the Prime Minister. Online. Available: http://thailand.prd.go.th/view_news.php?id=5525&a=2 (accessed 15 December 2014).

Tourism Authority of Thailand (TAT) (1998) *Statistical Report 1998*. Bangkok: TAT.

—— (2014) 'TAT to make "Thainess" and "Happiness" core themes of Tourism Marketing Plan for 2015,' *TAT Intelligence Center*. Online. Available: http://marketingdatabase.tat.or.th/ewt_news.php?nid=1751&filename=default_en (accessed 3 January 2015).

—— (2015a) 'Yearly international tourist arrivals to Thailand by nationality: international tourist arrivals to Thailand (port of entry),' TAT Intelligence Center. Online. Available: http://marketingdatabase.tat.or.th/ewt_news.php?nid=1612 (accessed 5 January 2015).

—— (2015b) 'Tourism receipts from international tourist arrivals: Tourism receipts from international tourists,' TAT Intelligence Center. Online. Available: http://marketingdatabase.tat.or.th/ewt_news.php?nid=1614 (accessed 5 January 2015).

—— (2015c) *Discover Thainess*. Online. Available: http://discoverthainess.tourismthailand.org/discoverthainessebook/FLASH/index.html (accessed 15 January 2015).

Turner, A. and Ash, J. (1975) *The Golden Hordes: International Tourism and the Pleasure Periphery*. New York: St. Martin's Press.

United Nations World Tourism Organization (UNWTO) (2014) *UNWTO Tourism Highlights, 2014 Edition*. Online. Available: http://mkt.unwto.org/publication/unwto-tourism-highlights-2014-edition (accessed 30 November 2014).

World Bank (2015) 'International tourism, number of arrivals,' World Development Indicators. Online. Available: http://data.worldbank.org/indicator/ST.INT.ARVL?order=wbapi_data_value_2010+wbapi_data_value+wbapi_data_value-first&sort=desc (accessed 10 January 2015).

World Tourism Organization (WTO) (1996) *Tourism Highlights 1996*. Madrid: WTO.

World Travel and Tourism Council (WTTC) (2014) 'Travel & tourism economic impact 2014 Thailand.' Online. Available: www.wttc.org/-/media/files/reports/economic%20impact%20research/country%20reports/thailand2014.pdf (accessed 20 December 2014).

—— (2015) 'Visitor exports,' Economic Data Search Tool. Online. Available: www.wttc.org/focus/research-for-action/economic-data-search-tool (accessed 11 January 2015).

Zander, R. (2014) 'Survey says … Chinese tourists wearing out their welcome in Chiang Mai,' *Siam and Beyond*. 20 February. Online. Available: http://siamandbeyond.com/survey-says-chinese-tourists-wearing-welcome-chiang-mai (accessed 20 January 2015).

12

TOURISM IN MALAYSIA

Ghazali Musa & Thinaranjeney Thirumoorthi

Introduction

Malaysia, formerly known as the Federation of Malaya, covers a land area of 329,847km², neighbouring Singapore, Thailand, Brunei and Indonesia, all of whose economies have been growing intensely in the recent decades. Its two main regions, Peninsular Malaysia and East Malaysia, consist of 13 states and three federal territories: Wilayah Persekutuan, Putrajaya and Labuan. A total of 29.8 million people live in Malaysia, represented by Malays (67.4%), Chinese (24.6%), Indians (7.3%) and others (0.7%) (Department of Statistics Malaysia 2011). Although Malay is the country's official language, English is widely used in daily life, especially in business communications, along with some Chinese and Indian dialects. Malaysia is a constitutional monarchy headed by the chief of state (the king) while the prime minister is the head of the ruling government.

The tourism industry is not only one of the biggest contributors to the country's economy, but also the second largest source of foreign exchange (Ismail & Lai 2015). Pemandu (2013) forecast that the industry would contribute MYR103.6 billion in gross national income (GNI) by 2020. Tourism National Key Economic Areas (NKEAs) defined tourism as leisure and tourism businesses which include the sub-sectors of accommodation, shopping, tourism products (i.e. ecotourism, cruise tourism and other related activities such as spa and wellness), food and beverage and inbound and domestic transportation (Pemandu 2013: 317). Under the Ministry of Tourism and Culture, the promotion board, which is widely known as Tourism Malaysia, promotes the country's tourism activities using the successful tagline of 'Malaysia Truly Asia'.

Malaysia recorded 25.7 million tourist arrivals in 2013, with the total receipt of MYR65.4 billion (Tourism Malaysia 2015). There was a 10.3% increase in tourist arrivals from January to August 2014, compared to the same period in 2013 (Arukesamy 2015). Despite facing major challenges, which will be discussed in detail later, the tourism industry continues to grow at a rapid pace, hosting 27.4 million tourists in 2014. Euromonitor International (2014b) ranked Kuala Lumpur as the sixth top city destination in 2012. The country was also ranked fourth for the World's Top Retirement Havens in 2015 (International Living 2015). Crescent Rating (2014) ranked Malaysia as a top halal-friendly destination ahead of the United Arab Emirates, Turkey, Indonesia and Saudi Arabia.

The tourism industry has grown in leaps and bounds from the 1960s, and today Malaysia is a well-known tourist destination that offers diverse natural and cultural attractions. Malaysia was ranked 12th on the international tourist arrivals list by country in 2014 (27.4 million), with a growth of 6.7% compared to 2013 (Khunton 2015). The economic crisis in the late 1990s only paved the way for both public and private sectors to creatively explore the tourism industry in terms of its resilience, development and potential expansion. Various factors have affected the healthy growth of the tourism industry over the years, such as policies by the government, development of infrastructure and facilities, transportation and tourism marketing and promotion.

Tourist arrivals

Tourist arrivals to Malaysia have continued to grow since 2010. A total of 27.4 million tourists visited the country in 2014 compared to 24.6 million in 2010, with a corresponding increase in tourism incomes (Table 12.1). Visit Malaysia Year 2014 was extended to Malaysia Year of Festivals (MyFest) in 2015, with the target to host 29.4 million tourists (*Malay Mail Online* 2015a). The tourism industry is expected to expand to three times its current size, targeting 36 million tourists in 2020, bringing in MYR3 billion income per week (Pemandu 2013).

In terms of tourist arrivals, Malaysia's top ten markets are Singapore, Indonesia, China, Thailand, Brunei, India, the Philippines, Japan, Australia and Britain (*Star Online* 2014a). Excellent transportation networks within the ASEAN region mean over 85% of tourists in the country are regional tourists who visit Malaysia mainly for short stays. The highest tourist arrival growth was also from regional ASEAN countries: Brunei (+41.5%), Vietnam (+28.9%), the Philippines (+21.3%), Indonesia (+17.9%), Laos (+14.4%), Thailand (+12.6%), Cambodia (+11.8%) and Singapore (+10.8%) (*Star Online* 2014a).

Table 12.1 Malaysian tourist arrivals and receipts

Year	Tourists arrivals (million)	Receipts (MYR) (billion)
2014	27.4★	–
2013	25.72	65.44
2012	25.03	60.6
2011	24.71	58.3
2010	24.58	56.5
2009	23.65	53.4
2008	22.05	49.6
2007	20.97	46.1
2006	17.55	36.3
2005	16.43	32.0
2004	15.70	29.7
2003	10.58	21.3
2002	13.29	25.8
2001	12.78	24.2
2000	10.22	17.6

Sources: Tourism Malaysia (2015a); Ismail and Lai (2015).
Note: ★Preliminary estimate.

Domestic tourism

Tourism Malaysia not only focuses on attracting international tourists but also strives to enhance domestic tourism. The Asian Economic Crisis in the late 1990s witnessed a change in the government initiative to develop and promote domestic tourism, efforts which not only reduced the flow of money to foreign countries, but also sustained tourism businesses within the country. The 'Cuti-Cuti Malaysia' campaign was launched in 1999 to encourage local people to travel domestically, particularly going back to their hometowns (balik kampung). It was later renamed Zoom Malaysia (2008) and further termed as the Cuti-Cuti 1Malaysia campaign (Gaya Travel 2015).

A total of 141.4 million domestic tourists were recorded in 2012, which increased to 152.9 million in 2013. This is in line with the number of trips which increased from 174.4 million trips in 2012 to 193.3 million trips in 2013 (Table 12.2). In 2013 domestic tourism contributed MYR54 billion to the economy. Visitors from urban areas (69.5%) constituted the majority of domestic tourists, while those from rural areas comprised 30.5%. From the total domestic visitors in 2013, the excursionists and tourists were 64.4% and 35.6% respectively (Department of Statistics Malaysia 2013).

The main travel purpose was to visit friends and family (44.0%), followed by shopping (30.1%), relaxation (14.1%), entertainment/special events (3.1%) and medical and personal care (2.8%). The breakdown of expenditures were shopping (29.0%), transportation (24.0%), food and beverages (13.9%) and accommodation (12.2%). The top five states visited by tourists are Perak (6,011 million), Johor (5,962 million), Selangor (5,563 million), Pahang (4,725 million) and Kedah (4,477 million) (Department of Statistics Malaysia 2013). The Kuala Lumpur City Hall forecasted 4.9 million domestic tourists to visit Kuala Lumpur in 2014, an increase from 4.7 million in 2012 (*Star Online* 2014b).

High-yield tourism

Perhaps the most striking characteristics of Malaysian inbound tourism are the relatively shorter stays by tourists and lower yield compared with their neighbouring countries of Singapore and Thailand (Malaysia's main tourism competitors). These aspects are among the main challenges in Malaysian tourism. Malaysia's yield per tourist is MYR2,260, much lower than the neighbouring countries of Singapore (MYR3,106) and Thailand (MYR3,785) (Pemandu 2013). Pemandu (2013) highlights the contributing factors to Malaysian tourism's low yield as a low average length of stay (Malaysia = 10 days, Thailand = 14 days), low spending per day (except for tourists from the Middle East) and the predominantly short-haul travel markets.

Table 12.2 Malaysian domestic tourism statistics

	2012	2013
Total domestic tourists	141.4 million	152.9 million
Urban	97.4 million	106.3 million
Rural	44.1 million	46.6 million
Number of trips	174.4 million	193.3 million
Receipts	MYR47.8 billion	MYR54.0 billion
Average length of stay	2.53 days	2.56 days
Average trips per visitor	1.23	1.26

Source: Department of Statistics Malaysia (2013).

Even though Malaysia attracts more tourists than the other two countries, the growth in terms of yield is relatively low. The ratio for tourist arrivals and yield is 1:3 for both Thailand and Singapore, while for Malaysia it is 1:2.

High-yield tourism could be achieved from efforts to attract more high-spending tourists and at the same time making sure they extend their stay in the country. Two well-established high-spending tourist markets for Malaysia are MICE (meetings, incentives, conventions and exhibitions) and the Middle Eastern markets. Complementary products to them are premium outlets for shopping and the availability of luxury and boutique hotels. Other tourists who stay longer are Malaysia My Second Home (MM2H) participants, medical tourists, ecotourists and elderly tourists. These are markets which should be emphasized in the development and marketing of high-yield tourism in Malaysia.

Perhaps the main market to be targeted for high-yield tourism is international business tourists who spend much more despite their usually short stay (*Malaysia Hotel News* 2011), spending MYR7,418 per trip compared with leisure tourists' spend of MYR2,257. They also spend over three times more per day (MYR1,268) as compared to the latter (MYR337). Malaysia received 1,278,014 business tourists in 2010 who spent a total of MYR10.6 billion.

Among the initiatives taken by the Ministry of Tourism and Culture was the establishment of the MyCEB (Malaysia Convention & Exhibition Bureau) in 2009, an effort to enhance tourism provision for the international MICE market (*Malaysia Hotel News* 2011; MyCEB 2013). The 'Malaysia – Asia's Business Events Hub' tagline promoted by MyCEB reflects the country as an excellent venue for events and meetings. In 2012, the country was ranked as 35th in the International Congress and Convention Association (ICCA) country rankings (ICCA 2012). In the same year, MyCEB secured 26 associations and 109 corporate incentive groups representing 61,086 delegates, with an economic value of RM634.6 million (US$209.4 million). It also assisted 112 meetings and conventions, 15 exhibitions and 128 corporate incentive groups, which contributed an estimated economic impact of RM1.2 billion (US$396 million) to Malaysia (MyCEB 2013). Among the main convention centres in the country are the Kuala Lumpur Convention Centre, the Borneo Convention Centre, the Putrajaya International Convention Centre and the Sunway Convention & Exhibition Centre. Recently, the Kuala Lumpur Convention Centre received the 'Best MICE Experience' award at the Best of Malaysia Awards 2014 (ICCA 2014a). Malaysia will be hosting the 9th World Urban Forum 2018 (WUF9) in April 2018 catering to about 10,000 international delegates (ICCA 2014b).

Another high-yield market segment targeted by Tourism Malaysia is tourists from Middle Eastern countries. They visit Malaysia for various reasons, such as the availability of halal food, sufficient amenities to perform prayers, it being a moderate Muslim country, abundance of shopping centres with air-conditioning and also the climate (*Travel and Tourism News* (TTN) 2010; Maelzer 2013). Maelzer (2013) reported that almost 33.3% of the total tourists visiting Malaysia (excluding those from Singapore) in 2012 were from Gulf countries. The number of tourists from the Gulf countries and Iran is growing rapidly, from fewer than 27,000 when Malaysia initially started receiving tourists from these countries (*Sunday Daily* 2014) to 324,437 tourists in 2013 (UAE = 19,830, Qatar = 7,264 and Jordon = 6,278) and 370,535 in 2012 (*Rakyat Post* 2014). In line with Tourism Malaysia's efforts, a guidebook was launched by the Penang state government for Muslim tourists. *Experience Penang: A Muslim Travel Guide 2014* consists of halal eateries and an accommodation list with halal-certified kitchens (*Rakyat Post* 2014). Tourism Malaysia acknowledges the emergence of global elites who are 'high-income consumers'. Melaka getaway, 1Malaysia Contemporary Art Tourism and the Johor Premium Outlet are among the projects organized to attract more high-end consumers (*Cultural Diplomacy News* 2014; Tourism Malaysia 2011).

Factors that affect the tourism industry in Malaysia

Airline transportation in Malaysia has seen intense competition between the Malaysian Airline System (MAS) and AirAsia. MAS is the national carrier, which operates to various countries throughout Asia, the Middle East, Europe and Australasia. The airline has suffered massive financial losses, and the major incidents involving MH370 (missing flight from Kuala Lumpur to Beijing) and MH17 (shot down near the Russia–Ukraine border) in 2014 have affected passengers' confidence and the airline's image, which subsequently considerably reduced its flights' load factors. At the time of writing MAS is undergoing major restructuring with actions which include slashing non-profitable international routes, cutting 6,000 jobs, pruning frequency patterns and aircraft sizes, trimming suppliers and eliminating other sources of losses (*New Straits Times Online* 2015). The new MAS CEO, Christoph Muller, whose track record of successful turnarounds includes Ireland's Aer Lingus and Lufthansa, stated that the airline is technically bankrupt, and expected it to take three years before it became profitable again (*New Straits Times Online* 2015).

On the other hand, AirAsia is a highly successful airline, contributing most to the growth of the tourism industry in Malaysia, and perhaps to several other Asian countries. It started operating in 1996, aiming to provide a cheaper air travel alternative, using the tagline 'Now Everyone Can Fly'. Skytrax awarded AirAsia the world's best low-cost carrier (LCC) award for seven consecutive years. AirAsia has sister companies in many countries under the names of AirAsia India, AirAsia Japan, Indonesia AirAsia, Philippines AirAsia and Thai AirAsia. Long-haul flights are operated under AirAsia X. The airline continues to expand its routes, mainly within Asia, which is partly responsible for the upsurge in tourist arrivals not only to Malaysia, but also other parts of the Asian region.

Malaysian Airports has formed partnerships with 55 airlines, offering 117 airline routes (Malaysian Airports Holdings Berhad 2015b). In 2014, a total of 48,930,409 passengers travelled via Kuala Lumpur International Airport (KLIA) from 340,821 aircraft movements (take-offs and landings) (Malaysian Airports Holdings Berhad 2015a). Within Malaysia, other airlines that have become competitors to AirAsia are Firefly and Malindo Airlines.

Among the latest airport infrastructure developments are the new low-cost terminal Kuala Lumpur International Airport 2 (KLIA2) in Sepang, which has the capacity of handling 45 million passengers yearly; the development of mass rapid transit; and the extension of the light rapid transport, which all increase the comfort and flexibility for both residents and tourists traveling around the city centre. Under the Greater Kuala Lumpur plan, walkways will be built linking Bukit Bintang and Kuala Lumpur City Centre, which houses many shopping malls.

Malaysia's strategic location within Southeast Asia enables tourists to easily visit the country, with many direct flights from various destinations. In addition, Singapore, Thailand, Indonesia and Brunei have access to the country via road. Access to public transport, such as bus, train and taxi, also enables tourists to travel easily into and within the country.

Malaysia is an economical option for tourists because it is affordable to travel in the country. Kuala Lumpur ranked as the seventh cheapest city in the world to travel to (*Telegraph* 2015). At the same time, CNN placed Kuala Lumpur as the fourth best shopping city in the world, after New York, London and Tokyo (Kim 2014). Thus, the city provides a wide range of options in terms of products and services that cater to both the budget-conscious and the high-end tourist.

Malaysia was ranked 33rd in the Global Peace Index for 2014 and second after Singapore among the ASEAN countries. The score has declined compared to 2012 (20th) due to terrorist activity and a series of kidnappings and political instability (*Malay Mail Online* 2014a). Some Malaysians are linked to the Islamic State of Iraq and Syria (ISIS) group, and Sulu militant activity in Lahad Datu, Sabah, contributed to the drop of the peace index score. Nevertheless, the country is generally regarded as safe for tourists and Malaysia is still considered as a moderate Islamic country.

The tourism industry is identified as one of the 12 NKEAs and the government is encouraging and supporting various tourism projects and developments. Tourism Malaysia, Malaysia Healthcare Tourism Council (MHTC) and MyCEB were formed to provide a wide range of tourism offerings to tourists. The government encourages the industry's development by providing tax exemptions. The hotel industry is given a 60% exemption on investment tax and 70% on statutory income (Ministry of International Trade and Industry (MITI) 2013). The establishment of hotels (budget and high-end), renovation and tourism projects are entitled to incentives based on the *Promotion of Investment Act* (1986) (Malaysian Investment Development Authority (MIDA) 2015).

Tourism products and services

Kuala Lumpur is one of the premier shopping destinations in the world. It has numerous shopping malls, among which are Mid Valley Mega Mall and The Gardens, Sunway Pyramid, One Utama, Suria KLCC, Pavilion, Lot 10, Fahrenheit 88, Star Hill Gallery, The Mines, Gurney Plaza and Plaza Lowyat. The main three shopping carnivals are 1Malaysia GP Sale (March), 1Malaysia Mega Sale Carnival (June) and 1Malaysia Year-End Sale (November). Shopping currently represents 28% of total tourist receipts, but Pemandu (2013) is aiming to increase it to 35% by 2020, which will contribute MYR9.9 billion to the country's economy. Pemandu (2013) added that duty-free shopping destinations need to be created as imported products are expensive compared to Singapore and Hong Kong due to import taxes. In addition, the major shopping malls will be better connected. Currently there is a lack of connectivity with poor traffic flow. Linking the malls through pedestrian walks and integrated transportation will provide a convenient atmosphere for the shoppers and tourists. Pemandu (2013) also expressed the need to establish premium outlets to provide more options and choices for shoppers.

Malaysia is rich with nature. Among the top ecotourism hotspots in the country are Mulu Caves National Park (Sarawak), Penang National Park, Teluk Bahang (Penang), Forest Research Institute Malaysia (FRIM) (Selangor), Royal Belum State Park (Perak), Taman Negara, Cameron Highlands (Pahang) and Pulau Perhentian (Terengganu) (*Star Online* 2014c). A total of 22 high-potential parks are promoted to create awareness of biodiversity available in both Peninsular Malaysia and Borneo (Gaya Travel 2015). Nature provides an opportunity for tourists to engage in various activities. Currently, many developments place emphasis on sites' protection to ensure sustainable tourism activities.

Malaysia is also well known for scuba diving destinations such as Sipadan, Layang Layang and Mabul (Musa 2002, 2011; Musa *et al.* 2006). Other secondary scuba diving attractions are Redang, Perhentian, Tioman, Tenggol and Langkawi (Ong & Musa 2012). The seas in Sabah and the east coast of Peninsular Malaysia are famous for white sandy beaches, crystal-clear underwater visibility and an abundance of marine life (Thirumoorthi *et al.* 2013). They are also known for underwater attractions such as deep dives, coral blocks, drift dives and sloping reefs (Tourism Malaysia 2014d).

The MM2H program was launched in 2002 to encourage foreigners to live or retire in the country. The successful candidates are given a ten-year renewable social visit pass. The applicants are expected to have a fixed deposit of MYR500,000 and a MYR10,000 monthly offshore income, for they will not be able to work while residing in Malaysia (Ministry of Tourism and Culture Malaysia 2014). However, they are allowed to invest and participate in businesses. Among the factors attracting foreigners to stay in Malaysia under the MM2H program are cheap living costs, warm weather, culture and language, government support, recreational and entertainment opportunities and political stability (Wong & Musa 2014). The top three nationalities who retire to Malaysia are Japanese, British and Australian (Wong 2015; Wong & Musa 2015; Abdul-Aziz *et al.* 2014). Among the Japanese, Malaysia is the number one retirement destination abroad (Ono 2008; Wong 2015; Lee 2014; Koh 2013).

Medical tourism boomed after the recession in 1997, soon after which the MHTC was formed to attract medical tourists to the country, to sustain ailing private hospital businesses. Thailand, Singapore and India are Malaysia's main competitors in the region, all of which offer first-class medical services at a relatively cheaper cost than is available in the West (Musa *et al.* 2012; Wong & Musa 2013). Numerous private hospitals with Joint Commission International and the Malaysian Society for Quality in Health accreditations have participated in medical tourism, such as Gleneagles, Pantai Hospital, Prince Court Medical Centre, Sunway Medical Centre, Mahkota Medical Centre and Penang Adventist Hospital. Medical tourists prefer to seek treatment in Malaysia due to low costs, qualified physicians and nurses, state-of-the-art technology, shorter waiting times and strategic location (Musa *et al.* 2011; Wong & Musa 2013). The majority of Malaysian medical tourists come from Indonesia owing to the geographical and cultural proximity (Ormond & Sulianti 2014).

Homestay is a program that was initiated along with the development of community-based tourism which encourages the involvement of local people. This program enables international tourists to experience local culture and way of life, while simultaneously improving the livelihood of local people by generating additional income (*Cultural Diplomacy News* 2014). The homestay program is also promoted aggressively to domestic tourists, offering a new experience of staying in traditional villages among those who live in urban areas (Gaya Travel 2015). The tourists stay with the hosts, who they regard as foster parents, and participate in activities such as visiting paddy fields, fruit and vegetable farms, fishing and attending traditional cultural performances (Musa *et al.* 2010).

Malaysia is also known for golf tourism and the number of golf facilities in the country has increased over the years. Among the well-known golf clubs are Kota Permai Golf and Country Club, The Royal Selangor Golf Club, Sultan Abdul Aziz Shah Golf Club, Gunung Raya Golf Resort, Saujana Golf and Country Club, Kelab Golf Sarawak and Sutera Harbour Golf and Country Club (Tourism Malaysia 2012). Recently, cycling tourism has been promoted by Tourism Malaysia through cycling packages with the aim to attract both domestic and international tourists. Cuti-Cuti 1Malaysia Bike Ride@Putrajaya has three categories – Family Fun Ride, Fun Ride Challenge and BMX Tourism Sprint – which attracted 2,500 cyclists (Tourism Malaysia 2014b).

The Malaysia Cruise Council (MCC) was established to develop cruise tourism. The MCC is planning to develop 'Straits Riviera', which consists of six ports – Penang, Port Klang, Kota Kinabalu, Langkawi, Melaka, Kuching – and other secondary ports (Tourism Malaysia 2014a). Malaysia also offers luxury holidays to high-end tourists. Among the famous luxury brands of hotels and resorts are Four Seasons, The Westin Langkawi Resort and Spa, Datai Langkawi, the Bon Ton, Hilton KL, Pangkor Laut Resort, Hilton Batang Ai Longhouse Resort, Palace of the Golden Horses, Shangri-La Kuala Lumpur, Shangri-La's Tanjung Aru Resort and Spa, Mandarin Oriental, Le Meridien (Tourism Malaysia 2012).

Tourism marketing and promotion

Tourism Malaysia engages in aggressive promotional activities to attract more tourists to visit the country. The Malaysia Truly Asia campaign has contributed immensely to the increase in arrivals. The tagline has been very successful and has continued to be relevant even though a decade has passed since it was initiated. Tourism Malaysia has participated in international travel trade events such as the World Travel Market (WTM), the Lord Mayor Show parade and the Arabian Travel Market to create awareness about Malaysia internationally. The Malaysia Year of Festivals ('MyFEST 2015') was launched at the London WTM 2014 and in Berlin on March 2015 (Tourism Malaysia 2014c). In London, double-decker buses and taxi exteriors were painted with the country's iconic destinations. The *Exploring Malaysia* documentary was also launched at the London WTM and aired by the National Geographic Channel. In addition, Tourism Malaysia participated in the Lord Mayor Show 2014 parade in conjunction with the appointment of the new mayor in London. This event was widely covered by the BBC and local newspapers such as the *Sunday Times, Evening Standard, Financial Times* and *Daily Telegraph* (Tourism Malaysia 2014c).

Apart from promoting the country using traditional media such as television, newspapers, magazines, events, radio, trade fairs, brochures and pamphlets, Tourism Malaysia also uses digital marketing extensively. Facebook, Twitter, Blog, Flickr, WebTV and YouTube are among the online tools used by Tourism Malaysia. Tourism Malaysia's website offers various information ranging from places, experiences, events, packages, travel agents, an image gallery, a tourism directory, mobile applications, packages and promotions, a trip planner, programs and travel bookings for flights, hotels, car rentals and buses. The website also contains information about other tourism offerings or products such as MM2H, medical tourism, education tourism, golf tourism, and conventions and exhibitions. Contact information of local tourism offices, marketing representatives, overseas offices and tourist information centres are provided on the website. Cuti-Cuti 1Malaysia (CC1M) Facebook page has reached two million likes or followers.

The Malaysia Trip Planner is a travel application introduced by Tourism Malaysia which assists and organizes travel plans and itineraries that can be shared with others through social networking sites like Facebook and Twitter (Tourism Malaysia 2013). Users with smartphones are able to download other applications such as Truly Asia and go2homestay.com from the Tourism Malaysia website (Gaya Travel 2015). Online tools such as Mobile and YouTube, Online Display and Google Search allow more people to receive Malaysian tourism promotions. Apart from the Cuti-Cuti 1Malaysia page on Facebook, ShareMy is another social networking platform created by Tourism Malaysia which enables one to share his/her experience(s), which indirectly becomes a source of information to others (Tourism Malaysia 2013). Similarly, WebTV (online TV) like TrulyAsia.TV and Malaysia Tourism TV (MyTTV) showcase events in Malaysia and provide other information pertaining to tourism, such as places to visit, events and festivals (Tourism Malaysia 2013).

Tourism policies and strategies

Malaysian policy is focused on increasing tourist arrivals. The country is considering waiving visas for tourists from China (Arukesamy 2015; *Malay Mail Online* 2015a). This move is necessary to increase Chinese tourists, who are currently the world's biggest tourism market. Other ASEAN competitors – Cambodia, Indonesia, Laos, Vietnam, Thailand and the Philippines – have already implemented this policy (*Malay Mail Online* 2015a). To achieve the targeted tourist number of 36 million in 2020, other than China focus should also be given to India, which has a large and growing middle-class population. One of the ways to attract these two major markets is to relax visa policies (*Sunday Daily* 2014).

The local airlines (MAS, AirAsia, Firefly) are expected to benefit from the ASEAN open sky agreement, which means they can determine flight frequency, capacity and types of aircraft without permission from the airline authorities (*Malaysian Insider* 2013). This will allow the airlines to increase the number of routes and flights, particularly to high-yield destinations.

The government supports domestic tourism and encourages Malaysians to travel within the country. Directives were issued in conjunction with the Cuti-Cuti 1Malaysia campaign. During the early 2000s, public sector employees were entitled to leave on the first and the third Saturday of every month. In July 2005, leave for five working days was announced by the government in an effort to boost domestic tourism (Gaya Travel 2015).

The high broadband penetration rate in Malaysia (Euromonitor International 2014a) has also contributed to the growing use of online distribution channels. Tourists increasingly purchase Malaysian airline tickets, hotels and tour packages online (*Malay Mail Online* 2015a).

Tourists from the Middle East are known as a high-yield market who travel in groups, particularly with family. Some hotels have extended the meal time and operation hours of retail outlets to cater to tourists from the Middle East (Chandran 2009). Unlike the older generation who opt for leisure and shopping, the younger generation from this region prefer to engage in golfing, jungle trekking and scuba diving. They are also open to travel to other parts of the country like Sabah and Sarawak rather than just spending time in Kuala Lumpur (Chandran 2009). This requires the service providers to adjust their services according to the demands of customers. Tourism packages offered to younger Middle Eastern tourists may emphasize nature and adventure activities. The Islamic Tourism Centre (ITC) was formed in 2009 to assist Tourism Malaysia, particularly on issues pertaining to Islamic tourism. The ITC is an initiative to market Malaysia as an Islamic tourism hub, a Muslim-friendly destination. Marketing intelligence will be conducted and appropriate strategies will be devised to cater to Muslim tourists (Islamic Tourism Centre of Malaysia 2015).

Based on the 10th Malaysia Plan, strategies to increase tourist arrivals are focused on promoting to various market segments (ecotourism, family fun, culture diversity) and establishing partnerships between the public sector and the private sector to develop tourism products such as Legoland and Kidzania. In addition, tourism sites need to be maintained and preserved, engage in promotional activities in the main markets and develop more iconic tourism products such as Geopark Langkawi, Georgetown, Sipadan Island, Kinabalu Park, Sarawak Cultural Village and Gunung Mulu National Park (Economic Planning Unit 2010).

Challenges and threats

Despite substantial growth, Malaysia faces many challenges. The attitude of service providers is vital as it affect tourists' perception of the country. Any negative experience affects the overall image of the country. For instance, taxi drivers top the list of unpleasant tourist experiences in the country, for over-charging (do not use the meter) and being selective in choosing customers according to their convenience (*Malay Mail Online* 2014c). Taxi touts are common at the airports and several locations in the Malaysian cities. The Road Transport Department, Land Public Transport Commission, Malaysia Airports Bhd and Transport Ministry must make a joint effort to prevent these damaging activities.

Many service providers such as hotels are hiring non-Malaysians to work in their establishments, mostly in the frontline. Some of these employees are not able to communicate in English fluently, and their existence is sometimes regarded as not representative of Malaysian hospitality. Tourists tend to share these negative experiences with others, particularly on social networking sites.

As noted above, 2014 was a difficult year for MAS. The MAS flight MH370 scheduled to Beijing with 239 passengers and crews disappeared on 8 March 2014. In January 2015, the

Department of Civil Aviation Malaysia declared the occurrence to be an accident (Ministry of Communications and Multimedia Malaysia 2015). Despite efforts taken by Australia, Malaysia and other countries to search for the missing plane, its location is yet to be identified. Additionally, flight MH17 (Amsterdam to Kuala Lumpur) was shot down on 17 July 2014 near the Ukraine–Russia border. All 298 passengers were killed in the incident. Arrivals from China declined (estimated at 540,000) after the MH370 incident (Arukesamy 2015). Efforts to increase the number of tourists and rebrand were dampened after the second air disaster. The safety of MAS became a concern to potential tourists not only from China but also from other parts of the world, which resulted in many flight cancellations that were later refunded by MAS (*Express Tribune* 2014a). There was international criticism over both crises, and they were considered to be poorly handled by both the airline and the Malaysian government (*Express Tribune* 2014b).

Another accident involved an AirAsia Indonesia flight (QZ8501) from Surabaya to Singapore which carried 162 passengers and crashed into the Java Sea on 28 December 2014. Even though the flight belonged to the sister company AirAsia, it is still linked to Malaysia. The CEO of AirAsia, Tony Fernandez, was commended on how he dealt with the crisis. Fernandez communicated with the victims' families and provided emotional support in addition to taking full responsibility after the incident (Burt 2015). Besides that, Fernandez utilized the social network Twitter (Einhorn 2015) to provide updates on the status of the crisis, keeping everyone informed. He took charge of crisis communication instead of assigning the crisis management task to public relations professionals. An information center was initiated after the crisis center was closed in order to assist victims' families (AirAsia Berhad 2015). Tony Fernandez's approach was compared with how MAS handled its crises. The latter's failure to provide accurate and timely information has tarnished its image and reputation as an airline.

Other non-tourism-related issues such as safety, natural disasters, government transparency and human rights also affect the destination image of Malaysia. Unsafe travel destinations are less likely to be visited by tourists. A few kidnapping cases were reported in Borneo which is recognized for its scuba diving. This resulted in the cancellation of 76 flights from China to Kota Kinabalu and travel guidance was issued by the United States, Germany and the United Kingdom warning of the danger of visiting Sabah (*Star Online* 2014d). In Kinabatangan, two armed robberies were reported in April 2015, followed by a kidnapping in Sandakan by armed assaulters (Chong 2015), and other criminal actions like the smuggling of illegal weapons and drugs. The increasing influx of illegal immigrants in West Malaysia may have contributed to the increase in crime rates.

Kelantan, Terengganu, Pahang, Perlis and Perak are the states in Malaysia hit by flooding in 2014. Annually, the north-eastern part of peninsular Malaysia is affected by the Northeast Monsoon. The flooding recorded in the area in 2014 was the worst in recorded history (*Malay Mail Online* 2014b). The train service was interrupted due to damaged tracks and platforms. In addition, some of the main roads were closed. Crisis management is vital as it affects the image of Malaysia internationally. A well-managed crisis portrays a positive picture and minimizes hostility from the affected parties; in this case both the affected local people and tourists. The flooding in this area not only affects the transport sector but also other stakeholders, like hotels and travel agencies.

Another issue that is affecting Malaysia's image internationally is the publicity surrounding 1Malaysia Development Berhad (1MDB), a government entity initiated to drive foreign direct investment, which made headlines due to debts of MYR42 billion (Channel News Asia 2015). Various issues include forming partnerships with new non-proven companies, the Tun Razak

Exchange project, falsifying documents and inconsistency in reporting to the media by the board of directors and the senior management team. A lack of transparency in financial dealings has caused an uproar among Malaysians and attracted international media attention as well as financial investigations in Singapore and Switzerland. The involvement of public funds such as the Employee Provident Fund and Tabung Haji (Malaysian hajj pilgrims fund board) in bailing out the loss incurred by 1MDB indirectly (e.g. purchasing land for more than the market rate) has only fuelled the controversy. All these issues reflect the poor credibility of the government. How the government deals with the issues not only reflects on governance capabilities but may also affect the overall image of the stability of the country.

Similarly, a country's tourism industry and image could suffer from awareness of human rights violations. In May 2015, more than 2,000 Rohingya and Bangladeshi migrants stranded in the Andaman Sea were shunned by the Malaysian, Thai and Indonesian governments. Malaysia received harsh criticism, especially in social media, for being a callous government, showing little sympathy to fellow Muslims. Pressured by various quarters such as the International Human Rights Commission and NGOs (Cochrane 2015), both Malaysia and Indonesia decided to give one year of temporary shelter to the migrants while waiting for third-country relocation. Soon after that, 139 graves of Rohingya and Bangladeshi refugees was unveiled, implicating Malaysia as a transit camp for human trafficking (Arulldas 2015). Malaysia was ranked in the lowest tier (Tier 3) for human trafficking by the United States' Trafficking in Persons report (Hodal 2014). The migrants were mainly from neighbouring countries like Indonesia, Myanmar and Cambodia. Lack of law enforcement, failure to take immediate action and corruption among the immigration officers, politicians, police officers and other relevant authorities contribute to the increase in human trafficking activities. The failure to prevent human trafficking and protect the refugees reflects badly on the country's image, and human right activists around the world are questioning Malaysia's stance on this issue.

In 1998, Anwar Ibrahim, the former deputy prime minister, was charged with corruption and sodomy (Havely 1998). Ibrahim pleaded not guilty and claimed that the evidence and medical reports were tampered with. The sodomy case was seen as politically motivated after the alleged victim was photographed with some senior political officers on various occasions. Anwar Ibrahim was leading the opposition coalition (Pakatan Rakyat) in both the 2008 and the 2013 elections. The ruling government (Barisan Nasional) lost its one-third majority for the first time in 50 years in the 2013 election and the opposition won 51% of the popular vote (ABC 2013). In 2014, Anwar was found guilty by the Court of Appeal and was sentenced to five years' imprisonment (*Straits Times* 2014). The sodomy case was seen as an attempt to end his political career so that he will not be able to take part in the 2018 general election. The independence of the judiciary system has been questioned, showing evidence of undermining democratic freedom, which may affect Malaysia's standing in some quarters.

The *Sedition Act of 1948* was instituted by the then colonial government with the aim of ensuring domestic harmony. Never purged from the list of statutes, the Malaysian government was criticized for revising the draconian law, which was seen as a threat to democracy and free expression by some commentators. The jail terms were increased from three years to seven years, with a maximum penalty of 20 years (*Guardian* 2015). This was followed by the *Anti-Terrorism Bill* which allows detention without trial. According to Amnesty International, the *Sedition Act* is an 'outdated and repressive piece of legislation' (cited in Pak 2014). Recently, opposition party candidates, activists, students, journalists and academics who have spoken out or criticized the government have been charged under this act. It is used to suppress the voices of those against the ruling government and is a threat to the freedom of speech. The growing transgression of basic human rights may paint a negative image of the country. Extensive human rights violations may also result in travel bans or boycotting by some travel agents or countries (Hall 1994). This may affect travel to Malaysia predominantly among more ethical travellers (Lovelock 2008) who are concerned about social issues.

Malaysia has always regarded itself as a moderate Islamic country. Nevertheless, there are efforts by PAS (Malaysian Islamic Party), a member of the opposition party (Pakatan Rakyat) (People's Pact/People's Alliance – People's Justice Party, Democratic Action Party and Pan-Malaysia Islamic Party) to introduce Islamic civil law in some parts of the country, with the future aim to impose it on the whole country. The *hudud bill* (Islamic Shariah Law) was passed in Kelantan and Terengganu, for example, to introduce an Islamic dress code for tourists (*Malay Mail Online* 2015b). Many concerts have been cancelled and banned due to various restrictions imposed by the authorities and radical religious groups (e.g. Malaysian Muslim Solidarity). This development has hindered many opportunities for the country to diversify its tourism product into entertainment and concert events.

The rising Islamic fundamentalism in Malaysia is evident in several recent incidents. For instance, more extreme Muslims have protested against: building other religions' places of worship (e.g. churches and temples) in Muslim majority areas; the LGBT (lesbian, bisexual, gay and transgender) movement; the 'I want to touch a dog' campaign; and even cross symbols on churches. Similarly, the connection of 70 army personnel with ISIS that was discovered by the Defence Ministry (Wright 2015) jeopardized the reputation of the army. Such developments may affect the current image of Malaysia of being a moderate Islamic country. This may have potential repercussions for tourism development and tourist arrivals. Even the high-yield Muslim tourists from the Middle East prefer to travel to other Muslim countries that are moderate in their political stance.

Conclusion

This chapter unveils the main aspects of the tourism industry in Malaysia which has grown tremendously over the years. The country has been successful in attracting a huge volume of tourists, mainly among those from neighbouring countries, although they stay for a short period and spend much less compared with tourists who visit Singapore and Thailand. The future target of the country is to attract higher-yield tourists, who are MICE participants, from the Middle Eastern countries, medical tourists, ecotourists, MM2H participants and mature tourists. Efforts are being made to provide tourism products and services required to cater to these markets. Tourism Malaysia, which is the marketing organization for the industry in Malaysia, has been successful in marketing the country worldwide using the tagline of 'Malaysia Truly Asia'. However, there have been several incidents and concerns which affect the tourism industry in Malaysia, especially those which tarnish Malaysia's image as a democratic country, a country which looks after human rights and one which is safe to travel to. But perhaps the greatest future challenge will be inhibiting the change in the political landscape of the country from the claimed moderate Islamic nation to one more fundamentalist in its stance. If the country is to enjoy the current status of tourism growth it should make every effort to maintain its image as a moderate Islamic country. The image is not only appealing to non-Islamic nations, but is also the preference among tourists from Islamic countries.

Key reading

Butler, G., Khoo-Lattimore, C. and Mura, P. (2014) 'Heritage tourism in Malaysia: Fostering a collective national identity in an ethnically diverse country', *Asia Pacific Journal of Tourism Research*, 19(2): 199–218.

Musa, G., Thirumoorthi, T. and Doshi, D. (2011) 'Travel behaviour among health tourists in Kuala Lumpur', *Current Issues in Tourism*, 15(6): 525–543.

Wong, K.M. and Musa, G. (2013) 'Medical tourism in Thailand, Singapore, Malaysia and India', in C.M. Hall (ed.), *Medical Tourism: The Ethics, Regulation, and Marketing of Health Mobility* (pp. 167–186). New York: Routledge.

Wong, K.M. and Musa, G. (2015) 'International second home retirement motives in Malaysia: Comparing British and Japanese retirees', *Asia Pacific Journal of Tourism Research*, 20(9): 1041–1062.

Zannierah S.M., Hall, C.M. and Ballantine, P.W. (2012) 'Restaurant managers' perspectives on Halal certification', *Journal of Islamic Marketing*, 3(1): 47–58.

References

ABC (2013) 'Ruling coalition wins Malaysians election amid fraud allegations'. Online. Available: www.abc.net.au/news/2013-05-06/an-barisan-wins-malaysia-election/4670904 (accessed 4 June 2015).

Abdul-Aziz, A-R., Loh, C.-L. and Jaafar, M. (2014) 'Malaysia's My Second Home (MM2H) programme: An examination of Malaysia as a destination for international retirees', *Tourism Management*, 40: 203–212.

AirAsia Berhad (2015) *AirAsia Indonesia flight QZ8501*. Online. Available: http://qz8501.airasia.com (accessed 29 May 2015).

Arukesamy, K. (2015) 'Malaysia looking to China for tourism target', *Sunday Daily*, 12 January. Online. Available: www.thesundaily.my/news/1293561 (accessed 17 January 2015).

Arulldas, S. (2015) 'Human trafficking kingpins identified', *Malay Mail Online*, 29 May. Online. Available: www.themalaymailonline.com/malaysia/article/human-trafficking-kingpins-identified (accessed 29 May 2015).

Burt, J. (2015) 'Indonesia AirAsia flight QZ8501 was "hardest part of my life", says QPR chairman Tony Fernandes', *Telegraph*, 21 February. Online. Available: www.telegraph.co.uk/sport/football/teams/queens-park-rangers/11427521/Indonesia-AirAsia-Flight-QZ8501-was-hardest-part-of-my-life-says-QPR-chairman-Tony-Fernandes.html# (accessed 29 May 2015).

Chandran, S. (2009) 'A new tourism strategy for Malaysia', *Travel and Tourism News Middle East*. Online. Available: www.ttnworldwide.com/Article/8931/A_new_tourism_strategy_for_Malaysia (accessed 16 January 2015).

Channel News Asia (2015) 'Malaysia's 1MDB to be dismantled under debt plan: Reuters'. Online. Available: www.channelnewsasia.com/news/asiapacific/malaysia-s-1mdb-to-be/1697218.html (accessed 29 May 2015).

Chong, R. (2015) '2 kidnapped from Sandakan restaurant', *Borneo Post Online*. Online. Available: www.theborneopost.com/2015/05/15/2-kidnapped-from-sandakan-restaurant (accessed 30 May 2015).

Cochrane, J. (2015) 'Indonesia and Malaysia agree to care for stranded migrants', *New York Times*, 20 May. Online. Available: www.nytimes.com/2015/05/21/world/asia/indonesia-malaysia-rohingya-bangladeshi-migrants-agreement.html?_r=0 (accessed 30 May 2015).

Crescent Rating (2014) 'Crescentrating's Halal Friendly Travel (CRaHFT) Ranking 2014'. Online. Available: www.crescentrating.com/crahft-ranking-2014/item/3602-crescentratings-top-halal-friendly-holiday-destinations-2014.html (accessed January 28 2015).

Cultural Diplomacy News (2014) 'A keynote speech by the Hon. YB Dato' Seri Mohamed Nazri Bin Abdul Aziz, Minister of Tourism and Culture Malaysia'. Online. Available: www.cd-n.org/index.php?the-hon-yb-dato-seri-mohamed-nazri-bin-abdul-aziz (accessed 28 January 2015).

Department of Statistics Malaysia (2011) 'Population distribution and basic demographic characteristic report 2010 (updated: 05/08/2011)'. Online. Available: www.statistics.gov.my/index.php?r=column/cthemeByCat&cat=117&bul_id=MDMxdHZjWTk1SjFzTzNkRXYzcVZjdz09&menu_id=L0pheU43NWJwRWVSZklWdzQ4TlhUUT09 (accessed 4 June 2015).

—— (2013) 'Domestic tourism survey'. Online. Available: www.statistics.gov.my/portal/download_Services/files/tourism/Penerbitan_Domestic_Tourism_Survey_2013.pdf (accessed 29 January 2015).

Economic Planning Unit (2010) *Tenth Malaysia Plan 2011–2015*. Putrajaya: Economic Planning Unit, Prime Minister's Department.

Einhorn, B. (2015) 'AirAsia CEO turns to Twitter for crisis management', *Bloomberg Business*, 5 January. Online. Available: www.bloomberg.com/bw/articles/2015-01-05/airasia-ceo-tony-fernandes-manages-crisis-with-social-media (accessed 29 May 2015).

Euromonitor International (2014a) 'Travel and tourism in Malaysia'. Online. Available: www.euromonitor.com/travel-and-tourism-in-malaysia/report (accessed 16 January 2015).

—— (2014b) 'Top 100 City destinations ranking'. Online. Available: http://blog.euromonitor.com/2014/01/euromonitor-internationals-top-city-destinations-ranking.html (accessed 28 January 2015).

Express Tribune (2014a) 'Twin air disasters threaten Malaysian tourism push', *Express Tribune*, 23 July. Online. Available: http://tribune.com.pk/story/739774/twin-air-disasters-threaten-malaysian-tourism-push (accessed 2 February 2015).

—— (2014b) 'Malaysia Airlines to refund cancellations after MH17', *Express Tribune*, 20 July. Online. Available: http://tribune.com.pk/story/738333/malaysia-airlines-to-refund-cancellations-after-mh17 (accessed 2 February 2015).

Gaya Travel (2015) 'Musa Yusof: Director domestic marketing division Tourism Malaysia'. Online. Available: www.gayatravel.com.my/articles/musa-yusof-director-domestic-marketing-division-tourism-malaysia (accessed 16 January 2015).

Guardian (2015) 'Malaysia strengthens sedition law in a "black day" for free speech', *Guardian*, 10 April. Online. Available: www.theguardian.com/world/2015/apr/10/malaysia-strengthens-sedition-law-in-a-black-day-for-free-speech (accessed 4 June 2015).

Hall, C.M. (1994) *Tourism and Politics*. Chichester: John Wiley.

Havely, J. (1998) 'The case against Anwar', BBC News, 5 October. Online. Available: http://news.bbc.co.uk/2/hi/special_report/1998/10/98/malaysia_crisis/186916.stm (accessed 4 June 2015).

Hodal, K. (2014) 'US penalises Malaysia for shameful human trafficking record', *Guardian*, 20 June. Online. Available: www.theguardian.com/global-development/2014/jun/20/malaysia-us-human-trafficking-persons-report# (accessed 29 May 2015).

International Congress and Convention Association (ICCA) (2012) 'Country & city rankings 2012: International association meetings market'. Online. Available: www.iccaworld.com/dcps/doc.cfm?docid=1612 (accessed 28 January 2015).

—— (2014a) 'Malaysia's expatriate community awards Kuala Lumpur Convention Centre inaugural "Best MICE Experience" accolade at best of Malaysia Awards 2014'. Online. Available: www.iccaworld.com/newsarchives/archivedetails.cfm?id=4414 (accessed 28 January 2015).

—— (2014b) 'Malaysia wins bid to host the 9th world urban forum 2018'. Online. Available: www.iccaworld.com/newsarchives/archivedetails.cfm?id=4473 (accessed 28 January 2015).

International Living (2015) 'The world's best places to retire in 2015'. Online. Available: http://internationalliving.com/2015/01/the-best-places-to-retire-2015/# (accessed 28 January 2015).

Islamic Tourism Centre of Malaysia (2015) 'Discover Malaysia: Your Muslim friendly destination'. Online. Available: http://itc.gov.my (accessed 2 February 2015).

Ismail, L. and Lai, A. (2015) 'Nation a top tourist draw', *New Straits Times*, 28 May. Online. Available: www6.lexisnexis.com/publisher/EndUser?Action=UserDisplayFullDocument&orgId=685&topicId=14285&docId=l:2372890694&Em=7&start=14 (accessed 1 June 2015).

Khunton, T. (2015) 'Thailand drops in global tourism rankings', *Bangkok Post*. Online. Available: www.bangkokpost.com/news/general/536583/thailand-drops-in-global-tourism-rankings (accessed 17 June 2015).

Kim, V. (2014) 'World's 12 best shopping cities', CNN, 19 February. Online. Available: http://edition.cnn.com/2013/11/18/travel/worlds-best-shopping-cities (accessed 28 January 2015).

Koh, J. (2013) 'Asia Weekly: Ease of living entices retirees to Malaysia', *China Daily Asia*, 6 December. Online. Available: www.chinadailyasia.com/business/2013-12/06/content_15104184.html (accessed 12 June 2015).

Lee, L. (2014) 'Malaysia is a big hit with Japanese retirees', *The Ant Daily*, 12 November. Online. Available: www.theantdaily.com/Main/Malaysia-a-big-hit-with-Japanese-retirees (accessed 12 June 2015).

Lovelock, B. (2008) 'Ethical travel decisions: Travel agents and human rights', *Annals of Tourism Research*, 35(2): 338–358.

Maelzer, R. (2013) 'Malaysia looks to entice tourists from Middle East', China Central Television. Online. Available: http://english.cntv.cn/program/cultureexpress/20130917/102384.shtml (accessed 29 January 2015).

Malay Mail Online (2014a) 'Terrorism dents Malaysia in global peace rankings again', *Malay Mail Online*, 19 June. Online. Available: www.themalaymailonline.com/malaysia/article/terrorism-dents-malaysia-in-global-peace-rankings-again-video (accessed 1 February 2015).

—— (2014b) 'Tourism Ministry cancels Malaysia Christmas do as floods deepen', *Malay Mail Online*, 26 December. Online. Available: www.themalaymailonline.com/malaysia/article/tourism-ministry-cancels-malaysia-christmas-do-as-floods-deepen (accessed 2 February 2015).

—— (2014c) 'Uber crackdown? Fix taxi services first, authorities told', *Malay Mail Online*, 27 September. Online. Available: www.themalaymailonline.com/malaysia/article/uber-crackdown-fix-taxi-services-first-authorities-told (accessed 2 February 2015).

—— (2015a) 'Tourism ministry: Dissemination of positive information on social media vital for local tourism', *Malay Mail Online*, 12 January. Online. Available: www.themalaymailonline.com/malaysia/article/tourism-ministry-dissemination-of-positive-information-on-social-media-vita (accessed 1 June 2015).

—— (2015b) 'Visiting Terengganu? Dress this way', *Malay Mail Online*, 2 March. Online. Available: www.themalaymailonline.com/malaysia/article/visiting-terengganu-dress-this-way# (accessed 31 May 2015).

Malaysia Convention & Exhibition Bureau (MyCEB) (2013) *MyCEB Fact Sheet Sep 2013*. Online. Available: www.myceb.com.my/sites/default/files/MyCEB%20Factsheet%20Sep%202013.pdf (accessed 16 January 2015).

Malaysia Hotel News (2011) 'Malaysia to attract more high yield international business travelers'. Online. Available: http://malaysiahotelnews.blogspot.com/2011/07/malaysia-to-attract-more-high-yield.html (accessed 28 January 2015).

Malaysian Airports Holdings Berhad (2015a) 'Kuala Lumpur International Airport'. Online. Available: www.malaysiaairports.com.my/?m=business&c=business_about&id=17 (accessed 4 June 2015).

—— (2015b) 'Airlines'. Online. Available: www.klia.com.my/index.php?m=corp_info&c=airline_list&type=1 (accessed 4 June 2015).

Malaysian Insider (2013) 'ASEAN open sky policy to benefit MAS, says transport ministry', *Malaysian Insider*, 18 November. Online. Available: www.themalaysianinsider.com/business/article/asean-open-sky-policy-to-benefit-mas-says-transport-ministry (accessed 2 February 2015).

Malaysian Investment Development Authority (MIDA) (2015) 'Hospitality'. Online. Available: www.mida.gov.my/home/hospitality/posts (accessed 1 February 2015).

Ministry of Communications and Multimedia Malaysia (2015) 'MH370 official site'. Online. Available: www.mh370.gov.my/index.php/en (accessed 2 February 2015).

Ministry of International Trade and Industry (MITI) (2013) 'Comments on the 2014 Budget by YB Dato' Sri Mustapa Mohamed Minister of International Trade and Industry'. Online. Available: www.miti.gov.my/cms/contentPrint.jsp?id=com.tms.cms.article.Article_fd28929b-c0a81573-98dbc960-53186c58&paging=0 (accessed 1 February 2015).

Ministry of Tourism and Culture Malaysia (2014) 'About MM2H programme'. Online. Available: www.mm2h.gov.my/index.php/en/home/programme/about-mm2h-programme (accessed 2 February 2015).

Musa, G. (2002) 'Sipadan: A SCUBA-diving paradise – an analysis of tourism impact, diver satisfaction and tourism management', *Tourism Geographies: An International Journal of Tourism Space, Place and Environment*, 4(2): 195–209.

—— (2011) 'Sipadan: A case study', in T. Hinch and J. Higham (eds), *Sport Tourism Development* (pp. 130–133) (2nd edn). Clevedon: Channel View Publications.

Musa, G., Kadir, S.L.S.A. and Lee, L., (2006) 'Layang-Layang: An empirical study on scuba divers' satisfaction', *Tourism in Marine Environments*, 2(2): 89–102.

Musa, G., Kayat, K. and Thirumoorthi, T. (2010) 'The experiential aspect of rural home-stay among Chinese and Malay students using diary method', *Tourism and Hospitality Research*, 10(1): 25–41.

Musa, G., Thirumoorthi, T. and Doshi, D. (2011) 'Travel behaviour among health tourists in Kuala Lumpur', *Current Issues in Tourism*, 15(6): 525–543.

Musa, G., Doshi, D., Wong, K.M. and Thirumoorthi, T. (2012) 'How satisfied are medical tourists in Malaysia? A study on private hospitals in Kuala Lumpur', *Journal of Travel & Tourism Marketing*, 29(7): 629–646.

New Straits Times Online (2015) 'Getting the house back in order', 2 June. Online. Available: www.nst. com.my/node/86685 (accessed 4 June 2015).

Ong, T.F. and Musa, G. (2012) 'Examining the influences of experience, personality and attitude on SCUBA divers' underwater behaviour: A structural equation model', *Tourism Management*, 33(6): 1521–1534.

Ono, M. (2008) 'Long stay tourism and international retirement migration: Japanese retirees in Malaysia', *Senri Ethnological Reports*, 77: 151–162.

Ormond, M. and Sulianti, D. (2014) 'More than medical tourism: Lessons from Indonesia and Malaysia on South–South intra-regional medical travel', *Current Issues in Tourism*, DOI:10.1080/13683500.201 4.937324.

Pak, J. (2014) 'What is Malaysia's sedition law?', BBC News, 27 November. Online. Available: www.bbc. com/news/world-asia-29373164 (accessed 4 June 2015).

Pemandu (2013) 'Revving up the tourism industry: Economic transformation programme – a roadmap for Malaysia'. Online. Available: http://etp.pemandu.gov.my/Download_Centre-@-Download_Centre. aspx (accessed 20 January 2015).

Rakyat Post (2014) 'Nazri in Middle East to promote "Visit Malaysia"', *Rakyat Post*, 7 May. Online. Available: www.therakyatpost.com/news/2014/05/07/nazri-middle-east-promote-visit-malaysia (accessed 20 March 2015).

Star Online (2014a) 'More tourist arrivals to Malaysia in comparison to last year', *Star Online*, 16 October. Online. Available: www.thestar.com.my/Travel/Malaysia/2014/10/16/More-tourist-arrivals-to-Malaysia-in-comparison-to-last-year (accessed 20 January 2015).

—— (2014b) 'Visit Malaysia 2014: KL targets 15 million tourists, RM24bil revenue', *Star Online*, 1 January. Online. Available: www.thestar.com.my/News/Nation/2014/01/01/visit-malaysia-year-kuala-lumpur-15-million-tourists (accessed 29 January 2015).

—— (2014c) 'Seven wonders of Malaysian eco-tourism', *Star Online*, 5 June. Online. Available: www. thestar.com.my/News/Nation/2014/06/05/Environment-7-wonders-of-Malaysian-ecotourism (accessed 1 February 2015).

—— (2014d) 'Nazri: Sabah kidnappings affecting tourism industry more than MH370', *Star Online*, 17 June. Online. Available: www.thestar.com.my/News/Nation/2014/06/17/Sabah-kidnappings-affecting-tourism-more-than-MH370 (accessed 2 February 2015).

Straits Times (2014) 'Anwar Ibrahim's sodomy cases: What you need to know', *Straits Times*, 28 October. Online. Available: www.straitstimes.com/news/asia/south-east-asia/story/anwar-ibrahims-sodomy-cases-what-you-need-know-20141028 (accessed 4 June 2015).

Sunday Daily (2014) 'Nazri to aggressively promote tourism traffic from major markets to M'sia', *Sunday Daily*, 2 February. Online. Available: www.thesundaily.my/news/945800 (accessed 29 January 2015).

Telegraph (2015) 'The world's cheapest cities', *Telegraph*, Online. Available: www.telegraph.co.uk/travel/picturegalleries/10112558/The-worlds-cheapest-cities.html?frame=2586722 (accessed 4 June 2015).

Thirumoorthi, T., Wong, K.M. and Musa, G. (2013) 'Scuba diving satisfaction', in G. Musa and K. Dimmock (eds), *SCUBA Diving Tourism* (pp. 152–158). Abingdon: Routledge.

Tourism Malaysia (2011) 'Ministry of Tourism Malaysia reveals another art wave to attract high-yield tourists'. Online. Available: http://corporate.tourism.gov.my/mediacentre.asp?page=news_desk&subpage=archive&news_id=582 (accessed 28 January 2015).

—— (2012) 'Golf holidays & other luxury indulgences in Malaysia'. Online. Available: http://corporate. tourism.gov.my/mediacentre.asp?page=feature_malaysia&subpage=archive&news_id=101 (accessed 28 January 2015).

—— (2013) 'Tourism Malaysia launches integrated digital marketing programme'. Online. Available: http://corporate.tourism.gov.my/mediacentre.asp?page=news_desk&subpage=archive&news_id=946 (accessed 16 January 2015).

—— (2014a) 'Malaysia committed to developing cruise tourism'. Online. Available: http://corporate. tourism.gov.my/mediacentre.asp?page=news_desk&subpage=archive&news_id=1091 (accessed 16 January 2015).

—— (2014b) 'CCIM bike ride @ Putrajaya 2014 sets the pace for cycling tourism'. Online. Available: http://corporate.tourism.gov.my/images/media/news/MR%20CCIM%20Bike%20Ride%20 English.pdf (accessed 16 January 2015).

—— (2014c) 'Tourism Malaysia launches year of festivals campaign at world travel market'. Online. Available: http://corporate.tourism.gov.my/images/media/news/WTM%202014%20MR%20 (final%20draft).pdf (accessed 16 January 2015).

—— (2014d) 'Diving'. Online. Available: www.tourismmalaysiausa.com/what-to-do/activities/diving (accessed 1 February 2015).

—— (2015) 'Tourist arrivals and receipts to Malaysia'. Online. Available: http://corporate.tourism.gov. my/research.asp?page=facts_figures (accessed 16 January 2015).

Travel and Tourism News (TTN) (2010) 'Malaysia emerging as hotspot for Middle East tourists'. Online. Available: www.ttnonline.com/Article/10280/Malaysia_emerging_as_hotspot_for_Middle_East_ tourists (accessed 29 January 2015).

Visit Malaysia Year (2014) 'Top 25 places to visit'. Online. Available: www.vmy2014.com/see-and-do/ places-to-visit/top-25-places-to-visit (accessed 28 January 2015).

Wong, K.M. (2015) 'Malaysia My Second Home' (MM2H): Retirees' motivations, satisfaction, and post-satisfaction intentions'. Unpublished doctoral thesis, University of Malaya, Kuala Lumpur.

Wong, K.M. and Musa, G. (2013) 'Medical tourism in Thailand, Singapore, Malaysia and India', in C.M. Hall (ed.), *Medical Tourism: The Ethics, Regulation, and Marketing of Health Mobility* (pp. 167–186). New York: Routledge.

—— (2014) 'Retirement motivation among "Malaysia My Second Home" participants', *Tourism Management*, 40: 141–154.

—— (2015) 'International second home retirement motives in Malaysia: Comparing British and Japanese retirees', *Asia Pacific Journal of Tourism Research*, 20(9): 1041–1062.

Wright, B. (2015) 'Malaysian army and ISIS: 70 soldiers have joined Islamic state, officials say', *International Business Times*, 13 April. Online. Available: www.ibtimes.com/malaysia-army-isis-70-soldiers-have-joined-islamicstate-officials-say-1879299 (accessed 31 May 2015).

13

TOURISM IN INDONESIA

Mark P. Hampton & Julian Clifton

Introduction

The tropical archipelago of Indonesia, with a population of 249 million people spread over a landmass of almost 2 million km² encompassing over 20,000 islands, visually dominates the map of Southeast Asia. Its immense diversity of landscapes, culture, built heritage and natural resources offers innumerable options for visitors. However, Indonesia seems to have languished behind its regional neighbours in terms of international tourism arrivals, accounting for just 9% of arrivals to Association of Southeast Asian Nations (ASEAN) member states in 2012. This figure is dwarfed by Malaysia and Thailand, which represented 28% and 25% of ASEAN overseas arrivals in 2012 respectively (ASEAN 2015). Yet, there is some discussion over the reliability of international arrivals data for Malaysia as the official published statistics do not separate arrivals from Singapore. If these are excluded (as Singapore does for Malaysian arrivals), the headline arrivals figures of 25.7 million in 2013 (United Nations World Tourism Organization (UNWTO) 2014) could be adjusted downwards by as much as 10–11 million. In that case, Indonesia's international arrivals figure of 8.8 million in 2013 appears less dramatic in comparison (UNWTO 2014). In this chapter we explore recent trends in international and domestic tourism in the context of national policy and planning in Indonesia, and discuss the prospects for enhancing the country's role as a regional tourist destination.

Organised international tourism to Indonesia commenced during the first half of the twentieth century under colonial rule. Following the final Dutch subjugation of Bali in 1908, an image of the island as a cultural and spiritual paradise was popularised in Europe. This was reinforced by the colonial power's preference for preserving chosen cultural assets as part of the Eastern equivalent of the European "Grand Tour" (Lewis & Lewis 2009). However, this aesthetic did not extend to other parts of the archipelago and the push for independence, coupled with the violent civil unrest of the 1960s, precluded any strategic development of tourism at the national level until General Suharto assumed power in 1967.

President Suharto's objectives in promoting international tourism appeared to rest largely with his desire to gain international recognition and financial support whilst reinforcing his own power base through offering development opportunities to members of the ruling elite and promoting economic stability through diversification and growth. The Suharto "New Order" regime perceived tourism as a way to also reduce the Indonesian economy's reliance upon primary product exports (Booth 1990). Tourism was thus envisaged on a grand scale at a selected number of sites, involving funding from international organisations including the World Bank to construct large-scale capital-intensive integrated resort developments targeted at the wealthier segments of the overseas tourist market (Dahles 2001). Once again, Bali was selected as the "shop window" for international tourism, commencing with the expansion of Ngurah Rai Airport in Denpasar to accommodate long-haul aircraft in 1969 and the development of nearby enclave destinations such as Nusa Dua. Little consideration appeared to have been given to the environmental or social consequences of this mode of development for the next three decades. For instance, the French consultants who authored the Bali Master Plan in the early 1970s had a clear economic brief, and did not consult with local Balinese over the social aspects of the new plans (Picard 1996). It destroyed extensive natural habitats on land and sea (Warren 2005), disrupted existing systems of land and water management within Balinese communities and placed severe stress on freshwater resources in particular (Cole 2012) and, in the case of Tanah Lot and other sacred sites, caused serious offence to religious and cultural values (Warren 1998). Whilst these early initiatives geared towards facilitating mass tourism were taking place, other types of tourists were already arriving in Indonesia, with growing numbers of hippies and overland travellers from the late 1960s onwards. Bali also began to attract surfers, and by the 1980s the island was hosting significant numbers of backpackers: the budget-travelling "descendants" of the hippies (Hampton 2013).

This model of centrally planned tourism development, with its focus on enclave tourism, was hugely to the benefit of the ruling elite and was implemented with little consideration given to the surrounding cultural or natural context (Lewis & Lewis 2009). This approach was characteristic throughout the Suharto era and was further exemplified by the large Bintan resort development close to Singapore that opened in the mid-1990s (Bunnell *et al.* 2006; Shaw & Shaw 1999). Smaller-scale resorts were also developed throughout the archipelago, mostly capitalising on coastal assets, but diversification was also evident through tourism focusing upon key built heritage sites such as the eighth-century Buddhist complex at Borobodur in Java, unique cultural practices such as those of the Toraja community of Sulawesi, and photogenic endemic species including the komodo dragon (*Varanus komodoensis*) of the Lesser Sunda Islands in eastern Indonesia.

For most of the 1980s and 1990s, international tourism increased slowly to around five million arrivals per year, constrained to a considerable extent by practical difficulties in travelling, little tourist infrastructure outside of the key destinations and weak overseas marketing coupled with strong competition elsewhere in Southeast Asia. Significant but short-term fluctuations in tourism arrivals were associated with major hazards and political disturbances, notably the Asian Financial Crisis and unrest associated with the fall of Suharto in 1997–98, the Bali bombings in 2002 (Hitchcock & Darma Putra 2005) and the Boxing Day tsunami of 2004 (Figure 13.1).

However, there has been a steady increase in international arrivals to the order of 12% per annum from 2006, to a total of 8.8 million in 2013. The largest single source market remains Singapore, accounting for 1.6 million travellers representing 18% of arrivals in 2013. The increase in arrivals from 2006 to 2013 owes much to the growth of Malaysia (1.6 million in 2013), Australia (1 million) and China (0.8 million) as source markets, which experienced increases of 86%, 340% and 450% respectively during this seven-year period. Bali dominates the internal market, with 3.3 million arrivals representing 35% of all overseas visitors in 2013. The key source market is Australia, which accounted for 25% of arrivals to Bali in 2013 (Bali Provincial Government Tourist Office 2014). Given the relatively positive economic situation in Australia along with the recent expansion of low-cost airlines, there is little prospect of a significant or long-term decline in the primacy of the Australian market for Bali (Tourism

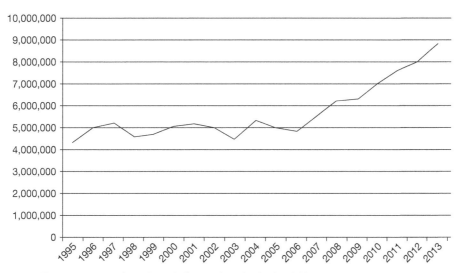

Figure 13.1 International tourist arrivals to Indonesia, 1995–2013.
Source: World Bank (2015).

Research Australia 2013). The average length of stay in 2013 for all tourists was 7.5 days with average expenditure per tourist being $1,042 (data from Statistics Indonesia 2014).

Data from the World Travel and Tourism Council (WTTC) indicates that tourism made a direct contribution of 3.1% of GDP in 2013, accounting for direct employment of around 3.04 million, representing 2.7% of the labour force in that year (WTTC 2014a). This can be compared with the direct contribution of tourism to GDP amounting to 9% and 7.2% of GDP in neighbouring Thailand and Malaysia respectively, directly supporting around 6.6% of the labour force in both countries (WTTC 2014b, 2014c).

Whilst accurate estimates of domestic tourist numbers are clearly difficult to obtain in such a large and populous country, recent government surveys indicate a total of around 248 million individuals made trips qualifying as domestic tourism in 2013, representing an increase of over 25% from the total of 196 million in 2001 (WTTC 2014a). The end of long-standing regional conflicts in Aceh and Maluku provinces, the construction of airports in major towns as well as provincial capitals (served by a growing number of low-cost airlines) and the relative prosperity of a growing proportion of middle-class Indonesians are clearly major drivers in this process. Furthermore, much of this travel takes place at key dates, including the two week Eid al-Fitr holiday wherein many family visits are undertaken. The sheer volume of internal travel is reflected in the fact that domestic tourism accounted for over three-quarters of tourism's direct contribution to GDP in Indonesia in 2013, as opposed to 28% and 45% in Thailand and Malaysia respectively (WTTC 2014a, 2014b, 2014c). With over 50% of Indonesian domestic tourism involving VFR (visiting friends and relatives), only around 10% of domestic visitors use rented accommodation.

The major economic contribution of domestic tourism is associated with the food and beverage sector, which accounted for almost half of the average total individual spend of 700,000 rupiah (approximately US$55) during domestic trips in 2010 (Statistics Indonesia 2012). These figures underline the importance of domestic tourism for alleviating poverty through channelling tourism activity to a wider range of destinations than international travel, whilst also presenting greater opportunities for local providers of food, beverages, transport and accommodation (Scheyvens 2007). However, the lack of data on Indonesian domestic tourism trends and impacts, coupled with a lack of focus from a government policy perspective, means that it is difficult to comment further upon this sector, other than noting that the following discussion focusing upon international travel is a small part of a broader and more diffuse picture.

Tourism policy and planning

In terms of government organisations, tourism is administered at two main levels. At the national level, the Ministry of Tourism and Creative Economy (MTCE) gives a strategic lead for national tourism planning, whilst the Tourism Promotion Board is responsible for international marketing. The current *National Tourism Development Master Plan* (MTCE 2011) covers the period 2010 to 2025 and is administered by the MTCE. Based upon principles of sustainable tourism, the plan focuses on the development of 16 Strategic National Tourism areas including Bali alongside other established marine, terrestrial and lakeside destinations across the archipelago (Pangestu 2012). Several niche tourism sectors are also targeted for development, including nature-based tourism, ecotourism, MICE (meetings, incentives, conventions and exhibitions) tourism and health tourism, amongst others. The plan also highlights mainly ASEAN countries, as well as China, South Korea and India as its future dominant source markets, facilitated by plans for visa-free travel within the region by ASEAN nationals, with an overall goal of increasing international arrivals by 5% per annum to 20 million in 2025.

However, the effectiveness of any such national strategy is limited by Indonesia's notoriously complex and inefficient bureaucracy (Kasim 2013). Over ten different national pieces of legislation relating to tourism have been enacted in the post-Suharto period, covering areas ranging from national planning, governance and environmental management to cultural heritage and civil rights (International Labour Organisation (ILO) 2012). Each of these acts is sponsored and implemented by different government ministries, with inevitable conflicts and confusion over policy priorities. To complicate this situation further, decision making in many policy arenas including tourism has been decentralised to lower government levels in the post-Suharto era in response to calls for greater accountability. Successive administrative tiers from province to municipality, district and village level may therefore identify tourism priorities and enact policies accordingly (Firman 2009). Hence, whilst national plans and strategies may exist, their translation into policy will very much reflect local or regional politics, history, power and local governance (Hadiz 2004; Hampton & Jeyacheya 2015).

'There is more to Indonesia than Bali': the spatial concentration of international tourism

This was the strap line of a government marketing campaign to persuade international visitors to travel beyond the iconic island destination. Aside from the well-documented environmental and social issues associated with Bali's rapid growth (Cole 2012; Minca 2000), noted earlier, an estimated 85% of Bali's tourist economy is owned by non-Balinese (MacRae 2010). Furthermore, provincial and district governments in Indonesia are now responsible for self-financing to a much greater extent than prior to decentralisation in 2002 (McCarthy 2004). Generating revenue through supporting the development of taxable trading activities along with the development of natural resources and assets is therefore of high priority to all administrative tiers (Larson & Soto 2008). Tourism offers clear opportunities to address these financial demands and consequently most provincial and many district governments are engaged in partnerships with overseas development corporations and promotional activities to develop their own tourism sector, often targeting niche markets (Clifton & Benson 2006; Hampton 2013).

Whilst consistent and reliable data regarding overseas visitors at the provincial level is difficult to obtain, port of entry data indicates that over 75% of all international visitors in 2013 entered Indonesia via Ngurah Rai International Airport in Bali (36%), Soekarno-Hatta International Airport, Jakarta (25%) and via the port of Batam in the Riau Islands near Singapore (15%) (Statistics Indonesia 2014). Similarly, analysis of accommodation data indicates that, of the 170,000 registered hotel rooms in 2013, the percentage located in Java (51%) and Bali (15%) far outweighed the proportion found in the larger islands of eastern Indonesia such as Kalimantan (6%) and Sulawesi (4%). The spatial distribution of international tourism therefore remains very much focused on the densely populated centres of power in western Indonesia. However, there have been several responses to address this spatial and economic imbalance within Indonesia, including planning economic corridors; encouraging resort development outside Bali and diversification into niche tourism forms.

Linking nearby islands to Bali: economic corridors

The *National Tourism Development Master Plan* (2011) presents a vision of the Bali–Nusa Tenggara Economic Corridor where tourism is seen as one of the three core economic sectors alongside fishing and animal husbandry. Bali is positioned as the tourism "gateway" with different types of tourism planned for different areas in the corridor located within an hour's flying time from Bali. This radius encircles Yogyakarta and central Java's UNESCO World Heritage Sites of Borobudur and Prambanan to the west, and the eastern side includes Lombok and Sumbawa, extending across to Komodo National Park and western Flores. The listed key subsectors include beach tourism (Bali, Lombok and East Nusa Tenggara); cultural tourism (Bali); "mountainous tourism" (East Java, Bali, Lombok); and "endangered species tourism" (Komodo island). This appears to be a classic "hub and spoke" model and the Master Plan states that air transport links will push tourism development as the 'key to success of this strategy is access and provision of adequate flight routes to tourism destinations beyond Bali, driven by a strong and targeted marketing strategy' (MTCE 2011: 144).

However, although national tourism planning in South-East Asia often includes economic "corridors" and "growth triangles" as seen in neighbouring Malaysia in the Ninth Malaysia Plan and the Indonesia–Malaysia–Singapore Growth Triangle (Bunnell *et al.* 2006; Hampton 2010; Hamzah 2004), there are questions over whether such ambitious plans will help reduce regional inequalities in Indonesia. Kuncoro (2013) argues that for the economic corridors in Indonesia to succeed there needs to be further reallocation of funds from the centre to the regions; increased public investment in infrastructure and central government should 'encourage the provincial and district governments to *implement pro-public budgeting rather than pro-bureaucratic budgeting*' (Kuncoro 2013: 32, emphasis added).

Resort development outside Bali

In addition to the sizeable Bintan resort development mentioned earlier, there are several new resorts planned or under construction outside Bali, such as the new $240 million Funtasy Island "eco-tourism" resort also in the Riau archipelago, just 16 kilometres from Singapore, that was originally due to open in late 2015; and the planned Mandalika Resort in southern Lombok being managed by the Bali Tourism Development Corporation (who led the development of Nusa Dua). The Mandalika Resort is approximately four times larger in land area than Nusa Dua (Nurhayati 2014) and will benefit from Lombok's new international airport.

Diversification: prospects for niche tourism

The dominant view in the literature is that ecotourism is considered to be an important sector for developing countries (Weaver 2006), but it can also be argued that for Indonesia – perhaps somewhat surprisingly – ecotourism may perhaps not prove as important as in other tropical developing countries. This is despite its impressive biodiversity in both terrestrial ecology (especially rainforest) and marine ecology due to its location in the "Coral Triangle" (Clifton 2009). Although Indonesia has significant ecotourism and cultural tourism attractions as noted earlier, the changing tourist market with the growing Chinese sector in particular implies a changing pattern of preferences from those typically associated with ecotourism (Galley and Clifton 2004). These include a growing demand for retail opportunities, typically luxury goods and modern shopping malls, certain types of catering including Chinese food, along with golf courses and gambling facilities such as casinos. Scuba diving is one possible exception. There is some evidence of demand from younger Chinese tourists wishing to dive in Indonesia in destinations such as Bali (Natahadibrata 2014). However, the broad market preference of Asian regional tourism so far appears to have limited interest in ecotourism in general.

Growing a sustainable and resilient tourism sector

The notion of a sustainable tourism sector, with its implicit balancing of economic, social and environmental components, has recently been supplemented by the concept of resilience, or capacity to withstand stress, which has its roots in ecological systems theory (Holling 1973). The goal of facilitating a sustainable and resilient tourism sector would therefore reflect the need to maintain tourism activities at a sustainable level whilst building capacity to absorb the impacts of unexpected or severe anthropogenic and natural disturbances (Lew 2014). There are several dimensions to this objective which can be identified in the case of Indonesia as discussed below.

Environmental hazards

Indonesia has the unenviable reputation of ranking first amongst countries worldwide in terms of predicted total deaths resulting from tsunamis and landslides, with high rankings in many other areas including earthquake, flood and drought (AIPA Secretariat 2010). This vulnerability reflects a host of environmental as well as social drivers which will influence the stability of both domestic and international tourism. The assets which led to tourism development are clearly lost following a major disaster, leading to long-term economic and social difficulties prolonging and exacerbating the period of recovery.

The tourism potential of Indonesia's many islands, inland areas and coastal environments will inevitably result in continued development and associated risks to visitors resulting from this variety of natural hazards. Whilst this may be construed as unsustainable, particularly from an environmental perspective, there is now greater recognition of the need to build resilience into the tourism sector, most notably following the Boxing Day tsunami of 2004. One of the many lessons learned in the wake of this disaster relates to the inter-dependence of vulnerability between coastal resorts and marine ecosystems, with healthy reefs and mangroves affording enhanced physical protection to inshore developed areas (Adger *et al.* 2005). Similarly, efforts are necessary to preserve local environmental knowledge in communities where tourism is replacing fishing, agriculture and other natural resource uses in order to maintain societal resilience and preparedness for natural disasters (Liu *et al.* 2005).

Human resources and training

In terms of human resources (HR) and training for tourism, there are differences between the formal and informal segments. For the formal sector in tourism, Indonesia has a growing HR "skills gap" and a shortage of experienced and sufficiently skilled labour for parts of the tourism industry (ILO 2012). This is despite a growing number of hotel and tourism schools across the archipelago as rising demand is still outpacing supply of trained staff, as well as issues of variable quality of the training staff have received. The ILO commented (2012: iv) that Indonesia's 'lack of skilled human resources in tourism and hospitality threatens to undermine national development goals and weaken the country's overall competitiveness'. For the informal sector, although Indonesia has a large and significant informal sector in tourism including beach vendors, mobile stalls, unlicensed guides and rickshaw drivers (Baker & Coulter 2007; Dahles & Susilowati 2013), it remains "off the radar" in government tourism planning, and so its potential for economic growth and poverty alleviation remains constrained (Hampton 2003; ILO 2012).

Transport and communications

Concerning tourism and transport, the air travel and cruise segments are both growing fast. Indonesia has a booming low-cost airline sector with rising passenger demand for flights to replace slow ferries across archipelago. However, Indonesia has a poor aircraft safety record, with one of the worst air crash rates in the Asia-Pacific region (Fuller & Bradsher 2014). More needs to be done by both government and the airline businesses, with a need for enhanced pilot training and more efficient safety and air traffic control systems. The other transport growth area is the cruise ship sector, with more than 203,000 passenger arrivals in 2014 (port data cited by Osman 2014) and industry players such as Princess Lines stating their vision that Indonesia could become the "Caribbean of the East" (Gustanto 2014). However, despite the growth rates of the cruise sector worldwide, and eye-catching "headline" passenger arrivals figures, the overall economic benefit for the destination is typically far smaller than for land-based tourism. Evidence from around the world shows that cruise passenger expenditure ashore is usually low compared with tourists who stay at the destination, and that sizeable infrastructure costs of deep-water harbours and terminals (as well as dredging channels and other environmental costs) can often significantly outweigh the localised and small spend of passengers ashore (Wood 2004).

Conclusion

After such a turbulent recent history, what are the likely trends for tourism in Indonesia? First, given the archipelago's sheer size and variety of tourist assets encompassing traditional beach and marine tourism, nature, built heritage and cultural assets, tourism is likely to continue its growth both in the international and domestic sectors. However, rising tourist numbers per se are not sufficient in themselves for the country to capture significant or rising economic development benefits. Crucially, length of stay and the corresponding tourist expenditure are key factors along with the employment opportunities (both direct and indirect) to meet rising demand for jobs in this nation with its large and growing population (World Bank 2015).

Second, it remains unclear how the imminent ASEAN Economic Community due to start in late 2015 will affect tourism in Indonesia, especially moves towards a "common market" including services such as tourism. It may be that common standards in training and the regulation of tourism may benefit Indonesia in the medium to long term but may generate costs in the short term as businesses and government bring services up to common ASEAN standards.

Third, regional tourism from ASEAN and other Asian countries is likely to continue growing in importance for Indonesia, especially given growing ASEAN trade and other links. This is associated with the role of low-cost airlines in the region, such as AirAsia, Lion Air and Jetstar Asia, but there are some questions over the impact of the ASEAN "open skies" and Single Air Market liberalisation (Abeyratne 2014).

Finally, there is the role of shocks such as large-scale natural disasters and major terrorist incidents. Indonesian tourism has been adversely affected by the 2004 Boxing Day tsunami, regular volcanic eruptions and earthquakes, as well as ongoing problems with Islamic extremist terrorism from the Bali bombings of 2002 and 2004 onwards. Although such shocks have affected tourist perceptions and resulted in short-term fluctuations in international arrivals figures, overall demand for tourism in Indonesia still appears to be rising. In addition, different generating markets' characteristics (Asian compared to European or North American) as well as different tourist segments (independent travellers versus package or group tours) can all affect tourists' decisions to travel or not. Domestic tourists' market characteristics are different again. Despite some complexities associated with the changing political economy of Indonesia and other ongoing challenges, all things being equal, it would seem that the outlook for tourism in the country is reasonably bright.

Key reading

Baker, K. and Coulter, A. (2007) 'Terrorism and tourism: The vulnerability of beach vendors' livelihoods in Bali', *Journal of Sustainable Tourism*, 15(3): 249–266.

Hampton, M.P. (2010) 'Enclaves and ethnic ties: Local impacts of Singaporean cross-border tourism in Malaysia and Indonesia', *Singapore Journal of Tropical Geography,* 31(2): 239–253.

Hampton, M.P. and Jeyacheya, J. (2015) 'Power, ownership and tourism in small islands: Evidence from Indonesia', *World Development*, 70: 481–495.

Hitchcock, M. and Darma Putra, I.N. (2005) 'The Bali bombings: Tourist crisis management and conflict avoidance', *Current Issues in Tourism*, 8(1): 62–76.

Lewis, J. and Lewis, B. (2009) *Bali's Silent Crisis: Desire, Tragedy and Transition*. Lanham: Rowman & Littlefield.

References

Abeyratne, R. (2014) 'ASEAN single aviation market and Indonesia: Can it keep up with the giants?' *Indonesian Law Review*, 2: 163–175.

Adger, W.N., Hughes, T.P., Folke, C., Carpenter, S.R. and Rockström, J. (2005) 'Social-ecological resilience to coastal disasters', *Science*, 309(5737): 1036–1039.

AIPA Secretariat (2010) *Indonesia's Country Report on Disaster Response Management*. Online. Available: www.aipasecretariat.org/wp-content/uploads/2011/07/Indonesia_Disaster-Response-Management.pdf (accessed 3 March 2015).

ASEAN (2015) 'Tourism statistics'. Online. Available: www.asean.org/news/item/tourism-statistics (accessed 20 February 2015).

Baker, K. and Coulter, A. (2007) 'Terrorism and tourism: The vulnerability of beach vendors' livelihoods in Bali', *Journal of Sustainable Tourism*, 15(3): 249–266.

Bali Provincial Government Tourist Office (2014) 'Direct foreign tourist arrivals to Bali 2013'. Online. Available: www.disparda.baliprov.go.id/en/Statistics2 (accessed 2 February 2014).

Booth, A. (1990) 'The tourism boom in Indonesia', *Bulletin of Indonesian Economic Studies*, 26(3): 45–73.

Bunnell, T., Muzaini, H. and Sidaway, J. (2006) 'Global city frontiers: Singapore's hinterland and the contested socio-political geographies of Bintan, Indonesia', *International Journal of Urban and Regional Research*, 30(1): 3–22.

Clifton, J. (2009) 'Science, funding and participation: Key issues for marine protected area networks and the Coral Triangle Initiative', *Environmental Conservation* 36(2): 91–96.

Clifton, J. and Benson, A. (2006) 'Planning for sustainable ecotourism: The case for research ecotourism in developing country destinations', *Journal of Sustainable Tourism* 14(3): 238–254.

Cole, S. (2012) 'A political ecology of water equity and tourism: A case study from Bali', *Annals of Tourism Research*, 39(2): 1221–1241.

Dahles, H. (2001) *Tourism, Heritage and National Culture in Java: Dilemmas of a Local Community*. Richmond: Curzon.

Dahles, H. and Susilowati, T. (2013) 'Entrepreneurship in the informal sector: The case of the pedicab drivers of Yogyakarta, Indonesia', *Journal of Small Business and Entrepreneurship*, 26(3): 241–259.

Firman, T. (2009) 'Decentralisation reform and local government proliferation in Indonesia: Towards a fragmentation of regional development', *Review of Urban and Regional Development Studies*, 21(2/3): 143–157.

Fuller, T. and Bradsher, K. (2014) 'Crash of AirAsia Flight 8501 spotlights Indonesia's poor air safety record', *New York Times*, 31 December. Online. Available: www.nytimes.com/2015/01/01/world/asia/airasia-flight-8501-indonesia-airline-safety.html (accessed 20 February 2015).

Galley, G. and Clifton, J. (2004) 'The motivations and demographic characteristics of research ecotourists: Operation Wallacea volunteers in south-east Sulawesi, Indonesia', *Journal of Ecotourism*, 3(1): 69–82.

Gustanto, P. (2014) 'Indonesia's cruise tourism potential', *Jakarta Post*, 11 September. Online. Available: www.thejakartapost.com/news/2014/09/11/indonesia-s-cruise-tourism-potential.html (accessed 19 December 2014).

Hadiz, V.R. (2004) 'Decentralisation and democracy in Indonesia: A critique of neo-institutionalist perspectives', *Development and Change*, 35(4): 697–718.

Hampton, M.P. (2003) 'Entry points for local tourism in developing countries: Evidence from Yogyakarta, Indonesia', *Geografiska Annaler B: Human Geography*, 85(2): 85–101.

—— (2010) 'Enclaves and ethnic ties: Local impacts of Singaporean cross-border tourism in Malaysia and Indonesia', *Singapore Journal of Tropical Geography*, 31(2): 239–253.

—— (2013) *Backpacker Tourism and Economic Development: Perspectives from the Less Developed World*. London: Routledge.

Hampton, M.P. and Jeyacheya, J. (2015) 'Power, ownership and tourism in small islands: Evidence from Indonesia', *World Development*, 70: 481–495.

Hamzah, A. (2004) 'Policy and planning of the tourism industry in Malaysia'. Paper presented at the 6th ADRF (Asian Development Research Forum) General Meeting, Bangkok. Online. Available: http://adrf.trf.or.th/ADRF6update/Full_Papers/Tourism_Product_Development/Amran_Hamzah/Amran_paper.pdf (accessed 6 February 2014).

Hitchcock, M. and Darma Putra, I.N. (2005) 'The Bali bombings: Tourist crisis management and conflict avoidance', *Current Issues in Tourism*, 8(1): 62–76.

Holling, C.S. (1973) 'Resilience and stability of ecological systems', *Annual Review of Ecological Systems*, 4: 1–23.

International Labour Organisation (ILO) (2012) *Strategic Plan: Sustainable Tourism and Green Jobs for Indonesia*. Jakarta: ILO.

Kasim, A. (2013) 'Bureaucratic reform and dynamic governance for combating corruption: The challenge for Indonesia', *International Journal of Administrative Science and Organization – Bisnis & Birokrasi, Jurnal Ilmu Administrasi dan Organisasi*, 20(1): 18–22.

Kuncoro, M. (2013) 'Economic geography of Indonesia: Can MP3EI reduce inter-regional inequality?' *South East Asia Journal of Contemporary Business, Economics and Law*, 2(2): 17–33.

Larson, A.M. and Soto, F. (2008) 'Decentralisation of natural resource governance regimes', *Annual Review of Environment and Resources*, 33(1): 213–239.

Lew, A.A. (2014) 'Scale, change and resilience in community tourism planning', *Tourism Geographies*, 16(1): 14–22.

Lewis, J. and Lewis, B. (2009) *Bali's Silent Crisis: Desire, Tragedy and Transition*. Lanham: Rowman & Littlefield.

Liu, P.L.-F., Lynett, P., Fernando, H., Jaffe, B.E., Fritz, H., Higman, B., Morton, R., Goff, J. and Synolakis, C. (2005) 'Observations by the international tsunami survey team in Sri Lanka', *Science*, 308(5728): 1595.

McCarthy, J.F. (2004) 'Changing to gray: Decentralisation and the emergence of volatile socio-legal configurations in Central Kalimantan, Indonesia', *World Development*, 32(7): 1199–1223.

MacRae, G. (2010) 'If Indonesia is too hard to understand, let's start with Bali', *Journal of Indonesian Social Sciences and Humanities*, 3: 11–36.

Minca, C. (2000) 'The Bali Syndrome: The explosion and implosion of "exotic" tourist spaces', *Tourism Geographies*, 2(4): 389–403.

Ministry of Tourism and Creative Economy (MTCE) (2011) *Master Plan of National Tourism Development 2010–2025*. Jakarta: MTCE.

Natahadibrata, N. (2014) 'Chinese tourists overtake Australian arrivals', *Jakarta Post*, 3 June. Online. Available: www.thejakartapost.com/news/2014/06/03/chinese-tourists-overtake-australian-arrivals. html (accessed 6 February 2014).

Nurhayati, D. (2014). 'BTDC starts developing Mandalika as new site', *Jakarta Post*, 15 April. Online. Available: www.thejakartapost.com/news/2014/04/15/btdc-starts-developing-mandalika-new-site. html (accessed 9 January 2015).

Osman, N. (2014) 'Indonesia's cruise tourism sees record growth', *Jakarta Post*, 4 December. Online. Available: www.thejakartapost.com/news/2013/12/04/indonesia-s-cruise-tourism-sees-record-growth.html (accessed 19 December 2014).

Pangestu, M.E. (2012) 'Unleashing tourism potential', *First Magazine* (Special report: Indonesia: Balanced growth, social justice, global cooperation). Online. Available: www.firstmagazine.com/ DownloadSpecialReportDetail.1337.ashx.

Picard, M. (1996) *Cultural Tourism and Touristic Culture* (translated by D. Darling). Singapore: Archipelago Press.

Scheyvens, R. (2007) 'Poor cousins no more: Valuing the development potential of domestic and diaspora tourism', *Progress in Development Studies*, 7(4): 307–325.

Shaw, B. and Shaw, G. (1999) '"Sun, sand and sales": Enclave tourism and local entrepreneurship in Indonesia', *Current Issues in Tourism*, 2(1): 68–81.

Statistics Indonesia (2012) *Indonesia Domestic Tourism: Household Approach*. Jakarta: Badan Pusat Statistik. Online. Available: www.bps.go.id (accessed 2 February 2014).

—— (2014) *Statistik Indonesia 2014*. Jakarta: Badan Pusat Statistik. Online. Available: www.bps.go.id (accessed 2 February 2014).

Tourism Research Australia (2013) *What is Driving Australians' Travel Choices?*. Canberra: Government of Australia.

United Nations World Tourism Organization (UNWTO) (2014) *Tourism Highlights 2014 Edition*. Madrid: UNWTO.

Warren, C. (1998) 'Tanah Lot: The cultural and environmental politics of resort development in Bali', in P. Hirsch and C. Warren (eds), *The Politics of Environment in Southeast Asia: Resources and Resistance* (pp. 229–261). London: Taylor & Francis.

—— (2005) 'Community mapping, local planning and alternative land use strategies in Bali', *Geografisk Tidsskrift – Danish Journal of Geography*, 105(1): 29–41.

Weaver, D. (2006) *Sustainable Tourism: Theory and Practice*. Oxford: Butterworth-Heinemann.

Wood, R. (2004) 'Global currents: Cruise ships in the Caribbean Sea', in D. Duval (ed.), *Tourism in the Caribbean: Trends, Developments, Prospects* (pp. 152–171). London: Routledge.

World Bank (2015) *Data by Country: Indonesia*. Online. Available: http://data.worldbank.org/country/ indonesia (accessed 20 February 2015).

World Travel and Tourism Council (WTTC) (2014a) *Travel and Tourism: Economic Impact Indonesia 2013*. London: WTTC.

—— (2014b) *Travel and Tourism: Economic Impact Thailand 2013*. London: WTTC.

—— (2014c) *Travel and Tourism: Economic Impact Malaysia 2013*. London: WTTC.

14

THE EVOLUTION OF TOURISM POLICY IN VIETNAM, 1960–2015

V. Dao Truong & Anh Le

Introduction

Since the *Renewal Process* was introduced by the Vietnamese government (GOV) in 1986, tourism in Vietnam has developed relatively quickly and become an important economic sector (Truong 2013, 2014a; Truong *et al.* 2014). Indeed, the number of domestic tourists increased from 11.2 million in 2000 to 35 million in 2013, while that of foreign tourists rose from 2.2 million to 7.5 million in the same period (Vietnam National Administration of Tourism (VNAT) 2009a, 2011, 2015). In terms of economic contribution, the tourism receipts generated totalled Vietnamese Dong (VND) 200 trillion (US$9.5 billion) in 2013, an 11-fold increase from VND17.4 trillion (US$809 million) in 2000 (VNAT 2009a, 2015). Vietnam's *Law on Tourism* affirms that tourism is a spearhead sector and an important contributor to poverty alleviation (GOV 2005). Given the economic significance of tourism, the GOV has enacted a number of policies to promote tourism development (Truong 2013).

Government involvement has a significant impact on tourism development, particularly in former and transitioning state socialist countries in Southeast Asia (Hall 1994). Jenkins and Henry (1982) argued that most developing countries are characterised by a scarcity of resources for development, where the private sector is generally non-existent or otherwise has minimal experience in tourism. As such, government involvement in tourism in these countries may be greater than that in those with a developed free market economy, not only to achieve long-term objectives but also to compensate for the absence of the private sector. Elliot (2002) claimed that only governments have the power to provide the political, legal, and financial frameworks as well as essential services and basic infrastructure that tourism requires. In addition, only governments can negotiate and arrange with other governments on issues pertaining to immigration procedures or the issuing of tourist visas. Governments are also interested in tourism because of the magnitude of its economic, social, and environmental impacts. In general, governments consider tourism a means of economic growth, particularly in developing countries (Truong 2014a, 2014b, 2015).

Vietnam is a state socialist-oriented developing country, where the participation of the private sector in tourism has been relatively limited. For example, the VNAT, established in 1978, was until 1994 responsible for managing all tourism activities nationwide. As of 2005, nearly half of international tour operators in Vietnam were state- and collective-owned (VNAT

2015). Given the rapid growth of tourism since 1990, most efforts can be attributed to the GOV, which has sought to address most aspects of tourism development through its policies and strategies (Truong 2013).

Although tourism has been recognised as an important economic sector in Vietnam, there is fairly limited understanding of the development of tourism policies and the types of role(s) that have been played by the GOV in the extant literature (Truong 2013, 2014a). Hall (1994) indicated that the role(s) of governments in tourism is an outcome of their tourism policy formulation and implementation, which is set in a wider policy agenda with individual and institutional arrangements, values, powers, and ideologies influencing tourism policies. Therefore, analysing tourism policies is central to understanding the roles and ideologies of governments in tourism development. Hall (1994) also suggested a model of the tourism policy-making process, which consists of four main components: demands, decisions, outputs, and impacts (see also Truong 2013, 2014a).

This chapter examines the development of tourism policies in Vietnam to identify the roles that have been played by the GOV. Attention is given to the post-1975 period when the Vietnam–US war had ended. The period 1960–1975 is also briefly reviewed to contextualise the subsequent periods. To this end, Hall's (1994) model of the tourism policy-making process is applied. The development of Vietnam's tourism policies is divided into three main periods. In the period 1976–1990, tourism was recognised as an economic sector, although political motivations were still strong. Between 1991 and 2004, tourism was considered an economic spearhead. From 2005 to the present, tourism has remained an economic spearhead while also being perceived as a contributor to poverty alleviation. This chapter may provide tourism scholars and practitioners with a systematic review of tourism policy development in Vietnam and assist the governments in Vietnam and elsewhere in addressing various aspects of tourism development through their policy initiatives and measures.

1960–1975: "politics-in" command

During this period, Vietnam was divided into two regions, the North and the South, as a result of the Vietnam–US war. Domestic tourism hardly existed. International tourism was solely developed to achieve political goals, with foreign tourists being political delegates (VNAT 2005). Leisure and business tourists were rare (Mok & Lam 1997). Therefore, the total international tourist arrivals were very limited, numbering only 6,130 in 1960 and 36,910 in 1975 (Tran 2005). The Vietnam Civil Aviation airline (the present flag carrier Vietnam Airlines), which was established by the Northern Vietnamese government in 1956, primarily served civilian purposes (Vinafour n.d.). The Vietnam Tourist Company was set up in 1960 in the North and was placed under the Ministry of Foreign Affairs (Tran 2005; VNAT 2005). Later it was managed by the Ministry of Public Security (Tran 2005). The evidence reflects an extremely close control of tourism activities by the central government. Although some tourist sites were already in place (e.g. Hanoi, Tam Dao), economic benefits were subordinated to national security. As a result, tourism was neither an economic activity nor an economic sector in this period (Truong 2013, 2014a).

1976–1990: from political command to economic demand

After the war, Vietnam was severely damaged. It was also worsened by the economic sanctions that were imposed by the American government (Truong 2014a). Politically, Vietnam entered a period of isolation from the West. As a result, until the mid-1980s Vietnam was one of the poorest countries in the world. It was very difficult to develop tourism in such a situation. However, tourist sites were gradually expanded to other areas throughout the country, such as Hue, Da Nang, Vung Tau, and Can Tho (VNAT 2005), where some state-owned tourist companies were established and managed by provincial people's committees. The VNAT was established in 1978 to manage all tourism activities nationwide. Foreign visitors were still few in number (e.g. 41,110 in 1980; Tran 2005) and these mainly consisted of those coming from the then Soviet Union (VNAT 2005). Tourism in the early years after 1975 was primarily developed to promote patriotism, enhance the mutual understanding between the North and the South, and introduce Vietnam as a peaceful country (VNAT 2005). It was only when the 1986 *Renewal Policy* was adopted that Vietnam shifted from a centrally planned economy to a market-oriented one, where tourism was gradually recognised as an economic sector (Table 14.1; Truong 2013, 2014a).

Demands for tourism policies

First, a state agency responsible for managing tourism was unavailable. The tourism sector lacked both well-trained human resources and professional facilities (Tran 2005). Second, the state management of tourism was ineffective. The VNAT undertook the roles of both a management agency and a business at the same time. These roles were not clearly separated. In addition, the VNAT was inexperienced in managing tourism (Tran 2005). Third, foreign tourists were increasing. Meanwhile, tourism infrastructure was poor, tourist sites were limited, and human resources untrained (Hobson *et al.* 1994).

Policy decisions and outputs

In 1978 the VNAT was established to undertake state management of tourism. It also managed over 30 state-owned tourist companies, hotels, guesthouses, and villas nationwide (Tran 2005). In 1983, the Vietnam Tourist Company was dissolved and its business activities were transferred to the VNAT. The evidence suggests that the GOV was playing the roles of operator and entrepreneur in tourism. However, the VNAT was inexperienced and thus it could not effectively implement both the state management and business functions. Therefore, *Decree No. 20* was issued to specify three main responsibilities of the VNAT: undertaking state management of tourism, managing tourism training institutions, and managing state-owned tourism businesses (VNAT 2005).

There was a significant transfer from state monopoly to joint-venture businesses. This transfer was most evident in the hotel sector. Before 1986, most state-owned hotels and guesthouses were of old styles and were equipped with very basic facilities and unskilled staff. After the *Law on Foreign Investment* was approved (1987), joint-venture hotels started to emerge. The Saigon Floating Hotel was opened in 1989 and was managed by Southern Pacific Hotels. It was the first five-star hotel in Ho Chi Minh City that offered international standards of services (Truong 2013). By the end of this period, 45 hotel investment projects were recorded (Hobson *et al.* 1994), indicating that the state monopoly over tourism was diminishing and that the GOV was starting to act as the coordinator of FDI in tourism.

In 1990, the *Vietnam's Tourism Year* campaign was launched. It aimed to promote Vietnam's image to the world (Hobson *et al.* 1994; Truong 2013) in order to accelerate economic growth. It suggested that the GOV was acting as the promoter of tourism. In addition, some tourism schools were established, including Hanoi Hospitality School, Vung Tau Hospitality School, and Centre for Tourism and Hospitality Training. They were managed by the VNAT, indicating that the GOV was also the provider of tourism education.

Table 14.1 Summary of Vietnam's tourism policy development, 1976–2015

Policy issues	1976–1990	1991–2004	2005–2015
Policy-making context	a. Local government's perception changed. b. 1986 *Renewal Policy* adopted. c. Tourism used for economic growth, although still politically driven.	a. Significant perceptual changes in government. b. Tourism development for economic growth over political purposes. c. Tourism should be developed in the context of the socialist-oriented market economy.	a. Change in the attitude of the Vietnamese government towards tourism. b. Recognition of the various social impacts of tourism, including its potential for poverty alleviation.
Demands for tourism policies	a. Lack of a state management agency. b. Ineffective state management. c. Poor infrastructure, unskilled human resources, limited tourist sites.	a. Tourists increased. b. Foreign investments required. c. Tourist sites needed expanding. d. Tourism quality needed improving.	The goals stated in the *Master Plan for Tourism Development to 2020, Vision2030*: a. Tourism becomes a spearhead sector. b. Tourism sector becomes more professional. c. Infrastructure improves for tourism development. d. Tourism products and services improve their quality.
Policy decisions	a. Formulating a state management agency. b. Separating business function from state management function. c. Transferring from state monopoly to joint ventures.	a. Separating state management from provincial management (1994). b. Coordinating tourism development among regions and industries. c. Regulating the tourism sector. d. Formulating tourism strategies and plans. e. Increasing tourism promotion. f. Intensifying tourism education.	a. Planning and development of tourist zones. b. Expansion of the areas of tourism business. c. Classification and standardisation of tourism businesses. d. Intensification of tourism education and training. e. Intensification of tourism promotion.

Policy outputs	a. The VNAT established (1978). b. The VNAT became a state management function. c. Joint-venture hotels emerged (post-1986). d. *Vietnam's Tourism Year* campaign launched (1990). e. Tourism schools established.	a. Local Departments of Tourism established (1994). b. National Steering Committee for Tourism Development established (1999), followed by provincial steering committees. c. Areas of tourism business specified; registration and approval of tourist guides introduced (1999). d. *Tourism Year* campaigns implemented. e. Promotional campaigns implemented. f. Visa exemption agreements signed. g. Tourism education and training at tertiary level.	a. Planning and development of seven tourist zones. b. Introduction of business in development of tourist resorts and spots. c. Regulation of the classification of tourist accommodation establishments. d. Formulation and implementation of promotion campaigns. e. Signing of more visa exemption agreements.
Policy impacts	a. Domestic tourism started to develop. b. Foreign tourists increased considerably. c. Tourism recognised as an industry. d. Tourist sites expanded. e. Lack of flights and hotels.	a. Tourism recognised as a spearhead industry. b. The number of foreign tourists increased to one million in 1994; total tourism receipts increased by 19 times between 1999 and 2004; state funding and foreign direct investment increased. c. The Master Plan's target of 3.5–3.8 million tourists by 2000 not achieved.	a. The target of 7.5 million foreign tourists achieved in 2013. The number of domestic tourists doubled from 16 million (2005) to 35 million (2013). b. Total tourism receipts grew from VND30 trillion (US$1.4 billion) (2005) to VND200 trillion (US$9.5 billion) (2013). c. In 2010, tourism contributed 5.8 per cent to Vietnam's GDP. e. Concerns: the sustainability of tourism development; the contribution of tourism to poverty alleviation.
Government's roles	Operator, regulator, entrepreneur, coordinator, promoter and educator.	Entrepreneur (weakened); regulator, coordinator, planner, promoter (intensified); and educator (weakened).	Entrepreneur (weakened); regulator, coordinator, planner, promoter (intensified); and educator (weakened).

Sources: GOV 1999, 2005; Hobson et al. 1994; Mok & Lam 1997; Tran 2005; VNAT 2005, 2009a, 2009b, 2010.

Impacts of tourism policies

Domestic tourism started to develop. In 1989, domestic tourists numbered 540,000, an approximate two-fold increase from 280,000 in 1986 (Tran 2005; Truong 2013). The Vietnam Civil Aviation airline made its first international flight to Beijing and then Vientiane in 1976. In 1978 it started to offer flights to Bangkok. By the end of this period, the airline expanded its network to Hong Kong, Manila, Kuala Lumpur, and Singapore (Vinafour n.d).

In terms of international tourism, the 1990 *Tourism Year* campaign led to a sharp increase in foreign tourists. Between 1975 and 1990, the number of foreign tourists increased more than six times, from 36,900 (Tran 2005) to 250,000 (Brennan & Nguyen 2000). The total tourism income generated was about US$140 million in 1989 (Truong 2013). To some extent, the campaign succeeded in introducing Vietnam to the world community. Nevertheless, it failed to handle the rapid influx of foreign tourists and provide sufficient hotels and flights. Added to this was the lack of well-trained human resources (Hobson *et al.* 1994; Truong 2013).

Tourist sites were expanded to include Hue, Nha Trang, Can Tho, and Ho Chi Minh City (VNAT 2005) among those previously developed. The local human resources in tourism were improved in terms of both quantity and quality (Tran 2005). From only 112 direct employees in the 1960s, the tourism sector created about 8,000 direct jobs in 1989 (Truong 2013). Although the nature of tourism had shifted from politics to economics, it was only a secondary sector (Truong 2014a) and was facing such difficulties as inadequate infrastructure, poor service quality, and ineffective inter-sectoral coordination. These challenges ushered the sector into a new period when a new legal framework was created.

Period 1991–2004: from a secondary sector to an economic spearhead

As a result of the *Renewal Policy*, barriers to private investments were gradually removed and foreign investments encouraged, with the issuance of the *Law on Private Companies* and the *Company Law* (1990), the *Law on the Promotion of Domestic Investment* (1994), and the amendment of the *Law on Foreign Investment* (1992, 1996) (Truong 2014a). Furthermore, the US trade embargo was lifted in 1994. These changes led to a rapid increase in foreign tourists, from about 300,000 in 1991 to 2.1 million in 2000 (Truong 2014a), who sought business and investment opportunities (Hobson *et al.* 1994). The *Renewal Process* also resulted in a significant change in the GOV's perception, from considering tourism a political means towards focusing more on its economic benefits. *Decree No. 46* of 1994 affirmed that tourism was a strategic component in the country's socio-economic development, industrialisation, and modernisation. In particular, the Ninth Party Congress of 2001 set the target of developing tourism into a spearhead sector (GOV 2002).

Demands for tourism policies

Effective tourism policies were required for three main reasons. First, the number of foreign tourists increased annually, coming from many other countries than those of the former Soviet Union (VNAT 2005). Second, the roles of foreign partners and investors were recognised, particularly in developing the hotel sector, which required intensive funding. Foreign investments were even more important because Vietnam aimed to construct some tourist sites of regional and international significance and to become a tourist centre in Asia (VNAT 2005). Third, the increase in foreign tourists required the expansion of tourist sites and the diversification of quality products and services (Tran 2005).

Policy decisions and outputs

The management of tourism was separated between the state and provincial level. *Decree No. 9* was issued in 1994, specifying the responsibilities of provinces and cities for managing their own tourism activities (GOV 1994). Departments of Tourism were thus established in 14 provinces and cities where tourism was more developed than in others. By the end of 2004, Departments of Tourism or Departments of Tourism and Trade were founded in 61 provinces and cities nationwide (VNAT 2005). Tourism coordination has been strengthened since the National Steering Committee for Tourism Development was established in 1999. Headed by the deputy prime minister, the committee assists the GOV in coordinating relevant ministries in developing tourism (GOV 1999). Local-level steering committees were then formed in 51 provinces and cities, where cooperation agreements were signed (VNAT 2005).

Tourism business was opened to various types of enterprises (e.g. collective, private-owned, family-run, and foreign-invested). Some state-owned enterprises were reformed, such as the Hanoi Tourist Company, Saigontourist Company, and Ben Thanh Tourist Company (VNAT 2005). The GOV's role of entrepreneur was thus slightly weakened, while its roles of regulator and promoter were intensified, which was demonstrated by the formulation and implementation of many strategies and plans. At the national level, the *Master Plan for Tourism Development 1995–2010* was made in 1994, setting the target of 3.5–3.8 million foreign tourists by the end of 2000 (VNAT 1994). The *Vietnam: A Destination for the New Millennium* campaign was launched in 2000, followed by the formulation of the *National Strategy for Tourism Development 2001–2010* in 2002 (GOV 2002). At the local level, tourism development plans were approved in 50 provinces and cities (VNAT 2005). *National Tourism Year* programmes were implemented in a number of provinces and cities (e.g. Quang Ninh, Quang Nam, Hanoi, Thua Thien Hue). By the end of 2004, visa exemption agreements were signed between Vietnam and about 40 countries worldwide (Truong 2014a).

Given the rapid growth of the tourism sector, the GOV saw the need to regulate the operations of tourism enterprises. In 1999, the *Tourism Ordinance* entered into force (GOV 1999), specifying four main areas of tourism business: domestic and international tour operations, tourist accommodation business, tourist transportation business, and other tourism business. The *Ordinance* also provided regulations covering matters such as operating conditions, approval procedures, and penalties for violations of rules and regulations. Furthermore, it regulated all tourist guides with provisions covering their qualifications and personality. Tourist guides were required to be Vietnamese citizens, have good ethical records and good health, be fluent speakers of at least one foreign language, and hold a tertiary degree in tourism or otherwise a tertiary degree in a close field of study, as well as a certificate of tourist guiding issued by a recognised education institution (GOV 1999).

In terms of education, tourism courses started to be offered at the tertiary level. The Department of Tourism and Hospitality was established in 1996 at the National Economics University in Hanoi. Tourism departments were also founded at Vietnam National University (both Hanoi and Ho Chi Minh City campuses). Tourism courses began to be offered by privately owned higher education institutions such as Dong Do University and Phuong Dong University. These institutions differ from early tourism and hospitality schools not only because they offer courses of higher levels but also because they are independent of the VNAT. Therefore, the GOV's role of tourism education provider was gradually weakened.

Impacts of tourism policies

In 1994, the number of foreign tourists to Vietnam was one million (Tran 2005; VNAT 2009a), a fourfold increase compared to 1990. From 1991 to 2004, the number of foreign tourists increased by nearly ten times, from 300,000 to 2.9 million (Tran 2005; VNAT 2009a), where Asian countries were the biggest international markets (Truong 2014a). Total tourism receipts grew by about 19 times, from VND1,350 billion (US$64.3 million) in 1999 to VND26,000 billion (US$1.2 billion) in 2004 (Truong 2014a; VNAT 2009a).

In late 2004 there were 5,847 tourist accommodation establishments nationwide, a 16-fold increase from 350 in 1990; and an estimated 400 international tour operators (VNAT 2011). State funding for infrastructure development was recorded at VND550 billion (US$26.2 million) in 2004, which doubled the 2001 figure of VND266 billion (US$12.6 million) (VNAT 2005). In terms of FDI, between 1988 and 1997 Vietnam attracted over US$30 billion, of which more than 20% was for tourism (Truong 2014a). From 2000 to 2004, FDI increased about eight times in terms of project numbers and five times in terms of capital amounts (General Statistics Office of Vietnam (GSOV) 2010).

Despite these achievements, the policies implemented failed to deliver the *Master Plan for Tourism Development*'s target of 3.5–3.8 million foreign tourists by 2000. The Plan was therefore revised to make tourist numbers and revenue figures more realistic and to better focus on the sustainable development of tourism. Accordingly, the revised copy of this Plan placed emphasis on the protection of natural and cultural resources that are essential for tourism and on the creation of benefits for destination communities (VNAT 1994).

2005–2015: tourism as an economic spearhead and a means of poverty alleviation

In 2005, the *Law on Tourism* entered into force (GOV 2005), replacing the 1999 *Tourism Ordinance*. It set out the goal of developing tourism as a spearhead industry that contributes significantly to raising people's intellectual standards and to poverty alleviation. In 2006 the GOV incorporated tourism as a key component of the *National Socio-economic Development Plan 2006–2010* that was approved at the Tenth Party Congress (VNAT 2005). These events were an important benchmark for tourism in Vietnam as there was a change in the attitude of the GOV towards the nature of tourism, from considering tourism as an important means of economic growth towards placing a greater focus on its contribution to poverty alleviation.

Demands for tourism policies

In developing tourism as a spearhead sector, the VNAT prepared the *Master Plan for Tourism Development to 2020, Vision 2030* (VNAT 2013). The overall goal of the Plan is to turn Vietnam into a country with a developed tourism industry, and as an attractive destination in Asia by 2030. Tourism is expected to become an economic spearhead by the end of 2020, and to be characterised by professionalism, advanced infrastructure, and diversified and high-quality products and services (VNAT 2013). In terms of tourist numbers, the Plan sets the target as 7.5 million foreign tourists and 37 million domestic tourists in 2015. In 2020, the number of foreign tourists is expected to increase to 10.5 million and domestic tourists 47.5 million. Tourism receipts are set to reach US$10.3 billion in 2015, US$18.5 billion in 2020, and US$26.6 billion in 2025 (VNAT 2013). The GOV has thus given attention to the planning of tourist zones, expansion of the areas of tourism business, classification of tourism businesses, intensification of tourism education, and intensification of promotional activities.

Policy decisions and outputs

Until the end of the 1990s, the main emphasis of the GOV was on historical and cultural tourism. The development policy for tourist attractions was mainly limited to major cities, particularly where historical and cultural attractions were located. There were three tourist zones: North, North Central, and South Central (VNAT 1994). Awareness was raised of the importance of diversifying tourism products and improving the receiving capacities of tourist attractions. The *Master Plan for Tourism Development to 2020, Vision 2030* provided guidance for the planning and development of seven tourist zones: Northern Midlands and Mountain Areas; Red River Delta and North-eastern Coastal Areas, North Central, South Central Coastal Areas, Central Highlands, South East, and South West (VNAT 2013). It also set out the organisation and development of 46 national tourist areas and 41 national tourist spots, where product development and marketing plans were outlined (VNAT 2013).

Before 2005 there were only four main areas of tourism business, as noted above. In order to make tourist attractions more adaptable to the needs of the international market, the *Law on Tourism* (GOV 2005) expanded the scope of tourism business to include business in development of tourist resorts and spots. The other areas are international and domestic tour business, tourist accommodation business, tourist transportation business, and business in other tourism services. The GOV allows both Vietnamese citizens and foreigners to invest in developing tourist resorts and spots; they are entitled to own their allocated land for up to 50 years and this right can be renewed (GOV 2013).

The *Law on Tourism* also classified tourist accommodation establishments into tourist hotels, tourist villages, tourist villas, tourist apartments, tourist campsites, houses for tourist rental, and other tourist accommodation establishments (GOV 2005). Tourist hotels are divided into city hotels, hotel resorts, motels, and floating hotels, and are ranked in terms of location and architecture, facilities and amenities, quantity and quality of services, quality of executive and service staff members, and security and environmental protection (VNAT 2009b). In addition, it set five conditions for international tourist guides: being Vietnamese citizens, having good ethics and personality, having good health, being fluent in at least one foreign language and holding a tertiary degree in tourist guiding (GOV 2005).

The growing importance of tourism has led to the increase in education institutions offering tourism and hospitality courses. About 40 universities and colleges and 30 vocational schools now offer tourism and hospitality programmes (VNAT 2005). Many of these are privately owned and hence are independent of the VNAT, such as FPT University. These institutions have also started to offer postgraduate programmes in tourism and hospitality. For example, the Faculty of Tourism Studies at Vietnam National University has provided a Master's Programme in Tourism since 2005. The National Economics University in Hanoi has offered both master's and doctoral programmes in tourism economics. Although these programmes meet the requirements of the local Ministry of Education and Training, they are hardly recognised by any international accreditation organisations.

With respect to promotional activities, the VNAT has actively engaged in tourism promotion, and the budget reached VND112 billion (US$5.3 million) in 2005 (VNAT 2005). The Department of Tourism Promotion was set up within the VNAT in 2004, indicating the GOV's recognition of the importance of professional tourism promotion. Three promotional campaigns have since been implemented to attract foreign tourists: *Welcome to Vietnam* (2004–2005), *Vietnam – the Hidden Charm* (2006–2011), and *Vietnam – the Timeless Charm* (2012 to present). In terms of domestic tourism, the VNAT has continued to implement *Vietnam's Tourism Year* campaigns, with a single theme being developed each year. The theme in 2006 was *One Destination – Two World Heritages* and was dedicated to the central province of Quang

Nam. In 2011, the campaign featured Phu Yen and other provinces in the South Central Coastal Areas in the theme of *Sea and Coastal Tourism*. The theme for 2015 is *Connecting the World Heritages* and is implemented in the central province of Thanh Hoa.

To effectively launch these promotional campaigns, the VNAT has collaborated with Vietnam Airlines, Vietnamese embassies overseas, and international media corporations (e.g. the BBC, CNN, NHK). It has also participated in international tourism promotion events such as ATF (ASEAN Tourism Forum), Top Resa (France), ITB (Germany), JATA (Japan), and WTM (UK) (VNAT 2005, 2011). Furthermore, the GOV has signed visa exemption agreements with about 80 countries worldwide (Truong 2014a).

Impacts of tourism policies

Tourism in this period has enjoyed sustained growth in both visitor numbers and total receipts. The 2015 target of 7.5 million foreign tourists was achieved in 2013 (VNAT 2015). The number of domestic tourists doubled from 16 million in 2005 to 35 million in 2013 (VNAT 2009a, 2015). Total tourism receipts grew by about six times, from VND30 trillion (US$1.4 billion) in 2005 to VND200 trillion (US$9.5 billion) in 2013 (VNAT 2009a, 2015). In 2010 tourism contributed 5.8% to Vietnam's GDP compared to 3.2% in 1995 (VNAT 2013).

As of June 2014 there were 15,998 tourist accommodation establishments and 1,383 international tour operators nationwide (VNAT 2015). About 50% of tourist hotels were ranked from one to five stars. Tourism created employment for about 1.4 million people, accounting for 3.8% of the local labour force (VNAT 2013). About 470,000 people were direct tourism workers, of which 9.7% were university graduates or higher and 51% were college graduates or lower (VNAT 2013). The growth of tourism also led to increased state funding for infrastructure development, from VND550 billion (US$26.2 million) in 2004 to VND700 billion (US$33 million) in 2009 (VNAT 2010). In terms of FDI in tourism, the number of projects rose from 15 in 2004 to 48 in 2007. However, it decreased to 26 projects in 2008 and 25 projects in 2011 (VNAT 2011).

In this third and current period, the GOV's roles of regulator, planner, coordinator, and promoter continued to intensify. Its role of entrepreneur slightly weakened, given that Vietnam was developing towards a market-oriented economy where state-owned enterprises were reformed. Similarly, the GOV's role of tourism educator was also weakened since a variety of education institutions offered tourism education and training at different levels. This period witnessed an important change in the GOV's attitudes towards tourism, from considering tourism an economic spearhead to placing greater focus on its potential for poverty alleviation. Implications for tourism policy development are discussed below.

Implications and conclusions

Elliot (2002) argued that the private sector is the basic sector in tourism. It is generally the most dynamic and responsive to market demand and the changing business environment. However, in a socialist-oriented developing country such as Vietnam, government involvement has played an important role in the development of tourism, particularly in its initial stages when the private sector was non-existent and when the GOV was more concerned about national security than the benefits of tourism. Over the past 55 years, the GOV has played different roles in developing tourism: operator/entrepreneur – owning and running state-owned tourism enterprises; regulator – providing a legal framework for tourism business; planner – leading the planning and development of tourist zones; coordinator – coordinating relevant ministries in tourism development; promoter – spending money on promotion campaigns; and educator – providing tourism education and training.

The past 55 years have also seen significant changes in the GOV's attitudes towards tourism. Tourism transformed from being a political tool in the 1960–75 period to an economic one in the 1976–1990 period. From 1991 to 2004, tourism emerged as an important economic sector. Since 2005, tourism has been perceived as a contributor to social development, especially to poverty alleviation. These changes can be attributed to many social, economic, and political reasons. Of these, the adoption of the 1986 *Renewal Policy* is arguably the most decisive because it was then that Vietnam transformed into a market-oriented economy from a centrally planned one. Given that Vietnam is under communist rule with strong central government control, it is understandable that the government has played a key role in shaping tourism development, which is demonstrated by the formulation and implementation of a series of policies, strategies, and plans.

Despite the GOV's efforts, tourism development in Vietnam faces challenges. It seems that the GOV has placed much focus on tourist numbers and revenue figures, some of which could not be achieved. The failure to deliver the *Master Plan for Tourism Development 1995–2010*'s target of 3.5–3.8 million foreign tourists is an example. Although in 2013 Vietnam had already achieved the goal of 7.5 million foreign tourists that was actually set for 2015, it is difficult to ensure that it can attract the 10.5 million foreign tourists in 2020 as set by the *Master Plan for Tourism Development to 2020, Vision 2030*. Indeed, foreign tourist numbers significantly decreased in the first quarter of 2015. In January, an estimated 700,692 foreign tourists visited Vietnam, a 9.7% decrease compared to the same period the previous year. Likewise, February and March saw a 10.2% and 12.9%, respectively, reduction in foreign tourists compared to the same period the previous year (VNAT 2015). This is mainly due to the dramatic decline in the Chinese and Russian markets following the dispute over the South China Sea for the former and the decline of the rouble for the later (see Case study 14.1).

Other barriers preventing Vietnam from generating repeat tourists include concerns over pollution in tourist destinations, limited tourism products, second-rate facilities and amenities, and poor customer service. For example, in Sapa, a well-known destination in the north-western province of Lao Cai, foreign tourists expressed their discomfort when being followed by local handicraft sellers (Truong *et al.* 2014). In other destinations, tourists were dissatisfied with the knowledge and personality of their guides, who even made up stories about historical relics or made inappropriate gestures towards tourists (Trung Hieu & Dieu Linh 2014). This is despite policies having been enacted regarding the qualifications of international tourist guides and tourism education and training having been intensified.

In addition, although the GOV has perceived tourism as an important means of poverty alleviation in tourist destinations, it has not taken any concrete policy measures to realise this. Nor has it been able to demonstrate the actual impact of tourism on poor people (Truong 2013). Truong *et al.* (2014) indicate that many of the poor in Sapa did not even believe tourism could lift them out of poverty, given that it primarily benefited privately owned tour operators. Therefore, policy initiatives and measures need to be taken if tourism is to be recognised as an actual contributor to poverty alleviation.

In conclusion, the analysis of tourism policy development in Vietnam has provided some interesting insights into the way a socialist-oriented developing country has transformed tourism from a political means into an economic spearhead that is now operated in a market economy. The GOV at different stages has played a decisive role in shaping the development of tourism. The insights gained from this chapter may also assist the governments in Vietnam and similar societies elsewhere in addressing various aspects of tourism development through their policy initiatives and measures.

Case study 14.1 Vietnam's tourism marketing strategy in a time of crisis

The number of foreign tourists to Vietnam has increased relatively quickly during the past years. In 2010, foreign tourists reached five million, a two-fold increase from 2.3 million in 2001 (VNAT 2011). The number increased to 6 million in 2011, 6.8 million in 2012, 7.5 million in 2013, and 7.8 million in 2014 (VNAT 2015). However, it dropped by 13.7% in the first quarter of 2015 compared to the same period last year (VNAT 2015). This is largely because of the significant decline in the number of tourists from China and Russia, two of Vietnam's main international markets. The number of Chinese tourists decreased by 40.4% in the first quarter of 2015 following the dispute over the South China Sea (also known as the East Sea in Vietnam). Meanwhile, Russian visitors had to terminate their travel plans since the value of the rouble declined as a result of the Ukraine incident.

A number of strategies were formulated by the VNAT. Primary amongst these was the "*Người Việt Nam du lịch Việt Nam – Mỗi chuyến đi thêm yêu Tổ quốc*" (Vietnamese people travel Vietnam – Every trip makes you love the country better) programme which aimed to promote domestic tourism. The programme was implemented from October 2014 to the end of 2015 (VNAT 2014). It sets the targets of over 35 million domestic tourists in 2014 and 37.5 million in 2015. The programme consists of two main components. First, Vietnamese citizens are encouraged to travel within Vietnam, particularly to rural, mountainous, and coastal areas. Second, overseas Vietnamese nationals are urged to visit the homeland to demonstrate their patriotism. A number of measures have been proposed to achieve the planned targets. For example, tourism enterprises participating in the programme are entitled to VAT discounts and/or late payment of corporate income tax. Provinces and cities strengthen their collaboration to create new and high-quality products. Enterprises draw-up promotion programmes while improving their customer service. Furthermore, the Ministry of Foreign Affairs coordinates with Vietnamese embassies overseas and the VNAT in disseminating the programme to overseas Vietnamese nationals in their respective countries (VNAT 2014).

A final evaluation report was not available at the time of writing since the programme is still in progress. In the first quarter of 2015 the number of domestic tourists was reportedly 19.5 million, which accounted for over half of the total number of domestic tourists in 2013 (VNAT 2015; personal communication with VNAT official, May 2015). Given that a number of promotional activities are being intensified by the VNAT as well as tourism enterprises, it is likely that the programme's target of 37.5 million domestic tourists will be achieved by the end of 2015.

Key reading

Cooper, M. (2000) 'Tourism in Vietnam: Doi Moi and the realities of tourism in the 1990s', in C.M. Hall and S. Page (eds), *Tourism in South and Southeast Asia: Issues and Cases* (pp. 167–177). Oxford: Butterworth-Heinemann.

Gillen, J. (2014) 'Tourism and nation building at the War Remnants Museum in Ho Chi Minh City, Vietnam', *Annals of the Association of American Geographers*, 104(6): 1307–1321.

Gillen, J., Kirby, R. and Riemsdijk, M. (2015) 'Tour guides as tourist products in Dalat, Vietnam: Exploring market freedoms in a communist state', *Asia Pacific Viewpoint*, 56(2): 237–251.

Hildebrandt, T. and Isaac, R. (2015) 'The tourism structures in Central Vietnam: Towards a destination management organisation', *Tourism Planning & Development*, 12(4): 463–478.

Trinh, T.T. and Ryan, C. (2015) 'Heritage and cultural tourism: The role of the aesthetic when visiting Mỹ Sơn and Cham Museum, Vietnam', *Current Issues in Tourism*, DOI:10.1080/13683 500.2015.1054269.

Truong, V.D. (2013) 'Tourism policy development in Vietnam: A pro-poor perspective', *Journal of Policy Research in Tourism, Leisure and Events*, 5(1): 28–45.

Truong, V.D., Hall, C.M. and Garry, T. (2014) 'Tourism and poverty alleviation: Perceptions and experiences of poor people in Sapa, Vietnam', *Journal of Sustainable Tourism*, 22(7): 1071–1089.

References

Brennan, M. and Nguyen, N.B. (2000) 'Vietnamese tourism: The challenges ahead'. Online. Available: http://ir.lib.oita-u.ac.jp/dspace/handle/10559/7058 (accessed 20 March 2013).

Elliot, J. (2002) *Tourism, Politics and Public Sector Management*. London: Routledge.

General Statistics Office of Vietnam (GSOV) (2010) *Statistical Yearbook of Vietnam 2010*. Hanoi: Statistical Publishers.

Government of Vietnam (GOV) (1994) *Decree No. 9 on the Organisation and Management of Tourism Businesses*. Online. Available: www.vietnamtourism.gov.vn (accessed 15 May 2013).

—— (1999) *Tourism Ordinance*. Hanoi: National Political.

—— (2002) *National Strategy for Tourism Development 2001–2010*. Hanoi: GOV.

—— (2005) *Law on Tourism*. Hanoi: National Political.

—— (2013) *Land Law*. Online. Available: www.chinhphu.vn (accessed 20 May 2015).

Hall, C.M. (1994) *Tourism and Politics: Policy, Power and Place*. Chichester: Wiley & Sons.

Hobson, P.J., Heung, V. and Chon, K.S. (1994) 'Vietnam's tourism industry: Can it be kept afloat?' *Cornell Hotel and Restaurant Administration Quarterly*, 35(5): 42–48.

Jenkins, C.L. and Henry, B.M. (1982) 'Government involvement in tourism in developing countries', *Annals of Tourism Research*, 9(4): 499–521.

Mok, C. and Lam, T. (1997) 'Hotel and tourism development in Vietnam', *Journal of Travel and Tourism Marketing*, 7(1): 85–91.

Tran, D.T. (2005) *Introduction to Tourism* (4th edn). Hanoi: VNU Publishers.

Trung Hieu and Dieu Linh (2014) 'Unprofessional tour guides ruin experience'. Online. Available: http://vietnamnews.vn/talk-around-town/254180/unprofessional-tour-guides-ruin-experience.html (accessed 15 May 2015).

Truong, V.D. (2013) 'Tourism policy development in Vietnam: A pro-poor perspective', *Journal of Policy Research in Tourism, Leisure and Events*, 5(1): 28–45.

—— (2014a) 'Tourism and poverty alleviation: A case study of Sapa, Vietnam'. Unpublished doctoral dissertation, University of Canterbury, New Zealand. Online. Available: http://ir.canterbury.ac.nz/handle/10092/9244.

—— (2014b) 'Pro-poor tourism: Looking backward as we move forward', *Tourism Planning & Development*, 11(2): 228–242.

—— (2015) 'Pro-poor tourism: Reflections on past research and directions for the future', in C.M Hall, S. Gössling and D. Scott (eds), *The Routledge Handbook of Tourism and Sustainability* (pp. 127–140), London: Routledge.

Truong, V.D., Hall, C.M. and Garry, T. (2014) 'Tourism and poverty alleviation: Perceptions and experiences of poor people in Sapa, Vietnam', *Journal of Sustainable Tourism*, 22(7): 1071–1089.

Vietnam National Administration of Tourism (VNAT) (1994) *Master Plan for Tourism Development 1995–2010*. Hanoi: VNAT.

—— (2005) '45 years of construction and development of Vietnam's tourism sector'. Online. Available: www.vietnamtourism.gov.vn (accessed 15 May 2013).

—— (2009a) 'Some achievements in the development of Vietnam's tourism sector'. Online. Available: www.vietnamtourism.gov.vn (accessed 15 May 2013).

—— (2009b) 'National standards for hotel classification'. Online. Available: www.vietnamtourism.gov.vn (accessed 15 May 2013).

—— (2010) 'Mobilising investments to construct tourism infrastructure, diversify tourist products and improve quality'. Online. Available: www.vietnamtourism.gov.vn (accessed 15 May 2013).

—— (2011) *Tourism Development 2011: Final Evaluation*. Online. Available: www.vietnamtourism.gov.vn (accessed 15 May 2013).

—— (2013) *Master Plan for Tourism Development*. Hanoi: VNAT.

—— (2014) 'Approval of the "Người Việt Nam du lịch Việt Nam – Mỗi chuyến đi thêm yêu Tổ quốc" program'. Online. Available: www.vietnamtourism.gov.vn (accessed 20 May 2015).

—— (2015) 'Tourist arrivals and tourism receipts'. Online. Available www.vietnamtourism.gov.vn (accessed 20 May 2015).

Vinafour (n.d.) 'Vietnam airlines'. Online. Available: www.vinafour.com (accessed 20 May 2015).

15

VISITING OPPRESSIVE STATES

Tourism in Laos, Cambodia and Myanmar

Andrea Valentin & Daniela Schilcher

Introduction

Different degrees of change have occurred in Lao People's Democratic Republic (PDR), the Kingdom of Cambodia and the Republic of the Union of Myanmar over the past decades. While civil war and ethnic unrest have been embedded in the recent histories of all three countries, the political situation is gradually improving. But it remains to be seen how the impacts of tourism will be absorbed in the local cultures and economies of Laos, Cambodia and Myanmar in the long term. The Community Learning Center Laos (2014) explains that in the 1970s Laos was ravaged by the US "Secret War", turning it into the most heavily bombed country on earth per capita. The Khmer Rouge created the state of "Democratic Kampuchea" in 1975 and ruled Cambodia until January 1979. Under the Khmer Rouge nearly two million people died, and those who lived through the genocide remain severely traumatised by their experiences. Myanmar entered a new period of governance in 2010 after half a century of military dictatorship, leading to the dropping of most economic sanctions and an opening up to the outside world. All three countries not only share a history of political unrest and civil war, they have also experienced dramatic increases in tourist arrivals since opening their borders to international visitors. In 2013, about 3.8 million tourists visited Laos, more than 4.2 million visited Cambodia, and about one million visited Myanmar. All three countries are experiencing substantial growth in tourist numbers, with tourism being a target industry in terms of employment generation and economic development. This chapter will provide an overview of the opportunities and challenges of tourism development in the three countries.

Laos

Lao PDR is a landlocked country bordering China, Vietnam, Cambodia, Thailand and Myanmar. With a mere 6.8 million people inhabiting Laos' 236,800km^2 (United Nations Development Programme (UNDP) 2015), the country's low population density and corresponding prevalence of relatively pristine natural areas offer various opportunities for tourism development. However, officially classified as a "least developed country", Laos faces several development challenges (UNDP 2015). Despite an increase of GDP from US$876 per capita in 2009 (Delang & Toro 2011) to US$1,660 in 2013 (World Bank 2015a), Laos still ranks among the poorest countries in South-East Asia. High poverty rates prevail particularly within the rural population (65% of the population live in rural areas) (World Bank 2015a). Unexploded ordnance, the remains of over two million tons of bombs dropped onto Laos during the 1964–1973 "Secret War", continues to pose a serious threat to villagers – as well as "off the beaten track" visitors – and is a main contributing factor to poverty in rural areas (UNDP 2015).

Tourism and economic development

The country's significant rate of economic growth in recent years is mainly the result of foreign direct investment in natural resource extraction and the export of hydropower to Thailand, China and Vietnam (World Bank 2014). The Lao government's hydropower development plan contains the construction of 72 major dams (Department of Energy Business 2012), despite opposition of displaced villagers and NGOs documenting negative human consequences (Delang & Toro 2011). 'Capital entered the country to transform its forests, orchards, upland rice fields and fallow areas, along with smallholder cash crop fields, into coffee plantations, rubber plantations, logging areas, mines and dammed reservoirs' (Delang & Toro 2011: 569). This shift away from traditional agriculture as the key sector of the economy is reflected in its changing economic contribution. In 2003 agriculture contributed 51% to GDP (Suntikul 2007), while ten years later it was reduced to 26% (World Bank 2015a). During the same period, the significance of the services sector, including tourism, increased from 26% to 40% (Suntikul 2007; World Bank 2015a).

This gradual restructuring of a former state socialist economic system towards a market economy has had a positive impact on the national economy; however, negative consequences in terms of social sustainability have been noted (Rehbein 2007). The gap has widened not only between rich and poor, but also between men and women and different ethnic groups (Organization for Economic Cooperation and Development (OECD) 2013; UNDP 2015). Lao is marked by a high degree of ethnic diversity, being home to 49 officially recognised ethnic groups. The largest group is the Tai-Kadai linguistic family, to which belong the Lao (Ministry of Information, Culture and Tourism 2014). Poverty rates are lowest among the Tai-Kadai, who are also referred to as the Lao-Lum (*Lowland Lao*). Members of this ethnic family are usually integrated into the cash economy and have access to basic services. The Lao-Suung (*Upland-Lao*), on the other hand, still live mostly subsistence lifestyles or work as labourers for the Tai-Kadai or Chinese on rubber plantations (Adams & Gillogly 2011). With limited or no access to healthcare and education, hard work on slash-and-burn upland rice fields, a lack of hygiene and nutritious food, life expectancy remains low and many Lao-Suung, such as the Akha and Khmu ethnic people, are locked in a poverty trap (Adams & Gillogly 2011; Ministry of Information, Culture and Tourism 2014).

Laos' various economic challenges combined with its natural areas and cultural resources derived from a multi-ethnic society rich in history means that tourism is considered as a development tool by the Lao government and international organisations (Ministry of Information, Culture and Tourism 2014). The government's encouragement of international tourism began in the late 1980s. Until 1986, Lao had a closed-door policy under its state socialist ideology and the few international visitors the country received were representatives of (mostly socialist) states or international organisations (Sosamphanh *et al.* 2013; Yamauchi & Lee 1999).

Tourism development

In 1995 the National Assembly of Laos identified tourism as a priority sector for national economic development. Investment in infrastructure development was increased and 1999 was officially declared "Visit Lao Year" – all of which encouraged growth in international visitor arrivals (Sosamphanh *et al.* 2013). In the 20-year period from 1993 to 2013 arrivals increased from 102,946 to 3,779,490, which corresponds to an impressive average annual growth rate of 19%. Simultaneously, tourist receipts grew from US$6.2 million to US$596 million, which renders tourism the country's main earner of foreign exchange (Ministry of Information, Culture and Tourism 2014). In 2013, the tourism industry directly contributed 4.7% to Laos' GDP and generated 4% of direct employment. Taking into account the industry's indirect effects on employment generation, this figure rises to 12.3% (World Travel and Tourism Council (WTTC) 2014).

In 2013, Laos was proclaimed "World's Best Tourist Destination" by the European Council on Tourism and Trade, honouring the combined efforts of the Lao government, development organisations and the private sector in preserving the country's natural and cultural heritage (ASEAN Secretariat 2013). The latter includes the UNESCO World Heritage site of Luang Prabang – the ancient capital city of the Lan Xang Kingdom (Southiseng & Walsh 2011); the twelfth-century Wat Phu temple; and the Plain of Jars with its Neolithic heritage (ASEAN Secretariat 2013). Moreover, the government has been actively promoting ecotourism and community-based tourism (CBT) in order to tap into the industry's development potential. Approximately 12% of Laos' landmass is under special protected area status (Schipani & Marris 2002; Zeppel 2006), and in 2004 the Lao National Tourism Administration presented its *National Ecotourism Strategy and Action Plan 2005–2010* (Zeppel 2006; Lao National Tourism Administration 2004), putting forward the following vision:

> Laos will become a world renowned destination specialising in forms of sustainable tourism that, through partnership and cooperation, benefit natural and cultural heritage conservation, local socio-economic development and spread knowledge of Laos' unique cultural heritage around the world.
>
> *(Lao National Tourism Administration 2004: 6)*

Indeed, the network of small-scale ecotourism or CBT ventures spans the entire country and includes the praised *Nam Ha* project in Luang Namtha province, which won the 2001 United Nations Development Award for its contribution to poverty reduction (Zeppel 2006). The *Nam Ha* project, implemented by the Lao National Tourism Administration and supported by UNESCO, features trekking tours and homestays in ethnic minority villages in a national protected area. In one of the key homestay villages, for instance, tourism's contribution to village income amounted to 17% in 2002 (Blache 2014). Due to being resettled by government to halt slash and burn agriculture among other reasons, this very village, however, no longer benefits from ecotourism activities (while continuing with slash and burn practices due to a lack of agricultural land available at the new site) (Blache 2014).

Donor support for CBT in Laos has been substantial. The Asian Development Bank (ADB) in particular has been promoting the sector with a US$10 million grant under the *Greater Mekong Subregion Tourism Development Project 2009–2014* (Lao National Tourism Administration 2014) and a US$40 million *GMS Tourism Infrastructure for Inclusive Growth Project 2015–2019* (ADB 2015). The latter focuses on improving access and market linkages, which is certainly needed given that Laos has a low income multiplier effect (Khanal 2011).

The trials of Lao tourism

The dependency on imports, lack of accessibility of destinations outside of the key tourist centres such as Luang Prabang and insufficient domestic skills and capital (ADB 2015; Khanal 2011; Southiseng & Walsh 2011) are just a few of the challenges which Laos' tourism industry is facing. For a destination that aims to specialise in sustainable tourism, the Lao government's vision to transform the country into the "battery of Southeast Asia" (Parameswaran 2014: 1) is bound to create tensions. While sustainable tourism is based upon the notion of preserving the natural and socio-cultural environment, the extensive promotion of dams, mining and rubber plantations threatens the very foundation of Laos' tourism industry. For instance, there have been protests against the controversial Don Sahong dam, which several NGOs and representatives of communities living downstream expect to severely affect fish migration, and also threaten the endangered Irrawaddy dolphin – a major ecotourism attraction (Parameswaran 2014).

The promotion of cash crops, particularly rubber, poses a further threat to Laos' tourism industry in rural areas. Frequently, the local population opts for the cultivation of rubber instead of "eco-" or community-based tourism due to expected higher financial returns. A prime example is the "Akha Experience" trekking and homestay project in Muang Sing, Luang Namtha province, which was developed by the German GTZ (Deutsche Gesellschaft für Technische Zusammenarbeit/German Agency for Technical Cooperation – now GiZ or Deutsche Gesellschaft für Internationale Zusammenarbeit). Although the Akha are known for their spiritual relationship with the forest and in spite of the project design including a "tourist forest fee" which was meant to encourage the Akha communities to preserve nature (for tourism), to a variety of community members 'the village's economic future mattered more than any sentimental or spiritual value of the forest' (Schilcher 2008: 12). In Laokhao village, for example, one needs to juxtapose an approximate US$3,000 annual income from the "Akha Experience" against about US$23,000 from cash crop cultivation (Schilcher 2008). Among others, tourists' disappointment with encountering a landscape marked by rows of rubber trees and hills, which slash-and-burn agriculture had deprived of any vegetation, caused the tour operator Exotissimo – which held the exclusive rights to the "Akha Experience" – to discontinue the tours in 2013 (Baumgartner 2014).

A further example illustrating the complexities governing Laos' tourism landscape is the small town of Vang Vieng. Situated by the Xong river and surrounded by breathtaking nature, the formerly quiet village has rapidly developed into one of South-East Asia's most infamous party hotspots for backpackers, hosting 177,000 visitors in 2012 (Sosamphanh *et al.* 2013). 'If teenagers ruled the world, it might resemble Vang Vieng' (Kennedy-Good 2009: 1), where until recently drugs used to be available on restaurant menus and the typical breakfast of bikini-clad backpackers consisted of a bucket with Lao whiskey (Haworth 2012). After 27 recorded deaths of young tourists in 2011, many of whom had drowned in the river during a "tubing" adventure (the town has become famous for floating down the river in inflatable tubes, while taking frequent breaks at riverside bars), as well as mounting complaints by ethnic communities due to the obvious socio-cultural impacts (Haworth 2012), the government closed the majority of riverside bars and enforced a variety of restrictions on tourist venues (Meyer 2013).

While these measures in Vang Vieng may be perceived as an attempt to increase the sustainability of Laos' tourism industry, the key question remains whether the vision of a "sustainable" tourism industry may be realised in an economy based upon natural resource extraction and dammed rivers. However, visitor arrivals to this multifaceted destination are expected to increase substantially (WTTC 2014), irrespective of the direction the industry's development takes in the near future.

Cambodia: from Kingdom of Sorrow to Kingdom of Wonder

The Kingdom of Cambodia is a Southeast Asian nation that borders Vietnam to the east, Laos to the north and Thailand to the west. The country's landscape includes the low-lying central plains, the uplands and its mountains, as well as the Mekong River and the Tonle Sap (Great Lake), the two major sources of water (Central Intelligence Agency (CIA) 2016). Cambodia's highest peak is Mount Aoral, which rises to 1,813 meters in the south-west of the country, while the southern coastal region connects to the Gulf of Thailand.

Although modern-day Cambodia benefits from 20 years of relative political stability, due to its volatile history it remains a country associated with land mines, killing fields and war (Documentation Center of Cambodia 2016). Having identified tourism as a potential panacea for the country's woes, since 2008 the Cambodian Ministry of Tourism promotes the country as the "Kingdom Of Wonder", to enormous success: today the tourism industry is one of the two main engines of economic growth, with over four million tourists having visited in 2013 (Ministry of Tourism Cambodia 2014). The country's major attraction is Angkor Wat, the glorious Buddhist and Hindu temple complex from ancient times, which draws more than two million visitors per year. However, today many tourists are also drawn to Cambodia due to the appeal of dark tourism (Winter 2008). Two major sites of death and disaster have become "must-see destinations" for tourists: the S21/Tuol Sling former torture centre in Phnom Penh, and the most venerated of the hundreds of killing fields in Cambodia, Choeung Ek, located about 10km from the capital.

History

From the Hindu–Buddhist kingdoms (first–eighth century), to the Khmer period (ninth–fifteenth century), what is today known as Cambodia reached its peak in the twelfth century when the temples of Angkor were constructed (Chandler 1983; Winter 2008). Since the peak of the Angkor period, hundreds of years of decline followed. Cambodia became a French colony in the nineteenth century, was occupied by the Japanese during World War II, gained independence in 1953, experienced the havoc of US carpet bombing during the Vietnam War and continued to suffer political turmoil afterwards (Khamboly Dy 2007; Documentation Center of Cambodia 2016). Yet nothing could have prepared the people for the genocidal Khmer Rouge regime, which devastated the country by killing an estimated 1.7 million of its eight million people in less than four years (April 1975 to January 1979) (Cambodia Tribunal Monitor 2016). The signing of the 1991 Peace Accord allowed the UN Peace Keeping Operations to arrange for general elections in 1993, which led to the establishment of a constitutional monarchy and a government mandating a plural democracy (CIA 2016).

Economic background

After Cambodian reforms began in the early 1990s, economic transformations led to the establishment of a market-based economy. Since then, Cambodia's economy has shown growth and stability, with tourism being the second largest income contributor after the garment industry (Ministry of Tourism Cambodia 2014). Tourism therefore plays a very important role in shaping Cambodia's development, for better or worse. Nowadays, tourism income is driving economic growth, poverty reduction and revival of a cultural identity that had been lost after the tragedy of the Khmer Rouge genocidal regime. Tourism's shadier side, however, particularly in relation to human trafficking of children, is creating a situation whereby the negative socio-cultural impacts of the tourism sector may arguably outweigh its benefits.

Decades of war and internal conflict have left Cambodia as one of the world's poorest countries (World Bank 2015a). Millions of land mines still remain hidden and unexploded today, causing incredible hardships to the local people due to the dangers of pastoral development in a country where 90% of rural people depend on agriculture for their livelihoods (Mines Advisory Group 2015). According to the International Fund for Agricultural Development (IFAD 2014), in Cambodia 'two thirds of the country's 1.6 million rural households face seasonal food shortages each year. Rural people are constantly looking for work or other income-generating activities, which are mainly temporary and poorly paid.' Cambodia's poor include subsistence farmers, fishing communities, landless people, rural youth, internally displaced persons and mine victims. The most disadvantaged, however, are ethnic minority peoples and women, not least due to their unequal access to education, employment and their lack of land and property rights.

Tourism growth

Since the country experienced peace over the past two decades, the tourism sector in Cambodia has also experienced significant growth. The Cambodian Ministry of Tourism identified tourism as a priority sector early in its development process. Given the variety of tourism experiences Cambodia has to offer, tourism is being promoted due to its potential to significantly contribute to employment creation and economic growth (Ministry of Tourism Cambodia 2014). The country experienced a steady increase in tourism numbers, with the Ministry of Tourism reporting more than four million tourist arrivals in 2013 (Table 15.1). Most tourists visiting Cambodia came from Asia; Vietnam, China, Korea, Lao PDR, Thailand and Japan are the most important source countries of travellers to Cambodia, followed by US, Australian, Russian and French tourists (Table 15.2). But although tourism has increased dramatically over the past two decades, tourism has also brought a range of negative impacts, reflecting the inherent tensions in the sector.

Everything for sale?

Although Cambodia is one of the poorest countries in the world, and is ranked as the 17th most corrupt country in the world by Transparency International (2014), tourism is booming. Currently Cambodia's economy is dominated by the garment industry and tourism (World Bank 2015b), but the government also hopes to tap into offshore oil and gas reserves that were only recently discovered (Asian Development Bank 2016), in a bid to reduce the country's

Table 15.1 International tourist arrivals to Cambodia

Year	International arrivals ('000)	Average length of stay (days)	Receipts (US$ m)
1993	118.2	–	–
1998	286.6	5.2	166
2003	701.0	5.5	347
2008	2,124.5	6.65	1,595
2013	4,210.2	6.75	2,547

Source: based on Ministry of Tourism Cambodia 2014.

Table 15.2 Top ten international arrivals markets for Cambodia

Market	Arrivals 2012 ('000)	Arrivals 2013 ('000)	Market share (%)	Change (%)
Vietnam	763.1	854.1	20.3	11.9
China	333.9	463.1	11.0	38.7
South Korea	411.5	435.0	10.3	5.7
Lao PDR	254.0	414.5	9.8	63.2
Thailand	201.4	221.3	5.3	9.8
Japan	179.3	206.9	4.9	15.4
USA	173.1	185.0	4.4	6.9
Australia	117.7	132.0	3.1	12.1
Russia	99.8	131.7	3.1	32.0
France	121.2	131.5	3.1	8.5

Source: derived from Ministry of Tourism Cambodia 2014.

dependency on aid (Sophal 2007). In this context, therefore, developing tourism in a sustainable way that minimises the negative impacts of tourism and generates equal benefits to a wide range of people remains an extremely daunting challenge (Chheang 2008). Not only does the general population lack education and skills needed for tourism, many locals feel excluded and vulnerable due to the pressure of the fast-growing population (IFAD 2014). Such rural poverty has caused the spread of HIV/AIDS, as woman migrate to either urban factories or become involved in Cambodia's booming sex tourism industry (UNICEF 2013a, 2013b). Cambodia has long been a destination for male sex tourists from Asia and Western countries as prostitution is rampant (although prohibited by law) and especially visible in the tourist hotspots. A relatively new trend is that Cambodia has also been identified as a leading country of child sexual exploitation in the world (Save the Children 2003; UNICEF 2013a). To the deep shame of Cambodians, child sex tourism has become a multi-million dollar industry.

In line with the changing developments of the tourism industry and the diversification of tourism, volunteer tourism emerged as an "alternative form of tourism" over the past decade (Wearing 2001; Raymond & Hall 2008). Today an increasing number of tourists come to Cambodia in order to volunteer at orphanages. Cambodia has an estimated 553,000 orphans, accounting for 8.8% of all children; however, according to UNICEF (2013a, 2013b) the majority of children in residential care are not orphans but children with parents. UNICEF (2013a, 2013b) estimates that 269 orphanages exist in Cambodia, but orphanages are rising alongside rising tourism numbers. Many critics point out that orphanage tourism leads to manifold issues: it can negatively impact the children and the community; it can add to the existing problems; and it can create a situation whereby children are kept in vulnerable situations for the visiting orphanage tourists. Sometimes it can also lead to the sexual exploitation of orphans by "volunteers" (Dombrowski 2015).

Contributing to the development of uncontrolled tourism is the fact that Cambodia has one of the most investor-friendly environments in ASEAN:

> no exchange controls, no restriction on repatriation of profits, no discrimination between foreign and local investors; ... corporate income tax is only 20% and there are tax holidays of up to nine years. Foreigners can also take out leases of land for up to 99 years.
>
> *(Bangkok Post 2012)*

In a macabre twist, the Cambodian government announced that even the Choeung Ek killing fields were to be privatised. Since 2005 the management of the killing fields has been leased out for profit to JC Royal, a Japanese company, under a 30-year contract (Mydans 2005).

As with everything else that seems to be up for sale in Cambodia, its natural resources are no exemption. Hall and Ringer (2000: 179) pointed out that

> so widespread and indiscriminate is the logging – legal and illegal – that some government officials and aid groups identify deforestation as Indochina's greatest environmental problem and lament that 'virtually all of Cambodia's primary resources are now under some kind of unaccountable foreign control'.

From forests to genocidal museum concessions to women, girls or boys – in Cambodia there are some things money cannot buy, but not many.

If political and social conditions stabilise, and if the encouraging poverty rate decline continues to exceed expectations (World Bank 2015b), Cambodia will not be a poor country for much longer. Tourism can play a constructive role in helping the people achieve some sense of normalcy after years of conflict. The real challenge may be to overcome the tarnished image derived from the shady side of the tourism sector (Leiper 1998). In the future, responsible tourism business conduct in Cambodia requires enhanced due diligence to determine the impacts of tourism on society, including on human rights. It must include robust approaches to manage the negative impacts of tourism in a way that provides benefits to Cambodia and its people.

Myanmar

Myanmar, divided into seven divisions and seven states, is the second largest country in Southeast Asia, with a total land area of $676,577km^2$ and a coastline of 2,832km along the Bay of Bengal and the Andaman Sea. The population is 52 million according to the 2014 census (Department of Population, Ministry of Immigration and Population 2014). Myanmar's landmass includes diverse ecosystems, with the government having officially prioritised ecotourism in 21 of Myanmar's total 36 protected areas (ADB 2013; Myanmar Ministry of Hotels and Tourism (MoHT) 2015). Currently, tourism is largely confined to a central band of Myanmar, creating many challenges relating to demand for hotels outstripping supply during peak season. The sudden influx of tourists over recent years has put considerable strain on Myanmar's underdeveloped hotel sector: in 2015 there were about 35,000 hotel rooms in total in the country, which is not enough to meet the rising demand. In turn, the imbalance between supply and demand sends room prices soaring, particularly during peak season. The "big four" flagship destinations are Yangon, Bagan, Mandalay and Inle Lake. Previously inaccessible areas have since 2013 been opened to tourism (Tourism Transparency 2013). This section discusses Myanmar's recent tourism boom, future tourism development plans and the pledge of the Myanmar government to develop tourism responsibly.

From boycott to tourism boom

Five decades of military rule, sanctions and difficult visa regulations had prevented many people from visiting the land of golden pagodas. In early 2010 the country was largely perceived as closed and unsafe. It was portrayed as an unethical destination to visit due to the allegation that tourists directly supported the ruling military junta and their cronies who owned most tourist infrastructure and wielded power with an iron fist. Five years on, and Myanmar tourism is booming like it never has before. The fact that much of tourism's infrastructure is still military- and crony-owned, and that hotels continue to be built on land grabbed from local communities, seems to have escaped the notice of most.

Tumultuous times lie ahead for tourism development in Myanmar. After nearly five decades of military rule, Myanmar moved to a civilian governance structure with the passing of the new Constitution in 2008 (Republic of the Union of Myanmar 2008) and elections held in 2010 (Burma Fund UN Office 2011) and November 2015. According to the 2008 Constitution, the military retains veto power over any decisions as the generals hold 25% of seats in parliament. The 2010 elections were regarded as deeply flawed by most actors, including the UN, and were boycotted by the main opposition party, the National League For Democracy (NLD). Since the April 2012 by-elections, in which the NLD won 43 out of 44 contested seats, Daw Aung San Suu Kyi (DASSK) and others are now represented in parliament. However, due to the 59f clause in the 2008 Constitution, DASSK as the Chairman of the NLD remained prohibited from partaking in the 2015 elections as presidential candidate.

Gone seem to be the days of the tourism boycott, which DASSK herself had called for in response to the military junta's announcement of the "Visit Myanmar Year 1996" (Hall & Ringer 2000; International Institute of Social History 1996). Supported by a range of NGOs, academics, journalists and guidebook authors, and debated by many people many times over, the "Burma/Myanmar tourism boycott" had an arguably massive impact on how the country was and continues to be perceived as a tourist destination in the world (Lonely Planet Thorntree Forum 2011; Ko Htwe 2011). Unlike Laos, China or Vietnam, for example, advocates had for a long time campaigned against visiting Myanmar due to the regime's violation of human rights. Following the military junta's announcement of the "Visit Myanmar Year 1996" and the ensuing "beautification campaigns" throughout the country, the Nobel Peace Laureate DASSK called for a tourism boycott in 1995, saying that 'tourists should not visit until democracy returns' (quoted in O'Brian 1996; Burma Campaign UK 1996; Info Birmanie 2011). Very little tourist money was said to trickle down to the population. Some disagreed with DASSK, but even official Myanmar tourism statistics reveal that many tourists stayed away, waiting for better times (MoHT 2014). With the publication of the Tourism Statement in May 2011, the NLD officially revoked the tourism boycott 15 years after its inception (Tourism Transparency 2013). Many previously apprehensive visitors changed their minds and began to visit the newly opened country.

Table 15.3 indicates tourist arrivals to Myanmar from 2003 to 2015, based on official data from Myanmar's own MoHT. The data shows that tourist arrivals slowly rose during the 2000s, with a sudden increase in 2012 when Myanmar gained considerable popularity. Since 2012, tourism has been booming and many things are needed to cope with the increase in demand after five decades of isolation. The year 2013 saw 2,044,307 tourists visiting Myanmar, a number that represents an astonishing 93% increase compared with 2012. MoHT (2014) estimate that three million visited in 2014 and that 4.5 million tourists will visit Myanmar in 2015. By 2020, 7.489 million tourists are forecast to visit in the high-growth scenario (MoHT 2014; Myanmar Eleven 2015), with the medium-range forecast having already been likely exceeded by 2015. The WTTC (2015) estimated tourism's direct contribution to employment in Myanmar from 2004 to 2014 and suggested that tourism contributed between 1% and 1.5% of directly related jobs, a figure which is set to increase, with 2% of the Myanmar population being directly employed in tourism in 2024.

Table 15.3 Tourist arrivals in Myanmar

Year	Arrivals ('000)	Year	Arrivals ('000)
2003	597	2010	792
2004	657	2011	816
2005	660	2012	1,059
2006	631	2013	2,044
2007	716	2014	3,000*
2008	731	2015	4,500*
2009	763	2020	7,489**

Sources: Myanmar Ministry of Hotels and Tourism 2014; Myanmar Eleven 2015; WTTC 2015.
Notes
* MoHT estimate.
** WTTC high-end estimate.

Nevertheless, some caution is required regarding the real extent of the proposed impact of tourism as it remains unclear how data is collected and who benefits from tourism. There is no doubt that a great deal more tourists are visiting Myanmar today – tourism is one of the visible changes in the country. But in Myanmar official tourism data has to be treated with care. Private members of the tourism sector lament the official statistics as being inflated (Democratic Voice of Burma (DVB) 2014), while others say the numbers do not add up (Valentin, audio interview in Maung 2014) and that they vary when compared with data from the Ministry of Immigration (Thu & Kean 2015). The suspicion is that the Myanmar government exaggerates the increase in tourists in an effort to enhance the image of the country as a tourist destination and to attract more investors.

Tourism planning and development

With positive views from the media and multiple appearances on top destination lists, Myanmar continues to attract a broad range of travellers. The once burdensome visa process has been streamlined to make the country more accessible (World Economic Forum South East Asia 2013). Travellers are allowed greater freedom to see more of the country, and the arrival of major electronic payment companies has made using credit cards possible at a number of hotels, restaurants and shops. ATMs now accept major credit cards, ending the need to carry large amounts of cash into the country. Travellers from Asian nations represent more than 60% of total arrivals, with Thai, Japanese, South Korean and Chinese visitors topping the list. As for the Westerners, French, German, British, Spanish and US travellers make up the majority of visitors. Myanmar is a country with great tourism potential, but how this potential will be realised will depend on a variety of factors, not least environmental management and political stability – the prerequisite of sustainable tourism development for any country in the world.

The 2012 drafting of the *Responsible Tourism Policy for Myanmar* (MoHT 2012; Hanns Seidel Foundation (HSF) 2012a, 2012b), the *Community-Involved Tourism Policy* of 2013, and the introduction of the *Myanmar Tourism Master Plan* marked a clear shift in the government's approach to tourism development. The official aim is to develop tourism sustainably and responsibly, promoting a form of travel that is more equitable. There seem to be high hopes for tourism among some of the key stakeholders, not least due to the nature of the industry and the broad changes it could theoretically bring.

The major challenges

Myanmar's tourism industry is becoming one of the fastest growing areas of the economy. When tourism income rose in 2012 to more than 70% compared with the previous year ($534 million in 2012 and $315 million in 2011 according to the MoHT (2012)), the government began expanding international airports and developing tourism infrastructure throughout the country. At the national government level, MoHT's series of policies were set to shape the way towards a more responsible form of tourism development, and were viewed as a potentially crucial step in the transition process. The long-term vision was for Myanmar to implement sustainable tourism development safeguards early on in its development cycle.

Today's picture is looking much bleaker. Proposals to construct more than 20 new hotel zones throughout the country have been announced by the Myanmar Tourism Federation (Slow 2015). Some of these hotel zones are planned in areas as isolated and politically fragile as Chin or Kachin state. In this context, therefore, urgent questions in relation to ethical and responsible tourism development emerge. MoHT policies state that tourism is to make the lives of the ordinary people more liveable and that development should be responsible. Unlike other ministries in Naypyitaw, MoHT stood out at the time as producing solid documents for building sustainable innovations. However, so far actions are ineffective and tourism authorities have to re-learn their lessons from the past. For example, the effects of the "beautification campaign" that preceded the Visit Myanmar Year 1996, displacing thousands of farmers, resulted in international awareness campaigns about the complexities of visiting Myanmar. Advocates supporting a boycott of tourism to Myanmar targeted tourists wanting to visit Myanmar. Offering Myanmar as a tourist destination brought reputational risks for many tour operators. The future's concern may be – once again – not too dissimilar: some tourism businesses continue to forcibly move local communities from their land in order to attract greater numbers of tourists to the newly built high-end tourist resorts that are to be located in so-called "hotel zones" (Myanmar Center for Responsible Business 2015).

While the Myanmar Tourism Master Plan mentions factors such as the need to develop partnerships that respect the rights and livelihoods of indigenous people, there is a wide gap between the language of responsible tourism found on paper in integrated tourism development plans and the reality on the ground. This situation is dangerous not only because it is likely to result in greater incidents of forced land displacement. It may also cause growing resentment from locals, leading possibly to instability and security problems in the destinations.

For Thett (2012) the Myanmar Responsible Tourism Policy remains contested because it is possible that responsible tourism will be abused as another "eco-cash-cow" for authorities and crony businesses, while ignoring basic land rights:

> The Myanmar Responsible Tourism Policy is likely to undermine the very essence of sustainable development if it continues to favour the current Myanmar economic dynamic dominated by crony capitalism and foreign investment at the expense of political, ecological and cultural sustainability.
>
> *(Thett 2012: 8)*

To balance sustainable tourism development with the need for infrastructure is no easy task in any country, but Myanmar has the added challenge that it only recently began its transition process. Rising tourist numbers and the increased pressures on land will likely exacerbate the already existing issues in the fragile socio-economic and political environment. The problems will increase further and faster if prevention mechanisms and consultation processes are not put in place soon. While tourism can create many jobs and income opportunities in Myanmar, the risk of unsustainable development is real and the problem of inequality needs to be addressed. Many of the benefits of the tourism industry remain in the hands of a smallish elite group who control large portions of land and resources in Myanmar. Therefore it remains unclear how much the increase in visitors will really impact the people on the ground, and whether the communities affected by tourism will begin to get a fair share.

Conclusion

Laos, Cambodia and Myanmar are stunning tourist destinations with rich heritages, unique traditions, arts and crafts, and a magnificent diversity of wildlife. The three countries are also the sites of some of the worst human tragedies of the twentieth century. For many years the respective leaders of Laos, Cambodia and Myanmar followed policies that disregarded human life and produced repressions and massacres. Today, all three countries are booming tourist destinations, with around ten million tourists having visited Laos, Cambodia and Myanmar in 2014.

This chapter has showed that Laos, Cambodia and Myanmar should not simply be viewed as idyllic tourist destinations. If they are viewed apolitically, then tourism development will likely be unsustainable in the future. In other words, if tourists do not demand sustainable business practices on their trip, governments will be slow to take up the cause. Laos, Cambodia and Myanmar are countries with concerning human rights records, and all three are becoming increasingly authoritarian again. The Tourism Ministries have made some good statements and taken some promising steps towards sustainability; however, so far they neither have their own, nor abide by any, environmental and social standards. Meanwhile the local population is regularly excluded from tourism development project discussions. In the absence of meaningful stakeholder consultations for planned tourism development projects, a largely elitist group reaps the economic benefits of tourism while the local population is left to absorb the negative environmental and socio-cultural implications.

A sustainable tourism future is possible; if well implemented, sustainable tourism could become a tool for trust building and unity among the nations. Such a future requires respectful government regulatory action in order to preserve the fragile ecosystem and local heritage. If tourism will not be used for sustainability, then development in all three countries may prove to be superficial, investments may remain risky, and none of the countries may move towards a truly peaceful future anytime soon. Tourism development plans should be adapted to allow rural communities to ensure their livelihoods and land. Environmental and social impact assessments, as well as meaningful stakeholder consultations with the affected population about planned tourism development projects, are the pillars of responsible tourism anywhere in the world, including Laos, Cambodia and Myanmar.

Key reading

Chheang, V. (2008) 'The political economy of tourism in Cambodia', *Asia Pacific Journal of Tourism Research*, 13(3): 281–297.

Hall, C.M. and Ringer, G. (2000) 'Tourism in Cambodia, Laos and Myanmar: From terrorism to tourism?' in C.M. Hall and S. Page (eds), *Tourism in South and Southeast Asia: Issues and Cases* (pp. 178–194). Oxford: Butterworth-Heinemann.

Henderson, J.C. (2015) 'The new dynamics of tourism in South East Asia: Economic development, political change and destination competitiveness', *Tourism Recreation Research*, 40(3): 379–390.

Koleth, M. (2014) 'Hope in the dark: Geographies of volunteer and dark tourism in Cambodia', *Cultural Geographies*, 21(4): 681–694.

Ong, L.T.J. and Smith, R.A. (2014) 'Perception and reality of managing sustainable coastal tourism in emerging destinations: The case of Sihanoukville, Cambodia', *Journal of Sustainable Tourism*, 22(2): 256–278.

Sophal, E. (2007) 'The political economy of aid and governance in Cambodia', *Asia Pacific Journal of Tourism Research*, 15(1): 68–96.

Sosamphanh, B., Yongvanit, S. and Apichatvullop, Y. (2013) 'Cultural landscape of the urban community of Vang Vieng in the context of tourism', *The Journal of Lao Studies*, 4(1): 87–99.

Southiseng, N. and Walsh, C. (2011) 'Study of tourism and labour in Luang Prabang Province', *The Journal of Lao Studies*, 2(1): 45–65.

Suntikul, W. (2007) 'The effects of tourism development on indigenous populations in Luang Namtha Province, Laos', in R. Butler and T. Hinch (eds), *Tourism and Indigenous Peoples* (pp. 128–140). Oxford: Butterworth-Heinemann.

References

Adams, K. and Gillogly, A. (2011) *Everyday Life in Southeast Asia*, Bloomington: Indiana University Press.

ASEAN Secretariat (2013) 'Lao PDR awarded World's Best Tourist Destination', *ASEAN Secretariat News*, 22 May. Online. Available: www.asean.org/news/asean-secretariat-news/item/lao-pdr-awarded-world-s-best-tourist-destination (accessed 20 January 2015).

Asian Development Bank (ADB) (2013) *Myanmar Tourism Master Plan*. Online. Available: http://adb.org/projects/details?page=overview&proj_id=46271–001.

—— (2015) 'ADB, Lao PDR launch new tourism infrastructure project', *News from Country Offices*, 16 February. Online. Available: www.adb.org/news/adb-lao-pdr-launch-new-tourism-infrastructure-project (accessed 28 February 2015).

—— (2016) 'Cambodia: Economy'. Online. Available: www.adb.org/countries/cambodia/economy (accessed 14 February 2016).

Bangkok Post (2012) 'Cambodia opening its door to investment', 10 September. Online. Available: www.bangkokpost.com/print/311715 (accessed 14 February 2016).

Baumgartner, C. (2014) 'The Akha Experience: Lessons from a finally failed successful project', *Innovations in Rural Tourism E-Learning Platform*. Online. Available: http://learn.inrutou.eu/module-6/case-study-3 (accessed 20 January 2015).

Blache, M. (2014) 'Ethnic tourism failures in northern Laos', in B. Debarbieux, M. Oiry Varacca, G. Rudaz, D. Maselli, T. Kohler and M. Jurek (eds), *Tourism in Mountain Regions: Hopes, Fears and Realities*, Geneva: UNIGE, CDE, SDC.

Burma Campaign UK (1996) 'Don't Visit Myanmar Year 1996', 27 March. Online. Available: http://burmacampaign.org.uk/dont-visit-burma-year-1996.

Burma Fund UN Office (2011) *Burma's 2010 Elections: A Comprehensive Report*. Online. Available: www.burmalibrary.org/docs11/BurmaFund-Election_Report-text.pdf.

Cambodia Tribunal Monitor (2016) 'Khmer Rouge history'. Online. Available: www.cambodiatribunal.org/history/cambodian-history/khmer-rouge-history (accessed 14 February 2016).

Central Intelligence Agency (CIA) (2016) *The World Fact Book: Cambodia*. Online. Available: www.cia.gov/library/publications/the-world-factbook/geos/cb.html (accessed 14 February 2016).

Chandler, D.M. (1983) *A History of Cambodia*. Boulder: Westview Press.

Chheang, V. (2008) 'The political economy of tourism in Cambodia', *The Asia Pacific Journal of Tourism Research*, 13(3): 282–297.

Community Learning Center Laos (2014) 'A brief history of Laos'. Available: www.communitylearninginternational.org/laos.

Delang, C. and Toro, M. (2011) 'Hydropower-induced displacement and resettlement in the Lao PDR', *South East Asia Research*, 19(3): 567–594.

Democratic Voice of Burma (DVB) (2014) 'DVB Debate clip: Tourism businesses should be 100% Burmese'. Online. Available: www.youtube.com/watch?v=3czg8RC2W2I.

Department of Energy Business. (2012) *Electric Power Plants in Laos August 2012*. Vientiane: Ministry of Energy and Mines.

Department of Population, Ministry of Immigration and Population (2014) *The Population and Housing Census of Myanmar 2014: Summary of the Provisional Results*. Online. Available: http://unstats.un.org/unsd/demographic/sources/census/2010_phc/Myanmar/MMR-2014-08-28-provres.pdf.

Documentation Center of Cambodia (2016) 'Publications'. Online. Available: www.dccam.org/#/theorganization/publications (accessed 14 February 2016).

Dombrowski, K. (2015) 'Sex tourism: Dubious reputation', *Development and Cooperation European Union*. Online. Available: www.dandc.eu/en/article/cambodia-seen-heaven-paedophiles-and-sex-tourists (accessed 14 February 2016).

Hall, C.M. and Ringer, G. (2000) 'Tourism in Cambodia, Laos and Myanmar: From terrorism to tourism?' in C.M. Hall and S. Page (eds), *Tourism in South and Southeast Asia: Issues and Cases* (pp. 178–194). Oxford: Butterworth-Heinemann.

Hanns Seidel Foundation (HSF) (2012a) 'Government of the Republic of the Union of Myanmar Ministry of Hotels & Tourism Responsible Tourism Policy'. Online. Available: www.hss.de/fileadmin/media/downloads/Berichte/121015_Myanmar_Tourism_English.pdf.

—— (2012b) 'The Draft Responsible Tourism Policy for Myanmar formulated successfully'. Online. Available: www.hss.de/southeastasia/en/myanmar/news-events/2012/the-draft-responsible-tourism-policy-for-myanmar-formulated-successfully.html.

Haworth, A. (2012) 'Vang Vieng, Laos: The world's most unlikely party town', *Guardian*, 7 April. Online. Available: www.theguardian.com/world/2012/apr/07/vang-vieng-laos-party-town (accessed 18 January 2015).

Info Birmanie (2011) *Report on Tourism in Burma*. Online. Available: www.burma.no/noop/file.php?id=4917.

International Fund for Agricultural Development (IFAD) (2014) 'Cambodia'. Online. Available: http://operations.ifad.org/web/ifad/operations/country/home/tags/cambodia (accessed 14 February 2016).

International Institute of Social History (1996) 'Visit Myanmar Year 1996'. Online. Available: www.iisg.nl/collections/tourism/d29-242.php.

Kennedy-Good, M. (2009) 'Vang Vieng: A tragedy waiting to happen', *New Zealand Herald*, 22 September. Online. Available: www.nzherald.co.nz/travel/news/article.cfm?c_id=7&objectid=10598855 (accessed 2 February 2015).

Khamboly Dy (2007) 'A history of Democratic Kampuchea (1975–1979)', Documentation Center of Cambodia. Online. Available: www.d.dccam.org/Projects/Genocide/DK_Book/DK_History--EN.pdf (accessed 14 February 2016).

Khanal, B. (2011) 'An economic analysis of the Lao PDR tourism industry', PhD thesis, Lincoln University, New Zealand.

Ko Htwe (2011) 'NLD welcomes responsible tourism, but warns against abuses', *The Irrawaddy*, 24 May. Online. Available: www2.irrawaddy.org/article.php?art_id=21352.

Lao National Tourism Administration (2004) *2005–2010 National Ecotourism Strategy Action Plan*. Vientiane: LNTA.

—— (2014) 'Laos ecotourism'. Online. Available: www.ecotourismlaos.com/laoecotourism.htm (accessed 1 February 2015).

Leiper, N. (1998) 'Cambodian tourism: Potential problems and illusions', *Pacific Tourism Review*, 1(4): 285–298.

Lonely Planet Thorntree Forum (2011) 'NLD condemn tourism in Burma'. Online. Available: www.lonelyplanet.com/thorntree/forums/asia-south-east-asia-mainland/myanmar/nld-condemn-tourism-in-burma?page=1#post_18532709.

Maung, M. (2014) 'Call for transparency in Myanmar's tourism industry', SBS Australia. Online. Available: www.sbs.com.au/news/article/2014/12/01/call-transparency-myanmars-tourism-industry.

Meyer, M. (2013) 'Party over for Vang Vieng', *The Nation*, 24 July. Online. Available: www.nationmultimedia.com/travel/Party-over-for-Vang-Vieng-30210992.html (accessed 18 January 2015).

Mines Advisory Group (MAG) (2015) 'MAG: Landmines, cluster bombs, UXO in Cambodia'. Online. Available: www.maginternational.org/where-mag-works/cambodia/#.VsIzgIvollI (accessed 14 February 2016).

Ministry of Information, Culture and Tourism (2014) *Lao People's Democratic Republic: Greater Mekong Subregion Tourism Infrastructure for Inclusive Growth Project – Indigenous Peoples Plan*. Vientiane: ADB.

Ministry of Tourism Cambodia (2014) *Tourism Statistics Report, December 2014*. Online. Available: www.nagacorp.com/eng/ir/tourism/tourism_statistics_201412.pdf (accessed 14 February 2016).

Myanmar Center for Responsible Business (2015) *Tourism Sector Wide Impact Assessment Myanmar*. Online. Available: www.myanmar-responsiblebusiness.org/pdf/SWIA/Tourism/05-Sector-Level-Impacts. pdf.

Myanmar Eleven (2015) 'Myanmar targets 4.5 million tourists in 2015', 5 February. Online. Available: www.nationmultimedia.com/aec/Myanmar-targets-4-5m-tourists-in-2015-30253420.html.

Myanmar Ministry of Hotels and Tourism (MoHT) (2012) 'Responsible tourism policy'. Online. Available: www.hss.de/fileadmin/media/downloads/Berichte/121015_Myanmar_Tourism_English. pdf.

—— (2014) 'Myanmar tourism statistics 2007–2014'. Online. Available: www.myanmartourism.org/ index.php?option=com_content&view=article&id=368&Itemid=359.

—— (2015) *Eco Tourism Policy Myanmar*. Yangoon: MOHT.

Mydans, S. (2005) 'Cambodia profits from Killing Fields and other symbols', *New York Times*, 6 November. Online. Available: www.nytimes.com/2005/11/06/world/asia/cambodia-profits-from-killing-fields-and-other-symbols.html (accessed 14 February 2016).

O'Brian, H. (1996) 'Suu Kyi urges Britons to boycott Burma', *The Independent*, 17 March. Online. Available: www.independent.co.uk/news/world/suu-kyi-urges-britons-to-boycott-burma-1342477. html.

Organization for Economic Co-operation and Development (OECD) (2013) *Southeast Asian Economic Outlook 2013*. Paris: OECD.

Parameswaran, P. (2014) 'Laos dam risks damaging Meking River, igniting tensions with Vietnam', *The Diplomat*, 19 December. Online. Available: http://thediplomat.com/2014/12/laos-dam-risks-damaging-mekong-river-igniting-tensions-with-vietnam (accessed 2 February 2015).

Raymond, E.M. and Hall, C.M. (2008) 'The development of cross cultural (mis)understanding through volunteer tourism', *Journal of Sustainable Tourism*, 16(5): 530–543.

Rehbein, B. (2007) *Globalization, Culture and Society in Laos*. London: Routledge.

Republic of the Union of Myanmar (2008) *Constitution of the Republic Union of Myanmar 2008*. Online. Available: www.burmalibrary.org/docs5/Myanmar_Constitution-2008-en.pdf.

Save the Children (2003) *A Last Resort: The Growing Concern about Children in Residential Care*. London: International Save the Children Alliance. Online. Available: http://resourcecentre.savethechildren.se/ content/library/documents/last-resort-growing- concern-about-children-residential-care (accessed 14 February 2016).

Schilcher, D. (2008) *Tourism to Akha Villages in Muang Sing: An Impact Study*. Vientiane: GTZ.

Schipani, S. and Marris, G. (2002) *Linking Conservation and Ecotourism Development: Lessons from the UNESCO–National Tourism Authority of Lao PDR Nam Ha Ecotourism Project*. Bangkok: UNESCO.

Slow, O. (2015) 'Myanmar is changing and people will continue to come: Interview with U Yan Win, Chairman of Myanmar Tourism Federation', *Mizzima Magazine*, January. Online. Available: www. mizzima.com/opinion/interviews/item/16554-myanmar-is-changing-and-people-will-continue-to-come.

Sophal E. (2007) 'The political economy of aid and governance in Cambodia', *Asia Pacific Journal of Tourism Research*, 15(1): 68–96.

Sosamphanh, B., Yongvanit, S. and Apichatvullop, Y. (2013) 'Cultural landscape of the urban community of Vang Vieng in the context of tourism', *The Journal of Lao Studies*, 4(1): 87–99.

Southiseng, N. and Walsh, C. (2011) 'Study of tourism and labour in Luang Prabang Province', *The Journal of Lao Studies*, 2(1): 45–65.

Suntikul, W. (2007) 'The effects of tourism development on indigenous populations in Luang Namtha Province, Laos', in R. Butler and T. Hinch (eds), *Tourism and Indigenous Peoples* (pp. 128–140). Oxford: Butterworth-Heinemann.

Thett, K.K. (2012) *Responsible Tourism in Myanmar: Current Situation and Challenges*. Prague: Burma Centre Prague. Online. Available: www.burma-center.org/en/publications/reports/item/347-responsible-tourism-in-myanmar-current-situation-and-challenges.

Thu, E.E. and Kean, T. (2015) 'Why Myanmar's tourist numbers don't add up', *Myanmar Times*, 19 January. Online. Available: www.mmtimes.com/index.php/in-depth/12828-why-myanmar-s-tourist-numbers-don-t-add-up.html.

Tourism Transparency (2013) *Evolution of the No Go Zones in the Republic of Myanmar*. Online. Available: www.tourismtransparency.org/no-go-zones-changes.

Transparency International (2014) 'Corruption by country: Cambodia'. Online. Available: www. transparency.org/country#KHM (accessed 14 February 2016).

UNICEF (2013a) *Findings from Cambodia's Violence against Children Survey 2013*. Online. Available: www. unicef.org/cambodia/results_for_children_23119.html (accessed 14 February 2016).

—— (2013b) *UNICEF Annual Report 2013: Cambodia*. Online. Available: www.unicef.org/cambodia/ UNICEF_Cambodia_annual_report_2013.pdf (accessed 14 February 2016).

United Nations Development Programme (UNDP) (2015) 'About Lao PDR'. Online. Available: www. la.undp.org/content/lao_pdr/en/home/countryinfo.html.

Wearing, S. (2001) *Volunteer Tourism: Experiences That Make a Difference*. Wallingford: CABI Publishing.

Winter, T. (2008) 'Post conflict heritage and tourism in Cambodia: The burden of Angkor', *Asia Pacific Journal of Tourism Research*, 14(6): 524–539.

World Bank (2014) *Managing Risks for Macroeconomic Stability: Lao PDR Economic Monitor*. Vientiane: World Bank.

—— (2015a) 'Data: Lao PDR'. Online. Available: http://data.worldbank.org/country/lao-pdr (accessed 1 April 2015).

—— (2015b) 'Countries: Cambodia – overview'. Online. Available: www.worldbank.org/en/country/ cambodia/overview (accessed 14 February 2016).

World Economic Forum South East Asia (2013) *High Level Tourism Meeting Naypyitaw, Report*. Online. Available: www3.weforum.org/docs/EA13/WEF_EA13_TT_HighLevelMeeting_Report.pdf.

World Travel and Tourism Council (WTTC) (2014) *Economic Impact 2014 Laos*. London: WTTC.

—— (2015) *Travel and Tourism Economic Impact Myanmar 2014*. London: WTTC.

Yamauchi, S. and Lee, D. (1999) *Tourism Development in the Lao People's Democratic Republic*. New York: United Nations.

Zeppel, H. (2006) *Indigenous Ecotourism: Sustainable Development and Management*. Wallingford: CABI.

PART 3

Tourism in South and Central Asia

16

DEVELOPING TOURISM IN SOUTH AND CENTRAL ASIA

Introduction

C. Michael Hall & Stephen J. Page

One of the darker sides of us, the South Asians seems to be our habit of thinking that we know what is right and nobody should bother to teach us. We are very good teachers but not necessarily good students. Now we should be learning from what other feels about us. We have to accept the fact that for long, we have been deceived by our own thought of greatness. For [sic] tourism industry to flourish and contribute to our national development we should learn to cater to the demands of the incoming tourists. The mere existence of almighty Himalayas, beautiful blue seas with their magnificent beaches, the grand palaces and forts left as heritage by our forefathers, the varied wild life, birth places of saints and lords or the archaeological heritage of 5000 years civilisation is not going to make foreigners with cash in their purse beg to be allowed to enter our countries.

(Vaidya 1996)

South Asia covers 3 percent of the world's land surface, contains 22 percent of the world's population, and shares 1 percent of the world's trade. The region is characterized by poverty, representing half of the world's poor, and frequently suffers from devastating natural calamities, border conflicts, and ethnic and religious disturbances.

(Harun 2010: 279)

Introduction

Travel and tourism have long been associated with south and central Asia. Religious pilgrimage has long provided the basis for tourism mobility in south Asia, up to and including these more secular times. Overlying the pilgrimage routes are the networks of travel from colonial times; Central Asia was integral to the historic Silk Road which also provides strong connections between south and central Asia. These travel linkages were strong up to the 1970s, with Afghanistan being the land connection between the two areas. The political instability of Afghanistan since the early 1980s has served to lessen these linkages but they are not entirely dormant.

Pre-existing patterns of colonial transport infrastructure remain utilised and developed for domestic travel along with the rapidly expanding air transport network, especially in India, and intensive network of railways and roads. Religious pilgrimage has been and is still an important factor in the domestic travel patterns in South Asia and, increasingly, international visitation, with the pilgrimage centres and routes which have developed over the past three thousand years remaining important to the present day. Yet despite the relatively early development of resort tourism under the British, international tourism received relatively little consideration as an economic development mechanism by the governments of the region until the late 1970s in the cases of the Maldives, Nepal and Sri Lanka, and in the case of India not until the early 1990s. In the case of central Asia international tourism was restricted during the Soviet era but they too are beginning to utilise tourism for economic development purposes (Kantarci *et al.* 2014; see also Chapter 20, this volume). Nevertheless, for an area with such a large population as well as so many iconic tourist attractions the proportion of global international arrivals is remarkably small. For example, in 2014 South Asia only accounted for 1.5% of the world's international tourist arrivals and 2.2% of international tourism receipts (UNWTO 2015). Table 16.1 provides an overview of international tourism arrivals to the region.

One reason for the moribund performance of the region may be the conflicting images and stereotypes of the exotic, the modern and the "begging bowl" which are all wrapped together in Western media portrayals of South Asia (Richter 1989). Regional images are also heavily dominated by the political instability and fraught international relations between countries in the region. This includes not just tensions between India and China along the Tibetan border, and India and Pakistan, but also the international sanctions on Iran that were only lifted in late 2015. In addition, ongoing civil war in Afghanistan, civil wars in Nepal and Sri Lanka and domestic political tensions in Bangladesh and Pakistan over the past two decades have served to build up an often negative inferred image of the area (Rasul & Manandhar 2009). Yet simultaneously the region is culturally vibrant, ethnically diverse, rich in heritage resources and has a growing middle class (see Chapters 17–21, this volume). As with southeast Asia, south and central Asia are characterised by high rates of population growth and urbanisation. However, unlike southeast Asia, the construction of regional identities is extremely limited. Indeed, in many countries the construction of national identities is arguably a more important task.

Box 16.1 Tourism in Afghanistan

C.M. Hall

Afghanistan was a significant international tourism destination (Grötzbach 1983) until civil war began to wrack the country in the late 1970s and led to several decades of substantial political and economic instability. Historically, Afghanistan linked the Indian sub-continent with the Silk Road, as well as to Central Asia. However, Afghanistan has also long been a battleground for imperial interests and the movement of peoples and ideas, although this has also provided a rich cultural heritage from different periods of history (Najimi 2011). Nevertheless, while the country's position as a "crossroads of culture" is a source of great pride and identity that resonates with its tradition of hospitality (Coulson *et al.* 2014), its built heritage is also under threat. As Najimi (2011) notes,

> authorities lack policies and resources for the preservation of the monuments and the protection of historic sites; communities lack awareness of the monuments' significance and need for their protection. Illicit excavations, inadequate renovations and damage to the historic fabric are taking place on many sites.

Furthermore, the desperate need for development and employment generation also creates significant conservation issues. Tourism can potentially be a major contributor to heritage conservation, although before that can occur there is a need for greater political stability and the generation of a more secure environment (Durko & Petrick 2015). As Euromonitor (2014) noted in their report on tourism in the country

> Most countries issue a warning to travelling into Afghanistan and most people understand the risk of travelling into the country. Only the brave and adventurous would venture into the pristine landscape with breathtaking mountain ranges and beautiful lakes.... A normal traveller would not consider visiting Afghanistan in case they meet with any danger during attacks and bombings.

Nevertheless, tourism to the country, although very small by international standards, does appear to be growing. In addition to business travellers, there are also visitors from neighbouring countries who are used to the insecure environment and who are visiting friends and relatives, and adventure tourists, usually as part of guided tours (Baynham 2013; Gordon 2014). The country's main air gateway, Hamid Karzai International Airport (formerly Kabul International Airport), has regular flights to Delhi, Dubai and Istanbul and, as well as low-cost carriers, and is also served by Air India, Emirates and Turkish Air. Yet the long-term development of tourism to the country, whether by air or by overland routes, will depend on political stability and security returning to the country.

One of the main reasons for the lack of a regional imaginary is the postcolonial legacy of political boundaries constructed along religious and ethnic lines. Another, and an interesting comparison with southeast Asia, is the relative failure of attempts to encourage regional cooperation via institutional means, which is discussed further below. Numerous constraints exist that have affected regional integration efforts in tourism, these include poor transport connectivity and infrastructure, restrictive bilateral air services agreements and visa regimes (Hall & Page 2000; Timothy 2003; de Alwis 2010; Harun 2010; Chanda 2015). The absence of an integrated transport infrastructure in south Asia in terms of cross-border road and rail links, limited air connectivity between major cities and lack of transit facilities within the region are a major constraint to developing intraregional tourism. The air service agreements between South Asian countries are more restrictive than their agreements with countries outside the region (Chanda 2015).

Table 16.1 International tourist arrivals in Central and South Asia

Country		1995	2000	2005	2010	2011	2012	2013
Afghanistan	Number of arrivals							
	Receipts (% of total exports)				3.84	3.51	3.16	2.49
	Number of departures							
	Expenditures (% of total imports)				1.29	1.59	0.69	0.89
Bangladesh	Number of arrivals	156,000	199,000	208,000	303,000	155,000	125,000	148,000
	Receipts (% of total exports)			0.73	0.44	0.38	0.39	0.41
	Number of departures	830,000	1,128,000	1,767,000				
	Expenditures (% of total imports)			2.46	2.61	2.21	2.38	3.12
Bhutan	Number of arrivals	5,000	8,000	14,000	41,000	66,000	105,000	116,000
	Receipts (% of total exports)				10.84	10.19	12.76	17.67
	Number of departures							
	Expenditures (% of total imports)				4.60	4.45	5.79	5.91
India	Number of arrivals	2,124,000	2,649,000	3,919,000	5,776,000	6,309,000	6,578,000	6,968,000
	Receipts (% of total exports)			4.95	4.16	3.97	4.13	4.07
	Number of departures	3,056,000	4,416,000	7,185,000	12,988,000	13,994,000	14,920,000	16,626,000
	Expenditures (% of total imports)			4.55	2.39	2.48	2.43	2.47
Iran, Islamic Rep.	Number of arrivals	489,000	1,342,000	1,889,000	2,938,000	3,354,000	3,834,000	4,769,000
	Receipts (% of total exports)							
	Number of departures		2,286,000					
	Expenditures (% of total imports)							
Kazakhstan	Number of arrivals		1,471,000	3,143,000	3,196,000	4,434,000	4,807,000	4,926,000
	Receipts (% of total exports)			2.64	1.89	1.70	1.71	1.94
	Number of departures		1,247,000	3,004,000	6,019,000	8,020,000	9,066,000	10,144,000
	Expenditures (% of total imports)			3.69	3.36	3.57	3.28	3.29
Kyrgyz Republic	Number of arrivals	36,000	59,000	319,000	855,000	2,278,000	2,406,000	3,076,000
	Receipts (% of total exports)			9.93	8.91	12.95	16.64	18.93
	Number of departures	42,000	47,000	201,000	597,000	931,000	1,326,000	1,401,000
	Expenditures (% of total imports)			6.73	7.27	8.00	8.15	7.51

Country / Indicator							
Maldives							
Number of arrivals	315,000	467,000	395,000	792,000	931,000	958,000	1,125,000
Receipts (% of total exports)			170.48	85.33	79.11	78.09	79.63
Number of departures	32,000	42,000	77,000				
Expenditures (% of total imports)			10.82	14.88	10.14	9.64	10.28
Nepal							
Number of arrivals	363,000	464,000	375,000	603,000	736,000	803,000	798,000
Receipts (% of total exports)			12.47	24.05	22.28	19.65	20.89
Number of departures	100,000	155,000	373,000	765,000	774,000	862,000	983,000
Expenditures (% of total imports)			8.15	8.98	6.51	8.21	7.89
Pakistan							
Number of arrivals	378,000	557,000	798,000	907,000	1,161,000	966,000	
Receipts (% of total exports)			4.33	3.56	3.58	3.24	3.09
Number of departures							
Expenditures (% of total imports)			5.99	3.42	3.95	3.79	3.29
Sri Lanka							
Number of arrivals	403,000	400,000	549,000	654,000	856,000	1,006,000	1,275,000
Receipts (% of total exports)			9.24	9.41	10.42	12.94	16.62
Number of departures	504,000	524,000	727,000	1,122,000	1,239,000	1,269,000	1,262,000
Expenditures (% of total imports)			5.48	5.44	4.16	5.61	8.41
Tajikistan							
Number of arrivals				160,000	183,000	244,000	208,000
Receipts (% of total exports)			0.73	3.66	3.44	3.67	4.87
Number of departures		6,400				15,000	15,000
Expenditures (% of total imports)			0.23	0.74	0.33	0.25	0.26
Turkmenistan							
Number of arrivals	218,000	3,000	12,000				
Receipts (% of total exports)							
Number of departures	21,000	78,000	33,000				
Expenditures (% of total imports)							
Uzbekistan							
Number of arrivals	92,000	302,000	242,000	975,000			1,969,000
Receipts (% of total exports)							
Number of departures		217,000	572,000	1,610,000			
Expenditures (% of total imports)							

Sources: World Bank 2016a, 2016b, 2016c, 2016d.

The South Asian Association for Regional Cooperation (SAARC)

One of the most important political and economic initiatives in South Asia is the South Asian Association for Regional Cooperation (SAARC) (Ahmed *et al.* 2010). Although it might surprise many readers, given the common colonial heritage of the countries in the region, the idea of regional cooperation in order to deal with common development problems did not take hold until the late 1970s, when the late President Ziaur Rehman of Bangladesh promoted the concept. Despite its significance with respect to population and economic size, even now intra-regional trade within South Asia is extremely limited compared to many other regional economic groupings. The lack of regional economic cooperation affects investment. For example, for India, which is the largest outward FDI source among the SAARC nations, intraregional FDI constitutes only 1.5% of its total outward FDI (Chanda 2015), while the lack of integration also affects wider foreign investment into the region as a whole.

Following a series of meetings of foreign secretaries in the early 1980s which identified areas of cooperation, the first summit of South Asian countries (the People's Republic of Bangladesh, the Kingdom of Bhutan, the Republic of India, Republic of Maldives, the Kingdom of Nepal, the Islamic Republic of Pakistan and the Democratic Socialist Republic of Sri Lanka) was held in Dhaka in December 1985 with the formal launching of SAARC. Afghanistan became a member at the end of 2013. Although Iran is grouped by the UNWTO as part of the south Asia region for statistical purposes, it is not a member of SAARC, although it does have observer status along with Australia, China, the European Union, Japan, Mauritius, Myanmar, South Korea and the United States. Myanmar is also a possible future candidate for membership.

Box 16.2 Tourism in Iran: poised for growth?

C.M. Hall

Iran received an estimated 4.77 million international arrivals in 2013 (UNWTO 2015), accounting for approximately 1% of exports (WTTC 2015a), with arrivals having increased from 2.94 in 2010. However, the removal of sanctions in late 2015 and the election of what appears to be a more reformist and liberal parliament in February 2016 appears to herald a potentially substantial increase in international arrivals to go with the robust domestic tourism industry (Alipour *et al.* 2013; Anabestani 2014). In 2014 94% of travel and tourism's contribution to GDP was estimated to come from domestic tourism (WTTC 2015a).

Iran has many cultural heritage sites that will potentially appeal to international travellers (Butler *et al.* 2012), as well as other tourism products such as ski tourism, medical tourism, Islamic tourism and a number of national parks and conservation areas (Goodarzi *et al.* 2015). Importantly, there is also a substantial Persian diaspora which, given the political changes in Iran's relations with the West, is also likely to contribute substantially to international arrivals. Nevertheless, there are also substantial tourism development issues to be overcome. In addition to the need to modernise infrastructure there is also a substantial rural–urban economic divide as well as concerns over the impacts of tourism development on the environment (Dadvar-Khani 2012; Khoshkam *et al.* 2016).

According to the WTTC (2015a) the direct contribution of travel and tourism to Iran's GDP was IRR237,121.0bn (2.3% of total GDP) in 2014, and is forecast to rise by 5.7% pa, from 2015 to 2025, to 2.9% of total GDP in 2025. The combined direct and indirect contribution is estimated to account for 7.8% of GDP by 2025. Given population growth and levels of unemployment and underemployment in Iran, the employment creation potential of tourism is significant. In 2014 travel and tourism directly supported 413,000 jobs (1.8% of total employment), with this expected to rise by 4.3% pa to 656,000 jobs (2.2% of total employment) in 2025 (WTTC 2015a). However, while tourism is expected to increase, it should be noted that the market and transport connections to the sub-continent are relatively poor, although they do show significant potential to grow post-sanctions.

The greatest challenges to tourism growth, however, are arguably not infrastructural but relate to perceptions of Iran and its regional relations in the market. Political instability in neighbouring countries and the competition with Saudi Arabia for regional influence in the Middle East will likely have a significant effect on Western perceptions of Iran as a destination. Internal stability and maintenance of policies that are more welcoming to the West and which also ensure that sanctions against Iran's nuclear developments are not renewed are also important, especially for much-needed investment and the development of business partnerships. The final challenge likely surrounds the price of oil and gas and the returns this brings to the country and its role in infrastructure, education and welfare. However, while low oil prices provide a significant economic challenge, they are also likely to bring renewed government focus on the potential role of tourism as a means of diversifying the economy and providing employment opportunities.

SAARC is significant because it not only provides a basis for economic cooperation and development between the various countries in the region, but also provides opportunities for trust building between several nations – India and Pakistan in particular – which have gone through periods of substantial conflict. Traditionally focused on issues of agriculture and rural development, and the development of Preferential Trading Arrangements, tourism was a latecomer to the areas of interest for SAARC. Although, thanks to the assistance of the World Tourism Organization, 1975 was promoted as Visit South Asia Year by the South Asia Regional Travel Commission, it was not until the late 1980s that intra-regional cooperation on tourism and travel began to develop in earnest (Hall & Page 2000).

A further initiative with implications for tourism is the development of a SAARC Agreement on Trade in Services (SATIS) (previously known as the SAARC Framework Agreement on Services, which had provided for tariff reductions between member states), which was signed at the 16th SAARC Summit in 2010. In addition to tourism, other areas of direct relevance that are included in services negotiations include aviation, transport, health services (because of the connection to medical tourism) and FDI. FDI in tourism is little restricted in south Asia; however, substantial FDI restrictions apply in transport and aviation, particularly in India, Pakistan and Sri Lanka.

SATIS resembles the General Agreement on Trade in Services (GATS) in terms of its provisions, carve-outs and scheduling modalities. The objective is progressive liberalisation of services, which is in line with national policy objectives, the level of development and size of the member economies. The general guidelines call for countries to make initial offers, which cover substantial sectoral and modal improvements over existing commitments to services in WTO negotiations (Chanda 2015). Not surprisingly given the state of the economy, India's offers are the most extensive, although the offers across member countries are quite limited in both scope and depth and are subject to conditions of foreign equity ceilings, minimum capital requirements, preferential treatment of domestic service providers and economic needs tests (Chanda 2015). As it currently stands offers in tourism and travel services are limited to hotels, transport services are minimally covered, and employment considerations are minimal. As Chanda (2015: 64) comments:

Lack of meaningful market access offers indicates an overall conservative stance towards regional services integration, even though member countries have undertaken unilateral liberalization in services. As argued next, this stance partly reflects the behind-the-border regulatory and institutional barriers, which undermine not only unilateral liberalization undertaken but also the process of regional services liberalization.

A number of tourism-specific initiatives have been undertaken. In August 1988 representatives of designated banks and agencies met to formulate recommendations regarding financial aspects of tourism (settlement of accounts and limited convertibility of national currencies for tourists from SAARC countries) under a scheme for the promotion of organised tourism in the region. A Technical Committee on Tourism within the framework of SAARC was established in 1991 and a SAARC Working Group on Tourism in 2004. The establishment of a Tourism Council by the SAARC Chamber of Commerce and Industry (SCCI), the apex organisation of business and industry of the region representing the private sector of all the countries of the region, had the objective of raising the level of regional co-operation and contributing to the development of the economy. The overall mission of the Tourism Council is to 'contribute to the development of tourism sector and through it to the economic development of the region and promote regional cooperation at private sector level'. Its objectives are to:

1 contribute to the development of the tourism sector of the SAARC countries by way of promotion of flow of tourists within the region and from outside the region;
2 provide recommendations to the governments for the policy changes for promotion of tourism business in the region;
3 act in a catalytic role for increasing cooperation on tourism-related activities at the private sector level;
4 work for easier travel procedures for citizens of the SAARC countries to travel inside the region;
5 find investment opportunities and promote investment in tourism-related business;
6 contribute to the development networking of tourism-related institutions of the region;
7 promote direct air and other transport linkages among members of SAARC;
8 facilitate in setting up a Tourism Information Network in the SAARC region;
9 promote South Asian tourism among clients outside the region;
10 organise regional events like seminars, training, fairs and workshops on tourism;
11 conduct and facilitate research on tourism-related issues in the region; and
12 promote development of human resources related to tourism in the region.
(SAARC Chamber of Commerce and Industry Tourism Council 1997)

Earlier attempts to promote regional co-operation in tourism in South Asia, such as the formation of the South Asia Tourism Association in 1984, were short-lived. However, the private–public partnerships involved in SAARC and SCCI would appear to hold promise for tourism development. In addition, there are bilateral agreements among some SAARC governments to promote hospitality and tourism (e.g. India and the Maldives via joint development of hospitality projects, increased flight frequency and cross-border cooperation between travel agents) (Chanda 2015). Nevertheless, the region faces substantial problems and issues. Vaidya (1996), in a report to the SCCI Tourism Council Seminar in Colombo, Sri Lanka, identified four major issues which the Council and the region as a whole needed to face, and which apply to the present day:

Political and economic stability and political commitment: in terms not only of a reduction in political conflict in the region but also in relation to issues such as passport and visa control, and concrete government commitment to regional cooperation.

Turning the potentials into reality: through cooperation at the regional level in order to compete more effectively with other destinations at the international level, through such mechanisms as common tour packages.

Making common sense prevail on pseudo-nationalism: one of the greatest threats to the promotion of tourism in the region was the dominance of perceived national interests over the interests of the region as a whole.

Getting away from the negative image of South Asia in the leading world tourism markets: the common image of South Asia in the international media was often negative. Therefore, one of the aims of the Tourism Council and the region's tourism industry should be to project a positive image of South Asia.

In addition to the four broad issues identified by Vaidya (1996), several specific policy items remain on the SAARC agenda:

- Better intra-regional air connectivity.
- Improved land transport linkages.
- Improvements in visa procedures and costs.
- Preferential treatment of tourists from the SAARC region.
- Infrastructure development and investment.
- Joint marketing initiatives.
- Human resource development and product standardisation.

Many of these policy proposals also fit closely with initiatives with respect to services trade discussed above (Chanda 2015). However, to bring these policy goals to fruition requires a reduction in the regional rivalry between India and Pakistan in particular. Paradoxically, tourism-related mobilities are likely to be an important part of any trust-building exercise. Nevertheless, the region-wide need of governments to accommodate increased economic expectations from their populations and the growing common environmental threats facing the region from climate change, increased risk of natural disaster and water security, potentially provide strong reasons for the SAARC members to improve levels of policy cooperation and implementation.

Box 16.3 Tourism in Bangladesh

C.M. Hall

Situated on the Bay of Bengal, Bangladesh is one of the world's most densely populated and least developed nations. It has a range of major environmental problems related to climate change and sea level rise, natural disaster and food and water security, as well as the loss of forest and natural vegetation cover through population pressures and environmental change. All of these issues contribute substantially to significant image issues for the country (Zahra 2012). Nevertheless, at the same time Bangladesh also has significant cultural and natural diversity, including the largest mangrove forest in the world in the Sundarbans, as well as other significant areas of marine and forest biodiversity (Tisdell 1997; Alam *et al.* 2009).

Following Bangladesh's (formerly East Pakistan) independence from Pakistan in 1971, tourism became the responsibility of the Bangladesh Parjatan Sangstha, restructured as the Bangladesh Parjatan Corporation (BPC) in 1973. The BPC drew up a series of plans for government involvement in promoting and developing the industry, but 'these plans have not been implemented … properly by the government due to various impediments including ministerial legacy problems' (Khondker & Ahsan 2015: 2). Over time greater private sector involvement in the industry has been encouraged, although government policy means that many key elements of the industry remain highly regulated and directly or indirectly owned by the state.

Like many countries in the region the tourism industry is dominated via domestic travel, with international arrivals being limited. The number of international arrivals has only shown limited growth since 1991 when it received 113,200 arrivals, to 148,000 in 2013. The highest number of arrivals in this period was 467,300 in 2008, followed by 303,400 in 2010, when Bangladesh was involved in hosting the World Cup of Cricket. These figures suggest that the BPC's (2007) 2020 vision for Bangladesh of 1.3 million visitor arrivals by 2020, given favourable market situations, is extremely optimistic, as is the supposedly more "realistic" forecast of 900,000 and even the lower-end forecast of at least 500,000 visitor arrivals. The forecast growth rates were generally above that forecast for South Asia by the UNWTO (2015) and reflect a lack of realism in assessment of the promotion and appeal of Bangladesh as a tourism destination, especially given issues of political instability that affect the country's image. Indeed, Al-Masud (2015: 18) identified the following as 'crucial for the development for implementing the marketing plan for tourism in Bangladesh':

- Lack of financial support from government.
- Inadequate education system.
- Absence of a training institute related to tourism.
- Lack of efficient infrastructure facilities.
- Lack of market information.
- Lack of contact with the market.
- Lack of appropriate tourism policy.
- Lack of safety and security.

Given this situation it is not surprising that tourism only directly contributes 1.9% of GDP, which the WTTC (2015b) estimate will increase to 2.0% by 2025. In 2014 travel and tourism directly supported 903,500 jobs – equivalent to 1.6% of total employment. This is expected to rise by 1.4% pa to 1,062,000 jobs in 2025, which in proportional terms will represent a slight drop in direct contribution to employment of 1.5%. The WTTC (2015b) estimates that leisure travel spending (inbound and domestic) generated 78.0% of direct travel and tourism GDP in 2014 (BDT389.0bn) compared with 22.0% for business travel spending (BDT110.0bn). Overall, domestic travel spending generated 97.9% of direct travel and tourism GDP in 2014 compared with 2.1% for visitor exports. Perhaps not surprisingly, therefore, the proportional contribution of international arrivals to exports is not expected to change between 2015 and 2025 (WTTC 2015b).

The majority of international arrivals come for leisure tourism purposes (approximately 46% in 2009, the year for which the most recent data is available), followed by business tourism (approximately 43%), with the remainder of arrivals for educational, religious and medical tourism reasons (Bangladesh Tourism Board data in Khondker & Ahsan 2015). Religious tourism is primarily associated with a pilgrimage event known as Bishwa Ijtema, which, it is estimated, attracted 3.4% of the total tourist inflow into Bangladesh in 2009.

The Biswa Ijtema is the annual congregation of the Tablighi Jama'at, a transnational Sunni fundamentalist Islamic reform and re-pietisation movement (Ali 2003; Gaborieau 2009; Burki 2013) that is held in Tongi, just outside the capital, Dhaka. The term Biswa Ijtema (or Viswa/Bishwa Ijtema) translates as "world congregation". Biswa is Sanskrit for "world". Ijtema is Arabic and means "public gathering". 'What is remarkable about the Biswa Ijtema as a pilgrimage is that the location where it is held, the township of Tongi, bears no connection to a holy person, nor is it a holy place in itself and as such it is not a typical pilgrimage site' (Björkman 2010: 14). The annual three-day congregation is one of the largest gatherings of Muslims outside of the Hajj (Sikand 2002), with Siddiqi (2010) estimating that it attracts up to five million people including 30,000 foreign participants. As Siddiqi (2010: 134) comments

> *ijtema* is not only popular among the TJ activists but also to the larger number of people who do not actively engage with TJ in Bangladesh. However, they take part with the annual *ijtema* to get the blessings and mercy of Allah. To many Bangladeshi, participation in *ijtema* acts as a significant pilgrimage outside *hajj*. However, *hajj* is a *farz*, compulsory for a financially solvent Muslim. On the other side, *ijtema* is not compulsory; rather this is an optional or voluntary action for the Muslims.

Although estimates of attendance vary (Björkman 2010; Khondker & Ahsan 2015) it is clear that the numbers are in the several millions, with the number of foreign attendees in the tens of thousands but growing. Understandably, attendees and organisers of the event would not tend to classify attendance as tourism, given its often pejorative meaning, yet it is clear that it is a significant pilgrimage occasion and has considerable potential to attract more foreign arrivals, given the transnational nature of Tablighi Jama'at. Nevertheless, as with international tourism in Bangladesh in general there are issues of accessibility and infrastructure capacity to accommodate increasing numbers of visitors. Indeed, a major issue for Bangladeshi tourism is that the number of departures by Bangladeshi residents is substantially higher than the number of arrivals. In 1995 and 2000 departures were over 5.5 times greater than arrivals; in 2005 they were almost seven times, and in 2009 over nine (see Table 16.1; Khondker & Ahsan 2015).

Khondker and Ahsan (2015) identify five entry-point projects that they believe would substantially boost the attractiveness and viability of Bangladesh as an international tourism destination:

1   Establishing three premium shopping outlets.
2   Developing an eco-nature integrated resort near Sundarbans.
3   Creating a Strait Riviera linking Teknaf to Sundarbans.
4   Promoting archaeological sites.
5   Establishing eco-parks in CHT and Sylhet.

Undoubtedly, such developments are potentially valuable. However, arguably the greatest problems facing tourism in Bangladesh relate to overall issues of infrastructure, transport and accommodation in general, which are only exacerbated by an overly complex set of institutional arrangements for tourism and a poorly developed, managed and funded destination marketing strategy. Overlapping with all of these is the country's competing political factions that serve, together with issues of vulnerability to climate change, to generate an image of instability. While there is great potential for halal and medical tourism, VFR (visiting friends and relatives) travel and ecotourism, unless broader political and tourism policy issues are engaged with, along the lines of many of the SAARC proposals, it is extremely unlikely that the country will achieve its targets for international tourism for 2020 and beyond.

Box 16.4 Tourism in Pakistan

Kashif Hussain

Compared to the wider situation of tourism in Asia the tourism industry in Pakistan is relatively fragile due to its current volatile political and economic situation, lack of proper transportation infrastructure, susceptibility to natural disasters, and terrorism and regional political instability. Nevertheless, Pakistan offers many tourism products ranging across history, adventure, desert, medical, wildlife, nature and educational tourism which attract tourists from all over the world and explore the hidden treasures of Mughal and Indian civilisations that have been nourished in time. In addition, tourism in Pakistan also benefits from the Pakistani diaspora that has developed since colonial times (Ali & Holden 2006).

Pakistan is a multi-cultural, multi-ethnic and predominantly Muslim society. Ninety-seven per cent of the almost 200 million people in Pakistan are Muslims. The population is made up of numerous ethnic groups, such as dominant Punjabis, Siraikis, Sindhis, Pakhtuns, Baloch, Brahvis, Kashmiris, Hazaras, Urdu-speaking immigrants from India or Mohajirs, Gojars, Kohistanis, Chitralis and a dozen or so Dardic languages-speaking lingo-ethnic groups, where the official language is English and the national language is Urdu.

The landscape of Pakistan ranges from beautiful mountains in the north, the Karakoram and the Himalayas, through dissected plateaus to the rich alluvial plains of the Punjab. The mountains are a significant special-interest tourism attraction as Pakistan is home to several mountain peaks over 7,000m, which attract adventurers and mountaineers from around the world, especially K2. The northern areas of Pakistan, spread over 72,496km², are as fascinating as its southern region. There are also the arid areas of Balochistan and Sindh as well as the beaches of the Mekran coast. The cultural heritage of Pakistan is also substantial. The ancient civilisations (2500 BC to 7000 BC) of the Indus Valley (Moenjodaro, Harappa, Kot Diji and Mehrgarh) and Gandhara (focused on Taxila, Peshawar, Charsadda, Shahbaz Garhi, Jamal Garhi, Takht Bahi, Swat and the rock carvings along the ancient Silk Road) are significant for archaeological tourism. The country also has a rich heritage of Muslim art and architecture, with shrines, mosques and forts associated with the Ghaznavids (AD 1021–1186), Ghoris (AD 1186–1202) and Slaves (AD 1206–1524), dynasties before the arrival of the Mughals (AD 1524–1764). The United Nations Educational, Scientific and Cultural Organization (UNESCO) recognises Moenjodaro, Takht Bahi and Sahr Bahlol, the ruins of Taxila, the Lahore Fort and Shalimar Gardens in Lahore, the historic monuments of the ancient city of Thatta and the ancient fort of Rohtas as World Heritage Sites (Ministry of Finance 2015; Pakistan Tourism Development Corporation 2016).

In relative terms tourism in Pakistan was most successful during the 1970s when the country received unprecedented numbers of foreign tourists. The main destinations were the Khyber Pass, Peshawar, Karachi, Lahore, Swat, Quetta, Gwadar and Rawalpindi. In the 1960s and 1970s, Pakistan was part of the overland Asia route (also sometimes referred to as the "hippie trail") where backpackers from Europe would cross the Khyber Pass and make their way through Peshawar, Chitral and Karachi (Zahid 2014).

According to the World Travel and Tourism Council (WTTC) (2014), Pakistan, with its diverse culture, people and landscapes, has attracted 822,000 international tourist arrivals with PKR704.2 billion as direct contribution to GDP and PKR1,632.2 billion as total contribution to GDP in 2013, creating 1,484,500 direct jobs and 3,562,500 total jobs. In 2014 this was expected to grow by 9.2%, and the country was expected to attract 905,000 international tourist arrivals. By 2024, international tourist arrivals are forecast to total 1,519,000, generating expenditure of PKR 180.8 billion, an increase of 6.7% pa with 1,920,000 direct jobs and 4,745,000 total jobs (WTTC 2014).

Figure 16.1 presents a snapshot of international tourist arrivals in Pakistan for the last two decades from 1995 to 2014. It can be observed that the number of tourist arrivals has seen progressive growth of 70.1% overall. However, the great recession periods can be seen between 2001–2003, 2007–2008 and 2012–2013. The reason for such recessions could be easily linked with economic and political instability of the country, floods, the Afghanistan War and terrorism.

Tourism is a promising growing industry in Pakistan but political issues pose a persistent problem in further developing the sector. Concerns over safety and security play a major role in limiting tourism numbers (Raza & Jawaid 2013; Saha & Yap 2014). Pakistan also faces problems in policy as well as implementation in exploiting the inherent tourist potential of the country due to social and religious constraints, ineffective promotional policies, lack of infrastructure and inadequate

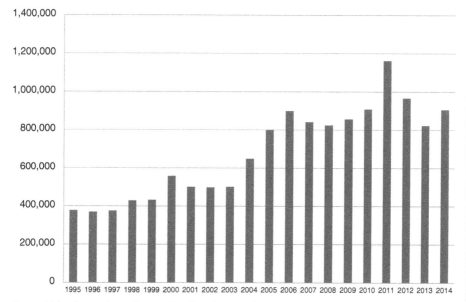

Figure 16.1   A snapshot of international tourist arrivals in Pakistan.
Sources: WTTC 2014; World Bank 2016a.

tourist services. The tourism potential of the country has not been realised and harnessed, arguably because of a lack of initiatives on the part of the relevant government departments, which also include inadequate knowledge and training of personnel in the tourism sector (Zahid 2014).

The position of tourism in Pakistan government policy is also a major issue in tourism development. According to *Dawn News* (2007), tourism in Pakistan has never been viewed as a major engine of economic growth by successive Pakistan governments. In fact, it has failed to regard tourism as equal to other industries capable of creating jobs, earning foreign exchange, improving terms of trade and regional development, overcoming economic disparities and for conservation purposes. Although the first master plan was conceived in 1967 it recognised environmental considerations only in general terms and placed no emphasis on conservation. As a result, hotels and tourists resorts were built close to natural attractions and archaeological monuments. From 1967 to the release of the National Tourism Policy in 1990, no policy-level attempts were made to develop tourism on the national level. The National Tourism Policy of 1990 stressed that government should ensure preservation of the environment and argued for government intervention given that market forces cannot be expected to ensure environmental degradation. It also proposed launching educational programmes to generate awareness and conservation efforts.

In 2001 the national government announced a new tourism policy that sought to promote year-round tourism. In addition, efforts were made for qualitative improvement, development in environment, human resources, tourist services and the tourist product. Federal and provincial governments were also to be asked to bring all legislation in consonance with demands from the tourist industry. The policy also aimed to stimulate private sector involvement in tourism through provision of industry support. To give effect to the tourism policy Pakistan developed the Tourism Master Plan 2002. Prepared jointly by the United Nations Development Programme, the WTO and the government of Pakistan, the Master Plan also noted several constraints that must be overcome to ensure the sustainable development of tourism services:

- lack of awareness amongst the general public about the structure, impact and benefits of tourism;
- limitations on adequately trained personnel in all sectors;
- outdated regulations and over-regulation of tourist services and facilities in certain areas and a lack of regulation in other areas;
- lack of investment in tourist facilities and services by both national and provincial authorities and few incentives for private investors;
- limited and outdated infrastructure all over the country.

In order to manage and promote tourism in Pakistan, an autonomous authority, the Pakistan Tourism Development Corporation (PTDC) was incorporated on 30 March 1970 under the repealed Companies Act 1913 (now the Companies Ordinance, 1984) as a public corporation limited by shares. Today, the PTDC generally promotes Pakistan in terms of adventure tourism, eco-tourism, spiritual tourism, heritage tourism and sports tourism. Fairs and festivals such as the Silk Route Festival and the Shandur Polo Festival are promoted along with other notable cultural events as Sibi Mela, Horse and Cattle Show, Folk Heritage Festival, Basant (Kite Flying Festival) and the Lok Virsa (Folk Festival).

Tourism promotion in Pakistan is also undertaken at the provincial level. Pakistan is subdivided into four provinces, one federal capital territory and a group of federally administered tribal areas. The four large provinces are what make up the majority of Pakistan which include Balochistan, Khyber Pakhtunkhwa, Punjab and Sindh. The Islamabad Capital Territory is home to the Pakistani capital, Islamabad. The Federally Administered Tribal Areas include Azad, Jammu and Kashmir, and Gilgit-Baltistan. Each province runs its own organisation that is responsible for tourism development and promotion of the sector in their province under the PTDC. These are:

- Tourism Development Corporation of Punjab (TDCP), working in Punjab for the promotion of the tourism sector.
- Culture Tourism and Antiquities Department – Sindh.
- Department of Tourism – Khyber Pakhtunkhwa.
- Secretary of Culture, Tourism & Archives – Baluchistan.
- Tourism, Sports, Culture and Youth Department – Gilgit-Baltistan.
- Department of Tourism – Azad Jammu and Kashmir.

For Pakistan to make progress in this sector, the government will need to continue to explore the links that exist between sustainable tourism development and natural and cultural resource management. Given the cultural context within which much tourism occurs in Pakistan, greater attempts need to be made to develop community-based tourism and recreational opportunities, especially for the very large domestic tourist market, which is an area in which policy is substantially lacking. Similarly, international tourism policies need to become much more relevant to the international market and especially the extensive Pakistan diaspora.

Conclusions

South and Central Asia are facing an increasingly competitive tourism marketplace in a global context. The immediate competition between the nations in south Asia and added range and choice of destinations in southeast Asia for tourist travel pose specific challenges for government and industry. It is somewhat ironic that the analysis of Pakistan's future market potential by Shaikh (1976) is still as relevant 50 years after it was written: that is, that the nation (and many of the other countries in the region) are not gaining their rightful share of international arrivals, although domestic tourism is beginning to grow substantially (Singh 2009). In central Asia international tourism is also beginning to grow, though it depends substantially on ties with Russia and the region's energy wealth (Kantarci *et al.* 2014).

Yet there are many obvious factors which account for the often erratic patterns of tourist arrivals in the region: the absence of political stability and confidence among volatile markets to visit destinations which have faced political turmoil, civil war and armed insurrections. Tourism cannot thrive unless there is regional political stability. There is also often a lack of political cooperation between the neighbouring governments to facilitate a free flow of visitors across the international borders with the minimum of restrictions. Improvements to infrastructure in many of the gateway cities are improving carrying capacity, although restrictions on aviation and trade connectivity continue to limit potential developments.

One theme that is common throughout south and central Asia is the great potential tourism has to create employment due to its labour-intensive nature. However, research and greater attention by policy makers and investors needs to be placed on generating tangible economic benefits for local people, particularly through the indirect benefits that visitor spending can yield. This is particularly the case in more remote and peripheral areas.

There is no doubt that the region has many jewels to be discovered and developed, but the increasing concern with the state of the environment in each country does not augur well for tourism. After all, tourism is one further human activity that can damage the environment if it is not managed correctly, with critical thresholds established for use by visitors. Although many countries have developed substantial master plans for tourism, effective environmental assessment and management systems seem to be far from the objectives of sustainable development. Yet rapidly growing populations and middle classes signal increases in expectations not only for the capacity for travel but also for ongoing economic development and employment; in this, the environment often appears to become an afterthought.

Key reading

Ahmed, S., Kelegama, S. and Ghani, E. (eds) (2010) *Promoting Economic Cooperation in South Asia: Beyond SAFTA*. Washington, DC: World Bank and Sage.

Alipour, H., Kilic, H. and Zamani, N. (2013) 'The untapped potential of sustainable domestic tourism in Iran', *Anatolia*, 24(3): 468–483.

Butler, R., O'Gorman, K.D. and Prentice, R. (2012) 'Destination appraisal for European cultural tourism to Iran', *International Journal of Tourism Research*, 14(4): 323–338.

Kantarci, K., Uysal, M. and Magnini, V. (eds) (2014) *Tourism in Central Asia: Cultural Potential and Challenges*. Toronto: Apple Academic Press.

Najimi, A.W. (2011) 'Built heritage in Afghanistan: Threats, challenges and conservation', *International Journal of Environmental Studies*, 68(3): 343–361.

Rasul, G. and Manandhar, P. (2009) 'Prospects and problems in promoting tourism in South Asia: A regional perspective', *South Asia Economic Journal*, 10(1): 187–207

Singh, S. (ed.) (2009) *Domestic Tourism in Asia: Diversity and Divergence*. London: Earthscan.

References

Ahmed, S., Kelegama, S. and Ghani, E. (eds) (2010) *Promoting Economic Cooperation in South Asia: Beyond SAFTA*. Washington, DC: World Bank and Sage.

Alam, M., Furukawa, Y. and Akter, S. (2009) 'Forest-based tourism in Bangladesh: Status, problems and prospects', *Tourismos: An International Multidisciplinary Journal of Tourism*, 5(1): 163–172.

Ali, J. (2003) 'Islamic revivalism: The case of the Tablighi Jamaat', *Journal of Muslim Minority Affairs*, 23(1): 173–181.

Ali, N. and Holden, A. (2006) 'Post-colonial Pakistani mobilities: The embodiment of the "myth of return" in tourism', *Mobilities*, 1(2): 217–242.

Alipour, H., Kilic, H. and Zamani, N. (2013) 'The untapped potential of sustainable domestic tourism in Iran', *Anatolia*, 24(3): 468–483.

Al-Masud, T.M.M. (2015) 'Tourism marketing in Bangladesh: What, why and how', *Asian Business Review*, 5(1): 13–19.

Anabestani, A. (2014) 'Effects of second home tourism on rural settlements development in Iran (case study: Shirin-Dareh Region)', *International Journal of Culture, Tourism and Hospitality Research*, 8(1): 58–73.

Bangladesh Parjatan Corporation (BPC) (2007) *Bangladesh Tourism Vision 2020*. Dhaka: BPC.

Baynham, J. (2013) 'The land the war ate: Tourism in Afghanistan', *Outside*, 14 January. Online. Available: www.outsideonline.com/1912746/land-war-ate-tourism-afghanistan (accessed 1 April 2015).

Björkman, N. (2010) 'The Biswa Ijtema', *Scripta Instituti Donneriani Aboensis*, 22: 9–23.

Burki, S.K. (2013) 'The Tablighi Jama'at: Proselytizing missionaries or Trojan horse?' *Journal of Applied Security Research*, 8(1): 98–117.

Butler, R., O'Gorman, K.D. and Prentice, R. (2012) 'Destination appraisal for European cultural tourism to Iran', *International Journal of Tourism Research*, 14(4): 323–338.

Chanda, R. (2015) 'Challenges to regional services integration in South Asia', *South Asia Economic Journal*, 16(2 suppl.): 19S–38S.

Coulson, A.B., MacLaren, A.C., McKenzie, S. and O'Gorman, K.D. (2014) 'Hospitality codes and social exchange theory: The Pashtunwali and tourism in Afghanistan', *Tourism Management*, 45: 134–141.

Dadvar-Khani, F. (2012) 'Participation of rural community and tourism development in Iran', *Community Development*, 43(2): 259–277.

Dawn News (2007) 'Time to review tourism policy', *Dawn News*, 22 October.

de Alwis, R. (2010) 'Promoting tourism in South Asia', in S. Ahmed, S. Kelegama and E. Ghani (eds), *Promoting Economic Cooperation in South Asia: Beyond SAFTA* (pp. 259–276). Washington, DC: World Bank and Sage.

Durko, A. and Petrick, J. (2015) 'The Nutella Project: An education initiative to suggest tourism as a means to peace between the United States and Afghanistan', *Journal of Travel Research*, DOI:10.1177/0047287515617300.

Euromonitor (2014) 'Country report: Travel and tourism in Afghanistan', Euromonitor International, October. Online. Available: www.euromonitor.com/travel-and-tourism-in-afghanistan/report (accessed 1 April 2015).

Gaborieau, M. (2009) 'South Asian Muslim diasporas and transnational movements: Tablîghî Jamâ'at and Jamâ'at-I Islâmî', *South African Historical Journal*, 61(1): 8–20.

Goodarzi, M., Haghtalab, N. and Shamshiry, E. (2015) 'Wellness tourism in Sareyn, Iran: resources, planning and development', *Current Issues in Tourism*, DOI:10.1080/13683500.2015.1012192.

Gordon, S. (2014) 'Bookings for adventure trips to Afghanistan DOUBLE as curious travellers defy Foreign Office advice and pay £5,000 each to visit troubled country', *Daily Mail*, 29 December. Online. Available: www.dailymail.co.uk/travel/travel_news/article-2889853/Bookings-adventure-trips-Afghanistan-DOUBLE-curious-travellers-defy-Foreign-Office-advice-pay-5-000-visit-troubled-country.html (accessed 1 April 2015).

Grötzbach, E. (1983) 'Der ausländertourismus in Afghanistan bis 1979: Entwicklung, struktur und räumliche problematik' (International tourism in Afghanistan until 1979), *Erdkunde*, 37(2): 146–159.

Hall, C.M. and Page, S. (2000) 'Developing tourism in South Asia: India, Pakistan and Bangladesh: SAARC and beyond', in C.M. Hall & S.J. Page (eds) *Tourism in South and South-East Asia: Critical Perspectives* (pp. 197–224). Oxford: Butterworth-Heinemann.

Harun, Y.A. (2010) 'Regional cooperation in South Asia: Bangladesh perspective', in S. Ahmed, S. Kelegama and E. Ghani (eds), *Promoting Economic Cooperation in South Asia: Beyond SAFTA* (pp. 279–299). Washington, DC: World Bank and Sage.

Kantarci, K., Uysal, M. and Magnini, V. (eds) (2014) *Tourism in Central Asia: Cultural Potential and Challenges*, Toronto: Apple Academic Press.

Khondker, B.H. and Ahsan, T. (2015) *Background Paper on Tourism Sector*. Dhaka: Planning Commission of Bangladesh.

Khoshkam, M., Marzuki, A. and Al-Mulali, U. (2016) 'Socio-demographic effects on Anzali wetland tourism development', *Tourism Management*, 54: 96–106.

Ministry of Finance (2015) 'Population, labor force and employment', in *Pakistan Economic Survey (2014–15)*, Ministry of Finance, Government of Pakistan. Online. Available: http://finance.gov.pk/survey/chapters_15/12_Population.pdf (accessed 14 February 2016).

Najimi, A.W. (2011) 'Built heritage in Afghanistan: Threats, challenges and conservation', *International Journal of Environmental Studies*, 68(3): 343–361.

Pakistan Tourism Development Corporation (2016) *Tourism in Pakistan*. Rawalpindi: Government of Pakistan.

Rasul, G. and Manandhar, P. (2009) 'Prospects and problems in promoting tourism in South Asia: A regional perspective', *South Asia Economic Journal*, 10(1): 187–207.

Raza, S.A. and Jawaid, S.T. (2013) 'Terrorism and tourism: A conjunction and ramification in Pakistan', *Economic Modelling*, 33: 65–70.

Richter, L. (1989) *The Politics of Tourism in Asia*. Hawaii: University of Honolulu Press.

SAARC Chamber of Commerce and Industry Tourism Council (1997) *SAARC Chamber of Commerce and Industry Tourism Council*, Kathmandu: SAARC Chamber of Commerce and Industry Tourism Council. Online. Available: http://south-asia.com/saarc-tourism/index.htm (accessed 3 October 1998).

Saha, S. and Yap, G. (2014) 'The moderation effects of political instability and terrorism on tourism development: A cross-country panel analysis', *Journal of Travel Research*, 53(4): 509–521.

Shaikh, P. (1976) 'The development of international tourism in Pakistan', Master's thesis, Cornell University, Ithaca.

Siddiqi, B. (2010) '"Purification of self": Ijtema as a new Islamic pilgrimage', *European Journal of Economic and Political Studies*, 3 (Special Issue: Transnational Islam): 133–150.

Sikand, Y. (2002) *The Origins and Development of the Tablighi Jama`at, 1920–2000: A Cross-Country Comparative Survey*. Hyderabad: Orient Longman.

Singh, S. (ed.) (2009) *Domestic Tourism in Asia: Diversity and Divergence*. London: Earthscan.

Timothy, D.J. (2003) 'Supranationalist alliances and tourism: Insights from ASEAN and SAARC', *Current Issues in Tourism*, 6(3): 250–266.

Tisdell, C. (1997) 'Tourism development in India and Bangladesh: General issues, illustrated by ecotourism in the Sunderbans', *Tourism Recreation Research*, 22(1): 26–33.

UNWTO (2015) *UNWTO Tourism Highlights 2015*. Madrid: UNWTO.

Vaidya, S. (1996) 'Tourism in SAARC region: Common policies for progress', Paper presented at SCCI Tourism Council Seminar at Colombo, Sri Lanka, 2–4 September 1996. Online. Available: http://south-asia.com/saarc-tourism/srilanka.htm (accessed 3 October 1998).

World Bank (2016a) 'World Bank data: International tourism, number of arrivals'. Online. Available: http://data.worldbank.org/indicator/ST.INT.ARVL (accessed 14 February 2016).

—— (2016b) 'World Bank data: International tourism, receipts (% of total exports)' Online. Available: http://data.worldbank.org/indicator/ST.INT.RCPT.XP.ZS (accessed 14 February 2016).

—— (2016c) 'World Bank data: International tourism, number of departures'. Online. Available: http://data.worldbank.org/indicator/ST.INT.DPRT (accessed 14 February 2016).

—— (2016d) 'World Bank data: International tourism, expenditures (% of total imports)' Online. Available: http://data.worldbank.org/indicator/ST.INT.XPND.MP.ZS (accessed 14 February 2016).

World Bank Database (2016) 'Country, series & time analysis', World Bank Group.

World Travel and Tourism Council (WTTC) (2014) *Economic Impact: Pakistan*. London: WTTC.

—— (2015a) *Economic Impact of Travel & Tourism 2015: Iran*. London: WTTC.

—— (2015b) *Economic Impact of Travel & Tourism 2015: Bangladesh*. London: WTTC.

Zahid, J. (2014) 'Tourism has fallen from great peaks', *Express Tribune*, 3 November. Online. Available: http://tribune.com.pk/story/785077/tourism-has-fallen-from-great-peaks (accessed 16 February 2015).

Zahra, I. (2012) 'Destination image and tourism: A case study of Bangladesh', *European Journal of Business and Management*, 4(6): 18–27.

17

TOURISM IN INDIA

Development, performance and prospects

Girish Prayag & Subhajit Das

Introduction

Tourism has emerged as an important sector of the Indian economy in the last ten years contributing significantly to GDP and foreign exchange earnings. By 2024, it is expected that tourism could contribute as much as 6.8% to GDP and create 48.37 million jobs, either directly or indirectly (WTTC 2014). In 2013, the direct contribution of tourism to GDP was way above the world average of US$18bn, but significantly lower than the Asia-Pacific average of US$163.5bn. The tourism industry in India is expected to grow at least 6.4% per annum over the period 2014–2024, placing the country in the top 15 destinations with the highest projected tourism growth (WTTC 2014). Despite the destination's economic, cultural, infrastructural and political landscape acting as enablers of tourism growth, these factors also create barriers to growth. Accordingly, the purpose of this chapter is to examine the performance of the tourism industry in India with respect to both the outbound and inbound tourism markets. Hence, the chapter also outlines some of the key challenges and opportunities facing the tourism industry. The chapter starts with a brief overview of the physical geography and a historical account of tourism development in India, followed by an analysis of the performance of the outbound and inbound tourism markets. Thereafter, three major enablers and barriers to tourism growth – namely, economic conditions, physical infrastructure and politics – are reviewed. The chapter concludes with a case study on the Incredible India campaign and its associated marketing strategies to boost tourism numbers.

The physical geography of India

India is a vast geographical territory that embraces several physical characteristics with their unique assemblages of landform features and climatic conditions. Spate (1954) considered four macro-regions of India taking into account factors like topography, climate and vegetation cover. His four categories are:

1   Natural regions of mountain.
2   Regions of northern plain.

3   Regions of peninsular India.
4   Regions of islands.

In such regionalization, eastern and western coastlines of India – which comprise about 5,700km (Singh 1971) – were incorporated under "regions of peninsular India", but in other schemes a separate macro-region is found to be assigned to the coasts and islands (Khullar 2011). Broadly speaking, India is dominated by monsoonal climate and thus the affected regions experience humid climatic conditions, e.g. North-east India, the Western Ghats and the south-eastern coast. India offers a multi-dimensional blend of tourism that is associated with different physico-climatic regions and inhabited by typical cultural communities. India has 20 states, six union territories and one National Capital Territory. Each state is unique enough in terms of its cultural, infrastructural, socio-economic and political aspects to be considered a separate tourist destination.

At a global level, the major tourist attractions may be clubbed into regions. In the north-east, tribal societies such as those in Assam, Tripura and Nagaland provide significant opportunities for cultural and heritage tourism. In the mountainous region of north India (e.g. Himachal Pradesh, Uttarakhand and Sikkim) nature-based tourism is often prioritized. In states such as Madhya Pradesh, part of Middle India, tourism on the basis of historical and archaeological resources is promoted. Western India can be experienced in deserts and palaces of states like Gujrat and Rajasthan. South India is famous for its excellent ambience and natural beauty, comprising Indian coasts and backwaters, mountains of the Western Ghats and residual hills of the Eastern Ghats. However, Indian states cannot be grouped on the basis of dominant tourism dimensions as individual states indeed have several niche tourism markets and products.

History and development of the tourism industry in India

The history of Indian tourism can be broadly charted into three major phases on the basis of significant changes in orientations and approaches for tourism development. The first phase, from pre-colonial India to 1982, is when the first tourism policy got framed. Tourism promotion started with the Sargent Committee in 1945 to examine tourism opportunities by assessing tourist traffic in India (Bhatia 2001). A significant shift occurred in the tourism sector with the establishment of the Indian Tourism Development Corporation (ITDC) in 1966 and the formation of the Ministry of Tourism and Civil Aviation in 1967, followed by the first Tourism Policy in 1982. These political actors mainly focused on promoting tourism as a major export industry, opening the way for private investment, developing tourism circuits and increasing the growth of foreign tourism. Yet, from an industrial perspective, the tourism policy failed to widen the scope of foreign investment and to promote domestic tourism on a larger scale (Kerr 2003).

The second phase began after 1982 and ended in 2002 when the second tourism policy of India was framed. During that time, the tourism industry was given several industrial incentives, concessions, tax rebates and other exemption facilities by the central government. The National Action Plan of 1992 emphasized increasing the flow of tourists, development of proper infrastructure for domestic tourism, diversification of tourism for foreign tourists and improving the socio-economic condition of tourist destinations (Srinivasan 2004; Ball *et al.* 2009). The third phase started after 2002 and continues to the present day. Since then, the basic endeavours of the Indian tourism sector have been to achieve strong coordination between public and private elements in the sector, the introduction of new forms of tourism such as rural tourism, the introduction of pro-poor tourism and publicizing India in the global tourism market through international campaigns like Incredible India in 2002 and "*Atithi Devo Bhava*" (Guests are like God) in 2005.

The competitiveness of the Indian tourism market

Given the diversity of products that exists in India, one would expect the destination to be highly competitive. According to the Travel and Tourism Competitiveness Index of 2013, India ranks only 11th in the Asia-Pacific region and 65th overall out of the 140 countries assessed. Several economic, political and socio-cultural issues dampen tourism growth, negatively affecting the destination's competitiveness in the region. In particular, the destination's tourism infrastructure remains underdeveloped and the policy environment is not necessarily conducive to start-ups. Coupled with a restrictive visa policy, few hotel rooms per capita by international standards, health and hygiene standards and the country's human resources base, which is ranked 96th in terms of competitiveness (WEF 2013), the destination has yet to achieve its full tourism potential.

The outbound tourism market

India is emerging as an important outbound tourism market on the global stage. According to UNWTO, India ranked 23rd in the world in terms of international tourism expenditure of about US$12.3bn, excluding transport (European Travel Commission 2014). The number of Indian outbound tourists has grown from 1.9m in 1991 to 14.9m in 2012, with a compounded annual growth rate of 10.2% (Ministry of Tourism 2012). Table 17.1 represents the number of Indian outbound tourist arrivals in major continents and reflects a pattern which can be used for categorizing outbound travel into four groups. The first group consists of destinations in South-East Asia, West Asia and East Asia, which attracts the most Indian tourists. The second group includes North America and Western Europe, with an increasing share of Indian visitors since 2005. Africa and South Asia fall under the third group, with a steady increase in the number of visitors only after 2007. The fourth group is composed of Australasia, Central and South America and Eastern Europe, among which Australasia shows a steady year-on-year growth. Countries belonging to South and Central America and Eastern Europe have the lowest number of visits by Indians.

Among the many factors that have contributed to growth in outbound tourism, a few are noteworthy. First, economic liberalization and globalization have significantly affected this sector by widening the scope for mobility of both pleasure and business travellers. Second, India possesses the largest number of middle-class people in the world (Singh 2001) and a substantial proportion have the disposable income to spend for travel purposes (Sarkar 2009). However, the continued devaluation of the Indian currency is inhibiting growth of outbound tourism (Euromonitor International 2013). Third, the ease of issuance of travel documents like passports to Indian citizens has also contributed to growth in outbound tourism. Fourth, aggressive campaigning by foreign countries with several new and attractive tourism packages is fuelling outbound tourism growth (World Tourism Organization (WTO) and European Travel Commission (ETC) 2009). It is predicted that this market will comprise approximately 50 million visitors, spending more than US$28bn by 2020 (WTO & ETC 2009).

Table 17.1 Departures of Indian outbound tourists to top ten continental regions of the world ('000)

Destinations	2000	2001	2002	2003	2004	2005	2006	2007	2008	2009	2010	2011
South-East Asia	777.1	786.2	901.3	767.0	1,041.9	1,258.3	1,503.1	1,853.3	2,038.8	2,129.0	2,493.7	2,715.3
West Asia	768.3	861.6	1,055.0	1,183.9	867.8	1,273.5	1,731.4	2,276.5	1,604.7	1,323.7	1,539.0	2,482.8
East Asia	363.5	431.2	530.3	517.6	695.8	785.8	871.8	982.0	1,031.0	1,074.3	1,427.5	1,450.5
Group 1 sub-total	*1,908.9*	*2,079.1*	*2,486.7*	*2,468.5*	*2,605.5*	*3,317.6*	*4,106.3*	*5,111.8*	*4,674.5*	*4,527.0*	*5,460.1*	*6,648.6*
North America	326.3	324.4	312.8	329.2	377.2	422.8	494.1	668.8	709.9	657.4	778.6	802.7
Western Europe	358.7	333.8	387.7	363.1	461.6	454.6	628.4	628.7	712.8	605.9	785.0	787.7
Group 2 sub-total	*685.0*	*658.2*	*700.4*	*692.3*	*838.8*	*877.4*	*1,122.5*	*1,297.5*	*1,422.7*	*1,263.3*	*1,563.6*	*1,590.4*
Africa	147.1	151.6	164.1	185.4	153.1	203.6	252.1	310.1	329.6	325.4	389.3	510.2
South Asia	279.8	242.6	230.1	280.5	306.1	365.1	360.0	338.5	240.1	256.4	284.6	384.2
Group 3 sub-total	*426.9*	*394.2*	*394.2*	*465.9*	*459.3*	*568.6*	*612.1*	*648.6*	*569.7*	*581.8*	*673.9*	*894.3*
Australasia	49.9	61.0	62.4	61.0	71.9	86.7	106.1	119.6	140.1	153.3	173.5	176.9
Central and South America	6.3	6.6	6.6	8.9	8.5	24.1	26.4	32.3	53.2	44.4	218.3	57.5
Eastern Europe	33.9	40.5	49.5	50.8	49.5	86.5	96.9	128.9	125.8	45.9	127.3	62.3
Group 4 sub-total	*90.1*	*108.2*	*118.4*	*120.7*	*129.9*	*197.3*	*229.4*	*280.8*	*319.1*	*243.6*	*519.0*	*296.7*
Total	**3,111.0**	**3,239.6**	**3,699.7**	**3,747.4**	**4,033.4**	**4,960.9**	**6,070.3**	**7,338.7**	**6,986.0**	**6,615.6**	**8,216.6**	**9,430.0**

Sources: Ministry of Tourism 2005, 2012.

The inbound tourism market

In 2013, the top five tourism-generating markets for India were the US, UK, Bangladesh, Sri Lanka and Russia. Most international tourists arrive by air, with Delhi, Mumbai and Chennai airports being the main ports of entry. Table 17.2 shows that the annual growth of foreign and domestic tourism has been erratic for the last 13 years with a peak of 26.8% in 2004 and 20.9% in 2009 respectively. As expected, the domestic tourism market has grown steadily since 2010. India remains a competitively priced tourism destination, ranked 20th out of 140 countries in price competitiveness (WEF 2013). However, several issues impact on the development of the domestic and international inbound markets. Despite improvements in air and ground transport, accessibility remains a key issue for the Indian tourism industry. Specifically, quality of roads and ports needs further improvement (WEF 2013). Safety and security, especially for women travellers, and extremist threats will continue to be major barriers to tourism growth for both the domestic and international markets (Euromonitor International 2013). Compared to the Asia-Pacific annual tourism growth rate, inbound tourism growth to India has been below average. For example, the Asia-Pacific annual growth rates were 12.7% in 2010 and 7.1% in 2012, while Indian tourism grew by only 11.8% and 4.3% respectively. Nevertheless, in 2010 the Ministry of Tourism put in place an action plan that incorporates, amongst others, the development of new products by creating "target destinations" with a cluster of attractions in specific regions, establishment of a tourism development board, a boost in advertising and promotion campaigns and human resource development (AC Nielsen 2010). This action plan should boost both inbound and outbound markets.

Table 17.2 Key tourism inbound statistics for India, 2000–2013

Year	Foreign tourist arrivals ('000)	Annual growth (%)	Domestic tourists ('000)	Annual growth (%)
2000	2,649.4	6.7	220,106.9	15.4
2001	2,537.3	−4.2	236,469.6	7.4
2002	2,384.4	−6.0	269,598.0	14.0
2003	2,726.2	14.3	309,038.4	14.6
2004	3,457.5	26.8	366,267.5	18.5
2005	3,918.6	13.3	392,014.3	7.0
2006	4,447.2	13.5	462,321.1	17.9
2007	5,081.5	14.3	526,564.5	13.9
2008	5,282.6	4.0	563,034.1	6.9
2009	5,167.7	−2.2	668,800.5	18.8
2010	5,775.7	11.8	747,703.4	11.8
2011	6,309.2	9.2	864,532.7	15.6
2012	6,577.7	4.3	1,045,047.5	20.9
2013★	6,967.6	5.9	1,145,280.4	9.6

Source: Ministry of Tourism 2014.
Note
★ Provisional figures.

Opportunities and challenges facing the Indian tourism industry

Despite an economic slow-down, sluggish demand and security concerns, the travel and tourism industry in India is growing. This growth is fuelled by several factors that can be considered as enablers. In this section, three such factors – economic, infrastructural and political – are reviewed. Yet, these factors also pose several challenges to tourism stakeholders in India.

The economic dimension of tourism

The importance of tourism for the Indian economy can be seen from the government's targeting of foreign tourist arrivals. The government has embarked on several initiatives to boost tourism revenues. Besides investing in the Incredible India campaign to create awareness of the destination on the global stage, the government has also extended the benefits of section 10(23G) of the *Income Tax Act, 1961* to institutions financing hotels of three stars and above. This had the effect of boosting the number and types of rooms available for both domestic and international markets. Another step in the right direction has been the divestment of the government's stake in government-run hotels and promotion of niche products. For example, the government has relaxed the criteria for a medical tourism visa. The annual growth rate of medical tourism is about 30%, contributing significantly to tourism revenues. Alongside this, several other niche tourism products, such as rural tourism, heritage and pilgrim tourism, and the creation of new tourist circuits, are purported to strengthen rural economy and reduce poverty (Ministry of Tourism 2011). Having realised the benefits of tourism, several state governments such as that of Kerala are also placing high importance on boosting tourism numbers and revenues. The Ministry of Tourism is also involving non-residential Indians in the tourism sector, with more flexible investment opportunities than were previously available (Hannam & Diekmann 2011). The public–private partnership model is being encouraged and implemented in sectors involving large revenue-generating projects such cruise vessels, tourist trains and golf courses. In these ways, the right economic climate is being created to boost tourism growth.

However, economically several factors have contributed to the poor performance of tourism in India when compared to world tourism and the Asia-Pacific region. The devaluation of the Indian currency is inhibiting tourism growth (Euromonitor International 2013). The "multiplicity of taxation system" on services to foreign tourists is another limiting factor. The struggling aviation industry is hindering accessibility, and competitors offering better-packaged products and value for money are some of the main factors hindering tourism growth (Ministry of Tourism 2011).

The physical infrastructure dimension of tourism

The Indian government is working to upgrade the physical infrastructure to achieve an overall successful development of the tourism industry to reap economic returns in the future (Dasgupta 2011). The completion of the golden quadrilateral project by the National Highway Authority of India at the end of 2014 is an example of physical infrastructure development that will boost tourist travel within the country. The aim is to establish an intra-state transport network that includes major economic and cultural centres of India (National Highway Authority of India 2013). The Ministry of Tourism has also started the implementation of five major schemes as part of the policy on tourism infrastructure development. For example, the Product/Infrastructure Development for Destinations and Circuits, Assistance to Central Agencies for Tourism Infrastructure Development and Incentives to Accommodation Infrastructure are noteworthy. Some tourism resources are directly maintained by central agencies such as the

ITDC and the Archaeological Survey of India. Funds are allocated to such agencies to develop infrastructure and maintain destinations (Ministry of Tourism 2011). Incentives for accommodation infrastructure is another scheme that will have a long-term effect on developing tourism infrastructure in India. The Indian government is also addressing the connectivity issue through upgrading existing airports and building new ones.

These schemes are certainly improving the physical infrastructure of the destination, but because of several issues related to price sensitivity, these schemes have not been successfully implemented. Indian tourism is still limited by several transport and accommodation infrastructure constraints, wayside amenities and public utilities that undermine tourism performance (Chaudhary 2000; Hannam & Diekmann 2011; Ministry of Tourism 2011).

The political dimension of tourism

Indian politics have always been a regulating and determining factor in the development of the tourism industry. The Department of Tourism has experienced several changes regarding its association with several ministries during different political phases of the Indian central government (Fazili & Ashraf 2006). The federal structure of India has substantially moulded the tourism sector both positively and negatively. On a positive note, for example, the federal structure encourages and promotes innovative tourism products and political stability. However, it is often affected by unnecessary delay and lack of coordination in policy implementation (Richter 1989; Singh & Singh 2011). The role of the Indian government has shifted over the years, from so-called "tourism facilitator" to a "powerful catalyst" in shaping the future of the tourism industry (Hannam & Diekmann 2011; Ministry of Tourism 2011).

However, Indian tourism has experienced significant ignorance, indifference and negligence, at least up to 2002, before the introduction of the new tourism policy (Fazili & Ashraf 2006; Hannam & Diekmann 2011; Ministry of Tourism 2011). Despite the government encouraging tourism growth, the ranking of India in comparison to other countries in terms of the government's prioritization of the travel and tourism industry is falling, from 59 in 2006 to 80 in 2010 and 91 in 2011 (Blanke & Chiesa 2011; Planning Commission 2013). Also, tourism-related data and reports have been criticized for being politically biased. Because other political spheres such as planning and policy making bodies (e.g. Planning Commission of India, National Development Council) depend on such reports and data, it "means that those supplying the information have vested interest in how it is perceived" (Richter 1989: 122). Dissonance has also been found between the representations of Indian tourism by Western countries and the Indian government (Bhagavan & Bari 2001; Bandyopadhyay & Morais 2005; Spivak 2010).

Case study 17.1 Incredible India: boosting tourism growth

Despite the challenges facing the tourism industry in India, the destination has been able to boost international tourism growth through the well-known "Incredible India" campaign. The case study highlights some of the major marketing strategies that were used by the Government of India and Ministry of Tourism to boost foreign tourist arrivals in India. In October 2002, "Incredible India", a branding and promotion campaign by India's central government, was launched to promote tourism in a consistent and coherent manner on the global tourism stage (Harish 2010). The objective of the campaign was to market the country as a high-end tourist destination with multiple attractions and world-class amenities (Kant 2009). The success of the campaign can be attributed to several factors, including the use of imagery, the positioning of niche products, the use of media channels and clever use of advertising logos/taglines.

The initial campaign drew upon familiar tourist imagery and global Indian icons such as the Bengal Tiger, the Taj Mahal and the luxurious backdrops in Rajasthan, rugged Himalayan mountain ranges, the beaches of Goa and the backwaters of Kerala to emphasize the diversity of products and experiences the country offers (Geary 2013). Traditionally, tourists to India have followed the conventional tourism route of what is known as "the golden triangle", comprising Delhi, Agra and Jaipur. The initial campaign used these images associated with the golden triangle to reinforce familiarity with the destination. The clever use of such imagery confirmed existing image stereotypes of the destination on the global stage and reassured tourists that India offered a unique experience.

Subsequent campaigns attempted to portray specific products and regions. For example, the 2003/2004 campaign showcased prominent yoga positions to reinforce the spiritual, transcendental, rejuvenating and wellness characteristics of the destination (Geary 2013). In particular, the niche markets of medical and wellness tourism as well as spiritual tourism are perceived by the government and tourism industry as lucrative, given India's pool of physicians, hospitals and treatment centres that are equipped with infrastructure and technology on par with Western countries but at a fraction of the cost (IBEF 2008). Also, tourism departments of several states were encouraged to adopt their own taglines (e.g. Andhra Pradesh – The Essence of Incredible India) to boost tourism numbers (Harish 2010).

Tourism growth has also been sought through a synchronized communication strategy to facilitate advertising in prime generating markets (Geary 2013). Worldwide channels such as CNN, the BBC and Discovery were used along with online contests on leading internet portals such as Yahoo, MSN and Google (Kant 2005). The campaign unequivocally changed the image of India in Western countries from poverty driven to a growing and vibrant destination (Bandyopadhyay & Morais 2005). Visually the use of the "!" symbol to convey the mind-boggling depth and intensity of the Indian experience was perceived as a powerful new way of shaping the identity of India in the twenty-first century (Kant, 2005; Geary, 2013). The symbol "!" represented India's accelerating GDP, extreme geography, cultural diversity and deep-rooted spirituality (Kant 2005). Witty advertising copy and tone transformed India into an optimistic and extroverted brand. For example, headlines such as "not all Indians are polite, hospitable and vegetarian" (with the image of a Bengal Tiger) and "And to think these days men get away with giving flowers and chocolates to their wives" (with the image of the Taj Mahal) are credited for their contribution to shaping the image of the destination in Western countries (Geary 2013).

The Incredible India campaign has resulted in a steady growth in foreign tourist arrivals and foreign exchange earnings over the years. For instance, tourism revenues increased from US$3,103 million in 2002 to US$18,445 million in 2013 (Ministry of Tourism 2014), partly attributable to the campaign due to increased global awareness of the destination. Tourist arrivals, which were hovering around two million per annum for many years, were boosted to five million in 2007 (Harish 2010). Despite the recognised success of the campaign, it has been criticized by many as being unfocused branding and positioning that has contributed to India's poor placement in travel and tourism competitiveness (Sharma 2007). The financial investment in the production and dissemination of India's brand image has become more important than the delivery of the destination experience (Geary 2013). The creative display of marketing talent through the country's image management may be self-defeating in the long term due to the political, social, economic and infrastructural challenges. These challenges have the potential to undermine the country's programme of tourism development (Geary 2013).

Key readings

Ball, S., Horner, S. and Nield, K. (2009) *Contemporary Hospitality and Tourism Management Issues in China and India*, Abingdon: Taylor & Francis.

Bindra, P. and Karanth, K.K. (2013) 'Tourism turf wars: Debating the benefits and costs of wildlife tourism in India', *Oryx*, 47(1): 15–16.

Geary, D. (2013) 'Incredible India in a global age: The cultural politics of image branding in tourism', *Tourist Studies*, 13(1): 36–61.

Hannam, K. and Diekmann, A. (2011) *Tourism and India: A Critical Introduction*. Abingdon: Routledge.

Harish, R. (2010) 'Brand architecture in tourism branding: The way forward for India', *Journal of Indian Business Research*, 2(3): 153–165.

Munjal, P. (2013) 'Measuring the economic impact of the tourism industry in India using the Tourism Satellite Account and input–output analysis', *Tourism Economics*, 19(6): 1345–1359.

Wong, K.M. and Musa, G. (2013) 'Medical tourism in Thailand, Singapore, Malaysia and India', in C.M. Hall (ed.), *Medical Tourism: The Ethics, Regulation, and Marketing of Health Mobility* (pp. 167–186). New York: Routledge.

References

AC Nielsen (2010) *Competitiveness of Tourism Sector in India with Selected Countries of World*. New Delhi: AC Nielsen India.

Ball, S., Horner, S. and Nield, K. (2009) *Contemporary Hospitality and Tourism Management Issues in China and India*. Abingdon: Taylor & Francis.

Bandyopadhyay, R. and Morais, D. (2005) 'Representative dissonance: India's self and western image', *Annals of Tourism Research*, 32(4): 1006–1021.

Bhagavan, M.B. and Bari, F. (2001) '(Mis) representing economy: Western media production and the impoverishment of South Asia', *Comparative Studies of South Asia, Africa and the Middle East*, 21(1–2): 99–109.

Bhatia, A.K. (2001) *International Tourism Management*. New Delhi: Sterling Publishers.

Blanke, J. and Chiesa, T. (2011) *The Travel & Tourism Competitiveness Report 2011*. Switzerland: World Economic Forum. Online. Available: www3.weforum.org/docs/WEF_TravelTourism Competitiveness_Report_2011.pdf (accessed 13 October 2014).

Chaudhary, M. (2000) 'India's image as a tourist destination: A perspective of foreign tourists', *Tourism Management*, 21(3): 293–297.

Dasgupta, D. (2011) *Tourism Marketing*. New Delhi: Dorling Kindersley (India).

Euromonitor International (2013) *Travel and Tourism in India*. Euromonitor International Passport Publications.

European Travel Commission (ETC) (2014) 'Market insights: India'. Online. Available: www.etc-corporate.org/?page=report&report_id=52 (accessed 24 November 2014).

Fazili, A.I. and Ashraf, S.H. (2006) *Tourism in India Planning & Development*. New Delhi: Sarup Book Publishers.

Geary, D. (2013) 'Incredible India in a global age: The cultural politics of image branding in tourism', *Tourist Studies*, 13(1): 36–61.

Hannam, K. and Diekmann, A. (2011) *Tourism and India: A Critical Introduction*. Abingdon: Routledge.

Harish, R. (2010) 'Brand architecture in tourism branding: The way forward for India', *Journal of Indian Business Research*, 2(3): 153–165.

India Brand Equity Foundation (IBEF) (2008) 'Tourism and hospitality'. Online. Available: www.ibef.org (accessed 18 January 2015).

Kant, A. (2005) 'The branding of India', *Incredible India Magazine*, April.

—— (2009) *Branding India: An Incredible Story*. Noida: Collins Business.

Kerr, W.R. (2003) *Tourism Public Policy, and the Strategic Management of Failure*. Oxford: Pergamon.

Khullar, D.R. (2011) *India: A Comprehensive Geography*. New Delhi: Kalyani Publishers.

Ministry of Tourism (2005) *India Tourism Statistics at a Glance 2005*. New Delhi: Govt. of India, Ministry of Tourism.

—— (2011) *Report of the Working Group on Tourism: 12th Five Year Plan (2012–2017)*. New Delhi: Govt. of India, Ministry of Tourism. Online. Available: http://planningcommission.nic.in/aboutus/committee/wrkgrp12/wgrep_tourism.pdf (accessed 15 October 2014).

—— (2012) *India Tourism Statistics at a Glance 2012*. New Delhi: Govt. of India, Ministry of Tourism. Online. Available: http://tourism.gov.in/writereaddata/CMSPagePicture/file/marketresearch/publications/India%20Tourism%20Statics(2012)%20new.pdf (accessed 24 September 2014).

—— (2014) *India Tourism Statistics at a Glance 2013*. New Delhi: Govt. of India, Ministry of Tourism. Online. Available: http://tourism.gov.in/writereaddata/CMSPagePicture/file/marketresearch/Incredible%20India%20final%2021-7-2014%20english.pdf (accessed 10 September 2014).

National Highway Authority of India (2013) 'Golden Quadrilateral: Overall progress corridor wise including completed length as on 31st May 2013'. Online. Available: www.nhai.org/goldenquadrilateral.asp (accessed 15 October 2014).

Planning Commission, Govt. of India (2013) *Twelfth Five Year Plan (2012–2017), Economic Sectors (volume II)*. New Delhi: Sage Publications India.

Richter, L.K. (1989) *The Politics of Tourism in Asia*. Hawai'i: University of Hawaii Press.

Sarkar, A.N. (2009) *Enhancing Global Competitiveness: Advantage India*. New Delhi: I.K. International Publishing House.

Sharma, R.T. (2007), 'Tourism in India has little to cheer'. Rediff News. Online. Available http://in.rediff.com/money/2007/apr/05tour.htm (accessed 13 January 2015).

Singh, R.L. (1971) *India: A Regional Geography*. Varanasi: National Geographical Society of India.

Singh, S. (2001) 'Indian tourism: Policy, performance and pitfalls', in D. Harrison (ed.), *Tourism and the Less Developed World: Issues and Case Studies* (pp. 137–149). Wallingford: CABI Publishing.

Singh, T.V. and Singh, S. (2011) 'Tourism in India: Development, performance and prospects', in C.M. Hall and S. Page (eds), *Tourism in South and Southeast Asia* (pp. 225–232). Abingdon: Routledge.

Spate, O.H.K. (1954) *India and Pakistan: A General and Regional Geography*. London: Methuen and Co.

Spivak, G.C. (2010) 'Can the subaltern speak?', in R. C. Morris (ed.), *Can the Subaltern Speak? Reflections on the History of an Idea* (pp. 237–292). New York: Columbia University Press.

Srinivasan, R. (2004) *Services Marketing: The Indian Context*. New Delhi: Prentice-Hall of India.

World Economic Forum (WEF) (2013) *The Travel and Tourism Competitiveness Report 2013*. Geneva: WEF.

World Tourism Organization (WTO) and European Travel Commission (ETC) (2009) *The Indian Outbound Travel Market: With Special Insight into the Image of Europe as a Destination*. Spain: WTO and ETC.

World Travel and Tourism Council (WTTC) (2014) *Travel and Tourism Economic Impact 2014: Asia Pacific*. London: WTTC.

18

TOURISM IN SRI LANKA

Sriyantha Fernando, Jayatilleke S. Bandara & Christine Smith

Introduction

Although Sri Lanka has a long history as a tourist destination, there have been ups and downs in the tourism industry in Sri Lanka in recent decades, particularly between 2003 and 2009 due to political violence and the separatist war interspersed with a number of periods of peace. Since the end of the separatist war in May 2009 tourism in Sri Lanka has been booming and it has been ranked as one of the top tourist destinations in the world for the past few years. The purpose of this chapter is to present an overview on tourism in Sri Lanka. The chapter mainly focuses on Sri Lanka's attractiveness to tourists, historical evolution of its policies towards modern-day tourism, the changing patterns of tourist arrivals during different episodes of war and peace and the recent tourism boom and the associated national tourism development strategy (TDS).

Location and tourism attractions

Sri Lanka is a beautiful tropical island in the Indian Ocean, situated at the southern tip of India between 6° and 10° north and 80° to 82° east. It is separated from India by the Palk Strait, which is 32km wide at its narrowest (UNDP & WTO 1993: 2). The land area of the island is 65,610km², with a maximum length of 432km and a maximum width of 224km (Sri Lanka Info 2011). The southern half of the island is dominated by rugged hill country, while the northern half is a large plain. It also has palm-fringed beautiful beaches on the south-western, southern and south-eastern coastlines (Lai 2002).

As a tourism destination, Sri Lanka competes successfully with other destinations partly because of its pivotal geographical position. Its strategic location in the Indian Ocean on the major air and sea routes between Europe and the Far East is an advantage for the country's positioning as a global logistics hub (Sri Lanka Info 2011). O'Hare and Barrett (1994: 43) pointed out 'the Island "controls" (as in colonial times) routes to the Far East as well as to other destinations in the Indian Ocean, the Middle East, Africa and Australasia'. This geographical location of Sri Lanka was the reason for colonisation by three Western powers: the Portuguese (1505–1656), the Dutch (1656–1796) and the British (1796–1948).

In addition to its location, Sri Lanka offers a plethora of attractions for tourists, among them beaches, favourable climate, rich cultural heritage, national parks and wildlife (Lai 2002). It has 1,585km of coastline, with Hikkaduwa and Unawatuna well known for excellent scuba diving. Mirissa has become famous for viewing of whales and dolphins, while Tangalle is being promoted as a diving destination. Meanwhile, Trincomalee is known for its natural harbour and has two relatively unexploited beaches.

It has an enormous amount of culture and heritage-based resources. Sri Lanka is home to eight UNESCO World Heritage Sites, including several Buddhist and Hindu temples. According to the World Tourism Organization, Sri Lanka has the advantage of having numerous sites classified as unique attractions, including World Heritage Sites and ancient monuments (de Silva 2000). These include the central highlands area, comprising the Horton Plains National Park and Knuckles Conservation Forest, the Sinharaja Forest Reserve, the Dutch Fort in Galle, the Golden Temple of Dambulla, the Temple of Tooth in Kandy and the Nallur Kandaswamy Temple in Jaffna. It has more than 2,500 years of history as a civilisation, including nine ancient kingdoms and ruins with temples of Buddhist heritage. It has designated a "Cultural Triangle" for heritage tourism which includes five out of seven World Heritage Sites (including the ancient cities of Anuradhapura, Polonnaruwa, Kandy and Sigiriya, a spectacular fortress build by King Kasyapa in the 5th century).

As a result of this unique mixture of golden beaches, rich cultural heritage, diverse landscapes and a significant amount of wildlife, Sri Lanka is classified as one of the most popular tourist destinations in the region (Lai 2002). Also, as noted by Kiriella (2011: 2), Sri Lanka is a well-known tourist destination because of its endowment of the three "S"s (sun, sea and sand).

A historical narrative on tourism in Sri Lanka

Sri Lanka has been a tourist destination for centuries because of its strategic location and uniqueness. At the end of the 13th century Marco Polo visited Sri Lanka, then known as Ceylon, and noted 'the traveller reaches Ceylon, which is the untouchably finest island of its size in all the World' (in UNDP & WTO 1993). It was known as "The Pearl of the Indian Ocean", Serendib, Ceylon and "Taprobane" among the explorers and merchants for many years (SLTDA 2011). The country has been exposed to Western influences since 1505 with the arrival of the Portuguese, and it became a British colony after the capture of Kandiyan Kingdom by the British in 1815, with Sri Lanka gaining independence from the British in 1948.

The earliest tourist arrivals recorded in the history of tourism in Sri Lanka were mainly related to religious tourism such as worshipping at shrines in the ancient capital of Anuradhapura and Polonnaruwa, or pilgrimages to Adam's Peak. However, during the colonial period, Sri Lanka was attractive to travellers who sailed between the West and the East through the port of Colombo on many cruise ships, freighters and other vessels because of its important location on the world's sea lanes. Therefore, the passengers used to enter the port of Colombo and enjoyed sightseeing in Colombo, Kandy and their surroundings. The Sri Lankan government set up its first Tourist Bureau in 1937 mainly to service these passengers and sailors travelling between the West and the East when they came ashore. Although accurate records are unavailable, 'it is estimated that approximately one hundred thousand to two hundred thousand passengers visited the country per annum' (SLTDA 2011: 1) during this period. However, the Tourist Bureau ceased its operations in 1940 due to the commencement of World War II. Due to the war there was little tourist activity in the 1940s.

After gaining independence in 1948, the new government decided to reorganise tourist activities by setting up the Government Tourist Bureau under the Ministry of Commerce. This

Bureau was entrusted with the function of undertaking tourist promotional works overseas. According to SLTDA information (SLTDA 2011: 1), a range of accommodation facilities were constructed throughout the country during British colonial rule. These facilities were not originally designed for the promotion of inbound tourism but for the use of planters, the business community and government officials. Some of these relatively luxurious accommodation facilities, which at that time were residences of colonial governors, were later converted into high-class hotels in Sri Lanka in order to facilitate the growing tourism industry. These included the Galle Face Hotel, the Grand Oriental Hotel and the Mount Lavinia Hotel in Colombo, the Queens Hotel in Kandy, the Grand Hotel and St. Andrews Hotel in Nuwara Eliya, and the New Oriental Hotel in Galle. These hotels were renovated and were used as prime accommodation facilities for foreign visitors. In addition to these hotels, some other accommodation facilities were built as tourist rest-houses. These accommodation establishments were developed in places of scenic beauty such as Ella, Belihul Oya, Horton Plains, Pussellawa, Polonnaruwa, Sigiriya, Dambulla, Tissa Wewa, Nuwara Wewa, Kitulgala, Bentota and Tissamaharama. As a result of this growing supply of facilities and the associated government promotion and foreign relations operation, the tourism industry gained enormous respect and confidence during the period of 1948–1953 and tourism receipts doubled from US$1.04 million to US$2.23 million (Due 1980). There was rapid growth in international tourism around the world during the 1950s (Nordström 2005), largely due to the introduction of jet aircraft for civilian transport after World War II. Therefore, Sri Lanka had a golden opportunity to establish a tourism hub between the East and West using its unique central location and relatively sufficient accommodation facilities. It was necessary to invest in infrastructure in developing countries for them to attract a share of this growth in international tourism. For example, new airports with wider and long runways, parking bays with large spaces and terminal buildings with modern facilities were required to facilitate inbound tourism. However, during the period 1954–1960 tourism arrivals in Sri Lanka declined rapidly, while leading hotels experienced low occupancy rates (ranging from 14 per cent to 32 per cent) as a result of the government's lack of support of tourism activities (Due 1980). Like other South Asian countries Sri Lanka implemented a protectionist import-substitution regime after independence, except for a brief episode in 1948–1956 (Athukorala 1998). Under this closed trade policy regime the government's main focus was to develop import-substitution industries to accelerate growth, and tourism was not considered a key ingredient in the national economic development strategy. In general, growth in tourism during this period was positively related to open economic policies (United Nations 1993). Therefore, the earlier tourism-oriented development failed to take root and Sri Lanka missed a golden opportunity to establish itself as a major tourism and transport hub between the East and the West. By contrast a significant competitor in this space – Singapore – was moving quickly and strategically by improving the infrastructure needed to develop and support international tourism during the 1960s; it became the major hub between the East and West. Sri Lankan policy makers missed this first opportunity to develop its tourism sector by not investing in tourism-related infrastructure and not considering tourism as an important sector in its national economic development policy. Table 18.1 provides a detailed chronology of national economic policies and TDSs in Sri Lanka.

Although the country is extremely rich in natural, cultural and heritage-based resources, as described above, it took about 18 years following independence for Sri Lankan policy makers to recognise a significant role for tourism in enhancing economic development (Brau *et al.* 2011).

After identifying tourism as a key sector for the first time, the Sri Lankan government commissioned a study to prepare a Ten-Year Master Plan for tourism in 1966. This plan was developed with funding from USAID (United Nations 1993). Following this study the Sri

Table 18.1 A chronology of national economic policies and tourism development strategy in Sri Lanka

Period	National economic policy regime	Tourism development strategies	Main features of strategies
Before 1948	The pre-independence open economic policy	1937 – First Tourism Bureau was established 1940 – Tourist Bureau ceased its operations due to the war	Provided services to the passengers who sailed between the West and East through the port of Colombo.
1948 –56	Continuation of pre-independence open economic policy	1948 – Revival of Government Tourist Bureau	Began to undertake tourism marketing and promotional strategies immediately after independence from the colonial rulers.
1956 –65	Closing up the economy with the import-substitution strategy	Under the closed economy tourism did not play an important role in the national development strategy	Under the directionless and loosely organised Tourist Bureau there were no tourism promotional and marketing activities.
1965 –70	Partial departure from the closed economy	1966 – The government legislative body was established for the tourism sector 1966 – Introduction of the first Ten-Year Master Plan for tourism	Revival of tourism promotion and marketing strategies. *Tourist Board Act No. 10 of 1966,* *Ceylon Hotel Corporation Act No 14 of 1966,* *Tourist Development Act No. 14 of 1968.* The plan became the blueprint for tourism development and witnessed the first tourism boom in Sri Lanka. The country witnessed a first wave of new hotel construction with five resort development zones.
1970 –77	Closing up the economy again	No new government initiative to develop tourism	Rate of investment growth in tourism fell due to the re-establishment of import control measures. However, tourism grew rapidly as a result of previous promotional activities and the peaceful environment.
1977 –96	Opening up the economy	1977 – Introduction of trade liberalisation, exchange rate reforms and incentives for FDI	Sri Lanka managed to attract a large number of tourists, especially from Europe under the open economic policies. Tourism was promoted. The progress continued until 1983. Tourism became a victim of war after 1983.
	The second wave of economic reforms in 1989	1992 – Introduction of the second Ten-Year Tourism Master Plan	Temporary rebound in the tourism sector and recovery of tourism arrivals with the second wave of trade reforms.
1996 to date	Continuation of opening economic policies with some limitations	2002 – Signing a cease fire agreement and creating a peaceful environment for the tourism sector	The relatively peaceful short-term environment gave rise to an increase in tourist arrivals to Sri Lanka.
		2005 – New *Tourism Act* 2008 – Introduction of the Third Tourism Master Plan	Closer relationship between government and private sector has built an integrated approach to tourism.
		End of war in 2009 – launching a new tourism promotion strategy 2011 – Implementation of the Tourism Development Strategy	The tourism sector has made a remarkable recovery and it is becoming one of the fastest growing and most dynamic industries in the country due to the peaceful environment.

Source: adapted from Fernando *et al.* (2013).

Lankan government passed two acts (*Tourist Board Act No. 10 of 1966* and *Tourist Development Act No. 14 of 1968*) to establish institutional arrangements such as the Ceylon Tourist Board, the Ceylon Hotel School and the Ceylon Hotels Corporation in order to actively engage in tourism promotion and development for Sri Lanka (United Nations 1993).

It was very difficult to attract private sector investors into this area of the economy without incentives since the number of tourist arrivals was at that point small relative to other destinations. Therefore, the Sri Lankan government offered an incentive package to the private sector including fiscal and financial concessions and land at concessional rates and provision of infrastructure. This created the first tourist boom in Sri Lanka and a first wave of new hotel construction mainly occurred along the southern coast. The period 1966–1977 saw a rapid growth in tourist arrivals in Sri Lanka (Table 18.2). The pro-Western United National Party (UNP) government introduced a far-reaching economic reform package in 1977 and commenced the process of opening the economy. This was a turning point in economic policy for Sri Lanka and this policy change not only stimulated export-led industries but also assisted in attracting international tourists. During this first post-war tourism boom Sri Lanka also managed to increase foreign exchange earnings and generate enhanced employment opportunities in tourism-related activities.

Table 18.2 documents historical trends in tourist arrivals in Sri Lanka for a period of over four decades (between 1966 and 2014). It illustrates a number of features and episodes of Sri Lankan tourism and indicators such as tourist arrivals, foreign exchange earnings from tourism, employment generation and the room occupancy rate. During the period from 1966 to 1970 the country witnessed an average increase of 23 per cent in tourist arrivals per annum (from 18,969 in 1966 to a peak of 407,230 in 1982). Although there was a negative annual growth of 14 per cent in 1971 as a result of the first Youth Uprising in the south, there was a further rapid rise in tourist arrivals between 1972 and 1982 at a rate of around 24 per cent per annum. The numbers of inbound tourists in Sri Lanka reached 100,000 in 1975 for the first time. With the introduction of open economic policies in Sri Lanka in 1977, the tourism industry enjoyed remarkable success until 1982, recording an increase in tourist arrivals from 153,665 in 1977 to 407,230 in 1982. The period 1978–1982 can thus be considered as a relatively prosperous period in the early history of Sri Lanka.

Unfortunately, the first tourism boom ended with the eruption of ethnic riots in July 1983 and the escalation of the separatist war in the north and east. During the next 27-year period Sri Lanka missed many opportunities to attract tourists and foreign direct investment (FDI) to the sector because of the so-called "twin wars" (namely the separatist war in the north and east coupled with youth violence in the south). As a result of these events all expectations of reaping the benefits of economic liberalisation in 1977 and Sri Lanka's dream of becoming another Singapore faded away.

As O'Hare and Barrett (1994) pointed out, the tourism sector has been sensitive to civil disturbances, and the number of tourist arrivals has fluctuated as a reaction to civil disturbance and violence, as well as to different episodes of peace talks (see Table 18.2). During the first episode of war (1983–1987), the number of tourist arrivals declined at an average annual rate of 15 per cent. Although the peace process started between the Sri Lankan government and the Eelam separatists in 1987 following intervention by the Indian government, tourist arrivals to Sri Lanka were low and stagnating (see Table 18.2) as a result of the above-mentioned "twin war". However, the elimination of the second Youth Uprising in the south in 1989 and the beginning of another round of peace talks between the Sri Lankan government and the Eelam separatists resulted in a temporary rebound in the tourism industry in 1990. This rebound was also supported by the second wave of economic reforms including further liberalisation of the trade regime (Kelagama & Danham 1995).

Table 18.2 Historical trends in tourism within the context of political phenomenon and its contributions to the economy

Different episodes of peace, war and violence	Year	Tourist arrivals	Year-on-year growth	Periodical average growth	Tourism receipts US$ (million)	Employment Direct	Employment Indirect	Annual room occupancy rate (graded)
First period of missing opportunities	1948–65	Data not available						
Closed economy (with partial liberalisation) Boom in tourism under peace, democracy and political stability and also starting promotion of tourism (first Ten-Year Tourism Master Plan 1967–76)	1966	18,969	–	25	1.3	n/a	n/a	n/a
	1967	23,666	25		1.2	n/a	n/a	35.0
	1968	28,272	19		1.8	n/a	n/a	40.7
	1969	40,204	42		2.9	n/a	n/a	44.3
	1970	46,247	15		3.6	5,138	6,940	42.8
First Youth Uprising in the south	1971	39,654	–14	–14	3.4	6,397	8,640	31.1
Closed economy Tourism was booming under democracy and political stability and promotion of tourism	1972	56,047	41	25	7.3	7,040	9,500	38.8
	1973	77,888	39		12.8	7,134	10,780	42.4
	1974	85,011	9		16.4	8,551	11,550	39.7
	1975	103,204	21		22.4	10,148	13,700	36.8
	1976	118,971	15		28.2	11,752	15,900	37.7
Opening up of the economy Tourism was booming with accumulation of the largest numbers of tourists (253,565)	1977	153,665	29	23	40.0	13,716	18,520	42.0
	1978	192,592	25		55.8	15,404	20,795	47.7
	1979	250,164	30		77.8	18,472	24,937	52.8

1980		321,780	29		110.7	19,878	28,022	57.8
1981		370,742	15		132.4	23,023	32,232	54.5
1982		407,230	10		146.6	26,776	37,486	47.8
1983	*Eelam War I* Well-known ethnic riots in 1983 and the escalation of civil war in the north and east	337,530	−17	−15	125.8	22,374	31,234	35.9
1984		317,734	−6		104.9	24,541	34,357	35.6
1985		257,456	−19		82.2	22,723	31,810	32.7
1986		230,106	−11		82.1	22,285	31,199	32.9
1987	*Period of "Twin War"* One war in the north and another in the south	182,620	−21	−10	82.0	20,388	28,473	31.5
1988		182,662	0		76.6	19,960	27,944	32.2
1989	*Peace Talk II (1989/90)* Peace talks between the Sri Lankan government and the LTTE	184,732	1	31	76.0	21,958	30,741	31.0
1990		297,888	61		132.0	24,964	34,950	47.2
1991	*Eelam War II* Implementation of the Second Ten-Year Tourism Master Plan (1992–2001) while starting Eelam War II	317,703	7	10	156.8	26,878	37,629	48.2
1992		393,669	24		201.4	28,790	40,306	55.3
1993		392,250	0		208.0	30,710	42,994	57.0
1994	*Peace Talks III and Eelam War III* Another round of peace talks and its collapse	407,511	4	−13	230.5	33,956	47,538	56.6
1995		403,101	−1		225.4	35,068	49,095	52.2
1996		302,265	−25		173.0	31,963	44,748	40.3
1997	*Searching for a political solution* Discussing constitutional changes as a result of ethnic problems during ongoing civil war	366,165	21	13	216.7	34,006	47,608	49.1

(Continued overleaf)

Table 18.2 continued

Different episodes of peace, war and violence	Year	Tourist arrivals	Year-on-year growth	Periodical average growth	Tourism receipts US$ (million)	Employment		Annual room occupancy rate (graded)
						Direct	Indirect	
	1998	381,063	4		230.5	34,780	48,692	52.8
	1999	436,440	15		274.9	36,560	51,184	57.6
LTTE attacked economic nerve centres in Colombo	2000	400,414	−8	−12	252.8	37,943	53,120	52.3
	2001	336,794	−16		211.1	37,710	47,194	42.1
Cease Fire Agreement (CFA) and Peace Talks IV Norway led peace talks and CFA	2002	393,171	17	19	253.0	38,821	54,349	43.1
	2003	500,642	27		340.0	46,761	65,465	53.2
	2004	566,202	13		416.8	53,766	75,272	59.3
Eelam War IV and the end of war	2005	549,308	−3	−4	362.3	52,085	72,919	45.4
Beginning of full-scale war and the end of war in May 2009. Implementation of the Third Tourism Master Plan (2008–12) in 2008	2006	559,603	2		410.3	55,649	77,909	47.8
	2007	494,008	−12		384.4	60,516	84,722	46.2
	2008	438,475	−11		319.5	51,306	71,828	43.9
	2009	447,890	2		349.0	52,071	72,899	48.4
The post-war tourism boom	2010	654,476	46	24	575.0	55,023	77,032	70.1
The end of the war in May 2009 begins a new chapter in Sri Lanka in general and for tourism in particular. The Sri Lankan economy bounced back strongly immediately after the war	2011	855,975	31		838.9	57,786	80,899	77.1
	2012	1,005,606	17		1,038.3	67,862	95,007	71.2
	2013	1,274,593	25		1,715.5	112,550	157,600	71.2
	2014	1,527,153	20		n/a	n/a	n/a	n/a

Source: derived from Sri Lanka Tourism Board Annual Reports, various.

The economic reforms associated with the second Ten-Year Tourism Master Plan witnessed a recovery in tourism arrivals from 184,732 in 1989 to 393,669 in 1992. However, the start of the Second "Eelam War" in 1990 and the assassination of the president of Sri Lanka by Eelam separatists in 1993 meant that Sri Lankan tourism growth again became negative. After 17 years in power, the right-of-centre UNP government lost power in the 1994 general elections and the left-of-centre People Alliance (PA) government led by the former president (Mrs Bandaranayake Kumaranatunga) came to power with new directions and expectations. The new government began a fresh round of peace talks with the Eelam separatists in 1994 and there was a small growth in tourist arrivals during this brief period. However, once again, peace talks collapsed and the war started again in earnest in 1996. The Sri Lankan security forces captured Jaffna (the heart of the northern province) and the Eelam separatists started to mount attacks on economic targets like tourist hotels, the Central Bank and the business district in Colombo.

The Eelam separatists attacked Colombo International Airport in 2001. The tourism sector faced a severe crisis and the economy recorded negative economic growth for the first time in three decades. As a result of the ensuing economic crisis, as well as an increase in the intensity of war in the north and east and attacks mounted by the Eelam separatists in Colombo and the southern part of the country, the PA government became unpopular. In 2002 the right-of-centre, pro-Western government led by the UNP came to power and began a fresh peace process in 2002 after signing a cease fire agreement with the Eelam separatists following international mediation led by Norway. Between 2002 and 2006 there was a relatively peaceful environment in the country and the government had six rounds of peace talks with the Eelam separatists. The relative optimism in relation to the possibility of the achievement of long-term peace and the relatively peaceful short-term environment gave rise to an increase in tourist arrivals to Sri Lanka during this period (see Table 18.2). This was a mini tourism boom. However, the war between the Eelam separatists and the Sri Lankan government security forces started again in 2006 and the tourism industry was badly affected once again between 2006 and 2009. During this period growth in tourist arrivals was negative, as expected. The war finally ended in May 2009 as a result of the government forces defeating the Eelam separatists and gaining full control of the entire island.

The post-war tourism boom in Sri Lanka

Although the tourism sector suffered immensely during nearly three decades of war, violence and disasters, it has shown resilience to all man-made and natural disasters and conflicts (see O'Hare & Barrett 1994; Tisdell & Bandara 2005). The sector survived and tourist hotels managed to operate even though the occupancy ratio was low for a long period. The end of war in May 2009 begins a new chapter in Sri Lanka in general, and tourism in particular. The Sri Lankan economy bounced back strongly immediately after the war. It also managed to achieve an impressive economic growth of 6–8 per cent for 2010 to 2013.

The post-war figures also demonstrate that the Sri Lankan tourism industry has made a remarkable recovery, and it is becoming one of the fastest growing and most dynamic industries in the country. After recognising the key role that the tourism industry can play in post-war development, the Sri Lankan government launched the TDS with a Five-Year Master Plan for 2011–2016. The TDS set a number of important targets centred on attracting a large number of international tourists. The targets include

an increase in tourist arrivals from 650,000 in 2010 to 2.5 million by 2016, attract US $3 billion of FDI within the planned period, an increase in direct and indirect tourism related employment opportunities from 125,000 in 2010 to 500,000 by 2016, distribution of the economic benefits of tourism to a larger cross-section of the society, increase in foreign exchange earnings from US$ 500 million to US$ 2.75 billion by 2016, contribute towards improving the global trade and economic linkages of Sri Lanka and position Sri Lanka as the world's most treasured island for tourism.

(Ministry of Economic Development 2011: 4)

These targets are almost four times the values of 2009 in pure numbers. This demonstrates that the Sri Lankan government is very keen to accelerate economic development in the country through tourism. It is also important for Sri Lanka to implement marketing and management strategies to rebuild its image as an attractive and safe tourist destination after decades of negative international publicity highlighting the ongoing political violence, war and persistent acts of terrorism prior to 2009.

In addition to the TDS, Sri Lanka has launched a massive marketing campaign under the tourism branding slogan of "Sri Lanka – the wonder of Asia". This strategy is important for Sri Lanka considering its effort to recreate its image and the competition it faces from other destinations in terms of attracting international tourists.

The number of international tourist arrivals to Sri Lanka has sharply increased breaking all previous historical annual and monthly tourist arrival records. The total number of arrivals has nearly tripled within four years (from 447,890 in 2009 to 1,274,593 in 2013). The experience of the short history of the post-war period shows that the tourism industry has now become a main driver of the Sri Lankan economy in terms of foreign exchange earnings, employment generation and attracting FDI. For example, in 2013 tourism generated 270,150 direct and indirect employment opportunities and US$1,715 million of foreign exchange earnings for the Sri Lankan economy (SLTDA 2014).

Composition of the tourism market in Sri Lanka

Tables 18.3 and 18.4 provide the composition of international tourist arrivals and the changing patterns of arrivals from different countries and regions during the period 1970–2014. India is the main source followed by the United Kingdom. It demonstrates that Sri Lanka's heavy dependence on traditional Western tourist markets has declined. Emerging Asian economies such as India and China are becoming important tourist markets for Sri Lanka, along with Russia.

Table 18.3 Composition of the international tourist arrivals in Sri Lanka from 1970 (as a percentage of total arrivals in each year)

Country	1970	1975	1980	1985	1990	1995	2000	2005	2010	2014
North America	*12.60*	*7.58*	*4.79*	*4.02*	*2.71*	*3.61*	*4.33*	*8.46*	*6.14*	*4.71*
Canada	1.45	1.16	1.00	0.84	0.82	1.36	1.87	3.86	3.23	2.23
United States	11.15	6.42	3.79	3.19	1.90	2.25	2.45	4.60	2.92	2.47
Western Europe	*49.57*	*58.78*	*67.02*	*59.43*	*56.83*	*62.06*	*65.14*	*41.36*	*39.25*	*31.51*
France	9.69	10.75	10.62	10.35	11.12	7.69	6.49	4.85	4.78	5.40
Germany	12.48	15.02	23.43	19.78	19.85	19.81	17.63	8.44	6.99	6.76

Country	1970	1975	1980	1985	1990	1995	2000	2005	2010	2014
Netherlands	0.00	1.83	2.43	1.85	2.92	3.55	5.65	2.76	1.75	1.66
United Kingdom	11.86	8.48	9.64	8.46	7.32	16.00	21.15	16.86	16.12	9.56
Eastern Europe	*1.05*	*4.85*	*1.50*	*1.20*	*2.54*	*1.14*	*1.71*	*1.69*	*5.43*	*9.63*
Russia	0.33	4.22	1.21	0.92	1.74	0.61	0.89	0.67	2.03	4.33
Asia	*32.18*	*23.04*	*22.38*	*30.71*	*33.57*	*29.35*	*22.86*	*40.57*	*37.30*	*42.64*
China	–	–	–	0.49	0.32	0.36	0.55	1.76	1.59	8.70
Japan	2.26	8.02	3.58	9.07	7.50	4.52	2.56	3.12	2.19	3.06
India	23.07	7.57	11.26	12.02	4.38	11.82	7.96	20.63	19.39	16.02
Maldives	0.66	2.51	0.92	1.25	2.46	1.63	1.98	4.47	5.47	5.20
Pakistan	0.93	1.58	0.79	1.85	2.55	2.81	2.50	2.01	1.40	1.70
Australasia	–	*3.53*	*2.71*	*3.14*	*2.99*	*2.54*	*4.55*	*5.41*	*5.70*	*3.92*
Australia	**2.58**	**3.06**	**2.29**	2.79	2.73	2.25	4.11	4.73	5.11	3.47

Source: based on various Annual Reports of Sri Lankan Tourist Board.

Table 18.4 International tourist arrivals in Sri Lanka, 1970–2014

Country	1970	1975	1980	1985	1990	1995	2000	2005	2010	2014
North America	**5,826**	**7,823**	**15,408**	**10,358**	**8,084**	**14,564**	**17,319**	**46,457**	**40,216**	**57,828**
Canada	671	1,194	3,214	2,158	2,432	5,496	7,503	21,185	21,123	27,425
USA	5,155	6,629	12,194	8,200	5,652	9,084	9,816	25,272	19,093	30,403
Western Europe	**22,924**	**60,660**	**215,650**	**153,004**	**169,294**	**250,152**	**260,824**	**227,191**	**256,861**	**387,215**
France	4,480	11,093	34,170	26,656	33,114	31,008	25,992	26,653	31,285	66,301
Germany	5,771	15,497	75,380	50,922	59,138	79,869	70,584	46,350	45,727	83,099
Netherlands	–	1,886	7,818	4,758	8,712	14,307	22,618	15,156	11,423	20,370
UK	5,484	8,756	31,014	21,788	21,812	64,491	84,693	92,629	105,496	117,442
Eastern Europe	**486**	**5,002**	**4,838**	**3,080**	**7,562**	**4,578**	**6,840**	**9,290**	**35,517**	**118,305**
Russia	151	4,354	3,884	2,356	5,188	2,472	3,552	3,704	13,278	53,157
Asia	**14,882**	**23,779**	**72,022**	**79,056**	**100,004**	**118,323**	**91,521**	**222,844**	**244,124**	**523,945**
China	–	–	–	1,260	948	1,440	2,208	9,668	10,430	106,888
Japan	1,043	8,281	11,526	23,356	22,344	18,207	10,266	17,148	14,352	37,577
India	10,668	7,808	36,234	30,938	13,056	47,654	31,860	113,323	126,882	196,819
Maldives	304	2,588	2,964	3,222	7,330	6,561	7,935	24,576	35,791	63,938
Pakistan	430	1,628	2,540	4,770	7,600	11,343	10,005	11,029	9,148	20,830
Australasia	–	**3,638**	**8,720**	**8,090**	**8,914**	**10,254**	**18,228**	**29,738**	**37,290**	**48,205**
Australia	1,193	3,156	7,368	7,182	8,128	9,069	16,443	25,986	33,456	42,679

Source: based on various Annual Reports of Sri Lankan Tourist Board.

Constraints and challenges

As described above, tourism in Sri Lanka is booming and the government is implementing TDS as a main driver of economic growth. However, the country is facing a number of challenges in terms of developing the tourism industry. First, the Sri Lankan tourism industry needs around 45,000 hotel rooms to accommodate the estimated 2.5 million tourists by 2016 (Ministry of Economic Development 2011). In other words, it has to double the number of hotel rooms currently available (as shown in Table 18.5). This represents a massive challenge. Clearly the existing accommodation capacity in the Sri Lankan tourism sector is inadequate to cater to anticipated tourism demand. The longer-term option is to build new high-quality hotels. The government has approved a number of new hotel development projects recently to meet this challenge.

Second, the tourism industry needs improved transport infrastructure facilities in order to meet the needs of the anticipated increased number of tourists. Despite the recent implementation of massive infrastructure development projects, Sri Lanka has a long way to go to catch up with other favoured Asian tourist destinations like Singapore and Thailand.

Third, the industry is facing a shortage of trained workers because of decades of neglect in training the tourism workforce due to civil disturbances. As highlighted in a 2011 industry report, the tourism sector needs five times the current workforce to cater for 2.5 million tourists by 2016 (Clearer Skies 2011). The current hospitality-related education and training facilities are not sufficient to train such high numbers of workers or to train workers at the level needed to compete effectively in the high end of the tourism sector. To train the workforce for the tourism industry, the Sri Lankan government established the Sri Lanka Institute of Tourism & Hotel Management in 1964. In addition, a few national universities and several private sector institutions are engaged in training the workforce for top- and middle-management positions in the industry. There are other supplementary short courses conducted by various government departments. At present, the tourism sector employs about 163,000 people (both directly and indirectly). However, there is currently a severe shortage of employees in the hotel sector. According to the tourism plan, Sri Lanka needs to expand employment in this sector by around 500,000 people over the next five years to cater for the expected 2.5 million tourists in 2016. This is a demanding task given the current state of tourism education in the country.

Fourth, it is important that the country moves away from low-cost tourism and focuses on the higher end of the tourism market (Ministry of Economic Development 2011). However, attracting quality tourists has been a major challenge given the state of existing tourism-related infrastructure and support.

Table 18.5 Accommodation capacity in Sri Lanka, 2013

Class of accommodation		Accommodation capacity			Room occupancy rate (%)
		No. units	No. rooms	No. beds	
Hotels		279	16,223	33,950	71.7
	5 star	14	3,152	6,265	71.9
	4 star	18	2,070	3,683	70.2
	3 star	14	1,061	2,142	70.3
	2 star	33	1,717	3,381	69.9
	1 star	33	1,325	2,627	73.1
	Unclassified	167	6,898	15,672	74.9
Supplementary establishments		688	7,373	14,750	77.1

Source: Sri Lanka Tourism Development Authority (2014).

Finally, rapidly increasing accommodation costs represent another constraint on meeting tourism targets. According to some recent reports, the pricing of hotel accommodation is not competitive and Sri Lankan hotel accommodation is over-priced for its quality compared with its rivals. While Sri Lanka is more expensive than many other countries for four-star and five-star accommodation, it has traditionally been competitive in terms of price for three-star-rated beach resort hotels – yet these are generally not of a standard that is attractive to high-end international tourists. The room rates for even three-star accommodation in Sri Lanka have increased dramatically because of the expansion in demand associated with the post-war tourism boom, such that comparable room rates in other tourist destinations like Thailand, Indonesia, Vietnam and Kenya are cheaper than Sri Lanka. Over the last few years, hotel charges have gone up by about 50 per cent. Some believe that the government regulation of these charges represents an unhealthy intrusion into the sector and that it is important to allow rates to be determined by the market (*The Nation* 2011). The tourist price index estimated by the Sri Lanka Tourism Development Authority (2011) shows that the index increased by 5.3 per cent in 2010.

Key reading

Buultjens, J.W., Ratnayake, I. and Gnanapala, W.A.C. (2015) 'Post-conflict tourism development in Sri Lanka: Implications for building resilience', *Current Issues in Tourism*, DOI:10.1080/1368 3500.2014.1002760.

Hyndman, J. (2015) 'The securitisation of Sri Lankan tourism in the absence of peace', *Stability: International Journal of Security and Development*, 4(1), DOI: http://doi.org/10.5334/sta.fa.

Hyndman, J. and Amarasingam, A. (2014) '"Touring terrorism": Landscapes of memory in post-war Sri Lanka', *Geography Compass*, 8(8): 560–575.

Pieris, A. (2014) 'Southern invasions: Post-war tourism in Sri Lanka', *Postcolonial Studies*, 17(3): 266–285.

Samaranayake, H.M.S., Lantra, N. and Jayawardena, C. (2013) 'Forty six years of organised tourism in Sri Lanka (1966–2012)', *Worldwide Hospitality and Tourism Themes*, 5(5): 423–441.

References

Athukorala, P. (1998) *Trade Policy Reforms and Industrial Restructuring in Sri Lanka: Trade Policy Issues in Asian Development*. London: Routledge.

Brau, R., Di Liberto, A. and Pigliaru, F. (2011) 'Tourism and development: A recent phenomenon built on old (institutional) roots?', *The World Economy*, 34(3): 444–472.

Clearer Skies (2011) 'Growth drivers of the Sri Lankan hotel industry', *Hotel Sector Report*, April.

de Silva, C. (2000) 'Tourism and sustainable development', *The Island*. Online. Available: www.island. lk/2000/06/13/islfetrs.html (accessed 13 June 2011).

Due, E. (1980) 'Tourism and development: Examining the case of Sri Lanka', MA thesis, McMaster University, Canada.

Fernando, S., Bandara, J.S. and Smith, C. (2013) 'Regaining missed opportunities: The role of tourism in post-war development in Sri Lanka', *Asia Pacific Journal of Tourism Research*, 18(7): 685–711.

Kelagama, S. and Danham, D. (1995) *Economic Reform and Governance: The Second Wave of Liberalisation in Sri Lanka, 1989–93*. Working Paper Series No. 203, International Institute of Social Studies.

Kiriella, M.B. (2011) 'Reaping the benefits of the peace: Selling destination Sri Lanka'. SLTDA Resources. Online. Available: www.sltda.gov.lk/home (accessed 26 July 2011).

Lai, T.W. (2002) 'Promoting sustainable tourism in Sri Lanka', in T. Hundloe (ed.), *Linking Green Productivity to Ecotourism: Experiences in the Asia-Pacific Region* (pp. 208–214). Tokyo: Asian Productivity Organization.

Ministry of Economic Development (2011) *Tourism Development Strategy 2011–2016*. Colombo: Ministry of Economic Development.

The Nation (2011) 'The boom in tourism: Great expectations', *The Nation*, 17 July. Online. Available: www.nation.lk/2011/07/17/newsfe4.htm (accessed 19 August 2011).

Nordström, J. (2005) 'Dynamic and stochastic structures in tourism demand modeling'. *Empirical Economics*, 30(2): 379–392.

O'Hare, G. and Barrett, H. (1994) 'Effects of market fluctuations on the Sri Lankan tourist industry: Resilience and change, 1981–1991', *Tijdschrift Voor Economische en Sociale Geografie*, 85(1): 39–52.

Sri Lanka Info (2011) 'Geographical location'. Sri Lanka Info. Online. Available: www.icta.lk/si/component/content/article/74.html (accessed 6 September 2011).

Sri Lanka Tourism Development Authority (SLTDA) (2011) 'Overview tourism: Early years'. Online. Available: www.sltda.lk/node/200 (accessed 12 July 2011).

—— (2014) *Annual Statistical Report of Sri Lanka Tourism*. Colombo: SLTDA.

Tisdell, C.A. and Bandara, R.R. (2005) 'Tourism and economic development in Sri Lanka', in N. Narayana (ed.), *Economic Development Issues and Policies* (pp. 109–137). New Delhi: Serials Publications.

United Nations (1993) *The Economic Impact of Tourism in Sri Lanka*. New York: Economic and Social Commission for Asia and Pacific, United Nations.

United Nations Development Program (UNDP) and World Tourism Organization (WTO) (1993) *Tourism Master Plan Sri Lanka*. Madrid: UNDP and WTO.

19

THE MALDIVES

Parallel paths of conventional and alternative tourism

Aishath Shakeela & David Weaver

Introduction

Due to natural resource limitations, island destination planners often direct attention to tourism as an engine for development, with many embracing the industry as an "economic miracle" capitalising on ample endowments of sun, sea and sand (Ioannides 2000; Nowak *et al.* 2007). This may create hyper-dependency, whereby traditional industries such as fishing or agricultural monocultures are replaced by tourism. Government pro-growth proclivities and investment in tourism, however, are based on the assumptions that this sector will mitigate the numerous development constraints they face (Wilkinson 1989). Indeed, tourism in island destinations is usually seen as a convenient and expeditious means for generating employment and foreign exchange earnings.

In focusing on tourism as a tool for economic growth, governments often ignore or downplay attendant environmental and sociocultural costs. Negligible local community participation in tourism development, a widespread phenomenon in small island tourism, can create a paradox whereby government and industry view tourism as sustainable on the basis of observed revenue and job creation, but locals regard it negatively due to perceptions of costs such as environmental degradation and social alienation (Shakeela & Weaver 2014). Acknowledgement of tourism as an effective generator of economic benefits may also be contested when significant variances in remuneration between local and expatriate employees are perceived. In some island destinations, culture and religion play a significant role as a barrier to female participation in tourism (Shakeela *et al.* 2010).

Industry and government attempts to maximise economic gains can result in stress on limited and fragile natural resources, reinforcing the view that attempting to balance development and sustainability is a game of trade-offs between the "triple bottom line" of economy, environment and society. As Weaver (2006) noted, tourism sustainability is particularly challenging in the context of small tropical island destinations within the global "pleasure periphery". This challenge is explored here in the context of the Maldives, a classic "3S" pleasure periphery destination-state that nonetheless has also attempted recently to cultivate localised forms of tourism. This chapter focuses on government policies that influence tourism development, how they have evolved and their implications for sociocultural, economic and environmental sustainability. Following an overview of the country and its basic tourism contours, the relevant policy environment and its impacts are presented. A discussion of implications for sustainability concludes the chapter.

Tourism context

The Maldives is the smallest Asian country, consisting of 1,192 coralline islands with a landmass of 298km^2 (roughly 1.7 times the size of Washington, DC). The country is dispersed over an Exclusive Economic Zone of 859,000km^2, extending 820km north to south, and 130km east to west at its widest point. Geographically formed as 26 natural atolls, this small island nation is administered as seven provinces (Shakeela 2015). On average, the islands are less than three metres above sea level. The local population of 341,000 resides on 188 of the islands (National Bureau of Statistics 2015).

The Maldives embodies classic features of 3S tourism (Shakeela & Weaver 2014), offering international visitors what Butler (1993: 71) referred to as the 'Robinson Crusoe factor' in isolated enclave resorts. Tourism, however, was not purposefully introduced due to practical constraints such as limited physical access to the destination. Indeed, in the late 1960s a 'UNDP consultant who visited the Maldives decided that tourism development was impractical' (Niyaz 2002: 18). Nevertheless, and as per the serendipity that often attends the onset of the "involvement" stage of the destination life cycle (Butler 1980), the Italian photographer and adventurer George Corbin and a group of tourists visited the Maldives in 1971, staying in local homes at the capital island of Malé, and visiting other islands within the atoll. Following opportunistic discussions between Corbin and three local elite entrepreneurs, in 1972 two uninhabited islands were developed as resorts (Ministry of Tourism and Civil Aviation (MTCA) 2008). These two resorts, with 280 beds, were owned and operated by Crescent Tourist Agency and Muman Agency, both government travel agencies (Ministry of Tourism (MOT) 1998). The president at the time, Mr Ibrahim Nasir, was a co-owner of these companies (MOT 1998), illustrating the extent to which politics and industry in the Maldives are intertwined.

Since its inception, tourism has grown exponentially and is now well ensconced in the "development" stage. As of 2015 there were 109 resorts, 18 hotels, 257 guesthouses, 123 safari *dhoni* and two yacht marinas in operation, with a capacity of 31,627 beds (MOT 2015c). An additional 112 properties, and over eight lagoons, are being developed as tourist facilities (MOT 2015b). Enclave resorts account for 76% of total accommodation in the country, with guesthouses accounting for 11.9% and hotels 4.6% (MOT 2015c).

This exponential growth in the accommodation sector reflects increased tourism demand, with international tourist arrivals demonstrating consistent growth since 1972 (Figure 19.1). The only significant decline (36%) in international tourist arrivals to the country followed the 2004 Asian tsunami. The resilience of the industry to recover from such disasters, however, was seen in the years following the tsunami. By December 2014 the Maldives received 1,204,857 international tourists (MOT 2015a), or 3.5 tourists for each resident. According to the Maldives visitor survey (MTAC 2013b) this destination is popular for honeymoons (23%) and diving (19%).

The average duration of stay fell from 8.6 days in 2009 to 6.3 days in 2013. In the same year, the average occupancy for resorts was 78.4%. Proximity and household income of generating markets influence duration of stay. International visitors from Asian countries, such as Chinese tourists, stay on average three or four days in comparison to 7–11 days for European tourists (MOT 2014). Traditionally, the top ten generating countries were from Europe. Although

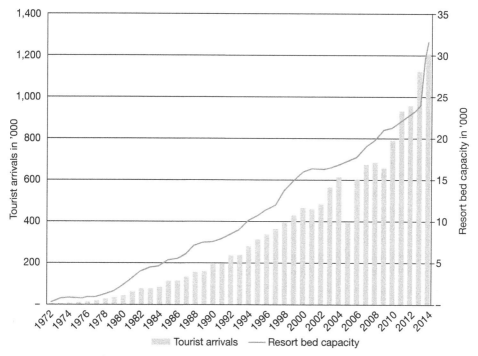

Figure 19.1   Resort bed capacity and international arrivals in the Maldives, 1972–2014.
Source: Ministry of Planning and National Development (MPND) 2005; Ministry of Tourism 2014; Ministry of Tourism, Arts and Culture 2009.

Europe collectively remains dominant, since 2009 China has become the number-one tourist-generating market. To reflect this change, tourism products which were largely targeted at the Europeans have been slowly modified to Asian preferences.

Similar to many small island states, the Maldivian economy has become hyper-dependent on tourism. In 2013 the sector contributed 27% to GDP and 38% to government revenue (MOT 2014), and it remains the largest foreign exchange earner and employer. With the introduction of the tourism land tax and goods and services tax on tourism in 2011, as well as revision of the airport service charge, in 2013 over 42% of government tax revenue was generated from tourism-related taxes (National Bureau of Statistics 2014), a tax revenue increase of 26% from 2008.

Policies governing tourism development

The dominant resort-based mode of tourism development in the Maldives depends almost exclusively on the leasing of uninhabited government-controlled islands for that purpose. To better understand this critical dynamic, a brief analysis of the development and implementation of national laws and regulations is provided. Since the abolition of the monarchy in 1953, the country (which became a republic) has been subject to a presidential/parliamentary system of governance. The sixth and present Constitution (Government of the Republic of Maldives 2008) instituted reforms including the separation of powers, a multi-party democratic system, decentralised local administrative structures and mechanisms for accountability and transparency. Nevertheless, entrenched political and business elites exercise enormous influence within the institutions of the state. All bills and regulations related to tourism and otherwise are passed through the Parliament, and ratified accordingly as an act or regulation.

Under the Constitution all islands are government-owned, and the *Decentralisation Act* (Ministry of Home Affairs 2010) confers on the president the power to proclaim an island "inhabited" or "uninhabited". The latter, in principle, are available for resort development, agriculture or manufacturing. Until the late 1970s there was no open bidding process to access such opportunities, and uninhabited islands were often leased to affluent citizens who pay "*varuvaa*" to the government. Historically, "*varuvaa*" was the annual or monthly rent paid in the form of coconuts and/or other agricultural produce. Today, the term applies to leasing an uninhabited island for agricultural and industrial purposes, with the annual rent paid in local currency. Following recent changes to the *Regulation on Uninhabited Islands* (Ministry of Fisheries and Agriculture (MFA) 2015), 700 metres surrounding an uninhabited island can be used by the lessee, who is required to pay an annual rent for the utilised area, thereby in effect allowing resorts to establish an "exclusive zone".

The MOT designates islands for tourism development, resulting in their transfer from MFA to MOT, which leases uninhabited islands and land for tourism purposes. Islands and land are in theory leased to the "best qualified" bidders identified by the MOT through a public tendering process. Although the maximum lease period for resort development was originally 21 years (Department of Tourism and Foreign Investment 1979), recent amendments to the *Tourism Act* (MOT 2015d) have increased this to 99 years. This highlights the Maldivian government focus on tourism as the driver of the national economy, but also the power of industry operators within Parliament to influence government policies.

Although a Government Tourist Board (now Ministry of Tourism) was established in 1976, the government was passive, leaving tourism policy, planning and development in the hands of investors and operators as informal processes. Such self-governance facilitated the establishment of a "Club Nature" nudist resort by Club Méditerranée (now Club Med) in 1973 (Shakeela *et al.* 2010). During this early period, a parallel trajectory of local or alternative tourism was also evidenced by a modest flow of tourists who travelled throughout the country, staying at local houses on the "inhabited islands", or visiting local islands on day-trip excursions from the enclave resorts.

The government indirectly facilitated tourism growth in 1977 by developing an international airport at Hulhulé, near the capital city of Malé. As the number of international arrivals increased, signs of unsustainable mass tourism (Weaver 2000) emerged. The nudist colony and tourists visiting inhabited islands were seen by some locals as personifying behaviour incompatible with local culture, customs and religion. To curtail social conflict, the government enacted the *Maldives Tourism Act* (1979), which prohibited nudity, gambling and guesthouses in inhabited islands other than Malé, and restricted safari *dhoni* (safari boat) movement to designated tourism zones. Yet, under a permit system which reinforced this two-tier (resort–local) pattern of tourism development, resorts were able to sell alcohol in this Islamic country, an allowance extended to safari operations in 1990.

This and other early policies were focused on ensuring that non-employee locals and tourists had as little interaction as possible, enforcing in practice sharp "backstage/frontstage" distinctions (MacCannell 2011) between inhabited and uninhabited islands. For example, until as recently as 2007 Ministry of Education rules prohibited students from visiting resorts unless accompanied by a parent or guardian (Shakeela *et al.* 2010). As of 2015, locals were still not allowed to visit a resort unless employed there or visiting as a domestic tourist. Local employees can now serve alcohol, but bartending is still restricted to expatriate employees.

Exposing residents to tourism again

With the government decentralisation policy and establishment of Atoll and Island Councils in 2008, a significant policy shift occurred, from keeping tourism operations away from local communities to opening the whole country for tourism. Accordingly, uninhabited islands continued to be leased for resort development, but local residents were once again permitted to develop guesthouses. Guesthouses are developed on land registered for residential use, while city hotels are typically high-rise hotels developed on public land on any inhabited island (MTAC 2013a). The aspiration of this policy reform is "to bring direct benefits to island communities" (MTAC 2013a: 40). With these changes in tourism policy, growth in city hotels and the guesthouses sector was seen. However, city hotels have remained largely concentrated at Malé, with only four hotels operating in outer atolls.

The guesthouse sector in particular expanded rapidly, with bed capacity increasing from 400 in 2008 to 3,769 in 2015 (MOT 2015c), such accommodation having 3–37 rooms. Over 60% of guesthouses are located in the core tourism hubs of Kaafu, Alif-Alif and Alif-Dhaalu Atolls (close to the capital city of Malé). This has resulted in a 'dilemma facing government as how to on the one hand encourage local councils to engage in tourism in constructive ways, but on the other hand limit the potential for inappropriate, non-viable and ill-advised developments' (MTAC 2013a: 42).

Despite such government concerns, a predisposition for expanding tourism to achieve widespread economic benefits is seen. The Second Tourism Master Plan (MOT 1996) policy strategy directed tourism to nearby atolls around Kaafu Atoll, as well as to the southern region, and promoted an equitable distribution of tourism within other regions. The development of a second international airport in the south as well as domestic airports and seaplane operations facilitated this decentralised spatial expansion. Indeed, air transport has been a key facilitator of tourism decentralisation. This diffusion of tourism to other atolls also coincided with the scarcity of suitable islands for tourism purposes within the core tourism atolls.

Although government policy aspires to provide tourism benefits to locals, tourism industry growth has not equated to income growth for average residents as they do not have the financial capacity to invest in the sector. Tourism statistics (MOT 2014) indicate a significant representation of foreign investors and operators. By late 2013, 14% of resort leases were held by foreign investors and a further 16% by local–foreign joint ventures. While 37% resorts were operated by foreign companies, 17% were operated through local–foreign joint ventures. Similarly, a significant proportion of resort management is by foreign companies, with 42% solely foreign managed and 16% managed through local–foreign joint ventures. Due to weak banking regulations, revenue generated from tourism is commonly transferred overseas by foreign investors and operators.

Sustainability implications

The dual resort–local mode of tourism development in the Maldives adds complexity to a sustainability equation which cannot in any circumstances be readily disaggregated into discrete economic, sociocultural or environmental dimensions. The two former dimensions, in particular, display some intriguing interrelationships. Essentially, the contemporary wellbeing of the Maldivian people is underwritten by revenue from resort-based tourism which, paradoxically, involves elements such as alcohol and revealing beachwear that run counter to the conservative religious and cultural sensibilities of the society. These were already evident in the 1970s with the development of a nudist colony. Yet, notwithstanding similarities in culture and geography among the inhabited islands, homogeneity of impact and perception should not be assumed (see Case study 19.1). The economic contribution, moreover, is neither evenly disbursed nor an unalloyed good, as evidenced by the disproportionate benefits – notwithstanding the rapid growth of the guesthouse industry – accruing to local elites and foreign interests.

The full economic benefits of tourism as an employer, additionally, are curtailed by reliance on expatriate labour and resulting leakages (Shakeela *et al.* 2012). Such reliance occurs because tourism is perceived by locals as an undesirable sector in which to work, and at best a necessary evil (Shakeela *et al.* 2010). While women are recognised as key contributors to national economies, they tend to avoid tourism employment in the Maldives and account for only 2% of resort employees (Shakeela *et al.* 2010). The industry is also challenged to recruit locals, females and males, due to an "enclave paradox" whereby residents support tourism because of the benefits they obtain from tourism revenue, but refuse to personally experience the spatial/ social isolation and low pay that attends employment in resorts (Shakeela & Weaver 2012).

The aforementioned marine exclusion zones around enclave resorts generate additional social impacts even as they boost operator profits. For many island communities, fishing still represents a viable food source and significant revenue source. Given how atolls are formed, it is in addition often cheaper and safer to commute through shallow lagoons in the atoll rather than through main ocean channels. Another issue is that lagoons are traditionally used for recreation by island communities. Thus, where a resort is located within the vicinity of locally inhabited islands (as is almost always the case), restricting local access creates conflicts of interest. Tourism thus indirectly contributes to a variety of societal challenges. It is so far unclear whether the relatively incipient guesthouse sector offers a viable and more sustainable alternative to the resorts or just exposes residents more directly to some of the social ills associated with tourism.

The environmental implications of tourism also deserve investigation. Over the years, various policies were enacted to protect natural habitat on uninhabited islands, including those designated for resort development. Thus, the Regulation on Protection and Conservation of Environment in the Tourism Industry (MOT 2006) permits only 20% of an uninhabited island to be developed, prohibits infrastructure within a five-metre buffer from the vegetation line and requires a two-metre distance between guestrooms. Such policies indicate that planners are aware of the need to provide high-yield tourist markets with a semblance of the pristine tropical marine environment that is promoted extensively.

However, these policies do not deter powerful members of the industry from circumvention to suit their development purposes. Due to island smallness, resorts are compelled to operate as self-contained enclaves on a one-island/one-resort basis. Initial resort investment in the Maldives is therefore relatively high as each resort requires its own power generators, telecommunication system, water desalination plant, sewage treatment system, transport facilities and souvenir shops (Shakeela 2015). To compensate for built-up land area limitations as well as to diversify accommodation opportunities, water villas have been built on reef beds since the mid-1980s. This necessitates extensive reef engineering and manipulation. Furthermore, land reclamation through dredging and residual sedimentation by sandbagging beaches is undertaken to maximise land area for accommodation construction, resulting in additional negative impacts on the fragile littoral environment. McElroy and de Albuquerque (2002) contend that tourism activities in environmentally sensitive coastal areas induce increased beach erosion, siltation of lagoons and reef damage. Today, water villas are a common feature of Maldivian resorts, with the associated iconic imagery attracting tourists.

The Maldives has also attracted attention for its predicament under climate change scenarios, because projected sea level rise will eventually inundate the low-lying islands. Already, 60% of the 188 inhabited islands are experiencing serious erosion and saline encroachment. Accelerated marine biodiversity loss is also predicted. However, while international audiences are cognisant of these climate change risks, several factors inspire more insouciant domestic reactions. Consequently, local tourism stakeholders are not incentivised to act immediately, and adaptation measures are woefully inadequate to cope with future climate risks (Shakeela & Becken 2015) that may dwarf any impacts from tourism per se in their severity.

Case study 19.1 Kaafu Atoll Huraa and Gnaviyani Atoll Fuvahmulah

The Maldivian government has shifted its policy from keeping tourism away from local communities to permitting locals to develop tourism within their island communities so that it can 'bring direct benefits to island communities' (MTAC 2013a: 40). Two contrasting island communities illustrate the relationship between residents and the private sector, and the extent to which local communities are involved in policy decisions – a factor that has implications for community support for and success of tourism.

Kaafu Atoll Huraa (local population 1,142, land area 25.1 hectares) is located within the main tourism hub of North-Malé atoll and has seven guesthouses (58 beds). Tourism is heavily concentrated in this atoll, with 25 resorts (5,844 beds), three of which share the same lagoon as Huraa. A further 17 resorts (3,132 beds) are located in South-Malé atoll. During the initial stage of tourism, Huraa was one out of four islands in Kaafu atoll which initiated local guesthouse development, allowing backpackers to stay at local houses. Although local guesthouse operations were banned in 1979, Huraa maintained a very close relationship with Kaafu Atoll resort operators, who sell day-trip excursions to tourists interested in local life. Islanders have proactively capitalised on these economic opportunities, establishing several souvenir shops and other tourist-oriented businesses. As such, this is a highly tourism-dependent community with a high tourist-to-host ratio, but one which harbours positive attitudes toward tourism. The local tourism strategy, moreover, can be situated here as *complementing* rather than *counteracting* the enclave sector through the provision of day-only excursions that benefit resort operators and locals.

The remote Gnaviyani Atoll Fuvahmulah (local population 8,579, land area 4.92km²), is the third largest Maldivian island and an independent atoll accommodating one guesthouse (eight beds). The opening of a domestic airport in 2011, and changes brought to tourism policy directives, has opened tourism potential for this island. However, acceptance of tourism as a local economic activity is highly resisted. For instance, land leased for a city hotel development by the government has generated protests from local residents (Hamdhoon 2005) on the basis that tourism will introduce alcohol to the community (Hamdhoon 2010). In response, the government demarcated two zones of Fuvahmulah as "uninhabited islands" (Jameel 2011), one highly contested by local community members. Due to local resistance, as of mid-2015, construction of the proposed city hotel had not yet proceeded.

According to Simons and de Groot (2015), balanced power relationships and empowerment of community members foster healthier public and private partnerships, and successful community tourism projects. Local attitudes toward tourism in Huraa demonstrate that community members are more tolerant toward tourism due partly to the longer exposure to and participation in tourism, notwithstanding the contention of the tourism area life cycle that increased intensity equates with increased resident ambivalence toward tourism. As tourism has grown, Huraa residents have been able to maximise tourism benefits while minimising associated social and environmental costs. In contrast, although some men from Fuvahmulah work in resorts, the island generally has not been exposed to tourists and tourism, and apparently fears such exposure. The reluctance of locals to engage in tourism development is also due to the alienation caused by a lack of involvement in local tourism policy decisions.

Conclusions

Applying elite theory (Darity 2008) to the Maldivian tourism context, it is noted that political and economic power is concentrated within a relatively small and cohesive group of wealthy residents from privileged backgrounds. Many resort owners and operators are also members of Parliament who influence the country's constitution to suit their interests. Examples include the extended resort lease period and the establishment of exclusive zones around leased islands. Such policies significantly reduce entry of potential new players to the industry and further concentrate power and wealth.

From a sustainability perspective, and as per social exchange theory (Thibaut & Kelley 1959), this economic outcome and other costs may be rationalised by locals as the "price to pay" for material quality of life benefits otherwise unrealised. The enclave economy, however, is not the sole manifestation of the contemporary Maldivian tourism industry. It is important to note the "two track" pattern of tourism development, whereby enclave resorts in the classic "frontstage", controlled by Maldivian elites and foreign interests, can be contrasted with "backstage" guesthouses accommodating seekers of a more alternative and localised destination experience. Local residents do benefit directly or indirectly from employment in the enclave resorts, but experience concomitant costs such as isolation from families and onerous working conditions. Concurrently, non-elite residents can more directly participate through the growing guesthouse sector, albeit on a much smaller scale and with its own accompanying risks, such as social intrusion and suboptimal management of waste and water. The capacity of small-scale entrepreneurs to succeed in this highly competitive service economy is also questionable, as is the ability of small inhabited islands to stimulate multiplier effects through the provision of sufficient goods and services. Regrettably, research into the actual impacts of this parallel tourism sector is not yet available.

Such considerations, finally, must be qualified by the reality that even the most enlightened tourism policies and intentions may be nullified by external factors such as climate change-induced sea level rises over which the sector and government have no control. With the Maldives positioned as an exceptionally vulnerable destination, destination resilience – environmental but also cultural and social – must be featured as a central tenet and objective of its sustainable tourism policy, planning and management as it applies to both tracks of development.

Key reading

Shakeela, A. (2015) 'Here today, gone tomorrow? Cultural and religious embeddedness of climate change risk perception', in L. Ruhanen (ed.), *Climate Change in the Asia-Pacific Region*. Madrid: UN World Tourism Organization.

Shakeela, A. and Becken, S. (2015) 'Understanding tourism leaders' perceptions of risks from climate change: An assessment of policy-making processes in the Maldives using the social amplification of risk framework (SARF)', *Journal of Sustainable Tourism*, 23(1): 65–84.

Shakeela, A. and Weaver, D. (2012) 'Resident reactions to a tourism incident: Mapping a Maldivian emoscape', *Annals of Tourism Research*, 39(3): 1337–1358.

Shakeela, A., Ruhanen, L. and Breakey, N. (2010) 'Women's participation in tourism: A case from the Maldives', in D. Scott and A. Jafari (eds), *Tourism in the Muslim World*, Bingley: Emerald Group Publishing Limited.

Relevant websites

Maldives Association of Travel Agents and Tour Operators: www.matato.org
Maldives Tourism Board: www.visitmaldives.com
Ministry of Tourism: www.tourism.gov.mv
National Bureau of Statistics: www.planning.gov.mv

References

Butler, R.W. (1980) 'The concept of a tourist area cycle of evolution', *Canadian Geographer*, 24(1): 5–12.
—— (1993) 'Tourism development in small islands: Past influences and future directions', in D.G. Lockhart, D. Drakakis-Smith and J. Schembri (eds), *The Development Process in Small Island States* (pp. 71–91), London: Routledge.
Darity, W.A. (2008) 'Elite Theory', in W.A. Darity (ed.), *International Encyclopedia of the Social Sciences*, vol. 2, (2nd edn) (p. 475). Detroit: Macmillan Reference USA.
Department of Tourism and Foreign Investment (1979) *Maldives Tourism Act (Law no 15/79)*. Malé: Government of Maldives.
Government of the Republic of Maldives (2008) *Dhivehiraajeyge Jumhooriyaage Qaanoon Asaasee*. Malé: Rayyithunge Majlis.
Hamdhoon, A. (2005) 'Fuvahmulah Hotalah Gina Bayaku Shauqveri Nuvee Keeve?', *Haveeru Daily*. Online. Available: www.haveeru.com.mv/?page=details&cat=cTrOPir&id=31709 (accessed 1 December 2005).
—— (2010) 'Banguralah Hulhuvifaivaa Enmme Dhorehves Huregen Nuvaane', *Haveeru Daily*. Online. Available: http://haveeru.com.mv/?page=details&id=93585 (accessed 21 March 2010).
Ioannides, D. (2000) 'The dynamics and effects of tourism evolution in Cyprus', in Y. Apostolopoulos, P.J. Loukissas and L. Leontidou (eds), *Mediterranean Tourism: Facets of Socioeconomic Development and Cultural Change* (pp. 112–128). New York: Routledge.
Jameel, A. (2011) 'Fuahmulakugai Dhe Falhu Rasheh Ufahdahifi', *Haveeru Daily*. Online. Available: http://haveeru.com.mv/?page=details&id=116343 (accessed 2 September 2011).
MacCannell, D. (2011) 'Staged authenticity today', in D. MacCannell (ed.), *Ethics of Sightseeing* (pp. 13–40). Berkeley, CA: University of California Press.
McElroy, J. and de Albuquerque, K. (2002) 'Problems for managing sustainable tourism in small islands', in Y. Apostolopoulos and D.J. Gayle (eds), *Island Tourism and Sustainable Development: Caribbean, Pacific, and Mediterranean Experiences* (pp. 15–31). Westport: Praeger.
Ministry of Fisheries and Agriculture (MFA) (2015) *Dhivehi Raajeyge Falhu Rahrashaabehey Qawaidh: Ibadhee Maadhaathah, 2015/R–126*. Malé: Government of Maldives.
Ministry of Home Affairs (2010) *Act on Decentralisation of the Administrative Dvisions of the Maldives*. Malé: Government of Maldives.
Ministry of Planning and National Development (MPND) (2005) '25 years of statistics Maldives', MPND. Online. Available: www.planning.gov.mv/publications/25yearsstats/default.htm (accessed 5 January 2008).
Ministry of Tourism (MOT) (1996) 'Maldives Tourism Master Plan 1996–2005: main report', MOT. Online. Available: www.tourism.gov.mv/pubs/MasterPlan/MasterPlan.htm (accessed 1 April 2015).
—— (1998) *Dhivehiraajeygai Tourism*. Malé: MOT.
—— (2006) *Regulation on the Protection and Conservation of Environment in the Tourism Industry*. Malé: MOT.
—— (2014) *Tourism Year Book 2014*. Malé: MOT.
—— (2015a) 'Arrival updates', MOT. Online. Available: www.tourism.gov.mv/wp–content/uploads/2015/01/December.pdf (accessed 18 May 2015).
—— (2015b) 'Facilities in development', MOT. Online. Available: www.tourism.gov.mv/facilities/facilities–development/ (accessed 13 May 2015).
—— (2015c) 'Registered facilities', MOT. Online. Available: http://tourism.gov.mv/facilities (accessed 1 April 2015).
—— (2015d) *Seventh Amendment to the Maldives Tourism Act (Law no 8/2015)*. Malé: Government of Maldives.

Ministry of Tourism and Civil Aviation (MTCA) (2008) *Fathuruverikamuge Tharageege 35 Aharu*. Malé: MTCA.

Ministry of Tourism, Arts and Culture (MTAC) (2009) *Tourism Year Book 2009*. Malé: MTAC.

—— (2013a) *Maldives Fourth Tourism Master Plan 2013–2017: Background and Analysis*. Malé: MTAC.

—— (2013b) *Maldives Visitor Survey 2013 February*. Malé: MTAC.

National Bureau of Statistics (2014) *Statistical Year Book of Maldives 2014*. Malé: National Bureau of Statistics, Ministry of Finance & Treasury.

—— (2015) *Population and Housing Census 2014*. Malé: National Bureau of Statistics, Ministry of Finance & Treasury.

Niyaz, A. (2002) *Tourism in Maldives: A Brief History of Development*. Malé: Novelty Printers and Publishers.

Nowak, J.J., Sahli, M. and Cortés-Jiménez, I. (2007) 'Tourism, capital good imports and economic growth: Theory and evidence for Spain', *Tourism Economics*, 13(4): 5115–5536.

Shakeela, A. (2015) 'Maldives', in J. Jafari and H. Xiao (eds), *Encyclopaedia of Tourism*. Dordtrecht: Springer. Online. Available: http://link.springer.com/referenceworkentry/10.1007%2F978-3-319-01669-6_281-1 (accessed 14 February 2016).

Shakeela, A. and Becken, S. (2015) 'Understanding tourism leaders' perceptions of risks from climate change: An assessment of policy-making processes in the Maldives using the social amplification of risk framework (SARF)', *Journal of Sustainable Tourism*, 33(1): 65–84.

Shakeela, A. and Weaver, D. (2012) 'Resident reactions to a tourism incident: Mapping a Maldivian emoscape', *Annals of Tourism Research*, 39(3): 1337–1358.

—— (2014) 'The exploratory social-mediatized gaze: Reactions of virtual tourists to an inflammatory YouTube incident', *Journal of Travel Research*, DOI:10.1177/0047287514532369.

Shakeela, A., Ruhanen, L. and Breakey, N. (2010) 'Women's participation in tourism: A case from the Maldives', in N. Scott and J. Jafari (eds), *Tourism in the Muslim World* (pp. 61–74). Bingley: Emerald Group.

—— (2012) 'Human resource policies: Striving for sustainable tourism outcomes in the Maldives?', *Tourism Recreation Research*, 37(2): 113–122.

Simons, I. and de Groot, E. (2015) 'Power and empowerment in community-based tourism: Opening Pandora's box?', *Tourism Review*, 70(1): 72–84.

Thibaut, J. and Kelley, H. (1959) *The Social Psychology of Groups*. New York: Wiley.

Weaver, D.B. (2000) 'A broad context model of destination development scenarios', *Tourism Management*, 21(3): 217–224.

—— (2006) *Sustainable Tourism: Theory and practice*. Oxford: Elsevier Butterworth-Heinemann.

Wilkinson, P.F. (1989) 'Strategies for tourism development in island microstates', *Annals of Tourism Research*, 16(2): 153–177.

20

TOURISM IN CENTRAL ASIA

Kemal Kantarci, Muzaffer Uysal, Vincent Magnini &
Murat Alper Başaran

Introduction

Restoring the independence of the Central Asian (CA) countries unlocked the door of the ancient Silk Road to the world as a tourism product. Central Asia's mysterious and magnificent "novel" formed through the centuries has started to open its pages and be read. The CA region has participated in the world tourism market not only as individual states but also as a whole with, what is for much of the world, its new, unique and exotic destinations. The CA region, the core of the Asian continent, has played the critical role of connecting East and West throughout history. The Silk Road that had started to develop in Roman times has created extraordinary heritage and tourism attractions for world tourism markets. The Silk Road project, initiated in 1991 and covering 28 countries across Asia to the Middle East and Europe, provides a crucial opportunity to promote and market their tourism products and services. Central Asia, in particular, has had a special role in this project (Kantarci *et al.* 2014; Kantarci & Develioglu 2013).

The five CA countries occupy a territory of nearly four million square kilometres and have a total population of nearly 66 million (Table 20.1 provides specific details on each country as well as tourism statistics). The region stretches from the Caspian Sea in the west to China in the east, and from Central Siberia in the north to Afghanistan, Iran and Pakistan in the south (Buyers 2003; Kantarci 2014).

The region has also been in a transition period since 1991. To better understand the conditions of the region through its history, it may be examined in three periods. The first period is before the Soviet Union; the second period is the Soviet Union era; and the third period is the disintegration of the Soviet Union (Pala 2014). Developments in the first period shaped a rich culture and human geography. The Silk Road was the main factor in the cultural and historical features of the region. During the years through 1917 to 1991, the Soviet regime changed almost everything and impacted the role of the government, education, architecture, art, transportation systems and city landscape and virtually created a new culture. Both domestic and international tourism were restricted by the state. The central state was the main controller and the owner of any kind of tourism activity. International tourism first emerged during the 1950s with the Khrushchev reforms. Inbound and outbound tourism was managed by a state

Table 20.1 Overview of the countries of Central Asia

Country	Area ('000 km²)	Population (million)	Tourist arrivals ('000)						Tourism receipts (US$ million)					
			2008	2009	2010	2011	2012	2013	2008	2009	2010	2011	2012	2013
Kazakhstan	2,724	16.4	3,211	2,944	3,196	4,434	4,807	4,926	1,255	1,185	1,236	1,524	1,572	1,717
Kyrgyzstan	200.0	5.5	1,844	1,394	855	2,278	2,406	3,076	569	300	212	405	486	585
Tajikistan	143.1	8.2	325	207	160	183	244	208	23.7	19.5	32.4	39.8	60.4	56.9
Turkmenistan	488.1	5.2	–	–	–	–	–	–	–	–	–	–	–	–
Uzbekistan	447.4	28.3	1,069	1,215	975	–	–	1,969	–	–	–	–	–	–

Sources: United Nations Development Program (UNDP) 2013; United Nations data 2015.

entity called Intourist. All the hotels, recreation centers, transport, services and guides working with foreign tourists were subordinate to Intourist (Shokirov *et al.* 2014). Today, the heritage of this period is very rich and colorful in terms of tourism products based on nostalgia, special interest and cultural tourism.

After the collapse of the Soviet Union, the CA countries struggled with many social, economic, political and cultural issues. While Kazakhstan better managed the transition period, the other countries have struggled from the perspective of tourism. The CA countries and other regional states have formed some international organisations such as the Shanghai Cooperation Organization, the Eurasian Economic Community, the Central Asia Regional Economic Cooperation and the Economic Cooperation in order to develop international cooperation in several areas, especially related to economic issues (Shanghai Cooperation Organization 2015; Central Asia Regional Economic Cooperation 2015; Economic Cooperation Organization 2015).

Tourism development in the region depends upon the confluence of numerous push and pull factors representing both the demand and supply sides of tourism planning and development. Road infrastructure, accommodation quality, tourism education, safety and security, image issues, service quality, protection of the environment and cultural heritage need to be improved in order to further promote tourism development. Government corruption and bureaucratic red tape are also other critical factors that need to be reduced in order to attract international investors that will encourage tourism development in the region (Kantarci *et al.* 2014; Horák 2014).

Stability and economic development in the CA region are vital for tourism. Due to its location and political realities, the whole CA region is perceived as risky and insecure in terms of political, economic and ethnic conflicts. This fact is one of the most important barriers that poses a challenge to expansion of tourism. Therefore, substantial efforts have been made to shape national branding and destination image (Marat 2009; Lee *et al.* 2012).

This chapter will provide general information about each country in the region and describe their tourism potential. The chapter then analyses the tourism competitiveness of Kazakhstan, Kyrgyzstan and Tajikistan using the Travel and Tourism Competitiveness Index Measures by the World Economic Forum (WEF), before discussing the policy implications and challenges.

The countries of Central Asia

Kazakhstan

Kazakhstan, with its capital city of Astana, is bordered by China, the Kyrgyz Republic, Russian Federation, Turkmenistan and Uzbekistan, as well as the Aral Sea and the Caspian Sea. The population consists of Kazakhs (63.1 percent), Russians (23.7 percent) and other minorities. Kazakhstan has two totally different climate regions (Middle Asia, Siberia) where the impacts of the air masses of the cold north and the hot south meet. Summers in Kazakhstan are hot and winters are cold (United Nations Educational, Scientific and Cultural Organization (UNESCO) 2015).

Since 1993, when Kazakhstan joined the United Nations World Tourism Organization (UNWTO) as a full member, the development of its travel and tourism industry has been based on three major tourism products: nature, culture/heritage and special interest. Four main attractions are on the UNESCO World Heritage List, which are: the Mausoleum of Khoja Ahmed Yasawi located at Yasi, built at the time of Timur (Tamerlane), from 1389 to 1405; petroglyphs within the archaeological landscape of Tamgaly house a remarkable concentration of some 5,000 rock carvings dating back to the second millennium BC; Silk Roads, the Routes

Network of Chang'an-Tianshan Corridor, is a 5,000km section of the extensive Silk Roads network; the final World Heritage Site is Saryarka, steppe and lakes of northern Kazakhstan, and is a wetland of outstanding importance for migratory water birds. In addition, Kazakhstan has 13 properties that are on the UNESCO Tentative List (UNESCO 2015).

A number of international tourism projects are under development, including "Zhana Ilye" on the coast of Kapshagai reservoir in the Almaty region; "Burabai" in the Akmola region; an international health resort "Kenderli" in Mangistau; "Ancient Otrar" and "Ancient Turkestan" in South Kazakhstan; a health hotel complex "Katon Karagai" in East Kazakhstan; an ethnogeographical complex "Korkyt Ata" and "Baikonur the first space port" in Kyzylorda; and "Kambash" and "Caravanserai Irgyz" in Aktyube. However, Porter (2005) and Baisakalova and Garkavenko (2014) point out that weakness in the physical infrastructure, shortage of managerial skills, lack of advanced technical skills in the business environment and tourism are the main concerns for tourism development.

The tourism sector is designated as a leading priority in the country's *Development Strategy 2030* (Tiberghien *et al.* 2014; UNESCO 2013). Tourist arrivals and tourism receipts for 2008–13 are shown in Table 20.1. There were 1,203 travel agencies and 1,235 hotels in Kazakhstan in 2009 with tourism businesses most developed in Eastern Kazakhstan. Tourism generates KZT629.0bn, 152,000 jobs and KZT421.2bn investment, which corresponds to 17 percent of total GDP, 1.8 percent of total employment and 4.9 percent of total investment in 2014. For 2025 the contribution to GDP, employment and investment are estimated to rise to KZT1,135.9bn, 237,000 jobs and KZT728.3bn investment, which corresponds to 1.7 percent of total GDP, 2.6 percent of total employment and 4.5 percent of total investment respectively (World Travel and Tourism Council (WTTC) 2015).

Uzbekistan

The republic of Uzbekistan, with its capital city of Tashkent, is bordered by Kazakhstan, Kyrgyzstan, Tajikistan, Turkmenistan and Afghanistan, and is ethnically very rich and diverse. The cities of Samarkand, Bukhara and Khiva have been central to the Silk Road since ancient times. The country has a rich cultural and historical heritage, as well as ancient artistic traditions that attract cultural, religious, archeological and ethnographical tourists. There are many unique sacred places that are valuable for people professing to follow Islam, Christianity and Buddhism, and there are abundant natural attractions such as lakes, mountains, rivers, steppes and desert landscapes serving ecological and adventure tourism.

Uzbekistan has four cultural attractions that are on the UNESCO World Heritage List: the Historic Centre of Bukhara; the Historic Centre of Shakhrisabz; Itchan Kala; and Samarkand Crossroad of Cultures. Bukhara is known as "the princess of cities"; situated on the Silk Road, it is more than 2,000 years old and provides the most complete example of a medieval city in CA (Sazak 2014). The Historic Centre of Shakhrisbaz contains a collection of exceptional monuments and ancient quarters which bear witness to the city's development. Itchan Kala is the inner town of the old Khiva oasis and is a coherent and well-preserved example of the Muslim architecture of CA (UNESCO 2015). Samarkand, also known as the "queen of all cities", is a crossroad and melting pot of world cultures (Yücel 2014).

Modern tourism in Uzbekistan began with the foundation of the national company "Uzbektourism" in 1992. There is no detailed legislation on hotel classification and collaboration of tourism market stakeholders. Yet, Soviet-style hotel infrastructure in Uzbekistan underwent dramatic change and new modern hotels were established in Tashkent, Samarkand and Bukhara that meet Western standards. Nevertheless, many experts believe that the tourism sector currently has only a limited impact on the national economy (UNDP 2007). Lack of a unified tourism policy and strategic planning are major problems and a new plan needs to be created that specifies the main directions of tourism sector development (UNDP 2007).

Although Uzbekistan has developed some educational institutions to meet international standards for tourism marketing and management, and service and hotel businesses, it still lags behind with respect to a skilled human resource base (Baum & Thompson 2007). In 2012 there were 294 hotels in Uzbekistan providing 8,460 rooms and a capacity of 15,661 beds. There were 1,969 million international tourists in 2013 and international tourism receipts amounted to $252 million in 2012 (Kapiki & Tarikulov 2014; United Nations data 2015).

Tourist arrivals and tourism receipts for 2008–13 are denoted in Table 20.1. Tourism in Uzbekistan generates UZS1,317.1bn, 118,500 jobs and UZS711.0bn investment, which corresponds to 0.9 percent of total GDP, 0.8 percent of total employment and 2.2 percent of total investment in 2014. For 2025 the contributions to GDP, employment and investment are estimated to rise to UZS2,468.0bn, 175,000 jobs and UZS1,321.0bn investment, which corresponds to 0.9 percent of total GDP, 0.8 percent of total employment and 2.1 percent of total investment, respectively (Saliev & Soliev 2015).

Kyrgyzstan

Kyrgyzstan, with its capital city of Bishkek, has a number of minority groups including Uzbeks, Russians, Dungans, Ukrainians, Uyghur and others, and is a small country sharing borders with the People's Republic of China to the east, Tajikistan to the south and west, Uzbekistan to the west and Kazakhstan to the north.

The country has a fast-growing tourism sector. Its mountains, a relatively unspoiled natural environment, provide for a wide range of fauna and flora as well as rivers, forests and many highland lakes which are key attractions (Capisani 2000; Gleason 2003; Akçalı 2014). Kyrgyzstan can be divided into six regions with potential for tourism development: Issyk-Kul, Chui, Osh, Talas, Naryn and Batken. Issyk-Kul is the second largest alpine lake at high altitude and one of the deepest lakes on earth; it never freezes due to hot springs flowing into the lake which enable people to swim. The lake was the country's first nature reserve (1948) and is listed on the Ramsar Convention and as part of a biosphere reserve. Kyrgyzstan has two sites listed in the UNESCO World Heritage List, which are the Silk Roads Routes Network of Chang'an-Tianshan Corridor and the Sulaiman-Too Sacred Mountain (Özcan 2010; Anderson 1999; Akçalı 2014; UNESCO 2015).

The Chui region offers eco- and mountain tourism. Osh is an urban settlement whose history dates to Roman times. Talas is a historical location which is very important for indigenous Kyrgyz; its association with the epic hero of Manas plays an important role in the construction of Kyrgyz identity. The Naryn region and Batken offer a variety of sporting activities such as horse riding, trekking, rafting and rock climbing (Akçalı 2014).

Kyrgyzstan lacks high-quality vocational training in tourism services and its infrastructure is in need of significant development. Obstacles to international tourism include insufficient power and water supplies; a low level of hygiene in public places; lack of signage and maps; and a lack of guides in internationally spoken languages. Nevertheless, tourism was declared a priority sector in the *National Strategy for Sustainable Development* in 2013 (Shokirov *et al.* 2014).

Statistics related to the number of hotels, rooms, employed people and tourism travel agencies are not available. However, web searches suggest that the total number of hotels across Kyrgyzstan that are connected to the international tourism system is just over 200, with Bishkek appearing to house more than 50 percent of these.

Tourist arrivals and tourism receipts for 2008–13 are shown in Table 20.1. Tourism in Kyrgyzstan is estimate to generate KGS4.9bn, 28,000 jobs and KGS3.8bn investment that corresponds to 1.3 percent of total GDP, 1.2 percent of total employment and 3.6 percent of total investment in 2014. For 2025 tourism is estimated to rise to KGS7.9bn contribution to GDP, 28,000 jobs and KGS5.7bn in investment, which corresponds to 1.1 percent of total GDP, 1.1 percent of total employment and 3.6 percent of total investment respectively (WTTC 2015).

Turkmenistan

Turkmenistan emerged as an independent state after the dissolution of the Soviet Union in 1991. Turkmenistan, with its capital city of Ashgabat, is located in Central Asia between the Caspian Sea in the west and the Amu Darya River in the east. Turkmenistan borders the Republic of Kazakhstan in the north, the Republic of Uzbekistan in the north-east, the Islamic Republic of Iran in the south and Afghanistan in the south-east. The Karakum Desert occupies approximately 80 percent of Turkmenistan (UNDP 2015).

Turkmenistan's economy largely depends on energy exports although it is trying to diversify its economy by developing new sectors such as tourism and agriculture. Inspired by resorts in Dubai and Turkey, the Awaza Tourist Zone is the most ambitious project yet launched in Turkmenistan aimed at attracting foreign leisure tourists. However, Awaza has displayed disappointing results due to low occupancy rates, charging high rates to local citizens, and being mainly used to host festivals, conferences and top-level meetings (United States Department of Commerce 2012).

Turkmenistan has historical attractions such as Kunya-Urgench, the Parthian Fortresses of Nisa and the State Historical and Cultural Park of "Ancient Merv" that are included in the UNESCO World Heritage List (UNESCO 2015). Significant sites of natural heritage include Dehistan/Mishrian, Badhyz State Nature Reserve, Syunt Hasardag State Nature Reserve and the Dinosaurs and Caves of Koytendag. The Karakum Desert has the potential for special-interest tourism. There is little international tourism data available for Turkmenistan.

Tajikistan

Tajikistan, with its capital city Dushanbe, is the smallest country of the region. To the west and the north, Tajikistan borders with Uzbekistan and Kyrgyzstan, in the south with Afghanistan, and in the east, with China. More than 90 percent of the country is occupied by mountains, including the Pamir and Tien Shan ranges. The climate of Tajikistan is moderate, continental and dry (PricewaterhouseCoopers 2011).

Tajikistan, the poorest of the former Soviet Republics, lags economically behind its neighbours. About 66 percent of the population is engaged in agriculture. Communication and transport networks in Tajikistan are poorly developed and not well maintained. The main gateway to Tajikistan is the Dushanbe Airport. Tajikistan has one natural site (Tajik National Park (Mountains of the Pamirs)) and one cultural site (Sarazm) that are included on the UNESCO World Heritage List, as well as several sites that are on the tentative list (UNESCO 2015).

Tajikistan's labor force is ill-equipped to provide international standards of customer service and management. The country has very little tourism-relevant legislation that forms a basis for the development of tourism infrastructure. Tourism underperforms economically when compared with its potential, with a need for substantial improvements in tourism planning and management (Shokirov *et al.* 2014). Tourist arrivals and tourism receipts for 2008–13 are shown in Table 20.1.

Competition factors of Central Asian countries

This section of the chapter focuses on the relative competitiveness of the CA countries using data generated by the Travel and Tourism Competitiveness Report issued by the WEF (2007, 2008, 2009, 2011, 2013). The WEF has been disseminating tourism competitiveness results of countries based on three sub-indexes and one aggregated index called the Overall Index. Each sub-index comprises a group of related variables. The three sub-indexes are: Tourism and Travel Regulatory Framework (RF); Tourism and Travel Business Environment and Infrastructure (BEI); and Tourism and Travel Human, Cultural and Natural Resources (HCNR). The variables grouped under the Tourism and Travel Regularity Framework sub-index are policy rules and regulations, environmental sustainability, safety and security, health and hygiene, and prioritisation of travel and tourism. The attributes grouped under Travel and Tourism Business Environment and Infrastructure are air transport infrastructure, ground transport infrastructure, tourism infrastructure, ICT infrastructure and price competitiveness in tourism and travel. The variables grouped under Travel and Tourism Human Cultural and Natural Resources are human resources, affinity for travel and tourism, natural resources, cultural resources and climate change.

This chapter uses data from 2007 to 2013 from the WEF and subjects it to multi-dimensional scaling (MDS) analysis in order to generate MDS maps to visually analyse and assess the relative positioning and competitiveness of the CA region countries. Data for Uzbekistan and Turkmenistan was not accessible. Therefore, the results cover Kazakhstan, Kyrgyzstan and Tajikistan only.

Figure 20.1 shows the result of MDS covering Kazakhstan, Kyrgyzstan and Tajikistan for 2007 through 2013, with the exception of the missing year, 2010, using three sub-indexes and the overall index in order to determine which index or indexes affect the overall index in the comparison of those countries. It is seen that while the RF is represented in one dimension, the HNCR is displayed in another. The RF index is positioned above all other indexes on dimension 2 indicating that its weight is the most important. On the other hand, HNCR is the most important one on dimension 1. The overall index representing the countries' comprehensive performances is located at the middle of the graph denoting that it is an average index affected mostly by BEI. Therefore, while the three countries of Kazakhstan, Kyrgyzstan and Tajikistan put emphasis on attributes of RF and HNCR, attributes related to BEI should be improved.

With respect to the RF, Tajikistan has made little progress since 2007 (Figure 20.2). Although Kazakhstan has the best RF performance its position is highly volatile. Kyrgyzstan, like Tajikistan, is located at the middle of the graph denoting that there is no advancement on the RF index attributes. Figure 20.3 illustrates the position of the countries on the BEI sub-index. Both Tajikistan and Kyrgyzstan share a similar pattern of decline over the study period. Even though Kazakhstan has a volatile trend during the years of analysis, it has better results in 2011 and 2013 in dimension 2. This is because Kazakhstan is better positioned having received massive investments into infrastructure and superstructure in recent years. Figure 20.4 shows the relative positions of the three countries with respect to the HCNR sub-index. All three countries achieved their best positions in 2007. With the exception of 2011, Kazakhstan has been declining since 2007. Although Tajikistan has been in continuous decline, Kyrgyzstan has begun to steadily improve its performance.

Displaying countries' relative positions on a graph consisting of two dimensions by MDS helps show that the attributes related to each sub-index are grouped under either of the dimensions. However, giving a representative title to either of the dimensions is difficult. Therefore, they are left as dimension 1 and dimension 2 in order to interpret the position of

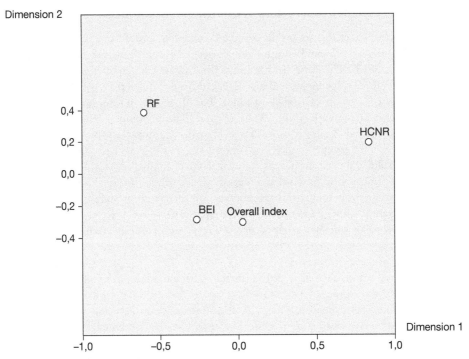

Figure 20.1 The position of the three sub-indices and overall index.

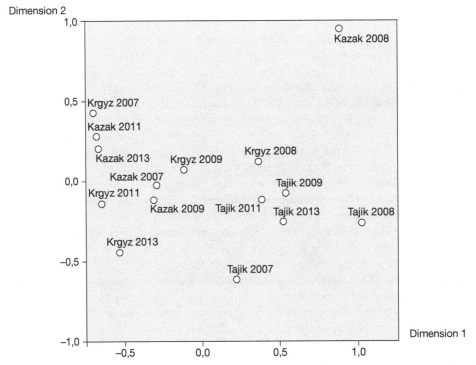

Figure 20.2 The positions of the countries in the Regularity Framework Index, 2007–2013.

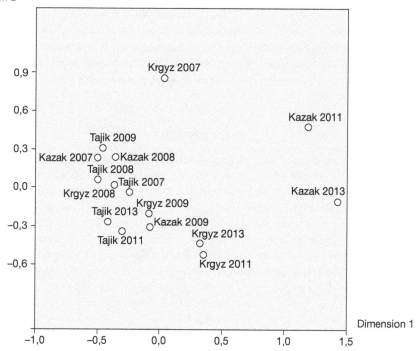

Figure 20.3 The position of the countries in the Business Environment and Infrastructure Index, 2007–2013.

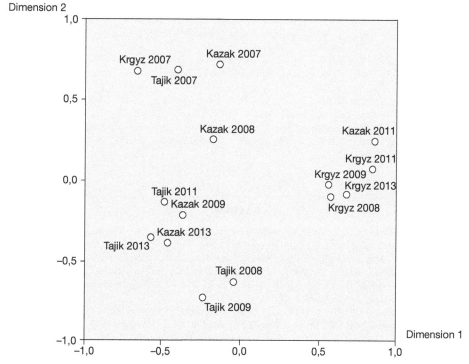

Figure 20.4 The position of the countries in the Human Natural and Cultural Resources Index, 2007–2013.

countries more easily. For each graph, being in a position in the upper part of the graph indicates progress with respect to the related attributes, while being in a position in the lower part of the graph means that the country has declined with respect to either of the dimensions. Therefore, even though Kazakhstan shows significant volatility, it demonstrates progress in all three sub-indexes. In contrast, both Kyrgyzstan and Tajikistan do not appear to have made any progress over the study period (2007–13), with Kyrgyzstan revealing a decline with respect to its overall competitiveness.

Conclusion

The CA countries have special importance not only for the great tourism potential they possess individually, but also because they are an important part of the Silk Road network. As such, they form a destination cluster that is a unique heritage and cultural product. However, as newly emerging destinations they also face significant developmental challenges. In order to be a competitive destination in the world tourism market, the countries of the CA region need to work on reducing and eliminating obstacles and barriers, including: lack of democratisation in tourism planning and development, including the development of stronger relationships to stakeholders; the need for a skilled workforce; the absence of a sufficiently developed tourism organisation and regulatory functions; and the need to get reliable information regarding the countries of CA to the world market. Finally, the prioritisation of international tourism by government officials needs to be complemented by greater recognition of the importance of domestic tourists in implementation plans and strategies.

Key reading

Hallé, J. and Raspaud, M. (2012) 'Sports tourism in Central Asia: Between the imaginary tourist and the production strategies of adventure tour operators', *Espaces, Tourisme & Loisirs*, 299: 39–47.

Kantarci, K. (2007) 'Perceptions of foreign investors on the tourism market in Central Asia including Kyrgyzstan, Kazakhstan, Uzbekistan, Turkmenistan', *Tourism Management*, 28(3): 820–829.

Kantarci, K., Uysal, M. and Magnini, V. (eds) (2014) *Tourism in Central Asia: Cultural Potential and Challenges*. Toronto: Apple Academic Press.

Ozturk, I. (2016) 'The relationships among tourism development, energy demand, and growth factors in developed and developing countries', *International Journal of Sustainable Development & World Ecology*, 23(2): 122–131.

References

Akçalı, P. (2014) 'Tourism in Kyrgyzstan', in K. Kantarci, M. Uysal and V. Magnini (eds), *Tourism in Central Asia: Cultural Potential and Challenges* (pp. 259–286). Toronto: Apple Academic Press.

Anderson, J. (1999). *Kyrgyzstan: An Island of Democracy in Central Asia*. Amsterdam: Harwood Academic.

Baisakalova, A. and Garkavenko, V. (2014) 'Competitiveness of tourism industry in Kazakhstan', in K. Kantarci, M. Uysal and V. Magnini (eds), *Tourism in Central Asia: Cultural Potential and Challenges* (pp. 15–40). Toronto: Apple Academic Press.

Baum, T. and Thompson, K. (2007) 'Skills and labour markets in transition: A tourism skills inventory of Kyrgyzstan, Mongolia and Uzbekistan', *Asia Pacific Journal of Human Resources*, 45(2): 235–255.

Buyers, L.M. (2003) *Central Asia in Focus: Political and Economic Issues*. New York: Nova Publishers.

Capisani, G.R. (2000) *The Handbook of Central Asia: A Comprehensive Survey of the New Republics*. London: IB Tauris.

Central Asia Regional Economic Cooperation (2015) 'CAREC program'. Online. Available: www.carecprogram.org (accessed 14 May 2015).

Economic Cooperation Organization (2015) 'Economic Cooperation Organization'. Online. Available: www.ecosecretariat.org/In2.Htm (accessed 14 May 2015).

Gleason, G. (2003) *Markets and Politics in Central Asia: Structural Reform and Political Change*. London: Routledge.

Horák, S. (2014) 'Visa regimes and regulatory documents as an obstacle for tourism development in Central Asia', in K. Kantarci, M. Uysal and V. Magnini (eds), *Tourism in Central Asia: Cultural Potential and Challenges* (pp. 233–258). Canada: Apple Academic Press.

Kantarci, K. (2014) 'Perceptions of foreign investors on the tourism market in Central Asia', in K. Kantarci, M. Uysal and V. Magnini (eds), *Tourism in Central Asia: Cultural Potential and Challenges* (pp. 307–330). Toronto: Apple Academic Press.

Kantarci, K. and Develioglu, K. (2013) 'The impact of travel & tourism competitiveness factors on tourism performance: The case of Silk Road countries'. Paper presented at the International Conference on Economic and Social Studies, 10–11 May 2013, Sarajevo, International Burch University.

Kantarci, K., Uysal, M. and Magnini, V. (2014) 'Exploring tourism potential in Central Asia', in K. Kantarci, M. Uysal and V. Magnini (eds), *Tourism in Central Asia: Cultural Potential and Challenges* (pp. 1–14). Toronto: Apple Academic Press.

Kapiki, S.T. and Tarikulov, M. (2014) 'Development prospects of Uzbekistan's tourism and hospitality industry by utilizing the EU experience'. Paper presented at the International Conference on Tourism Milestones – Preparing for Tomorrow, Sharjah, United Arab Emirates.

Lee, C.K., Kang, S., Reisinger, Y. and Kim, N. (2012) 'Incongruence in destination image: Central Asia region', *Tourism Geographies*, 14(4): 599–624.

Marat, E. (2009) 'Nation branding in Central Asia: A new campaign to present ideas about the state and the nation', *Europe–Asia Studies*, 61(7): 1123–1136.

Özcan, G.B. (2010) *Building States and Markets: Enterprise Development in Central Asia*. London: Palgrave Macmillan.

Pala, A. (2014) 'A chronology of Central Asia', in K. Kantarci, M. Uysal and V. Magnini (eds), *Tourism in Central Asia: Cultural Potential and Challenges* (pp. 331–360). Toronto: Apple Academic Press.

Porter, M.E. (2005) *Kazakhstan's Competitiveness: Roadmap Towards a Diversified Economy*. Institute for Strategy and Competitiveness, Harvard Business School. Online. Available: www.hbs.edu/faculty/Publication%20Files/Kazakhstan_Competitiveness_2005.01.26_35321255-da68-4cb9-a97b-1cba5f2535f5.pdf (accessed 14 May 2015).

PricewaterhouseCoopers (2011) *Doing Business Guide: Tajikistan 2012–2013*. Online. Available: www.pwc.kz/en/about-us/dbg-eurasia/dbg-tajikistan-2011-2012.pdf (accessed 14 May 2015).

Saliev, F. and Soliev, M. (2015) 'Economic advancement of tourism industry in Uzbekistan', *Global Disclosure of Economics and Business*, 4(1): 43–54.

Sazak, G. (2014) 'Bukhara: The Princess of Cities', in K. Kantarci, K.M. Uysal and V. Magnini (eds), *Tourism in Central Asia: Cultural Potential and Challenges* (pp. 67–90). Toronto: Apple Academic Press.

Shanghai Cooperation Organization (2015) 'The Shanghai Cooperation Organization'. Online. Available: www.sectsco.org/EN123 (accessed 14 May 2015).

Shokirov, Q., Abdykadyrova, A., Dear, C. and Nowrojee, S. (2014) *Mountain Tourism and Sustainability in Kyrgyzstan and Tajikistan: A Research Review*. MSRI Background Paper No. 3. Online. Available: http://msri.ucentralasia.org/publications.asp (accessed 14 May 2015).

Tiberghien, G., Garkavenko, V. and Milne, S. (2014) 'Authenticity and ecocultural tourism development in Kazakhstan: Potential and challenges', in K. Kantarci, K.M. Uysal and V. Magnini (eds), *Tourism in Central Asia: Cultural Potential and Challenges* (pp. 41–66). Toronto: Apple Academic Press.

United Nations data (2015) 'Tourism'. Online. Available: http://data.un.org/Search.aspx?q=tourism (accessed 14 May 2015).

United Nations Development Program (UNDP) (2007) *Policy Brief: Uzbekistan's Tourism Sector – An Unrealized Potential*. Tashkent: UNDP.

—— (2013) *World Population Prospects: The 2012 Revision*. Online. Available: http://esa.un.org/wpp/Documentation/pdf/WPP2012_%20KEY%20FINDINGS.pdf (accessed 14 May 2015).

—— (2015) 'About Turkmenistan'. Online. Available: www.tm.undp.org/content/turkmenistan/en/home/countryinfo (accessed 14 May 2015).

United Nations Educational, Scientific and Cultural Organization (UNESCO) (2013) *Country Programming Document Republic of Kazakhstan 2013–2014*. Almaty: UNESCO. Online. Available: http://unesdoc.unesco.org/images/0022/002239/223965E.pdf (accessed 14 May 2015).

—— (2015) 'UNESCO'. Online. Available: http://whc.unesco.org/en (accessed 14 May 2015).

United States Department of Commerce (2012) *Doing Business in Turkmenistan: 2012 Country Commercial Guide for U.S. Companies*. Online. Available: http://photos.state.gov/libraries/turkmenistan/49351/pdf/Doing%20Business%20in%20Turkmenistan%202012%20CCG.pdf (accessed 14 May 2015).

World Economic Forum (WEF) (2007) *The Travel & Tourism Competitiveness Report 2007*. Geneva: WEF.

—— (2008) *The Travel & Tourism Competitiveness Report 2008*. Geneva: WEF.

—— (2009) *The Travel & Tourism Competitiveness Report 2009*. Geneva: WEF.

—— (2011) *The Travel & Tourism Competitiveness Report 2011*. Geneva: WEF.

—— (2013) *The Travel & Tourism Competitiveness Report 2013*. Geneva: WEF.

World Travel and Tourism Council (WTTC) (2015) *Economic Impact 2015: Kazakhstan*. London: WTTC. Online. Available: www.wttc.org/-/media/files/reports/economic%20impact%20research/countries%202015/kazakhstan2015.pdf (accessed 14 May 2015).

Yücel, M.U. (2014) 'Samarkand: Queen of all Cities', in K. Kantarci, M. Uysal and V. Magnini (eds), *Tourism in Central Asia: Cultural Potential and Challenges* (pp. 149–172). Toronto: Apple Academic Press.

21

TOURISM IN BHUTAN AND NEPAL

Sanjay Nepal & Heidi Karst

Introduction

The purpose of this chapter is to briefly examine contemporary tourism trends in Bhutan and Nepal. The chapter begins with a brief overview of tourism history, followed by tourism plans and policies, and concludes with brief remarks on development trajectories, strategies and links to sustainable development goals.

Bhutan

Bhutan is a relative newcomer to global tourism that has long been romanticised by travellers keen to explore remote destinations. As an independent state in the Eastern Himalaya that has never been colonised, Bhutan remained in self-imposed isolation until the mid-1960s. The kingdom focused on cultural preservation as a way to strengthen its sovereignty and security due to its lack of military and economic power (Crosette 1995 in Brunet *et al.* 2001). The third king took gradual steps towards modernisation, opening up the country to the world after the nearby kingdoms of Tibet and Sikkim and Ladakh were annexed by China and India respectively in the early 1960s (Brunet *et al.* 2001).

Tourism was introduced as a means of attaining foreign currency and a source of direct income to help achieve economic development and autonomy from donor aid (Dorji 2001). Bhutan was initially promoted as "Eden" and "the last Shangri-la", capitalising on a culture imbued with Mahayana Buddhist spirituality and lush, biodiverse landscapes (Brunet *et al.* 2001). Small groups of tourists were allowed in to visit cultural and religious sites around Paro and Thimphu following the coronation of the fourth king in 1974 (Basu 1996). Tours were designed as higher-end, all-inclusive packages to discourage backpacking, mass and low-budget tourism (Brunet *et al.* 2001). Officials and industry stakeholders still express widespread concern over the potential development of a "hippie" drug culture and depletion of natural resources, as evidenced in neighbouring Nepal during the 1960s and 1970s (Brunet *et al.* 2001).

Strict government regulation, geographical isolation, lack of infrastructure and few seasonal attractions have traditionally restricted tourism access. For nearly a decade, Bhutan was accessible only by road through the southern town of Phuentsholing via India. A few *dzongkhags* (districts) were gradually opened to tourism. Punhakha and Wagdue Phodrang were accessible in 1978 and central Bhutan in 1982, while several areas were purposely closed for national security reasons (Dorji 2001). Off-limit areas included the border region with China and the southern areas that had been occupied by Indian separatist groups from 1990 until a Bhutanese military campaign in 2003 (Schroeder 2014: 52). Visitor numbers remained low until the Paro airport opened in 1983 and Drukair, the new national airline, started to operate flights from Calcutta (Brunet *et al.* 2001).

Nepal

The development of tourism in Nepal has been rapid, considering that Nepal opened its borders to the outside world only in 1949. Unlike the cautious approach of Bhutan, tourism grew rapidly through the 1970s, followed by a levelling-off period until 1985; a second phase of steady growth until 1988 followed by a slump in 1989; a third phase of growth until 1992 followed by a second slump in 1993; a fourth phase of rapid growth until the end of 1999; a fifth phase of dramatic decline in visitor numbers between 1999 and 2006; and the current phase of dramatic growth since 2006 (Nepal 2010). Roughly 800,000 tourists had visited Nepal during 2013. Tourism has been an important source of revenues for the government, for example, in 2013 total earnings from tourism were US$429 million, which is 4.9 per cent of total foreign exchange of the country (Ministry of Culture, Tourism and Civil Aviation (MoCTCA) 2013). Thousands of businesses providing services to the tourism industry create jobs and income for people who directly or indirectly work in this sector. For many local residents in Nepal's major tourism destinations such as the Annapurna and Everest regions, tourism is the only source of income and employment opportunities (Nepal *et al.* 2002). The early period of tourism focused on mountaineering-related tourism, which quickly paved the way for trekking tourism in the 1970s. Currently, while a significant part of tourism is still driven by adventure activities in the mountains and in national parks and reserves, there has been a steady growth in sight-seeing and pleasure travel, mostly due to the rise in inbound tourists from India and China. There have been concerted efforts to promote alternative forms of tourism such as ecotourism, village tourism (Nepal 2007) and pro-poor tourism, and in expanding tourism opportunities to areas that are off the beaten track (e.g., in the Manaslu region) and in remote locations (e.g., in the upper Dolpo and Mustang regions).

Tourism policy and planning

Bhutan

Policy, development philosophy and organisation

Tourism development in Bhutan, which incorporates the principle of gross national happiness (GNH), has been cautious and tightly controlled to mitigate negative impacts on society and environment (Rinzin 2006). As Bhutan's overarching development philosophy, GNH entails sustainable development that assumes a holistic approach towards the concept of progress and accords equal value to non-economic aspects of well-being (Centre for Bhutan Studies (CBS) 2012). The concept of GNH encompasses four pillars (good governance, sustainable socio-economic development, cultural preservation and environmental conservation), which are categorised into nine domains that reflect GNH values: psychological wellbeing, health, education, time use, cultural diversity and resilience, good governance, community vitality, ecological diversity and resilience, and living standards (CBS 2012).

Through a "high value, low volume" policy, the Royal Government of Bhutan (RGoB) established an annual quota of 200 tourists travelling in groups of six or more at a daily tariff of US$130 per person in 1974, thereby excluding budget travellers and curtailing the capacity for extended stays (Nyaupane & Timothy 2010). National standards were developed for hotels and guides to provide quality amenities and experience, and the tariff incorporated a government royalty that was used to fund healthcare, infrastructure and other public programmes (Schroeder & Sproule-Jones 2012).

Recognising the potential for economic development and private sector growth in tourism, the RGoB shifted from the "high value, low volume" policy to one of "high value, low impact" (Rinzin 2006). This subtle modification ended the fixed quota but increased the daily tariff to US$165–200, depending on the season. A one-time US$10 fee per visitor was introduced in 2000 that would go to a Tourism Development Fund to support the development of tourism marketing and activities. Although the tariff has fluctuated according to season, activity and geography over the years, it has had no effect on the type of tourism (Rinzin *et al.* 2007).

What began as a state-controlled monopoly has evolved into a 'semi-controlled/semi-liberalised' market (Rinzin *et al.* 2007: 112). As a result of pressure from the private sector, RGoB opened the market to Bhutanese tour operators and privatised the industry in 1991 (Rinzin *et al.* 2007).

The administrative body of the industry was renamed and shifted ministries several times until 2009 when it became the Tourism Council of Bhutan (TCB), an autonomous organisation under the leadership of the prime minister (Schroeder 2014). The industry is dominated by a few key private tour operators: in 2011 there were 741 licensed local tour operators, of which only 318 were operational and most were small-scale; the top 12 tour operators accounted for around 41.46 per cent of total tariff-paying arrivals (Gross National Happiness Commission (GNHC) 2013: 177). Since the new millennium, tour operators and the Association of Bhutanese Tour Operators (ABTO) have emerged as powerful players and beneficiaries (Schroeder 2014), and some critics state that complacency with the tariff system has led to the subsequent lack of innovation of tourism products. The government still holds sway over the operating practices and monetary flows of the tourism industry (Rinzin 2006) and collects US$65 in government royalty from the daily tariff (T. Nadik, pers. comm. 17 February 2015).

Impact of GNH philosophy on the tourism industry

Royal edicts and RGoB directives have shaped the tourism industry and fostered GNH by prioritising cultural and environmental interests over economic gain. In 1986, the fourth king agreed to a request by a monastic body to consider prohibiting foreign tourism in certain religious and historical places to retain their sacred stature (Nishimizu 2008). Further mitigation measures were taken in 2010, when the Ministry of Agriculture and Forests (MOAF) and TCB signed a bilateral agreement to partner on the progress and promotion of tourism in protected areas (PAs) (Schroeder 2014). A separate division was created as the focal agency, which has since inaugurated guidelines for ecotourism initiatives in Bhutanese parks (Nature Recreation and Ecotourism Division 2012). Moreover, the lucrative sport of mountaineering has been almost entirely banned in Bhutan because mountains are considered the sacred abodes of local deities (Burns 2011). The RGoB even declined an offer of US$1 million from an alpine club that wished to summit Gangkhar Puensum, the highest unclimbed peak in the world (Tashi 2009 in Burns 2011).

The voice of the private sector and civil society organisations can also balance government opinions and support the GNH vision. In 2009–10, the RGoB planned to fully liberalise the sector by abolishing the daily tariff and setting an ambitious target of 250,000 annual tourist arrivals by the end of 2012, based on recommendations from the international consulting firm McKinsey & Company (Schroeder 2014). Many tourism stakeholders, including ABTO, the Guide Association of Bhutan and private tour operators and guides, largely opposed this proposal: the vast majority were concerned about the adverse impact on GNH, citing potential ecological damage, cultural erosion and loss of image as a niche tourism destination (Schroeder 2014). In response, the RGoB reversed its decision, lowered the target to 100,000 tourist arrivals and raised the tariff to US$200–250 per day, contingent on season (Schroeder & Sproule-Jones 2012; TCB 2012). This case not only demonstrates the influence of the private sector and civil society, but the RGoB's desire to achieve equilibrium between the economic, cultural and environmental pillars of GNH (Schroeder 2014: 165).

Nepal

Tourism in national development plans

Tourism is prominently featured in all development plans. Tourism was accorded a departmental status during the First Plan (1956–60), while the *Tourism Act of 1964* was enacted for the first time during the Second Plan (1962–65; this was a three-year plan). For the first time, tourism development objectives were explicitly stated in the Third Plan (1965–70), while during the Fourth Plan the country's First Tourism Master Plan was formulated.

Tourism received a separate ministry-level status during the Fifth Plan (1975–80). During the Sixth Plan (1980–85), major tourism infrastructure projects were launched, but these were mostly concentrated within Kathmandu Valley and Pokhara, two primary tourism destinations in the country. The Seventh Plan (1985–90) stressed the need for high-value tourism and development of heritage tourism. The Eighth Plan (1991–96) called for greater public–private participation in tourism development, and deregulated the airline industry with a view to expanding international and domestic air passenger capacities. The Ninth Plan (1997–2002) had targeted the development of forward and backward linkages, and conservation of existing and proposed World Heritage Sites and their promotion as tourist destinations. Similarly, it had aimed to tie conservation of the national heritages to income-earning opportunities and their institutionalisation through community management. It was during this period that the "Visit Nepal 1998" year was launched to generate national and international awareness of tourism opportunities in Nepal. The same year the Nepal Tourism Board (NTB) was established to bolster greater public–private cooperation in branding and marketing tourism.

The Tenth Plan (2002–7) emphasised expansion of tourism to rural areas through qualitative improvement of tourism-related services, and projected tourist numbers to increase to 1.2 million by the year 2015, which is unlikely to be realised. One of the strategies mentioned explicitly in the Tenth Plan was to develop Nepal as one of the major destinations for ecotourism. Similar to Visit Nepal 1998, the Destination Nepal Campaign 2002–03 Year was implemented during this Plan. An important project completed during this period was the Tourism for Rural Poverty Alleviation Program, launched as a pilot project in six districts targeting employment and income generation opportunities for backward castes (Dalit) and women. One outcome of this campaign was the destination branding through the slogan "Naturally Nepal: Once is not Enough", which continues to be promoted today. This period saw tremendous political volatility which greatly affected tourism and resulted in a major decline in tourist numbers. The Eleventh Plan (2007–10; three-year interim plan) saw emphasis placed on human resources development, particularly in travel and tourism education within the country. This period saw the formulation of the new Tourism Policy 2008. The policy focused on developing rural tourism and encouraging domestic tourism, and identified 13 tourism types: business and events, mountaineering, trekking, rafting, adventure and extreme sports, culture, pilgrimage, sports, casino, film, educational, health and agri-tourism.

A long-term (2020) tourism vision was prepared in 2009 with a view to attract two million visitors by 2020. The Twelfth Plan (2010–12) stressed the need to concentrate its efforts in neighbouring countries, mainly India and China. Similar to previous national campaigns, Nepal Tourism Year 2011 was launched with the goal of attracting one million tourists. One of the strategies was to strengthen and expand domestic air transport systems. The emphasis in the Thirteenth Plan (2013–15) is on increasing the flow of tourists both in quantity and quality, and diversifying and expanding tourism to rural areas by improving infrastructure.

Regional distribution through product diversification

Tourism development since the 1990s has focused on three thematic issues: (1) achieving a balance in regional distribution of tourists; (2) identifying alternative tourism products and markets; and (3) the role of tourism in addressing rural poverty and youth employment. The Nepalese government has promoted new areas as alternatives to established tourism destinations like Kathmandu, Pokhara, Annapurna and Everest regions. In the early 1990s, the Upper Mustang region and the Upper Dolpo region in central and western Nepal respectively were developed as high value, low volume destinations. New products including ecotourism (e.g., Ghale Kharka-Sikles trail; see Nepal 2007), village tourism (e.g., in Sirubari; Nepal 2007) and pro-poor tourism (Saville 2001) were promoted in various rural communities throughout the country. Attention has been focused also on the nascent domestic tourism market. There has been a concerted effort in marketing in India and China too; tourist numbers from both countries have risen significantly in the last ten years. However, the majority of tourists from the two countries are concentrated in cities and more accessible areas, which is also giving a boost to luxury tourism.

An interesting and ambitious initiative was launched in 2008 that had the goal of establishing the Great Himalayan Trail, which traverses the entire country east to west, and links all major trekking destinations, providing opportunities to villages that are off the beaten track. This is another example of thinking about tourism development away from more established destinations, but one that takes full advantage of the network and connectivity that these destinations provide as a whole (Pradhan 2014).

Opportunities and constraints

Bhutan

Although tourism is divided into culture- and nature-based tours, Bhutan is primarily seen as a cultural destination. Most tourists visit in spring (February–April) and autumn (August–October) to attend *tsechus* (festivals) (Gurung & Seeland 2008). Tours to Bhutan are booked through an international or Bhutanese agent and are implemented by a nationally registered tour operator. Since 2012, the daily minimum package includes the cost of internal land transportation, accommodation in a three-star hotel, three meals per day, an English-speaking local guide and necessary equipment for groups of three foreign tourists or more; a surcharge is levied on single travellers (US$40) and couples (US$30 per person) (TCB 2015). Citizens of India, Bangladesh and the Maldives are not required to pay the all-inclusive tariff or take a tour package (TCB

2014). This exception appears to be inconsistent with tourism policy but Schroeder (2014) argues that compromise and balance are necessary to achieve GNH values of state sovereignty and peaceful co-existence, particularly in the case of India and Bhutan, who share a long history of close relations through economic partnership and development assistance (Nyaupane & Timothy 2010).

The steadily growing tourism industry is the major source of foreign exchange earnings and employment in Bhutan. Gross earnings in 2012 were US$62.80 million and approximately 22,045 employment opportunities were created in 2011 (GNHC 2013). Tourist arrivals in 2013 rose to 116,209, increasing over 10 per cent compared to 2012 (TCB 2014). Most tourists hail from Europe (e.g., Germany, France), the United States and Japan, but there has been a rise in regional tourists from China, India and Thailand in recent years (TCB 2014). On average, most international tourists fall in the 45 and above age category and tend to stay just under seven days (TCB 2014).

Some core challenges facing the industry include lack of tourist facilities and amenities, high seasonality, few tourism products, insufficient professional expertise and regional spread (TCB 2012). Most tourist activities are centred around multi-day cultural events and religious sites within western and central regions, with four out of 20 *dzongkhags* benefiting most (TCB 2014). Local hotels are unable to accommodate the influx of tourists during such events, which exhibit signs of mass tourism and arguably are not low-impact nor sustainable (Gurung & Seeland 2008: 494). To address these concerns, the RGoB is focused on four key areas: (1) accessibility; (2) product diversification; (3) institutional development; and (4) seasonality (GNHC 2013).

Accessibility

Travelling to and around Bhutan can be difficult and contributes to the limited regional spread of tourism. In-country travel along winding roads takes time and few functioning airports and aircraft carriers exist. The international airport at Paro and domestic Jakar airport are currently in operation, while two new airports for domestic travel in Gelephu and Yongphulla are still under construction. International air transport connectivity has improved with the arrival of the private carrier Bhutan Airlines in 2013, and the RGoB has approved construction of new tourist-grade hotels in central and eastern regions as well as widening and building new roads to meet anticipated demand and to increase the geographic spread of tourism (GNHC 2013).

Product diversification

The RGoB has adopted a sustainable development approach to product diversification and creating new attractions. New priority products and target markets include cultural tours that embrace regional festivals, Bhutanese heritage sites and local arts and crafts; and meetings, incentives, conferences and exhibitions (MICE) tourism. Nature-based sports and activities are also under exploration, such as rafting, cycle tours and mountain-biking; hiking tours in parks and along transit corridors to experience flora and fauna (e.g., flower tours, birdwatching); and well-being tours that embrace spirituality, wellness and traditional medicine (TCB 2012).

There has been a growing trend towards nature-based, community-based and ecotourism initiatives to spread the benefits of tourism to rural areas in recent years. Government funds have supported the construction of campsites, rest sites, farmstays, agri-tourism and homestays, and training for community members to provide local goods and services. Sites like the formerly restricted Sakteng Wildlife Sanctuary were opened to foreign tourists in 2010 as a community-based ecotourism project and other PAs, such as Royal Manas National Park near the Indian border, are developing ecotourism activities. In 2014, the RGoB initiated a "project finance for permanence" approach in which Bhutanese PAs will be able to self-finance through revenue generated from ecotourism and other means (Karst & Gyeltshen 2016).

The emergence of ecotourism activities in PAs presents new challenges and opportunities in Bhutan. The term "ecotourism" is fluid and vague, having been used in the *2001 Ecotourism Strategy* to broadly encompass all tourism activities (Gurung & Seeland 2008). Furthermore, it is frequently conflated with "community-based tourism" and potential for local economic benefits, which can consequently heighten expectations and cause dissatisfaction in communities (Karst & Gyeltshen 2016). Litter along trails and in local villages has disappointed trekkers who come to Bhutan to enjoy "pristine" landscape (Nyaupane & Timothy 2010), signalling the need for local-level waste management systems and greater community action. While MOAF has developed ecotourism guidelines for PAs, the tourism sector would greatly benefit from a similar set of universal principles and ensuing regulation.

Institutional development

Institutional development is one of the tourism sector's greatest hurdles, given the shortage of adequately trained guides and qualified professionals in hospitality and tourism-related services in an industry still largely dependent on international tour agents for arrivals (TCB 2012). The RGoB aims to strengthen the Royal Institute of Tourism and Hospitality, which provides training for professionals and plans to become a regionally renowned centre (GNHC 2013). The tour operator licensing system is currently open, and the quality and quantity of the products and practice of most tour operators is not well known (TCB 2012). To reduce the over-supply of tour operators, build professional competency and stimulate innovation, the *Tourism Strategy and Development Plans* (TCB 2012: 56) recommends new industry-wide guidelines and licensing requirement procedures, and a classification and certification system that will help monitor tour quality. For Bhutanese tour operators to become more globally competitive, more research and capacity building on the dynamics and trends of international tourism would translate into creative tours as well as improved connections with businesses and niche markets abroad (TCB 2012).

Seasonality

Tourism in Bhutan requires creative solutions to bridge seasonality constraints. One of the most successful initiatives has been the 2011 launch of www.makemytrip.com, a website that enables high-spending Indian tourists to book chartered flights and book selected hotels during off-peak seasons (TCB 2012). Other ideas under exploration include the development of winter tourism activities and treks, wellness and spiritual tourism that promotes Bhutan as a Buddhist circuit destination and encourages longer stays (TCB 2012). The RGoB has also undertaken aggressive tourism marketing and promotion strategies, such as the 2012 branding slogan "Happiness is a Place" and coining 2015 as "Visit Bhutan Year". Marketing strategies have focused on emerging regional markets among high-end tourists in China and India (Dema 2013a, 2013b), which pose a new challenge. Visitors from India, the biggest source market for Bhutanese tourism, tend to stay in cheaper hotels, bargain for food and lodging and often travel overland in their own vehicles, yet this unbridled tourist stream jeopardises the integrity of the policy as well as cultural and natural resources (Nyaupane & Timothy 2010).

Nepal

Many of the challenges associated with tourism in Bhutan are also common to Nepal – for example, distinct seasonality, poor infrastructure and unbalanced regional distribution continue to undermine tourism. In comparison to Bhutan, access to Nepal's tourism locations is relatively easy as the country is connected nationally via several highways and Short Take Off and Landing airports, but poorly developed local infrastructure means few tourists visit remote rural locations. Numerous new highways and rural roads have been constructed in the last two decades, which offer new opportunities to tourists not willing to hike on foot (for example, domestic tourists). However, the presence of such roads also pose a threat to established trekking destinations such as the Annapurna Conservation Area, where the classic sense of adventure associated with trekking has been diminished by the prospect of traversing the region on buses plying the rural roads (Loleng 2010). The negative impacts on social and environmental conditions in destinations like Everest and Annapurna are significant as well (Nepal 2003).

One of the major challenges in realising the goal of attracting two million tourists to Nepal by the end of 2020 has to do with tourism infrastructure. A major effect of a decade-long political commotion and frequent changes in government was that Nepal's national airline suffered dire consequences; not that the national airline was efficient and had a good reputation before the insurgency, but its reputation took a big hit after 2000 (Nepal 2010). It is depressing to note that NAC was founded in 1958, almost at the same time when Thailand's national carrier, Thai Airways, was founded (1957). During its peak years it carried almost 150,000 tourists; in 2008 it carried 21,000 tourists only, and sharply reduced its international operations thereafter. More recently, the NAC has decided to purchase two Airbus planes to resume its international operations. On the domestic front, plans to encourage tourists to lesser-known regions are thwarted by the fact that the vast majority of airports are in need of urgent repairs and upgrades; only 33 out of 54 airports are operational (eKantipur.com 2014). Plans are underway to build a second international airport 175km south of the capital city, made more urgent by the recent closure of the only international airport for five days due to an accident (eKantipur.com 2015).

A second challenge is the institutional instability created as a result of ongoing political contests between the major national parties, which has often led to street protests and bandhs that cripple daily lives, especially in Kathmandu. These protests disrupt essential services like transportation and give the impression of a country that is agitated, faced with an uncertain future and unsafe for travel. The politicisation of national institutions including the NTB, which was supposed to be an autonomous body, has meant that commercial enterprises related to tourism are managed in a similarly way to government bureaucracy, encouraging a culture of corruption, nepotism and inefficiency. Indeed, one of the former NTB chief executive officers has recently been questioned over financial improprieties and abuse of power.

The third challenge includes addressing social and environmental justice issues. In many areas, tourism has been developed without giving much consideration to local social and cultural disruption, lack of a supporting economic base (e.g., integrating tourism as part of the local economy) and environmental impacts. In rural areas, there is a greater discrepancy between those who benefit from tourism and those who do not, even though many benefits of tourism are derived from what essentially are common societal goods (e.g., national parks, mountain peaks, cultural heritage). Air pollution and haphazard town planning in Kathmandu Valley have greatly undermined the value of its cultural heritage, which includes seven UNESCO designated sites and hundreds of nationally important ancient monuments. It is likely that if air quality, sanitation and aesthetics in the Valley are improved, the length of stay of many leisure-class tourists would increase.

Conclusions

Bhutan and Nepal share many common characteristics. These include land-locked location, mountainous topography, rich biodiversity, agricultural economy, diverse culture and growing population. In the case of Bhutan, political relations with China have been historically tense compared to close relations with India, upon whom Bhutan is largely dependent for development projects. Nepal has taken a more balanced approach in its foreign policies towards China and India. Both Bhutan and Nepal have tremendous potential for energy development (i.e., hydropower), one which they are eager to exploit. The political economy of these two countries and the geopolitical strategies of their larger and more powerful neighbours severely limit the kinds of development and opportunities to expand. Tourism is perceived as a development strategy. Tourism is highly regulated and controlled in Bhutan, with an emphasis on a high value, low volume tourism policy. In Nepal, it is largely low value, high volume tourism, but there are some exceptions to that rule (e.g., in upper Mustang and Dolpo regions).

Tourism in Bhutan continues to be a slowly evolving, carefully engineered process, but its future remains open to possibilities and change. Although the "high value, low impact" policy is unlikely to change in the near future, the policy and concept of deregulation are subjects of ongoing scrutiny and debate. Some stakeholders argue for a free market approach that will generate business and revenue, drive competition and innovation that can elevate industry standards and, in turn, advance genuine sustainable tourism. Others are sceptical about a liberalised system, the motives of certain actors and the negative impacts on culture and natural ecosystems that it would likely cause. Opening the country up to mass tourism not only contradicts the values of GNH and sustainable tourism but would have severe social and environmental consequences and undoubtedly destroy Bhutan's image as an unspoiled, exclusive niche destination.

In contrast, tourism in Nepal has reached a stage of maturation; more ambitious plans are in place to extend the luxury aspect of tourism. Another interesting development is the growing domestic tourism, a market that the local tourism industry has seen evolving and is eager to capture. The target of attracting two million tourists, however, is not likely to be met due to poor infrastructure development and uncertainty in international markets.

Accountability and action in terms of building strong partnerships and support systems, establishing clear and suitable industry guidelines, conducting research, regular monitoring and evaluation of tourism developments, linkages and initiatives would enable the sector to thrive in a sustainable manner in Bhutan and Nepal. While the paths the two countries have taken are similar (i.e., to make tourism an important part of their national economic development), approaches to tourism policies are different. There are certain strengths and limitations to these approaches.

Key reading

Dorji, T. (2001) 'Sustainability of tourism in Bhutan', *Journal of Bhutan Studies*, 3(1): 84–104.

Pradhan, K.M. (2014) 'Cultural tourism and Nepal', *Transnational Corporations Review*, 6(3): 238–247.

Schroeder, K. and Sproule-Jones, M. (2012) 'Culture and policies for sustainable tourism: A South Asian comparison', *Journal of Comparative Policy Analysis: Research and Practice*, 14(4): 330–351.

References

Basu, G.K. (1996) *Bhutan: The Political Economy of Development*. New Delhi: South Asian Publishers.

Brunet, S., Bauer, J., De Lacy, T. and Tshering, K. (2001) 'Tourism development in Bhutan: Tensions between tradition and modernity', *Journal of Sustainable Tourism*, 9(3): 243–263.

Burns, G.W. (2011) 'Gross National Happiness: A gift from Bhutan to the world', in R. Biswas-Diener (ed.), *Positive Psychology as Social Change* (pp. 73–87). Dordrecht: Springer.

Centre for Bhutan Studies (CBS) (2012) 'GNH Index'. Online. Available: www.grossnationalhappiness. com/articles (accessed 1 February 2015).

Dema, K. (2013a) 'Casting the net closer to home'. *Kuensel*, 2 February: 10.

—— (2013b) 'Boom in Chinese tourist numbers'. *Kuensel*, 7 September. Online. Available: www. kuenselonline.com/boom-in-chinese-tourist-numbers/#.VOOfLcbfJJM (accessed 13 February 2015).

Dorji, T. (2001) 'Sustainability of tourism in Bhutan', *Journal of Bhutan Studies*, 3(1): 84–104.

eKantipur.com (2014) '33 of 54 airports operational'. Online. Available: www.ekantipur.com/2014/01/03/top-story/33-of-54-airports-operational/383357.html (accessed 2 March 2015).

—— (2015) 'Turkish Airlines jet crash-lands at TIA'. Online. Available: www.ekantipur.com/2015/03/05/editors-pick/turkish-airlines-jet-crash-lands-at-tia/402422.html (accessed 8 March 2015).

Gross National Happiness Commission (GNHC) (2013) *Eleventh Five Year Plan 2013–2018. Volume 1: Main Document*. Thimphu: GNH Commission.

Gurung, D.B. and Seeland, K. (2008) 'Ecotourism in Bhutan: Extending its benefits to rural communities', *Annals of Tourism Research*, 35(2): 489–508.

Karst, H. and Gyeltshen, N. (2016) 'The politics of community-based ecotourism in Sakteng Wildlife Sanctuary, Bhutan', in S. Nepal and J. Saarinen (eds), *Political Ecology and Tourism*. Abingdon: Routledge.

Loleng, S.G. (2010) 'Road construction to change popular Nepal trekking route?'. Online. Available: www.ethicaltraveler.org/2010/07/road-construction-to-change-popular-nepal-trekking-route (accessed 10 March 2015).

Ministry of Culture, Tourism and Civil Aviation (2013) *Nepal Tourism Statistics 2013*. Kathmandu: Ministry of Culture, Tourism and Civil Aviation.

Nature Recreation and Ecotourism Division (2012) *Ecotourism Development in the Protected Areas Network of Bhutan: Guidelines for Planning and Management*. Thimphu: Ministry of Agriculture and Forests, Royal Government of Bhutan.

Nepal, S.K. (2003) *Tourism and the Environment: Perspectives from the Nepalese Himalaya*. Innsbruck and Kathmandu: Studien Verlag and Himal Books.

—— (2007) 'Indigenous perspectives on ecotourism in Nepal: The Ghale Kharka-Sikles and Sirubari experience', in J. Higham (ed.), *Critical Issues in Ecotourism* (pp. 349–367). Oxford: Butterworth-Heinemann.

—— (2010) 'Tourism and political change in Nepal', in R.W. Butler and W. Suntikul (eds), *Tourism and Political Change* (pp. 147–160). Oxford: Butterworth-Heinemann.

Nepal, S.K., Kohler, T. and Banzhaf, B.R. (2002) *Great Himalaya: Tourism and the Dynamics of Change in Nepal*. Berne: Swiss Foundation for Alpine Research.

Nishimizu, M. (2008) *Portrait of a Leader: Through the Looking-Glass of His Majesty's Decrees*. Thimphu: Centre for Bhutan Studies.

Nyaupane, G. and Timothy, D. (2010) 'Power, regionalism and tourism policy in Bhutan', *Annals of Tourism Research*, 37(4): 969–988.

Pradhan, K.M. (2014) 'Cultural tourism and Nepal', *Transnational Corporations Review*, 6(3): 238–247.

Rinzin, C. (2006) *On the Middle Path: The Social Basis for Sustainable Development in Bhutan*. Utrecht: Copernicus Institute for Sustainable Development and Innovation.

Rinzin, C., Vermeulen, W. and Glasbergen, P. (2007) 'Ecotourism as a mechanism for sustainable development: The case of Bhutan', *Journal of Integrative Environmental Sciences*, 4(2): 109–125.

Saville, N. (2001) *Practical Strategies for Pro-Poor Tourism: Case Study of Pro-Poor Tourism and SNV in Humla District, West Nepal*. Pro-poor Tourism Working Paper No. 3, Centre for Responsible Tourism, International Institute for Environment and Development and Overseas Development Institute.

Schroeder, K. (2014) 'The politics of Gross National Happiness: Image and practice in the implementation of Bhutan's multidimensional development strategy', PhD thesis, University of Guelph.

Schroeder, K. and Sproule-Jones, M. (2012) 'Culture and policies for sustainable tourism: A South Asian comparison', *Journal of Comparative Policy Analysis: Research and Practice*, 14(4): 330–351.

Tourism Council of Bhutan (TCB) (2012) *Tourism Strategy and Development Plans (2013–2018)*. Thimphu: Tourism Council of Bhutan.

—— (2014) *Bhutan Tourism Monitor Annual Report 2013*. Thimphu: Tourism Council of Bhutan.

—— (2015) 'Minimum daily package'. Online. Available: www.tourism.gov.bt/plan/minimum-daily-package (accessed 1 February 2015).

PART 4

Tourism in East and North-East Asia

22

TOURISM IN EAST AND NORTH EAST ASIA

Introduction

C. Michael Hall & Stephen J. Page

Tourism in east and northeast Asia includes some of the world's most important countries for inbound and outbound tourism, as well as areas that are either extremely isolated or which are only now beginning to be substantially opened for tourism. Tourism in the region has arguably been dominated by successive "waves" of pent-up travel demand for international travel from the major economies in the region, although inbound tourism has acquired substantially different characteristics.

Although the ability to travel internationally is now often taken for granted by consumers within the region, this has not always been the case. For example, in much the same way as Japan arrived on the international tourist scene with the 1964 Summer Olympics in Tokyo, for many people around the globe the arrival of South Korea into the world tourist market was marked by the hosting of the 1988 Olympic Games in Seoul, while the Beijing Olympics were similarly important for China. In all three cases the Olympics were used to "announce" a newfound economic and political position in the world. However, in the case of both the Tokyo and Seoul Games the hosting of the Olympics also coincided with the removal of outbound travel restrictions for nationals from Japan and South Korea respectively (Hall 1997). Similarly, Taiwan also only reduced the restrictions on its nationals travelling overseas in the late 1980s. In the case of Korea, according to the then Assistant Foreign Minister, Hong Soon-Young, 'The liberalisation of overseas travel is designed to meet the growing trend of internationalisation of people's lifestyles, at the same time a new government is inaugurated' (in Crean 1988: 30). With the lifting of travel restrictions for certain groups in 1988, the number of outbound Korean travellers grew to 725,000. In 1989, the first full year without restrictions, 1.2 million South Koreans travelled overseas (Hall 1997). In 2013 South Korea had almost 15 million international departures (Table 22.1). Of course, North Korea is marked by very little outbound travel, given that international travel from the country is highly restricted.

The economic development of East Asia has led to dramatic improvements in per capita disposable income and to marked changes in spending patterns. Rapid economic growth has had substantial implications for tourism. The improvement of transport services and associated infrastructure as part of the countries' industrialisation programmes; increased interest in the outside world, especially diasporas; lessening in restrictions on overseas travel; increased disposable income; and greater leisure time have meant that east and north-east Asia have long

Table 22.1 International tourism in East and North-East Asia

Country		1995	2000	2005	2010	2011	2012	2013
China	Number of arrivals	20,034,000	31,229,000	46,809,000	55,664,000	57,581,000	57,725,000	55,686,000
	Receipts (% of total exports)			4.13	3.04	2.68	2.51	2.39
	Number of departures	4,520,000	10,473,000	31,026,000	57,386,000	70,250,000	83,183,000	98,185,000
	Expenditures (% of total imports)			3.83	4.20	4.37	5.62	6.50
Hong Kong SAR, China	Number of arrivals		8,814,000	14,773,000	20,085,000	22,316,000	23,770,000	25,661,000
	Receipts (% of total exports)			4.22	5.80	6.27	6.54	6.97
	Number of departures			72,300,000	84,442,000	84,816,000	85,276,000	84,414,000
	Expenditures (% of total imports)			4.43	3.81	3.66	3.56	3.48
Japan	Number of arrivals	3,345,000	4,757,000	6,728,000	8,611,000	6,219,000	8,358,000	10,364,000
	Receipts (% of total exports)			2.31	1.77	1.35	1.77	2.03
	Number of departures	15,298,000	17,819,000	17,404,000	16,637,000	16,994,000	18,491,000	17,473,000
	Expenditures (% of total imports)			7.98	4.96	4.10	4.04	3.37
Korea, Dem. Rep.	Number of arrivals							
	Receipts (% of total exports)							
	Number of departures							
	Expenditures (% of total imports)							
Korea, Rep.	Number of arrivals	3,753,000	5,322,000	6,023,000	8,798,000	9,795,000	11,140,000	12,176,000
	Receipts (% of total exports)			2.47	2.63	2.57	2.67	2.67
	Number of departures	3,819,000	5,508,000	10,080,000	12,488,000	12,694,000	13,737,000	14,846,000
	Expenditures (% of total imports)			5.41	4.05	3.36	3.46	3.72

Macao SAR, China	Number of arrivals	4,202,000	5,197,000	9,014,000	11,926,000	12,925,000	13,577,000	14,268,000
	Receipts (% of total exports)			73.43	93.90	95.15	94.71	94.70
	Number of departures			629,000	753,000	908,000	1,291,000	1,446,000
	Expenditures (% of total imports)			8.37	8.75	7.53	7.68	7.67
Mongolia	Number of arrivals	108,000	137,000	338,000	456,000	460,000	476,000	418,000
	Receipts (% of total exports)			13.69	8.49	4.74	8.98	4.58
	Number of departures							
	Expenditures (% of total imports)			11.00	8.25	5.32	5.25	6.02
Taiwan	Number of arrivals	2,331,934	2,624,037	3,378,118	5,567,277	6,087,484	7,311,470	8,016,280
	Receipts (% of total exports)							
	Number of departures	5,188,658	7,328,784	8,208,125	9,415,074	9,583,873	10,239,760	11,052,908
	Expenditures (% of total imports)							

Sources: Tourism Bureau 2016; World Bank 2016a, 2016b, 2016c, 2016d.

been two of the fastest growing tourist-generating regions in the world, although led by different countries, initially Japan, then Korea and Taiwan, and now China.

The newly industrialised economies (NIEs) of east and northeast Asia have been the focus of a massive shift in the centre of gravity of world production. Although world attention was primarily on the Japanese "economic miracle" until the 1990s, other East Asian economies, particularly those of Korea, Taiwan and especially China, have asserted themselves in the global marketplace. For example, measured in terms of current national accounts data and exchange rates, the share of Japan, the People's Republic of China (PRC), the Republic of Korea, Taiwan and Hong Kong in world production rose from 8 per cent in 1960 to over 20 per cent in the early 1990s (Garnaut 1990). In terms of GDP the changes are even more pronounced. Between them they account for about one-quarter of world GDP, although there have been substantial shifts between them. China, now the world's largest economy accounting for 16.32 per cent of GDP at PPP in 2014, only accounted for 4.07 per cent in 1989, while the world's third largest economy at 4.4 per cent in 2014 accounted for 8.79 per cent in 1989 (International Monetary Fund (IMF) 2015). The implications of these changes for inbound and outbound tourism are borne out in the various chapters in this section.

However, one of the changes occurring in north-east Asia is the increasing significance of cross-border tourism between China and Russia, as well as Russian positioning of Vladivostok as a leisure tourism destination, especially for the Chinese market. Although the border region between China and Russia has been subject to territorial disputes, the two countries have increasingly begun to engage in cross-border initiatives (Akaha 2004). In particular, the cross-border area located between the Russian Far East (RFE) and the north-east of China (the provinces of Heilongjiang, Liaoning and Jilin) has become increasingly important for border tourism related to trade, shopping and leisure (Ryzhova & Ioffe 2009). Lee (2013), for example, reports that while trade with China accounts for 28 per cent of RFE provinces total trade and 10.3 per cent of gross regional product, for some locations in the RFE it is much higher. In the Jewish Autonomous Oblast (JAO) trade with China accounts for 99 per cent of total trade, Amur 90 per cent, Primorye 50 per cent and Khabarovsk 43 per cent (Lee 2013).

Case study 22.1 Vladivostok: the northern Macao?

C.M. Hall

Vladivostok is the administrative centre of the Primorsky Krai region which, as a Russian naval base, was for many years closed to international visitors. In 2009, Russia declared gambling illegal except in four (later expanded to five) integrated entertainment zones, including a gambling–hotel–entertainment zone in Primorsky Krai, near the Vladivostok airport. Its first integrated casino resort, Tigre de Cristal, opened its doors in October 2015 after several delays (Leung 2015). Tigre de Cristal will enjoy a monopoly until the next casino property is scheduled to open in the region in 2018. Strong government support, an under-penetrated gaming market in North Asia and a weak currency will all be factors in the growth of the gaming industry in the region. In an attempt to attract investors, the Russian government has offered a low gaming tax rate of around 1–2 per cent, compared with 39 per cent in Macau and 12 to 22 per cent in Singapore.

One group of investors, the Hong Kong-listed casino operator NagaGroup, will spend US$350 million to build a casino resort complex in the zone, featuring 100 gaming tables, 500 slots and 1,000 hotel rooms, as well as assorted bars and restaurants. A second group, comprising Macao tycoon Lawrence Ho's Melco International/Summit Ascent Holdings and two Russian partners,

---

will invest US$630 million in a two-stage project to build its own complex in the zone, adding an additional 235 tables, 1,300 slots and 720 hotel rooms to the overall total (Lee 2013). This venture has been described by the local government as 'Russia's largest and best-equipped casino' (Leung 2015). Global Market Advisors, a US-based research firm, has estimated that the gambling zone near Vladivostok could generate as much as US$5.2 billion by 2022 (Leung 2015), while the governor of Primorye, Vladimir Mikliuchevsky, predicts that the new casinos will attract four million tourists each year (Lee 2013).

Approximately 400 million people in northern China, South Korea and Japan live within a three-hour flight radius of the zone. However, a key factor in the success of Vladivostok's integrated entertainment zone will likely be Russian visa policy and the ease, for the Chinese market in particular, of crossing the border. As of late 2015, South Korean citizens can get visa-free entry into Russia for 60 days, while Hong Kong citizens can enter for up to 14 days. Vladivostok's new "Free Port" status from 1 January 2016 will enable mainland Chinese to visit the area for eight days visa-free (Leung 2015). In addition, unlike many other integrated resorts in northeast Asia, the Vladivostok resort will allow local players access, therefore encouraging domestic tourism. However, given the poor domestic economy, there are doubts as to how much revenue the casinos in Russia can generate from local visitors, although the weakness of the currency will likely attract the Chinese market, especially from the northeast provinces (Leung 2015). In the first six months of 2015 the Primorsky Krai region had 135,894 tourists – a 13.6 per cent increase compared to the same period the previous year (Leung 2015).

An additional new dimension to tourism in north-east Asia is the opening up of the northern sea route from Europe through to East Asia as a result of the impacts of climate change. Improved shipping access to the northern sea route (NSR) would connect nodes within the wider Asian–Arctic region like Busan (Korea), Vladivostok and Reykjavík (Iceland) (Bennett 2014). These gateways to the Arctic route bear similarities to the "wormholes" described by Sheppard (2002) as rapid connections between geographically distant parts of the globe. Undoubtedly, the potential opening up of the NSR as a result of climate change and the need to secure access to resources is creating new sets of place competitiveness in north-east Asia and also in Russia as cities seek to position themselves as the gateways to the route (Hong 2012; Hall 2015; Huntington *et al.* 2015) (although note the caution of Stephenson *et al.* (2014) with respect to navigational uncertainties). However, it is likely that it will not be until the 2020s, as the level of shipping grows further and intermodal linkages are developed further, that the regional impact on tourism in terms of connectedness to global transport networks becomes clearer (although see the more cautious appraisals by Farré *et al.* 2014; Moe 2014). Nevertheless, even though considerable uncertainty remains with respect to the near-term length and variability of the navigation season, and the critical constraint that shelf bathymetry presents in relation to vessel draft (Stephenson *et al.* 2014), it is clear that capacity for growth exists, with significant implications for new tourism linkages, especially as oil and mineral development further opens up Asian Russia's high north. For example, in 2014, although passenger ship voyages made up only 5.5 per cent of all NSR voyages (3 of 55), they accounted for 17.6 per cent of voyage days spent in the NSR (139 of 791 days) (Hall 2015).

Conclusions

Tourism in east and northeast Asia appears set to grow well into the foreseeable future. The Japanese and Korean outbound markets remain important, while the Chinese outbound market now underpins much of the tourism growth in east and southeast Asia. Yet, as the example of cross-border tourism with Russia illustrates, there is substantial further potential for growth in the future. Areas of Mongolia, Western China and Asian Russia also show potential for future tourism development, especially as new transport connectivities are established not only by air but also rail and sea routes. However, a key issue for the region will remain ongoing political stability, especially given the re-emergence of strong expressions of nationalism in relation to some of the long-standing territorial disputes that exist in the region, as well as ongoing post-conflict and post-colonial issues between China and Japan.

Key reading

Chen, C.M. (2010) 'Role of tourism in connecting Taiwan and China: Assessing tourists' perceptions of the Kinmen–Xiamen links', *Tourism Management*, 31(3): 421–424.

Funck, C. and Cooper, M. (2013) *Japanese Tourism: Spaces, Places and Structures*. New York: Berghahn Books.

Ryzhova, N. and Ioffe, G. (2009) 'Trans-border exchange between Russia and China: The case of Blagoveshchensk and Heihe', *Eurasian Geography and Economics*, 50(3): 348–364.

Timothy, D.J. and Kim, S.S. (2015) 'Understanding the tourism relationships between South Korea and China: A review of influential factors', *Current Issues in Tourism*, 18(5): 413–432.

References

Akaha, T. (2004) 'Cross-border migration as a new element of international relations in Northeast Asia: A boon to regionalism or a new source of friction?' *Asian Perspective*, 28(2): 101–133.

Bennett, M.M. (2014) 'North by Northeast: Toward an Asian–Arctic region', *Eurasian Geography and Economics*, 55(1): 71–93.

Crean, J. (1988) 'Lifting the lid on outbound travel', *Asia Travel Trade*, July: 30–31.

Farré, A., Stephenson, S., Chen, L., Czub, M., Dai, Y., Demchev, D., Efimov, Y., Graczyk, P., Grythe, H., Keil, K., Kivekäs, N., Kumar, N., Liu, N., Matelenok, I., Myksvoll, M., O'Leary, D., Olsen, J., Pavithran, S., Petersen, E., Raspotnik, A., Ryzhov, I., Solski, J., Suo, L., Troein, C., Valeeva, V., van Rijckevorsel, J. and Wighting, J. (2014) 'Commercial Arctic shipping through the Northeast Passage: Routes, resources, governance, technology, and infrastructure', *Polar Geography*, 37(4): 298–324.

Garnaut, R. (1990) *Australia and the Northeast Asian Ascendancy*. Canberra: Australian Government Publishing Service.

Hall, C.M. (1997) *Tourism in the Pacific Rim*. Chichester: Wiley.

Hall, C.M. (2015) 'Polar gateway cities: Issues and challenges', *Polar Journal*, 5(2): 257–277.

Hong, N. (2012) 'The melting Arctic and its impact on China's maritime transport', *Research in Transportation Economics*, 35(1): 50–57.

Huntington, H.P., Daniel, R., Hartsig, A., Harun, K., Heiman, M., Meehan, R., Noongwook, G., Pearson, L., Prior-Parks, M., Robards, M. and Stetson, G. (2015) 'Vessels, risks, and rules: Planning for safe shipping in Bering Strait', *Marine Policy*, 51: 119–127.

International Monetary Fund (IMF) (2015) *World Economic Outlook*. Washington, DC: IMF.

Lee, R. (2013) 'The Russian Far East and China: Thoughts on cross-border integration', Foreign Policy Research Institute – E Notes. Online. Available: www.fpri.org/docs/Lee_-_Russia_and_China.pdf (accessed 1 April 2015).

Leung, B. (2015) Vladivostok gambling zone: Opportunities and challenges', 4 December. Online. Available. www.ejinsight.com/20151204-vladivostok-gambling-zone-opportunities-and-challenges.

Moe, A. (2014) 'The Northern Sea Route: Smooth sailing ahead?' *Strategic Analysis*, 38(6): 784–802.

Ryzhova, N. and Ioffe, G. (2009) 'Trans-border exchange between Russia and China: The case of Blagoveshchensk and Heihe', *Eurasian Geography and Economics*, 50(3): 348–364.

Sheppard, E. (2002) 'The spaces and times of globalization: Place, scale, networks, and positionality', *Economic Geography*, 78: 307–330.

Stephenson, S.R., Brigham, L.W. and Smith, L.C. (2014) 'Marine accessibility along Russia's Northern Sea Route', *Polar Geography*, 37(2): 111–133.

Tourism Bureau (2016) 'Tourism Bureau, MOTC Republic of China (Taiwan)'. Online. Available: http://admin.taiwan.net.tw/statistics/market_en.aspx?no=16 (accessed 1 February 2016).

World Bank (2016a) 'World Bank data: International tourism, number of arrivals'. Online. Available: http://data.worldbank.org/indicator/ST.INT.ARVL (accessed 14 February 2016).

—— (2016b) 'World Bank data: International tourism, receipts (% of total exports)'. Online. Available: http://data.worldbank.org/indicator/ST.INT.RCPT.XP.ZS (accessed 14 February 2016).

—— (2016c) 'World Bank data: International tourism, number of departures'. Online. Available: http://data.worldbank.org/indicator/ST.INT.DPRT (accessed 14 February 2016).

—— (2016d) 'World Bank data: International tourism, expenditures (% of total imports)' Online. Available: http://data.worldbank.org/indicator/ST.INT.XPND.MP.ZS (accessed 14 February 2016).

23

CHINA

A growth engine for world tourism

Alan A. Lew & Zhifei Li

The opening of international tourism in China

China was essentially closed to foreign visitors soon after the Chinese Communist Party (CCP) came to rule the country in 1949. The few foreigners who did manage to visit China in the 1950s and 1960s were mostly from communist bloc countries, including the Soviet Union, Eastern Europe, North Korea and North Vietnam. Some early efforts at resurrecting a tourism industry were made in the mid-1950s, but these were set back by the political instability of the Great Leap Forward in the late 1950s (Lew 1987). Following that period of widespread starvation in rural China, interest in tourism grew modestly, with the eventual creation of the Bureau of Travel and Tourism in 1964. A small number of international tourists from Western countries (4,500 in 1966) were allowed to visit China during this period just before the start of the Cultural Revolution (late 1960s to early 1970s) when tourism again became almost non-existent.

International travel to China up to the mid-1970s was limited to official political, trade and professional delegations from selected countries. They were typically taken on highly managed visits to model communes and factories, supplemented by cultural performances (Zhang 1995). The only category of visitors who were not limited to these narrowly defined delegations were Chinese "compatriots" from Hong Kong and Macau, who were given relatively free entry to visit their relatives in China. Until 1971, many countries, including the US, had made it illegal for their citizens to visit communist China. In that year, however, the US (and other countries) lifted this ban and the US national table tennis team made its historic "ping-pong diplomacy" tour of China. This was followed in June 1971 by Secretary of State Henry Kissinger making the first official visit to the People's Republic of China (PRC) by a US government diplomat. In January 1972, President Richard Nixon visited China and established formal ties between the world's most populous country and its wealthiest. These events marked the beginning of the era of modern tourism to China.

Foreign tourist travel in the early 1970s remained tightly controlled by China's central government. Between 1971 and 1977 China granted only about 15,000 foreign tourist visas (excluding compatriot Chinese). The few who were admitted paid a premium price and traveled in professional groups of 15–25 persons. Remnants of the Cultural Revolution still fostered antiforeign sentiments and local Chinese were frequently cautioned by government authorities against any dealings with foreign visitors. Tourism was considered a "bourgeois" endeavor that was allowed only with considerable apprehension by Maoist elements in the Chinese bureaucracy (Tan 1986). Thus, the form of tourism was very similar to what had gone on in the 1960s, except that the new visitors came in slightly greater numbers and from more non-communist countries than in the past. In the mid-1970s, foreign tourists averaged around 30,000 per year (Lew 1987). Domestic travel was also limited, with anything other than work-related activities being criticized as "revisionist" and against communist socialist values.

Mao Zedong died in September 1976 and within a month moderate supporters of Deng Xiaoping took control of the CCP and China's central government. By the end of 1977, with the new moderate leaders in firm control, the Chinese government announced the beginning of a concerted effort to make tourism a major sector of the Chinese economy. The official goals of this policy shift were (1) to promote friendship and (2) to accumulate funds for the speeding up of China's socialist modernization (*Beijing Review* 1978a). In 1978 the Bureau of Travel and Tourism was upgraded to the State General Administration of Travel and Tourism and foreign airlines and travel agents were, for the first time, given authority to develop their own tours to China, instead of relying solely on tours packaged by the Chinese government. Major cities and provinces also established their own tourism agencies, independent of the central government (Xue 1982). Within a few months of the 1977 official "opening-up" of China, 100 sites had been designated as "open" to foreign tourists and 30 new hotels were under construction (*Beijing Review* 1979a). The country's first tourism training school was also opened in 1978 in Jiangsu province (*Beijing Review* 1978b). By the end of that year, 229,646 foreign tourists had come to China, up from only 30,000 in 1977 (*Beijing Review* 1979b). That number shot up another 50% in 1979 and again in 1980 as the industry began to take off (Table 23.1). Over three decades later, in 2014, China received 128.5 million international visitors (including day-

Table 23.1 China's international tourist and day-tripper arrivals ('000s)

Year	Arrivals*	% Change	Foreigners	Compatriots		
				Hong Kong	Macau	Taiwan
2013	129,077.8	-2.5	26,290.3	102,787.5	20,740.3	5,162.5
2012	132,405.3	-2.2	27,191.6	105,213.7	21,160.6	5,340.2
2011	135,423.5	1.2	27,112.0	108,311.5	23,690.8	5,263.0
2010	133,760.9	5.8	26,124.1	107,636.8	23,174.0	5,143.6
2005	120,292.3	10.3	20,255.1	100,037.2	25,734.1	4,109.2
2000	83,443.9	14.6	1,016.0	70,099.3	–	3,108.6
1990	27,461.8	12.1	1,858.4	25,623.4	–	948.0
1980	5,702.5	35.6	573.5	5,139.0	–	–
1978	1,809.2	665.5	237.7	1,561.5	–	–

Sources: Lew 2000; National Bureau of Statistics of China (NBSC) 2002; China National Tourism Administration (CNTA) 1998, 2008a, 2008b, 2009a, 2010a, 2011a, 2012a, 2013a, 2014a.
Notes
*Arrivals include day-trippers and overnight visitors, which is historically how China has counted its tourists. This cannot be compared with data from the UNWTO, which does not include day-trippers. Foreigners includes overseas ethnic Chinese (mostly from South-East Asia), who were a separate category in the 1970s to 1990s when they consistently comprised over 5% of all foreign visitors. Hong Kong compatriots for 1978 and 1980 include Macau and Taiwan; Hong Kong compatriots for 1990 and 2000 include Macau; Taiwan compatriots were negligible prior to 1988, when their official numbers increased dramatically, growing from fewer than 2,500 to 438,000 in one year.

trippers and compatriot Chinese), and 55.6 million overnight international tourists (Travel China Guide 2015) (the overnight visitors number is used by the UN World Tourism Organization (UNWTO) for international comparisons).

The opening of China to tourism was an integral part of Deng Xiaoping's "Four Modernizations" policy, designed to rapidly bring China's economy into the global marketplace. China's tourism sector was targeted by central planners for major investments and development from the start of the Four Modernizations (Zhang 1995). However, despite considerable expansion during the first few years of the reforms (up to 1982), education and diplomacy remained the primary objectives of international tourism in China. A major shift occurred in government policy in 1982 when the tourism industry was officially transformed from a political service to an economic activity (Zou 1993).

China's tourism boom continued throughout the 1980s as it became the newest destination in the world – big, exotic and unknown. Infrastructure problems were a constant challenge, despite the increasing number of hotels that dotted the post-World War II skyline in China's major cities. The whole country was in the throes of change in the late 1980s when, in June of 1989, the Chinese military attacked pro-democracy demonstrators in Beijing's Tiananmen Square. International arrivals to China plummeted and it took two years for their numbers to return to pre-1989 levels. Roehl (1995), however, has shown that China's visitors had actually started to change prior to the Tiananmen Square incident, with a proportional decline in purely recreational visitors and a rise in business travelers, as well as a shift in international arrivals from the West (Europe and North America) to Asian countries. These trends became more prominent through the 1990s, with China's continued economic growth and integration into the global (and Asian) economy being the main engine driving international visitor numbers.

Even taking into account the Tiananmen Square incident, China's international tourism grew almost five times in total arrivals from 1990 to 2010 (Table 23.1). The UNWTO (2014) ranked China as the fourth most visited international destination in 2013, based on its 55.69 million overnight international visitors (NBSC 2014a), and international tourism has become one of China's major sources of foreign currency earnings, with receipts from international tourism contributing US$56.9 billion in foreign currency exchange earnings in 2014 (Travel China Guide 2015). The total value of international tourism to the Chinese economy has consistently grown on an annual basis (see below), despite a downturn in actual arrival numbers (NBSC 2014a; see also Table 23.1). However, the contribution of international tourism to China's overall export earnings has consistently dropped from year to year, down from 4.1% in 2005 to 2.5% in 2012 (Knoema 2015).

In the late 1990s, the UNWTO had projected that China would become the most visited country in the world by 2020 (Newsweek 1998). That optimistic projection has been tempered, especially in recent years, by a slowing of international arrivals and even annual declines since as early as mid-2011 (Table 23.1). Several potential causes are likely to have contributed to a decline in almost all categories of tourist types. These include, in no particular order (Feng 2014; Watt 2013; Wang 2015):

- Consistently negative news stories that discuss the high air pollution problems in China, especially in Beijing, which contains China's most iconic tourist attractions.
- Growing geopolitical tensions between China and some of its East and Southeast Asian neighbours, mostly in disputes over small but potentially resource-rich islands.
- Concerns over China's handling of the pro-democracy movement in Hong Kong, which has created unease within the broader compatriot Chinese community.

- The previous successes of international tourism and a decrease in the number of potential visitors with a strong desire to visit China for the first time.
- The growing modernization of mainland China's cities and commodification of rural landscapes, making them less exotic and less interesting to some international visitor markets.
- A large growth in the number of domestic tourists, who often overwhelm more popular attractions, reducing the quality of the tourist experience. Both international and domestic tourists complain about this issue.
- Negative news stories about food safety problems, government corruption, poor public security and a widening wealth gap within China that make potential visitors less enthusiastic about visiting.
- Slowdowns in the global economy, especially Europe and the US, and more recently China's own economy, that result in fewer business and long-haul travellers.
- A gradual but consistent increase in the value of the Chinese RMB currency in comparison to other international currencies, making China more expensive for international travellers.
- The relatively high cost of visas for visitors to China from some major tourism source countries.

Regional patterns in this decline are evident in Tables 23.2 and 23.3, with only somewhat smaller and emerging countries, including those of Africa, experiencing recent growth in visitation to China. China's government has responded to this decline with new visa-free programs for short-term visitors from some countries and major new marketing campaigns to counter the flow of negative news; however, this has not yet proven to be effective (Feng 2014). The problem of international visitor arrivals is an indicator of the maturing of China's unprecedented economic growth since the late 1970s, which has resulted in a need to reassess that growth in terms of the social, cultural, and environmental costs that have often accompanied it.

Table 23.2 China's inbound foreign visitor markets: world regions, 2004 to 2013 ('000s)

Year	Asia	Europe	Americas	Oceania	Africa	Others
2013	118,875.8	5,660.0	3,123.8	863.4	552.7	2.2
2012	121,862.5	5,921.6	3,179.5	914.9	524.9	1.9
2011	124,961.7	5,910.8	3,201.0	859.3	488.8	1.9
2010	123,825.5	5,687.8	2,995.4	789.3	463.6	2.1
2009	118,317.7	4,591.2	2,491.2	672.4	401.2	2.2
2008	120,263.8	6,112.7	2,581.9	688.7	378.4	1.9
2007	121,833.9	6,207.3	2,721.0	728.5	379.1	3.4
2006	116,325.5	5,271.8	2,405.8	638.6	293.8	4.3
2005	112,543.5	4,784.9	2,145.8	573.6	238.0	6.5

Sources: CNTA 2008c, 2008d, 2008e, 2009b, 2010b, 2011b, 2012b, 2013b, 2014b.
Notes
Asia excludes compatriot Chinese.
Europe includes Russia.

Table 23.3 China's inbound markets: leading countries, 2005 to 2013 ('000s)

Country	2005	2006	2007	2008	2009	2010	2011	2012	2013
1. South Korea	3,545.3	3,924.0	4,776.8	3,960.4	3,197.5	4,076.4	**4,185.4**	4,069.9	3,969.0
2. Japan	3,390.0	3,745.9	**3,977.5**	3,446.1	3,317.5	3,731.2	3,658.2	3,518.2	2,877.5
3. Russia	2,223.9	2,405.1	3,003.9	3,123.4	1,743.0	2,370.3	**2,536.3**	2,426.2	2,186.3
4. United States	1,555.5	1,710.3	1,901.2	1,786.5	1,709.8	2,009.6	2,116.1	**2,118.1**	2,085.3
5. Malaysia	899.6	910.5	1,062.0	1,040.5	1,059.0	**1,245.2**	1,245.1	1,235.5	1,206.5
6. Mongolia	642.0	631.2	682.0	705.3	576.7	794.4	994.2	1,010.5	**1,050.0**
7. Philippines	654.0	704.2	833.0	795.3	748.9	828.3	894.3	962.0	**996.7**
8. Singapore	755.9	827.9	922.0	875.8	889.5	1,003.7	**1,063.0**	1,027.7	966.6
9. Australia	483.0	538.7	607.4	571.5	561.5	661.3	726.2	**774.3**	723.1
10. Canada	429.8	499.7	577.2	534.7	550.3	685.3	**748.0**	708.3	684.2
11. India	356.5	405.1	462.5	436.6	448.9	549.3	606.5	610.2	**676.7**
12. Thailand	586.3	592.0	611.6	554.3	541.8	635.5	608.0	647.6	**651.7**
13. Germany	454.9	500.6	556.7	528.9	518.5	608.6	637.0	**659.6**	649.3
14. United Kingdom	499.6	552.6	605.1	551.5	528.8	575.0	595.7	618.4	**625.0**
15. Indonesia	377.6	433.0	477.1	426.3	469.0	573.4	608.7	**622.0**	605.3
16. France	372.0	402.2	463.4	430.0	424.8	512.7	493.1	524.8	**533.5**
17. Kazakhstan	186.6	270.4	438.9	300.7	279.9	380.3	**506.2**	491.4	393.5
18. Italy	177.0	195.3	215.2	194.4	191.4	229.2	235.0	252.0	**251.2**
19. North Korea	125.8	110.1	113.7	101.8	103.9	116.4	152.3	180.6	**206.6**
20. Kyrgyzstan	37.5	37.8	50.1	43.5	32.8	35.4	47.6	48.1	**49.9**

Sources: CNTA 2008c, 2008d, 2008e, 2009b, 2010b, 2011b, 2012b, 2013b, 2014b.
Note
Peak year of visitation is highlighted in **bold**.

Major tourism markets

The vast majority (80% in 2013) of China's international visitors (including day-trippers) come from Hong Kong, Macau, and Taiwan, referred to either as "compatriot Chinese" or as "HMT" visitors (Table 23.1). Historically, most of these visitors travelled to China to visit friends and relatives (VFR) and their travel patterns differed considerably from those of other international travellers (Lew 1995). For example, HMT visitors are almost twice as likely to visit either Guangdong Province (adjacent to Hong Kong) or Fujian Province (across from Taiwan) than the average foreign visitor. Business travel is also often associated with family ties for these visitors.

Excluding compatriot visitors, over 90% of the "foreign visitors" (i.e., not from a territory claimed by mainland China) to China come from Asian countries (Table 23.2). This is a significant increase from the later 1990s when they comprised about two-thirds of foreign visitors to China (Lew 2000). These foreign visitors are more likely to come to China for leisure (38.5%), meetings and business (23.6%), and work (12.2%) (2013 data, from NBSC 2014b). The recent downturn in international tourist arrivals to China is evident in Table 23.2 for all regions, except for Africa and Others. Also evident is the impact of the economic recession that had its strongest impacts on

Europe and the US, but which had ripple effects across the globe. European tourists to China, in particular, have still not recovered to pre-2008 recession levels.

In the 1980s and 1990s, Japan consistently ranked as the leading source of foreign visitors to China, while the US gradually fell from second to fourth place (Lew 2000). Australia and the UK were regularly ranked third and fourth in visitor arrivals to China until 1989 when major global changes shifted China's predominant arrival patterns from developed Western countries toward its immediate neighbours in Asia (Yu 1992). Since the mid-2000s, South Korea and Japan, both of which have strong economic ties with China, have been the leading sources of international visitors to the country, followed by Russia and the US (Table 23.3). China and Russia share one of the longest land borders in the world (3,645km) and border crossings and trade developed rapidly after Mikhail Gorbachev, the last leader of the Soviet Union, visited China in 1989. By 1997, Russia had become the second largest source of visitors to China (Zhang & Lew 1997). Mongolia, the central Asian states of Kazakhstan and Kyrgyzstan, and North Korea also comprise a set of countries with significant cross-border travel to China, driven by economic and social connections.

Southeast Asian countries comprise the next largest Asian grouping that has come to dominate foreign travel to China. A major reason for the rapid rise in Southeast Asians visiting China in the 1990s was due to new laws adopted by Southeast Asian countries, making travel to China more accessible to their citizens (Zhang 1990). This also occurred in Taiwan at the same time and mainland China quickly become the new place to go for business interests and wealthy travellers from these countries. In Southeast Asia this trend began in the Philippines, which was China's fourth largest market in 1991, followed by Singapore and Thailand (Sun 1992). Rapid growth in visitors from Russia, Southeast Asia, and Taiwan helped China recover from the decline in Western (North America, Europe, and Australasia) visitors following the 1989 Tiananmen Square incident (Chang 1992; He 1991; Zhang 1990). The growth in arrivals from Southeast Asia continued through the 1990s and 2000s, reflecting improving political and economic relationships between China most Southeast Asian countries, as well as the growing middle and upper economic classes in these countries.

Domestic tourism and tourism development in China

Many, although clearly not all, of China's enormous population of 1.36 billion people (2013 estimate) have moved from poverty to varying levels of prosperity as a result of the country's economic growth since 1978. In 2013, China was about 89th in per capita GDP (US$11,868, based on purchasing power parity), and its growing middle class is estimated to number about 500 million (Barton 2013). Tourism has played a major part in increasing the country's prosperity, especially in the densely populated coastal provinces, while also prompting an explosion in domestic tourism demand. Domestic trips numbered 3.26 billion in 2013, and the income they generate dwarfs that of international travel to China (Table 23.4).

To meet the desires of this emerging population, eager to see the famous sites of their homeland, Chinese officials at all levels of government have promoted tourism development in even the most remote parts of the country. China's domestic hotel chains, for example, did not emerge significantly until the mid-2000s, but are now found throughout the country, with economy budget chains doubling in number almost every year (Lew 2007a). Meanwhile, the conservation of cultural and natural heritage sites has been a major challenge as urban environments have been razed and replaced by futuristic architectural wonders and commercial replicas of Chinese and international culture themed shopping districts, all in the name of progress and modernity (Liang & Bao 2015).

Table 23.4 Annual number of domestic travel trips and earnings from domestic and international travel in China

	Domestic trips (bn*)	Domestic travel earnings (US$ bn*)	International visitor earnings (US$ bn)
2013	3.262	426.414	51.66
2012	2.957	368.481	50.03
2011	2.641	313.292	48.46
2010	2.103	204.147	45.86
2009	1.903	165.263	39.68
2005	1.212	85.781	29.30
2000	0.744	51.533	16.22
1995	0.629	22.325	8.73

Sources: National Tourism Administration of China and UNWTO in Yang *et al.* 2010; NBSC 2014a.
Note
* 1 billion = 1,000 million; domestic earning values based on Chinese RMB to US dollar exchange rate of 0.162282.

Traditional rural countrysides are also being developed into leisure recreation attractions that can enhance the value of surrounding land for ex-urban residential development. In the process, traditional authenticity is replaced by staged commodities that, while well able to absorb the teaming masses of domestic tourists, bear little of the sense-of-place that their original renown might have been based on (Xu *et al.* 2014). In the decades since the death of Mao Zedong, the Chinese consumer has evolved from a Maoist pre-consumer, to an emerging consumer-based society, to a post-/hyper-modern consumer society of McDisneyfied shoppertainment and eatertainment (Lew 2007b). This is especially tragic due to the disintegration of tradition rural cultures in which tourism and development have caused the creation of placeless communities and local disempowerment (Han *et al.* 2014; Zhang 2014).

In a country that is as large and diverse as China, there are also alternative tourists who are more adventure-seeking and may be more interested in the authentic than the staged and spectacular. *Donkey Friends* (lyu you) is a practice in China whereby small groups of Chinese organize themselves online to share a trip together (Chen & Weiler 2014). Most have never met before their online introductions, and their preferred manner of travel is with a backpack and wearing jeans. These cyber-backpackers are typically young and from the highly developed metropolitan areas of eastern China. They seek out the more remote and ethnically diverse destinations in China's south and west. As in other parts of the world, these backpacker tourists are often credited with opening up new territories for mass tourism to emerge.

An additional issue with tourism development in China is the transfer of management rights and profits from nature resource-based attractions to private interests. The privatization of nature-based attractions is not new, and does not necessarily have negative impacts. It is widely used, for example, in South Africa, Namibia and Botswana to create a variety of private non-profit and for-profit organizations that either own or lease tracts of land for wildlife conservation and viewing (Spenceley 2008). Although the most famous scenic areas in China are fully controlled by government agencies of one form or another (some operate as publicly listed companies), a growing number of less developed lands have been leased to completely private developers (Huang *et al.* 2011). These leases are typically for 25–30 years, although some reach 50–70 years and are found in most of China's provinces, though they are more common in the less developed regions of the country. Government interest in privatization is driven by inadequate revenue sources and is usually managed by a large profit-driven corporation that is headquartered in the more developed eastern parts of the country, because local firms lack sufficient capital resources to undertake such an operation. While in theory this model can sustainably support local communities, corporate interests and the natural resource base, in practice, corrupt relationships, which are more entrenched in less developed parts of China, have had major negative impacts on all stakeholders, and threaten the conservation of many nature-based resources.

China is a developing country where limited government resources in some parts of the country have given rise to a wide range of public–private structures to oversee natural and cultural areas on government-owned land (which includes almost all of the land in China). In this way, private development interests are closely intertwined with government policy and the oversight of these public resources. At the same time, China has a massive domestic population, which makes many places relatively easy to commodify for tourism. This also gives rise to a greater potential for unethical business dealings, and irreversible environmental and cultural change due to tourism (Wang & Buckley 2010). Despite these differences, China's public resources areas share many of the same tourism management issues seen elsewhere, including how to balance the various roles of local government, national/state government, private investors, non-profit/non-governmental organizations, the local community and the natural resource base (Nelson 2010).

Chinese outbound tourism

The problems of domestic tourism in China essential stem from the very high demand for leisure travel by China's large, and increasingly diverse, population. That population also has a high demand for international travel, which is impacting tourism on a global scale as well.

For most of its recorded history, few Chinese left China proper. By the 3rd century (the Three Kingdoms period), military expansion, followed by migration out of the north China cultural hearth, had extended the area of Han Chinese settlement into what is today central and southern China. China became a major sea trading nation in the Indian Ocean during the Tang Dynasty (618–906), though it was still rare, and at times illegal, for Chinese to leave their homeland (Pan 1990). Most of those who did leave were traders (or more likely pirates) from the southern coastal province of Fujian plying the route through Southeast Asia to South Asia and beyond. This situation changed considerably in the late 1800s when European warships forced the Qing Dynasty leaders to allow freedom of travel for its citizens, many of whom then migrated to become coolie workers on European plantations in Southeast Asia.

China's doors were closed within a few years following the Chinese Communist Party's victory and Mao Zedong's rise to leadership in 1949. Up to the 1980s it was very rare for Chinese nationals to travel abroad. Since the opening up of China in 1978, the central government has gradually eased its control over outbound travel. Each year since the early 1980s larger numbers of Chinese have been granted permission to leave the country for short business or private trips, or to become a permanent resident in a foreign country (Table 23.5).

Hong Kong and Macau became the first international destinations for Chinese tourists in 1983 when travel to these territories of China was opened up to Chinese citizens on an experimental basis. This was the first time China allowed residents to leave the country for non-official, leisure purposes since the early 1950s (Lew 1995). In 1990 the status of Hong Kong and Macau became formalized as officially approved destinations at the same time that Thailand, Malaysia and Singapore became the first "tourism liberalizing countries" (Yatsko & Tasker 1998). These countries were selected because of their close geographic proximity, growing

Table 23.5 China outbound travel, 2005 to 2014 ('000s)

Year	Trips	% annual change
2014	116,000.0★	18.1
2013	98,185.2	18.0
2012	83,182.7	18.1
2011	70,250.0	22.4
2010	57,386.5	20.4
2009	47,656.3	4.0
2008	45,844.4	11.9
2007	40,954.0	18.6
2006	34,523.6	11.3
2005	31,026.3	7.5
2000	10,472.6	13.4
1995	7,139.0	16.9
1985	529.9	–

Sources: NBSC 2002; CNTA 2008a, 2008b, 2009a, 2010a, 2011a, 2012a, 2013a, 2014a; China Outbound Tourism Research Institute (COTRI) 2015.
Note
★ Projected.

trade relationships with China, and large numbers of ethnic Chinese citizens. In the early 1990s, international travel was encouraged with the goal of advancing the knowledge and skills of China's professionals and government officials (Zhang & Lew 1997). Most international outbound travel at that time was somehow business or government related, as it was far beyond the budgets of the vast majority of mainland Chinese.

It was expected that non-business travellers would primarily be VFR travelers, in the same manner that many of the visitors from these four countries travel to China. As such, when the first set of "tourism liberalizing countries" was designated in 1990, potential leisure travelers were required to certify that a relative in the destination country would pay for the trip before a passport or visa would be issued (Yatsko & Tasker 1998). This greatly limited the number of people traveling to these countries. However, by 1994 most travel agents were ignoring this requirement and in 1997 it was dropped completely. Still, the process was not easy, requiring approvals from one's place of work first, followed by China's Public Security Bureau, who would issue the exit visa, and then an entry visa from the destination country, many of which were still a little wary of mainland visitors (Brady 1998). Only about 40% of exit visa applications were approved by the Public Security Bureau in 1997 and 1998.

Outbound travel grew steadily in the 1990s and 2000s at rates that were closely monitored by the central government (Table 23.5). By 2012, Chinese travellers made over 83 million international trips, surpassing Germany and the US for the first time to make them the world's largest outbound travel market (*Want China Times* 2013). They also became the world's largest spending market that year, reaching US$102 billion (UNWTO 2014). By 2014, Chinese travellers were estimated to have surpassed 100 million outbound trips (*China Daily* 2014; Larson 2014).

Historically, the emphasis on employment-related travel meant that most outbound travellers were Communist Party officials and employees of government-owned companies. In 1993, the number of trips made by these business travellers accounted for more than 61% of total outbound travel (Liu 1995). Because the money used to pay for these trips came from the country's foreign currency reserves, the Chinese central government became increasingly critical of individuals using public funds for unnecessary or unauthorized trips abroad, which have gradually been curtailed over the years. By 2011, international business trips from China were estimate to account for 46% of all travel, which is closer to international norms for many countries, with pure leisure travel comprising 31% of trips, and overseas student and government travel making up the rest (Philip 2012).

Two-thirds of mainland Chinese trips are to Hong Kong and Macau; another 10% are to other areas of East Asia; and 10% are to Southeast Asia (Table 23.6). Thus, close to 90% of Chinese outbound travel trips are within the East and Southeast Asia region. Excluding the China Special Autonomous Regions of Hong Kong and Macau, South Korea and Thailand were, by far, the two most visited international destinations for mainland Chinese travellers in 2013. Chinese travellers are attracted to Thailand because they find it affordable, somewhat modern, and culturally exotic. South Korea benefits from its geographic proximity to China and the widespread success of its popular culture products, including music, movies and television shows. These destinations are followed by Taiwan, the US, Japan and Vietnam, which, with the exception of the US, are proximate neighbours and business partners of mainland China. Most of the countries in Asia view China as a significant part of their international tourism development strategies, which has resulted in relaxed visa requirements for Chinese tourists in recent years, the creation of special promotional campaigns in China, and the pursuit of direct flights from Chinese cities.

By 2010, countries throughout the world were pitching to the China market, most of whom traveled overseas on a tour package, which allowed greater control on the part of the Chinese government and destinations as they assessed the characteristics and impacts of this new, and potentially massive, market. In the early 2010s, countries gradually opened up to independent tourists from China, both as a sign that the Chinese tourist market was becoming more mature, and in hopes of receiving more tourist expenditures from high-end Chinese travelers. Since 2011, Japan, South Korea and Taiwan have made it easier for Chinese tourists to obtain visas and travel independently, and all three are consistently among the most popular destinations for mainland tourists (*Jing Daily* 2015; Qian 2015).

China is a country of 1.36 billion people, and 116 million outbound trips only account for perhaps as much as 7% of China's population traveling overseas. The potential for growth remains significant. For most of the mass of Chinese outbound tourists, it is their first time outside of China. Partly because of this, along with the level of national development that China is currently at (rapidly growing middle and upper classes emerging from poverty), their travel behavior has often been pointed to as problematic for destinations (*New York Times* 2013; Abad-Santos 2013). Traveling in somewhat loud and culturally insensitive groups with limited awareness of local behavioral norms, they have become the new "ugly tourists", replacing the British of the early 1900s, Americans of the post-World War II period, and Japanese of the 1970s. It is common for resorts in Southeast Asia, for example, to separate mainland Chinese tourists from European tourists in the location of their rooms to reduce potential conflicts and enhance the experience of their full range of guests.

Part of both the behavior and its resulting perceptions of Chinese tourists is engendered in the nature of group travel, which is the way most travel both within and outside of China is currently organized. As more mainland Chinese travel independently and otherwise become more aware of global cultural diversity, their negative image is likely to diminish. This is already happening as more wealthy and sophisticated Chinese travelers seek ever more remote corners

Table 23.6 China's outbound destinations to regions and leading destinations in 2013 ('000s)

	('000)	Average annual percentage change 2005–13	Market share (%)
Hong Kong	40,303.3	24.7	41.05
Macau	25,239.4	24.7	25.71
Asia-Pacific			22.51
S. Korea	4,253.4	22.3	
Thailand	4,010.3	29.0	
Taiwan	2,918.9	77.3*	
Japan	1,834.6	11.4	
Vietnam	1,772.7	14.9	
Cambodia	1,690.6	65.4	
Malaysia	1,351.6	20.2	
Singapore	1,322.8	13.6	
Indonesia	879.2	41.9*	
Australia	822.7	13.1	
Burma/Myanmar	561.3	14.1	
Philippines	446.5	34.4	
Mongolia	236.4	13.6*	
Europe			2.77
Russia	915.3	3.4*	
UK	490.6	16.1*	
Italy	478.0	21.1*	
France	422.1	16.0*	
Germany	415.1	7.6	
Americas			2.51
USA	1,966.9	20.8*	
Canada	497.7	19.5**	
Africa			1.46
Guinea-Bissau	1,143.9	–	
South Asia and the Middle East		0.06	
Maldives	302.4	65.0**	
UAE	263.3	17.54*	
*Other countries***	3,356.2		4.42
Total worldwide	98,185.2	14.69	100.00

Source: China National Tourism Administration (CNTA 2014a).
Notes
Based on the top 25 country trip destinations for Chinese outbound travellers in 2013.
*Average annual percentage change 2009–13.
**Average annual percentage change 2010–13.
*** Mostly to Africa, South Asia, the Middle East, and Latin America.

of the globe to explore, such as Antarctica (Boehler 2013). At the same time, with the very large population of China that is still waiting to see the rest of the world for the first time, there are likely to be many more culture-shock encounters in the years to come.

Conclusions

The history of contemporary international tourism in China began cautiously, coming after a long period of considerable internal social turmoil through the first half of the 20th century. Since the 1980s, however, both international and domestic tourism have expanded rapidly, along with the liberalization of economic and social policies in virtually every sector of Chinese society. While foreign international hotels played a major role in helping China to emerge from decades of inwardly focused development in the 1980s, it has been the explosion in domestic tourism in the 1990s and 2000s that has most reshaped and commodified China's urban and rural landscapes. International outbound tourism from China has grown consistently and steadily, reaching new highs in the 2010s even as foreign visitations to China have stalled and even declined.

Despite continuing steps toward decentralizing and opening China's tourism industry to outside investors, and its borders to international travelers, there is no doubt that China remains a more highly centralized society than is found in most of the countries from which its visitors come. Large areas of China, especially in its western regions, remain closed or have limited access to foreign travel. Chinese citizens still face some challenges in selecting travel destinations, while top-down tourism development can disempower local populations (Han *et al.* 2014), and bureaucratic rules and regulations can hinder the competition and efficiency of tourism services (Lew 2001; Huang *et al.* 2011).

China is the largest country in the Asia-Pacific region and one of the most important tourism countries in the world, both as a destination and a generator of tourists. Since the 1970s China may have reached a level of destination maturity for international travelers, which means that growth will continue, but at a slower pace than in the first 30 years following opening up.

The growth of domestic tourism has come to overwhelm international tourism in China, and the country is still searching for better ways of developing and using travel and tourism to further the welfare of its citizens and the country as a whole. Much of the focus in the past has been on infrastructure development and modernization, both of which have been largely achieved for both the domestic and international markets. This, however, has been at the expense of the conservation of traditional cultural diversity and natural resources, both of which have been highly commodified (Xu *et al.* 2014). The degradation and destruction of tourism resources by careless development and uncontrolled tourist use is destroying the core drawing power of its human and natural heritage attractions.

As a tourist generator, even with over 100 million outbound trips in 2014, there is still considerable pent-up demand by China's 1.36 billion citizens to see the world. China will continue to be a major factor in the future development of tourism in Asia. Chinese tourists are transforming both the intra-Asian and global patterns of travel and tourism (Philip 2012). How this vast country will continue to maintain its economic growth (which was slowing in the mid-2010s), and its concurrent social stability, is a key issue that will make, break or at least reshape the pattern of tourism development throughout Asia well into the foreseeable future.

In summary, international travel to China has probably matured. It was the first form of modern tourism to emerge in the 1970s and 1980s, and may be facing similar challenges to those the larger Chinese economy is currently struggling with. Domestic tourism, on the other hand, has grown so fast over such a short period of time (the 1990s and 2000s) that it challenges the ability of resource and infrastructure managers to moderate its impacts. Those impacts are a growing concern among many groups of stakeholders, including both local residents and tourists. For the rest of the world, it is the emergence of the international outbound traveller from China that is just beginning to reshape the contemporary patterns of global travel. As large as that number already is, this phenomenon is still in an emergent phase, and is likely to have impacts, both good and bad, that have yet to be fully realized by global tourism businesses and destination policy makers.

Key reading

Han, G., Wu, P., Huang Y. and Yang, Z. (2014) 'Tourism development and the disempowerment of host residents: Types and formative mechanism', *Tourism Geographies*, 16(5): 717–740.

Huang, X., Bao, J. and Lew, A.A. (2011) 'Nature-based tourism resources privatization in China: A system dynamic analysis of opportunities and risks', *Tourism Recreation Research*, 36(2): 99–111.

Liang, Z.-X. and Bao, J.-G. (2015) 'Tourism gentrification in Shenzhen, China: Causes and socio-spatial consequences', *Tourism Geographies*, 17(3): 461–481.

Ryan, C. and Huang, S. (eds) (2013) *Tourism in China: Destinations, Planning and Experiences*. Bristol: Channelview.

Xu, H., Zhang, C. and Lew, A.A. (2014) 'Tourism geography research in China: Institutional perspectives on community tourism development', *Tourism Geographies*, 16(5): 711–716.

References

Abad-Santos, A. (2013) 'How Chinese tourists usurp the ugly Americans', *The Atlantic*, 28 May. Online. Available: http://news.yahoo.com/chinese-tourists-usurped-ugly-americans-224046888.html (accessed 8 April 2015).

Barton, D. (2013) 'Half a billion: China's middle-class consumers', *The Diplomat*. Online. Available: http://thediplomat.com/2013/05/half-a-billion-chinas-middle-class-consumers (accessed 7 April 2015).

Beijing Review (1978a) 'More tourists', *Beijing Review*, 21(35): 3.

—— (1978b) 'Tourist news', *Beijing Review*, 21(38): 30–31.

—— (1979a) 'China's tourist service', *Beijing Review*, 22(2): 38.

—— (1979b) 'Expanding tourism', *Beijing Review*, 22(11): 6–7.

Boehler, P. (2013) 'Antarctica: The new hot destination', *South China Morning Post*, 23 December. Online. Available: www.scmp.com/news/china/article/1388514/antarctica-new-hot-destination (accessed 15 April 2015).

Brady, S. (1998) 'China's outwardly mobile', *Time* (Asia edition), 21 September: 10.

Chang, P.H. (1992) 'China's relations with Hong Kong and Taiwan', *The Annals of the American Academy of Political and Social Science*, 519 (January): 127–139.

Chen, H. and Weiler, B. (2014) 'Chinese donkey friends in Tibet: Evidence from the cyberspace community', *Journal of China Tourism Research*, 10(4): 475–492.

China Daily (2014) 'Chinese travelers to neighboring countries surge (Xinhua)', *China Daily*, 5 December. Online. Available: www.chinadaily.com.cn/business/2014-12/05/content_19028886.htm (accessed 14 January 2015).

China National Tourism Administration (CNTA) (1998) 'Tourist statistic data'. Online. Available: www.cnta.com/HTMLE/news/news.htm (accessed 11 December 1998).

—— (2008a) 'China tourism statistics bulletin' (in Chinese). Online. Available: www.cnta.gov.cn/html/2008-9/2008-9-10-11-35-98624.html (accessed 15 January 2015).

—— (2008b) 'China tourism statistics bulletin' (in Chinese). Online. Available: www.cnta.gov.cn/html/2008-6/2008-6-2-14-52-59-212.html (accessed 15 January 15, 2015).

—— (2008c) 'Tourist arrivals to China by way of entry points' (in Chinese). Online. Available: www.cnta.gov.cn/html/2008-6/2008-6-2-21-29-4-325.html (accessed 15 January 2015).

—— (2008d) 'Tourist arrivals to China by way of entry points' (in Chinese). Online. Available: www.cnta.gov.cn/html/2008-6/2008-6-2-14-53-4-262.html (accessed 15 January 2015).

—— (2008e) 'Tourist arrivals to China by way of entry points' (in Chinese). Online. Available: www.cnta.gov.cn/html/2008-6/2008-6-2-21-28-46-108.html (accessed 15 January 15, 2015).

—— (2009a) 'China Tourism Statistics Bulletin' (in Chinese). Online. Available: www.cnta.gov.cn/html/2009-9/2009-9-28-9-30-78465.html (accessed 15 January 2015).

—— (2009b) 'Tourist arrivals to China by way of entry points' (in Chinese). Online. Available: www.cnta.gov.cn/html/2009-2/2009-2-18-9-34-95871.html (accessed 15 January 2015).

—— (2010a) 'China Tourism Statistics Bulletin' (in Chinese). Online. Available: www.cnta.gov.cn/html/2010-11/2010-11-25-9-42-64682.html (accessed 15 January 2015).

—— (2010b) 'Tourist arrivals to China by way of entry points' (in Chinese). Online. Available: www.cnta.gov.cn/html/2010-1/2010-1-19-10-48-20174.html (accessed 15 January 2015).

—— (2011a) 'China Tourism Statistics Bulletin' (in Chinese). Online. Available: www.cnta.gov.cn/html/2011-11/2011-11-1-9-50-68041.html (accessed 15 January 2015).

—— (2011b) 'Tourist arrivals to China by way of entry points' (in Chinese). Online. Available: www.cnta.gov.cn/html/2011-3/2011-3-25-10-15-28226.html (accessed 15 January 2015).

—— (2012a) 'China tourism statistics bulletin' (in Chinese). Online. Available: www.cnta.gov.cn/html/2012-10/2012-10-25-9-0-71726.html (accessed 15 January 2015).

—— (2012b) 'Tourist arrivals to China by way of entry points' (in Chinese). Online. Available: www.cnta.gov.cn/html/2012-2/2012-2-21-19-9-54985.html (accessed 15 January 2015).

—— (2013a) 'China tourism statistics bulletin' (in Chinese). Online. Available: www.cnta.gov.cn/html/2013-9/2013-9-12-%7B@hur%7D-39-08306.html (accessed 15 January 2015).

—— (2013b) 'Tourist arrivals to China by way of entry points' (in Chinese). Online. Available: www.cnta.gov.cn/html/2013-1/2013-1-17-17-10-20496.html (accessed 15 January 2015).

—— (2014a) 'China tourism statistics bulletin' (in Chinese). Online. Available: www.cnta.gov.cn/html/2014-9/2014-9-24-%7B@hur%7D-47-90095.html (accessed 15 January 2015).

—— (2014b) 'Tourist arrivals to China by way of entry points' (in Chinese). Online. Available: www.cnta.gov.cn/html/2014-1/2014-1-16-15-52-71196.html (accessed 15 January 2015).

China Outbound Tourism Research Institute (COTRI) (2015) 'China outbound tourism 2000–2015'. Online. Available: www.china-outbound.com/fileadmin/COTRI_graph_2000–2015_Feb.15.jpg (accessed 7 April 2015).

Feng, B. (2014) 'Beijing battles decline in tourism', *New York Times: Sinosphere*, 19 December. Online. Available: http://sinosphere.blogs.nytimes.com/2014/12/19/beijing-battles-decline-in-tourism (accessed 15 March 2015).

Han, G., Wu, P., Huang Y. and Yang, Z. (2014) 'Tourism development and the disempowerment of host residents: Types and formative mechanism', *Tourism Geographies*, 16(5): 717–740.

He, G. (ed.) (1991) *The Yearbook of China Tourism Statistics 1991*. Beijing: China Travel and Tourism Press.

Huang, X., Bao, J. and Lew, A.A. (2011) 'Nature-based tourism resources privatization in China: A system dynamic analysis of opportunities and risks', *Tourism Recreation Research*, 36(2): 99–111.

Jing Daily (2015) 'Destination Asia: Chinese tourists plan to stay close to home in 2015', *Jing Daily*, 9 January. Online. Available: https://jingdaily.com/destination-asia-chinese-tourists-plan-to-stay-close-to-home-in-2015 (accessed 15 April 2015).

Knoema (2015) 'World data atlas, China: International tourism receipts % of total exports'. Online. Available: http://knoema.com/atlas/China/Tourism-receipts-percent-of-total-exports (accessed 4 April 2015).

Larson, C. (2014) 'Chinese tourists make more than 100 million overseas trips in 2014', *Bloomberg Businessweek*, 5 December. Online. Available: www.businessweek.com/articles/2014-12-05/theyre-coming-chinese-tourists-will-make-100-million-trips-abroad-this-year (accessed 14 January 2015).

Lew, A.A. (1987) 'The history, policies and social impact of international tourism in the Peoples Republic of China', *Asian Profile*, 15(2): 117–128.

—— (1995) 'Overseas Chinese and compatriots in China's tourism development', in A.A. Lew and L. Yu (eds), *Tourism in China: Geographical, Political, and Economic Perspectives* (pp. 155–175), Boulder: Westview Press.

—— (2000) 'China: A growth engine for Asian tourism', in C.M. Hall and S.J. Page (eds), *Tourism in South and South East Asia: Issues and Cases* (pp. 269–285). Oxford: Butterworth-Heinemann.

—— (2001) 'Tourism development in China: The dilemma of bureaucratic decentralization and economic liberalization', in D. Harrison (ed.), *Tourism in the Less Developed World*, 2nd edn (pp. 109–120), Wallingford: CAB International.

—— (2007a) 'China's growing wander lust', *Far Eastern Economic Review*, 170(8): 60–63.

—— (2007b) 'Pedestrian shopping streets in the restructuring of the Chinese city', in T. Coles and A. Church (eds), *Tourism, Power and Place* (pp. 150–170). London: Routledge.

Liang, Z.-X. and Bao, J.-G. (2015) 'Tourism gentrification in Shenzhen, China: Causes and socio-spatial consequences', *Tourism Geographies*, 17(3): 461–481.

Liu, Y. (ed.) (1995) *The Yearbook of China Tourism*. Beijing: National Tourism Administration of the People's Republic of China.

National Bureau of Statistics of China (NBSC) (2002) 'China Statistical Yearbook 2002, table 18–1 development of tourism'. Online. Available: www.stats.gov.cn/english/statisticaldata/yearlydata/YB2002e/ml/indexE.htm (accessed 6 April 2015).

—— (2014a) 'China Statistical Yearbook 2014, table 17–9 development of tourism'. Online. Available: www.stats.gov.cn/tjsj/ndsj/2014/indexeh.htm (accessed 6 April 2015).

—— (2014b) 'China Statistical Yearbook 2014, table 17–12 number of overseas arrivals by sex, age and purpose'. Online. Available: www.stats.gov.cn/tjsj/ndsj/2014/indexeh.htm (accessed 6 April 2015).

Nelson, F. (2010) 'Democratizing natural resource governance: Searching for institutional change', in F. Nelson (ed.), *Community Rights, Conservation and Contested Land: The Politics of Natural Resource Governance in Africa* (pp. 310–333). London: Earthscan.

Newsweek (1998) 'Go east, young man', *Newsweek*, 6 April, 17.

New York Times (2013) 'Chinese tourists: The new ugly Americans', *The Chronicle Herald*, 17 September. Online. Available: http://thechronicleherald.ca/world/1154671-chinese-tourists-the-new-ugly-americans (accessed 8 April 2015).

Pan, L. (1990) *Sons of the Yellow Emperor: A History of the Chinese Diaspora*. Boston: Little, Brown and Co.

Philip (2012) 'What's the difference between Chinese business travelers and leisure tourists?' *Marketing China*, 11 July. Online. Available: http://marketingtochina.com/chinese-business-travelers-and-leisure-tourists-difference/ (accessed 14 January 2015).

Qian, R. (2015) 'Chinese tourists swarming into Japan', *ECNS.CN*, 7 April. Online. Available: www.ecns.cn/2015/04-07/160763.shtml (accessed 15 April 2015).

Roehl, W.S. (1995) 'The June 4, 1989, Tiananmen Square incident and Chinese tourism', in A. Lew and L. Yu (eds), *Tourism in China: Geographic, Political, and Economic Perspectives* (pp. 19–39), Boulder: Westview Press.

Spenceley, A. (ed.) (2008) *Responsible Tourism: Critical Issues for Conservation and Development*. London: Earthscan.

Sun, G, (ed.) (1992) *The Yearbook of China Tourism Statistics 1992*. Beijing: China Travel and Tourism Press.

Tan, M. (1986) 'China tourism: Big growth, immediate problems', *China Reconstructs*, 35(6): 8–10.

Travel China Guide (2015) 'China tourism'. Online. Available: www.travelchinaguide.com/tourism (accessed 4 April 2015).

United Nations World Tourism Organization (UNWTO) (2014) *UNWTO 2014 Tourism Highlights*. Online. Available: www.e-unwto.org/content/r13521/fulltext.pdf (accessed 14 January 2015).

Wang, C.-H. and Buckley, R. (2010) 'Shengtai Anquan: Managing tourism and environment in China's forest parks', *AMBIO: A Journal of the Human Environment*, 39(6): 451–453.

Wang, N. (2015) 'Tourists avoiding China because of pollution, corruption, and bad food', *The Nan Fang*, 23 January. Online. Available: https://thenanfang.com/pollution-corruption-and-food-safety-killing-tourism-to-china (accessed 4 April 2015).

Want China Times (2013) 'China is the world's largest outbound tourism market', *Want China Times*, 28 April. Online. Available: www.wantchinatimes.com/news-subclass-cnt.aspx?id=20130428000008&cid=1102 (accessed 14 January 2015).

Watt, L. (2013) 'China's tourism industry is spiraling, thanks in part to air pollution', *The Huffington Post*. Online. Available: www.huffingtonpost.com/2013/08/13/china-tourism-pollution-smog_n_3747289.html (accessed 4 April 2015).

Xu, H., Zhang, C. and Lew, A.A. (2014) 'Tourism geography research in China: Institutional perspectives on community tourism development', *Tourism Geographies*, 16(5): 711–716.

Xue, M. (ed.) (1982) 'Rapid development of tourism', in *Almanac of China's Economy 1981* (pp. 677–683). Hong Kong: Modern Language Company.

Yang, C.H., Lin, H.L. and Han, C.C. (2010) 'Analysis of international tourist arrivals in China: The role of World Heritage Sites', *Tourism Management*, 31(6): 827–837.

Yatsko, P. and Tasker, R. (1998) 'Outward bound: Just in time, ordinary Chinese catch the travel bug', *Far Eastern Economic Review*, 26 March: 66–67.

Yu, L. (1992) 'Emerging markets for China's tourism industry', *Journal of Travel Research*, 31(1): 10–13.

Zhang, G. (1995) 'China's tourism development since 1978: Policies, experiences, and lessons learned', in A. Lew and L. Yu (eds), *Tourism in China: Geographic, Political, and Economic Perspectives* (pp. 3–17), Boulder: Westview Press.

Zhang, J. (1990) 'Down but not out: Taiwan and Southeast Asia are keeping China's wounded tourism industry alive', *The China Business Review*, 17 (November–December): 12–14, 16.

Zhang, Y. (2014) 'Tourism and the "villagers without history": The case of Yubeng', *Tourism Geographies*, 15(5): 741–756.

Zhang, Y. and Lew, A.A. (1997) 'The People's Republic of China: Two decades of tourism', *Pacific Tourism Review*, 1(2): 161–172.

Zou, T. (1993) *Tourism Development and Planning*. Beijing: Tourism Education Press.

24

TOURISM AND THE "OTHER CHINAS"

Hong Kong, Macao and Taiwan

Wantanee Suntikul

Introduction

The continual loosening of Chinese governmental restrictions on its citizens' travel since the inauguration of the open door policy in the late 1970s presents current generations of Chinese with unaccustomed opportunities to travel abroad, while the rapid growth of the Chinese economy has meant that at least a portion of the Chinese population is acquiring the financial means, and the global outlook, to undertake international travel. Consequently, the past two decades have seen a massive influx of Chinese tourists to many of the far-flung popular tourism destinations of the world as the People's Republic of China (PRC or "mainland China") has become the world's largest source market for international tourists (see Chapter 23, this volume).

As mainland Chinese tour groups become an increasingly familiar sight in Paris, New York and Dubai, they have also been gaining new opportunities to travel to destinations within what can be termed "greater China," yet which for various historical reasons have been politically disenfranchised from the mainland for decades or even centuries and have only recently become accessible to mainland Chinese travelers due to processes of rapprochement or re-appropriation. These "other Chinas" include the former European colonial outposts of Hong Kong and Macao, both of which were repatriated as "Special Administrative Regions" (SARs) of China in the closing years of the 20th century, and the island nation of Taiwan, which splintered off from China in 1949 but which has been gradually re-establishing channels of contact with the "motherland" in recent years. As with destinations further afield, Chinese tourists have also been taking advantage of the newfound opportunity to visit these places in droves.

This chapter will examine the ways in which the development of mainland Chinese tourism to these three destinations has been implicated in the complex and interrelated political, social, cultural and economic dimensions of the ongoing process of negotiation of the relationship between the Chinese mainland and these distinct entities whose identities are deeply connected to, yet distinct from, any greater Chinese identity that may be said to exist.

Hong Kong

Background

Hong Kong is located in eastern Asia, bordering the South China Sea and the Chinese mainland, with a total area of 1,104km². The population of Hong Kong was 7.24 million in 2014. In the same year, the population density reached 6,690 people per square kilometre, making Hong Kong one of the most densely populated places in the world. Most Hong Kong residents are either natives of, or trace their ancestry to, the neighbouring Guangdong Province.

Hong Kong was a colony of Britain for 156 years, and was returned to China on 1 July 1997, to become a Special Administrative Region (SAR) of China under "one country, two systems" as a constitutional principle formulated by then President of the PRC, Deng Xiaoping. Hong Kong is governed by the *Basic Law of Hong Kong*, ensuring that it will retain its own currency, parliamentary system and legal system until 2047. The chief executive of Hong Kong (equivalent to the governor during the British period) is appointed by a Beijing-picked committee. The Executive Council (ExCo) assists the Chief Executive in policy making, while the Legislative Council (LegCo) is in charge of approval of law making and government budgeting.

The Hong Kong SAR (HKSAR) promotes itself as an international and cosmopolitan city with a business-friendly environment, rule of law, free market economy and liberalization of investment, with no trade barriers. It is also the main gateway to mainland China for both business and international tourism. Around 60 million tourists came to Hong Kong in 2014, and visitor arrivals are projected to reach 70 million by 2017 and 100 million by 2023 (Nip & Chan 2014).

Issues with Hong Kong identity

Even though 95% of Hong Kong's population is ethnic Chinese, most either came to Hong Kong to flee Chinese communist rule or are the descendants of such migrants (Flowerdew 2004). Under colonial rule, contact with mainland China was minimized, which gave Hong Kong people space to create their own identity. Ma and Fung (1999) stated that Hong Kong people tend to see themselves as Westernized and more sophisticated than the less "civilized" mainland Chinese.

The Chinese government has worked with the government of Hong Kong on nation-building and the gradual reintegration of Hong Kong into China. However, there is also concern about the consequences if Hong Kong should eventually lose the legal and societal underpinnings that still distinguish it from the mainland. According to Anson Chan Fang On-sang, former chief secretary of the HKSAR, in an interview with the *South China Morning Post* (2013), 'Hong Kong must determine for itself the role it plays in the development of the nation, but should not be content to become just another Chinese city.'

Various scholars such as Chun (1996), Flowerdew (2004), Fong (2010) and Mathews *et al.* (2008) have discussed Hong Kong identity issues. Chun (2000: 300) stated,

> The promotion of utilitarianism and consumerism as a way of life … broke down rigid distinctions between Chinese and Western culture. Thus, Hong Kong's hybrid culture which seems to effortlessly fuse East and West was brought about by unrestrained capitalism's wholesale demystification of those cultural barriers that has been fostered by an earlier "colonialism."

Chun (1996) also predicted that Hong Kong would continue to search for its identity; given that youth brought up in Hong Kong's apolitical culture were also now forced to ask how they were Chinese.

Growth of Chinese mainland tourism to Hong Kong

In 1980 the visible trade deficit of Hong Kong was HK$13,547 million, and tourist expenditure was HK$6,060 million. At that time, tourism was the territory's third largest export industry after clothing (HK$23,258) and electronics (HK$12,816 million). In accordance with Hong Kong's free economic system, the government chose to intervene selectively rather than extensively in the development of tourism (Lin & Sung 1984). In 1983 Hong Kong and Macao became the first two foreign destinations to which mainland Chinese were permitted to travel (Liu & McKercher 2014), and after the Hong Kong handover in 1997, Chinese tourists were allowed to visit Hong Kong as part of packaged tours. In 2002, the Hong Kong government abolished limits on the allowable number of Chinese visitors.

Tourist arrivals to Hong Kong declined drastically with the outbreak of severe acute respiratory syndrome (SARS) in 2003. During this time, the Hong Kong government inaugurated an "Individual Visit Scheme" (IVS) to encourage mainlanders to travel to Hong Kong. This scheme allowed visitors to apply for permission to enter on an individual basis, rather than being required to be part of a group tour or a business delegation, as was previously stipulated. The IVS has enabled large numbers of mainland Chinese tourists to visit and has been a primary factor in the significant development of Hong Kong's tourism sector, stimulating the local economy. It is estimated that IVS tourism added 110,000 jobs and 1.3% to Hong Kong's GDP in 2012 (Commerce and Economic Development Bureau 2013).

On its initiation on 28 July 2003, the IVS was applied only to four cities (Dongguan, Foshan, Jiangmen and Zhongshan) in Guangdong Province, which borders directly with Hong Kong. Eligibility was gradually extended through 2007. At the time of writing the IVS applies to 49 mainland Chinese municipalities, including all cities in Guangdong Province, as well as major Chinese cities beyond Guangdong. Since April 2009, eligible permanent residents of Shenzhen, the mainland city lying directly across the border from Hong Kong, have been able to apply for one-year multiple-entry Individual Visit Endorsements to visit Hong Kong as often as they like. By June 2013, 27.2 million visitors had come to Hong Kong under this provision. In the first half of 2013, 67.1% of mainland visitors were IVS travellers (compared to 34.8% in 2004) and the cumulative number of IVS visitors was over 100 million (Commerce and Economic Development Bureau 2013).

In a 2015 report, Credit Suisse cautioned Hong Kong on over-reliance on mainland tourists (*Wall Street Journal* 2015), but the fact is that the Hong Kong tourism industry relies on Chinese tourists, and China, in turn, relies on Hong Kong's unique social, economic and political status to maintain its value as an economic engine that could not be duplicated elsewhere in China (*The Economist* 2014). The hybrid nature of Hong Kong's identity, emerging from its distinctive historical and geopolitical circumstances, is therefore at the core of its tourism image (Zhang *et al.* 2015).

Impacts and local perception of Chinese tourists in Hong Kong

Despite the Hong Kong Tourism Board's declared intention to 'maintain a balanced portfolio of visitors and thus healthy growth in arrivals from all key markets' (Legislative Council Panel on Economic Services 2006), the Hong Kong tourism industry has come to heavily rely on

Chinese tourists, the number of which increased tenfold between 2000 and 2015 (*The Economist* 2015). IVS visitors spent an average of HK$3,593 per day in 2013, compared to HK$1,970 daily for non-mainland tourists (Research Office Legislative Council Secretariat 2014), and mainland Chinese visitors accounted for over 70% of arrivals.

Shopping is a primary activity for mainland tourists in Hong Kong. The three most important motivations for these tourists to shop in Hong Kong are lower prices (no sales tax compared to 17% in the mainland), better quality assurance and a wider and more exclusive range of products (*Hong Kong Business* 2011). This applies not only to luxury goods, but also to daily necessities such as shampoo and milk powder for infants. The huge demand from Chinese tourists for the imported milk powder available in Hong Kong, inspired by incidents of melamine tainting Chinese-produced milk powder that led to six infant deaths in China, caused severe shortages of milk powder for the local market and led the SAR government in 2008 to institute a strictly enforced limit of two cans per tourist.

The retail environment of the city has metamorphosed to address these tourists' consumption demand. In 2004 there were 90 cosmetic and toiletries shops in Hong Kong. In 2013 there were 1,440. During the same period, the number of clothing and footwear stores grew by 42% (to 15,410) and the number of jewellery and watch shops increased by 31% (to 3,850) (Nip 2014). Meanwhile, book and stationery shops decreased by over 25% during the same period (Research Office Legislative Council Secretariat 2014). Whole districts of the city, such as Causeway Bay and Tsim Sha Tsui, have shifted from a traditional mix of shops to one dominated by stores catering to mainland tourists.

The police force has also experienced added demands due to the need to keep order and to control the ever-growing crowds in these areas, as well as at border crossings, ferry terminals and the airport, as well as dealing with cases of theft, exploitation and deception of mainland visitors by unscrupulous individuals and businesses (Commerce and Economic Development Bureau 2013). Reports and videos of public spitting, urination, defecation and other "uncivilized" behaviour by certain Chinese tourists in Hong Kong are circulated via the Internet. Visitors practicing "parallel trading" (acquiring goods in Hong Kong to be sold on the black market in the mainland), and pregnant mainlanders who come to Hong Kong to give birth to take advantages of the SAR's superior healthcare and gain their offspring the automatic right to Hong Kong permanent residency, with all of its attendant privileges (LaFraniere 2012), are examples of sources of irritation. Angry locals refer to these visitors as "locusts," swarming into the city and sapping its resources.

Hong Kongers are very vocal and public in expressing their negative views of the Beijing government, as well as of Chinese tourists. A 2015 survey of 743 Hong Kong people found that two-thirds would favour a reduction in the number of individual Chinese visitors and more than three-fifths felt that their lives had been inconvenienced by these tourists (Li & Lin 2015).

The Hong Kong government response

Manifestations of political tensions in Hong Kong, including demonstrations in favour of local suffrage and against imposition of the Chinese "national curriculum" on Hong Kong schools, protests against mainland shoppers and harassment of individual tourists, have contributed to an unwelcoming atmosphere for mainland tourists, which has discouraged some from visiting. The 2015 May Day holiday saw a 20% decrease in the number of mainland tourists visiting Hong Kong, even as Chinese visitors to Japan and Korea increased, in part due to these countries' efforts to attract Chinese tourists (Zou 2015). Contrary to this public sentiment, the Hong Kong government has re-affirmed its desire to maintain and indeed increase the number of mainland Chinese visitors. Expressing dismay at the drop in visitor numbers, the current chief executive, Leung Chun-ying, has sought to dissuade Hong Kongers from future protests against tourists (Lai & Lam 2015).

A 2013 study (Commerce and Economic Development Bureau 2013) appraising Hong Kong's future tourism carrying capacity concentrated more on the city's physical carrying capacity than the social carrying capacity of the local society. The study found that the city was well capable of receiving the projected expanded number of guests in 2017, necessitating some specific measures such as expansion of Hong Kong's two theme parks (Hong Kong Disney and Ocean Park) as well as a significantly expanded supply of tourist accommodation, in response to which the government is instituting a number of planning and revitalisation programmes to facilitate hotel development. An increase in guest rooms is thus foreseen, from 68,000 in 2013 to 84,000 in 2017 (Hong Kong's Information Service Department 2014).

However, there are some recent indications that governments on both sides of the Hong Kong–Chinese border are not oblivious to the strain on Hong Kong's social carrying capacity. Both the Chinese central government and the government of Hong Kong have become cautious about the further development of cross-border tourism. The number of IVS-eligible cities has not been increased since 2007, and in 2013 the Chinese central government and the government of Hong Kong agreed to cap this number at the existing 49 in order to 'maintain the stable and orderly development of our tourism industry' (Commerce and Economic Development Bureau 2013), and Beijing has imposed specific limits on visits to Hong Kong by residents of the neighbouring city of Shenzhen (*Guardian* 2015).

Taiwan

20th-century development of Taiwan–China relations and tourism

In 1949, when Communists took power in mainland China, Chinese nationalists declared an independent nation on the island of Taiwan. As Taiwan and the PRC were on hostile terms, sometimes verging on military confrontation, for nearly three decades thereafter, travel between the two nations was seriously restricted until 1978, when Taiwanese were granted the right to visit the mainland as part of the PRC's economic reform (open door) policy. However, it was not until 1979 that Taiwan allowed its citizens to travel abroad, and not until November 1987 that they were allowed to visit their family members in mainland China (albeit not directly, only via Hong Kong). The following year, the Chinese government began allowing its citizens to visit their direct relatives in Taiwan, and Taiwan also made provisions to allow Chinese visitors, but at first only to visit sick relatives or attend funerals (Guo *et al.* 2006).

Another step in the rapprochement occurred with the Cross-Straits Talks of 1992, which led to the "1992 Consensus," the agreement between the PRC and Taiwan that there exists "one China," without constraining how this is interpreted. Subsequently, in 1993 further provisions were made by Taiwan for Chinese to attend educational, cultural and media events, mainly involving high-profile travellers such as scholars, actors, scientists and journalists (Guo *et al.* 2006).

Until 2001 there were no direct flights between the two Chinas, and travel was only possible via a "gateway" such as Hong Kong, Macau or Manila. Despite this restriction, more Taiwanese visited China during this period than did residents of any other country, accounting for nearly one out of four tourists to the PRC throughout the 1990s (Guo *et al.* 2006).

Governmental attitudes towards cross-strait tourism

The PRC government has promoted tourism as a component in its plan of eventual reunification with Taiwan (Liu 2011), and in 1979 formally proposed the creation of "Three Links" between the mainland and Taiwan, to allow or direct flights, shipping and postal connections. However, it was not until 1 January 2001 that the small-scale Mini Three Links policy was initiated (*Taiwan Yearbook* 2007), allowing for seaborne passenger cargo and post transportation between three cities in China's Fujian Province and Kinmen and Matsu, two small islands belonging to Taiwan but located just two kilometres off the coast of mainland China. This small-scale contact was found to have positive effects on island residents' impressions of mainland China (Chen 2010), re-affirming earlier findings from a study on the two Koreas, that contact between individuals from mutually "hostile" countries can reduce negative views (Kim *et al.* 2007). The fully-fledged Three Links agreement was finally established on 15 December 2008: an indication of the slow-but-steady gradual thawing of relations between the two nations.

The Taiwanese government has been relatively apprehensive about encouraging the exchange of tourists, and restrictions on travel from the PRC to Taiwan have been mainly due to the Taiwanese government's limits on Chinese tourist numbers, not PRC restrictions on its own citizens' travel (Yu 1997). Taiwan has only allowed mainland Chinese tourists to visit directly since the signing of the *Cross-Strait Agreement Concerning Mainland Tourists Travelling to Taiwan* in July 2008, just half a year before the launch of the Three Links agreement. Taiwan initially restricted numbers to 4,000 tourists per day, by tour groups only. From no direct tourist movement between China and Taiwan before 2008, in 2009 there were 972,123 arrivals from the PRC to Taiwan, and over 1.5 million from Taiwan to the PRC (Tourism Bureau 2010).

Despite Taiwan's population being less than 2% of that of its huge neighbour, and in spite of the increasing mobility and propensity for overseas travel among mainland Chinese, every year from 2009 – the year following the Three Links Agreement – to 2013, more Taiwanese visited the PRC than vice versa. In 2014, for the first time, the Taiwan Tourism Bureau recorded more mainland visitors to Taiwan than Taiwanese visiting the mainland, with 3.27 million Taiwanese travelling to mainland China (6.3% increase from the previous year) as compared with 3.99 million tourist arrivals to Taiwan from mainland China (an increase of 38.7%) (Tourism Bureau 2015).

With increasing political dialogue and improving relations between Taiwan and the PRC, tourism between the two countries has also continuously increased. The ongoing development of tourism has in turn had a positive effect on cross-strait relations (Zhuang 1993), and has been a significant factor in encouraging peaceful relations (Liu 2011).

Irritation and backlash

In Taiwan, as in Hong Kong, with the growing number of mainland tourists has come increasing irritation among a local population who consider themselves more refined than mainlanders and balk at the indoor smoking, public urination and price haggling even over tiny purchases, which are commonly practiced in China but are seen as irritants by many in the host society. Tour operators, dependent on the mainland market, are wary of being perceived by their clients as too constraining (Jennings 2015), but there has been local backlash against the impacts of these tourists as well. For example, the town of Sizhiwan Bay, a popular oceanfront destination in Taiwan's south that has recently been receiving over 4,000 tourists per day, has threatened to ban tourists unless the government takes measures to limit the number of mainland tourists (Jackson 2015).

Tourism industry operators in Taiwan have also complained about Chinese mass tourism from an economic perspective, decrying the purported monopolization of this market by Hong Kong investors, their inordinate control over tourism service providers in Taiwan, the preponderance of shopping in their itineraries rather than patronizing other sights and attractions, the reputation of Chinese tour groups for paying late, and other factors that lead many to doubt the real economic benefits of such tourists.

Taiwan introduced an individual permit scheme for independent travellers in June 2011. Originally restricted to 500 people each day from Beijing, Shanghai and Xiamen, the limit on the number of people has been raised incrementally over the years, most recently from 4,000 to 5,000 in September 2015. In 2014, 1.18 million Chinese travelled to Taiwan under this scheme, more than double the number in the previous year, and in March 2015 a further 11 Chinese cities were added to the eligibility list for the scheme (Jackson 2015). Allowing more independent travellers from China is widely seen as a way to circumvent many of the above-mentioned problems brought by mass group tours (Chung 2013).

In 2015 the Taiwanese government inaugurated a new scheme for "high-end tour groups," who were granted expedited entry permit processing (rather than the typical 40-day wait), and other concessions such as a guarantee that their tours will not include mandatory shopping stops. In exchange, these tourists stay primarily in five-star hotels and conform to an upper limit of coach travel distance per day (to give more time to purchase and consume) and a lower limit of NT$1,500 (about US$46) per day spending on lunch and dinner (Jennings 2015). It is hoped that this initiative will allow Taiwan to increase its gains from tourism while reducing irritation and negative impacts, by attracting smaller numbers of more culturally refined, higher-spending tourists.

Political issues and Chinese tourism to Taiwan

A recent trend is travel from the PRC to Taiwan to experience the "carnival atmosphere" of shows, food and giveaways that surround campaigns for municipal elections, which are particularly exotic for tourists from mainland China, where elections are not held. In advance of the November 2014 round of local elections, Chinese online forums kept tourists apprised of the itineraries of the different campaigns, while warning about the threat of deportation if one should become actively involved in a particular campaign (BBC 2014). Elections are a sensitive issue for the PRC government, and Beijing warned Chinese tourists and travel agencies to exercise caution when visiting Taiwan during the lead-up to the presidential and legislative elections in January 2016, though rumours of intentions to cut the number of visitors by 95% were vehemently denied (Hsiao 2015).

There have, however, been recent events for which the Beijing government has put decisive and explicit restrictions on its citizens' travel to Taiwan. At least 200 tour reservations at hotels were cancelled after the Chinese government instructed tour companies not to travel to Kaohsiung following a visit by the Dalai Lama to that city in September 2009. The screening of a documentary about exiled Chinese Uyghur activist Rebiya Kadeer at a film festival in Kaohsiung later that year, in defiance of the protests of local tourism operators, also affected Chinese visitor numbers (Kastner 2011).

A series of deadly road accidents that killed or injured dozens of mainland tourists to Taiwan was followed by a 20% year-on-year drop in the number of Chinese visitors to Taiwan during the "Golden Week" holiday of 2011, when tourism is normally at its most intense. Without explicitly acknowledging any governmental machinations behind this decrease, China National Tourism director Shao Qiwei responded to queries by stating, "If there is no safety, then there is no tourism" (Kastner 2011).

Macao

Background

Macao is a city of about half a million population, located about 60 kilometers from Hong Kong, at the opposite, west, side of the Pearl River Delta. Although it was a Portuguese colony from 1557 until its handover to China in 1999, over 96% of the population is ethnic Chinese. Also like Hong Kong, Macao has the status of an SAR within China, with its own currency and legal system. For much of its 400-year history, the Portuguese colony of Macao was the only Western outpost in China and a primary point through which technology, culture and goods from the West entered China, and vice versa (Peterson 1994). Macao is currently perhaps best known as the only place in China in which gambling is legalized.

The desire for a more democratic form of government that is evident in Hong Kong and Taiwan is not mirrored in the population of Macao, who have been found to be politically apathetic, content to accept the delegation of broad powers to a government that also takes broad responsibility for seeing to their interests and welfare (Ho 2011). This corresponds to a more "traditional" Chinese (Confucian) concept of the respective roles of government and citizens. Correspondingly, Macao society also remained very hierarchical and highly stratified through the colonial era, with only 8% of citizens having acquired a high school education as of the 1999 handover (Tan 1999).

History of gambling in Macao

Gambling has been legal in Macao since 1847, and even in the early years it offered types of gambling unknown elsewhere in China, such as (horse and dog) racecourse betting and Western table games (du Cros 2009). Macao's casinos have operated under a franchise arrangement since 1934, but casino development long remained small-scale, with only three established casino hotels in 1950 (Pao 2004). The franchise has been held by the *Sociedade de Turismo e Diversoes de Macau* since 1962.

The subsequent rapid growth of Macao's casino industry, as well as the attendant hotels, restaurants and other recreation facilities, in the 1970s and 1980s was fueled primarily by an increasing influx of visitors from Hong Kong. The Macao government liberalized the SAR's casino industry in 2003, and casino earnings rose rapidly, surpassing those of Las Vegas by 2006 (Ho 2011). This is nearly completely driven by a huge influx of mainland Chinese tourists made possible by the "individual free travel scheme."

In a manner reminiscent of the sanitization of Las Vegas' image in the 1980s, recent casino development in Macao has been characterized by megaresort developments, with shopping malls, stage shows and other more diversified and "family-friendly" attractions (Monaghan 2014), spearheaded by the development of the Venetian Macao, which opened in 2007, by the Las Vegas Sands group. However, Macao's resorts still receive only 5% of their revenue from non-gaming activities, as compared with 65% for Las Vegas (Cohen 2015). Macao remains precariously dependent on gambling.

Macao gaming tourism

With the launch of the "Individual Traveller Scheme" in 2002, mainland China immediately overtook Hong Kong as Macao's largest tourist source market, and has driven a steady increase in visitor arrivals. Even during 2003, the year of the SARS outbreak, visitor arrivals increased by 3.1%, including 5.7 million mainland visitors, as compared with fewer than one million in 1998 (Lo 2005). In 2014, Macao received over 31.5 million visitors, 28.6 million (90.8%) of whom came from mainland China, Hong Kong and Taiwan. Of these three groups, mainland Chinese are the biggest spenders, inside and outside of casinos. Constituting just over 65% of visitors in 2014, they accounted for 81% of the total of 61.75 billion Macao patacas (around US$7.7 billion) in non-gambling tourist spending, mainly on shopping (Government of Macao Statistics and Census Service 2015).

However, it is in casinos that most of Macao's tourism revenue is earned. As mentioned above, Macao's economy has become nearly completely dependent on the gambling sector, and although casinos have brought an economic boom to the city, making it into one of Asia's richest municipalities (and the world's fourth wealthiest territory per capita (Monaghan 2014)) within a matter of years, they have also brought social ills, such as an exacerbation of income inequality between those profiting from the gaming industry and those who do not, an influx of foreign labour, worsening traffic, pollution and corruption (Ho 2011). Average gamblers in Macao bet much larger sums than typical gamblers in Las Vegas. Even for mass-market Chinese gamblers, the average bet is over US$100 (Kaiman 2014). Most of Macao's casino income is brought by affluent "high roller" Chinese gamblers, with these VIP gamblers accounted for 70% of Macao casinos' takings up to 2014. However, gambling revenue in Macao fell for the second year in a row in 2015, by 34.3% to $28.93 billion as a result of a prolonged anti-corruption campaign and slowing economic growth (*Reuters* 2016).

The Chinese government limits the amount of money each of its citizens can bring into Macao to CNY20,000 (around US$3,150) per trip. There is also a daily limit of CNY10,000 per day for bank card withdrawals abroad, which in January 2016 became further restricted to a maximum of CNY100,000 per year (Hombrebueno 2015). The high-roller gambling tourism on which Macao relies is thus dependent upon the organizers of the junkets that bring big-spending VIP tourists to Macao providing ways to circumvent these limits on importing of cash. This is done through various (illegal) means, such as organizing advance payments and easy credit, which is then paid back to the organizer in Chinese currency upon return to the mainland (Kaiman 2014).

Crime and corruption in Macao's gambling sector

In order to consolidate the government-granted monopoly on Macao's casino industry, Stanley Ho, who remains owner of the *Sociedade de Turismo e Diversoes de Macau* and the wealthiest man in Macao to this day, overcame threats and sabotage from the local triads (organized crime syndicates) who had traditionally controlled gambling in Macao (Lo 2005). Despite prevailing over the triads, Ho unwittingly provided an opportunity for them to once again infiltrate casinos by contracting out the running of high-stakes gambling saloons from the mid-1980s to early 1990s, which is seen as allowing the triads to once again expand their power and influence in Macao, prompting the Chinese government, which had been monitoring criminal activity in the SAR in advance of the handover, to station an advance garrison of the People's Liberation Army (PLA) in Macao just hours after the official transfer of the territory from Portugal to China (Lo 2005). Indeed, gambling in Macao remains deeply infiltrated by criminal activities such as money laundering, governmental corruption and organized crime (*Guardian* 2015). It has been estimated that over US$200 billion in illicit funds from China are laundered in Macao each year (Kaiman 2014).

While triad involvement in Macao's casinos has declined, especially since the sector came to be dominated by megaresorts run by US-based firms that forbid triads operating within their walls (*Guardian* 2015), the rapid rise of the hugely lucrative mainland Chinese VIP market has provided organized crime with a new niche in Macao's gambling tourism system. As mentioned, junket organizers are very resourceful in finding ways to give their clients access to gambling funds while in Macao, despite governmental restrictions on bringing cash into the SAR. However, because gambling is illegal in China outside of Macao, junket operators cannot appeal to formal law enforcement authorities and legal mechanisms to force recalcitrant customers to repay their debts. In such cases, triads are engaged to enforce repayment through threats, intimidation and violence. In addition, the gambling sector in Macao is also under threat as a direct or indirect consequence of changes in mainland Chinese governmental culture. Although Chinese visitor numbers continue to increase, their spending has declined since the inauguration of Chinese President Xi Jinping's sweeping anti-corruption measures in mid-2014, which have made government officials wary of conspicuously profligate spending. Casino revenues for the 2015 Chinese New Year holiday season, normally a high point in the year for gambling, were only half of what they were in the previous year (*Guardian* 2015).

Conclusion

The political relations between mainland China and the "other Chinas" discussed in this chapter demonstrate that each is conditioned by history and economics. The common factor in these three cases is a tourism economy that has come to rely on mainland Chinese tourists: a situation which is at times used by Beijing to provide leverage in exercising political influence locally.

The frictions and debates that surround the policy and practice of mainland Chinese tourism to Hong Kong mirror the broader ongoing negotiations and disputes surrounding the sovereignty and uniqueness of Hong Kong as a city, the role of the Hong Kong government in protecting this sovereignty and uniqueness, and the social and cultural values that are at the heart of Hong Kong people's sense of identity. The handover of Hong Kong from the UK to China in 1997 has changed the city in many ways. Losing the status that it had under British rule as a cheap manufacturing centre and uniquely accessible point of entry to Asia for Western nations' financial institutions, companies and tourists, since the 1997 handover nearly all of Hong Kong's manufacturing has moved to the much cheaper and suddenly much more accessible Chinese mainland, and other Chinese cities have become more accessible to trade and tourism. Although certainly not "just another Chinese city," Hong Kong has nonetheless had to discover its role as a "special case" among Chinese cities.

The discourse that accompanies China's rapprochement with Taiwan is characterized by an appeal to shared identity, "common heritage" and "cultural proximity" (Zhang 2013). The development of touristic exchange that has paralleled the political process has at times served to validate such claims, but as tourism has evolved from a mechanism of political reconciliation to a significant economic sector in Taiwan, the nature of the situations within which Taiwanese and mainland Chinese come into contact in the context of tourism appear to increasingly encourage Taiwanese to perceive these tourists as irritating "others" rather than compatriot guests.

The relationship between mainland China and Macao is the least politically charged of the three cases here, but in some ways the most economically charged. Even at the level of non-gambling earnings, mainland Chinese tourists are the cornerstone of Macao's tourism economy, but this income is dwarfed by the immense dividends from gambling, which is nearly completely dependent on Chinese VIP tourists. Moreover, this economy has been fed in large part by demand and a supply of cash generated by government corruption and facilitated by organized crime. Perhaps Xi Jinping's current crackdown on governmental impropriety will provide impetus for Macao, like Las Vegas three decades earlier, to speed its transition from the "shadow side" of a burgeoning economy to a more diversified destination.

In a study of how local Taiwanese people's views of mainland Chinese were affected by the first trickle of tourists allowed by the Mini Three Links Agreement, Chen (2010) found that experiences from interpersonal contact played more of a role in forming people's opinions than broad political realities, and that people's opinions on tourism could be affected positively without having any influence – positive or negative – on their opinion on reunification. What binds together the various "Chinas" examined here must be understood not only in political terms, but also in cultural, social and indeed economic terms. The three cases discussed in this chapter serve to illuminate the different collusive, mutually antagonistic or ambivalent ways in which the relationships between these different facets are playing out in the realm of tourism.

Key reading

Chen, C.M. (2010) 'Role of tourism in connecting Taiwan and China: Assessing tourists' perceptions of the Kinmen–Xiamen links,' *Tourism Management*, 31(3): 421–424.

Liu, A. and McKercher, B. (2014) 'The impact of visa liberalization on tourist behaviors: The case of China outbound market visiting Hong Kong,' *Journal of Travel Research*, DOI:10.1177/0047287514564599.

Zhang, C., Decosta, P.L.E. and McKercher, B. (2015) 'Politics and tourism promotion: Hong Kong's myth making,' *Annals of Tourism Research*, 54: 156–171.

References

BBC (2014) 'Taiwan: Chinese tourists flock to see elections,' BBC, 25 November. Online. Available: www.bbc.com/news/blogs-news-from-elsewhere-30194773 (accessed 12 August 2015).

Chen, C.M. (2010) 'Role of tourism in connecting Taiwan and China: Assessing tourists' perceptions of the Kinmen–Xiamen links,' *Tourism Management*, 31(3): 421–424.

Chun, A. (1996) 'Discourses of identity in the changing spaces of public culture in Taiwan, Hong Kong and Singapore,' *Theory, Culture & Society*, 13(51): 51–75.

—— (2000) *Unstructuring Chinese Society: The Fictions of Colonial Practice and the Changing Realities of 'Land' in the New Territories of Hong Kong*. Reading: Harwood Academic Publishers.

Chung, J. (2013) 'Tourism industry asks government to help fix issues,' *Taipei Times*, 21 January. Online. Available: www.taipeitimes.com/News/taiwan/archives/2013/01/21/2003553060/2 (accessed 12 August 2015).

Cohen, M. (2015) 'Risky business: Revenue slump highlights Macau's reliance on mainland China visitors,' *Forbes*. Online. Available: www.forbes.com/sites/muhammadcohen/2015/04/24/risky-business-revenue-slump-highlights-macaus-reliance-on-mainland-china-visitors (access 25 September 2015).

Commerce and Economic Development Bureau (2013) *Assessment Report on Hong Kong's Capacity to Receive Tourists*. Hong Kong: Legislative Council. Online. Available: www.legco.gov.hk/yr13-14/english/panels/edev/papers/edevcb1-765-e.pdf (accessed 12 September 2015).

du Cros, H. (2009) 'Emerging issues for cultural tourism in Macau,' *Journal of Current Chinese Affairs*, 38(1): 73–99.

The Economist (2014) 'Why Hong Kong remains vital to China's economy,' *The Economist*, 30 September. Online. Available: www.economist.com/blogs/economist-explains/2014/09/economist-explains-22 (accessed 15 August 2015).

—— (2015) 'Aisles apart', *The Economist*, 21 March. Online. Available: www.economist.com/news/china/21646794-protests-about-mainland-shoppers-reveal-graver-problems-aisles-apart (accessed 15 August 2015).

Flowerdew, J. (2004) 'Identity politics and Hong Kong's return to Chinese sovereignty: Analysing the discourse of Hong Kong's first Chief Executive,' *Journal of Pragmatics*, 36: 1551–1578.

Fong, A. (2010) 'Playing up our international and Chinese advantages,' *The Bulletin: Talking Points*, 13.

Government of Macao: Statistics and Census Service (2015) 'Statistics' [in Chinese]. Online. Available: www.dsec.gov.mo/Statistic.aspx?NodeGuid=7b23463a-d253-4750-bd12-958030df5ccb (accessed 15 August 2015).

Guardian (2015) 'Beijing to limit Hong Kong visits by mainland Chinese,' *Guardian*, 12 April. Online. Available: www.theguardian.com/world/2015/apr/12/beijing-to-limit-hong-kong-visits-by-mainland-chinese (accessed 20 August 2015).

Guo, Y., Kim, S.S., Timothy, D.J. and Wang, K.C. (2006) 'Tourism and reconciliation between mainland China and Taiwan,' *Tourism Management*, 27(5): 997–1005.

Ho, B. (2011) 'Political culture, social movements, and governability in Macao', *Asian Affairs: An American Review*, 38(2): 59–87.

Hombrebueno, C. (2015) 'China limits overseas union pay cash withdrawals,' *Casino News*, 29 September. Online. Available: http://calvinayre.com/2015/09/29/casino/china-limits-overseas-unionpay-cash-withdrawals (accessed 5 October 2015).

Hong Kong Business (2011) 'Three reasons why mainland tourists shop in Hong Kong,' *Hong Kong Business*, 2 September. Online. Available: http://hongkongbusiness.hk/retail/news/three-reasons-why-mainland-tourists-shop-in-hong-kong (accessed 12 August 2015).

Hong Kong's Information Service Department (2014) 'HK has capacity to welcome more tourists,' Online. Available: www.news.gov.hk/en/categories/finance/html/2014/01/20140117_171114.shtml (accessed 12 August 2015).

Hsiao, A. (2015) 'China not sharply cutting tourist numbers: Official,' *Taipei Times*, 14 October. Online. Available: www.taipeitimes.com/News/taiwan/archives/2015/10/14/2003630027 (accessed 12 August 2015).

Jackson, D. (2015) 'Town in Taiwan threatens blockade against mainland tourists,' Online. Available: http://shanghaiist.com/2015/03/20/taiwan-town-threatens-blockade-mainland-tourists.php (accessed 25August 2015).

Jennings, R. (2015) 'Taiwan tests the high-end mainland Chinese tourism market,' *South China Morning Post*, 5 July. Online. Available: www.scmp.com/business/china-business/article/1832782/taiwan-tests-high-end-mainland-chinese-tourism-market (accessed 12 August 2015).

Kaiman, J. (2014) 'Macau is betting on a new kind of Chinese tourism,' *Guardian*, 5 January. Online. Available: www.theguardian.com/business/2014/jan/05/macau-gambling-tourism-money-laundering (accessed 5 August 2015).

Kastner, J. (2011) 'Crash course in political risk for Taiwan's tourism,' *Asia Times*, 19 May. Online. Available: www.atimes.com/atimes/China_Business/ME19Cb01.html (accessed 5 August 2015).

Kim, S.S., Timothy, D.J. and Han, H.C. (2007) 'Tourism and political ideologies: A case of tourism in North Korea,' *Tourism Management*, 28(4): 1031–1043.

LaFraniere, S. (2012) 'Mainland Chinese flock to Hong Kong to give birth,' *New York Times*, 22 February. Online. Available: www.nytimes.com/2012/02/23/world/asia/mainland-chinese-flock-to-hong-kong-to-have-babies.html?_r=0 (accessed 5 August 2015).

Lai, Y.K. and Lam, J. (2015) 'Stop attacking Chinese tourists: Hong Kong leader says protests are threatening city's "hospitable" image as visitor numbers drop,' *South China Morning Post*, 1 September. Online. Available: www.scmp.com/news/hong-kong/economy/article/1854349/hong-kong-localists-are-driving-mainland-chinese-tourists?page=all (accessed 12 August 2015).

Legislative Council Panel on Economic Services. (2006) *2006–07 Business Plan of the Hong Kong Tourism Board*. Online. Available: www.legco.gov.hk/yr05-06/english/panels/es/papers/es0626cb1-1805-5e.pdf (accessed 12 August 2015).

Li, F. and Lin, L. (2015) 'China limits Shenzhen visits to Hong Kong to curb day trips,' *Bloomberg Business*, 13 April. Online. Available: www.bloomberg.com/news/articles/2015-04-13/china-limits-shenzhen-visitors-to-hong-kong-to-curb-day-trippers (accessed 12 August 2015).

Lin, T. and Sung, Y. (1984) 'Tourism and economic diversification in Hong Kong,' *Annals of Tourism Research*, 11(2): 231–247.

Liu, A. and McKercher, B. (2014) 'The impact of visa liberalization on tourist behaviors: The case of China outbound market visiting Hong Kong', *Journal of Travel Research*, DOI:10.1177/0047287514564599.

Liu, F.K. (2011) 'The dynamics of cross-strait relations: Heading for peace or unknown ground?' *Brookings Northeast Asia Commentary*. Online. Available: www.brookings.edu/articles/2011/0719_cross_strait_relations_liu.aspx (accessed 12 August 2015).

Lo Shiu Hing (2005) 'Casino politics, organized crime and the post-colonial state in Macau,' *Journal of Contemporary China*, 14(43): 207–224.

Ma, E. and Fung, A. (1999) 'Re-sinicization, nationalism and the Hong Kong identity,' in C. So and J. Chan (eds), *Press and Politics in Hong Kong: Case studies from 1967 to 1997* (pp. 497–528). Hong Kong: Chinese University Press.

Mathews, G., Ma, E. and Lui, T. (2008) *Hong Kong, China: Learning to Belong to a Nation.* New York: Routledge.

Monaghan, A. (2014) 'China's gambling capital Macau is world's fourth-richest territory,' *Guardian*, 2 July. Online. Available: www.theguardian.com/world/2014/jul/02/macau-china-gambling-capital-fourth-richest-in-world-per-capita (accessed 16 August 2015).

Nip, A. (2014) 'Government urged to consider impact of surging tourism on Hong Kong', *South China Morning Post*. Online. Available: www.scmp.com/news/hong-kong/article/1506926/government-urged-consider-social-impact-visitors (accessed 16 August 2015).

Nip, A. and Chan, T. (2014) 'Annual tourists to Hong Kong could rise to 70 million in three years, commission says,' *South China Morning Post*, 17 January. Online. Available: www.scmp.com/news/hong-kong/article/1407779/visitor-numbers-can-rise-70m-three-years-commission-says?page=all (accessed 26 August 2015).

Pao, J. (2004) 'Recent developments and prospects of Macao's tourism industry,' Monetary Authority of Macao. Online. Available: www.amcm.gov.mo/publication/quarterly/Oct2004/Macao_en.pdf (accessed 12 August 2015).

Peterson, W. (1994) 'Why did they become Christians? Yang Tingjun, Li Jizao and Xu Guangqi,' *Review of Culture*, 2(21): 95–110.

Research Office Legislative Council Secretariat (2014) *Research Brief Issue No. 6: Individual Visit Scheme.* Online. Available: www.legco.gov.hk/research-publications/english/1314rb06-individual-visit-scheme-20140507-e.pdf (accessed 12 August 2015).

Reuters (2016) 'Macau gambling revenue tumbles for second year in row,' Markets, 1 January. Online. Available: www.reuters.com/article/macau-revenues-idUSENNFCO0SJ20160101 (accessed 25 January 2016).

South China Morning Post (2013) 'Anson Chan says Hong Kong must set its own role in developing nation,' *South China Morning Post*, 28 October. Online. Available: www.scmp.com/news/hong-kong/article/1341539/anson-chan-says-hong-kong-must-set-its-own-role-developing-nation?page=all (accessed 1 April 2015).

Taiwan Yearbook (2007) 'Taiwan–China relations.' Online. Available: www.taiwan.gov.tw/ct.asp?xItem=18662&ctNode=1638&mp=9 (accessed 15 August 2015).

Tan, Z.M. (1999) 'Post-handover economic positioning and developmental pathways for Macau,' *Academic Forum*, 137: 7–10.

Tourism Bureau (2010) *Annual Report.* Online. Available: http://admin.taiwan.net.tw/statistics/year_en.aspx?no=15 (accessed 12 August 2015).

—— (2015) *Annual Report.* Online. Available: http://admin.taiwan.net.tw/statistics/year_en.aspx?no=15 (accessed 12 August 2015).

Wall Street Journal (2015) 'Waning Chinese tourist enthusiasm could hurt Hong Kong, Credit Suisse warns,' *Wall Street Journal*, 18 March. Online. Available: http://blogs.wsj.com/chinarealtime/2015/03/18/waning-chinese-tourist-enthusiasm-could-hurt-hong-kong-credit-suisse-warns (accessed 15 August 2015).

Yu, L. (1997) 'Travel between politically divided China and Taiwan,' *Asia Pacific Journal of Tourism Research*, 2(1): 19–30.

Zhang, J. (2013) '"Crossing borders": Cultural-geo-politics of rapprochement tourism between China and Taiwan,' unpublished PhD thesis, Durham University. Online. Available: http://etheses.dur.ac.uk/7368 (accessed 20 August 2015).

Zhang, C., Decosta, P.L.E. and McKercher, B. (2015) 'Politics and tourism promotion: Hong Kong's myth making,' *Annals of Tourism Research*, 54: 156–171.

Zhuang, G.R. (1993) 'Tourism across the Taiwan Straits,' *Tourism Management*, 14(3): 228–231.

Zou, M. (2015) 'Number of mainland Chinese visitors to Hong Kong "falls" over holiday weekend, says Beijing tourism authority,' *South China Morning Post*, 4 May. Online. Available: www.scmp.com/news/china/economy/article/1785606/number-mainland-visitors-hk-falls-over-holiday-weekend-says (accessed 20 August 2015).

25

TOURISM IN MONGOLIA

Dallen J. Timothy

Introduction

Mongolia is a land of mystery, a place that for decades has stimulated the imaginations of astute schoolchildren and history buffs. Mongolia's unique cultures and natural landscapes have long wielded considerable appeal among outsiders and drawn in explorers and travel writers (Montagu 1957). Nomadic herders, their dwellings and animals against a backdrop of dramatic steppe grasslands and deserts have created an inseparable natural and anthropic landscape unlike any other. Mongolia's landscape engendered many of the legends and stories associated with the reign of Genghis Khan (Chinggis Khan) and was the hearth from which the massive Mongol Empire spread.

Images of this enigmatic place were etched into the minds of baby boomers and Generation X through *National Geographic* articles, motion pictures and documentaries shown in school. Likewise, travel writing in the nineteenth and twentieth centuries extolled the virgin landscapes of Mongolia, effectively congealing the mystique of this inimitable place by emphasizing the improbable reality that such traditional nomadism could still exist in the modern world (Tavares & Brosseau 2006). In the Western mind, the country is an imaginary land of mystery, isolation and tradition. Stewart's (2012: n.p.) personal account of visiting Mongolia captures well the country's prevailing mystique and extraordinary aura:

> Mongolia shaped my life years before I set foot in the country…Mongolia was the journey that I had always wanted to make…[It] was a rare place—virtually the last place—where nomadic life still thrived….I saw the journey as a matter of loyalty to my 12-year-old self. This is the journey he had dreamed of making: by horse in a virgin landscape. Other destinations came and went, but the dream of Mongolia persisted…Childhood dreams can be dangerous things. But Mongolia was everything I had hoped.

Today, Mongolia is an emerging tourist destination with many hopes for development. However, with all its successes and strides to overcome its difficult past, it faces considerable challenges in its efforts to develop tourism, more so than many other Asian countries.

The country's past century has been tumultuous to say the least. However, in 1990, together with the tides of change occurring in many other communist states, change also came to Mongolia. Since the onset of democratic reforms in the 1990s there have been many political, economic and development advancements. Tourism has grown and remained steady, spurred by the romanticism of the idyllic Mongolian landscapes described above, and is now one of the most salient sectors of the country's economy. This chapter describes tourism in Mongolia under the communist regime, its current demand and supply trends, and issues surrounding the industry in a nation that was until the 1990s almost entirely off-limits to Westerners.

Tourism in modern Mongolia

In 1924, following its Soviet-backed independence from China, Mongolia became a satellite state with strong military, political and trade connections with the USSR. This alliance introduced a strict form of communism that suppressed many personal freedoms, emphasized development through heavy industry, collectivized herding and agriculture, prompted urban growth as nomads were enticed into towns and cities to work in manufacturing and kept national borders closed to most Mongolians and foreigners.

In the late 1930s, many of Mongolia's elites, educated classes, nationalists, ethnic minorities and Buddhist priests were executed on Stalin's orders during the Great Repression, or the 'purge'. Buddhism was especially hard hit. In 1934, religious teaching was outlawed, and children were prohibited from entering monasteries. The Soviet-led purge destroyed most of the country's 800 monasteries and took the lives of upwards of 17,000–18,000 Buddhist priests (Kaplonski 2004). In total, 4–5 percent of Mongolia's population was slaughtered. The Great Repression destroyed much of what was idyllic about the country, particularly its colorful religious heritage.

Following Stalin's death in 1953, the socialist system relaxed somewhat, and in the 1970s Mongolia became an increasingly attractive tourist destination for the privileged elites of the USSR and socialist states of Europe (Hall 2001). With the Soviet-inspired growth of cities and towns, urban-to-rural domestic tourism began to gain a foothold and, in common with other communist states, party-sponsored holidays were provided and encouraged in the countryside as a way of maintaining good health and loyalty to the Mongolian People's Party. Domestic tourism overwhelmingly focused on holiday camps for urban workers' groups and youth organizations, although even nomadic herders vacationed with their collectives at holiday camps (Dorjsuren 2009). These served to unite the country's citizens and instruct them in the dogma of the party.

Beginning in the late 1950s, relations with China improved, increasing initial cross-border travel between the two neighboring countries. Other communist countries began to encourage inbound tourism in the 1970s and 1980s as a means of earning hard currency (Hall 2001). However, Mongolia's hardline leadership continued to downplay international tourism until the late 1980s when Gorbachev's *perestroika* and *glasnost* policies spread to the satellite state as well. These principles of openness and limited freedom ushered in a new era of self-determination, which in 1990 resulted in public demonstrations in Ulaanbaatar and other towns in support of political reforms and the country's first democratic elections the same year (Pomfret 2000). In 1992, the Mongolian People's Republic ceased to exist, being replaced by a multi-party democracy and market economy.

These momentous changes had profound implications for tourism. Mongolia, which had essentially been off-limits to most of the world's population, opened its doors for tourism in 1992, and private enterprise was allowed and encouraged (Hall 2001). Tourism was identified early as a potentially powerful tool for economic development. However, the fledgling government, without its long-time support from the USSR, had no resources for marketing itself abroad, developing the needed tourism infrastructure or training human resources (Rossabi 2005). Marketing and development efforts were left to the mercy of the newly embraced free market. Mongolia has seen substantial increases in tourist arrivals since the turn of the new millennium, but its relative isolation, lack of widespread overseas promotion and underdeveloped infrastructure continue to see international arrivals lower than the tourism industry hopes to achieve.

Demand for Mongolian tourism

As already noted, tourism in Mongolia has grown a great deal since its multi-party and capitalist transition in 1990–1992 (Aramand 2013; Yu & Goulden 2006). In 1988, international tourist arrivals primarily from other communist states numbered approximately 240,000. The collapse of state socialism in the USSR and Central and Eastern Europe in 1990–1991 severely affected Mongolia's tourism. Tumultuous politics and its economic uncertainties, as well as the democratic protests and free elections in Mongolia in 1990, saw a dramatic drop in arrivals to 150,000 in 1990. This volatile climate prevailed throughout much of the 1990s with only 71,000 foreign arrivals being recorded in 1996 and 55,000 in 1997. However, in 1998 foreign arrivals peaked at 165,000, declining again in the following two years, followed by an upsurge to 229,000 in 2002, only to be affected in 2003 by the SARS outbreak in Asia. Growth in arrivals since 2004 has been reasonably steady (see Table 25.1), with the exception of modest declines in 2007–2009 due to the global economic crisis.

In 2014, tourism was estimated to have supported 16,400 jobs directly in tourism and 33,600 jobs in total, or about 2.8 percent of total employment. Tourism amounted to approximately US$200 million the same year in direct spending and US$400 million in indirect and induced

Table 25.1 Tourist arrivals in Mongolia by country of origin, 2005–2013

Country	2005	2006	2007	2008	2009	2010	2011	2012	2013
China	170,345	178,941	211,007	196,832	229,451	193,730	200,010	228,547	n/a
Russia	57,926	79,163	98,759	109,975	108,105	121,647	102,738	83,707	n/a
South Korea	30,787	39,930	43,930	43,396	38,273	42,231	43,994	44,360	n/a
Japan	12,952	16,707	17,238	14,939	11,401	14,140	14,988	17,119	n/a
United States	10,153	11,377	12,223	12,474	11,344	12,808	15,423	15,587	n/a
Germany	8,168	8,576	8,250	8,027	6,867	8,095	8,545	8,909	n/a
France	5,822	5,237	6,341	6,688	6,706	7,527	7,570	7,553	n/a
United Kingdom	5,206	5,893	6,717	6,781	5,872	6,209	7,120	6,804	n/a
Kazakhstan	3,928	4,185	4,882	5,473	5,053	5,757	7,973	10,523	n/a
Australia	3,454	4,053	4,502	4,466	3,725	5,443	7,093	7,480	n/a
Canada	2,300	2,528	2,422	2,645	2,259	2,864	3,173	2,828	n/a
Sweden	1,926	1,509	2,112	1,894	1,665	1,625	1,463	1,407	n/a
Other	25,748	27,890	33,405	32,856	62,115	34,014	40,270	41,068	n/a
Total	338,715	385,989	451,788	446,446	433,136	456,360	460,360	475,892	418,000

Sources: National Statistical Office (2015); World Bank (2015).

spending. Expected growth for the near future has been forecasted at about 4–6 percent per year in visitor arrivals and expenditures (World Travel & Tourism Council (WTTC) 2015).

Despite Mongolia's democratic transition, the country is still closely linked to Russia in many ways, including tourism. China is Mongolia's largest trading partner, followed by Russia, including tourism as an export commodity. With improved Sino-Mongolian relations in the late 1980s and 1990s, there has been an upsurge in cross-border travel between the two countries. Since 1990, China has surpassed Russia as Mongolia's main tourist market source, although Russia remains the second largest market.

Other countries are also important sources of tourists, for example South Korea (Republic of Korea, or ROK). While there are documented ethnic connections between Koreans and Mongolians, ROK's prominence as a source country derives largely from the high number of Mongolian laborers in the ROK, the rising popularity of Korean culture in Mongolia and the fact that the ROK is Mongolia's third largest trading partner (Campi 2012). The Mongolian diaspora in the ROK is the largest Mongolian population outside the homeland. In the late 1990s, the ROK opened its doors to Mongolian low-wage laborers, and today estimates suggest there are approximately 40,000 legal Mongolian resident-workers in ROK and thousands of illegal migrants (Campi 2012). Increasing trade and commerce, including sizable investments in tourism services (e.g. hotels), by Korean groups and the mounting popularity of Korean culture (e.g. soap operas and music), known as the 'Korean wave' (Timothy & Kim 2015), have resulted in an impressive Korean market growth.

Aside from other, more generic tourist purposes, Mongolia is also a burgeoning destination for business travel (Buckley 2010). Since the collapse of communism and the country's overdependence on Russia, Mongolia has turned toward its Asian neighbors for increasing trade and tourism. In 2012, 47.5 percent of total foreign arrivals came for official and work purposes (National Statistical Office 2015). Koreans and Chinese account for the majority of this business traffic; much of the country's business travel is related to mining, manufacturing and infrastructure development.

Domestic travel is an important part of tourism and focuses overwhelmingly on rural experiences. Although they have lost their socialist philosophical mandates, holiday camps in the form of ger (yurt) compounds are extremely popular among the increasingly affluent urban population, and they mingle freely with foreign tourists at these camps. Visiting friends and relatives (VFR) is a critical element of domestic tourism, as many urbanites still have relatives who remain in the countryside to tend their animals. Since the re-establishment of religious freedom in 1990, pilgrimages to the few remaining famous monasteries that were not destroyed in the purge have also become fashionable (Dorjsuren 2009).

Tourism resources

Living culture and natural landscapes are both important resources for Mongolian tourism. However, as mentioned earlier, it is the exceptional harmonization of the two heritage realms that underlies most of the country's tourist appeal (Buckley 2010; Buckley *et al.* 2008; Lew *et al.* 2015; Sanjmyatav *et al.* 2012), in much the same way remote and fabled places such as Tibet, Bhutan and Greenland appeal to outsiders.

Mongolia's physical geography comprises high mountains, deserts and steppes. It is home to more than 38 national parks and nature preserves, and approximately 85 percent of the country is grasslands (Buckley 2010). These natural resources have played a major role in the country's tourism development strategy (Saffery 2000). The Uvs Nuur Basin straddling the Mongolia–Russia border was inscribed on UNESCO's World Heritage List in 2003 for its extraordinary natural landscapes that typify Mongolia's topographic diversity. Similarly, noteworthy paleontological discoveries have created a distinctive element of nature-based tourism (Laws & Scott 2003; Lew *et al.* 2015).

The cultural heritage of Mongolia is equally noteworthy. While most of the citizenry are Mongolic, there are Kazakh (4 percent of the national population) and other minorities in the western part of the country who, like their Mongolic compatriots, practice traditional transhumance and nomadism. Today, between one-quarter and one-third of Mongolia's population is nomadic, living in family groups in gers in the countryside. Their livelihoods and diets are based almost entirely on sheep, camels, goats, yaks and horses. The nomadic history of Mongolia has meant that, unlike many other parts of Asia, built heritage is overall lacking from the cultural landscape (Timothy *et al.* 2009). Exceptions to this are the living monasteries, monastery ruins from the purge and a modest number of archaeological sites, such as the ancient capital of Karakorum. The Orkhon Valley Cultural Landscape and the Petroglyphic Complexes of the Mongolian Altai are the nation's two designated cultural World Heritage Sites.

Perhaps more important than the built environment in the Mongolian context is the living, intangible heritage, which UNESCO has also recognised as being worthy of global distinction (Timothy *et al.* 2009). The popularity of Kazakh falconry led to the establishment of a falconry festival (Soma & Sukhee 2014) and is listed by UNESCO as an Intangible World Heritage (IWH). Eleven additional elements of intangible heritage have been inscribed. These elements of living culture have their roots in the country's nomadic society and revolve around singing, musical instruments, games, craftsmanship, traditional sport, dance and epic stories. The most iconic intangible heritage element and IWH is the Naadam festival, which Case study 25.1 describes in more detail.

Case study 25.1 The Naadam festival

Naadam, or the festival of three manly sports, has a centuries-old tradition in Mongolia and focuses on three ancient nomadic sports—wrestling, horseracing and archery—and games associated with the reign of Genghis Khan. These three sports demonstrate 'manly' courage, strength and endurance as exhibited by traditional herders and warriors, and celebrate good health and prosperity. Each summer, the three-day games are celebrated at the national level in Ulaanbaatar and in towns and villages throughout the country. The event typically corresponds with the July National Holiday, which commemorates Mongolia's independence from China in 1921, and attracts thousands of city dwellers and rural herders to observe and participate. Naadam gives practicing nomads an opportunity to come together each year to renew acquaintances and make new friends, urban residents a chance to return to their nomadic roots and Mongolians of the diaspora an excuse to return to the homeland.

Traditionally, game participation was limited to men, but recent years have seen the inclusion of women in the archery and horseback portions of the games. The first two days are generally devoted to opening ceremonies and sports, with the final day having a more relaxed atmosphere focused largely on relationship building, eating and drinking. The opening ceremonies include much more than sport; they are also demonstrations of traditional music, dance and religion, with monks, 'warriors' and athletes donning traditional clothing and weaponry providing the inaugural entertainment. Naadam is the country's most celebrated event, and the winners in Ulaanbaatar are regarded as national celebrities.

Naadam has become an important attraction for foreign tourists and is widely promoted by Mongolia's tourism officials as representative of authentic Mongolian culture. Many package tours are planned to correspond with the summer celebration, and the fête features prominently in organized tours that also take in natural and cultural elements of the country. International tourists attending the competition appreciate most its authenticity, uniqueness and representativeness of national culture, and they enjoy the opening ceremony, horsemanship and wrestling above all other elements of the celebration. For most foreigners, Naadam represents much of what it means to visit Mongolia, and the overall cultural experience weighs much heavier than does the element of the sport itself. For Mongolians, it is foundational to their national identity and represents what it means to be Mongolian.

Sources: O'Gorman & Thompson 2007; Schofield & Thompson 2007; Thompson & Matheson 2008; Thompson & Schofield 2009; Timothy et al. 2009

To appreciate the simultaneity of culture and nature in the landscape, the most common tourist activities in the country are horseback riding and staying in a ger. Ger camps developed rapidly in the 1990s and early 2000s with the privatization of lands and herds. There are currently hundreds of ger camps and ger resorts scattered throughout Mongolia, with their isolation and authentic design providing most of their appeal (Dorjsuren 2009; Karthe *et al.* 2013; Timothy & Teye 2009). There, tourists can stay in a traditional ger, eat local foods, participate in traditional music and sport and trek by horseback. Increasing numbers of equestrian adventure companies are materializing as entrepreneurs begin to realize the potential of profitability of using their horses, herds and homes for tourism services (Ollenburg 2006).

Issues and challenges

Despite the unmistakable allure of Mongolia, the country faces several challenges as its tourism industry continues to mature. Many issues derive from its communist legacy and former association with the USSR. Hall (2001: 98–99) explained several ways in which tourism changed, or was utilised, in post-communist societies, including Mongolia. Of particular interest among these are encouraging international investments in tourism services, infrastructure development and enlarging human resource skills for the tourism sector.

At the time of writing there were many hotels in the country, but only a handful of international starred hotels in Ulaanbaatar. There were no international-standard hotels in regional centers, with the exception of a few ger resorts. Most tours of Mongolia spend only a couple of days in Ulaanbaatar. Thus, the capital's hotels are used primarily for short stays and business travel. As Mongolia is still considered an allocentric destination, most tourist bed-nights are spent in the countryside in gers and tents (Karthe *et al.* 2013).

The three international lodging brands represented in Ulaanbaatar in 2015 are Ramada, Kempinski and Shangri La. The Ulaanbaatar Shangri La will open on June 3, 2015. Negotiations have been ongoing for years with investors for a Hilton, but this has yet to come to fruition. Investments from other Asian countries, mainly South Korea, the People's Republic of China and Taiwan, have been crucial in developing other lodging facilities in the capital and regional centers (Cheng 2008).

One of the country's main concerns is its relative isolation from existing and potential markets. Besides land border crossings, Chinggis Khaan International Airport is the country's only international gateway, with limited air services to Beijing, Berlin, Hong Kong, Istanbul,

Moscow, Seoul and Tokyo on only five international carriers. The time and cost associated with getting to Mongolia add to its functional distance from main markets and it is widely considered a 'long-haul' destination (Mwaura *et al.* 2013). Funded by loans from Japan, construction on a new international airport near Ulaanbaatar started in 2013 and is planned for completion in 2017, with a higher passenger and aircraft capacity (Cheng 2008).

Adding to the country's relative isolation is an insufficient infrastructure. This, more than any other tourism challenge, has plagued Mongolia since 1992 owing to limited funds, harsh environments and government bureaucracy. Only a small percentage of the country's roads are paved, requiring most tours to be offered in small groups using four-wheel-drive vehicles. While this has some benefits, such as keeping the countryside pristine and limiting mass tourism development, it is a salient concern of the Ministry of Nature, Environment and Tourism in its regional development efforts. In recent years, however, foreign investments in road construction have improved the situation noticeably. The prominence of unsurfaced roads and resultant lengthy travel times necessarily restrict the places tourists can visit. Internal air travel is also complicated, as almost all flights between provincial and district capitals must connect through Ulaanbaatar (Timothy *et al.* 2009).

Long-term infrastructure plans have included a multi-lane, 1,000km highway leading from the border of China at Zamiin Üüd to the border of Russia at Altanbulag, via Ulaanbaatar—the busiest travel and trade route. As of 2015, the highway was not completed, and funding was still being sought from other Asian sources. Besides roadworks, additional railway lines have been planned to increase trade and tourism throughout Asia (Cheng 2008). The Trans-Mongolian Railway was built between 1949 and 1955 and connected with the Trans-Siberian Railway in the USSR. During the 1970s and 1980s, one of the only ways Western tourists were permitted to visit Mongolia was in transit from the Soviet Union to Beijing, China, on this famous train, stopping briefly in Ulaanbaatar. Today, there is a desperate need for additional rail lines.

As with other countries under the former influence of the Soviet Union, human resources and skills shortages plague the tourism industry of Mongolia (Baum & Thompson 2007). Labor costs are still low, but skills are low too. With support from the national government, several tourism educational programs have been developed at universities throughout the country, although the National University of Mongolia has had a tourism training program since the late 1990s. Such endeavours are important, for since the privatization of grazing lands and livestock in the early 1990s, many herders have begun supplementing their meager incomes through tourism enterprises much the same way as has been done by farmers and ranchers in the Western world for years in agritourism operations and farmstays. To encourage greater public participation in the benefits of tourism, nomadic entrepreneurs desperately need guidance and training to be able to get the most benefit from their rural enterprises while maintaining their traditional livelihoods and harmony with nature.

Fifteen years ago Saffery (2000) noted that tourism had already grown too quickly for adequate planning and policies to be implemented. This is an endemic problem in transitioning economies everywhere (Hall 2001). While one of the goals of the Ministry of Nature, Environment and Tourism is to implement sustainability practices, the country faces difficulties in leading with community-based directives that so often accompany international funding. This stems largely from the top-down socialist model Mongolia is just now recovering from, resulting in people not appreciating their grassroots role in tourism development (Nault & Stapleton 2011), their own entrepreneurial abilities and the simple fact that their nomadic lifestyles are sometimes difficult to reconcile with the stability needs of tourism.

Chinese and Russian tourists will continue to dominate the market owing to their geographic proximity, upwardly mobile middle classes and historical connections with Mongolia. Also,

Koreans will continue to be a large market owing to their ethnic, diasporic and commercial connections. Mongolia's curiosity factor will also continue drawing Americans, Canadians, Europeans and Australians, but Mongolia is striving to reach new markets which, it hopes, will be aided by a vastly improved infrastructure. In the past few years, new markets, including India, Taiwan, Ukraine and Indonesia, have been identified as important for Mongolian tourism.

Conclusion

During the state communist era, tourism in Mongolia was characterized by domestic travel by party members, workers' cooperatives and youth groups. Most international arrivals came from the Soviet Union and the communist states of Central and Eastern Europe. With the collapse of state socialism in 1990–1992, however, Mongolia, one of the last vestiges of unexplored *terra nova* for tourism, opened its doors to the outside world. This allowed adventurous tourists to explore a mystic land of legends and exceptional landscapes, where being among the earliest to conquer or collect this latecomer to tourism was a coveted accolade (Timothy 1998).

Breathtaking natural landscapes overlaid with nomadic encampments form the core of Mongolia's charm. Living culture is paramount in the heritage milieu, followed by a sparse built urban environment, much of which is of recent vintage. The country's tourism markets are well defined, although new markets are beginning to emerge, which national leaders hope will continue to be stimulated by a larger airport, better roads and the addition of international hotel chains.

While Mongolia faces many of the same challenges other transitioning and isolated nations face—including an overdependence on foreign investments; deficiencies in infrastructure, tourism skills and training, and appropriate planning; and a limited market—it also has many opportunities for the future. New efforts are being made to expand supply and demand, such as: the country's collaborative efforts to develop the Silk Road as a multi-nation, pan-Central Asian cultural resource (Timothy & Boyd 2015); expanding its market beyond East Asia through infrastructure development and increased promotional efforts; and extending visa exemptions.

Mongolia's own heritage identity, separately from its former masters of Russia and China, is now strong. Its people have once again embraced Buddhism, and pilgrimage tourism is growing. Mongolians demonstrate their own national consciousness through sport, events and festivals, ger stays, horse riding and appreciating their own intangible inheritance. Many ancient traditions, some of which had been suppressed by the Soviets (including the original Mongolian alphabet, which was replaced by Cyrillic in 1941), are being resurrected, honoured, protected and promoted. These are a great source of pride for the Mongolian people, something they seek in their domestic experiences and desire to share with their international guests.

Key reading

Dorjsuren, A. (2009) 'From community to holiday camps: The emergence of a tourist economy in Mongolia', in S. Singh (ed.), *Domestic Tourism in Asia: Diversity and Divergence* (pp. 107–128). London: Earthscan.

Rossabi, M. (2005) *Modern Mongolia: From Khans to Commissars to Capitalists*. Berkeley: University of California Press.

Timothy, D.J., Wu, B. and Luvsandavaajav, O. (2009) 'Heritage and tourism in East Asia's developing nations: Communist-socialist legacies and diverse cultural landscapes', in D.J. Timothy and G.P. Nyaupane (eds), *Cultural Heritage and Tourism in the Developing World: A Regional Perspective* (pp. 93–108). London: Routledge.

Relevant websites

Ministry of Nature, Environment and Tourism: www.mongoliatourism.org
Mongolian Tourism Association: www.travelmongolia.org
Visit Mongolia: www.visitmongolia.com/index_1.html

References

Aramand, M. (2013) 'Women entrepreneurs in Mongolia: The role of culture on entrepreneurial motivation', *Equality, Diversity and Inclusion*, 32(1): 68–82.

Baum, T. and Thompson, K. (2007) 'Skills and labour markets in transition: A tourism skills inventory of Kyrgyzstan, Mongolia and Uzbekistan', *Asia Pacific Journal of Human Resources*, 45(2): 235–255.

Buckley, R. (2010) *Conservation Tourism*. Wallingford: CABI.

Buckley, R., Ollenburg, C. and Zhong, L. (2008) 'Cultural landscape in Mongolian tourism', *Annals of Tourism Research*, 35(1): 47–61.

Campi, A. (2012) 'Expanding prospects for ROK–Mongolian relations: The view from Ulaanbaatar', *Korea Compass*, December: 1–6.

Cheng, G. (2008) 'A brief discussion on Mongolia's tourism development', *Journal on the Mongolian and Tibetan Current Situation*, 17(5): 1–21.

Dorjsuren, A. (2009) 'From community to holiday camps: The emergence of a tourist economy in Mongolia', in S. Singh (ed.), *Domestic Tourism in Asia: Diversity and Divergence* (pp. 107–128). London: Earthscan.

Hall, D.R. (2001) 'Tourism and development in communist and post-communist societies', in D. Harrison (ed.), *Tourism and the Less Developed World: Issues and Case Studies* (pp. 91–108). Wallingford: CABI.

Kaplonski, C. (2004) *Truth, History and Politics in Mongolia: The Memories of Heroes*. London: Routledge.

Karthe, D., Londong, J., Reeh, T. and Hufert, F. (2013) 'Wassermanagement in mongolischen Tourist Ger Camps: Eine interdisziplinäre Aufgabe', *Zeitschrift für Tourismuswissenschaft*, 5(2): 215–221.

Laws, E. and Scott, N. (2003) 'Developing new tourism services: Dinosaurs, a new drive tourism resource for remote regions?', *Journal of Vacation Marketing*, 9(4): 368–380.

Lew, A.A., Hall, C.M. and Timothy, D.J. (2015) *World Regional Geography: Human Mobilities, Tourism Destinations, Sustainable Environments*, 2nd edn. Dubuque, IA: Kendall Hunt.

Montagu, I. (1957) 'A recent visit to Mongolia', *Journal of the Royal Central Asian Society*, 44(1): 6–16.

Mwaura, D., Acguaye, D. and Jargal, S. (2013) 'Marketing implications of the destination image of Mongolia', *Worldwide Hospitality and Tourism Themes*, 5(1): 80–91.

National Statistical Office (2015) 'Tourism: Inbound and outbound passengers'. Online. Available: http:// en.nso.mn (accessed 3 April 2015).

Nault, S. and Stapleton, P. (2011) 'The community participation process in ecotourism development: A case study of the community of Sogoog, Bayan-Ulgii, Mongolia', *Journal of Sustainable Tourism*, 19(6): 695–712.

O'Gorman, K. and Thompson, K. (2007) 'Tourism and culture in Mongolia: The case of the Ulaanbaatar Nadaam', in R. Butler and T. Hinch (eds), *Tourism and Indigenous Peoples: Issues and Implications* (pp. 161–175). Oxford: Butterworth-Heinemann.

Ollenburg, C. (2006) 'Horse riding', in R. Buckley (ed.), *Adventure Tourism* (pp. 305–323). Wallingford: CABI.

Pomfret, R. (2000) 'Transition and democracy in Mongolia', *Europe–Asia Studies*, 52(1): 149–160.

Rossabi, M. (2005) *Modern Mongolia: From Khans to Commissars to Capitalists*. Berkeley: University of California Press.

Saffery, A. (2000) 'Mongolia's tourism development race: Case study from the Gobi Gurvansaikhan National Park', in P.M. Godde, M.F. Price and F.M. Zimmermann (eds), *Tourism and Development in Mountain Regions* (pp. 255–274). Wallingford: CABI.

Sanjmyatav, G., Sumdangdej, K. and Khamkhong, S. (2012) 'Development and management model for cultural tourism in Mongolia based on the model in Thailand', *European Journal of Social Sciences*, 35(1): 32–38.

Schofield, P. and Thompson, K. (2007) 'Visitor motivation, satisfaction and behavioural intention: The 2005 Naadam Festival, Ulaanbaatar', *International Journal of Tourism Research*, 9(5): 329–344.

Soma, T. and Sukhee, B. (2014) 'Altai Kazakh falconry as "heritage tourism": The Golden Eagle Festivals of western Mongolia', *International Journal of Intangible Heritage*, 9: 135–147.

Stewart, S. (2012) 'Steppe by steppe in Mongolia', *National Geographic Traveler*, November. Online. Available: http://travel.nationalgeographic.com/travel/countries/mongolia/altay-hentiy-stanley-stewart-traveler (accessed 1 April 2013).

Tavares, D. and Brosseau, M. (2006) 'The representation of Mongolia in contemporary travel writing: Imaginative geographies of a travellers' frontier', *Social & Cultural Geography*, 7(2): 299–317.

Thompson, K. and Matheson, C.M. (2008) 'Culture, authenticity and sport: A study of event motivations at the Ulaanbaatar Naadam Festival, Mongolia', in J. Cochrane (ed.) *Asian Tourism: Growth and Change* (pp. 233–243), Oxford: Elsevier.

Thompson, K. and Schofield, P. (2009) 'Segmenting and profiling visitors to the Ulaanbaatar Naadam festival by motivation', *Event Management*, 13(1): 1–15.

Timothy, D.J. (1998) 'Collecting places: Geodetic lines in tourist space', *Journal of Travel and Tourism Marketing*, 7(4): 123–129.

Timothy, D.J. and Boyd, S.W. (2015) *Tourism and Trails: Cultural, Ecological and Management Issues*. Bristol: Channel View Publications.

Timothy, D.J. and Kim, S.S. (2015) 'Understanding the tourism relationships between South Korea and China: A review of influential factors', *Current Issues in Tourism*, 18(5): 413–432.

Timothy, D.J. and Teye, V.B. (2009) *Tourism and the Lodging Sector*. Oxford: Butterworth Heinemann.

Timothy, D.J., Wu, B. and Luvsandavaajav, O. (2009) 'Heritage and tourism in East Asia's developing nations: Communist-socialist legacies and diverse cultural landscapes', in D.J. Timothy and G.P. Nyaupane (eds), *Cultural Heritage and Tourism in the Developing World: A Regional Perspective* (pp. 93–108). London: Routledge.

World Bank (2015) 'International tourism, number of arrivals'. Online. Available: http://data.worldbank.org/indicator/ST.INT.ARVL (accessed 20 April 2015).

World Travel and Tourism Council (WTTC) (2015) *Travel and Tourism Economic Impact: Mongolia 2015*. London: WTTC.

Yu, L. and Goulden, M. (2006) 'A comparative analysis of international tourists' satisfaction in Mongolia', *Tourism Management*, 27(6): 1331–1342.

26

TOURISM IN SOUTH AND NORTH KOREA

Timothy Jeonglyeol Lee

Overview of the South Korean tourism industry

The Republic of Korea (South Korea) has a population of 51 million people and is one of the most industrialized countries in Asia. It is often called the "second Japan". South Korea's GDP soared at an average of 10% annually in a period called the "Miracle on the Han River" that rapidly and successfully transformed it into a high-income advanced economy and the world's 11th largest economy by 1995. South Korea is presently the world's fifth largest exporter and seventh largest importer, and a G-20 and OECD member. Since the first free election in 1987, South Koreans have enjoyed high levels of civil liberty. Its popular culture has considerable influence in Asia, and is expanding globally as a phenomenon often called the "Korean Wave". South Korea is East Asia's most developed country in the Human Development Index. Driven by high-tech *chaebols* such as Samsung, the world's largest technology company, Hyundai-Kia and LG, South Korea has one of the highest levels of research and development spending per unit of GDP (Choi & Ahn 2014).

South Korea had more than 12 million international arrivals in 2013, a 9.3% growth compared to the previous year. The number of foreigners visiting Korea, which only amounted to 11,109 in 1961, has therefore achieved rapid growth since. After the International Tourism Corporation (currently called the Korea Tourism Organization (KTO)) was established in 1962, one million foreign visitors arrived in Korea in 1978 as the tourism industry was promoted as an international strategic business. Thereafter, there were over two million visitors in 1988, eight million visitors in 2010, nine million visitors in 2011 and ten million visitors in 2012 (KTO 2014).

If the decline of tourism due to major negative events such as domestic political instability, including the Gwangju Democratization Movement in 1980, the September 11 US terror attack in 2001, the Iraq War in 2003 and the outbreak of SARS are excluded, inbound tourism in Korea has seen continuous growth. The number of foreign visitors to Korea grew for the ten consecutive years following the SARS epidemic. Owing to the attraction of shopping tourism and the spread of Korean culture after the weakening of the Korean won in 2008, there was a record growth of more than 10% for four consecutive years from 2009 (KTO 2014).

The income from tourism had grown consecutively for seven years since 2007 (KTO 2014). Until 2007, the income from tourism remained at US$5–6 billion; however, as the currency became attractive following the weakening of the Korean won, in 2008 there was a rapid increase of shopping tourists resulting in the increase of income from tourism to US$9 billion. In 2010 and 2012, the total income from tourism was US$10.3 billion and US$13.4 billion, respectively; and in 2013 there was a record income of US$14.1 billion, a 5.8% increase compared with the previous year.

The number of outbound travelers has increased 1,300 times, from 11,245 travelers in 1961 to 14,846,485 travelers in 2013 (KTO 2014). Due to consumer sentiment following the SARS epidemic and the weakening of the Korean won, the number of outbound travelers from Korea decreased in 2003, 2008 and 2009; however, it increased in all other years. In the years following 1995, the number of outbound travelers surpassed the number of inbound foreign visitors. Following the liberalization measures on international travel in 1989, the number of outbound travelers increased from one million to five million in 2000 and ten million in 2005. The number of outbound travelers first exceeded the number of inbound foreign visitors in 1995 (Choi & Ahn 2014).

Tourism expenditures also increased again after 2010. Excluding the decline in 2003 due to the SARS epidemic, tourism expenditure showed an annual increase of over 10% until 2007; however, after the weakening of the Korean won in 2008 there was a two-year decrease in tourism expenditures. With the restoration of demand for overseas travel in 2010, expenditure has increased again, and in 2011 the growth trend resulted in an increase of 8.8% compared with the previous year. The tourism expenditure of 2013 recorded an increase of 7.8% compared with the previous year, up to US$17.8 billion due to the increase in consumption by domestic overseas tourists resulting from the increase of outbound travelers and the strengthening of the Korean won in respect to the US dollar and Japanese yen. Average consumption per capita was US$1,197 (Choi & Ahn 2014).

Trend of foreigners visiting Korea

There was a record 12,175,550 international visitor arrivals in 2013. Despite the rapid decline of Japanese visitors, the 9.3% increase in the number of foreign visitors was achieved due to increased numbers from China and Southeast Asia (Tables 26.1 and 26.2). Overall, arrivals from Asia are the mainstay of the tourism economy and showed increases of 13.6% in 2011, 16.0% in 2012 and 10.8% in 2013 compared with previous years (Choi & Ahn 2014; KTO 2014). There has also been a continuous increase in the number of foreign visitors from Asia, 74.5% in 2005, 77.7% in 2010 and 82.0% in 2013. In comparison, the number of foreign visitors from Europe has decreased over time, 8.4% in 2005, 7.3% in 2010 and 6.3% in 2013. The number of foreign visitors from North America has decreased as well, 10.6% in 2005, 9.3% in 2010 and 7.5% in 2013. Of the overall foreign visitors to Korea, the three major countries – Japan, China and the US – accounted for 64% in 2013. Japan, the country that once accounted for over 40% of foreign visitors to Korea, has greatly decreased, to 34.4% in 2010 and 22.6% in 2013. On the other hand, the percentage of visitors from China has increased significantly from 11.8% in 2005 to 21.3% in 2010 and 35.5% in 2013 (KTO 2014).

Table 26.1 International visitor arrivals to South Korea

	2005 ('000)	2010 ('000)	2013 ('000)	Growth rate (%) (2013)	Market share (%) (2013)
Asia	4,489.9	6,838.5	9,978.6	10.8	82.0
North America	640.0	813.9	915.6	4.5	7.5
Europe	508.9	645.8	768.2	7.1	6.3
Oceania	85.2	146.1	160.0	−3.8	1.3
Africa	18.2	33.8	43.4	5.3	0.4
Overseas Koreans	280.5	319.5	309.5	−6.1	2.5
Total	6,022.8	8,797.7	12,175.6	9.3	100

Source: KTO 2014.

Table 26.2 International arrivals to South Korea by country

Country	2012 ('000)	2013 ('000)	Growth rate (%)	Market share (%)
China	2,836.9	4,326.9	52.5	35.5
Japan	3,518.8	2,747.8	−21.9	22.6
United States	697.9	722.3	3.5	5.9
Taiwan	548.2	544.7	−0.7	4.5
Philippines	331.3	400.7	20.9	3.3
Hong Kong	360.0	400.4	11.2	3.3
Thailand	387.4	372.9	−3.8	3.1
Malaysia	178.1	207.7	16.6	1.7
Indonesia	149.2	189.2	26.8	1.6
Russia	166.7	175.4	5.2	1.4
Singapore	154.1	174.6	13.3	1.4
Canada	128.4	133.6	4.1	1.1
Australia	128.8	123.6	−4.1	1.0
India	91.7	123.2	34.4	1.0
United Kingdom	110.2	120.9	9.7	1.0
Vietnam	106.5	117.1	9.9	1.0
Germany	102.3	100.8	−1.4	0.8
France	71.1	75.9	6.8	0.6
Turkey	19.3	19.7	2.1	0.2

Source: KTO 2014.

Background of the division between the two Koreas

The division of North Korea and South Korea generates one typical image of South Korea that it is an unstable nation with the danger of aggression from the People's Democratic Republic of Korea (North Korea) (Kim & Morrison 2005). Such a negative stereotype image cannot easily be eliminated or positively changed, although South Korea has endeavored to present the image of a stable or peaceful nation by hosting sporting mega-events (the FIFA World Cup Finals in 2002) (Kim & Morrison 2005; Lee *et al.* 2005), encouraging the *Korean wave* – the growing popularity of South Korean culture (Choi *et al.* 2011), and seeking to cooperate in economic and tourism development projects with the North.

Prior to the liberation of Korea from Japanese rule immediately after World War II had ended, the decision of two conferences, the Cairo Declaration in 1943 and the Moscow Conference of Foreign Ministers in December 1945, determined the destiny of the Korean peninsula. In the former conference, the Allies (Great Britain, the US and China) discussed the division of Korea along the 38th parallel and the placement of Korea under the trusteeship of the Allies for a considerable period of time (up to 35 years) (Kirkbride 2011). The latter provided the agreement that arranged South and North Korea under the rules of the US and USSR for five years. This is arguably one of the main starting points of the severe political and ideological conflict, which has lasted till now, and which brings the constant state of tension and hostility to the Korean peninsula. The division formed by the trusteeship or for political reasons unfortunately became a permanent political, cultural, and economic division of Korea (Lee & Mjelde 2007). The South adopted capitalism and, eventually, democracy, while the North adopted the State Stalinist Communist model of economic and social development (Kim & Prideaux 2003).

The division of South and North Korea was reinforced by the Korean War that broke out on 25 June 1950 and lasted till the armistice agreement on 27 July 1953. The war destroyed almost all the infrastructure in the peninsula and left a large number of divided families, refugees and prisoners of war (POWs) (Kim & Prideaux 2003). It also changed the mid-peninsula boundary from the 38th parallel to the truce line that refers to the Military Demarcation Line (MDL) and produced the Demilitarized Zone (DMZ) to the Korean peninsula (Henderson 2002; Kang *et al.* 2012; Yoon & Park 2010).

Since the truce agreement in 1953, a constant state of tension and aggression based on mutual suspicion and mistrust remains in the peninsula. Several dangerous military conflicts between the Koreas in the Yellow Sea and near the DMZ have occurred. North Korea dug several tunnels under the MDL, found in the DMZ of South Korea, and continuously sent spies or terrorists to South Korea (Kirkbride 2011). These tensions or hostile relations dramatically changed for ten years when South Korea's national government was formed by the left wing (Ahn 2010). The president, Dae-jung Kim (Millennium Party), introduced the "Sunshine Policy" designed to draw South and North closer together, based on mutual development and cooperation in economic and tourism development. As a consequence, Koreans could have opportunities to cross the DMZ through joining the Mt. Geumgang tour (Kim & Prideaux 2003), participating in the reunion of separated family and establishing a special economic zone at Gaeseong, just north of the DMZ (Harden 2008).

Such a peaceful approach changed rapidly after 2008, when the South Korean national government shifted to the right under President Myung-bak Lee, who developed a new policy toward the North, focused on a realistic-pragmatic approach rather than on humanitarian assistance (CNN 2009). Tension in the peninsula increased following negative events: a middle-aged South Korean housewife who joined the Mt. Geumgang tour was killed by a North Korean soldier; the South Korea's *Cheonan* ship sinking in 2010; and the bombardment of Yeonpyeong Island in late 2010 by North Korea. As a consequence, several economic development and tourism projects, where South and North Korea cooperated, are currently suspended, with the operation of the Gaeseong Industrial Complex in North Korea being the final visible area of cooperation to be suspended (see Kang *et al.* 2012).

The effect of the division of South and North Korea on tourism

The division of South and North Korea has produced some distinctive or unique tourism phenomena in terms of DMZ tourism: the Mt. Geumgang resort project, the reunion of the divided families, visiting the DMZ by refugees or defectors and visiting friends or relatives (VFR) who serve in the military. The following sections discuss these phenomena in South Korea, specifically focusing on the tourism activities around the DMZ (Ministry of Unification 2011; Paju Municipal Government 2011).

The DMZ has various meanings in terms of political, ideological, ecological and tourism perspectives. First, the DMZ is a political or geographical boundary resulting from the 1953 armistice agreement between the UN forces and North Korea. The agreement stipulates that the DMZ would consist of a two kilometer-wide (1.3 mile) strip of land on both sides of the MDL, which extends 250km (155 miles), crossing the Korean Peninsula through the 38th parallel (Ahn 2010; John *et al.* 2003; Kim 2011). The DMZ serves as a buffer zone to prevent further hostility between the two Koreas. Hence, the DMZ is one of the most heavily militarized areas in the world and a forbidden region. More than one million heavily armed soldiers, one million land mines, artillery and barbed wire surround the zone (Healy 2007; Yoon & Park 2010). With respect to the ideological perspective, the DMZ is a symbol of one of the last severe ideological conflicts remaining in the world. Some commentators have referred to the DMZ as the "last Cold War frontier" (Escobar 2010), a "hot spot" of the last remaining Cold War (Efron 2000) or a symbol of the US's Cold War (Healy 2007). In other words, the DMZ is a reminder to the world that the Cold War has not technically ended on the peninsula (Ahn 2010).

From an ecological perspective, the DMZ is a sanctuary for wildlife, because human access has been strictly limited for nearly six decades (Healy 2007; John *et al.* 2003; Lee & Mjelde 2007; Yoon & Park 2010). The Civilian Control Zone (CCZ), 5–20km from the DMZ's southern boundary, has also allowed some limited human access. Consequently, these forbidden zones have completely preserved natural ecosystems and are a sanctuary for rare species, including 1,597 species of plant, 201 species of bird, 52 species of mammals and 106 species of fish (Korea National Tourism Organization 2004). Not surprisingly, these unique and distinct characteristics of the DMZ have attracted attention from all around the world (Healy 2007; John *et al.* 2003; Lee & Mjelde 2007; Yoon & Park 2010).

War-related tourism around the DMZ and CCZ

There are several tourist or visitors sites around the DMZ, such as Panmunjeom, tunnels, several observatories, Dorasan station, Imjingak and Freedom Bridge. These sites can provide tourists or visitors with the opportunity to experience the Korean War of the past and the tension or aggression created by the two Koreas in the present. Thus, some of these sites are often referred to as "live" education sites about war and the outcome of political and ideological conflicts (Yoon & Park 2010). Panmunjeom and the tunnels are considered as the most representative sites of the Korean War given their unique or special characteristics (Hwang 2010).

Panmunjeom

The *Panmunjeom*, officially known as the JSA (Joint Security Area), is sited on the MDL in the center of the DMZ (Yoon & Park 2010). It is located 62km north-west of Seoul, the capital of South Korea and 215km south of Pyongyang, the capital of North Korea. The circular JSA, with a diameter of 800 meters, includes a total of 24 buildings for various offices and conference rooms of the Military Armistice Commission and the UN Freedom House. As a special zone, the JSA is the only place where UN troops and North Korean soldiers jointly conduct security duties and the North and South representatives can meet each other unarmed. Hence, the JSA is officially used as the meeting venue of the Military Armistice Commission and South–North contacts, and the point of passage for South–North travel (Kirkbride 2011; Yoon & Park 2010).

The JSA is also the site of an incident in which a group of North Korean soldiers hacked a US official to death in August 1976 (Gyeonggi Province 2011). This incident totally changed the relationship between North Korea's soldiers and the UN security troops within the area. Since the incident, the North Korean and UN security troops and other relevant personnel cannot move freely in the area and have been banned from accessing the opposite side of the MDL (Kirkbride 2011; Yoon & Park 2010). Given its location and positional aspect, the strong restrictions for the JSA tour are reasonable for the safety of tourists and preventing any further incidents occurring between the North Korean and UN security troops. The JSA tour is only available through the travel agents officially appointed by the UN or the South Korean government. All tourists or visitors should provide their identification or passport number for the ID check, which takes at least ten days for foreigners and at least one month for domestic visitors. Some tourist restrictions include an appropriate dress code and being limited to visitor or tourist access areas, or limited photo-taking sites (Gyeonggi Province 2011). Despite such restrictions or inconveniences, the JSA remains one of the famous tourist sites in South Korea. This may be related to the extraordinary experience that is produced by the unique or special characteristics of the JSA. The strong restrictions in place regarding the JSA may also enhance the tourist's or visitor's interest or curiosity in the area (Shin 2012).

Tunnels

There may be more than ten tunnels either completed or under construction along the DMZ, but of these only four tunnels were discovered by South Korean soldiers (Kirkbride 2011). Some of the fortifications, the construction of minefields and the movements of artillery forward are for the purpose of defence. However, there is no other purpose for these tunnels, except for a surprise attack against South Korea, sending spies and to gather military intelligence. The first three tunnels were discovered in the 1970s and the fourth was discovered in March 1990, just 1.2km from the MDL. These tunnels have sufficient width and height for North Korea to infiltrate an entire regiment into the South within one hour. In particular, the third tunnel, 1.7km in length, 2m in width and 2m in height, would allow 30,000 fully armed North Korean soldiers and their vehicles and weapons to pass through in one hour (Gyeonggi Province 2011; Kirkbride 2011; Yoon & Park 2010).

The Inter-Korean project: Mt. Geumgang resort

There are very few inter-Korean joint projects, although one of the most representative projects is the development of Mt. Geumgang, located on the east coast of North Korea close to the DMZ (Cho 2007). The natural scenery and the positive image of Mt. Geumgang are sufficient to appeal to Korean tourists. Thus, the Hyundai Group, the largest conglomerate corporation in South Korea, presented a proposal for the development of a resort at Mt. Geumgang. The proposal consisted of a three-phase development, including South Korea's cruise tour to Mt. Geumgang and the construction of tourism-related facilities in addition to infrastructure, such as hotels, casino, golf resort, convention hall, cultural center, a human resource training institute and an international airport (Hyundai Asan Corporation 2001).

The proposal project was accelerated with government support during the presidency of Dae-Jung Kim and Moo-hyun Roh. At that time the national government was left wing and its policy was to reduce the hostility between the two nations and reach a mood of rapprochement through enthusiastically supporting the Hyundai proposal (Kim & Prideaux 2003). As a part of the project, the Mt. Geumgang cruise tour began in 1998 and included an itinerary of acrobats, several bars, shopping and hiking several trails in Mt. Geumgang. With the limited itinerary and tourist access areas, tourists were dissatisfied with the tour. Moreover, tourists were not allowed contact with North Koreans, except as guides or some staff working at the tourist attractions (Cho 2001). Despite the strong restrictions, poor tourism facilities and high price for the tour event, a substantial number of South Koreans applied to do the tour. Approximately 147,391 South Koreans and 69 non-Koreans joined the tour in 1999 and the number of tourists increased in 2000 to 212,202, including 762 non-Korean visitors; 498 tourists had the opportunity to undertake the coach tour program for Mt. Geumgang (Kim & Prideaux 2003).

The project seemed to be well operated and played an important role for the South and the North. The Mt. Geumgang tour was considered as the only way for South Korean civilians to reach the North. It was also notably meaningful for the first or second generation of migrants from North Korea, who had not been in touch with the North for six decades. Moreover, the project was promised to be a confidence-building exercise between the two hostile nations. Despite the important roles of the Mt. Geumgang resort project, there was some opposition. For instance, some conservative politicians in South Korea were worried about substantial financial support to the North, given South Korea's economic recession (Lee 2014).

The Mt. Geumgang project was suspended owing to the incident described above, in which a South Korean housewife was killed by a North Korean soldier's gunshot in July 2008 (Harden 2008). The present national government is also to the right politically and is not as enthusiastic as the previous government about supporting the project because it is against the new policy toward the North. This indicates, explicitly, that tourism does not play a critical role in providing peaceful relations between the two hostile nations. Tourism is also characterized as weak, fragile and changeable according to government policy. The South have used tourism as one of several methods for achieving a political agenda, while the North accepted tourism as the means to gain foreign currency in addition to financial support from the South (Kim & Prideaux 2003).

North Korean foreign tourism policies and attraction trends

Overview of North Korean foreign tourism policies

Since the 1980s, the People's Democratic Republic of Korea, or North Korea, began to show interest in the tourism industry in order to increase holdings of foreign currencies. The domestic tourism policies of North Korea, with respect to welfare such as leisure and recreation for the general citizens, are strong, but there are almost no international tourism policies. Since the 1980s there has been an active change in position, with the aim to acquire foreign currencies. In the 1960s and 1970s, North Korea fostered small recreational tourism parties in order to maintain a friendly relationship among communist nations and began fostering international tourism by targeting overseas Koreans. Measures were taken as part of an important foreign tourism policy in the 1980s: expansion of the relevant administrative bodies (expanded and restructured the National Travel Office to the National Tourism Directorate General in 1986); applied to the World Tourism Organization (WTO) (1987); and declared a grand opening of nine tourist areas (1987) (Korea Culture and Tourism Institute 2011; Lee 2014).

After enacting the joint-venture law, the importance of tourism as a means to earn foreign currencies was recognized and it was included as a target industry for joint ventures. However, up to the present it has been evaluated as not satisfying the desired performance of foreign investors. North Korea faced a limit on opening its doors to international tourism businesses as possible internal impacts of opening doors to foreign countries were taken into consideration. The measures taken by North Korea in order to attract foreign visitors are still focused on tourism-based expansion and marketing of areas limited to Pyongyang, Mt. Geumgang and Shinuiju. North Korea, focusing on China, is working harder on tourism promotional activities through overseas travel agencies in order to attract more foreign tourists and is gradually expanding its boundaries to the west (Shin 2012).

Attracting foreign visitors

There is active exchange of tourism products between North Korea and China as most of the tourists that visit North Korea are Chinese, and tourists of other countries must go through China in order to enter into North Korea. Statistics of outbound travelers from China show that 131,200 travelers visited North Korea in 2010, making it the 19th most visited country from China. There was an approximate increase of 47% from 130,000 travelers in 2010 to 190,000 in 2011 (Korea Culture and Tourism Institute 2011; Shin 2012).

Improvements in accommodating foreign visitors

Improvement in entry

North Korea agreed to allow Chinese and Russians to enter its boundaries without a visa in 2010. The agreement of the three nations has made entry more convenient resulting in less time being required for the travel planning process. Travelers are required to send a copy of their passport and identification by fax two days before their departure. In 2010, the limit in the length of stay for Americans was lifted. In the past, the length of stay for Americans was limited to five days and four nights; however, Americans are now allowed to visit and stay for up to one year. As a result, many American travel agencies have begun providing tourism products to North Korea (Park 2012).

North Korea approved a foreign investor in the Mt. Geumgang International Special Tourist Zone in December 2010. A foreign company with capital from Hong Kong and China received approval from the Management Board of Mt. Geumgang Special International Tourist Zone. As Mt. Geumgang tourism faced difficulties due to the conflict between North and South Korea, there was a need for the provision of conditions to attract international investors. Connecting transport routes that link North Korea to the rest of the world and approval of car tours are improving and acting as a means of diversification. Previously, tourism in North Korea required transportation by chartered planes and buses. However, there is a trend to develop routes via trains, private cars, cruise ships and walking, instead of only planes being possible (Shin 2012).

Currently, North Korea is in the process of creating new routes to allow direct international flights to Pyongyang Sunan International Airport. In the case of China, the Pyongyang–Shanghai route was created in July 2009; in addition, there are regular and charter flights to Xian and Harbin. Air Koryo, the state carrier, also has regular flights to Kuala Lumpur and Kuwait City, as well as charter services. In 2011 North Korea allowed Chinese tourists to sightsee with private cars. As procedures to enter North Korea have become more convenient, the number of tourists with personal cars has increased and is expected to continue to increase.

North Korea has also approved a frontier tour, beginning from Dandong, that visits the border areas of the country with China. Seventy percent of the trade between North Korea and China takes place in Dandong and support for quick customs clearance has been put in place (Korea Culture and Tourism Institute 2011; Park 2012; Shin 2012).

Diversification of tourism products

North Korea is in the process of attempting to increase the demand for tourism through the construction of tourism and economic districts and the development of tourism routes. The tourism products of North Korea are becoming increasingly diversified and more numerous. Expectancy of continuous development through specialization of cultural tourism, sports tourism, bicycle tourism and golf tourism is increasing. To attract tourists by celebrating the 100th birth anniversary of Kim Il Sung in April 2012, North Korea prepared many tourism products for foreign visitors. As a 100-year anniversary event, a travel agency in the US released package products of over US$15,000 in value for ten days as a luxury product (Park 2012).

A former British ambassador in Pyongyang has been permitted to introduce a political tourism itinerary. This tour route, which first began in October 2011, was planned as a tourism product that traveled to the major cities of North Korea for ten days. The second largest city of North Korea, Hamheung, and cities and towns distant to the capital city and rural areas were also included in the itinerary. A tourism product called "Juche study" was permitted. This product was first suggested by North Korea and is a product that explains the history and background of the Juche ideology to traveling trainees by experts on the Labor Party Juche ideology in agreement with the Korea International Travel Company of North Korea. As it targets young Westerners, the tourism product was named "Young Pioneer Tours" and is sold by travel agencies. Economic (Industrial) Tourism Product was planned as a program that visited sites such as the Cheollima steelworks of Nampo where the Cheollima Movement began. Planned by a British travel agency called "Political Tours", it was an economic tourism product that visited the factories of Nampo (Lee 2014; Shin 2012).

In June 2012, "Young Pioneer Tours", a travel agency which specializes in tours to North Korea, posted an advertisement on its homepage promoting golf tour products in Pyongyang. In May 2011, North Korea held an amateur golf tournament with foreign players for the first time in Pyongyang by conducting a joint venture with Chinese and British travel agencies. In 2012 and 2013, North Korea conducted a joint venture with a British travel agency to hold amateur golf tournaments in Pyongyang. North Korea also enabled foreigners to travel within the country on bicycles for the first time from 2012. For the attraction of tourists to Mt. Geumgang, the development plans of the "Geumgang International Tourism Zone" were announced in March 2012. As a Mt. Geumgang–Pyongyang–Beijing course that utilized railroad tracks and highways, it was created for the purpose of attracting Chinese tourists.

In order to attract more foreign tourists, North Korea is expending much energy in activities such as creation of promotional websites, publication of tourism booklets and shooting of promotional videos. In celebration of the 90th anniversary of Kim Il Sung, North Korea first showcased the "Arirang" performance in 2002, and by permitting foreigners to join, benefitted both the propaganda system and the inflow of foreign currency. In 2008, a website to introduce the "Arirang" performance and recruit spectators was created, and booklets for individual tours were published. North Korea actively attracted Chinese tourists, and in 2011 dispatched promotional teams to Dandung, Dalian and Shenyang of China to explain the country's tourism resources (Shin 2012).

Visits between North and South Korea

In 2013 the number of visitors from South Korea to North Korea (entering via Pyongyang) was 77,028, with 76,956 returning in that period, a decline compared to 241,368 the previous year (Ministry of Justice 2014). There were no visitors to South Korea from the North. After the murder that occurred in July 2008 at Mt. Geumgang, tours to the mountain and individual tours were stopped, and due to incidents such as the shooting of the *Cheonan* in March 2010 and North Korea's bombardment of the Yeonpyeong Island in November, 2010, the North–South exchanges drew to a standstill (Korea Culture and Tourism Institute 2011; Shin 2012).

Case study 26.1 Mt. Geumgang and Gaeseong Tour Business

The North–South Mt. Geumgang tourism business, together with the Gaeseong Industrial Complex business, formed the two major axes of tourism related to North–South economic cooperation projects. The Mt. Geumgang Tour as a business has faced extreme ups and downs. Table 26.3 provides a timeline for the business. In 2004, the number of visitors increased to 260,000, and by August 2005 the accumulated number of visitors to Mt. Geumgang was over ten million visitors. By June 2007 the total amount of visitors per 12-month period was 1.5 million (Korea Culture and Tourism Institute 2011; Lee 2014).

Table 26.3 Timeline of the Mt. Geumgang tour business

Stage	Elements
Stage 1 (1998–2000) Trial and error due to insufficient preparation	• This was a period of trial and error as the business abruptly began without sufficient preparation. • Business began with a minimal institutional framework based on agreements of the governing bodies of the North and South. • Began with poor tourism infrastructure and programme content on 18 November 1998. The first Mt. Geumgang tour began: 826 people including separated families and displaced people. As the infrastructure facilities of the North Korean Mt. Geumgang tourism district were in poor condition, the Hyundai Group utilised cruise ships for transportation and accommodation. • Incidents of forced detention of visitors from the South: a tourist was forced into detention due to remarks on the system of the North (21 June 1999). • As a result of the incident, the Mt. Geumgang tour ceased for 40 days, and problems of safety in the Mt. Geumgang tour business were raised. • The tour resumed (5 August 1999) as tourism laws and safety agreements were set up (30 July 1999).
Stage 2 (2001–2003) Decrease in business profitability and government support	• Excessive demand forecast by the Hyundai Group. The forecast made by the Hyundai Group predicted approximately 500,000 visitors per year; however, only 150,000–200,000 visitors travelled there. • Decline in visitors beginning in 2001. • As problems such as the weakening of the early novelty effect of the Mt. Geumgang tours, overpricing of products and monotonous tours arose, the number of visitors dropped to approximately 100,000. • The government decided to support the business as an economic cooperation between the North and the South.

Stage 3 (2004–July 2008) Stabilisation of land route tours and full-scale growth	• Decrease in the price of products and diversification as a result of the settlement of land route tours. • Land route tours were conducted daily in October 2003; in 2004 overnight tours (June) and one-day tours (September) were conducted.
Stage 4 (July 2008–present) Halting of business due to tourist murder	• 11 July 2008, a female South Korean tourist was murdered by a North Korean sentry. • 12 July 2008, suspension of all tours to North Korea. • Due to the prolonged conflict between the North and South, business was suspended • Until suspension, a total of 1.93 million visitors to Mt. Geumgang had been recorded.
Stage 5 (July 2008–July 2009) End and absence of communication	• After the incident, the South immediately halted the Mt. Geumgang tourism business and requested a joint investigation with the North; however, this was rejected. • The South determined that resuming tourism without a joint investigation would be impossible and afterwards requested personal security measures to prevent recurrence of similar incidents.
Stage 6 (August 2008– February 2010) North Korea's period of appeasement measures	• In August 2009 the chairman of Hyundai Group at the time through a meeting with Kim Jung Il came to an agreement on five matters regarding the resumption of tourism and traffic exchange. • According to the agreement, Kim Jung Il guaranteed the personal safety of tourists from the South. However, the Southern government pointed out that the agreement was not made between governments but with Hyundai, a private company. • Failure to come to an agreement regarding tourism in Mt. Geumgang. • A meeting was held on 8 February 2010 looking at the resumption of tourism; however, due to differences in position an agreement could not be reached.
Stage 7 (March 2010–July 2011) North Korea's period of strong action	• As the meeting could not reach an agreement, the North began to formulate pressure strategies for the Mt. Geumgang tourism business. • Increased tension in the North–South relationship due to the sinking of the *Cheonan* (March 2010) and bombardment of the Yeonpyeong Island (November 2010). • In January 2011, as a temporary appeasement gesture, the North proposed a meeting on Mt. Geumgang tourism in the following month. • North Korea's second strong measures began: threats regarding the enactment and property disposal of the Mt. Geumgang International Special Tourist Zone Act.
Stage 8 (March 2010–present) North Korea's strategic efforts for Mt. Geumgang tourism	• Efforts to attract foreign investors. • In 2012, the North announced development plans of the "Mt. Geumgang International Special Tourist Zone" to build hotels, duty-free shops, international nursing centres, an international cancer centre, international finance centre, international restaurants and golf courses around the Geumgang area within five years, investing US\$8.6 billion. • After permitting Chinese tourists to Mt. Geumgang, Western tourists were permitted as well. • Tours of Mt. Geumgang became possible to Europeans and, in 2012, permitted to Americans as well. • A demonstration tour of Chinese tourists to Mt. Geumgang was carried out in 2011 and the North decided to attract Chinese tourists instead of tourists from the South.

In July 2005, the chairman of Hyundai and Kim Jung Il came to an agreement to carry out tourism in Gaeseong; and in August 18, 2005 agreed to conduct demonstration tours that were carried out three times (August 26, September 2, and September 9, 2005). The tour was a one-day tour visiting Gaeseong on a bus and returning to the South on the same day. The actual Gaeseong tours began in December 2007.

Tours were conducted six times per week (excluding Mondays), and an average of 370 tourists visited, reaching 10,000 visitors per month, including approximately 2,600 foreigners (non-Koreans). The popularity of the tour was due to being able to see all the cultural artifacts in Gaeseong in a single day. In June 2008 the greatest number of tourists visited (12,168 visitors). After the Mt. Geumgang murder in 2008, the tension between the North and South continued to intensify. As a result, the Gaeseong tours came to a halt on November 29, 2008. In August 2009 the chairman of Hyundai visited Pyongyang in order to discuss the issues and, following the normalization of the land route passages of the MDL, it was assumed that an early resumption of the Gaeseong tours would be possible with agreements to resume the Gaeseong tour and activate the Gaeseong Industrial District (Ahn 2010). Accordingly, beginning on August 21, 2009, North Korea completely released the limitation measures on land passages and residence that were put in place after the halting of the Gaeseong tours and withdrew all limitation measures. However, since the agreement was not made between governments but with Hyundai, a private company, the Southern government pointed out that it would be difficult to guarantee the safety of the people. Afterwards, as the North and South could not come to an agreement, the Gaeseong tours, together with the Mt. Geumgang tours, could not resume, and the total number of tourists that visited Gaeseong until the day it halted was 110,549 visitors (Lee 2014; Shin 2012).

Conclusion

The Korean truce has been maintained for a long period, more than half a century, and the second and the third generations of Koreans may not know the cruelty or atrocity of war. In this respect, the DMZ and CCZ are reminders that the war is not yet completely over. The DMZ is also a living educational site about the war and the importance of peace, and also the conservation of natural ecology. Tourism is also referred to as a channel for achieving peace in divided countries such as the Korean peninsula. However, in the case of the Korean peninsula, tourism seems to produce a reduction in the tension or hostility between the two nations and has not been one of the crucial factors that may potentially lead to the reunification of Korea. Instead, tourism has become a tool for the implementation of the political agenda in the case of South Korea and for foreign currency earnings in the North.

Key reading

Kang, E.J., Scott, N., Lee, T.J. and Ballantyne, R. (2012) 'Benefits of visiting a "dark tourism" site: The case of the Jeju April 3rd Peace Park, Korea', *Tourism Management*, 33(2): 257–265.

Kim, S. (2012) 'The production and consumption of experience: Inter-Asian responses to small screen tourism in Korea', *European Journal of Tourism Research*, 5(1): 76–79.

Kim, S. and Jamal, T. (2015) 'The co-evolution of rural tourism and sustainable rural development in Hongdong, Korea: Complexity, conflict and local response', *Journal of Sustainable Tourism*, 23(8–9): 1363–1385.

Lee, T. and Nan, J.-H. (2016) 'Regional economic development through food tourism: The case of Asio Gusto in Namyangju City, South Korea', in C.M. Hall and S. Gössling (eds), *Food Tourism and Regional Development*. Abingdon: Routledge.

Lim, C.C. and Bendle, L.J. (2012) 'Arts tourism in Seoul: Tourist-orientated performing arts as a sustainable niche market', *Journal of Sustainable Tourism*, 20(5): 667–682.

References

Ahn, I. (2010) 'Deconstructing the DMZ: Derrida, Levinas and the phenomenology of peace', *Cooperation and Conflict*, 45(2): 205–223.

Cho, M. (2001) 'Inter-Korean efforts to activate the Mt. Gumgang tour business', in *Proceedings of an Academic Forum of Mt. Gumgang Tour Project and Inter-Korean Economic Cooperation*. Seoul: Hyundai Economy Institute.

—— (2007) 'A re-examination of tourism and peace: The case of the Mt. Gumgang tourism development on the Korean Peninsula', *Tourism Management*, 28(2): 556–569.

Choi, J.G., Tkachenko, T. and Sil, S. (2011) 'On the destination image of Korea by Russian tourists', *Tourism Management*, 32(1): 193–194.

Choi, K.E. and Ahn, H.J. (2014) *Recent Trends of the Korean Tourism Industry*. Seoul: Culture & Tourism Institute Press.

CNN (2009) 'Long-separated Korean families have reunion', CNN, 26 September. Online. Available: http://articles.cnn.com/2009-09-26/world/koreas.reunion_1_south-koreans-korean-war-korean-border?_s=PM:WORLD (accessed 25 July 2011).

Efron, S. (2000) 'Cold War still hot in Korea's DMZ', *Los Angeles Times*, 11 June. Online. Available: http://articles.latimes.com/2000/jun/11/news/mn-39962/3 (accessed 20 July 2011).

Escobar, P. (2010) 'The last frontier of the Cold War', *Asia Times*, 27 February. Online. Available: www.atimes.com/atimes/Korea/LB27Dg01.html (accessed 20 July 2011).

Gyeonggi Province (2011) 'Demilitarized zone'. Online. Available: http://dmz.gg.go.kr/ENG/index.asp (accessed 26 July 2011).

Harden, B. (2008) 'South Korean Tourist is shot dead in North', *Washington Post Foreign Service*, 12 July.

Healy, H. (2007) 'Korean demilitarized zone peace and nature park'. Paper presented at the DMZ Forum.

Henderson, J.C. (2002) 'Tourism and politics in the Korean Peninsula', *Journal of Tourism Studies*, 13(2): 16–27.

Hwang, J. (2010) 'Defector's nostalgia: When we can visit North Korea?', *Daily NK*, 19 September. Online. Available: www.dailynk.com/korean/read.php?cataId=nk00100&num=86740 (accessed 25 July 2011).

Hyundai Asan Corporation. (2001) *Summary of Mt. Gumgang Project*. Seoul: Hyundai Asan Corporation.

John, K.H., Youn, Y.C., and Shin, J.H. (2003) 'Resolving conflicting ecological and economic interests in the Korean DMZ: A valuation based approach', *Ecological Economics*, 46(1): 173–179.

Kang, E.J., Scott, N., Lee, T.J. and Ballantyne, R. (2012) 'Benefits of visiting a "dark tourism" site: The case of the Jeju April 3rd Peace Park, Korea', *Tourism Management*, 33(2): 257–265.

Kim, J.H. (2011) 'Comparative analysis of DMZ area tourist motivations by destination', *Journal of Tourism Sciences*, 35(4): 95–112.

Kim, S.S. and Morrison, A.M. (2005) 'Change of images of South Korea among foreign tourists after the 2002 FIFA World Cup', *Tourism Management*, 26(2): 233–247.

Kim, S.S. and Prideaux, B. (2003) 'Tourism, peace, politics and ideology: Impacts of the Mt. Gumgang tour project in the Korean Peninsula', *Tourism Management*, 24(6): 675–685.

Kirkbride, W.A. (2011) *Panmunjeom*. Seoul: Hollym Publishing.

Korea Culture and Tourism Institute (2011) *KCTI Analysis of the Cultural and Art Tourism Industry: Changes in the North Korean Political Situation and Task of South Korean Tourism Industry*. Seoul: Korea Culture and Tourism Institute Press.

Korea National Tourism Organization (2004) *Master Plan for Development of Peace Tourism Belt in the DMZ and its Vicinity*. Seoul: Government Printer.

Korea Tourism Organization (KTO) (2014) *Analysis of the Inbound Tourism Market to Korea*. Seoul: KTO Press.

Lee, C.K. and Mjelde, J.W. (2007) 'Valuation of ecotourism resources using a contingent valuation method: The case of the Korean DMZ', *Ecological Economics*, 63(2/3): 511–520.

Lee, C.K., Lee, Y.K. and Lee, B. (2005) 'Korea's destination image formed by the 2002 World Cup', *Annals of Tourism Research*, 32(4): 839–858.

Lee, H.J. (2014) *The Current Issues and Future Tasks of the Mt. Geumgang Tour Program*. Seoul: Hyundai Research Institute Press.

Ministry of Justice (MoJ) (2014) *2013 Annual Report of the Ministry of Justice (MoJ)*. Seoul: MoJ Press.

Ministry of Unification (2011) 'Integrated information system for separated families'. Online. Available: https://reunion.unikorea.go.kr/reunion/index (accessed 25 July 2011).

Paju Municipal Government (2011) 'The official website of Paju city'. Online. Available: http://en.paju.go.kr/index.do (accessed 10 August 2011).

Park, Y.J. (2012) *Directions and Tasks for Establishing Common Cultural Community Between the Two Koreas*. Seoul: The Korea Culture & Tourism Institute Press.

Shin, Y.S. (2012) *Analysis of the Tourism Between the Two Koreas and Policy Plan*. Seoul: The Korea Culture & Tourism Institute Press.

Yoon, J.S. and Park, J.H. (2010) *Peaceful Area DMZ*. Seoul: Yeseong Publishing.

27

PARADIGM SHIFT IN THE 21ST CENTURY?

Tourism in Japan

Carolin Funck

Introduction

Japan stands out among other Asian nations through its early economic development, and this is mirrored in tourism. The highly mature tourism market developed based on historical precedents like pilgrimages, visits to hot springs and regular official travel between the provinces and the capital. However, due to its geographic location far from other industrialized countries and the economic gap with neighbouring areas, until the 1990s this market catered mainly for domestic tourists and in consequence saw few intrusions by foreign investment. Only in the 21st century has "inbound" become the buzzword of tourism policies and industries, although the inbound tourism consumption ratio in 2012 was still a mere 5.7%, the lowest among countries that run a Tourism Satellite Account (TSA) (Japan Tourism Agency 2014a: 277).

The increase in visitors from abroad has not been the only change in the 21st century. Since an active inbound promotion policy was introduced in 2003 (Soshiroda 2005: 1100), the implementation of the revised *Tourism Nation Promotion Basic Law* in 2007, the approval of the *Tourism Nation Promotion Basic Plan* (2007, renewed 2012) and the inauguration of the Japan Tourism Agency in 2008, the latter responsible for an overhaul of the tourism statistics system, all point in direction of a paradigm shift in Japanese tourism policies. On the demand side, domestic tourism patterns have changed profoundly, which is reflected in a surge in tourism research on "new" forms of tourism like art (Klien 2010; Funck *et al.* 2013), volunteer (Nakamura *et al.* 2008), food (Kim & Ellis 2015), dark tourism (Funck 2014), ecotourism (Shikida *et al.* 2008; Jones 2012) and media-induced tourism, called "contents tourism" in Japanese (Yamamura 2009). After a brief outline of developments up to the 20th century, this chapter will therefore focus on the paradigm shift in Japanese tourism in the 21st century.

When Japan emerged from more than 200 years of relative seclusion in the late 19th century, it possessed an elaborate road and post-station system with the peculiarity that all forms of carriages had been forbidden – walking, riding and ships were the only means of transport, which put all travellers on an equal footing. This, in combination with political stability, had led to what Ishimori calls the 'popularization of tourism' (1989: 192), where broad parts of the population visited shrines and temples for religious reasons and hot springs for health reasons. Starting from the 1870s, the introduction of politics, ideas and industries from Western industrialized countries also had implementations for tourism. Hiking, golf, skiing, sailing and other Western-style leisure activities became popular and the government promoted the construction of hotels to cater for Western travellers in famous destinations. However, tourism development came to a halt in the years leading to and during World War II.

After World War II, tourism patterns changed in close connection with economic cycles (Funck & Cooper 2013: 77). Periods of high economic growth and substantial tourism development alternate with stagnation. The first growth period coincided with post-war recovery and high economic growth from the 1960s up to the first oil-crisis in 1973. Small-scale family-run inns sprang up across the countryside, traditional Japanese-style inns (*ryokan*) were rebuilt in concrete and equipped with modern facilities, hotels started to dot scenic locations and leisure facilities diversified. The second phase saw the development of resort hotels, golf and ski courses, marinas and theme parks during the so-called "bubble economy" in the late 1980s, partly based on the *Law for the Development of Comprehensive Resort Areas* ("Resort Law") passed in 1987 (Rimmer 1992; Funck & Cooper 2013). The current third phase of expansion in the tourism sector for the first time is strongly influenced by economic growth in surrounding countries and even some foreign investment.

The tourism market

Before analyzing the current tourism market in Japan, it should be noted that reliable statistics on this subject have been introduced rather recently starting from 2003. This proves that tourism has not been high on the agenda of economic policies, as the statistical system in general is highly elaborated. A range of surveys now cover the number of nights in accommodation (from 2007), the amount of domestic travel/tourism consumption (from 2003) and the number of inbound tourists and tourism consumption by prefecture (from 2010) (Japan Tourism Agency (JTA) 2013).

The TSA is based on the latter two surveys. In 2012 the Japanese domestic tourism consumption was 20.8 trillion yen and its rate in GDP reached 4.4%. However, consumption has dropped continually for six years, mainly due to a decrease in the average number of day-trips. The inbound tourism consumption in 2012 saw a steep increase to 1.3 trillion yen and contributed 1.9% of the exports of goods and services. On the other hand, the rate of outbound tourism consumption in imports of goods and services with 3.3 trillion yen was 4.1%, compared to 6.4% in 2004. Overall, internal tourism consumption consisted of 68.2% from domestic overnight trips, 19.8% from domestic day-trips, 6.3% from expenses for outbound trips made within Japan and 5.7% from inbound tourism. National tourism consumption showed a similar distribution, with 62.6% from domestic overnight trips, 18.2% from domestic day-trips, 5.8% from expenses for outbound trips made within Japan and 13.4% from those made outside Japan (JTA 2014a).

The TSA uses two different ways of calculating the number of jobs created from tourism. One method is based on employment numbers in tourism industries and the other on calculations based on tourism consumption. According to the former, in 2012 tourism industries accounted for 6.9% of all jobs; the latter method results in 2.8% (JTA 2014a: 271). In the Economic Census 2012, employment in accommodation alone made up 1.25% of total employment (Ministry of Internal Affairs and Communications Statistics Bureau 2013); therefore, the former estimate seems closer to reality.

According to the UNWTO (2014), Japan welcomed 10,364,000 visitors in 2013, up 24% from the year before. Despite this impressive growth, due mainly to a sharp devaluation of the Japanese yen starting from 2012, Japan still only occupied sixth position in the whole Asia-

Pacific region. On the other hand, in 2012 it lost its place among the top ten tourism spenders of the world, which it had occupied for decades. Compared to other countries that developed a TSA, Japan ranks high on absolute internal consumption but low on share of tourism in GDP, share of tourism in general employment and inbound tourism consumption rate (JTA 2014a). Japan's characteristic pattern of strong domestic and outbound tourism and a weak inbound sector is certainly changing in the 21st century, but is still clearly visible.

Outbound and inbound

Japanese outbound travel made a significant leap in the late 1980s, when numbers doubled in just five years between 1986 and 1991. However, from 1997 on, wars, terrorism, SARS and other health scares and a prolonged recession have taken their toll and numbers have been oscillating between 13.3 and 18.5 million trips per year (Figure 27.1). In 2012, the US received the highest number of Japanese visitors, 3.7 million, with 40% of them visiting Hawaii. China and Korea were visited by 3.5 million each, but trips to China have been declining since 2011 due to political tensions between the two countries. Hong Kong, Taiwan and Thailand also each welcomed more than one million Japanese tourists (JTA 2014d).

The 21st century has seen one much discussed change in outbound tourism, which is a decline in young travellers, especially women. Factors contributing to this decline are the decrease in the number of younger people, less disposable income of young workers and their lack of interest in foreign countries and overseas travel (Funck & Cooper 2013). From 1995 to 2010, the number of Japanese in their twenties travelling abroad has decreased by one-third. In contrast, although neighbouring Korea faces a similar decline in population, the number of young outbound tourists has increased significantly (An 2011).

Inbound tourism has also had its share of ups and downs since 2008, but since 2012 is considered an economic success story. Figure 27.2 illustrates the distribution of origin for foreign tourists in 2013. South Koreans (23.7%), Chinese (21.3%) and Taiwanese (12.7%) together account for more than half of all visitors. The number of tourists from South-East Asia, especially Thailand,

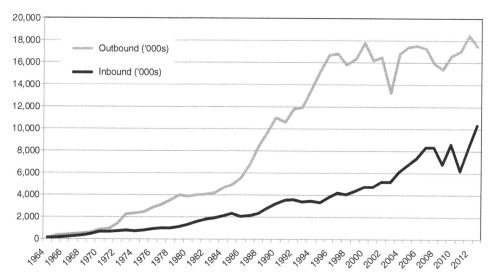

Figure 27.1 Inbound and outbound tourism in Japan, 1964–2013.
Source: based on JTA 2014d.

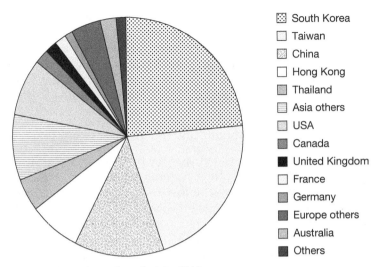

Figure 27.2 Foreign visitors by region of origin, 2013.
Source: based on JTA 2014d.

Singapore, Malaysia and Indonesia, has increased due to visa deregulation in 2013. However, Japan's very small Muslim resident population has not yet created a food infrastructure of its own that could cater to tourists. Therefore, tourism facilities are striving to provide *halal* food for Muslim visitors.

While arrivals have increased and finally surpassed the goal of ten million in 2013, the length of stay has decreased. Flights have become cheaper and travelling to Japan is no longer a once-in-a-lifetime voyage, but a convenient short trip from neighbouring countries. Economic effects differ by nationality. For spending inside Japan, Chinese rank highest with 24.7% of the total, followed by Taiwanese (15.2%), Koreans (13.5%) and US Americans (9.0%). Per capita, Australians spent most, followed by Chinese, Russians and French. Visitors from Chinese-speaking areas show a strong interest in shopping, with over 70% of them visiting supermarkets and shopping centres to buy cosmetics, food and fashion items (JTA 2014c).

After the latest change in government in 2012, the Japanese government has actively engaged in selling Japanese hospitality (*omotenashi*) and "Cool Japan". In 2013, it set up a public–private "Cool Japan Fund" with the aim of supporting and promoting the development of demand overseas for Japanese products and services across a variety of areas, including media, food, services, fashion and lifestyle (Cool Japan Fund 2014). Critics have pointed out that tourists might have different, less exotic interests, and that Japan should engage more actively in the conservation of important tourism resources, namely nature and traditional Japanese townscapes.

Regional patterns

While a share of just 5.7% (2012) in internal tourism consumption and 7.2% in night-stays (2013) does not support the hype about inbound tourism in the Japanese media in recent years, a different picture emerges based on regional distribution (Figure 27.3), because foreign tourists are concentrated in certain destinations where they can have a strong impact (Funck 2012). The same is true for domestic tourism, because the short average trip length of 2.27 nights (JTA 2014a: 24) leads to a concentration of tourists in locations accessible by car for a weekend trip from the major metropolitan areas or in places considered worth a flight for their unique nature

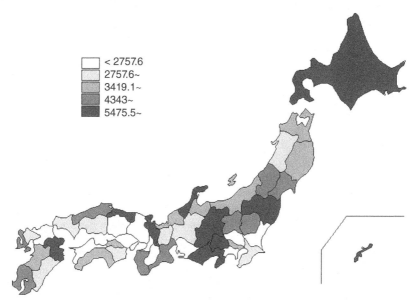

Figure 27.3   Tourism intensity in 2013 (nights/population ('000s)).
Source: based on JTA 2014b; Population data: Portal site of official statistics of Japan e-stat: www.e-stat.go.jp/SG1/estat/List.do?lid=000001118081.

and culture, like the islands of Hokkaido in the north and Okinawa in the south. Japan is made up of 47 prefectures, which also form the regional unit for tourism statistics. The prefectures with high numbers of nights spent in accommodation overlap for domestic and inbound tourism. They include the axis from Tokyo to Osaka/Kyoto, where most of Japan's population is concentrated, and the outliers Hokkaido, Okinawa and Fukuoka. On the other hand, all except the top eight prefectures receive less than 4% of night-stays. However, while the top ten prefectures account for only about half of all nights for Japanese tourists, they receive 80% of all nights spent by foreigners, showing a higher degree of concentration for inbound tourists. Also, prefectures surrounding the metropolitan areas of Kanto (Tokyo) and Kansai (Osaka, Kyoto) and those hit by the triple catastrophe of earthquake, tsunami and nuclear disaster in 2011 accommodate a 2–3% lower percentage of foreign tourists than Japanese (based on JTA 2014b). It can be concluded that regional patterns for domestic and inbound tourism overlap in large part, but differ in some aspects.

The distribution of domestic tourism has long been shaped by traditional tourism attractions like famous shrines, temples, castles and hot springs. In addition, nature-based tourism like hiking, sea-bathing, retreats from the summer heat and skiing have created a "pleasure periphery" in rural areas surrounding the capital metropolitan area, where 28% of Japan's population is concentrated. This periphery has been extended constantly through the development of highways and *shinkansen*. As a result, since Japanese tourists still account for 92.8% of all nights, prefectures with a high tourism intensity (number of nights per 1,000 inhabitants) form a half circle around the capital metropolitan area, extending into the Tohoku area (Figure 27.3). They also include prefectures with famous hot spring locations like Beppu (Oita Prefecture) in Kyushu and the nature-based resort destinations of Hokkaido and Okinawa.

Although inbound tourists concentrate around the major cities, differences occur according to nationality. Tokyo and Osaka alone accommodate 42.2% of all nights spend by foreigners in

Japan, followed by destinations located between these two hubs. This strong degree of concentration has contributed to a severe shortage of hotel rooms in Tokyo, Osaka and Kyoto, where occupancy rates reach over 80% on average (JTA 2014d). However, visitors from nearby China, Korea, Hong Kong and Taiwan concentrate to a lesser degree than tourists from other areas and stay more nights in a variety of prefectures, probably because a high percentage of repeat visitors are exploring new destinations outside the well-trodden foreign tourist paths. Some places like Tottori or Kagawa Prefecture, although far off the usual tourist circuit, have even seen a doubling in the number of nights by foreigners between 2007 and 2013. Such patterns are partly due to an increase in Asian charters and LCCs, which fly to regional airports around the country (JTA 2014d: 26; Wu *et al.* 2012). Some groups show clear destination preferences. Kyushu has become a short-trip destination easily accessible by boat or plane for South Koreans who want to soak in a hot spring, play golf or enjoy shopping. Taiwanese and Australians travel to Hokkaido to admire the landscape and look for powder snow. Although statistics prove that inbound tourism in Japan is still in its development phase, which is characterized by a strong reliance on major international gateways and golden routes, these more specific patterns have drawn the attention of mass media and created the impression that foreign tourists have an important economic impact all over the country. This impact, however, is mainly punctual, as some locations have succeeded in attracting limited groups of tourists through special attractions like *ninja* tours, direct marketing or comprehensive inbound strategies (Funck 2012).

Policies and politics

In his discussion of Japan's outbound promotion policy started in 1987, Leheny (2003: 135) emphasizes that few countries would promote outbound travel as it basically translates into economic loss. This illustrates that tourism and leisure policies in Japan have been less an economic strategy than a tool for social policies and image improvement. This is true even for domestic tourism. A big impact on tourism development was supposed to come from the Resort Law of 1987 mentioned above (Rimmer 1992; Funck & Cooper 2013). Attractions, golf and ski courses, marinas, theme parks, leisure and accommodation facilities were planned throughout the country and promoted through generous loans and relaxation of planning and conservation regulations. The aim was to show the world that Japan was not only an economic, but also a social super-power where citizens have ample opportunities to enjoy leisure. It was also hoped that tourism development in peripheral areas would counterbalance the continuous concentration of people and money in the capital metropolis. However, the bursting of Japan's famous bubble economy in 1991 brought an end to most projects. After that, domestic tourism stayed lacklustre through the prolonged recession, hampered as before by limited free time and paid holidays.

The promotion of inbound tourism, started by the Koizumi government on the occasion of the 2002 Football World Cup, followed a similar double purpose: to create a positive image of Japan and to revive regional economies. It proved successful because it coincided with strong economic growth in surrounding countries.

It is interesting that after the start of Koizumi's "Visit Japan Campaign", tourism moved up on the agenda of economic policies and stayed in the limelight throughout a series of fast-changing governments. In 2007, the Tourism Nation Promotion Basic Law replaced the Basic Tourism Law of 1963. Based on this legislation, the Tourism Nation Promotion Basic Plan set out specific numerical targets to be reached in 2016, as well as government measures to achieve those targets. Targets were set for the number of foreign travellers to Japan, the number of Japanese tourists travelling overseas, the value of tourism consumption, the number of overnight stays per person in domestic travel and the number of international conferences held in Japan each year. The second plan from 2012 increased numbers for these targets and added two more, to increase satisfaction of domestic and inbound tourists (JTA 2012). These targets could only be introduced because since 2003 a system of statistical surveys has been developed to measure consumption and satisfaction, as explained above. For the future, to prepare for the 2020 Tokyo Olympics and Paralympics will be the priority for tourism policies on the national, regional and local level.

The establishment of tourism as a sector worthy of attention has been symbolized by the creation of the JTA in 2008. An external agency of the Ministry of Land, Infrastructure, Transport and Tourism, the JTA is involved in tourism promotion, destination and industry development, training, vacation policies and safety measures for Japanese travellers abroad.

Even after the triple disaster in March 2011, tourism has been discussed from several aspects. Tour buses and hotels paid an important role during evacuation. Safety for tourists during disasters became an issue. Volunteers flocked to the area, leading to the creation of agencies and programmes for volunteer tourism. Possible use as future tourist attractions paid an important role in discussions about the preservation of disaster sites. Finally, tourism to the affected areas was promoted as an important tool for revitalization and a show of compassion. The attention these issues received proves that tourism has been firmly established in public discussion and policies.

Behind the curtain of hot-spring steam

Since tourism in Japan is discussed as an important sector of the economy, with special emphasis on regional development, a review of tourism industries as an employer has become a necessary but neglected task. Although often seen as a job in a dream world, tourism is infamous for seasonal employment, irregular and long working hours, and low wages, and Japan is no exception. It has been pointed out that accommodation facilities in Japan employ more part-time workers with a lower salary than other service industries, and that women over 50 form an important part of the workforce (Funck 1999). In 2013 the percentage of employees who enjoyed two days off each week was lowest in two major industry sectors connected to tourism: transportation (35.0%) and accommodation, eating and drinking services (40.8%). In the latter sector, employees take only about one-third of their holidays (32.6%), the lowest percentage of all major industry groups and 20% below the already low average of 52.9% (Ministry of Health, Labour and Welfare 2014). Also, companies pay the lowest amount of salary per employee among all major industry groups except agriculture (Ministry of Internal Affairs and Communications Statistics Bureau 2013).

If we look at the sub-sector of accommodation, 42.2% of employees work part-time and 11.8% non-regularly compared to 31.0% and 5.5% in all other industries. At 58.8%, the percentage of women working in accommodation facilities is much higher than the average of 43.5%. Among these, 52.4% are part-time (46.7% in all industries) and 14.6% (7.1%) are non-regularly employed (Ministry of Internal Affairs and Communications Statistics Bureau 2013).

In hot-spring resorts there are severe working conditions hidden behind the curtain of steam. The dominant types of facilities in hot-spring resorts are Japanese-style inns called *ryokan*. They offer Japanese rooms with *futon* that will be laid out for the guests on *tatami* mats and elaborate meals served in the guest room. Although services have been simplified to include breakfast buffets and meals in restaurants, this type of service requires a workforce available from early morning to late at night. Since many hot-spring resorts are tucked away in the mountains, personnel have to live in simple accommodation facilities provided by the employers. On the positive side, employment in hot-spring *ryokan* is a welcome addition to a mix of jobs in rural economies (McMorran 2008). Until the 1990s, it was also a winter option for women from the north of Japan, who moved to the hot-spring resorts surrounding the capital while their men worked in construction industries nearby. Ski resorts too offer part-time jobs in winter, when few other jobs are available in rural areas. On the negative side, working for low pay in a remote mountain area is not an attractive option for young people. In a very drastic way, it could be said that, because they offer staff accommodation and don't require specific skills, these kind of jobs are the only ones available for single or divorced women over 40 with or without children who cannot afford their own flat. In recent years, population decreases in rural areas in combination with deregulation of the dispatched temporary work sector have brought a shift from locally based employment to short-term temporary workers. In contrast to other countries, foreigners account for a very small part of the tourism labour force, because Japan poses strict limitations on the influx of unskilled or low-skilled foreign workers. Labour shortage due to a shrinking population might therefore be the only effective pressure to improve working conditions in tourism industries.

"New tourism"

In the Tourism Nation Promotion Basic Plan, "new tourism" forms an important pillar (JTA 2012: 41). New tourism here includes eco, green, cultural, industrial, health, sport and other types of tourism that boost regional characteristics and offer elements of experience and exchange. Like the individual foreign tourists attracting the curiosity of mass media, these new forms of tourism are still niche markets; however, they can support individual destinations. For example, since it was registered as a World Heritage Site in 1993, Yakushima Island to the South of Kyushu has developed as an ecotourism destination, where visitors take guided hikes to see the deep forests and thousand-year-old cedar trees in the mountains. Most of the guides have moved to the island from other areas in Japan. On Naoshima Island in the Seto Inland Sea, a company has created a comprehensive art and architecture resort by adding new facilities over several years. It has become the core of a tri-annual art festival and has spread art tourism to other islands in the area (Funck *et al.* 2013).

Rural areas were discovered as tourism destinations from the 1980s, when they became the symbol of traditional lifestyle and community ties (Moon 2002). The government promoted green tourism to revitalize mountain and coastal villages in the 1990s. As many villages try to diversify their agricultural base, green tourism can now be found in locations around the country. Farmers' markets, rice planting and fruit picking form the majority of rural tourism experiences; rental fields and homestay in farmhouses provide deeper involvement.

"New tourism" also includes new media for publicity and new forms of communication. Content spread through media like books, films and television has long played an important role in tourism promotion. In Japan, two programmes run by the public broadcaster NHK are potent and reliable creators of tourism demand for the location sites. One is a 15-minute drama series run every morning for six months, the other a history drama showing on Sunday evenings for one year. In 2013 the area affected by the 2011 disaster was chosen as the location for the morning drama and the city of Aizu in Fukushima Prefecture for the history drama; as anticipated, both are connected to an increase in domestic tourists. While the NHK series created a rather predictable tourism boom, because travel agencies started offering tours as soon as the programme started, the effects of new media like *manga*, *anime* or video games are difficult to predict. The question of location as such can be tricky to answer. "Location" might include a place that inspired an oeuvre, as the forest of Yakushima did for Miyazaki Hayato's famous *Princess Mononoke*. It could also be an exact depiction of a completely vernacular scene like a train station, leaving it to the fans to search for and discover the original place. Often, it involves a long-term strategy by municipalities to attract authors, have them create a series of works on different types of media and develop spin-off products and events in cooperation with fans. This type of tourism offers diverse forms of emotional networking created by sub-cultures making full use of individual information technologies (Yamamura 2009). Media-content tourism has thus extended from TV series that are watched by almost the entire nation to multiple forms of content taken up by different sub-groups not only inside Japan, but also worldwide. For destinations, this offers various possibilities for direct marketing. On the other hand, constant efforts to keep the attention of fickle online consumers are required.

Case study 27.1 *Shimanami Kaido*: cycling across the sea

Shimanami Kaido, literally translated as "island-scape sea route", is the name of a set of bridges linking the main islands of Honshu and Shikoku, passing over six islands along the way. In contrast to other bridge systems across the Seto Inland Sea, these bridges are equipped with foot and bicycle paths. Although some of the islands feature famous shrines or temples and had built up some tourism attractions like beaches and museums, none of them was a major national tourism destination. When all bridges were completed in 1999, the islands experienced a fierce but short-lived tourism boom of package tours that left behind quite a few closed restaurants and leisure facilities. It took another ten years for them to be rediscovered as a Mecca for cyclists and a retirement and relocation destination for tired urbanites. What started off as a group of rental cycle stations with very basic, three-gear cycles has developed into an elaborate system. Cyclists now have a space set aside in front of the nearest train station to put their bikes together; they can rent a variety of bikes, stay at a hotel with their bike in the room, use a cycle bus, take part in guided tours and combine cycling with boat trips on a special cycle pass. In an international cycling event in October 2014 more than 8,000 participants cycled along the bridges, which were closed to traffic that day. More tourists have created chances for new business, and some of the islands have attracted new inhabitants engaging in organic agriculture, accommodation, cafes or specialized shops.

Plate 27.1 A cyclist takes a picture of her bike in front of one of the bridges of *Shimanami Kaido*.

Conclusion

While domestic tourism remains a short-trip market and tourism industries an unstable workplace, tourism in Japan has diversified at a rapid pace in the 21st century, supported by an increasing influx of foreign tourists and, to a smaller degree, investment. Changes in society have been reflected too. A larger gap in income has been mirrored in an expansion of accommodation facilities, with international luxury chains and high-end *ryokan* at one end of the market and budget hostels at the other – neither available in the 1990s.

Depopulation could be the biggest challenge Japan will face. It means fewer domestic tourists and a smaller workforce. On the other hand, it opens up space, takes pressure off the environment and land and could contribute to nature conservation. At present, Japan's urban population is gazing at its rural periphery for relaxation and nostalgia; in the future, tourists from fast-developing Asian countries might gaze at Japan the same way.

Key reading

Funck, C. and Cooper, M. (2013) *Japanese Tourism: Spaces, Places and Structures*. New York: Berghahn Books.
Guichard-Anguis, S. and Moon, O. (eds) (2009), *Japanese Tourism and Travel Culture*. London: Routledge.
Hendry, J. and Raveri, M. (eds) (2002) *Japan at Play*. London: Routledge.
Leheny, D. (2003) *The Rules of Play: National Identity and the Shaping of Japanese Leisure*. Ithaca: Cornell University Press.

References

An J. (2011) 'A comparative study of views on overseas travel between Japanese and Korean university students', *The Tourism Studies*, 24(1): 69–79. (In Japanese.)
Cool Japan Fund (2014) 'What is Cool Japan Fund?' Online. Available: www.cj-fund.co.jp/en/about/cjfund.html (accessed 4 January 2015).
Funck, C. (1999) *Tourismus und Peripherie in Japan: Über das Potential touristischer Entwicklung zum Ausgleich regionaler Disparitäten*. Bonn: Verlag Dieter Born.
—— (2012) 'The innovative potential of inbound tourism in Japan for destination development: A case study of Hida Takayama', *Contemporary Japan*, 24(2): 121–147.
—— (2014) 'Mourn, rebuild, remember, prepare: Messages of the 1995 Great Hanshin-Awaji Earthquake', *Asia Pacific World*, 5(2): 12–31.
Funck, C. and Cooper, M. (2013) *Japanese Tourism: Spaces, Places and Structures*. New York: Berghahn Books.
Funck, C., Otsuka, H. and Chang, N. (2013) 'Chances and problems of development based on art tourism: From the example of Naoshima', *Environmental Studies* (Bulletin of the Graduate School of Integrated Arts and Sciences Hiroshima University), 8: 77–90. (In Japanese.)
Ishimori, S. (1989) 'Popularization and commercialization of tourism in early modern Japan', *Senri Ethnological Studies*, 29: 179–194.
Japan Tourism Agency (JTA) (2012) 'The Tourism Nation Promotion Basic Plan'. Online. Available: www.mlit.go.jp/kankocho/en/kankorikkoku/kihonkeikaku.html (accessed 4 January 2015).
—— (2013) *General Information of Tourism Statistics in Japan*. Online. Available: www.mlit.go.jp/common/000991725.pdf (accessed 30 December 2014).
—— (2014a) *Research Study on Economic Impacts of Tourism in Japan*. Online. Available: www.mlit.go.jp/common/001040524.pdf (accessed 3 October 2014).
—— (2014b) *Accommodation Survey 2013*. Online. Available: www.mlit.go.jp/kankocho/siryou/toukei/shukuhakutoukei.html (accessed 30 December 2014). (In Japanese.)

—— (2014c) *Consumption Trend Survey for Foreigners Visiting Japan 2013*. Online. Available: www.mlit. go.jp/kankocho/en/siryou/toukei/syouhityousa.html (accessed 4 January 2015).

—— (2014d) *White Paper on Tourism in Japan, 2014 (Japanese Edition)*. Online. Available: www.mlit.go.jp/ common/001042911.pdf (accessed 4 January 2015).

Jones, T. (2012) 'A life cycle analysis of nature-based tourism policy in Japan', *Contemporary Japan* (Journal of the German Institute for Japanese Studies, Tokyo), 24(2): 179–211.

Kim, S. and Ellis, A. (2015) 'Noodle production and consumption: From agriculture to food tourism in Japan', *Tourism Geographies*, 17(1): 151–167.

Klien, S. (2010) 'Contemporary art and regional revitalisation: Selected artworks in the Echigo-Tsumari Art Triennial 2000–6', *Japan Forum*, 22(3–4): 513–543.

Leheny, D. (2003) *The Rules of Play: National Identity and the Shaping of Japanese Leisure*. Ithaca: Cornell University Press.

McMorran, C. (2008) 'Understanding the "heritage" in heritage tourism: Ideological tool or economic tool for a Japanese hot springs resort?', *Tourism Geographies*, 10(3): 334–354.

Ministry of Health, Labour and Welfare (2014) *General Survey on Working Conditions*. Online. Available: www.e-stat.go.jp/SG1/estat/NewList.do?tid=000001014004 (accessed 4 January 2015). (In Japanese.)

Ministry of Internal Affairs and Communications Statistics Bureau (2013) *2012 Economic Census for Business Activity*. Online. Available: www.stat.go.jp/english/data/e-census/2012/index.htm (accessed 4 January 2015).

Moon, O. (2002) 'The countryside reinvented for urban tourists: Rural transformation in the Japanese Muraokoshi movement', in J. Hendry and M. Raveri (eds), *Japan at Play* (pp. 228–244). London: Routledge.

Nakamura, K., Matsumoto, H. and Shikida, A. (2008) 'Volunteer tourism: Integration of work and tourism', *Proceedings of JITR Annual Conference 2008* (pp. 425–428). (In Japanese.)

Rimmer, P.J. (1992) 'Japan's "Resort Archipelago": Creating regions of fun, pleasure, relaxation, and recreation', *Environment and Planning A*, 24: 1599–1625.

Shikida, A., Morishige, M., Takagi, H. and Miyamoto, H. (2008) *Komyunitii ekotsuurizumu* [Community Ecotourism]. Kyoto: Gakugei-Shuppansha. (In Japanese.)

Soshiroda, A. (2005) 'Inbound tourism policies in Japan from 1859 to 2003', *Annals of Tourism Research*, 32(4), 1100–1120.

UNWTO (2014) *Tourism Highlights 2014 Edition*. Online. Available: http://mkt.unwto.org/publication/ unwto-tourism-highlights-2014-edition (accessed 30 December 2014).

Yamamura, T. (2009) 'Kankô jôhô kakumei to bunka sôshutsugata kankô no kanôsei: anime seichi junrei ni miru jisedai tsûrizumu no hôga' [The revolution of tourism information and possibilities of creative cultural tourism], *Chiikikaihatsu*, 533: 32–36. (In Japanese.)

Wu, C., Hayashi, Y. and Funck, C. (2012) 'The role of charter flights in Sino-Japanese tourism', *Journal of Air Transport Management*, 22: 21–27.

PART 5

Conclusion

28

CONCLUSION

Prospects for tourism in Asia

C. Michael Hall & Stephen J. Page

Introduction: researching Asian tourism

The chapters contained in this book are by no means a complete assessment of tourism in Asia. Arguably the tendency in much Western tourism literature when discussing tourism in Asia has been to focus on east and southeast Asia and ASEAN member countries and to neglect south Asia (Hall & Page 2000a). Yet, as the chapters within this book undeniably show, there are complex inter-relationships which exist in terms of the tourism markets, regions and activities within Southeast and South Asia. Importantly, the residents in neighbouring Asian countries are increasingly providing major tourism markets for each other. This is reflected in the complex web of airline and cruise routes that are intra-regional in nature, often short-haul or medium-haul cross-border trips. For example, the growth of the Indian and the Chinese middle class has had substantial implications for intraregional travel as well as intercontinental travel, which is where much Western business and academic research is focused. What is also often overlooked is the extremely important domestic tourism market in Asian countries (see Singh 2009 for an important exception). In one sense of course this is understandable when framed in terms of the importance given to the attraction of foreign exchange by many governments in the region, and which is therefore also reflective of a number of chapters in the present volume. Nevertheless, it is also worth noting that despite most national tourism organisations' emphasising inbound tourism due to balance of trade and investment benefits, in some cases (e.g. Sri Lanka and Malaysia), tourism authorities have also tried to use domestic tourism as a substitute for a decline in international visitor arrivals, especially during periods of economic and financial crisis (Lew & Hall 1999; Hall 2010).

One of the immediate problems the researcher faces in reconstructing patterns of tourism visitation, activity and expenditure is the absence of up-to-date, reliable and consistent tourism statistics. Whilst the United Nations World Tourism Organization (UNWTO) and the Pacific Asia Tourism Association (PATA) perform a valuable role in collating visitor statistics and in encouraging destinations to adapt appropriate methodologies to enumerate tourism arrivals, the authors of the chapters in this book frequently faced problems in accessing reliable, up-to-date and meaningful tourism data. At a time when many destinations seek to encourage inward investment, governments need to acknowledge the necessity of accurate and authoritative tourism statistics to improve business confidence in major tourism investment destinations. Without easy access to such data, investors are likely to require additional inducements to make any contribution to inward investment, while assessments of the wider social and environmental impacts of tourism will also occur within a research vacuum – assuming it occurs at all outside of academic research. There are a number of tourism concerns in the region which are clearly under-researched. These include not only issues of tourism impacts raised throughout this book and applied concerns such as marketing and governance, but also such issues as the role of multinational corporations in tourism in the region, the contribution of mobility to health issues for both tourists and host populations, the ongoing relationships between tourism and politics, and the inter-relationships between tourism and other forms of development. Significantly, there is a growing awareness of the emergence of Asian interpretations and understandings of tourism (Winter *et al.* 2008; Winter 2009a, 2009b, 2013; Chang 2015; Dolezal & Trupp 2015), although there is considerable debate over the uniqueness or even appropriateness of such framings and their implications for tourism (Hall 2011a; Cohen *et al.* 2014; Chen & Chang 2015; Coles 2015; Cohen & Cohen 2015a, 2015b, 2015c; Hall 2015; King 2015; Dioko 2016).

Hybridity and hegemony in Asian tourism research

The possibilities of uniquely Asian academic interpretations of tourism are highly debatable, as opposed to the development of hybrid or postcolonial positionings or what should perhaps be more accurately described as "transplanted" framings (Hall & Tucker 2004). In the same way that Zhu *et al.* (2015) noted with respect to a group of Chinese consumers that the deeper "tourist gaze" of trust and brand admiration upon Western goods is a result of the long Chinese modernisation process and is very much influenced by the global consumer culture. So it can also be argued that that the deeper "tourist research gaze" of academics upon Asian tourism that is reported in the international literature is also a result of a long academic modernisation process dominated by Western thought and theory and is very much influenced by the hegemony of an Anglo-American research culture that is currently very much geared to the neoliberal project. As Hall (2013a: 604) observed, 'The phenomenological relationship between the geographical contexts of being somewhere and knowledge acquisition reflects a concern not just with where things matter but also how they matter'. For example, Hall went on to note

> No matter how important local and national knowledge is within a specific spatial context, unless it is conveyed in English it has little chance to enter the global marketplace and be reproduced and recirculated. Somewhat ironically, given the desire to give voice to local and indigenous perspectives, unless that voice can be spoken in English it is likely not to be heard.
>
> *(Hall 2013a: 608)*

Indeed, an analysis of research in tourism geography found that China accounted for over 10 per cent of all tourism geography publications in Scopus, although only a little over one-quarter of these are actually in Chinese (Hall 2013b). Chapter 1 problematised the issue of what constitutes Asia; in the same way questions about what constitutes an Asian perspective on tourism also need to be asked, especially when graduate training, publishing outlets, research frameworks, the circulation and mobility of staff and visiting professors, and institutional focus are often very much geared to current Western modes of academic knowledge production and their evaluation.

Themes and issues

The chapters in this book report a range of common themes affecting the governments of many countries that have influenced the organisation and management of tourism. Probably the most widespread change affecting the region is the privatisation of former state-owned tourism assets and the privatisation of capital-intensive plant and infrastructure associated with hotels and airlines. Yet many tourism destinations in South Asia have retained state control of their flag-carrier to continue to retain an influence over arrivals (see Chapter 3, this volume). This is often a complex decision based on domestic and external economic and political factors, including the financial and political instability affecting the region, which can easily affect tourist arrivals and the profitability of commercial airline activities. In contrast, more established destinations have encouraged privatisation and greater competition in aviation to improve access and market penetration and to reduce levels of government borrowings and debt. The real difficulty that many governments in the region have faced is managing the complex political and economic change that privatisation, competition and the removal of varying degrees of protectionism may bring.

Chapters within this book provide numerous examples of governments relying on inward investment to fund tourism development. At a strategic level, many governments throughout Southeast and South Asia view the economic development benefits of tourism as providing much needed sources of potential employment at a time of substantial population growth. Nevertheless, many of the chapters are critical of the cyclops mentality of a focus on growth, without considerations of the structural economic problems such as debt, unemployment and underemployment, as well as issues of income distribution. In addition, the growth focus is also accompanied by concerns over the environment and climate change (see Chapter 6). Nevertheless, despite some concerns over the long-term impacts of continuing growth in tourism, few governments actually question their ongoing focus on visitor growth, rather than using a broader basket of measures of the contribution that tourism makes. These issues are only likely to become even more important for the region given growth forecasts.

Growth forecasts

The UNWTO (2011) forecasts for 2030 suggest that international tourist arrivals to Asia and the Pacific are projected to increase by 331 million in the period from 2010 (204 million) to 535 million in 2030 (Tables 28.1 and 28.2). As a consequence, there will be increases in the global market shares of Asia and the Pacific to 30 per cent of international arrivals in 2030, up from 22 per cent in 2010. The UNWTO believes that South Asia will be the fastest growing sub-region in the world in relative terms (6.0 per cent per annum), but from a low base (Table 28.3). In absolute numbers, North-East Asia is the fastest growing sub-region (4.9 per cent), adding almost nine million arrivals per year. By 2030 it will become the sub-region to receive the most international arrivals, with an estimated 293 million each year (UNWTO 2011). Southeast Asia is estimated to grow at 5.5 per cent per annum to 2030, to reach 187 million arrivals. Tables 28.4 and 28.5 provide an interesting alternative framing of tourism in the region by illustrating the relative growth of arrivals and outbound tourism with respect to the permanent population. These two tables also indicate that Asia clearly has substantial room to grow even further as both a destination and source for international tourism beyond 2030. However, in addition it is also vital that much greater attention be given in all countries to the importance of domestic tourism and the contributions that can make to regional economic development (e.g. Dorjsuren 2009), along with improved levels of statistical gathering and research.

Table 28.1 International tourism arrivals and forecasts, 1950–2030 (millions)

Year	World	Africa	Americas	Asia and Pacific	Europe	Middle East
1950	25.3	0.5	7.5	0.2	16.8	0.2
1960	69.3	0.8	16.7	0.9	50.4	0.6
1965	112.9	1.4	23.2	2.1	83.7	2.4
1970	165.8	2.4	42.3	6.2	113.0	1.9
1975	222.3	4.7	50.0	10.2	153.9	3.5
1980	278.1	7.2	62.3	23.0	178.5	7.1
1985	320.1	9.7	65.1	32.9	204.3	8.1
1990	439.5	15.2	92.8	56.2	265.8	9.6
1995	540.6	20.4	109.0	82.4	315.0	13.7
2000	687.0	28.3	128.1	110.5	395.9	24.2
2005	799.0	34.8	133.3	153.6	440.7	36.3
2010	940.0	50.2	150.7	204.4	474.8	60.3
Forecast						
2020	1,360	85	199	355	620	101
2030	1,809	134	248	535	744	149

Sources: WTO 1997; UNWTO 2006, 2012.

Table 28.2 Average annual growth rates in international tourism arrivals and forecasts over selected time periods, 1950–2030 (%)

Year	World	Africa	Americas	Asia and Pacific	Europe	Middle East
1950–2000	6.8	8.3	5.8	13.1	6.5	10.1
1950–2005	6.5	8.1	5.4	12.5	6.1	10.1
1950–1960	10.6	3.7	8.4	14.1	11.6	12.3
1960–1970	9.1	12.4	9.7	21.6	8.4	11.5
1970–1980	5.3	11.6	4.0	13.9	4.7	14.3
1980–1990	4.7	7.8	4.1	9.3	4.1	3.1
1980–1985	2.9	6.1	0.9	7.4	2.7	2.7
1985–1990	6.5	9.5	7.3	11.3	5.4	3.5
1980–1995	4.4	6.7	3.8	8.9	3.7	4.5
1990–2000	4.6	6.4	3.3	7.0	4.1	9.6
1990–1995	4.2	6.1	3.3	8.0	3.5	7.3
1995–2000	4.9	6.7	3.3	6.0	4.7	12.0
1995–2010	3.9	6.7	2.1	6.3	3.0	10.5
2000–2005	3.3	5.7	0.8	7.1	2.2	10.0
Forecast						
2010–2030	3.3	5.0	2.6	4.9	2.3	4.6
2010–2020	3.8	5.4	2.9	5.7	2.7	5.2
2020–2030	2.9	4.6	2.2	4.2	1.8	4.0

Sources: UNWTO 2006, 2012.

Table 28.3 Estimated and actual international tourist arrivals to Asia by sub-region of destination (millions)

Sub-region	1995	2010	2030
Northeast Asia	41	112	293
South Asia	4	11	36
Southeast Asia	28	70	187

Source: derived from UNWTO 2011.

Table 28.4 International tourist arrivals by region per 100 population, 1995–2030

(Sub-)region	1995	2010	2030
Western Europe	62	81	114
Southern/Mediterranean Europe	47	71	103
Northern Europe	42	63	80
Caribbean	38	48	65
Central/Eastern Europe	15	25	47
Middle East	9	27	47
Southern Africa	9	22	46
Oceania	28	32	40
Central America	8	19	38
North Africa	6	15	28
Southeast Asia	6	12	27
North America	21	21	26
North-East Asia	3	7	18
South America	4	6	13
East Africa	2	4	7
West and Central Africa	1	2	3
South Asia	0	1	2

Source: after UNWTO 2011.
Note
Figures are rounded off.

Table 28.5 Generation of outbound tourism (trips) by region per 100 population, 1980–2030

Year	World	Africa	Americas	Asia and Pacific	Europe	Middle East
1980	6	1	12	1	21	6
1995	9	2	14	3	36	6
2010	14	3	17	5	57	17
Forecast						
2030	22	6	24	12	89	25

Source: after UNWTO 2011.

Employment generation and human resources

Underemployment in Southeast and South Asia can be partly addressed through the development of labour-intensive industries such as tourism, but all too often such strategies are not accompanied by integrated labour planning and human resource management strategies for the tourism and hospitality sector (see Chapter 4), while linkages between tourism and other sectors, such as agriculture, are also often not given sufficient attention (Hall & Gössling 2013, 2016). In many cases, governments have promoted growth in inbound tourism but failed to see the synergistic relationship with investing in people and their education and training needs to ensure the long-term viability of the tourism sector.

Cross-border and local tourism development

Rather belatedly, many Asian governments have recognised the benefits of regional cooperation in tourism, as the recent experience of ASEAN (see Chapter 9) and the Mekong Basin imply (Verbiest 2013; see also responses from Capannelli 2013 and Sussangkarn 2013). But evaluating the tangible benefits of regional marketing co-operation, multi-destination marketing and greater private sector participation in overseas marketing has not necessarily led to immediate plans and activities that promote these objectives. Although many countries share common borders and similar inbound markets, greater cooperation to extend the length of visitation through dual-destination marketing has yet to be realised, especially within the SAARC framework in south Asia. To date, many countries, even within ASEAN, have been overly protective and nervous about cross-border cooperation. In some cases (e.g. India, China, Bangladesh and Pakistan) political problems and ideology are unlikely to be overcome in the short term to promote a South Asian tourism experience. However, cross-border regional interactions based on economic linkages, such as tourism, does not necessarily indicate convergence of "neighbouring" areas (Lundquist & Trippl 2009). Nevertheless, many peripheral border areas in Asia would welcome improved cross-border tourism as a way to overcome their relative remoteness from metropolitan areas as well as to improve communication and transport networks. Indeed, cross-border differences may help open new economic opportunities, via increases in local and cross-border consumption, competition and labour mobility. As Chapter 22 noted, this has certainly been the case on the eastern Russia–China border – an area in which border disputes have been put to one side and there are no political independence movements. Yet this is in stark contrast to the situation in western China, where many Uyghurs in Xinjiang oppose the increasing numbers of Han Chinese and growing impositions on their culture (Culpepper 2012; Mackerras 2012; Joniak-Lüthi 2015), and which has less tight border controls. Similarly, in Chinese-occupied Tibet there remains resistance to the Han Chinese interventions in religion and culture (Mukherjee 2015). In both locations tourism has a mixed role and is often perceived as a means of commodifying certain aspects of local culture while denying other more political dimensions of cultural expression (Vasantkumar 2009).

One of the emerging issues in tourism development in the region is also the relative weight to be given to the national and regional development goals as compared to the benefits sought at the local and individual level. While Western tourism planning models provide for participation in the tourism development process, such models may have little relevance to situations in which legislative and political structures put power in the hands of undemocratically elected elites and authoritarian regimes (e.g. China, Kazakhstan, North Korea, Tajikistan, Turkmenistan, Uzbekistan) or where power has been attained by military coup (e.g. Thailand). Even in countries where governments have been elected, considerable concerns may exist over the independence of the judicial system and the potential for political corruption (e.g. Kyrgyzstan, Malaysia). Indeed, considerable debate exists as to what relevance Western notions of human rights, democracy and participation have in many parts of Asia at all, with much discussion of tourism planning in the region typically ignoring such basic issues and instead focusing on spatial planning issues.

Case study 28.1 Tourism in Tibet

C.M. Hall

> The only people free to travel around Tibet are the Han Chinese.
>
> *(Interview, Sichuan Province, March 2013 in Hillman 2014: 58)*

Tibet holds a particular place in the Western imagination; it is Shangri-La, it is the spectacular landscape of the Himalayas, it is the land of His Holiness the 14th Dalai Lama Tenzin Gyatso (who is in exile in northern India), it is a land of enormous cultural heritage and religious significance, and it has been occupied by the Chinese since 1951. Tibet is therefore an area of contested political, academic and tourism space which plays out in many dimensions of tourism (Shepherd 2006; Kolas 2008; Llamas & Belk 2011; Hannam 2013). Tibet is a political space claimed by the Tibetan government in exile in Dharamsala, India, and it is, according to the People's Republic of China, an autonomous region of China (Smith 2008).

Since the exile of the Tibetan government and the Dalai Lama in 1959, Lhasa in Tibet was strictly closed to tourists until 1984 (Guangrui 1989). However, the initial opening up of Tibet to Western visitors through the reforms of the Chinese government in 1979 had a number of unintended effects. Rather than support Chinese-backed tourism developments and images of Tibet as part of China, the policy only served to reinforce indigenous and refugee motivations to free Tibet from China, and to heighten the sacredness of the country for Westerners. As Klieger (1992) noted

> As distorted presentations of Tibet crafted by Chinese agencies appeared increasingly incredulous to many Westerners, the official tourist infrastructure built at great expense by China was increasingly ignored. Westerners wanted to experience Shangri-La, and Tibetans were more than happy to share their vision of the sacred landscape. Lost on the tourist audience was the Chinese managed impression that Tibet has been, since the days of Khubilai Khan, an integral part of the motherland.
>
> *(Klieger 1992: 124)*

Klieger's observations arguably still hold true to the present day as there remains significant contestation between Han Chinese portrayals of Tibet versus the experience and desires of ethnic Tibetans (Hillman 2009, 2010; Liu 2013; Saxer 2013). These occasionally come to the surface for Westerners when there are reactions to the Chinese human rights and economic regime, as in 2008 when there were street protests and rioting by Tibetan monks (Saxer 2013). The explanation for the Chinese government response to the Tibetan opposition is also well identified by Hillman (2014):

The Chinese Communist Party leadership's framework for interpreting the unrest is rooted in Maoist-era approaches to identifying friends and foes of the Communist revolution, and by the rhetoric of class struggle. A key reference is Mao Zedong's 1937 essay on the distinction between "contradictions among the people" and "contradictions against the people". According to Mao contradictions among the people are the result of ignorance or false consciousness and can be resolved through education and persuasion. Contradictions against the people, however, represent a threat that must be eliminated or subjected to absolute control.

Because the Chinese Communist Party's position is that unrest is orchestrated by Tibetan "splittists" and their anti-China supporters in the West, incidents of unrest are now routinely identified as contradictions against the people. The Party's categorisation of the unrest as hostile provides the political justification needed for a harsh response. China has responded to the 2008 unrest by dramatically expanding its internal security apparatus. Since 2008 Chinese government expenditure on internal security has grown so dramatically that it now exceeds expenditure on external defense. China's "stability maintenance" (*weiwen*) approach to governing Tibet has involved a dramatic scaling up of security forces and surveillance infrastructure. Police numbers have been increased in all Tibetan areas and People's Armed Police reinforcements that were sent as a response to the 2008 riots have been made permanent.

(Hillman 2014: 53)

Interestingly, both sides of the Tibetan debate see tourism as a potential positive, with tourists as observers of

human rights abuses and exploitation or economic development… In essence, the fight here contains a symbolic aspect in which the key participants in the debate – the Chinese state, Western tourists, and exiled Tibetans – not only struggle for control, but also compete for possession of the image of Tibet.

(Cingcade 1998: 1)

Nevertheless, it should be emphasised that the Tibetan opposition to the Chinese presence is as much related to economic opportunities as it is to cultural issues, especially among younger generations (Yeh 2009; Hillman & Tuttle 2016). This is especially the case as China's remote western regions have the highest concentrations of rural poverty, while there is also evidence that non-Tibetan economic migrants have out-competed Tibetans in urban labour markets (Hillman 2014).

In many ways the Tibetan situation reflects several of the wider issues with respect to tourism in Asia. Most importantly decisions regarding tourism development, including as a means of poverty reduction, can have far-reaching political implications. Furthermore, in different locales, different activities, concerns and mechanisms will be salient. The positionality of the researcher can have a significant effect on interpretation of research framing and results while ideally, but often little followed through, there is a need for substantially more attention to dynamic change over time and the factors that are influencing change.

References

Cingcade, M.L. (1998) 'Tourism and the many Tibets: The manufacture of Tibetan "tradition"', *China Information*, 13(1): 1–24.

Guangrui, Z. (1989) 'Ten years of Chinese tourism: Profile and assessment', *Tourism Management*, 10(1): 51–62.

Hannam, K. (2013) '"Shangri-La" and the new "great game": Exploring tourism geopolitics between China and India', *Tourism Planning & Development*, 10(2): 178–186.

Hillman, B. (2009) 'Ethnic tourism and ethnic politics in Tibetan China', *Harvard Asia Pacific Review*, 10(1): 3–6.

—— (2010) 'China's many Tibets: Diqing as a model for "development with Tibetan characteristics"?' *Asian Ethnicity*, 11(2): 269–277.

—— (2014) 'Interpreting the post-2008 wave of protest and conflict in Tibet', *Dálný Východ* (Far East), 4(1): 50–60.

Hillman, B. and Tuttle, G. (eds) (2016) *Ethnic Conflict and Protest in Tibet and Xinjiang: Unrest in China's West*. New York: Columbia University Press.

Kolas, A. (2008) *Tourism and Tibetan Culture in Transition: A Place Called Shangrila*. Abingdon: Routledge.

Klieger, P.C. (1992) 'Shangri-La and the politicization of tourism in Tibet', *Annals of Tourism Research*, 19(1): 122–125.

Liu, T.K. (2013) 'Re-constructing cultural heritage and imagining Wa primitiveness in the China/ Myanmar borderlands', in T. Blumenfield and H. Silverman (eds) *Cultural Heritage Politics in China* (pp. 161–184). New York: Springer.

Llamas, R. and Belk, R. (2011) 'Shangri-La messing with a myth', *Journal of Macromarketing, 31*(3), 257–275.

Saxer, M. (2013) 'The moral economy of cultural identity: Tibet, cultural survival, and the safeguarding of cultural heritage', *Civilisations*, 61(2), 65–82 (English version available at www. cairn-int.info/article.php?ID_ARTICLE=E_CIVI_611_0065).

Shepherd, R. (2006) 'UNESCO and the politics of cultural heritage in Tibet', *Journal of Contemporary Asia*, 36(2), 243–257.

Smith, W.W. (2008) *China's Tibet? Autonomy or Assimilation*. New York: Rowman & Littlefield.

Yeh, E. (2009) 'Tibet and the problem of radical reductionism', *Antipode*, 41(5): 903–1010.

Planning

As Chapter 1 highlighted, many destinations in Asia are based on a growing urbanised experience related to the principal gateways in the region. It is ironic that with the exception of Singapore, many of these increasingly urbanised countries continue to strongly promote images of rural and relatively natural areas in their tourist promotion. The problem here is that with the emergence of highly urbanised regions with an array of environmental problems, the tourist experience of entering each country may be tarnished by wider problems of a lowering of environmental quality (e.g. overcrowding, pollution and severe congestion in the absence of appropriate transport infrastructure), that in the long-run can affect economic development. In addition to the need for improved urban planning and design, one of the principal explanations is that infrastructure needs significant investment, redevelopment and replacement to meet the demands now being placed upon it through that of a growing middle-class population as well as tourist use. In this context, tourism planning and management needs to be included in many of the centralised five-year plans still in vogue in many countries in the region, so that tourist expenditure is used to reinvest in vital physical and social infrastructure for urban centres as a whole. Given the continued growth in urbanisation, the need for improved planning and investment is paramount, especially given additional challenges of environmental and social change.

In a social and cultural context, the rapid growth of tourism in Southeast and South Asia has generated a complex, diverse and often controversial range of impacts. The impact on indigenous culture, the loss of cultural identity and commodification of culture to generate economic benefits has not been without its critics. In a similar vein, there is also a growing concern that rapid tourism development has not been accompanied by adequate planning to ameliorate short- and long-term environmental impacts. While general short-term impacts of visitors on the environment can often be ameliorated through the application of visitor management techniques and strategies, the effects of longer-term indirect impacts, e.g. inadequate sewage disposal from resort developments, may have substantial implications for the quality of life of local residents, the health of residents and visitors alike, and the continued attractiveness of destinations (Hall & Lew 2009).

Ecotourism

Ecotourism has become an increasingly important part of the product mix of the region, along with marine and cultural tourism, and often under the umbrella of pro-poor tourism or poverty reduction (Truong *et al.* 2014; Carter *et al.* 2015). Nearly all countries in the region are seeking to develop ecotourism attractions, usually national parks and reserves, in order to attract high-yield tourism, although in the search for the tourist dollar the temptation to attract more and more tourists to environmentally sensitive sites seems to be unstoppable. The relationship between tourism and the environment is therefore problematic. Tourism has as much provided the justification for the conservation of cultural and natural heritage, and the conservation of biodiversity, throughout the region, e.g. through the creation of national parks and reserves, as it has led to its destruction. While appropriate environmental strategies for tourism are important, probably the most significant factor is the development of integrated planning and management strategies that seek to manage the synergistic and cumulative relationships within and between environmental uses. In this sense planning for tourism must be able to encompass more than just tourism. Indeed, one of the biggest drawbacks in tourism planning and development in the region is such a tunnel-vision towards tourism.

Asian identity and otherness

In this age of globalisation questions of power, rights, cultural representation, "otherness" and identity have become part of the vernacular of at least some students of tourism (Winter *et al.* 2008; Hall 2011a). However, it would be true to say that they are not part of the industry lexicon or even a large part of tourism academia. Instead, most concerns surround such issues as infrastructure capacities (particularly transport and accommodation capacities), levels of repeat visitation, effective marketing and promotional campaigns, efficient use of resources and presenting the best possible image to the outside world of a place where the locals are friendly, interesting and a little bit different (but not too different), and where the destination is safe, peaceful and attractive (Hall & Page 2000b). Such uncritical perspectives have often been reinforced by some academics and researchers who have not wanted to rock the government and tourism industry boat, perhaps because they do not want to be seen to bite the hand that feeds or because they wish to conduct more research (Hall 2011b). Yet, more wide-ranging research and debate of tourism in the region have become more vital than ever before, particularly when factors often regarded on the periphery of tourism research, e.g. political and socio-cultural issues, become central to industry interests at times of economic and governmental instability. This, though, requires a willingness of government, industry and academics to step outside the box and be willing to communicate and listen to alternative perspectives on tourism even if they may be regarded as critical of the hitherto received view.

It is therefore extremely appropriate that this book is being completed at a time when, in many countries throughout the region, the need for more open policy debate and an end to political corruption is being conveyed more than ever before. Academic commentators have their part to play in such a debate in a tourism context, given the significance of tourism development for economic, environmental and social wellbeing in many parts of the region. It is therefore hoped that some of the perspectives and insights contained in this book will help lead to improved policy making and the development of more sustainable forms of tourism in a century in which Asian concerns will likely dominate economically and politically.

References

Capannelli, G. (2013) 'Comment on "Regional Cooperation and Integration in the Mekong Region"', *Asian Economic Policy Review*, 8(1): 167–168.

Carter, R.W., Thok, S., O'Rourke, V. and Pearce, T. (2015) 'Sustainable tourism and its use as a development strategy in Cambodia: A systematic literature review', *Journal of Sustainable Tourism*, 23(5): 797–818.

Chang, T.C. (2015) 'The Asian wave and critical tourism scholarship', *International Journal of Asia-Pacific Studies*, 11: 83–101.

Chen, J. and Chang, T.C. (2015) 'Mobilising tourism research in emerging world regions: Contributions and advances', *Current Issues in Tourism*, 18(1): 57–61.

Cohen, E. and Cohen, S.A. (2015a) 'A mobilities approach to tourism from emerging world regions', *Current Issues in Tourism*, 18(1): 11–43.

—— (2015b) 'Tourism mobilities from emerging world regions: A response to commentaries', *Current Issues in Tourism*, 18(1): 68–69.

—— (2015c) 'Beyond Eurocentrism in tourism: A paradigm shift to mobilities', *Tourism Recreation Research*, 40(2): 157–168.

Cohen, S.A., Prayag, G. and Moital, M. (2014) 'Consumer behaviour in tourism: Concepts, influences and opportunities', *Current Issues in Tourism*, 17(10): 872–909.

Coles, T. (2015) 'Tourism mobilities: Still a current issue in tourism?' *Current Issues in Tourism*, 18(1): 62–67.

Culpepper, R. (2012) 'Nationalist competition on the internet: Uyghur diaspora versus the Chinese state media', *Asian Ethnicity*, 13(2): 187–203.

Dioko, L.D.A. (2016) 'Services management and the growing number of Asian travelers: What needs re-thinking?' *Worldwide Hospitality and Tourism Themes*, 8(1): 4–11.

Dolezal, C. and Trupp, A. (2015) 'Tourism and development in Southeast Asia', *Austrian Journal of South-East Asian Studies*, 8(2): 117–124.

Dorjsuren, A. (2009) 'From community to holiday camps: The emergence of a tourist economy in Mongolia', in S. Singh (ed.), *Domestic Tourism in Asia: Diversity and Divergence* (pp. 107–128). London: Earthscan.

Hall, C.M. (2010) 'Crisis events in tourism: Subjects of crisis in tourism', *Current Issues in Tourism*, 13(5): 401–417.

—— (ed.) (2011a) *Fieldwork in Tourism: Methods, Issues and Reflections*. Abingdon: Routledge.

—— (2011b) 'Researching the political in tourism: Where knowledge meets power', in C.M. Hall (ed.), *Fieldwork in Tourism: Methods, Issues and Reflections* (pp. 39–54). London: Routledge.

—— (2013a) 'Framing tourism geography: Notes from the underground', *Annals of Tourism Research*, 43: 601–623.

—— (2013b) 'Development(s) in the geographies of tourism: Knowledge(s), actions and cultures', in J. Wilson and S. Anton Clavé (eds), *Geographies of Tourism: European Research Perspectives* (pp. 11–34). London: Emerald.

—— (2015) 'On the mobility of tourism mobilities', *Current Issues in Tourism*, 18(1): 7–10.

Hall, C.M. and Gössling, S. (eds) (2013) *Sustainable Culinary Systems: Local Foods, Innovation, and Tourism & Hospitality*. Abingdon: Routledge.

—— (eds) (2016) *Food Tourism and Regional Development*. Abingdon: Routledge.

Hall, C.M. and Lew, A. (2009) *Understanding and Managing Tourism Impacts: An Integrated Approach*. London: Routledge.

Hall, C.M. and Page, S.J. (ed.) (2000a) *Tourism in South and Southeast Asia*. Oxford: Butterworth-Heinemann.

—— (2000b) 'Conclusion: Prospects for tourism in South and Southeast Asia in the new millennium', in C.M. Hall and S.J. Page (eds), *Tourism in South and South-East Asia: Critical Perspectives* (pp. 286–290). Oxford: Butterworth-Heinemann.

Hall, C.M. and Tucker, H. (2004) 'Introduction', in C.M. Hall and H. Tucker (eds), *Tourism and Postcolonialism: Contested Discourses, Identities and Representations* (pp. 1–24). London: Routledge.

Joniak-Lüthi, A. (2015) 'Xinjiang's geographies in motion', *Asian Ethnicity*, 16(4): 428–445.

King, V.T. (2015) 'Encounters and mobilities: Conceptual issues in tourism studies in Southeast Asia', *SOJOURN: Journal of Social Issues in Southeast Asia*, 30(2): 497–527.

Lew, A.A. and Hall, C.M. (1999) 'The impacts of the Asian Crisis on tourism', *Current Issues in Tourism*, 2(4): 277–278.

Lundquist, K.-J. and Trippl, M. (2009) *Towards Cross-Border Innovation Spaces: A Theoretical Analysis and Empirical Comparison of the Öresund Region and the Centrope Area*, SRE – Discussion Papers, 2009/05. Vienna: Institut für Regional- und Umweltwirtschaft, WU Vienna University of Economics and Business.

Mackerras, C. (2012) 'Causes and ramifications of the Xinjiang July 2009 disturbances', *Sociology Study*, 2(7): 496–510.

Mukherjee, K. (2015) 'Comparing China and India's disputed borderland regions: Xinjiang, Tibet, Kashmir, and the Indian Northeast', *East Asia*, 32(2): 173–205.

Singh, S. (ed.) (2009) *Domestic Tourism in Asia: Diversity and Divergence*. London: Earthscan.

Sussangkarn, C. (2013) 'Comment on "Regional Cooperation and Integration in the Mekong Region"', *Asian Economic Policy Review*, 8(1): 165–166.

Truong, V.D., Hall, C.M. and Garry, T. (2014) 'Tourism and poverty alleviation: Perceptions and experiences of poor people in Sapa, Vietnam', *Journal of Sustainable Tourism*, 22(7): 1071–1089.

United Nations World Tourism Organization (UNWTO) (2006) *International Tourist Arrivals, Tourism Market Trends, 2006 Edition – Annex*. Madrid: UNWTO.

—— (2011) *Tourism Towards 2030 Global Overview, UNWTO General Assembly 19th Session, Gyeongju, Republic of Korea, 10 October 2011*. Madrid: UNWTO.

—— (2012) *UNWTO Tourism Highlights, 2012 Edition – Annex*. Madrid: UNWTO.

Vasantkumar, A. (2009) '"Domestic" tourism and its discontents: Han tourists in China's "Little Tibet"', in S. Singh (ed., *Domestic Tourism in Asia: Diversity and Divergence* (pp. 129–150). London: Earthscan.

Verbiest, J.P.A. (2013) 'Regional cooperation and integration in the Mekong region', *Asian Economic Policy Review*, 8(1): 148–164.

Winter, T. (2009a) 'Asian tourism and the retreat of Anglo-Western centrism in tourism theory', *Current Issues in Tourism*, 12(1): 21–31.

—— (2009b) 'The modernities of heritage and tourism: Interpretations of an Asian future', *Journal of Heritage Tourism*, 4(2), 105–115.

—— (2013) 'Going places: challenging directions for the future of heritage studies', *International Journal of Heritage Studies*, 19(4): 395–398.

Winter, T., Teo, P. and Chang, T.C. (eds) (2008) *Asia on Tour: Exploring the Rise of Asian Tourism*. London: Routledge.

World Tourism Organization (1997) *Tourism 2020 Vision*. Madrid: World Tourism Organization.

Zhu, D., Xu, H. and Jiang, L. (2015) 'Behind buying: The Chinese gaze on European commodities', *Asia Pacific Journal of Tourism Research*, 21(3): 293–311.

INDEX

Items in **bold** refer to Tables, items in *italic* refer to Figures.